MODERN PORTFOLIO THEORY AND INVESTMENT ANALYSIS

MODERN PORTFOLIO THEORY AND INVESTMENT ANALYSIS

Third Edition

EDWIN J. ELTON
MARTIN J. GRUBER

New York University
Graduate School of Business Administration

JOHN WILEY & SONS
New York • Chichester • Brisbane • Toronto • Singapore

Library of Congress Cataloging in Publication Data:

Elton, Edwin J.
  Modern portfolio theory and investment analysis.

  Includes bibliographies and index.
  1. Portfolio management.   2. Investment analysis.
I. Gruber, Martin Jay, 1937–   II. Title.

HG4529.5.E47   1987   332.6   86-19070
ISBN 0-471-85113-2

Printed in the United States of America

10 9 8 7 6 5 4 3 2 1

To Jonathan, Stacey, Joelle, and Ellie Gruber
and
To Annette, Ned, Kathryn, John Paul, and Diane Elton

About the Authors

Edwin J. Elton is Nomura Professor of Finance at the Graduate School of Business of New York University. He has authored or coauthored five books and over 55 articles. These articles have appeared in such journals as *The Journal of Finance, Review of Economics and Statistics, Management Science, Journal of Financial Economics, Journal of Business, Oxford Economic Papers* and *Journal of Financial and Quantitative Analysis*. He is coeditor of the *Journal of Finance*. He has been a member of the Board of Directors of the American Finance Association and an Associate Editor of *Management Science*. Professor Elton has served as a consultant for many major financial institutions.

    Martin J. Gruber is Nomura Professor of Finance at the Graduate School of Business of New York University. He has published seven books and over 50 journal articles in such journals as *The Journal of Finance, Review of Economics and Statistics, Journal of Financial Economics, Journal of Business, Management Science, Journal of Financial and Quantitative Analysis, Operations Research, Oxford Economic Papers* and *The Journal of Portfolio Management*. He is coeditor of the *Journal of Finance*. He has been a Director of the American Finance Association, the Computer Applications Committee and the Investment Technology Symposium, both of the New York Society of Security Analysts. He was formerly Department editor for Finance of Management Science. Professor Gruber has consulted in the areas of Investment Analysis and Portfolio Management with many major financial institutions.

Preface

This book, as the title suggests, is concerned with the characteristics and analysis of individual securities as well as with the theory and practice of optimally combining securities into portfolios. The first and longest part of the book discusses modern portfolio theory. We begin with a detailed presentation of the theory of modern portfolio analysis and show that the characteristics of portfolios are significantly different from those of the individual securities from which they are formed. In fact, portfolio analysis is the recipe for one of the few "free lunches" in economics. By the end of Chapter 4, the reader will have learned the basis of portfolio theory from the relationship of portfolio characteristics to security characteristics to the method of computing sets of portfolios that investors will find desirable.

Although the theory presented at the beginning of the book is relatively new (any economic theory less than 30 years old is new!), it has been around long enough so that major breakthroughs have occurred in its implementation. These involve simplification of the amount and type of inputs to the portfolio problem (Chapters 5 and 6) as well as simplification of the computational procedure to find sets of desirable portfolios (Chapter 7). The major advantage in the latter simplification is that the portfolio selection process and the final portfolios selected have a structure that has a clear-cut economic rationale; one to which both the practicing security analyst and economist can relate.

The reader might note that up to now we have discussed sets of portfolios. These sets contain portfolios that would be desirable to any investor. Chapters 8 and 9 examine how an individual investor might choose the one optimal portfolio (for him or her) from among the sets of portfolios designed to appeal to any investor. We conclude Part 1 with a discussion of the potential benefits derived from diversifying portfolios internationally.

Part 2 is concerned with a discussion of equilibrium in the capital markets. This material usually is included under the rubric of the capital asset pricing model or arbitrage pricing theory and shows how portfolio theory can be used to infer what equilibrium returns and prices will be for individual securities. Much of the theory here is new and knowledge in this area is changing rapidly. But, as the reader will see, empirical tests suggest that the theory as it now stands provides great insight into the functioning of security markets and the pricing of individual issues.

The third part of this book deals with the characteristics and evaluation of individual securities. In this section we discuss whether security markets are efficient, the valuation of common stocks, the characteristics of earnings and their role in the valuation process, the valuation of bonds, the nature and valuation of options and finally, the valuation and uses of futures.

The final part of the book is a discussion of the evaluation of the investment analysis and portfolio management process. In writing this section we have stressed techniques for evaluating every stage of the process from the forecasting of earnings by security analysts to the performance of portfolios that are finally selected. It seems fitting that a book that deals primarily with investment analysis and portfolio management should end with a discussion of how to tell if these functions are performed well.

The book was designed to serve as a text for courses both in portfolio theory and in investment analysis that have a heavy emphasis on portfolio theory. We have used it for these purposes at New York University for several years. For the course in portfolio analysis we use the first 14 chapters plus Chapter 22. This thoroughly introduces the student to modern portfolio theory and general equilibrium or capital asset pricing models.

The book can also be used in a course in investments where both portfolio analysis and security analysis are discussed. For these purposes the security analysis chapters of Part 3, as well as Chapter 23 on the Evaluation of Security Analysis are appropriate, and some of the advanced portfolio theory and general equilibrium chapters of Part 1 and 2 can be deleted. Each professor's preference and the dictates of the course will ultimately determine the final choice. One possible choice that has been successfully utilized was the replacement of much of Chapter 4 and Chapters 6, 9, 12, 13, and 14 with the chapters on security analysis contained in Part 3. Courses covering portfolio theory and investments vary greatly in their content. We have included in this book those areas that we view as most relevant. Depending on the level and type of course being taught, the reader might well wish to supplement this book with descriptive material on securities or markets.

We believe that this book will be an aid to the practicing security analyst and portfolio manager. It is remarkable how quickly the ideas of modern portfolio theory have found their way into investment practice. The manager who wishes an overview of modern portfolio theory and investment analysis will find that Chapters 1, 2, 3, 5, 7, 10, and 15 through 23 will provide a thorough and readable understanding of the issues. Specialists who are concerned with issues on implementation will find that the other chapters will equip them with the most modern tools available.

As the reader may know, New York University not only has the normal M.B.A. and undergraduate student, but also has courses intended for full-time portfolio managers and security analysts. The professional reader can be assured that the book has been utilized in these courses and that some of our most enthusiastic responses came from the practicing manager who learned not only the ideas of modern portfolio theory and investment analysis but also its strengths and weaknesses.

In writing this book we have attempted to make all the material accessible to students of portfolio analysis and investment management, both at the undergraduate and graduate levels. To the extent possible, the text stresses the economic intuition behind the subject matter. Mathematical proofs involving more than simple algebra are placed in footnotes, appendixes, or specially noted sections of the text. They can be deleted without losing the general thrust of the subject matter. In addition, we have included problems both in the text and at the end of each chapter. We have tried to capture in this book the frontier of the state of the art of modern portfolio analysis, general equilibrium theory, and investment analysis while presenting it in a form that is accessible and has intuitive appeal.

A book must, of necessity, present material in a certain order. We have tried to present the material so that much of it can be used in alternative sequences. For example, we tend to teach formal utility analysis after many of the concepts of portfolio analysis. However, we realize that many professors prefer to begin with a discussion of utility analysis. Thus, this chapter in particular could be read immediately after the introductory chapter.

Many people have helped with the preparation of this book. We owe a lot to our students who suffered through early versions and helped find many errors. Excellent reviews of the entire manuscript were prepared by Nancy Jacob of the University of Washington, Charles Jones of North Carolina State, Dorothy Koehl of Maryland, and Richard McEnally of the University of North Carolina. Reviews and suggestions on individual chapters were provided by Bob Klemkosky at Indiana, Don Tuttle at Indiana, Joel Rentzler at Columbia, Jerry Levine at Temple, Maurice Joy at Kansas, Richard Kolodny at Maryland, Cheol S. Eun at Maryland, Bob Ferguson at L.O.R. Associates, Ron Singer at Houston, Ed Friedmann at City College of New York, and Jim Farrell at MPT Associates. Many of our own colleagues at New York University helped with the manuscript. We would like to thank Steve Figlewski, Tom Ho, Avner Kalay, Jerry Kallberg, Mike Keenan, Richard Levich, Prafulla Nabar, Marti Subrahmanyam, Mustafa Gultekin, now at North Carolina, and Ramasastry Ambarish, now at Wisconsin. In addition we would like to thank Jack Shelton at U.C.L.A., Gregg Brauer at Iowa, and Tom Conine at Fairfield University for help in eliminating many errors that were contained in the first printing. Ed Blomeyer of Louisiana State, Cheol Eun of Maryland, Stuart Wood of Tulane, Bob Klemkosky of Indiana, Gabriel Hawawini of INSEAD, Virgil Brewer of Eastern Kentucky University, and Joseph Liberman of the University of Illinois at Chicago Circle all provided helpful comments for the revision.

We would like to thank four of our doctoral students, Kirk Vandezande, Finbarr Bradley, Steve Freund, and Seth Grossman for special help with the manuscript. In addition, we owe special thanks to Anna F. Acocella, whose help in deciphering notes and typing this manuscript we greatly appreciate. Finally, we wish to thank Dr. Watson. We have noted her contribution to utility analysis and security valuation in previous books. Her contribution to early versions of this book were substantial. Her untimely death meant that we did not have the benefit of her excellent advice on the final version.

E.J. Elton
M.J. Gruber

A Brief Note on the Third Edition

In revising the second edition we have added one new chapter on the valuation and uses of financial futures. In addition, we have substantially rewritten eight other chapters to recognize advances in the literature and to make them more readable.

Contents

MODERN PORTFOLIO THEORY AND INVESTMENT ANALYSIS

Chapter 1
Introduction

Almost everyone owns a portfolio (group) of assets. This portfolio is likely to contain real assets such as a car, a house, or a refrigerator, as well as financial assets such as stocks and bonds. The composition of the portfolio may be the result of a series of haphazard and unrelated decisions or it may be the result of deliberate planning. In this book we discuss the basic principles underlying rational portfolio choice and what this means for prices determined in the marketplace. We confine our attention to financial assets, although much of the analysis we develop is equally applicable to real assets.

An investor is faced with a choice from among an enormous number of assets. When one considers the number of possible assets and the various possible proportions in which each can be held, the decision process seems overwhelming. In the first part of this book we analyze how decision makers can structure their problems so that they are left with a manageable number of alternatives. Later sections of the book deal with rational choice among these alternatives, methods for implementing and controlling the decision process, and equilibrium conditions in the capital markets to which the previous analysis leads.

Let us examine the composition of this book in more detail.

OUTLINE OF THE BOOK

This book is divided into five parts. The first and longest part deals with the subject of portfolio analysis. Portfolio analysis is concerned with finding the most desirable group of securities to hold, given the properties of each of the securities. This part of the book is itself divided into four sections. The first of these sections is entitled "Mean Variance Portfolio Theory." This section deals with determining the properties of combinations (portfolios) of risky assets given the properties of the individual assets, delineating the characteristics of portfolios that make them preferable to others, and, finally, showing how the composition of the preferred portfolios can be determined.

At the end of this section the reader will know almost all that he needs to know about the theory of portfolio selection. This theory is almost 30 years old. In the ensuing years, a tremendous amount of work has been devoted to implementing this theory. The second section of Part 1 is concerned with the implementation and simplification of portfolio theory. The topics covered include simplifying the quantity and type of input needed to do portfolio analysis, and simplifying the computational procedure used to find the composition of the efficient portfolios.

The third section of Part 1 deals with the selection of that one portfolio that best meets the needs of an investor. This section has two chapters. The first one discusses selection from the viewpoint of maximizing expected utility. This concept should be familiar to any student who has had a basic course in economics. The second chapter discusses alternative ways to select the best alternative. The assumption here is that the investor will not go through the arithmetic of expected utility maximization, but will employ one of the alternative and simpler decision-making criteria suggested in the economic literature.

The final section of Part 1 deals with the impact of the opportunity to diversify a stock portfolio across international boundaries. As the reader might suspect, any increase in the set of possible investment opportunities should increase portfolio performance.

Part 2 deals with models of equilibrium prices and returns in the capital markets. If investors behave as portfolio theory suggests they should, then their actions can be aggregated to determine prices at which securities will sell.

The first two chapters of Part 2 deal with alternative forms of equilibrium relationships. Different assumptions about the characteristics of capital markets and the way investors behave lead to different models of equilibrium. The final chapter in this part of the book deals with empirical tests of how well these theoretical models describe reality.

The third part of the book deals with some issues in investment analysis. The first question examined is the speed with which new information is incorporated into the share price. If new information is immediately and accurately incorporated into the share price, then there can be no payoff from security analysis, while if information is more slowly incorporated into the share price, it may pay to engage in certain types of analysis. The key to security analysis is the method used to turn forecasts of fundamental firm characteristics into forecasts of price performance. This is the subject of the second chapter in Part 3, entitled "Valuation Process." Virtually every valuation process employs forecasts of earnings as one important input. A detailed analysis of earnings is presented as an example of methods of forecasting inputs to valuation models. The final two chapters in Part 3 deal with the valuation of options and financial futures. The markets for security options and for futures are among the fastest growing markets in the country. In addition, the theory of option pricing has important implications for generating the inputs to portfolio analysis. Futures, because of their low transaction costs, are an important tool for modifying portfolio composition.

The fourth part of the book is concerned with evaluating the investment process. The first chapter in this section deals with the evaluation of portfolio performance. In this chapter we discuss the best methods of evaluating portfolio performance and how well-managed portfolios have performed. In contrast to the voluminous literature on portfolio performance, almost nothing has been written about how to evaluate the other steps in the investment process. For example, very little has been written about how to evaluate forecasts of security analysts or how to evaluate the valuation process. The second chapter in this part of the book deals with these problems. The final part of the book integrates the material contained in the earlier parts.

THE ECONOMIC THEORY OF CHOICE: AN ILLUSTRATION UNDER CERTAINTY

All decision problems have certain elements in common. Any problem involves the delineation of alternatives, the selection of criteria for choosing among those alternatives, and, finally, the solution of the problem. Futhermore, individual solutions can often be aggregated to describe equilibrium conditions that prevail in the marketplace. A large part of this book will be concerned with following these steps for the selection of risky assets. But before we start this problem, let us examine a simpler one, under certainty, to illustrate the elements of the solution to any economic problem.

Consider an investor who will receive with certainty an income of $10,000 in each of two years. Assume that the only investment available is a savings account yielding 5% per year. In addition, the investor can borrow money at a 5% rate.

How much should the investor save and how much should he consume each year? The economic theory of choice proposes to solve this problem by splitting the analysis into two parts. First, specify those options that are available to the investor. Second, specify how to choose among these options. This framework for analysis carries over to more complex problems.

The Opportunity Set

The first part of the analysis is to determine the options open to the investor. One option available is to save nothing and consume $10,000 in each period. This option is indicated by the point B in Figure 1.1.

Scrooge would choose another option. He would save all income in the first period and consume everything in the second. In the second period his savings account would be worth the $10,000 he saved in period 1 plus interest of 5% on the $10,000 or $10,500. Adding this to his second-period income of $10,000 gives him a consumption in period 2 of $10,500 + $10,000 = $20,500. This is indicated by point A in Figure 1.1.

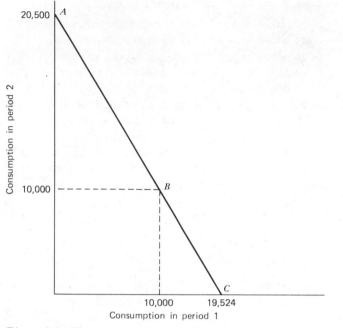

Figure 1.1   The investor's opportunity set.

Another possibility is to consume everything now and not worry about tomorrow. This would result in consumption of $10,000 from this period's income plus the maximum the investor could borrow against next period's income. If X is the amount borrowed, then X plus the interest paid for borrowing X equals the amount paid back. Since the investor's income in the second period is $10,000, the maximum amount is borrowed if X plus the interest on X at 5% equals $10,000.

$$X + 0.05X = 10,000$$

or

$$X = \frac{10,000}{1.05} = \$9,524$$

Thus, the maximum the investor can consume in the first period is $19,524. This is indicated by point C in Figure 1.1. Note that points A, B, and C lie along a straight line. This did not happen by accident. In fact, all of the enormous possible patterns of consumption in periods 1 and 2 will lie along this straight line. Let us see why.

The amount the investor consumes in the two periods is constrained by the amount of income the investor has available in the two periods. Let C_1 be the consumption in period 1 and C_2 be the consumption in period 2. The amount consumed in period 2 is the income in period 2 of $10,000 plus the period 2 value of the savings in period 1. Remember that the value of period 1 savings can be negative for the investor could have dissaved. That is, he could have borrowed in period 1 and consumed more than his period 1 income. As of period 2, the value of the savings in period 1 is the amount saved in period 1 ($10,000 minus what is consumed) plus accumulated interest. Putting this in equation form we have

$$\begin{bmatrix} \text{Period 2} \\ \text{consumption} \end{bmatrix} = \begin{bmatrix} \text{Period 2} \\ \text{income} \end{bmatrix} + \begin{bmatrix} \text{Amount} \\ \text{saved in 1} \end{bmatrix} \begin{bmatrix} 1 + 0.05 \end{bmatrix}$$

$$C_2 = \$10,000 + (10,000 - C_1)(1.05)$$

$$C_2 = \$20,500 - (1.05)C_1$$

This is, of course, the equation for a straight line and is the line shown in Figure 1.1. It has an intercept of $20,500, which results from zero consumption in period 1 ($C_1 = 0$) and is the point A we determined earlier. It has a slope equal to -1.05 or minus the quantity one plus the interest rate. The value of the slope reflects the fact that each dollar the investor consumes in period 1 is a dollar he cannot invest and, hence, reduces period 2 consumption by one dollar plus the interest he could earn on the dollar or a total of $1.05. Thus an increase in period 1's consumption of a dollar reduces period 2's consumption by $1.05.

The investor is left with a large number of choices. We usually refer to the set of choices facing the investor as the opportunity set. Let us now examine how an investor selects the optimum consumption pattern from the opportunity set.

The Indifference Curves

The economic theory of choice states that an investor chooses among the opportunities shown in Figure 1.1 by specifying a series of curves called utility functions or indifference curves. A representative set is shown in Figure 1.2. These curves represent the investor's preference for income in the two periods. The name "indifference curves" is used because the curves are constructed so that everywhere along the same curve the investor is assumed to be equally happy. In other words, the investor does not care whether he obtains point A, B, or C along curve I_1.

Choices along I_1 will be preferred to choices along I_2, and choices on I_2 will be preferred to choices on I_3, and so on. This ordering results from an assumption that the investor prefers more to less. Consider the line OM. Along this line the amount of consumption in period 1 is held constant. As can be seen from Figure 1.2, along the line representing equal consumption in period 1, I_1 represents the most consumption in period 2, I_2 the next most, and so on. Thus, if investors prefer more to less, I_1 dominates I_2, which dominates I_3.

The curved shape results from an assumption that each additional dollar of

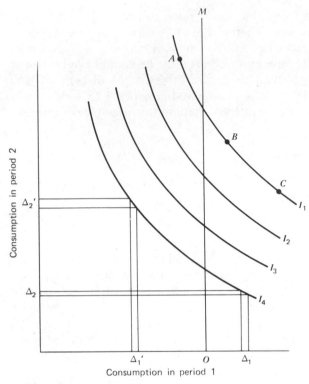

Figure 1.2 Indifference curves.

consumption forgone in period 1 requires greater consumption in 2. For example, if consumption in period 1 is large relative to consumption in period 2, the investor should be willing to give up a dollar of consumption in period 1 in return for a small increase in consumption in period 2. In Figure 1.2 this is illustrated by Δ_1 for the amount the investor gives up in period 1 and Δ_2 for the amount the investor gains in period 2. However, if the investor has very few dollars of consumption in period 1, then a large increase in 2 is required in order to be indifferent about giving up the extra consumption in period 1. This is represented by the Δ_1' in period 1 (which is the same size as Δ_1) and the Δ_2' in period 2, which is much larger than Δ_2.

The Solution

The indifference curves and the opportunity set represent the tools necessary for the investor to reach a solution. The optimum consumption pattern for the investor is determined by the point at which a member of the set of indifference curves is tangent to the opportunity set (point D in Figure 1.3). Let us see why. The investor can select either of the two consumption patterns indicated by the points where I_3 intersects the line ABC in Figure 1.3. But we have argued that the investor is better off selecting a consumption pattern lying on an indifference

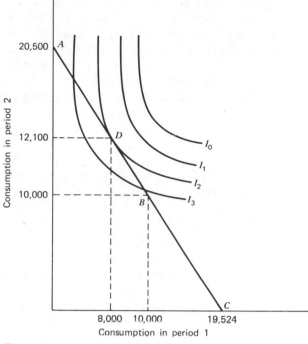

Figure 1.3   Investor equilibrium.

curve located above and to the right of I_3 if possible. The investor will move to higher indifference curves until the highest one that contains a feasible consumption pattern is reached. That is the one just tangent to the opportunity set. This is I_2 in Figure 1.3 and the consumption pattern the investor will choose is given by the point of tangency point D. The question might be asked why doesn't the investor move up to a point along I_0 since this would be preferable to a point along I_2. The answer is that there is no investment opportunity available on line I_0.

An Example: Determining Equilibrium Interest Rates

We take another look at the investor's possible decision to see how it can help in determining equilibrium conditions in the market. The optimum decision could occur in three sections of Figure 1.3: A to B, point B, or B to C. If the optimum occurs in the segment AB, then the investor lends money at the 5% rate. If the optimum occurs at point B, then the investor is neither a borrower nor a lender. Finally, if the optimum occurs in segment BC, the investor borrows against future income at the 5% rate.

In this simple framework, equilibrium in the marketplace is easy to determine. At a 5% interest rate this investor wishes to lend $2,000, the difference between $10,000 in income and $8,000 in consumption. Summing across all investors who wish to lend when the interest rate is 5% gives one point on the supply curve.

Similarly summing across investors who wish to borrow at a 5% interest rate gives one point on the demand curve. As the interest rate changes, the amount our hypothetical investor wishes to lend also changes. In fact, if the interest rate is low enough, the investor may change from a lender to a borrower. By varying the interest rate, the supply and demand curve can be traced out and the equilibrium interest rate determined. The equilibrium interest rate is that rate at which the amount investors wish to borrow is equal to the amount investors wish to lend. This is often called a "market clearing condition." The equilibrium interest rate depends on what each investor's decision problem looks like or the characteristics of a figure like 1.3 for each investor. Figure 1.3 depends on the investor's income in the two periods and his tastes or preferences. Thus, in this simple world, equilibrium interest rates are also determined by the same influences: investors' tastes and investors' income.

CONCLUSION

What we have learned from this simple example is the elements that are necessary to analyze a portfolio problem. We need two components to reach a solution: a representation of the choices available to the investor — called the opportunity set — and a representation of the investor's tastes or preferences — called indifference or utility curves. With these two components we solved this simple problem and can solve the more realistic problems that follow. In addition, this simple example taught us that by aggregating across investors we can construct models of equilibrium conditions in the capital markets. Now we turn to an examination of why and how this framework must be modified to deal realistically with multiple investment alternatives.

MULTIPLE ASSETS AND RISK

If everyone knew with certainty the returns on all assets, then the framework just presented could easily be extended to multiple assets. If a second asset existed that yielded 10%, then the opportunity set involving investment in this asset would be the line $A'BC'$ shown in Figure 1.4. Its intercept on the vertical axis would be $10,000 + (1.10)(10,000) = \$21,000$ and the slope would be $-(1.10)$. If such an asset existed, the investor would surely prefer it if lending and prefer the 5% asset if borrowing. The preferred opportunity set would be A', B, C. Additional assets could be added in a straightforward manner. But this situation is inherently unstable. Two assets yielding different certain returns cannot both be available since everyone will want to invest in the higher yielding one and no one will purchase the lower yielding one. We are left with two possibilities: either there is only one interest rate available in the marketplace or returns are not certain.[1] Since we observe many different interest rates, uncertainty must play

---

[1]Transaction costs, or alternative tax treatment of income from different securities, can explain the existence of some differential rates but nothing like the variety and magnitude of differentials found in the marketplace.

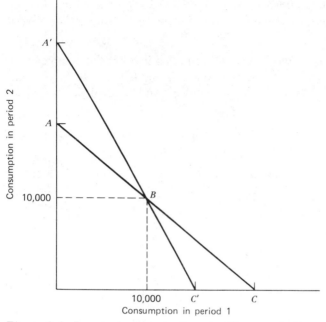

Figure 1.4   Investor's opportunity set with several alternatives.

an important role in the determination of market rates of return. To deal with
uncertainty, we need to develop a more complex opportunity set.

   The remainder of this book is concerned with the development of the framework necessary to solve the more complex asset choice problems in the presence
of risk. In the next two chapters we deal with the basic notions of the investor's
opportunity set under risk.

QUESTIONS AND PROBLEMS

1. Walking down an unfamiliar street one day, you come across an old-fashioned
   candy store. They have red hots 5 for 1 penny, and rock candy — 1 small
   piece for one penny. You decide to purchase some for yourself and your
   friends, but you find that you only have $1.00 in your pocket. Construct your
   opportunity set both geometrically and algebraically. Draw in your indifference map (set of indifference curves). Explain why you have drawn your
   indifference curves as you have drawn them.

2. Let us solve a two-period consumption investment decision similar to the
   one presented in the text. Assume that you have income equal to $20 in each
   of two periods. Furthermore, you have the ability to both lend and borrow
   money at a 10% rate. Draw the opportunity set and your indifference map.
   Show the optimum amount of consumption in each period.

3. Assume you can lend and borrow at 10% and have $5,000 in income in each
   of two periods. What is your opportunity set?

4. Assume you can lend and borrow at 5% and have $20,000 in income in each of two periods. Further assume you have current wealth of $50,000. What is your opportunity set?

5. An individual has two employment opportunities involving the same work conditions, but different incomes. Job 1 yields $Y_1 = 50$, $Y_2 = 30$. Job 2 yields $Y_1 = 40$, $Y_2 = 40$. Given that markets are perfect and bonds yield 5%, which should be selected?

6. Assume you have income of $5,000 in each of two periods and can lend at 10% but pay 20% on borrowing. What is your opportunity set?

7. Assume your preference function P is $P = C_1 + C_2 + C_1C_2$. Plot the location of all points with $P = 50$, $P = 100$.

8. In Problem 3 what is the preferred choice if the preference function discussed in Problem 7 holds?

BIBLIOGRAPHY

1. Hirshleifer, Jack. *Investment, Interest, and Capital.* (Englewood Cliffs, N.J.: Prentice-Hall, 1969).
2. Markowitz, Harry. *Portfolio Selection: Efficient Diversification of Investments.* (New York: John Wiley & Sons, 1959).
3. Sharpe, William. *Portfolio Theory and Capital Markets.* (New York: McGraw-Hill, 1970).

PART 1
PORTFOLIO ANALYSIS

SECTION 1
Mean Variance Portfolio Theory

Chapter 2

The Characteristics of the Opportunity Set Under Risk

In Chapter 1 we introduced the elements of a decision problem under certainty. The same elements are present when we recognize the existence of risk; however, their formulation becomes more complex. This is the first of two chapters dealing with the opportunity set under risk. We start by characterizing the nature of the opportunities open to the investor.

In the certainty case the investor's decision problem can be characterized by a certain outcome. In the problem analyzed in the previous chapter, the 5% return on lending (or the 5% cost of borrowing) was known with certainty. Under risk, the outcome of any action is not known with certainty and outcomes are usually represented by a frequency function. A frequency function is a listing of all possible outcomes along with the probability of the occurrence of each. Table 2.1 shows such a function. This investment has three possible returns. If event 1 occurs, the investor receives a return of 12%; if event 2 occurs, 9% is received; and if event 3 occurs, 6% is received. In our examples each of these events is assumed to be equally likely. Table 2.1 shows us everything there is to know about the return possibilities.

Table 2.1

Return	Probability	Event
12	$\frac{1}{3}$	1
9	$\frac{1}{3}$	2
6	$\frac{1}{3}$	3

Usually we do not delineate all of the possibilities as we have in Table 2.1. The possibilities for real assets are sufficiently numerous that developing a table like Table 2.1 for each asset is too complex a task. Furthermore, even if the investor decided to develop such tables, the inaccuracies introduced would be so large that he would probably be better off just trying to represent the possible outcomes in terms of some summary measures. In general, it takes at least two measures to capture the relevant information about a frequency function: one to measure the average value and one to measure dispersion around the average value.

DETERMINING THE AVERAGE OUTCOME

The concept of an average is standard in our culture. Pick up the newspaper and you will often see figures on average income, batting averages, or average crime rates. The concept of an average is intuitive. If someone earns $11,000 one year and $9,000 in a second, we say his average income in the two years is $10,000. If three children in a family are age 15, 10, and 5, then we say the average age is 10. In Table 2.1 the average return was 9%. Statisticians usually use the term "expected value" to refer to what is commonly called an average. In this book we use both terms.

An expected value or average is easy to compute. If all outcomes are equally likely, then to determine the average, one adds up the outcomes and divides by the number of outcomes. Thus, for Table 2.1 the average is $(12 + 9 + 6)/3 = 9$. A second way to determine an average is to multiply each outcome by the probability that it will occur. When the outcomes are not equally likely, this facilitates the calculation. Applying this procedure to Table 2.1 yields $\frac{1}{3}(12) + \frac{1}{3}(9) + \frac{1}{3}(6) = 9$.

It is useful to express this intuitive calculation in terms of formula. The symbol Σ should be read sum. Underneath the symbol we put the first value in the sum and what is varying. On the top of the symbol we put the final value in the sum. We use the symbol R_{ij} to denote the jth possible outcome for the return on security i. Thus,

$$\frac{\sum_{j=1}^{3} R_{ij}}{3} = \frac{R_{i1} + R_{i2} + R_{i3}}{3} = \frac{12 + 9 + 6}{3}$$

Using the summation notation just introduced and a bar over a variable to indicate expected return, we have for the expected value of the M equally likely returns for asset i

$$\overline{R}_i = \sum_{j=1}^{M} \frac{R_{ij}}{M}$$

If the observations are not equally likely and if P_{ij} is the probability of the jth return on the ith asset, then expected return is[1]

$$\overline{R}_i = \sum_{j=1}^{M} P_{ij}R_{ij}$$

We have up to this point used a bar over a symbol to indicate expected value. This is the procedure we adopt throughout most of this book. However, occasionally, this notation proves awkward. An alternative method of indicating expected value is to put the symbol E in front of the expression for which we wish to determine the expected value. Thus $E(R_i)$ should be read as the expected value of R_{ij} just as $\overline{R}_i$ is the expected value of R_{ij}.

Certain properties of expected value are extremely useful. These properties are:

1. The expected value of the sum of two returns is equal to the sum of the expected value of each return, that is,

$$E(R_{1j} + R_{2j}) = \overline{R}_1 + \overline{R}_2$$

2. The expected value of a constant "C" times a return is the constant times the expected return, that is,

$$E[C(R_{1j})] = C\overline{R}_1$$

These principles are illustrated in Table 2.2 For any event the return on asset 3 is the sum of the return on assets 1 and 2. Thus, the expected value of the return on asset 3 is the sum of the expected value of the return on assets 1 and 2. Likewise, for any event the return on asset 3 is three times the return on asset 1. Consequently, its expected value is three times as large as the expected value of asset 1.

These two properties of expected values will be used repeatedly and are worth remembering.

Table 2.2 Return on Various Assets

Event	Probability	Asset 1	Asset 2	Asset 3
A	⅓	14	28	42
B	⅓	10	20	30
C	⅓	6	12	18
	Expected Return	10	20	30

---

[1]This latter formula includes the formula for equally likely observations as a special case. If we have M observations each equally likely, then the odds of any one occurring are $1/M$. Replacing the P_{ij} in the second formula by $1/M$ yields the first formula.

A MEASURE OF DISPERSION

Not only is it necessary to have a measure of the average return, it is also useful to have some measure of how much the observations differ from the average. The need for this second characteristic can be illustrated by the old story of the mathematician who believed an average by itself was an adequate description of a process and drowned in a stream with an average depth of two inches.

Intuitively a sensible way to measure how much the observations differ from the average is simply to examine this difference directly; that is, examine $R_{ij} - \overline{R}_i$. Having determined this for each observation, one could obtain an overall measure by taking the average of this difference. Although this is intuitively sensible, there is a problem. Some of the differences will be positive and some negative and these will tend to cancel out. The result of the canceling could be such that the average difference for a highly variable return need be no larger than the average difference for an asset with a highly stable return. In fact, it can be shown that the average value of this difference must always be precisely zero. The reader is encouraged to verify this with the example in Table 2.2. Thus, the sum of the differences from the mean tells us nothing about dispersion.

Two solutions to this problem suggest themselves. First, we could take absolute values of the difference between an observation and its mean by ignoring minus signs when determining the average difference. Second, since the square of any number is positive, we could square all differences before determining the average. For ease of computation, when portfolios are considered, the latter procedure is generally followed. In addition, as we will see when we discuss utility functions, the average squared deviations have some convenient properties.[2] The average squared deviation is called the variance, and the square root of the variance is called the standard deviation. In Table 2.3 we present the possible returns from several hypothetical assets as well as the variance of the return on each asset. The alternative returns on any asset are assumed equally likely. Examining asset 1, we find the deviations of its returns from its average return are $(15 - 9)$, $(9 - 9)$, and $(3 - 9)$. The squared deviations are 36, 0, and 36, and the average squared deviation or variance is $(36 + 0 + 36)/3 = 24$.

To be precise, the formula for the variance of the return on the ith asset (which we symbolize as σ_i^2) when each return is equally likely is[3]

$$\sigma_i^2 = \sum_{j=1}^{M} \frac{(R_{ij} - \overline{R}_i)^2}{M}$$

---

[2]Many utility functions can be expressed either exactly or approximately in terms of the mean and variance. Futhermore, regardless of the investor's utility function, if returns are normally distributed, the mean and variance contain all relevant information about the distribution. An elaboration of these points is contained in later chapters.

[3]Sometimes the formula is divided by M and sometimes it is divided by $M - 1$. The choice is a matter of taste. However, the reader may be curious why some choose one or the other. The technical reason authors choose one or the other is as follows. σ_i^2 calculated above is an estimate of the true

If the observations are not equally likely, then, as before, we multiply by the probability with which they occur. The formula for the variance of the return on the ith asset becomes

$$\sigma_i^2 = \sum_{j=1}^{M} P_{ij}(R_{ij} - \overline{R}_i)^2$$

Occasionally, we will find it convenient to employ an alternative measure of dispersion called standard deviation. The standard deviation is just the square root of the variance and is designated by σ_i.

The variance tells us that asset 3 varies considerably more from its average than asset 2. This is what we intuitively see by examining the returns shown in Table 2.3. The expected value and variance or standard deviation are the usual summary statistics utilized in describing a frequency distribution.

There are other measures of dispersion that could be used. We have already mentioned one, the average absolute deviation. Other measures have been suggested. One such measure considers only deviations below the mean. The argument is that returns above the average return are desirable. The only returns that disturb an investor are those below average. A measure of this is the average (over all observations) of the squared deviations below the mean. For example, in Table 2.3 for asset 1 the only return below the mean is 3. Since 3 is 6 below the mean, the square of the difference is 36. The other two returns are not below the mean so they have 0 deviation below the mean. The average of (0) + (0) + (36) is 12. This measure is called the semivariance.

Intuitively, the semivariance is a reasonable measure and some portfolio theory has been developed using it. However, it is difficult to use when we move from single assets to portfolios. Furthermore, since empirical evidence shows most assets existing in the market have returns that are reasonably symmetrical, semivariance is not needed. If returns on an asset are symmetrical, the semivariance is proportional to the variance. Thus, in most of the portfolio literature the variance or, equivalently, the standard deviation is used as a measure of dispersion.

In most cases, instead of using the full frequency function such as that presented in Table 2.1, we use the summary statistics mean and variance or equivalent mean and standard deviation to characterize the distribution. Consider two assets. How might we decide which we prefer? First, intuitively one would think that most investors would prefer the one with the higher expected return if standard deviation was held constant. Thus, in Table 2.3 most investors would prefer asset

---

value based on sample evidence. Employing M as the denominator gave the best estimate of the true value or the so-called maximum likelihood estimate. Although it is the best estimate as M gets large, it does not converge to the true value (it is too small). Dividing by $M - 1$ produces a σ_i^2 that converges to the true value as M gets large (technically unbiased) but is not the best estimate for a finite M. Some people consider one of these properties more important than the other while some use one without consciously realizing why this might be preferred.

Handwritten notes:

$(16-10)$ $(16-10)^2 =$ 36
$(10-10)$ $(10-10)^2 =$ 0
$(4-10)$ $(4-10)^2 =$ 36

.58   1.16
.55   1.10
.52   1.09

.624
.476

Table 2.3 Returns on Various Investments[a]

| | Asset 1 | | Asset 2 | | Asset 3 | | Asset 4 | | Asset 5 | |
	Market Condition	Return	Market Condition	Return	Market Condition	Return	Rainfall	Return	Condition of Market	Return
	Good	15	Good	16	Good	1	Plentiful	16	Good	16
	Average	9	Average	10	Average	10	Average	10	Average	10
	Poor	3	Poor	4	Poor	19	Poor	4	Poor	4
Mean Return		9		10		10		10		10
Variance		24		24		54		24		24
Standard Deviation		4.90		4.90		7.35		4.90		4.90

[a]The alternative returns on each asset are assumed equally likely and, thus, each has a probability of ⅓.

2 to asset 1. Similarly, if expected return were held constant, investors would prefer the one with the lower variance. This is reasonable because the smaller the variance the more certain an investor is that she will obtain the expected return and the fewer poor outcomes she has to contend with.[4] Thus, in Table 2.3 the investor would prefer asset 2 to asset 3.

VARIANCE OF COMBINATIONS OF ASSETS

This simple analysis has taken us part way toward an understanding of the choice between risky assets. However, the options open to an investor are not to simply pick between assets 1, 2, 3, 4, or 5 in Table 2.3 but also to consider combinations of these five assets. For example, an investor could invest part of his money in each asset. While this opportunity vastly increases the number of options open to the investor and hence the complexity of the problem, it also provides the raison d'être of portfolio theory. The risk of a combination of assets is very different from a simple average of the risk of individual assets. Most dramatically, the variance of a combination of two assets may be less than the variance of either of the assets themselves. In Table 2.4 there is combination of asset 2 and asset 3 that is less risky than asset 2.

Let us examine this property. Assume an investor has $1 to invest. If he selects asset 2 and the market is good, he will have at the end of the period $1 + 0.16 = $1.16. If the market's performance is average, he will have $1.10, and if it is poor $1.04. These outcomes are summarized in Table 2.4 along with the corresponding values for the third asset. Consider an alternative. Suppose the investor invests $0.60 in asset 2 and $0.40 in asset 3. If the condition of the market is good, the investor will have $0.696 at the end of the period from asset 2 and $0.404 from asset 3, or $1.10. If the market conditions are average, he will recieve $0.66 from asset 2, $0.44 from asset 3, or a total of $1.10. By now the reader might suspect that if the market condition is poor the investor still receives $1.10, and this is, of course, the case. If the market condition is poor the investor receives $0.624 from his investment in 2 and $0.476 from his investment in asset 3, or $1.10. These possibilities are summarized in Table 2.4.

Table 2.4 Dollars at Period 2 Given Alternative Investments

Condition of Market	Asset 2	Asset 3	Combination of Asset 2 (60%) and Asset 3 (40%)
Good	$1.16	$1.01	$1.10
Average	1.10	1.10	1.10
Poor	1.04	1.19	1.10

[4]We will not formally develop the criteria for making a choice from among risky opportunities until the next chapter. However, we feel we are not violating common sense by assuming at this time that investors prefer more to less and act as risk avoiders. More formal statements of the properties of investor choice will be taken up in the next chapter.

   This example dramatically illustrates how the risk on a portfolio of assets can differ from the risk of the individual assets. The deviations on the combination of the assets was zero because the assets had their highest and lowest returns under opposite market conditions. This result is perfectly general and not confined to this example. When two assets have their good and poor returns at opposite times, an investor can always find *some* combination of these assets that yields the same return under all market conditions. This example illustrates the importance of considering combinations of assets rather than just the assets themselves and shows how the distribution of outcomes on combinations of assets can be different than the distributions on the individual assets.

   The returns on asset 2 and asset 4 have been developed to illustrate another possible situation. Asset 4 has three possible returns. Which return occurs depends on rainfall. Assuming that the amount of rainfall that occurs is independent of the condition of the market, then the returns on the assets 2 and 4 are independent of one another. Therefore, if the rainfall is plentiful we can have good, average, or poor security markets. Plentiful rainfall does not change the likelihood of any particular market condition occurring. Consider an investor with $1.00 who invests $0.50 in each asset. If rain is plentiful he receives $0.58 from his investment in asset 4, and any one of three equally likely outcomes from his investment in asset 2: $0.58 if the market is good, $0.55 if it is average, and $0.52 if the market is poor. This gives him a total of $1.16, $1.13, or $1.10. Similarly, if the rainfall is average, the value of his investment in asset 2 and 4 is $1.13, $1.10, or $1.07, and if rainfall is poor, $1.10, $1.07, or $1.04. Since we have assumed that each possible level of rainfall is equally likely as is each possible condition of the market, there are nine equally likely outcomes. Ordering then from highest to lowest we have $1.16, $1.13, $1.13, $1.10, $1.10, $1.10, $1.07, $1.07, and $1.04. Compare this to an investment in asset 2 by itself, the results of which are shown in Table 2.3. The mean is the same. However, the dispersion around the mean is less. This can be seen by direct examination and by noting that the probability of one of the extreme outcomes occurring ($1.16 or $1.04) has dropped from ⅓ to ⅑.

   This example once again shows how the characteristics of the portfolio can be very different than the characteristics of the assets that comprise the portfolio. The example illustrates a general principle. When the returns on assets are independent such as the returns on assets 2 and 4, a portfolio of such assets can have less dispersion than either asset.

   Consider still a third situation, one with a different outcome than the previous two. Consider an investment in assets 2 and 5. Assume the investor invests $0.50 in asset 2 and $0.50 in asset 5. The value of his investment at the end of the period is $1.16, $1.10, or $1.04. These are the same values he would have obtained if he invested the entire $1.00 in either asset 2 or asset 5 (See Table 2.3). Thus, in this situation the characteristics of the portfolios were exactly the same as the characteristics of the individual assets, and holding a portfolio rather than the individual assets did not change the investor's risk.

   We have analyzed three extreme situations. As extremes they dramatically illustrated some general principles that carry over to less extreme situations. Our first example showed that when assets have their good and bad outcomes at different times (assets 2 and 3), then investment in these assets can radically reduce the dispersion obtained by investing in one of the assets by itself. If the good outcomes of an asset are not always associated with the bad outcomes of a second asset, but the general tendency is in this direction, then the reduction in dispersion still occurs but the dispersion will not drop all the way to zero as it did in our example. However, it is still often true that appropriately selected combinations of the two assets will have less risk than the least risky of the two assets.

Our second example illustrated the situation where the conditions leading to various returns were different for the two assets. More formally, this is the area where returns are independent. Once again, dispersion was reduced but not in as drastic a fashion. Note that investment in asset 2 alone can result in a return of $1.04 and that this result occurs ⅓ of the time. The same result can occur when we invested an equal amount in asset 2 and asset 4. However, a combination of asset 2 and 4 has nine possible outcomes, each equally likely, and $1.04 occurs only ⅑ of the time. With independent returns, extreme observations can still occur. They just occur less frequently. Just as the extreme values occur less frequently, outcomes closer to the mean become more likely so that the frequency function has less dispersion.

Finally, our third example illustrated the situation where the assets being combined had their outcomes affected in the same way by the same events. In this case, the characteristics of the portfolio were identical to the characteristics of the individual assets. In less extreme cases this is no longer true. Insofar as the good and bad returns on assets tend to occur at the same time, but not always exactly at the same time, the dispersion on the portfolio of assets is somewhat reduced relative to the dispersion on the individual assets.

We have shown with some simple examples how the characteristics of the return on portfolios of assets can differ from the characteristics of the returns on individual assets. These were artificial examples designed to dramatically illustrate the point. To reemphasize this point it is worthwhile examining portfolios of some real securities over a historical period.

Three securities were selected: IBM, General Motors, and Alcoa Aluminum. The monthly returns, average return, and standard deviation from investing in each security is shown in Table 2.5. In addition, the return and risk of placing one half of the available funds in each pair of securities is shown in the table. Finally, we have plotted the returns from each possible pair of securities in Figure 2.1. In this figure we have the return from each of two securities as well as the return from placing one half of the available funds in each security. Both Figures 2.1 and the Table 2.5 make it clear how diversification across real securities can have a tremendous payoff for the investor. For example, a portfolio composed of 50% IBM and 50% Alcoa had the same return as each stock but less risk than either stock over the period studied. Earlier we argued that an investor is better off working with summary characteristics rather than full frequency functions.

Table 2.5 Monthly Returns on IBM, Alcoa, and GM (in percent)

	R_1	R_2	R_3	R_4	R_5	R_6	R_7	R_8	R_9	R_{10}	R_{11}	R_{12}	$\overline{R}$	σ
IBM	12.05	15.27	-4.12	1.57	3.16	-2.79	-8.97	-1.18	1.07	12.75	7.48	-.94	2.95	7.15
Alcoa	14.09	2.96	7.19	24.39	0.06	6.52	-8.75	2.82	-13.97	-8.06	-0.7	8.80	2.95	10.06
GM	25.20	2.86	5.45	4.56	3.72	0.29	5.38	-2.97	1.52	10.75	3.79	1.32	5.16	6.83
½ IBM + ½ Alcoa	13.07	9.12	1.54	12.98	1.61	1.87	-8.86	0.82	-6.45	2.35	3.39	3.93	2.95	6.32
½ GM + ½ Alcoa	19.65	2.91	6.32	14.48	1.89	3.41	-1.69	-0.08	-6.23	1.35	1.55	5.06	4.05	6.69
½ GM + ½ IBM	18.63	9.07	0.67	3.07	3.44	-1.25	-1.80	-2.08	1.30	11.75	5.64	0.19	4.05	6.02

Correlation Coefficient: IBM and Alcoa = 0.05; GM and Alcoa = 0.22; IBM and GM = 0.48

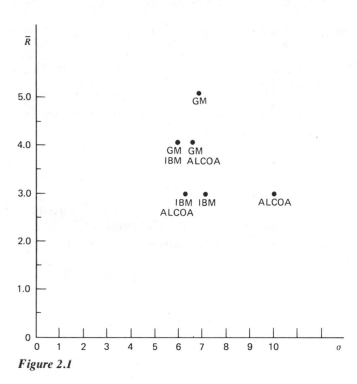

Figure 2.1

We used two summary measures: average return and variance or standard deviation of return. We will now examine analytically how the summary characteristics of a portfolio are related to those of individual assets.

CHARACTERISTICS OF PORTFOLIOS IN GENERAL

The return on a portfolio of assets is simply a weighted average of the return on the individual assets. The weight applied to each return is the fraction of the portfolio invested in that asset. If R_{Pj} is the jth return on the portfolio and X_i is the fraction of the investor's funds invested in the ith asset, then

$$R_{Pj} = \sum_{i=1}^{N} X_i R_{ij}$$

The expected return is also a weighted average of the expected returns on the individual assets. Taking the expected value of the expression just given for the return on a portfolio yields

$$\bar{R}_P = E(R_P) = E\left(\sum_{i=1}^{N} X_i R_{ij}\right)$$

But we already know that the expected value of the sum of various returns is the sum of the expected values. Therefore, we have

$$\bar{R}_P = \sum_{i=1}^{N} E(X_i R_{ij})$$

Finally, the expected value of a constant times a return is a constant times the expected return, or

$$\bar{R}_P = \sum_{i=1}^{N} X_i \bar{R}_i$$

This is a perfectly general formula and we use it throughout the book. To illustrate its use, consider the investment in assets 2 and 3 discussed earlier in Table 2.3. We determined that no matter what occurred, the investor would receive \$1.10 on an investment of \$1.00. This is a return of $0.10/1.00 = 10\%$.

Let us apply the formula for expected return. In the example discussed earlier, \$0.60 was invested in asset 2 and \$0.40 in asset 4; therefore, the fraction invested in asset 4 is $0.40/1.00$. Furthermore, the expected return on asset 2 and asset 4 is 10%. Applying the formula for expected return on a portfolio yields

$$\bar{R}_P = \left(\frac{0.60}{1.00}\right)(0.10) + \left(\frac{0.40}{1.00}\right)(0.10) = 0.10$$

The second summary characteristic was the variance. The variance on a portfolio is a little more difficult to determine than the expected return. We start out with a two-asset example. The variance of a portfolio P, designated by σ_P^2, is simply the expected value of the squared deviations of the return on the portfolio from the mean return on the portfolio, or $\sigma_P^2 = E(R_p - \bar{R}_P)^2$. Substituting in this expression the formulas for return on the portfolio and mean return yields in the two-security case

$$\sigma_P^2 = E(R_p - \bar{R}_P)^2 = E[X_1 R_{1j} + X_2 R_{2j} - (X_1 \bar{R}_1 + X_2 \bar{R}_2)]^2$$
$$= E[X_1(R_{1j} - \bar{R}_1) + X_2(R_{2j} - \bar{R}_2)]^2$$

where $\bar{R}_i$ stands for the expected value of security i with respect to all possible outcomes. Recall that

$$(X + Y)^2 = X^2 + XY + XY + Y^2 = X^2 + 2XY + Y^2$$

Applying this to the previous expression we have

$$\sigma_P^2 = E[X_1^2(R_{1j} - \bar{R}_1)^2 + 2X_1 X_2(R_{1j} - \bar{R}_1)(R_{2j} - \bar{R}_2) + X_2^2(R_{2j} - \bar{R}_2)^2]$$

Applying our two rules that the expected value of the sum of a series of returns is equal to the sum of the expected value of each return, and that the expected value of a constant times a return is equal to the constant times the expected return, we have

$$\sigma_P^2 = X_1^2 E[(R_{1j} - \overline{R}_1)^2] + 2X_1 X_2 E[(R_{1j} - \overline{R}_1)(R_{2j} - \overline{R}_2)]$$
$$+ X_2^2 E[(R_{2j} - \overline{R}_2)^2]$$
$$= X_1^2 \sigma_1^2 + 2X_1 X_2 E[(R_{1j} - \overline{R}_1)(R_{2j} - \overline{R}_2)] + X_2^2 \sigma_2^2$$

$E[(R_{1j} - \overline{R}_1)(R_{2j} - \overline{R}_2)]$ has a special name. It is called the covariance and will be designated as σ_{12}.[5] Substituting the symbol σ_{12} for $E[(R_{1j} - \overline{R}_1)(R_{2j} - \overline{R}_2)]$ yields

$16 - 10 = 6$

$4 - 10 = -6$

$$\sigma_P^2 = X_1^2 \sigma_1^2 + X_2^2 \sigma_2^2 + 2X_1 X_2 \sigma_{12}$$

Notice what the covariance does. It is the expected value of the product of two deviations: the deviations of the returns on security 1 from its mean $(R_{1j} - \overline{R}_1)$ and the deviations of security 2 from its mean $(R_{2j} - \overline{R}_2)$. In this sense it is very much like the variance. However, it is the product of two different deviations. As such it can be positive or negative. It will be large when the good outcomes for each stock occur together and when the bad outcomes for each stock occur together. In this case, for good outcomes the covariance will be the product of two large positive numbers, which is positive. When the bad outcomes occur, the covariance will be the product of two large negative numbers, which is positive. This will result in a large value for the covariance and a large variance for the portfolio. In contrast, if good outcomes for one asset are associated with bad outcomes of the other, the covariance is negative. It is negative because a plus deviation for one asset is associated with a minus deviation for the second and the product of a plus and a minus is negative. This was what occurred when we examined a combination of assets 2 and 3.

The covariance is a measure of how returns on assets move together. Insofar as they have positive and negative deviations at similar times, the covariance is a large positive number. If they have the positive and negative deviations at dissimilar times, then the covariance is negative. If the positive and negative deviations are unrelated, it tends to be zero.

For many purposes it is useful to standardize the covariance. Dividing the covariance between two assets by the product of the standard deviation of each asset produces a variable with the same properties as the covariance but with a range of -1 to $+1$. The measure is called the correlation coefficient. Letting ρ_{ij}

CC

---

[5]Note that when all joint outcomes are equally likely, the covariance can be expressed as

$$\sum_{j=1}^{M} \frac{(R_{1j} - \overline{R}_1)(R_{2j} - \overline{R}_2)}{M} \qquad 0$$

where M is the number of equally likely joint outcomes.

stand for the correlation between securities i and j, the correlation coefficient is defined as

$$\rho_{ij} = \frac{\sigma_{ij}}{\sigma_i \sigma_j}$$

24

Dividing by the product of the standard deviations does not change the properties of the covariance. It simply scales it to have values between -1 and $+1$. Let us apply these formulas. First, however, it is necessary to calculate covariances. Table 2.6 shows the intermediate calculations necessary to determine the covariance between securities 1 and 2 and securities 1 and 3. The sum of the deviations between securities 1 and 2 is 72. Therefore, the covariance is $72/3 = 24$ and the correlation coefficient is $24/\sqrt{24}\sqrt{24}$. For assets 1 and 3 the sum of the deviations is -108. The covariance is $-108/3 = -36$ and the correlation coefficient is $-36/\sqrt{24}\sqrt{54}$. Similar calculations can be made for all other pairs of assets and the results are contained in Table 2.7.

Table 2.6 Calculating Covariances

Condition of Market	Deviations Security 1	Deviations Security 2	Product of Deviations	Deviations Security 1	Deviations Security 3	Product of Deviations
Good	$(15 - 9)$	$(16 - 10)$	36	$(15 - 9)$	$(1 - 10)$	-54
Average	$(9 - 9)$	$(10 - 10)$	0	$(9 - 9)$	$(10 - 10)$	0
Poor	$(3 - 9)$	$(4 - 10)$	36	$(3 - 9)$	$(19 - 10)$	-54
			72			-108

Table 2.7 Covariance and Correlation Coefficients (in brackets) Between Assets

	1	2	3	4	5
1		24	-36	0	24
		$(+1)$	(-1)	(0)	$(+1)$
2			-36	0	24
			(-1)	(0)	$(+1)$
3				0	-36
				(0)	(-1)
4					0
					(0)
5					

Earlier we examined the results obtained by an investor with \$1.00 to spend who put \$0.60 in asset 2 and \$0.40 in asset 3. Applying the expression for variance of the portfolio we have

How is this determined?   *.48*   *?*   *How?*

$$\sigma_p^2 = \left(\frac{0.60}{1.00}\right)^2 24 + \left(\frac{0.40}{1.00}\right)^2 54 + 2\left(\frac{0.60}{1.00}\right)\left(\frac{0.40}{1.00}\right)(-36) = 0$$

8.64 + 8.64   -17.28

This was exactly the result we obtained when we looked at the combination of the full distribution. The correlation coefficient between securities 2 and 3 is -1.

This meant that good and bad returns of assets 2 and 3 tended to occur at opposite times. When this situation occurs, a portfolio can always be constructed with zero risk.

Our second example was an investment in securities 1 and 4. The variance of this portfolio is

$$\sigma_P^2 = (\tfrac{1}{2})^2 24 + (\tfrac{1}{2})^2 24 = 12$$

In this case where the correlation coefficient was zero, the risk of the portfolio was less than the risk of either of the individual securities. Once again, this is a general result. When the return patterns of two assets are independent so that the correlation coefficient and covariance are zero, a portfolio can be found that has a lower variance than either of the assets by themselves.

As an additional check on the accuracy of the formula just derived, we calculate the variance directly. Earlier we saw there were nine possible returns when we combined assets 2 and 4. They were $1.16, $1.13, $1.13, $1.10, $1.10, $1.10, $1.07, $1.07, and $1.04. Since we started with an investment of $1.00, the returns are easy to determine. The returns are 16%, 13%, 13%, 10%, 10%, 10%, 7%, 7%, and 4%. By examination it is easy to see that the mean return is 10%. The deviations are 6, 3, 3, 0, 0, 0, -3, -3, -6. The squared deviations are 36, 9, 9, 0, 0, 0, 9, 9, 36, and the average squared deviation or variance is $108/9 = 12$. This agrees with the formula developed earlier.

The final example analyzed previously was a portfolio of assets 1 and 5. In this case the variance of the portfolio is

$$\sigma_P^2 = (\tfrac{1}{2})^2 24 + (\tfrac{1}{2})^2 24 + 2(\tfrac{1}{2})(\tfrac{1}{2})24$$

$$= \tfrac{1}{4}(24) + \tfrac{1}{4}(24) + \tfrac{1}{2}(24)$$

$$= 24$$

As we demonstrated earlier, when two securities have their good and bad outcomes at the same time, the risk is not reduced by purchasing a portfolio of the two assets.

The formula for variance of a portfolio can be generalized to more than two assets. Consider first a three-asset case. Substituting the expression for return on a portfolio and expected return of a portfolio in the general formula for variance yields

$$\sigma_P^2 = E(R_P - \overline{R}_P)^2$$

$$= E[X_1 R_{1j} + X_2 R_{2j} + X_3 R_{3j} - (X_1 \overline{R}_1 + X_2 \overline{R}_2 + X_3 \overline{R}_3)]^2$$

Rearranging,

$$\sigma_P^2 = E[X_1(R_{1j} - \overline{R}_1) + X_2(R_{2j} - \overline{R}_2) + X_3(R_{3j} - \overline{R}_3)]^2$$

Squaring the right-hand side yields

$$\sigma_P{}^2 = E[X_1{}^2(R_{1j} - \overline{R}_1)^2 + X_2{}^2(R_{2j} - \overline{R}_2)^2 + X_3{}^2(R_{3j} - \overline{R}_3)^2$$
$$+ 2X_1X_2(R_{1j} - \overline{R}_1)(R_{2j} - \overline{R}_2) + 2X_1X_3(R_{1j} - \overline{R}_1)(R_{3j} - \overline{R}_3)$$
$$+ 2X_2X_3(R_{2j} - \overline{R}_2)(R_{3j} - \overline{R}_3)]$$

Applying the properties of expected return discussed earlier yields

$$\sigma_P{}^2 = X_1{}^2E(R_{1j} - \overline{R}_1)^2 + X_2{}^2E(R_{2j} - \overline{R}_2)^2 + X_3{}^2E(R_{3j} - \overline{R}_3)^2$$
$$+ 2X_1X_2E[(R_{1j} - \overline{R}_1)(R_{2j} - \overline{R}_2)] + 2X_1X_3E[(R_{1j} - \overline{R}_1)(R_{3j} - \overline{R}_3)]$$
$$+ 2X_2X_3E[(R_{2j} - \overline{R}_2)(R_{3j} - \overline{R}_3)]$$

Utilizing $\sigma_i{}^2$ for variance of asset i and σ_{ij} for the covariance between assets i and j, we have

$$\sigma_P{}^2 = X_1{}^2\sigma_1{}^2 + X_2{}^2\sigma_2{}^2 + X_3{}^2\sigma_3{}^2 + 2X_1X_2\sigma_{12} + 2X_1X_3\sigma_{13} + 2X_2X_3\sigma_{23}$$

This formula can be extended to any number of assets. Examining the expression for the variance of a portfolio of three assets should indicate how. First note that the variance of each asset is multiplied by the square of the proportion invested in it. Thus, the first part of the expression for the variance of a portfolio is the sum of the variances on the individual assets times the square of the proportion invested in each, or

$$\sum_{i=1}^{N} X_i{}^2\sigma_i{}^2$$

The second set of terms in the expression for the variance of a portfolio is covariance terms. Note that the covariance between each pair of assets in the portfolio enters the expression for the variance of a portfolio. With three assets the covariance between 1 and 2, 1 and 3, and 2 and 3 entered. With four assets, covariance terms between 1 and 2, 1 and 3, 1 and 4, 2 and 3, 2 and 4, and 3 and 4 would enter. Further note that each covariance term is multiplied by two times the product of the proportions invested in each asset. The following double summation captures the covariance terms:

$$\sum_{j=1}^{N} \sum_{\substack{k=1 \\ k \neq j}}^{N} X_j X_k \sigma_{jk}$$

The reader concerned that a 2 does not appear in this expression can relax. The covariance between securities 2 and 3 comes about both from $j = 2$ and $k = 3$

and from $j = 3$ and $k = 2$. This is how the term "2 times the covariance between 2 and 3" comes about. Furthermore, examining the expression for covariance shows that order does not matter; thus $\sigma_{jk} = \sigma_{kj}$. The symbol $\neq$ means k should not have the same value as j. To reemphasize the meaning of the double summation, we examine the three-security case. We have

$$\sum_{\substack{j=1 \\ k \neq j}}^{3} \sum_{k=1}^{3} X_j X_k \sigma_{jk} = X_1 X_2 \sigma_{12} + X_1 X_3 \sigma_{13} + X_2 X_1 \sigma_{21}$$

$$+ X_2 X_3 \sigma_{23} + X_3 X_1 \sigma_{31} + X_3 X_2 \sigma_{32}$$

Since the order does not matter in calculating covariance and thus $\sigma_{12} = \sigma_{21}$, we have

$$\sum_{\substack{j=1 \\ k \neq j}}^{3} \sum_{k=1}^{3} X_j X_k \sigma_{jk} = 2 X_1 X_2 \sigma_{12} + 2 X_1 X_3 \sigma_{13} + 2 X_2 X_3 \sigma_{23}$$

Putting together the variance and covariance parts of the general expression for the variance of a portfolio yields

$$\sigma_P^2 = \sum_{j-1}^{N} X_j^2 \sigma_j^2 + \sum_{\substack{j=1 \\ k \neq j}}^{N} \sum_{k=1}^{N} X_j X_k \sigma_{jk}$$

This formula is worth examining further. First, consider the case where all assets are independent and, therefore, the covariance between them is zero. This was the situation we observed for assets 2 and 4 in our little example. In this case $\sigma_{jk} = 0$ and the formula for variance becomes

$$\sum_{j=1}^{N} X_j^2 \sigma_j^2$$

Furthermore, assume equal amounts are invested in each asset. With N assets the proportion invested in each asset is $1/N$. Applying our formula yields

$$\sigma_P^2 = \sum_{j=1}^{N} (1/N)^2 \sigma_j^2 = 1/N \left[\sum_{j=1}^{N} \frac{\sigma_j^2}{N} \right]$$

The term in the brackets is our expression for an average. Thus our formula reduces to $\sigma_P^2 = (1/N)\bar{\sigma}_j^2$, where $\bar{\sigma}_j^2$ represents the average variance of the stocks in the portfolio. As N gets larger and larger, the varaince of the portfolio gets smaller and smaller. As N becomes extremely large, the variance of the portfolio approaches zero. This is a general result. If we have enough *independent* assets, the variance of a portfolio of these assets approaches zero.

In general, we are not so fortunate. In most markets the correlation coefficient and the covariance between assets is positive. In these markets the risk on the portfolio cannot be made to go to zero but can be much less than the variance of an individual asset. The variance of a portfolio of assets is

$$\sigma_P^2 = \sum_{j=1}^{N} X_j^2 \sigma_j^2 + \sum_{\substack{j=1 \\ k \neq j}}^{N} \sum_{k=1}^{N} X_j X_k \sigma_{jk}$$

Once again, consider equal investment in N assets. With equal investment, the proportion invested in any one asset X_j is $1/N$ and the formula for the variance of a portfolio becomes

$$\sigma_P^2 = \sum_{j=1}^{N} (1/N)^2 \sigma_j^2 + \sum_{\substack{j=1 \\ k \neq j}}^{N} \sum_{k=1}^{N} (1/N)(1/N) \sigma_{jk}$$

Factoring out $1/N$ from the first summation and $(N - 1)/N$ from the second yields

$$\sigma_P^2 = (1/N) \sum_{j=1}^{N} \left[\frac{\sigma_j^2}{N} \right] + \frac{(N - 1)}{N} \sum_{\substack{j=1 \\ k \neq j}}^{N} \sum_{k=1}^{N} \left[\frac{\sigma_{jk}}{N(N - 1)} \right]$$

Both of the terms in the brackets are averages. That the first is an average should be clear from the previous discussion. Likewise the second term in brackets is also an average. There are N values of j and $(N - 1)$ values of k. There are $N - 1$ values of k since k cannot equal j so that there is one less value of k than j. In total there are $N(N - 1)$ covariance terms. Thus the second term is the summation of covariances divided by the number of covariances and it is, therefore, an average. Replacing the summations by averages, we have

$$\sigma_P^2 = \frac{1}{N} \overline{\sigma_j^2} + \frac{N - 1}{N} \overline{\sigma_{jk}}$$

This expression is a much more realistic representation of what occurs when we invest in a portfolio of assets. The contribution to the portfolio variance of the variance of the individual securities goes to zero as N gets very large. However, the contribution of the covariance terms approaches the average covariance as N gets large. The individual risk of securities can be diversified away, but the contribution to the total risk caused by the covariance terms cannot be diversified away.

Table 2.8   Effect of Diversification

Number of Securities	Expected Portfolio Variance
1	46.619
2	26.839
4	16.948
6	13.651
8	12.003
10	11.014
12	10.354
14	9.883
16	9.530
18	9.256
20	9.036
25	8.640
30	8.376
35	8.188
40	8.047
45	7.937
50	7.849
75	7.585
100	7.453
125	7.374
150	7.321
175	7.284
200	7.255
250	7.216
300	7.190
350	7.171
400	7.157
450	7.146
500	7.137
600	7.124
700	7.114
800	7.107
900	7.102
1000	7.097
Infinity	7.058

Table 2.8 illustrates how this relationship looks when dealing with U.S. equities. The average variance and average covariance of returns were calculated using monthly data for all stocks listed on the New York Stock Exchange. The average variance was 46.619. The average covariance was 7.058. As more and more securities are added, the average variance on the portfolio declines until it approaches the average covariance. Rearranging the previous equation clarifies this relationship even further. Thus,

$$\sigma_P^2 = 1/N(\overline{\sigma_j^2} - \overline{\sigma}_{kj}) + \overline{\sigma}_{kj}$$

The first term is $1/N$ times the difference between the variance of return on

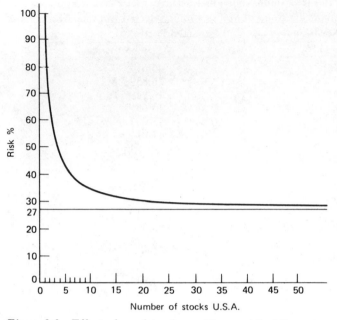

Figure 2.2   Effect of number of securities on risk of the portfolio [12].

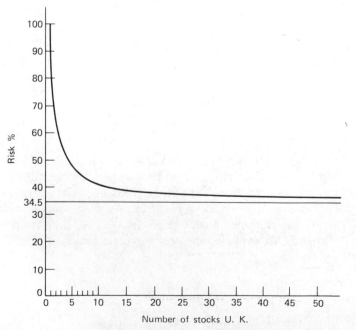

Figure 2.3   The effect of securities on risk in the U.K. [12].

Read Heading Very Carefully !

Table 2.9   Percentage of the Risk on an Individual Security that Can Be Eliminated by Holding a Random Portfolio of Stocks within Selected National Markets and among National Markets [12]

U.S.A.	73
U.K.	65.5
France	67.3
Germany	56.2
Italy	60.0
Belgium	80.0
Switzerland	56.0
Netherlands	76.1
International stocks	89.3

individual securities and the average covariance. The second term is the average covariance. This relationship clarifies the effect of diversification on portfolio risk. The minimum variance is obtained for very large portfolios and is equal to the average covariance between all stocks in the population. As securities are added to the portfolio, the effect of the difference between the average risk on a security and the average covariance is reduced.

Figures 2.2 and 2.3 and Table 2.9 illustrate this same relationship for common equities in a number of countries. In Figure 2.3 the vertical axis is the risk of the portfolio as a percentage of the risk of an individual security for the U.K. The horizontal axis is the number of securities in the portfolio. Figure 2.2 presents the same relationship for the United States. Table 2.9 shows the percentage of risk that can be eliminated by holding a widely diversified portfolio in each of several countries as well as an internationally diversified portfolio. As can be seen, the effectiveness of diversification in reducing the risk of a portfolio varies from country to country. From the previous equation we know why. The average covariance relative to the variance varies from country to country. Thus, in Switzerland and Italy securities have relatively high covariance, indicating that stocks tend to move together. On the other hand, the security markets in Belgium and the Netherlands tend to have stocks with relatively low covariances. For these latter security markets, much more of the risk of holding individual securities can be diversified away. Diversification is especially useful in reducing the risk on a portfolio in these markets.

CONCLUSION

In this chapter we have shown how the risk of a portfolio of assets can be very different from the risk of the individual assets comprising the portfolio. This was true when we selected assets with particular characteristics such as those shown in Table 2.3. It was also true when we simply selected assets at random such as those shown in Table 2.8 and 2.9.

In the following chapter we examine the relationship between the risk and return on individual assets in more detail. We then show how the characteristics of combinations of securities can be used to define the opportunity set of investments from which the investor must make a choice. Finally, we show how the properties of these opportunities taken together with the knowledge that the investor prefers return and seeks to avoid risk can be used to define a subset of the opportunity set that will be of interest to investors.

QUESTIONS AND PROBLEMS

1. Assume that you are considering selecting assets from among the following four candidates:

Asset 1		
Market Condition	Return	Probability
Good	16	1/4
Average	12	1/2
Poor	8	1/4

Asset 2		
Market Condition	Return	Probability
Good	4	1/4
Average	6	1/2
Poor	8	1/4

Asset 3		
Market Condition	Return	Probability
Good	20	1/4
Average	14	1/2
Poor	8	1/4

Asset 4		
Rainfall	Return	Probability
Plentiful	16	1/3
Average	12	1/3
Light	8	1/3

Assume that there is no relationship between the amount of rainfall and the condition of the stock market.

A. Solve for the expected return and the standard deviation of return for each separate investment.

B. Solve for the correlation coefficient and the covariance between each pair of investments.

C. Solve for the expected return and variance of each of the portfolios shown below.

Portfolio	Portions Invested in Each Asset			
	Asset 1	Asset 2	Asset 3	Asset 4
a	$X_1 = 1/2$	$X_2 = 1/2$		
b	1/2		1/2	
c	1/2			1/2
d		1/2	1/2	
e			1/2	1/2
f	1/3	1/3	1/3	
g		1/3	1/3	1/3
h	1/3		1/3	1/3
i	1/4	1/4	1/4	1/4

D. Plot the original assets and each of the portfolios from Part C in expected return standard deviation space.

2. Below is actual price and dividend data for three companies for each of 7 months.

	Security *A*		Security *B*		Security *C*	
Time	Price	Dividend	Price	Dividend	Price	Dividend
1	57 6/8		333		106 6/8	
2	59 7/8		368		108 2/8	
3	59 3/8	.725[a]	368 4/8	1.35	124	.40
4	55 4/8		382 2/8		122 2/8	
5	56 2/8		386		135 4/8	
6	59	.725	397 6/8	1.35	141 6/8	.42
7	60 2/8		392		165 6/8	

[a] A dividend entry on the same line as a price indicates that the return between that time period and the previous period consisted of a capital gain (or loss) and the receipt of the dividend.

A. Compute the rate of return for each company for each month.

B. Compute the average rate of return for each company.

C. Compute the standard deviation of the rate of return for each company.

D. Compute the correlation coefficient between all possible pairs of securities.

E. Compute the average return and standard deviation for the following portfolios:

$\frac{1}{2}A + \frac{1}{2}B$
$\frac{1}{2}A + \frac{1}{2}C$
$\frac{1}{2}B + \frac{1}{2}C$
$\frac{1}{3}A + \frac{1}{3}B + \frac{1}{3}C$

3. Assume that the average variance of return for an individual security is 50 and that the average covariance is 10. What is the expected variance of an equally weighted portfolio of 5, 10, 20, 50, and 100 securities?

4. In Problem 3 how many securities need to be held before the risk of a portfolio is only 10% more than minimum?

5. For the Italian data and Belgium data of Table 2.9, what is the ratio of the difference between the average variance minus average covariance and the average covariance? If the average variance of a single security is 50, what is the expected variance of a portfolio of 5, 20, and 100 securities?

BIBLIOGRAPHY

1. Brennan, Michael J. "The Optimal Number of Securities in a Risky Asset Portfolio When There are Fixed Costs of Transacting: Theory and Some

Empirical Results," *Journal of Financial and Quantitative Analysis,* **X,** No. 3 (Sept. 1975), pp. 483–496.

2. Elton, Edwin J., and Gruber, Martin J. "Risk Reduction and Portfolio Size: An Analytical Solution," *Journal of Business,* **50,** No. 4 (Oct. 1977), pp. 415–437.

3. Epps, Thomas W. "Necessary and Sufficient Conditions for the Mean-Variance Portfolio Model with Constant Risk Aversion," *Journal of Financial and Quantitative Analysis,* **XVI,** No. 2 (June 1981), pp. 169–176.

4. Evans, L. John, and Archer, N. Stephen. "Diversification and the Reduction of Dispersion: An Empirical Analysis," *Journal of Finance,* **XXIII,** No. 5 (Dec. 1968), pp. 761–767.

5. Fisher, Lawrence, and Lorie, James. "Some Studies of Variability of Returns on Investments in Common Stocks," *Journal of Business,* **43,** No. 2 (April 1970), pp. 99–134.

6. Jennings, Edward. "An Empirical Analysis of Some Aspects of Common Stock Diversification," *Journal of Financial and Quantitative Analysis,* **VI,** No. 2 (March 1971), pp. 797–813.

7. Johnson, K., and Shannon, D. "A Note of Diversification and the Reduction of Dispersion," *Journal of Financial Economics,* **1,** No. 4 (Dec. 1974), pp. 365–372.

8. Markowitz, Harry. "Markowitz Revisited," *Financial Analysts Journal,* **32,** No. 4 (Sept.–Oct. 1976), pp. 47–52.

9. Rubinstein, Mark. "The Fundamental Theorem of Parameter-Preference Security Valuation," *Journal of Financial and Quantitative Analysis,* **VIII,** No. 1 (Jan. 1973), pp. 61–69.

10. Wagner, W., and Lau, S. "The Effect of Diversification on Risk," *Financial Analysts Journal,* **27,** No. 5 (Nov.–Dec. 1971), pp. 48–53.

11. Whitmore, G.A. "Diversification and the Reduction of Dispersion: A Note," *Journal of Financial and Quantitative Analysis,* **V,** No. 2 (May 1970), pp. 263–264.

12. Solnick, Bruno. "The Advantages of Domestic and International Diversification," in Elton and Gruber, *International Capital Markets.* (Amsterdam: North Holland, 1975).

Chapter 3

Delineating Efficient Portfolios

In Chapter 2 we examined the return and risk characteristics of individual securities and began to study the attributes of combinations or portfolios of securities. In this chapter we look at the risk and return characteristics of combinations of securities in more detail. We start off with a reexamination of the attributes of combinations of two risky assets. In doing so we emphasize a geometric interpretation of asset combinations. It is a short step from the analysis of the combination of two or more risky assets to the analysis of combinations of all possible risky assets. After making this step we can delineate that subset of portfolios that will be preferred by all investors who exhibit risk avoidance and who prefer more return to less.[1] This set is usually called the efficient set or efficient frontier. Its shape will differ according to the assumptions that are made with respect to the ability of the investor to sell securities short as well as his ability to lend and borrow funds.[2] Alternative assumptions about short sales and lending and borrowing are examined.

COMBINATIONS OF TWO RISKY ASSETS REVISITED: SHORT SALES NOT ALLOWED

In Chapter 2 we began the analysis of combinations of risky assets. In this chapter we continue it. Previously, we treated the two assets as if they were individual assets, but nothing in the analysis so constrains them. In fact, when

---

[1] In this chapter and most of those that follow, we assume that mean variance is the relevant space for portfolio analysts. See Chapter 9 for an examination of other portfolio models.

[2] Short selling is defined at a later point in this chapter.

we talk about assets, we could equally well be talking about portfolios of risky assets.

Recall from Chapter 2 that the expected return on a portfolio of two assets is given by

$$\overline{R}_P = X_A \overline{R}_A + X_B \overline{R}_B \tag{3.1}$$

where

X_A is the fraction of the portfolio held in asset A
X_B is the fraction of the portfolio held in asset B
$\overline{R}_P$ is the expected return on the portfolio
$\overline{R}_A$ is the expected return on the asset A
$\overline{R}_B$ is the expected return on the asset B

In addition, since we require the investor to be fully invested, the fraction she invests in A plus the fraction she invests in B must equal one, or

$$X_A + X_B = 1$$

We can rewrite this expression as

$$X_B = 1 - X_A \tag{3.2}$$

Substituting Equation (3.2) into Equation (3.1), we can express the expected return on a portfolio of two assets as

$$\overline{R}_P = X_A \overline{R}_A + (1 - X_A)\overline{R}_B$$

Notice that the expected return on the portfolio is a simple-weighted average of the expected returns on the individual securities, and that the weights add to one. The same is not necessarily true of the risk (standard deviation of the return) of the portfolio. In Chapter 2 the standard deviation of the return on the portfolio was shown to be equal to

$$\sigma_P = (X_A^2 \sigma_A^2 + X_B^2 \sigma_B^2 + 2X_A X_B \sigma_{AB})^{1/2}$$

where

σ_P is the standard deviation of the return on the portfolio
σ_A^2 is the variance of the return on security A
σ_B^2 is the variance of the return on security B
σ_{AB} is the covariance between the returns on security A and security B

If we substitute Equation (3.2) into this expression, we obtain

$$\sigma_P = [X_A^2 \sigma_A^2 + (1 - X_A)^2 \sigma_B^2 + 2X_A(1 - X_A)\sigma_{AB}]^{1/2} \tag{3.3}$$

Recalling that $\sigma_{AB} = \rho_{AB}\sigma_A\sigma_B$ where ρ_{AB} is the correlation coefficient between securities A and B, then Equation (3.3) becomes

$$\sigma_P = [X_A^2\sigma_A^2 + (1 - X_A)^2\sigma_B^2 + 2X_A(1 - X_A)\rho_{AB}\sigma_A\sigma_B]^{1/2} \qquad (3.4)$$

The standard deviation of the portfolio is not, in general, a simple-weighted average of the standard deviation of each security. Cross-product terms are involved and the weights do not, in general, add to one. In order to learn more about this relationship, we now study some specific cases involving different degrees of co-movement between securities.

We know that a correlation coefficient has maximum value of $+1$ and minimum value of -1. A value of $+1$ means that two securities will always move in perfect unison, while a value of -1 means that their movements are exactly opposite to each other. We start with an examination of these extreme cases; then we turn to an examination of some intermediate values for the correlation coefficients. As an aid in interpreting results, we examine a specific example as well as general expressions for risk and return. For the example we consider two stocks: a large manufacturer of automobiles ("Colonel Motors") and an electric utility company operating in a large eastern city ("Separated Edison"). Assume the stocks have the following characteristics:

	Expected Return	Standard Deviation
Colonel Motors (C)	14%	6%
Separated Edison (S)	8%	3%

As you might suspect, the car manufacturer has a bigger expected return and a bigger risk than the electric utility.

Case 1 — Perfect Positive Correlation ($\rho = +1$)

Let the subscript C stand for Colonel Motors and the subscript S stand for Separated Edison. If the correlation coefficient is $+1$, then the equation for the risk on the portfolio, Equation (3.4), simplifies to

$$\sigma_P = [X_C^2\sigma_C^2 + (1 - X_C)^2\sigma_S^2 + 2X_C(1 - X_C)\sigma_C\sigma_S]^{1/2} \qquad (3.5)$$

Note that the term in square brackets has the form $X^2 + 2XY + Y^2$ and, thus, can be written as

$$[X_C\sigma_C + (1 - X_C)\sigma_S]^2$$

Since the standard deviation of the portfolio is equal to the positive square root of this expression, we know that

$$\sigma_P = X_C\sigma_C + (1 - X_C)\sigma_S$$

$$14\left(\sigma_P/3 \cdot 1\right) + 8\left(1 - \left(\sigma_P/3 \cdot 1\right)\right) =$$

$$8 + 6\left(\sigma_P/3 \cdot 1\right)$$

$$\tfrac{6}{1}\left(\tfrac{\sigma_P}{3}\right) \qquad \tfrac{6\,\sigma_P}{3}$$

$$= 8 + 2\sigma_P - 6$$
$$= 2 + 2\sigma_P$$

While the expected return on the portfolio is

$$\overline{R}_P = X_C\overline{R}_C + (1 - X_C)\overline{R}_S$$

Thus with the correlation coefficient equal to +1, both risk and return of the portfolio are simply linear combinations of the risk and return of each security. In footnote 3 we show that the form of these two equations means that all combinations of two securities that are perfectly correlated will lie on a straight line in risk and return space.[3] We now illustrate that this is true for the stocks in our example. For the two stocks under study

$$\overline{R}_P = 14X_C + 8(1 - X_C) = 8 + 6X_C$$

$$\sigma_P = 6X_C + 3(1 - X_C) = 3 + 3X_C$$

Table 3.1 presents the return on a portfolio for selected values of X_C and Figure 3.1 presents a graph of this relationship. Note that the relationship is a straight line. The equation of the straight line could easily be derived as follows. Utilizing the equation presented above for σ_P to solve for X_C yields

$$\tfrac{\sigma_P}{X_C} = 3 + 3$$

$$X_C = \sigma_P/3 - 1 \qquad \sigma_P = 3 + 3 X_C$$

Substituting this expression for X_C into the equation for $\overline{R}_P$ and rearranging yields[4]

$$\overline{R}_P = 2 + 2\sigma_P$$

In the case of perfectly correlated assets, the return and risk on the portfolio of the two assets is a weighted average of the return and risk on the individual

---

[3]Solving for X_C in the expression for standard deviation yields

$$X_C = \frac{\sigma_P - \sigma_S}{\sigma_C - \sigma_S}$$

$$\begin{array}{c|cc}
 & \overline{R} & \sigma \\
C & 14 & 6 \\
S & 8 & 3
\end{array}$$

Substituting this into the expression for expected return yields

$$\overline{R}_P = \frac{\sigma_P - \sigma_S}{\sigma_C - \sigma_S}\overline{R}_C + \left(1 - \frac{\sigma_P - \sigma_S}{\sigma_C - \sigma_S}\right)\overline{R}_S$$

$$\overline{R}_P = \left(\overline{R}_S - \frac{\overline{R}_C - \overline{R}_S}{\sigma_C - \sigma_S}\sigma_S\right) + \left(\frac{\overline{R}_C - \overline{R}_S}{\sigma_C - \sigma_S}\right)\sigma_P$$

which is the equation of a straight line connecting security C and security S in expected return standard deviation space.

[4]An alternative way to derive this equation is to substitute the appropriate values for the two firms into the equation derived in footnote 3. This yields

$$\overline{R}_P = 8 + 6\frac{(\sigma_P - 3)}{3} = 2 + 2\sigma_P$$

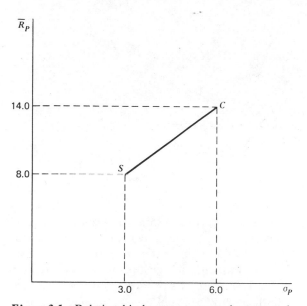

Figure 3.1 Relationship between expected return and
standard deviation when $\rho = +1$.

assets. There is no reduction in risk from purchasing both assets. This can be
seen by examining Figure 3.1 and noting that combinations of the two assets lie
along a straight line connecting the two assets. Nothing has been gained by
diversifying rather than purchasing the individual assets.

Table 3.1 Expected Return and Standard Deviation of a Portfolio of Colonel Motors
and Separated Edison When $\rho = +1$

X_C	0	0.2	0.4	0.5	0.6	0.8	1.0
$\overline{R}_P$	8.0	9.2	10.4	11	11.6	12.8	14.0
σ_P	3.0	3.6	4.2	4.5	4.8	5.4	6.0

Case 2 — Perfect Negative Correlation ($\rho = -1.0$)

We now examine the other extreme: two assets that move perfectly together
but in exactly opposite directions. In this case the standard deviation of the
portfolio is [from Equation (3.4) with $\rho = -1.0$]

$$\sigma_P = [X_C^2\sigma_C^2 + (1 - X_C)^2\sigma_S^2 - 2X_C(1 - X_C)\sigma_C\sigma_S]^{1/2} \qquad (3.6)$$

Once again the equation for standard deviation can be simplified. The term in
the brackets is equivalent to either of the following two expressions:

$$[X_C\sigma_C - (1 - X_C)\sigma_S]^2$$

or

$$[-X_C\sigma_C + (1 - X_C)\sigma_S]^2 \tag{3.7}$$

Thus σ_P is either

$$\sigma_P = X_C\sigma_C - (1 - X_C)\sigma_S$$

or

$$\sigma_P = -X_C\sigma_C + (1 - X_C)\sigma_S \tag{3.8}$$

Since we took the square root to obtain an expression for σ_P and since the square root of a negative number is imaginary, either of the above equations holds only when its right-hand side is positive. A further examination shows the right-hand side of one equation is simply -1 times the other. Thus, each equation is valid only when the right-hand side is positive. Since one is always positive when the other is negative (except when both equations equal zero), there is a unique solution for the return and risk of any combination of securities C and S. These equations are very similar to the ones we obtained when we had a correlation of $+1$. Each also plots as a straight line when σ_P is plotted against X_C. Thus, one would suspect that an examination of the return on the portfolio of two assets as a function of the standard deviation would yield two straight lines, one for each expression for σ_P. As we observe in a moment, this is, in fact, the case.[5]

The value of σ_P for Equation (3.7) or (3.8) is always smaller than the value of σ_P for the case where $\rho = +1$ [Equation (3.5)] for all values of X_C between 0 and 1. Thus the risk on a portfolio of assets is always smaller when the correlation coefficient is -1 than when it is $+1$. We can go one step further. If two securities are perfectly negatively correlated (that is, they move in exactly opposite directions), it should always be possible to find some combination of these two securities that has zero risk. By setting either Equation (3.7) or (3.8) equal to 0, we find that a portfolio with $X_C = \sigma_S/(\sigma_S + \sigma_C)$ will have zero risk. Since $\sigma_S > 0$ and $\sigma_S + \sigma_C > \sigma_S$, this implies that $0 < X_C < 1$ or that the zero risk portfolio will always involve positive investment in both securities.

Now let us return to our example. Minimum risk occurs when $X_C = 3/(3 + 6) = \frac{1}{3}$. Furthermore, for the case of perfect negative correlation,

$$\overline{R}_P = 8 + 6X_C$$

$$\sigma_P = 6X_C - 3(1 - X_C)$$

$$\sigma_P = -6X_C + 3(1 - X_C)$$

---

[5]This occurs for the same reason that the analysis for $\rho = +1$ led to one straight line and the mathematical proof is analogous to that presented for the case of $\rho = +1$.

there are two equations relating σ_P to X_C. Only one is appropriate for any value of X_C. The appropriate equation to define σ_P for any value of X_C is that equation for which $\sigma_P \geqslant 0$. Note that if $\sigma_P > 0$ from one equation, then $\sigma_P < 0$ for the other. Table 3.2 presents the return on the portfolio for selected values of X_C and Figure 3.2 presents a graph of this relationship.[6]

Table 3.2 The Expected Return and Standard Deviation of a Portfolio of Colonel Motors and Separated Edison When $\rho = -1$

X_C	0	0.2	0.4	0.6	0.8	1.0
$\overline{R}_P$	8.0	9.2	10.4	11.6	12.8	14.0
σ_P	3.0	1.2	0.6	2.4	4.2	6.0

Notice that a combination of the two securities exists that provides a portfolio with zero risk. Employing the formula developed before for the composition of the zero-risk portfolio, X_C should equal $3/(3 + 6)$ or ⅓. We can see this is correct from Figure 3.2 or by substituting ⅓ for X_C in the equation for portfolio risk

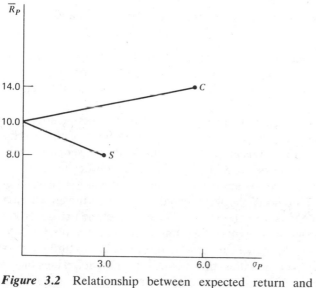

Figure 3.2 Relationship between expected return and standard deviation when $\rho = -1$.

[6]The equation for $\overline{R}_P$ as a function of σ_P can be obtained by solving the expression relating σ_P and X_C for X_C and using this to eliminate X_C in the expression for $\overline{R}_P$. This yields

$$\overline{R}_P = 8 + 6\left(\frac{\sigma_P + 3}{6 + 3}\right) = 10 + \tfrac{2}{3}\sigma_P$$

or

$$\overline{R}_P = 8 + 6\left(\frac{\sigma_P - 3}{-6 - 3}\right) = 10 - \tfrac{2}{3}\sigma_P$$

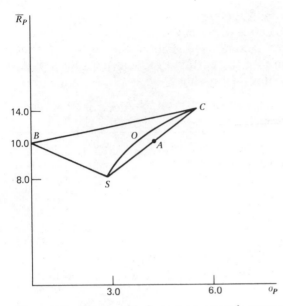

Figure 3.3   Relationship between expected return and standard deviation for various correlation coefficients.

given previously. We have once again demonstrated the most powerful result of diversification: the ability of combinations of securities to reduce risk. In fact, it is not uncommon for combinations of two securities to have less risk than either of the assets in the combination.

We have now examined combinations of risky assets for perfect positive and perfect negative correlation. In Figure 3.3 we have plotted both of these relationships on the same graph. From this graph we should be able to see intuitively where portfolios of these two stocks should lie if correlation coefficients took on intermediate values. From the expression for the standard deviation [Equation (3.4)] we see that for any value for X_C between 0 and 1 the lower the correlation the lower is the standard deviation of the portfolio. The standard deviation reaches its lowest value for $\rho = -1$ (curve SBC) and its highest value for $\rho = +1$ (curve SAC). Therefore, these two curves should represent the limits within which all portfolios of these two securities must lie for intermediate values of the correlation coefficient. We would speculate that an intermediate correlation might produce a curve such as SOC in Figure 3.3. We demonstrate this by returning to our example and constructing the relationship between risk and return for portfolios of our two securities when the correlation coefficient is assumed to be 0 and $+0.5$.

Case 3 — No Relationship between Returns on the Assets ($\rho = 0$)

The expression for return on the portfolio remains unchanged; but noting that the covariance term drops out, the expression for standard deviation becomes

$$\sigma_P = [X_C^2\sigma_C^2 + (1 - X_C)^2\sigma_S^2]^{1/2}$$

For our example this yields

$$\sigma_P = [(6)^2 X_C^2 + (3)^2(1 - X_C)^2]^{1/2}$$

$$\sigma_P = [45X_C^2 - 18X_C + 9]^{1/2}$$

Table 3.3 presents the returns and standard deviation on the portfolio of Colonel Motors and Separated Edison for selected values of X_C.

Table 3.3   The Expected Return and Standard Deviation for a Portfolio of Colonel Motors and Separated Edison with $\rho = 0$

X_C	0	0.2	0.4	0.6	0.8	1.0
$\overline{R}_P$	8.0	9.2	10.4	11.6	12.8	14.0
σ_P	3.00	2.68	3.00	3.79	4.84	6.0

A graphical presentation of the risk and return on these portfolios is shown in Figure 3.4. There is one point on this figure that is worth special attention: the portfolio that has minimum risk. This portfolio can be found in general by looking at the equation for risk:

$$\sigma_P = [X_C^2\sigma_C^2 + (1 - X_C)^2\sigma_S^2 + 2X_C(1 - X_C)\sigma_C\sigma_S\rho_{CS}]^{1/2}$$

To find the value of X_C that minimizes this equation, we take the derivative of it with respect to X_C, set the derivative equal to zero, and solve for X_C. The

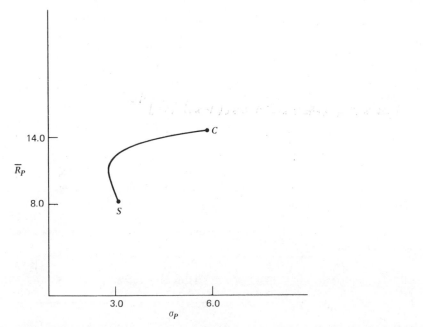

Figure 3.4   Relationship between expected return and standard deviation when $\rho = 0$.

derivative is

$$\frac{\partial \sigma_P}{\partial X_C} = \left(\frac{1}{2}\right) \frac{[2X_C\sigma_C^2 - 2\sigma_S^2 + 2X_C\sigma_S^2 + 2\sigma_C\sigma_S\rho_{CS} - 4X_C\sigma_C\sigma_S\rho_{CS}]}{[X_C^2\sigma_C^2 + (1 - X_C)^2\sigma_S^2 + 2X_C(1 - X_C)\sigma_C\sigma_S\rho_{CS}]^{1/2}}$$

Setting this equal to zero and solving for X_C yields

$$X_C = \frac{\sigma_S^2 - \sigma_C\sigma_S\rho_{CS}}{\sigma_C^2 + \sigma_S^2 - 2\sigma_C\sigma_S\rho_{CS}} \tag{3.9}$$

(handwritten: $\frac{9 - (6)(3)(.5)}{36 + 9 - 2(6)(3)(.5)}$)

In the present case ($\rho_{CS} = 0$) this reduces to

$$X_C = \frac{\sigma_S^2}{\sigma_C^2 + \sigma_S^2}$$

Continuing with the previous example, the value of X_C that minimizes risk is

$$X_C = \frac{9}{9 + 36} = \frac{1}{5} = 0.20$$

This is the minimum risk portfolio that was shown in Figure 3.4.

Case 4 — Intermediate Risk ($\rho = 0.5$)

The correlation between any two actual stocks is almost always greater than 0 and considerably less than 1. To show a more typical relationship between risk and return for two stocks, we have chosen to examine the relationship when $\rho = +0.5$.

The equation for the risk of portfolios composed of Colonel Motors and Separated Edison when the correlation is 0.5 is

(handwritten: $[36 x_c^2 + 9 - 9 x_c^2 + 2x_c(1-x_c)(9)]^{1/2}$)

$$\sigma_P = [(6)^2X_C^2 + (3)^2(1 - X_C)^2 + 2X_C(1 - X_C)(3)(6)(\tfrac{1}{2})]^{1/2}$$

$$\sigma_P = (27X_C^2 + 9)^{1/2}$$

Table 3.4 presents the returns and risks on alternative portfolios of our two stocks when the correlation between them is 0.5.

Table 3.4   The Expected Return and Standard Deviation of a Portfolio of Colonel Motors and Separated Edison When $\rho = 0.5$

X_C	0	0.2	0.4	0.6	0.8	1.0
R_P	8.0	9.2	10.4	11.6	12.8	14.0
σ_P	3.00	3.17	3.65	4.33	5.13	6.00

This risk-return relationship is plotted in Figure 3.5 along with the risk-return

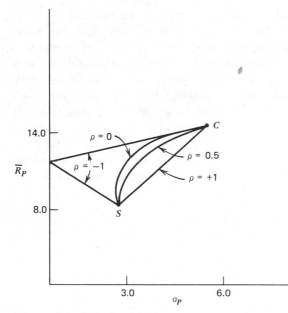

Figure 3.5   Relationship between expected return and standard deviation of return
for various correlation coefficients.

relationships for other intermediate values of the correlation coefficient. Notice
that in this example if $\rho = 0.5$, then the minimum risk is obtained at a value of
$X_C = 0$ or where the investor has placed 100% of his funds in Separated Edison.
This point could have been derived analytically from Equation (3.9). Employing
this equation yields

$$X_C = \frac{9 - 18(0.5)}{9 + 36 - 2(18)(0.5)} = 0$$

In this example (i.e., $\rho_{CS} = 0.5$) there is no combination of the two securities
that is less risky than the least risky asset by itself, though combinations are still
less risky than they were in the case of perfect positive correlation. The particular
value of the correlation coefficient for which no combination of two securities is
less risky than the least risky security depends on the characteristics of the assets
in question. Specifically, for all assets there is some value of ρ such that the risk
on the portfolio can no longer be made less than the risk of the least risky asset
in the portfolio.[7]

---

[7]The value of the correlation coefficient where this occurs is easy to determine. Equation (3.9) is the
expression for the fraction of the portfolio to be held in X_C to minimize risk. If σ_S is the least risky
asset, then the portfolio is less risky than the least risky asset as long as the equation for standard
deviation evaluated at the value of X_C determined by (3.9) is less than σ_S. These relationships can
be used to determine the critical value for ρ_{CS}.

We have developed some insights into combinations of two securities or port-folios from the analysis performed to this point. First, we have noted that the lower (closer to -1.0) the correlation coefficient between assets, all other attri-butes held constant, the higher the payoff from diversification. Second, we have seen that combinations of two assets can never have more risk than that found on a straight line connecting the two assets in expected return standard deviation space. Finally, we have produced a simple expression for finding the minimum variance portfolio when two assets are combined in a portfolio. We can use this to gain more insight into the shape of the curve along which all possible com-binations of assets must lie in expected return standard deviation space. This curve, which is called the portfolio possibilities curve, is the subject of the next section.

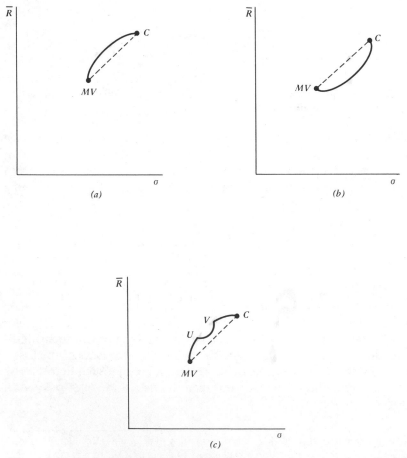

Figure 3.6   Various possible relationships for expected return and standard deviation when the minimum variance portfolio and Colonel Motors are combined.

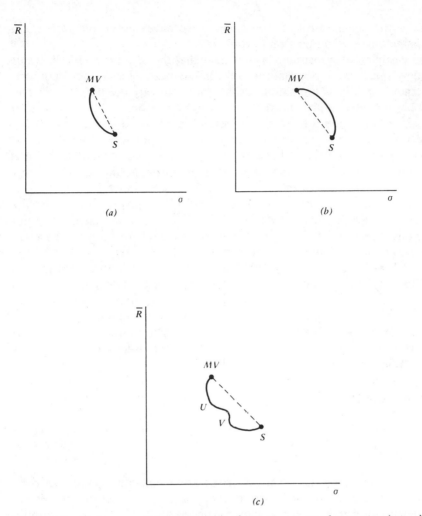

Figure 3.7   Various possible relationships between expected return and standard deviation of return when the minimum variance portfolio is combined with portfolio S.

THE SHAPE OF THE PORTFOLIO POSSIBILITIES CURVE

Reexamine the earlier figures in this chapter and note that the portion of the portfolio possibility curve that lies above the minimum variance portfolio is concave while that which lies below the minimum variance portfolio is convex.[8] This

---

[8]A concave curve is one where a straight line connecting any two points on the curve lies entirely under the curve. If a curve is convex a straight line connecting any two points lies totally above the curve. The only exception to this is that a straight line is both convex and concave and so can be referred to as either.

is not due to the peculiarities of the examples we have chosen but rather is a general characteristic of all portfolio problems.

This can easily be demonstrated. Remember that the equations and diagrams we have developed are appropriate for all combinations of securities and portfolios. We now examine combinations of the minimum variance portfolio and an asset that has a higher return and risk.

Figures 3.6a, 3.6b, and 3.6c represent three hypothesized shapes for combinations of Colonel Motors and the minimum variance portfolio. The shape depicted in 3.6b cannot be possible since we have demonstrated that combinations of assets cannot have more risk than that found on a straight line connecting two assets (and that only in the case of perfect positive correlation). But what about the shape presented in Figure 3.6c? Here all portfolios have less risk than the straight line connecting Colonel Motors and the minimum variance portfolio. However, this is impossible. Examine the portfolios labeled U and V. These are simply combinations of the minimum variance portfolio and Colonel Motors. Since U and V are portfolios, all combinations of U and V must lie either on a straight line connecting U and V or above such a straight line.[9] Hence 3.6c is impossible and the only legitimate shape is that shown in 3.6a, which is a concave curve. Analogous reasoning can be used to show that if we consider combinations of the minimum variance portfolio and a security or portfolio with higher variance and lower return, the curve must be convex, that is, it must look like Figure 3.7a rather than 3.7b or 3.7c.

Now that we understand the risk–return properties of combinations of two assets, we are in a position to study the attributes of combinations of all risky assets.

The Efficient Frontier with No Short Sales

In theory we could plot all conceivable risky assets and combinations of risky assets in a diagram in return standard deviation space. We used the words "in theory," not because there is a problem in calculating the risk and return on a stock or portfolio, but because there are an infinite number of possibilities that must be considered. Not only must all possible groupings of risky assets be considered, but all groupings must be considered in all possible percentage compositions.

If we were to plot all possibilities in risk–return space, we would get a diagram like Figure 3.8. We have taken the liberty of representing combinations as a finite number of points in constructing the diagram. Let us examine the diagram and see if we can eliminate any part of it from consideration by the investor. In Chapter 2 we reasoned that an investor would prefer more return to less and

---

[9]If the correlation between U and V equals $+1$, they will be on the straight line. If it is less than $+1$, the risk must be less, so combinations must be above the straight line.

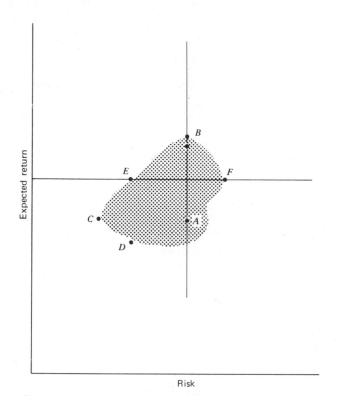

Figure 3.8   Risk and return possibilities for various assets and portfolios.

would prefer less risk to more. Thus, if we could find a set of portfolios that

1.   offered a bigger return for the same risk, or

2.   offered a lower risk for the same return,

we would have identified all portfolios an investor could consider holding. All other portfolios could be ignored.

Let us take a look at Figure 3.8. Examine portfolios A and B. Note that portfolio B would be preferred by all investors to portfolio A because it offers a higher return with the same level of risk. We can also see that portfolio C would be preferred to portfolio A because it offers less risk at the same level of return. Notice that at this point in our analysis we can find no portfolio that dominates portfolio C or portfolio B. It should be obvious at this point that an efficient set of portfolios cannot include interior portfolios. We can reduce the possibility set even further. For any point in risk–return space we want to move as far as possible in the direction of increasing return and as far as possible in the direction of decreasing risk. Examine the point D, which is an exterior point. We can eliminate D from further consideration since portfolio E exists, which has more return for the same risk. This is true for every other portfolio as we move up the outer

$\overline{R}_P$

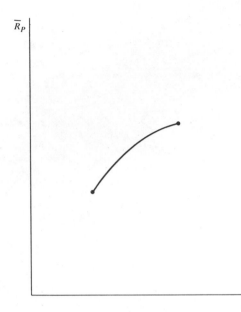

σ_P

Figure 3.9   The efficient frontier.

shell from D to point C. Point C cannot be eliminated since there is no portfolio that has less risk for the same return or more return for the same risk. But what is point C? It is the global minimum variance portfolio.[10] Now examine point F. Point F is on the outer shell, but point E has less risk for the same return. As we move up the outer shell curve from point F, all portfolios are dominated until we come to portfolio B. Portfolio B cannot be eliminated for there is no portfolio that has the same return and less risk or the same risk and more return than point B. Point B represents that portfolio (usually a single security) that offers the highest expected return of all portfolios. Thus the efficient set consists of the envelope curve of all portfolios that lie between the global minimum variance portfolio and the maximum return portfolio. This set of portfolios is called the efficient frontier.

Figure 3.9 represents a graph of the efficient frontier. Notice that we have drawn the efficient frontier as a concave function. The proof that it must be concave follows logically from the earlier analysis of the combination of two securities or portfolios. The efficient frontier cannot contain a convex region such as that shown in Figure 3.10 since as argued earlier U and V are portfolios and combinations of two portfolios must be concave.[11]

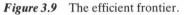

[10]The global minimum variance portfolio is that portfolio that has the lowest risk of any feasible portfolio.

[11]Furthermore, there can be linear segments if the two efficient portfolios are perfectly correlated. Since a linear relationship is both concave and convex, we can still refer to the efficient frontier as concave.

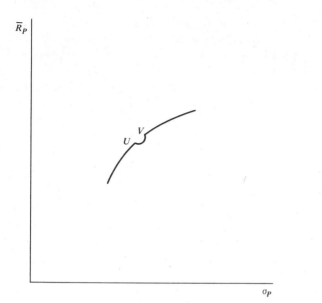

Figure 3.10   An impossible shape for the efficient frontier.

Up to this point we have seen that the efficient frontier is a concave function in expected return standard deviation space that extends from the minimum variance portfolio to the maximum return portfolio. The portfolio problem, then, is to find all portfolios along this frontier. The computational procedures necessary to do so will be examined in Chapter 4.

The Efficient Frontier with Short Sales Allowed

In the stock market (and many other capital markets), an investor can often sell a security that he or she does not own. This process is called short selling. It involves in essence taking a negative position in a security. Short sales exist in sizable amounts on the New York Stock Exchange (as well as other securities markets) and the amount of short sales in New York Stock Exchange stocks is reported in the New York *Times* every Monday. In a moment we will discuss the incorporation of short sales into our analysis. Before we do so, however, it is worthwhile pointing out that we have not been wasting our time by studying the case where short sales are disallowed. There are two reasons why this is true. The first is that most institutional investors do not short sell. Many institutions are forbidden by law from short selling, whereas still others operate under a self-imposed constraint forbidding short sales. The second is that the incorporation of short sales into our analysis involves only a minor extension of the analysis we have developed up to this point.

In this section we shall employ a simplified description of the way short sales work. This has been the general description of short sales in the literature, but in footnotes and in Chapter 4 we present both the deficiencies of this description and an alternative, more realistic description of short sales. Our description of short sales, which treats short sales as the ability to sell a security without owning it, assumes that there are no special transaction costs involved in this process. Let us see how this process might work.

Let us assume an investor believed that the stock of ABC company, which currently sells for $100 per share, is likely to be selling for $95 per share (expected value) at the end of the year. In addition, the investor expects ABC company to pay a $3.00 dividend at the end of the year. If the investor bought one share of ABC stock, the cash flow would be $-\$100.00$ at time zero when the stock is purchased and $+\$3.00$ from the dividend, plus $+\$95.00$ from selling the stock at time 1. The cash flows are

	Time	
	0	1
Purchase Stock	-100	
Dividend		$+ 3$
Sell Stock		$+95$
Total Cash Flow	-100	$+98$ $-\$2$

Unless this stock had very unusual correlations with other securities, it is unlikely that an investor with these expectations would want to hold any of it in his own portfolio. In fact, an investor would really like to own negative amounts of it. How might the investor do so? Assume a friend, Joelle, owned a share of ABC company and that the friend had different expectations and wished to continue holding it. The investor might borrow Joelle's stock under the promise that she will be no worse off lending him the stock. The investor could then sell the stock, receiving $100. When the company pays the $3.00 dividend, the investor must reach into his own pocket and pay Joelle $3.00. He has a cash flow of $-\$3.00$. He has to do this because neither he nor Joelle own the stock and he promised that Joelle would be no worse off by lending her the stock. Now at the end of the year, the investor could purchase the stock for $95 and give it back to Joelle. The cash flows for the investor are:

	Time	
	0	1
Sell Stock	$+100$	
Pay Dividend		$- 3$
Buy Stock		-95
Total Cash Flow	$+100$	-98

Notice in the example that the lender of the stock is no worse off by the process and the borrower has been able to create a security that has the opposite characteristics of buying a share of the ABC company. In the real world Joelle might require some added compensation for lending her stock, but we will continue to use this simplified description of short selling in analyzing portfolio possibilities.[12]

It was clear that when an investor expected the return on a security to be negative, short sales made sense. Even in the case where returns are positive, short sales can make sense, for the cash flow received at time zero from short selling one security can be used to purchase a security with a higher expected return. Return to an example employing Colonel Motors and Separated Edison. Recall that the expected return for Separated Edison was 8% while it was 14% for Colonel Motors. If we disallow short sales, the highest return an investor can get is 14% by placing 100% of the funds in Colonel Motors. With short sales higher returns can be earned by short selling Separated Edison and placing the investor's original capital plus the initial cash flow from short sales in Colonel Motors. In doing so, however, there is a commensurate increase in risk. To see this more formally we return to the case where the correlation coefficient between the two securities is assumed to be 0.5 and see what happens when we allow short sales. The earlier calculations in Table 3.4 and the diagram in Figure 3.5 are still valid, but now they must be extended to consider values of X greater than 1 and less than 0. Some sample calculations are shown in Table 3.5.

Table 3.5

X_C	-1	-0.8	-0.6	-0.4	-0.2	$+1.2$	$+1.4$	$+1.6$	$+1.8$	$+2.0$
$\overline{R}$	2.0	3.2	4.4	5.6	6.8	15.2	16.4	17.6	18.8	20.0
σ	6.0	5.13	4.33	3.65	3.17	6.92	7.87	8.84	9.82	10.82

The new diagram with short sales is shown in Figure 3.11. The reader should note that with short sales, portfolios exist that give infinite expected rates of return. This should not be too surprising since with short sales one can sell securities with low expected returns and use the proceeds to buy securities with high expected returns. For example, suppose an investor had $100 to invest in Colonel Motors and Separated Edison. The investor could place the entire $100 in Colonel Motors and get a return of $14, or 14%. On the other hand, the investor could sell $1,000 worth of Separated Edison stock short and buy $1,100 worth of Colonel Motors. The expected earnings on the investment in Colonel Motors is $154 while the expected cost of borrowing Separated Edison is $80. Therefore, the expected return would be $74, or 74%, on the original $100 investment. Is this a preferred position? The expected return would increase from 14% to 74% but the standard deviation would increase from 6% to 57.2%.

---

[12]In the case of actual short sales a broker plays the role of the friend and he demands that funds be put up as security for the loan of the stock. These funds are in addition to the proceeds from the short sale. Since, in most cases, the amount of the funds that must be put up is quite large and the broker pays no return on these funds, the description of short sales commonly used in the literature overstates the return from short sales.

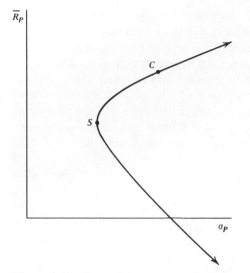

Figure 3.11   Expected return standard deviation combinations of Colonel Motors and
Separated Edison when short sales are allowed.

Whether an investor should take the position offering the higher expected return
would depend on the investor's preference for return relative to risk. We have
more to say about this in Chapter 8.

In Figure 3.11 we have constructed the diagram for combinations of Colonel
Motors and Separated Edison, assuming a correlation coefficient of 0.5. Notice
that all portfolios offering returns above the global minimum variance portfolio
lie along a concave curve. The reasoning for this is directly analogous to that
presented when short sales were not allowed.

When we extend this analysis to the efficient frontiers of all securities and

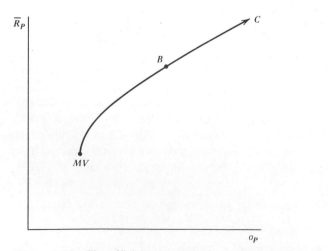

Figure 3.12   The efficient set when short sales are allowed.

portfolios, we get a figure such as Figure 3.12, where $MVBC$ is the efficient set. Since combinations of two portfolios are concave, the efficient set is concave. The efficient set still starts with the minimum variance portfolio, but when short sales are allowed it has no finite upper bound.[13]

THE EFFICIENT FRONTIER WITH RISKLESS LENDING AND BORROWING

Up to this point we have been dealing with portfolios of risky assets. The introduction of a riskless asset into our portfolio possibility set considerably simplifies the analysis. We can consider lending at a riskless rate as investing in an asset with a certain outcome (e.g., a short-term government bill or savings account). Borrowing can be considered as selling such a security short, thus borrowing can take place at the riskless rate.

We call the certain rate of return on the riskless asset R_F. Since the return is certain, the standard deviation of the return on the riskless asset must be zero.

We first examine the case where investors can lend and borrow unlimited amounts of funds at the riskless rate. Initially assume that the investor is interested in placing part of the funds in some portfolio A and either lending or borrowing. Under this assumption we can easily determine the geometric pattern of all combinations of portfolio A and lending or borrowing. Call X the fraction of original funds that the investor places in portfolio A. Remember that X can be greater than 1 because we are assuming that the investor can borrow at the riskless rate and invest more than his initial funds in portfolio A. If X is the fraction of funds the investor places in portfolio A, $(1 - X)$ must be the fraction of funds that were placed in the riskless asset. The expected return on the combination of riskless asset and risky portfolio is given by

$$\overline{R}_C = (1 - X)R_F + X\overline{R}_A$$

The risk on the combination is

$$\sigma_C = [(1 - X)^2\sigma_F^2 + X^2\sigma_A^2 + 2X(1 - X)\sigma_A\sigma_F\rho_{FA}]^{1/2}$$

Since we have already argued that σ_F is zero,

$$\sigma_C = (X^2\sigma_A^2)^{1/2} = X\sigma_A$$

Solving this expression for X yields

$$X = \frac{\sigma_C}{\sigma_A}$$

---

[13]Merton [13] has shown that the efficient set is the upper half of a hyperbola.

Substituting this expression for X into the expression for expected return on the combination yields

$$\overline{R}_C = \left(1 - \frac{\sigma_C}{\sigma_A}\right) R_F + \frac{\sigma_C}{\sigma_A} \overline{R}_A$$

Rearranging terms,

$$\overline{R}_C = R_F + \left(\frac{\overline{R}_A - R_F}{\sigma_A}\right) \sigma_C$$

Note that this is the equation of a straight line. All combinations of riskless lending or borrowing with portfolio A lie on a straight line in expected return standard deviation space. The intercept of the line (on the return axis) is R_F and the slope is $(\overline{R}_A - R_F)/\sigma_A$. Furthermore, the line passes through the point $(\sigma_A, \overline{R}_A)$. This line is shown in Figure 3.13. Note that to the left of point A we have combinations of lending and portfolio A, whereas to the right of point A we have combinations of borrowing and portfolio A.

The portfolio A we selected for this analysis had no special properties. Combinations of any security or portfolio and riskless lending and borrowing lie along a straight line in expected return standard deviation of return space. Examine Figure 3.14. We could have combined portfolio B with riskless lending and borrowing and held combinations along the line $R_F B$ rather than $R_F A$. Combinations along $R_F B$ are superior to combinations along $R_F A$ since they offer greater return for the same risk. It should be obvious that what we would like to do is to rotate

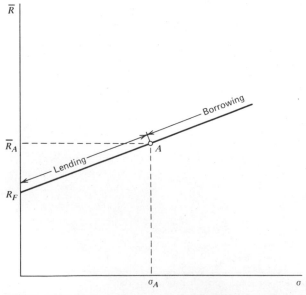

Figure 3.13   Expected return and risk when the risk-free rate is mixed with portfolio A.

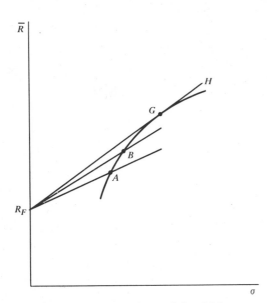

Figure 3.14   Combinations of the riskless asset and various risky portfolios.

the straight line passing through R_F as far as we can in a counterclockwise direction. The furthest we can rotate it is through point G.[14] Point G is the tangency point between the efficient frontier and a ray passing through the point R_F on the vertical axis. The investor cannot rotate the ray further because by the definition of the efficient frontier there are no portfolios lying above the line passing through R_F and G.

All investors who believed they faced the efficient frontier and riskless lending and borrowing rates shown in Figure 3.14 would hold the same portfolio of risky assets — portfolio G. Some of these investors who were very risk-averse would select a portfolio along the segment R_F–G and place some of their money in a riskless asset and some in risky portfolio G. Others who were much more tolerant of risk would hold portfolios along the segment G–H, borrowing funds and placing their original capital plus the borrowed funds in portfolio G. Still other investors would just place the total of their original funds in risky portfolio G. All of these investors would hold risky portfolios with the exact composition of portfolio G. Thus, for the case of riskless lending and borrowing, identification of portfolio G constitutes a solution to the portfolio problem. The ability to determine the optimum portfolio of risky assets without having to know anything about the investor has a special name. It is called the separation theorem.[15]

Let us for a moment examine the shape of the efficient frontier under more restrictive assumptions about the ability of investors to lend and borrow at the risk-free rate. There is no question about the ability of investors to lend at the

---

[14]In this section we have drawn the efficient frontier as it would look if short sales were not allowed. However, the analysis is general and applies equally well to the case where short sales are allowed.

[15]The words "separation theorem" have, at times, been used to describe other phenomena in finance. We continue to use it in the above sense throughout this book.

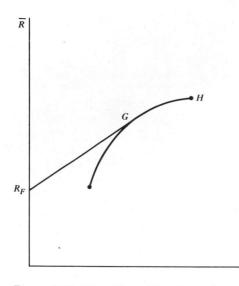

Figure 3.15   The efficient frontier with lending but not borrowing at the riskless rate.

risk-free rate (buy government securities). If they can lend but not borrow at this rate, the efficient frontier becomes R_F–G–H in Figure 3.15. Certain investors will hold portfolios of risky assets located between G and H. However, any investor who held some riskless asset would place all remaining funds in the risky portfolio G.

Another possibility is that investors can lend at one rate but must pay a different and presumably higher rate to borrow. Calling the borrowing rate R'_F the efficient frontier would become R_F–G–H–I in Figure 3.16. Here there is a small range of risky portfolios that would be optional for investors to hold. If R_F and R'_F are

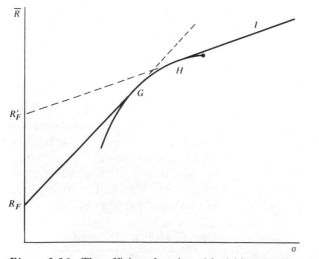

Figure 3.16   The efficient frontier with riskless lending and borrowing at different rates.

not too far apart, the assumption of riskless lending and borrowing at the same rate might provide a good approximation to the optimal range *G–H* of risky portfolios that investors might consider holding.

CONCLUSION

In this chapter we have defined the geometric properties of that set of portfolios all risk-avoiding investors would hold regardless of their specific tolerance for risk. We have defined this set — the efficient frontier — under alternative assumptions about short sales and the ability of the investor to lend and borrow at the riskless rate. Now that we understand the geometric properties of the efficient frontier, we are in a position to discuss solution techniques to the portfolio problem. This is done in the following chapter.

QUESTIONS AND PROBLEMS

1. Return to the example presented in Problem 1, Chapter 2.

    A.   Assuming short selling is not allowed:

        (1)   For securities 1 and 2 find the composition, standard deviation, and expected return of that portfolio that has minimum risk.

        (2)   On the same graph plot the expected return and standard deviation for all possible combinations of securities 1 and 2.

        (3)   Assuming that investors prefer more to less and are risk avoiders, indicate in red those sections of the diagram in Part 2 that are efficient.

        (4)   Repeat steps 1, 2, and 3 for all other possible pairwise combinations of the securities shown in Problem 1 of Chapter 2.

    B.   Assuming short selling is allowed:

        (1)   For securities 1 and 2 find the composition, standard deviation, and expected return of that portfolio that has minimum risk.

        (2)   On the same graph plot the expected return and standard deviation for all possible combinations of securities 1 and 2.

        (3)   Assuming that investors prefer more to less and are risk avoiders, indicate in red those sections of the diagram in Part 2 that are efficient.

        (4)   Repeat steps 1, 2, and 3 for all other possible pairwise combinations of the securities shown in Problem 1 of Chapter 2.

    C.   Assuming that the riskless lending and borrowing rate is 5%, and short sales are allowed, find the location of the optimal portfolio from among those considered. Repeat for a rate of 8%.

2.   Answer the questions to Problem 1 with data from Chapter 2, Problem 2.

3. For Problem 2 find the composition of the portfolio that has minimum variance for each two security combination you considered.

4. Derive the expression for the location of all portfolios of two securities in expected return standard deviation space when the correlation between the two securities is -1.

BIBLIOGRAPHY

1. Bawa, Vijay. "Admissible Portfolios for All Individuals," *Journal of Finance,* **XXXI,** No. 3 (Sept. 1976), pp. 1169–1183.
2. Ben-Horim, Moshe, and Levy, Haim. "Total Risk, Diversifiable Risk and Non-Diversifiable Risk: A Pedagogic Note," *Journal of Financial and Quantitative Analysis,* **XV,** No. 2 (June 1980), pp. 289–298.
3. Brennan, Michael J., and Kraus, Allan. "The Geometry of Separation and Myopia," *Journal of Financial and Quantitative Analysis,* **XI,** No. 2 (June 1976), pp. 171–193.
4. Brumelle, Shelby. "When Does Diversification between Two Investments Pay?" *Journal of Financial and Quantitative Analysis,* **IX,** No. 3 (June 1974), pp. 473–483.
5. Buser, Stephen. "A Simplified Expression for the Efficient Frontier in Mean-Variance Portfolio Analysis," *Management Science,* **23** (April 1977), pp. 901–903.
6. Cass, Davie, and Stiglitz, Joseph. "The Structure of Investor Preferences and Asset Returns, and Separability in Portfolio Allocation: A Contribution to the Pure Theory of Mutual Funds," *Journal of Economic Theory,* **2,** No. 2 (June 1970), pp. 122–160.
7. Dalal, Ardeshir J. "On the Use of a Covariance Function in a Portfolio Model," *Journal of Financial and Quantitative Analysis,* **XVIII,** No. 2 (June 1983), pp. 223–228.
8. Elton, Edwin J., and Gruber, Martin J. "Portfolio Theory When Investment Relatives Are Lognormally Distributed," *Journal of Finance,* **XXIX,** No. 4 (Sept. 1974), pp. 1265–1273.
9. ———. "Dynamic Programming Applications in Finance," *Journal of Finance,* **XXVI,** No. 2 (May 1971), pp. 473–505.
10. Friedman, Harris. "Real Estate Investment and Portfolio Theory," *Journal of Financial and Quantitative Analysis,* **VI,** No. 2 (March 1971), pp. 861–873.
11. Hakansson, Nils. "Risk Disposition and the Separation Property in Portfolio Selection," *Journal of Financial and Quantitative Analysis,* **IV,** No. 4 (Dec. 1969), pp. 401–416.
12. ———. "An Induced Theory of the Firm under Risk: The Pure Mutual Fund," *Journal of Financial and Quantitative Analysis,* **V,** No. 2 (May 1970), pp. 155–178.
13. Merton, Robert. "An Analytic Derivation of the Efficient Portfolio Fron-

tier," *Journal of Financial and Quantitative Analysis,* **VII,** No. 4 (Sept. 1972), pp. 1851–1872.

14. Mossin, Jan. "Optimal Multiperiod Portfolio Policies," *Journal of Business,* **41,** No. 2 (April 1968), pp. 215–229.

15. Ohlson, J.S., and Ziemba, W.T. "Portfolio Selection in a Lognormal Market When the Investor Has a Power Utility Function," *Journal of Financial and Quantitative Analysis,* **XI,** No. 1 (March 1976), pp. 57–71.

16. Ohlson, James. "Portfolio Selection in a Log-Stable Market," *Journal of Financial and Quantitative Analysis,* **X,** No. 2 (June 1975), pp. 285–298.

17. Pye, Gordon. "Lifetime Portfolio Selection in Continuous Time for a Multiplicative Class of Utility Functions." *American Economic Review,* **LXIII,** No. 5 (Dec. 1973), pp. 1013–1020.

18. Rosenberg, Barr, and Ohlson, James. "The Stationarity Distribution of Returns and Portfolio Separation in Capital Markets: A Fundamental Contradiction," *Journal of Financial and Quantitative Analysis,* **XI,** No. 3 (June 1973), pp. 393–401.

19. Smith, Keith. "Alternative Procedures for Revising Investment Portfolios," *Journal of Financial and Quantitative Analysis,* **III,** No. 4 (Dec. 1968), pp. 371–403.

Chapter 4

Techniques for Calculating the Efficient Frontier

In Chapters 2 and 3 we discussed the properties of the efficient frontier under alternative assumptions about lending and borrowing and alternative assumptions about short sales. In this chapter we describe and illustrate methods that can be used to calculate efficient portfolios. By necessity this chapter is more mathematically complex than those that preceded it and most of those that follow. The reader who is only concerned with a conceptual approach to portfolio management can skip this chapter and still understand later ones. However, we believe that knowledge of the solution techniques to portfolio problems outlined here yields a better understanding and appreciation of portfolio management.

We have not followed the same order in presenting solution techniques for portfolio problems as was followed in describing the properties of the efficient set (Chapter 3). Rather, we have rearranged the order so that solution techniques are presented from the simplest to the most complex. The four sections of this chapter discuss the solution to the portfolio problem when it is assumed in turn that:

1. Short sales are allowed and riskless lending and borrowing is possible.
2. Short sales are allowed but riskless lending or borrowing is not permitted.
3. Short sales are disallowed but riskless lending and borrowing exists.
4. Neither short sales nor riskless lending and borrowing are allowed.

The solution techniques discussed here are the ones used in actual applications. For most problems the calculations are lengthy enough that computers are used. Indeed computer programs exist for each of the techniques discussed. In addition, in Chapter 7 we present simplifications of the procedures discussed in the present chapter that are useful in solving most real problems. This chapter is necessary for an understanding of the computer programs and an appreciation of the simple rules discussed later. Thus although this chapter is more demanding than some others, it is well worth the effort needed to understand it.

SHORT SALES ALLOWED WITH RISKLESS LENDING AND BORROWING

The derivation of the efficient set when short sales are allowed and there is a riskless lending and borrowing rate is the simplest case we can consider. From Chapter 3 we know that the existence of a riskless lending and borrowing rate implies that there is a single portfolio of risky assets that is preferred to all other portfolios. Furthermore, in return standard deviation space, this portfolio plots on the ray connecting the riskless asset and a risky portfolio that lies furthest in the counterclockwise direction. For example, in Figure 4.1 the portfolio on the ray R_F–B is preferred to all other portfolios of risky assets. The efficient frontier is the entire length of the ray extending through R_F and B. Different points along the ray R_F–B represent different amounts of borrowing and/or lending in combination with the optimum portfolio of risky assets portfolio B.

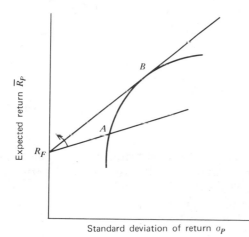

Figure 4.1

An equivalent way of identifying the ray R_F–B is to recognize that it is the ray with the greatest slope. Recall that the slope of the line connecting a riskless asset and risky portfolio is the expected return on the portfolio minus the risk-free rate divided by the standard deviation of the return on the portfolio. Thus, the efficient set is determined by finding that portfolio with the greatest ratio of excess return (expected return minus risk-free rate) to standard deviation that satisfies the constraint that the sum of the proportions invested in the assets equals 1. In equation form we have: maximize the objective function

$$\theta = \frac{\overline{R}_P - R_F}{\sigma_P}$$

subject to the constraint[1]

$$\sum_{i=1}^{N} X_i = 1$$

This is a constrained maximization problem. There are standard solution techniques available for solving it. For example, it can be solved by the method of Lagrangian multipliers. There is an alternative. The constraint could be substituted into the objective function and the objective function maximized as in an unconstrained problem. This latter procedure will be followed below. We can write R_F as R_F times 1. Thus we have

$$R_F = 1R_F = \left(\sum_{i=1}^{N} X_i\right) R_F = \sum_{i=1}^{N} X_i R_F$$

Making this substitution in the objective function and stating the expected return and standard deviation of return in the general form, derived in Chapter 2, yields

$$\theta = \frac{\sum_{i=1}^{N} X_i(\bar{R}_i - R_F)}{\left[\sum_{i=1}^{N} X_i^2 \sigma_i^2 + \sum_{i=1}^{N} \sum_{\substack{j=1 \\ j \neq i}}^{N} X_i X_j \sigma_{ij}\right]^{1/2}}$$

The problem stated above is a very simple maximization problem and as such can be solved using the standard methods of basic calculus. In calculus it is shown that to find the maximum of a function you take the derivative with respect to each variable and set it equal to zero.[2] Thus the solution to the maximization problem just presented involves finding the solution to the following system of

---

[1]Lintner [21] has advocated an alternative definition of short sales, one that is more realistic. He assumes correctly that when an investor sells stock short, cash is not received but rather is held as collateral. Furthermore, the investor must put up an additional amount of cash equal to the amount of stock he or she sells short. The investor generally does not receive any compensation (interest) on these funds. However, if the investor is a broker-dealer, interest can be earned on both the money put up and the money received from the short sale of securities. As shown in Appendix A, this leads to the constraint, $\Sigma|X_i| = 1$, and leaves all other equations unchanged.

[2]Solving the problem without constraining the solution by

$$\sum_{i=1}^{N} X_i = 1$$

does not work in every maximization problem. It works here because the equations are homogeneous of degree zero.

simultaneous equations:

$$1. \quad \frac{d\theta}{dX_1} = 0$$

$$2. \quad \frac{d\theta}{dX_2} = 0$$

$$3. \quad \frac{d\theta}{dX_3} = 0$$

$$\vdots$$

$$N. \quad \frac{d\theta}{dX_N} = 0$$

In Appendix B at the end of this chapter we show that

$$\frac{d\theta}{dX_i} = -(\lambda X_1\sigma_{1i} + \lambda X_2\sigma_{2i} + \lambda X_3\sigma_{3i} + \cdots + \lambda X_i\sigma_i^2 + \cdots$$

$$+ \lambda X_{N-1}\sigma_{N-1i} + \lambda X_N\sigma_{Ni}) + \overline{R}_i - R_F = 0$$

where λ is a constant.[3] A mathematical trick allows a useful modification of the derivative. Note that each X_k is multiplied by a constant λ. Define a new variable $Z_k = \lambda X_k$. The X_k are the fraction to invest in each security and the Z_k are proportional to this fraction. Substituting Z_k for the λX_k simplifies the formulation. To solve for the X_k after obtaining the Z_k, one divides each Z_k by the sum of the Z_k. Substituting Z_k for $\lambda_k X_k$ and moving the variance covariance terms to the right-hand side of the equality yields

$$\overline{R}_i - R_F = Z_1\sigma_{1i} + Z_2\sigma_{2i} + \cdots + Z_i\sigma_i^2 + \cdots + Z_{N-1}\sigma_{N-1i} + Z_N\sigma_{Ni}$$

We have one equation like this for each value of i. Thus the solution involves solving the following system of simultaneous equations.

$$\overline{R}_1 - R_F = Z_1\sigma_1^2 + Z_2\sigma_{12} + Z_3\sigma_{13} + \cdots + Z_N\sigma_{1N}$$

$$\overline{R}_2 - R_F = Z_1\sigma_{12} + Z_2\sigma_2^2 + Z_3\sigma_{23} + \cdots + Z_N\sigma_{2N}$$

$$\overline{R}_3 - R_F = Z_1\sigma_{13} + Z_2\sigma_{23} + Z_3\sigma_3^2 + \cdots + Z_N\sigma_{3N} \qquad (4.1)$$

$$\vdots$$

$$\overline{R}_N - R_F = Z_1\sigma_{1N} + Z_2\sigma_{2N} + Z_3\sigma_{3N} + \cdots + Z_N\sigma_N^2$$

---

[3]The constant is equal to $(\overline{R}_P - R_F)$ divided by σ_P^2.

The Z's are proportional to the optimum amount to invest in each security. To determine the optimum amount to invest, we first solve the equations for the Z's. Note that this does not present a problem. There are N equations (one for each security) and N unknowns (the Z_k for each security). Then the optimum proportions to invest in stock k is X_k, where

$$X_k = Z_k \bigg/ \sum_{i=1}^{N} Z_i$$

Let us solve an example. Consider three securities: Colonel Motors with expected return of 14% and standard deviation of return of 6%, Separated Edison with average return of 8% and standard deviation of return of 3%, and Unique Oil with mean return of 20% and standard deviation of return of 15%. Furthermore, assume that the correlation coefficient between Colonel Motors and Separated Edison is 0.5, between Colonel Motors and Unique Oil is 0.2, and between Separated Edison and Unique Oil is 0.4. Finally assume that the riskless lending and borrowing rate is 5%. Equation (4.1) for three securities is

$$\overset{14}{\underset{8}{\overline{R}_1}} - \overset{5}{\underset{5}{R_F}} = \overset{36}{Z_1\sigma_1^2} + Z_2\sigma_{12} + Z_3\sigma_{13}$$

$$\overset{}{\underset{20}{\overline{R}_2}} - \overset{}{\underset{5}{R_F}} = Z_1\sigma_{12} + Z_2\sigma_2^2 + Z_3\sigma_{23}$$

$$\overline{R}_3 - R_F = Z_1\sigma_{13} + Z_2\sigma_{23} + Z_3\sigma_3^2$$

Substituting in the assumed values, we get the following system of simultaneous equations:

$$14 - 5 = 36Z_1 + (0.5)(6)(3)Z_2 + (0.2)(6)(15)Z_3$$

$$8 - 5 = (0.5)(6)(3)Z_1 + 9Z_2 + (0.4)(3)(15)Z_3$$

$$20 - 5 = (0.2)(6)(15)Z_1 + (0.4)(3)(15)Z_2 + 225Z_3$$

Simplifying,

$$9 = 36Z_1 + 9Z_2 + 18Z_3$$

$$3 = 9Z_1 + 9Z_2 + 18Z_3$$

$$15 = 18Z_1 + 18Z_2 + 225Z_3$$

Further simplifying,

$$1 = 4Z_1 + Z_2 + 2Z_3$$

$$1 = 3Z_1 + 3Z_2 + 6Z_3$$

$$5 = 6Z_1 + 6Z_2 + 75Z_3$$

The solution to this system of simultaneous equations is

$$Z_1 = \frac{14}{63}, \quad Z_2 = \frac{1}{63}, \quad \text{and} \quad Z_3 = \frac{3}{63}.$$

The reader can verify this solution by substituting these values of Z_k into the foregoing equations.[4] The proportion to invest in each security is easy to determine. We know that each Z_k is proportional to X_k. Consequently, all we have to do to determine X_k is to scale the Z_k so that they add to 1.[5] For the foregoing problem

$$\sum_{i=1}^{3} Z_i = \frac{18}{63}$$

Thus the proportion to invest in each security is

$$X_1 = \frac{14}{18}, \quad X_2 = \frac{1}{18}, \quad \text{and} \quad X_3 = \frac{3}{18}$$

The expected return on the portfolio is

$$\overline{R}_P = \frac{14}{18}(14) + \frac{1}{18}(8) + \frac{3}{18}(20) = 14\tfrac{2}{3}\%$$

The variance of the return on the portfolio is[6]

$$\sigma_P^2 = \left(\frac{14}{18}\right)^2 (36) + \left(\frac{1}{18}\right)^2 9 + \left(\frac{3}{18}\right)^2 (225) + 2\left(\frac{14}{18}\right)\left(\frac{1}{18}\right)(6)(3)(0.5)$$

$$+ 2\left(\frac{14}{18}\right)\left(\frac{3}{18}\right)(6)(15)(0.2) + 2\left(\frac{1}{18}\right)\left(\frac{3}{18}\right)(3)(15)(0.4) = \frac{203}{6} = 33\tfrac{5}{6}$$

---

[4] See Appendix C at the end of this chapter for a description of solution techniques for systems of simultaneous equations.

[5] In the case of Lintnerian short sales, simply scale so that

$$\sum_{i=1}^{3} |X_i| = 1.$$

[6] The variance of the portfolio could have been determined in another way. Recall that λ is the ratio of the excess return on the optimum portfolio divided by the variance of the optimum portfolio. Thus

$$\lambda = \frac{\overline{R}_P - R_F}{\sigma_P^2} = \frac{14\tfrac{2}{3} - 5}{\sigma_P^2}$$

Also recall that $Z_i = \lambda X_i$ so that $\Sigma Z_i = \lambda \Sigma X_i = \lambda$. Earlier we determined that $\Sigma Z_i = \lambda = 18/63$. Equating these two equations and solving for σ_P^2 yields the value presented above.

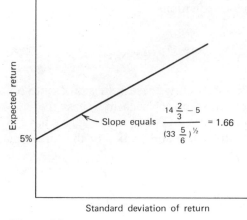

Figure 4.2

The efficient set is a straight line with an intercept at the risk-free rate of 5% and a slope equal to the ratio of excess return to standard deviation. (See Figure 4.2.) There are standard computer packages for the solution of a system of simultaneous equations. Appendix C at the end of this chapter presents some methods of solving them when the number of securities involved is limited so that hand calculations are reasonable.

SHORT SALES ALLOWED: NO RISKLESS LENDING AND BORROWING

When the investor does not wish to make the assumption that he can borrow and lend at the riskless rate of interest, the solution developed in the last section must be modified. However, much of the analysis can still be utilized. Consider Figure 4.3. The riskless lending and borrowing rate of 5% led to the selection of portfolio B. If the riskless lending and borrowing rate had been 4%, the investor would invest in portfolio A. If the investor's lending and borrowing rate was 6%, the investor would select portfolio C. These observations suggest the following procedure. Assume that a riskless lending and borrowing rate exists and find the optimum portfolio. Then assume that a different riskless lending and borrowing rate exists and find the optimum portfolio that corresponds to this second rate. Continue changing the assumed riskless rate until the full efficient frontier is determined.

In Appendix D we present a general solution to this problem. We show that the optimal proportion to invest in any security is simply a linear function of R_F. Furthermore, since the entire efficient frontier can be constructed as a combination of any two portfolios that lie along it, the identification of the characteristics of the optimal portfolio for any two arbitrary values of R_F is sufficient to trace out the total efficient frontier.

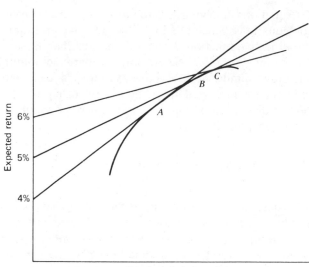

Figure 4.3

RISKLESS LENDING AND BORROWING WITH SHORT SALES NOT ALLOWED

This problem is analogous to the case of riskless lending and borrowing with short sales allowed. One portfolio is optimal. Once again, it is the one that maximizes the slope of the line connecting the riskless asset and a risky portfolio. However, the set of portfolios that is available to combine with lending and borrowing is different because a new constraint has been added. Investors cannot hold securities in negative amounts. More formally, the problem can be stated as

$$\text{Maximize } \theta = \frac{\overline{R}_P - R_F}{\sigma_P}$$

Subject to

$$(1) \quad \sum_{i=1}^{N} X_i = 1$$

$$(2) \quad X_i \geqslant 0 \quad \text{all } i$$

This is a mathematical programming problem because of the inequality restriction on X_i. At first glance this might look like a linear programming problem. In fact, the constraints (1) and (2) are linear constraints. The problem is that the objective function (the expression we are maximizing) is not linear. σ_P contains terms involving X_i^2 and X_iX_j. Equations involving squared terms and cross-product terms are called quadratic equations. Since this looks like a linear programming problem except that the objective function is quadratic rather than linear, it is called a quadratic programming problem. There are standard computer packages for solving quadratic programming problems just as there are for linear programming problems, and the reader interested in solving a large-scale problem would utilize one of them. Some discussion of solution techniques is contained in Appendix E at the end of this chapter.

NO SHORT SELLING AND NO RISKLESS LENDING AND BORROWING

Recall that an efficient set is determined by minimizing the risk for any level of expected return. If we specify the return at some level and minimize risk, we have one point on the efficient frontier. Thus, to get one point on the efficient frontier, we minimize risk subject to the return being some level plus the restriction that the sum of the proportions invested in each security adds to 1 and that all securities have positive or zero investment. This yields the following problem:

$$\text{Minimize} \sum_{i=1}^{N} X_i^2 \sigma_i^2 + \sum_{i=1}^{N} \sum_{\substack{j=1 \\ j \neq i}}^{N} X_i X_j \sigma_{ij}$$

Subject to

$$(1) \quad \sum_{i=1}^{N} X_i = 1$$

$$(2) \quad \sum_{i=1}^{N} X_i \overline{R}_i = \overline{R}_P$$

$$(3) \quad X_i \geq 0, \qquad i = 1, \cdots, N$$

Varying $\overline{R}_P$ between the return on the minimum variance portfolio and the return on the maximum return portfolio traces out the efficient set. Once again, the problem is a quadratic programming problem because of the presence of terms like X_i^2 and X_iX_j (squared and cross-product terms). However, there are standard packages available that solve this problem.

CONCLUSION

In this chapter we discussed and illustrated the use of techniques that can be employed to solve for the set of all possible portfolios that are efficient. All of the solution techniques discussed are feasible and have been used to solve problems. However, the techniques require gigantic amounts of input data and large amounts of computation time. Furthermore, the input data is in a form to which the security analyst and portfolio manager cannot easily relate. For this reason it is difficult to get estimates of the input data or to get practitioners to relate to the final output.

The next logical step is to simplify the number and type of input requirements for portfolio selection and, in turn, to see if this reduction in data complexity can also be used to simplify the computational procedure. This is the subject of the next three chapters.

APPENDIX A

An Alternative Definition of Short Sales

Modeling short sales from the viewpoint of the broker-dealer, we first note that the broker-dealer has a fixed sum of money to invest. A short sale involves putting up an amount of money equal to the short sale. Thus, the short sale is a use rather than a source of funds to the short seller. The total funds the broker-dealer invests short, plus the funds invested long, must add to the original investment. Since for short sales $X_i < 0$, the proportion of the funds invested in the short sale is $|X_i|$. In addition, the short seller (if a broker-dealer) receives interest on both the money put up against short sales and the money received from the short sale. Thus, the expected return from short selling .10 of stock i is $-.1\overline{R}_i + .2R_F$. Since X_i is negative for short sales, this can be written as $X_i(\overline{R}_i - 2R_F)$. Assume stocks 1 to k are held long and stocks $k + 1$ to N are sold short. Then

$$\overline{R}_P = \sum_{i=1}^{k} X_i(\overline{R}_i) + \sum_{i=k+1}^{N} X_i(\overline{R}_i - 2R_F)$$

$$\overline{R}_P = \sum_{i=1}^{N} X_i\overline{R}_i - 2 \sum_{i=k+1}^{N} X_i(R_F)$$

The constraint with the Lintner definition of short sales is

$$\sum_{i=1}^{N} |X| = 1.$$

Substituting this for 1 times R_F yields

$$R_F = \sum_{i=1}^{N} |X_i| R_F = \sum_{i=1}^{k} X_i R_F - \sum_{i=k+1}^{N} X_i R_F \qquad (A.1)$$

This is the expression used for R_F. Subtracting R_F from both sides of the equation for $\overline{R}_P$ and using (A-1) for R_F on the right-hand side of the equation yields

$$\overline{R}_P - R_F = \left[\sum_{i=1}^{N} X_i \overline{R}_i - 2 \sum_{i=k+1}^{N} X_i R_F \right] - \left[\sum_{i=1}^{k} X_i R_F - \sum_{i=k+1}^{N} X_i R_F \right]$$

$$\overline{R}_P - R_F = \sum_{i=1}^{N} X_i \overline{R}_i - \sum_{i=1}^{N} X_i R_F = \sum_{i=1}^{N} X_i (\overline{R}_i - R_F)$$

This is identical to the equation given in the text. The reader should note two points. In the Lintnerian definition of short sales, the final portfolio weights must be scaled so that the sum of the absolute value of the weights, rather than their sum, adds to 1. In addition, when short sales are defined in this manner, the efficient frontier no longer extends to infinity but rather resembles, in general shape, the efficient frontier when short sales are not allowed.

APPENDIX B

Determining the Derivative

In the text we discussed that in order to solve the portfolio problem when short sales are allowed the derivative of θ with respect to X_k was needed.[7] In the text we presented the value of the derivative. In this appendix we will derive its value. To determine the derivative rewrite the θ shown in the text as

$$\theta = \left[\sum_{i=1}^{N} X_i (\overline{R}_i - R_F) \right] \left[\sum_{i=1}^{N} X_i^2 \sigma_i^2 + \sum_{i=1}^{N} \sum_{\substack{j=1 \\ j \neq i}}^{N} X_i X_j \sigma_{ij} \right]^{-1/2}$$

Two rules from calculus are needed:

1. *The product rule:* θ is the product of two functions. The product rule states that the derivative of the product of two functions is the first function times the derivative of the second function plus the second times the derivative of the first. In symbols,

$$\frac{d}{dx} \left[[F_1(x)][F_2(x)] \right] = [F_1(x)] \frac{dF_2(x)}{dx} + [F_2(X)] \frac{dF_1(x)}{dx} \qquad \text{(B.1)}$$

---

[7]To ensure a maximum, the second derivative should be negative. The structure of this problem guarantees this.

Let

$$F_1(X) = \sum_{i=1}^{N} X_i(\overline{R}_i - R_F) \tag{B.2}$$

$$F_2(X) = \left(\sum_{i=1}^{N} X_i^2\sigma_i^2 + \sum_{i=1}^{N} \sum_{\substack{j=1 \\ j \neq i}}^{N} X_i X_j \sigma_{ij} \right)^{-1/2} \tag{B.3}$$

Consider first the derivative of $F_1(X)$. At first glance the reader may believe it is difficult. However, it turns out to be trivial. An expression like

$$\sum_{i=1}^{N} X_i(\overline{R}_i - R_F)$$

involves a lot of terms that do not contain an X_k and one term involving X_k. The derivative of the terms not involving X_k are zero (they are constants as far as X_k is concerned). The derivative of the term involving X_k is $\overline{R}_k - R_F$. Thus

$$\frac{dF_1(X)}{dX_k} = \overline{R}_k - R_F \tag{B.4}$$

Now consider the derivative of $F_2(X)$. To determine this a second rule from calculus is needed.

2.   *The chain rule:* $F_2(X)$ involves a term in brackets to a power (the power $-\frac{1}{2}$). The chain rule states that its derivative is the power, times the expression in parenthesis to the power minus one, times the derivative of what is inside the brackets. Thus,

$$\frac{dF_2(X)}{dX_k} = (-\tfrac{1}{2}) \left(\sum_{i=1}^{N} X_i^2\sigma_i^2 + \sum_{i=1}^{N} \sum_{\substack{j=1 \\ j \neq i}}^{N} X_i X_j \sigma_{ij} \right)^{-3/2}$$

$$\times \left(2X_k\sigma_k^2 + 2\sum_{\substack{j=1 \\ j \neq k}}^{N} X_j \sigma_{jk} \right) \tag{B.5}$$

The only term that requires comment is the last one. The derivative of

$$\sum_{i=1}^{N} X_i^2\sigma_i^2$$

follows the same principles discussed earlier. All terms not involving k are constant as far as k is concerned and thus their derivative is zero. The term involving k is $X_k^2 \sigma_k^2$ and has a derivative of $2X_k \sigma_k^2$. The derivation of the double summation is more complex. Consider the double summation term

$$\left(\sum_{\substack{i=1}}^{N} \sum_{\substack{j=1 \\ j \neq i}}^{N} X_i X_j \sigma_{ij} \right)$$

We get X_k twice, once when $i = k$ and once when $j = k$. When $i = k$, we have

$$\sum_{\substack{j=1 \\ j \neq k}}^{N} X_k X_j \sigma_{kj} = X_k \left[\sum_{\substack{j=1 \\ j \neq k}}^{N} X_j \sigma_{kj} \right]$$

The derivative of this is, of course

$$\sum_{\substack{j=1 \\ j \neq k}}^{N} X_j \sigma_{kj}$$

Similarly, when $j = k$ we have

$$\sum_{\substack{i=1 \\ i \neq k}}^{N} X_i X_k \sigma_{ik} = X_k \left(\sum_{\substack{i=1 \\ i \neq k}}^{N} X_i \sigma_{ik} \right)$$

The derivative of this is also

$$\left(\sum_{\substack{i=1 \\ i \neq k}}^{N} X_i \sigma_{ik} \right)$$

i and j are simply summonds. It does not matter which we use. Further, $\sigma_{ik} = \sigma_{ki}$. Thus,

$$\sum_{\substack{j=1 \\ j \neq k}}^{N} X_j \sigma_{kj} = \sum_{\substack{i=1 \\ i \neq k}}^{N} X_i \sigma_{ik}$$

and we have the expression shown in the derivative, namely,

$$2 \sum_{\substack{j=1 \\ j \neq k}}^{N} X_j \sigma_{kj}$$

Substituting (B.2), (B.3), (B.4) and (B.5) into the product rule, expression (B.1) yields

$$
\frac{d\theta}{dX_k} = \left[\sum_{i=1}^{N} X_i(\overline{R}_i - R_F) \right] \left[(-\tfrac{1}{2}) \left(\sum_{i=1}^{N} X_i^2\sigma_i^2 + \sum_{i=1}^{N}\sum_{\substack{j=1\\j\neq i}}^{N} X_iX_j\sigma_{ij} \right)^{-3/2} \right.
$$

$$
\left. \times \left(2X_k\sigma_k^2 + 2\sum_{\substack{j=1\\j\neq k}}^{N} X_j\sigma_{kj} \right) \right] + \left[\sum_{i=1}^{N} X_i^2\sigma_i^2 + \sum_{i=1}^{N}\sum_{\substack{j=1\\j\neq i}}^{N} X_iX_j\sigma_{ij} \right]^{-1/2}
$$

$$
\times \left[(\overline{R}_k - R_F) \right] = 0
$$

Multiplying the derivative by

$$
\left(\sum_{i=1}^{N} X_i^2\sigma_i^2 + \sum_{i=1}^{N}\sum_{\substack{j=1\\j\neq i}}^{N} X_iX_j\sigma_{ij} \right)^{1/2}
$$

and rearranging yields

$$
-\left[\frac{\sum_{i=1}^{N} X_i(\overline{R}_i - R_F)}{\sum_{i=1}^{N} X_i^2\sigma_i^2 + \sum_{i=1}^{N}\sum_{\substack{j=1\\j\neq i}}^{N} X_iX_j\sigma_{ij}} \right] \left[X_k\sigma_k^2 + \sum_{\substack{j=1\\j\neq k}}^{N} X_j\sigma_{kj} \right] + \left[\overline{R}_k - R_F \right] = 0
$$

Defining λ as

$$
\frac{\sum_{i=1}^{N} X_i(\overline{R}_i - R_F)}{\sum_{i=1}^{N} X_i^2\sigma_i^2 + \sum_{i=1}^{N}\sum_{\substack{j=1\\j\neq i}}^{N} X_iX_j\sigma_{ij}}
$$

yields

$$
-\lambda \left[X_k\sigma_k^2 + \sum_{\substack{j=1\\j\neq k}}^{N} X_j\sigma_{kj} \right] + (\overline{R}_k - R_F) = 0
$$

Multiplying the terms in the brackets by λ yields

$$-\left[\lambda X_k \sigma_k^2 + \sum_{\substack{j=1 \\ j \neq k}}^{N} \lambda X_j \sigma_{kj}\right] + (\overline{R}_k - R_F) = 0$$

This is the expression shown in the text.

APPENDIX C

Solving Systems of Simultaneous Equations

In order to solve large systems of simultaneous equations, one would use any of the large number of standard computer packages that exist for this purpose. However, small systems can be solved by hand. The simplest way is by repetitive substitution. Consider the following system of simultaneous equations:

$$4X_1 + X_2 = 7 \tag{C.1}$$

$$3X_1 + 2X_2 = 5 \tag{C.2}$$

Equation (C.1) can be rearranged so that X_2 is expressed as a function of X_1. This rearrangement yields

$$X_2 = 7 - 4X_1$$

Substituting this into Equation (C.2) yields

$$3X_1 + 2(7 - 4X_1) = 5$$
$$3X_1 + 14 - 8X_1 = 5$$
$$-5X_1 = -9$$
$$X_1 = \tfrac{9}{5}$$

Substituting the value for X_1 into rearranged Equation (C.1) yields

$$X_2 = 7 - 4(\tfrac{9}{5}) = 7 - \tfrac{36}{5} = -\tfrac{1}{5}$$

This technique is extremely easy and can be applied to solving any number of simultaneous equations, although with lots of equations it becomes extremely time consuming. For a second example consider the problem analyzed in the section "Short Sales Allowed":

$$1 = 4Z_1 + Z_2 + 2Z_3 \tag{C.3}$$

$$1 = 3Z_1 + 3Z_2 + 6Z_3 \tag{C.4}$$

$$5 = 6Z_1 + 6Z_2 + 75Z_3 \tag{C.5}$$

Solving Equation (C.3) for Z_2 and eliminating Z_2 from Equation (C.4) yields

$$Z_2 = 1 - 4Z_1 - 2Z_3 \tag{C.3'}$$

$$1 = 3Z_1 + 3(1 - 4Z_1 - 2Z_3) + 6Z_3 \tag{C.4'}$$

Simplifying (C.4') yields

$$-2 = -9Z_1$$

Following the same procedure for equation (C.5) yields

$$5 = 6Z_1 + 6(1 - 4Z_1 - 2Z_3) + 75Z_3 \tag{C.5'}$$

Simplifying (C.5') yields

$$-1 = -18Z_1 + 63Z_3$$

Equation (C.4') gives an immediate solution for Z_1; it is $Z_1 = \frac{2}{9}$. Substituting this into Equation (C.5') allows us to solve for Z_3,

$$-1 = -4 + 63Z_3$$

$$Z_3 = \frac{3}{63}$$

Substituting the value of Z_3 and Z_1 into (C.3') yields for Z_2

$$Z_2 = 1 - \frac{8}{9} - \frac{6}{63} = \frac{1}{63}$$

This is the solution stated in the text. When the number of equations and variables becomes large, it is usually more convenient to solve the problem by working on a tableau. A tableau for the last problem is presented below:

Z_1	Z_2	Z_3	= constant
4	1	2	= 1
3	3	6	= 1
6	6	75	= 5

Under each of the variables is the coefficient shown in the system of equations (C.3), (C.4), and (C.5). If c_1, c_2, c_3 are arbitrary constants, the solution is reached when the tableau looks like

Z_1	Z_2	Z_3	= constant
1	0	0	c_1
0	1	0	c_2
0	0	1	c_3

To move from the first tableau to the second, three operations are allowed:

1. You can multiply or divide any row by a constant.
2. You can add or subtract a constant times one row from another row.
3. You can exchange any two rows.

Let us apply this to the problem discussed earlier. Subtracting twice row 2 from row 3 yields

Z_1	Z_2	Z_3	constant
4	1	2	1
3	3	6	1
0	0	63	3

Dividing row 3 by 63 yields

Z_1	Z_2	Z_3	constant
4	1	2	1
3	3	6	1
0	0	1	$3/63$

Subtracting two times row 3 from row 1 and 6 times row 3 from row 2 yields

Z_1	Z_2	Z_3	constant
4	1	0	$57/63$
3	3	0	$45/63$
0	0	1	$3/63$

Subtracting ⅓ of row 2 from row 1 yields

Z_1	Z_2	Z_3	constant
3	0	0	$42/63$
3	3	0	$45/63$
0	0	1	$3/63$

Taking ⅓ of row 1 and ⅓ of row 2 yields

Z_1	Z_2	Z_3	constant
1	0	0	$14/63$
1	1	0	$15/63$
0	0	1	$3/63$

Subtracting row 1 from row 2 yields the final tableau

Z_1	Z_2	Z_3	constant
1	0	0	$14/63$
0	1	0	$1/63$
0	0	1	$3/63$

The now familiar solution can be read directly from this tableau. It is

$$Z_1 = \frac{14}{63}, \qquad Z_2 = \frac{1}{63}, \qquad \text{and} \qquad Z_3 = \frac{3}{63}$$

Either of these methods can be used to solve a system of simultaneous equations.

APPENDIX D

A General Solution

While we have just outlined a feasible procedure for identifying the efficient frontier, there is a simpler one. When we assumed a particular riskless lending and borrowing rate, we determined that the optimum portfolio is the one that solves the following system of simultaneous equations:

$$\overline{R}_1 - R_F = Z_1\sigma_1^2 + Z_2\sigma_{12} + Z_3\sigma_{13} + \cdots + Z_N\sigma_{1N}$$

$$\overline{R}_2 - R_F - Z_1\sigma_{12} + Z_2\sigma_2^2 + Z_3\sigma_{23} + \cdots + Z_N\sigma_{2N}$$

$$\overline{R}_3 - R_F = Z_1\sigma_{13} + Z_2\sigma_{23} + Z_3\sigma_3^2 + \cdots + Z_N\sigma_{3N}$$

$$\vdots$$

$$\overline{R}_N - R_F = Z_1\sigma_{1N} + Z_2\sigma_{2N} + Z_3\sigma_{3N} + \cdots + Z_N\sigma_N^2$$

When we solved this system of simultaneous equations we substituted, in particular, values of $\overline{R}_i$, R_F, σ_i^2, and σ_{ij}. However, we do not have to substitute in a particular value of R_F. We can simply leave R_F as a general parameter and solve for Z_k in terms of R_F. This results in a solution of the form

$$Z_k = C_{0k} + C_{1k}R_F$$

where C_{0k} and C_{1k} are constants. They have a different value for each security k but that value does not change with changes in R_F. Once the Z_k are determined as functions of R_F, we could vary R_F to determine the amount to invest in each security at various points along the efficient frontier. Let us apply this to the previous example. The system of simultaneous equations for a general R_F is

$$14 - R_F = 36Z_1 + 9Z_2 + 18Z_3 \qquad \text{(D.1)}$$

$$8 - R_F = 9Z_1 + 9Z_2 + 18Z_3 \qquad \text{(D.2)}$$

$$20 - R_F = 18Z_1 + 18Z_2 + 225Z_3 \qquad \text{(D.3)}$$

The solution to this system of simultaneous equations is

$$Z_1 = \frac{42}{189} \qquad \text{(D.4)}$$

$$Z_2 = \frac{118}{189} - \frac{23}{189} R_F \qquad \text{(D.5)}$$

$$Z_3 = \frac{4}{189} + \frac{1}{189} R_F \qquad \text{(D.6)}$$

This solution can be confirmed by substituting these values into Equations (D.1), (D.2), and (D.3). Also, as a further check, note that the substitution of $R_F = 5$ (which was the value we assumed in the last section) into Equations (D.4), (D.5), and (D.6) yields

$$Z_1 = \frac{42}{189} = \frac{14}{63}$$

$$Z_2 = \frac{118}{189} - \frac{23}{189}(5) = \frac{118 - 115}{189} = \frac{3}{189} = \frac{1}{63}$$

$$Z_3 = \frac{4}{189} + \frac{1}{189}(5) = \frac{9}{189} = \frac{3}{63}$$

the same solution we obtained earlier. The values of Z_k just determined can be scaled to sum to 1 exactly as was done before so that the optimum proportions can be determined.

Determining the General Coefficient from Two Portfolios

In the last section we determined that

$$Z_2 = \frac{118}{189} - \frac{23}{189} R_F$$

Assume that we had not determined this general expression. Rather we simply solved the system of simultaneous equations for two arbitrary values of R_F. The value of Z_2 corresponding to R_F of 5 is $\frac{1}{63}$ and the Z_2 corresponding to an R_F of 2 is $\frac{72}{189}$. Can we determine the general expression? The answer is clearly *yes*. As an example, assume we had solved the equations for an R_F of 2 and 5. We know the general expression has the form

$$Z_2 = C_{02} + C_{12}R_F$$

Further, we know that

$$Z_2 = \frac{1}{63} \quad \text{if } R_F = 5$$

$$Z_2 = \frac{72}{189} \quad \text{if } R_F = 2$$

Utilizing this in the previous equation we have

$$\frac{1}{63} = C_{02} + C_{12}(5)$$

$$\frac{72}{189} = C_{02} + C_{12}(2)$$

This is a system of two equations and two unknowns. We can use it to solve for $C_{02} = \frac{118}{189}$ and $C_{12} = -\frac{23}{189}$. Thus, if we have the optimum portfolio for any two values of R_F, we can obtain the value for C_{0k} and C_{1k} and then by varying R_F obtain the full efficient frontier.

This is an extremely powerful result. It means that the solution of the system of simultaneous equations for any two values of R_F allows us to trace out the full efficient frontier.

The tracing out of the efficient frontier can be done in two ways. First, we could solve for the general expression for Z_k in terms of R_F by determining Z_k for any two arbitrary values of R_F. Then, by varying R_F over the relevant range, we could trace out the efficient frontier.

A second procedure is suggested by the previous discussion. We showed that solving the system of simultaneous equations for any two values of R_F allowed us to obtain a general expression for Z_k in terms of R_F, thus enabling us to trace out the efficient frontier. This suggests that the efficient frontier can be determined directly by simply calculating any two optimum portfolios rather than indirectly by first determining Z_k as a function of R_F. It can be shown that this direct procedure is appropriate.[8] Thus, the entire efficient frontier can be traced out by determining the composition of any two portfolios and then determining all combinations of these two portfolios. This is an extremely powerful result and is the preferred way to determine the efficient set.

In the previous chapter we showed how to trace out all combinations (portfolios) of two assets. Nothing prevents the two assets from being efficient portfolios. Thus, given that the efficient frontier can be traced out by combining two efficient portfolios, if we find two efficient portfolios, we can utilize the proce-

---

[8]See Black [6] for a rigorous proof that this holds.

dures discussed in the last chapter to trace out the full efficient frontier. Let's see how this is done.

Tracing Out the Efficient Frontier

The Z_k that correspond to an $R_F = 2$ are from Equations (D.4) and (D.5), and (D.6):

$$Z_1 = \frac{42}{189}, \quad Z_2 = \frac{72}{189}, \quad Z_3 = \frac{6}{189}$$

The proportions to invest in each security are

$$X_1 = \frac{42}{120} = \frac{7}{20}$$

$$X_2 = \frac{72}{120} = \frac{12}{20}$$

$$X_3 = \frac{6}{120} = \frac{1}{20}$$

The expected return associated with this portfolio is

$$\overline{R}_P = \left(\frac{7}{20}\right)(14) + \left(\frac{12}{20}\right)(8) + \left(\frac{1}{20}\right)(20) = 10\frac{7}{10}$$

The variance of return on this portfolio is

$$\sigma_P^2 = \left(\frac{7}{20}\right)^2 (36) + \left(\frac{12}{20}\right)^2 9 + \left(\frac{1}{20}\right)^2 (225)$$

$$+ 2\left(\frac{7}{20}\right)\left(\frac{12}{20}\right)9 + 2\left(\frac{7}{20}\right)\left(\frac{1}{20}\right)(18) + 2\left(\frac{12}{20}\right)\left(\frac{1}{20}\right)18 = \frac{5481}{400}$$

If we knew the covariance between the portfolios associated with an $R_F = 5$ and the one associated with an $R_F = 2$, we could trace out the full efficient frontier by treating each portfolio as an asset and utilizing the method discussed in Chapter 3. The covariance is determined as follows. Consider a portfolio consisting of ½ of each of the two portfolios already determined. The investment proportions are

$$X''_1 = \frac{1}{2}\frac{7}{20} + \frac{1}{2}\frac{14}{18} = \frac{203}{360}$$

$$X''_2 = \frac{1}{2}\frac{12}{20} + \frac{1}{2}\frac{1}{18} = \frac{118}{360}$$

$$X''_3 = \frac{1}{2}\frac{1}{20} + \frac{1}{2}\frac{3}{18} = \frac{39}{360}$$

Its variance is

$$\sigma_P{}^2 = \left(\frac{203}{360}\right)^2 36 + \left(\frac{118}{360}\right)^2 9 + \left(\frac{39}{360}\right)^2 225$$

$$+2 \left(\frac{203}{360}\right)\left(\frac{118}{360}\right) 9 + 2 \left(\frac{203}{360}\right)\left(\frac{39}{360}\right) 18$$

$$+2 \left(\frac{118}{360}\right)\left(\frac{39}{360}\right) 18 = 21.859$$

But we know that this portfolio is a weighted average of the other two portfolios. In Chapter 3 we showed that the variance of a portfolio comprised of two assets or portfolios was

$$\sigma_P{}^2 = X_1{}^2\sigma_1{}^2 + X_2{}^2\sigma_2{}^2 + 2X_1X_2\sigma_{12}$$

Thus, the variance of a portfolio consisting of ½ of portfolio 1 and ½ of portfolio 2 is

$$\sigma^2 = \left(\frac{1}{2}\right)^2 \left(\frac{203}{6}\right) + \left(\frac{1}{2}\right)^2 \left(\frac{5481}{400}\right) + 2 \left(\frac{1}{2}\right)\left(\frac{1}{2}\right) \sigma_{12}$$

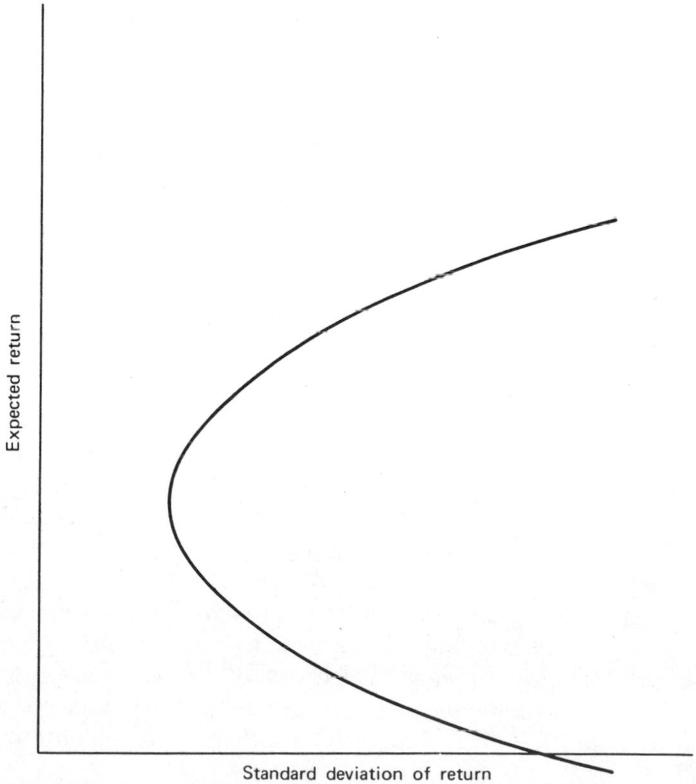

Figure 4.4

We know the variance of this portfolio is 21.859. Thus, σ_{12} can be determined from

$$21.859 = \left(\frac{1}{2}\right)^2 \left(\frac{203}{6}\right) + \left(\frac{1}{2}\right)^2 \left(\frac{5481}{400}\right) + 2\left(\frac{1}{2}\right)\left(\frac{1}{2}\right)\sigma_{12}$$

and

$$\sigma_{12} = 19.95$$

Knowing the expected returns variance and covariance, we can trace out the efficient frontier exactly as we did for combinations of two assets in Chapter 3. We have done so in Figure 4.4.

The Number of Securities Included

Before leaving this section, some observations are in order. First, when short sales are allowed, the investor takes a position in almost all securities. Each security will have, in general, one value of R_F for which it is not held. Namely, when $C_{0k} + C_{1k}R_F = 0$. But for all other values of R_F, it will be held either long or short. In fact, for all values of R_F above this value, the security will be held only long or short and vice versa for values of R_F below the value. Let us examine the expressions for Z_k as a function of R_F from our previous example.

$$Z_1 = \frac{42}{189}$$

$$Z_2 = \frac{118}{189} - \frac{23}{189}R_F$$

$$Z_3 = \frac{4}{189} + \frac{1}{189}R_F$$

Security 1 is always held long. Security 2 is held long if R_F is less than $^{118}\!/_{23}$ and is held short for all values of R_F greater than $^{118}\!/_{23}$. Finally, security 3 is held long if R_F is greater than -4 and held short for values of R_F below -4. The various values of Z_i as a function of R_F are shown in Figure 4.5.

The inclusion of almost all or all securities in the optimum portfolio makes intuitive sense. If a security's characteristics make it undesirable to hold, then the investor should issue it by selling it short. Thus, "good" securities are held and "bad" securities are issued to someone else. Of course, for someone else to be willing to take "bad" securities, there has to be a difference of opinion of what is good and bad.

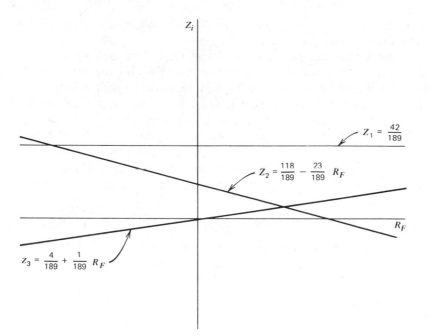

$$Z_1 = \frac{42}{189}$$

$$Z_2 = \frac{118}{189} - \frac{23}{189} R_F$$

$$Z_3 = \frac{4}{189} + \frac{1}{189} R_F$$

Figure 4.5

APPENDIX E

Quadratic Programming and Kuhn-Tucker Conditions

These quadratic programming algorithms are based on a technique from advanced calculus called Kuhn-Tucker conditions. For small-scale problems these conditions may be able to be used directly. Furthermore, an understanding of

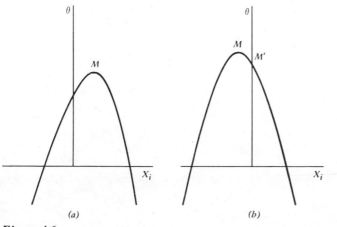

Figure 4.6

the nature of the solution to this type of portfolio problem can be gained by understanding the Kuhn-Tucker conditions.

Earlier we simply took the derivative of θ with respect to each X_i and set it equal to zero to find a maximum value of θ. This maximum is indicated by point M in Figure 4.6a or 4.6b. When X_i must be non-negative, a problem can occur because the unconstrained maximum may be at a value of X_i, which is infeasible. θ as a function of X_i might look like Figure 4.6b rather than Figure 4.6a. In this case (Figure 4.6b) the maximum feasible value of θ occurs at point M' rather than M. Notice that if the maximum value for X_i occurs at M', then $d\theta/dX_i < 0$ at the maximum feasible value ($X_i = 0$), whereas if it occurs when X_i is positive, then $d\theta/dX_i = 0$. Thus, in general, with X_i constrained to be larger than or equal to zero, we can write

$$\frac{d\theta}{dX_i} \leq 0$$

We could make this an equality by writing

$$\frac{d\theta}{dX_i} + U_i = 0$$

This is the first Kuhn-Tucker condition for a maximum.

Note two things about U_i. If the optimum occurs when X_i is positive, then the $d\theta/dX_i = 0$ and U_i is zero. Furthermore, if the optimum occurs when the maximum occurs at $X_i = 0$, then $d\theta/dX_i < 0$ and U_i is positive. To summarize at the optimum we have

$$X_i > 0, \qquad U_i = 0$$

$$X_i = 0, \qquad U_i > 0$$

This is the second Kuhn-Tucker condition. It can be written compactly as

$$X_i U_i = 0$$

$$X_i \geq 0$$

$$U_i \geq 0$$

The four Kuhn-Tucker conditions are

(1) $\dfrac{d\theta}{dX_i} + U_i = 0$

(2) $X_i U_i = 0$

(3) $X_i \geq 0$

(4) $U_i \geq 0$

If someone suggested a solution to us and it satisfied the Kuhn-Tucker conditions, then we could be sure that he had indeed given us the optimum portfolio.[9]

For example, assume the lending and borrowing rate was 6% and the securities being considered are the three securities considered throughout this chapter. Furthermore, assume the solution was

$$X_1 = \frac{43}{53}, \qquad U_1 = 0$$

$$X_2 = 0, \qquad U_2 = \frac{5}{8},$$

$$X_3 = \frac{10}{53}, \qquad U_3 = 0$$

Since this solution meets all the Kuhn-Tucker conditions, it is optimal.

To see that this solution meets the Kuhn-Tucker conditions, consider the following. First, all X's and U's are positive, thus conditions 3 and 4 are met. U_1, X_2, and $U_3 = 0$, thus either X or U is zero for any pair of securities and condition 2 is met. Finally, recall that

$$\frac{d\theta}{dX_i} = \bar{R}_i - R_F - \lambda \left[X_i \sigma_i^2 + \sum_{\substack{j-1 \\ j \neq i}}^{N} X_j \sigma_{ij} \right]$$

Adding U_i to this equation and substituting in the returns, variances, and covariances for the various securities, we have

$$8 - \lambda[36X_1 + 9X_2 + 18X_3] + U_1$$

$$2 - \lambda[9X_1 + 9X_2 + 18X_3] + U_2$$

$$14 - \lambda[18X_1 + 18X_2 + 225X_3] + U_3$$

$\lambda = (\bar{R}_P - R_F)/\sigma_P^2$. A little calculation shows that $\lambda = {}^{53}\!/_{216}$.
Substituting for X_1, X_2, and X_3 yields

$$8 - \frac{53}{216} \left[36 \left(\frac{43}{53}\right) + 9(0) + 18 \left(\frac{10}{53}\right) \right] + 0$$

$$2 - \frac{53}{216} \left[9 \left(\frac{43}{53}\right) + 9(0) + 18 \left(\frac{10}{53}\right) \right] + \frac{5}{8}$$

$$14 - \frac{53}{216} \left[18 \left(\frac{43}{53}\right) + 18(0) + 225 \left(\frac{10}{53}\right) \right] + 0$$

Since all three equal zero, the Kuhn-Tucker conditions are met.

---

[9]There are conditions on the shape of θ for this to be optimum, but they are always met for the portfolio problem and so can be safely ignored here.

QUESTIONS AND PROBLEMS

1. Assume analysts provide the following types of information. Assume (standard definition) short sales are allowed. What is the optimum portfolio if the lending and borrowing rate is 5%?

Security	Mean Return	Standard Deviation	Covariance with A	B	C
A	10	4		20	40
B	12	10			70
C	18	14			

2. Given the following information, what is the optimum portfolio if the lending and borrowing rate is 6% 8% or 10%? Assume the Lintner definition of short sales.

Security	Mean Return	Standard Deviation	Covariance with A	B	C
A	11	2		10	4
B	14	6			30
C	17	9			

3. Assume the information given in Problem 1, but that short sales are not allowed. Set up the formulation necessary to solve the portfolio problem.

4. Consider the following data. What is the optimum portfolio, assuming short sales are allowed (standard definition). Trace out the efficient frontier.

Number	$\overline{R}_i$	σ_i
1	10	5
2	8	6
3	12	4
4	14	7
5	6	2
6	9	3
7	5	1
8	8	4
9	10	4
10	12	2

$\rho_{ij} = 0.5$ for all ij
$R_F = 4$

5. Assume that the data below apply to two efficient portfolios. What is the efficient frontier? Assume the standard definition of short sales.

Portfolio	$\overline{R}_i$	σ_i
A	10	6
B	8	4

$\sigma_{ij} = 20$

BIBLIOGRAPHY

1. Alexander, Gordon. "Mixed Security Testing of Alternative Portfolio Selection Models," *Journal of Financial and Quantitative Analysis,* **XII,** No. 4 (Dec. 1977), pp. 817–832.
2. ———. "The Derivation of Efficient Sets," *Journal of Financial and Quantitative Analysis,* **XI,** No. 5 (Dec. 1976), pp. 817–830.
3. ———. "A Reevaluation of Alternative Portfolio Selection Models Applied to Common Stocks," *Journal of Financial and Quantitative Analysis,* **XIII,** No. 1 (March 1978), pp. 71–78.
4. Bawa, Vijay, "Mathematical Programming of Admissible Portfolios," *Management Science,* **23,** No. 7 (March 1977), pp. 779–785.
5. Bertsekas, Dimitris. "Necessary and Sufficient Conditions for Existence of an Optimal Portfolio," *Journal of Economic Theory,* **8,** No. 2 (June 1974), pp. 235–247.
6. Black, Fisher. "Capital Market Equilibrium with Restricted Borrowing," *Journal of Business,* **45,** No. 3 (July, 1972), pp. 444–445.
7. Bowden, Roger. "A Dual Concept and Associated Algorithm in Mean-Variance Portfolio Analysis," *Management Science,* **23,** No. 4 (Dec. 1976), pp. 423–432.
8. Breen, William, and Jackson, Richard. "An Efficient Algorithm for Solving Large-Scale Portfolio Problems," *Journal of Financial and Quantitative Analysis,* **VI,** No. 1 (Jan. 1971), pp. 627–637.
9. Buser, Stephen. "Mean-Variance Portfolio Selection with Either a Singular or Non-Singular Variance-Covariance Matrix," *Journal of Financial and Quantitative Analysis,* **XII,** No. 3 (Sept. 1977), pp. 436–461.
10. Chen, Andrew. "Portfolio Selection with Stochastic Cash Demand," *Journal of Financial and Quantitative Analysis,* **XII,** No. 2 (June 1977), pp. 197–213.
11. Chen, Andrew, Jen, Frank, and Zionts, Stanley. "Portfolio Models with Stochastic Cash Demands," *Management Science,* **19,** No. 3 (Nov. 1972), pp. 319–332.
12. ———. "The Optimal Portfolio Revision Policy," *Journal of Business,* **44,** No. 1 (Jan. 1971), pp. 51–61.
13. Chen, Andrew, Kim, Han, and Kon, Stanley. "Cash Demands, Liquidation Costs and Capital Market Equilibrium Under Uncertainty," *Journal of Financial Economics,* **2,** No. 3 (Sept. 1975), pp. 293–308.
14. ———. "Cash Demand . . . Reply," *Journal of Financial Economics,* **3,** No. 3 (June 1976), pp. 297–298.
15. Constantinides, George. "Comment on Chen, Kim and Kon," *Journal of Financial Economics,* **3,** No. 3 (June 1976), pp. 295–296.
16. Faaland, Bruce. "An Integer Programming Algorithm for Portfolio Selection," *Management Science,* **20,** No. 10 (June 1974), pp. 1376–1384.
17. Fishburn, Peter, and Porter, Burr. "Optimal Portfolios with One Safe and One Risky Asset: Effects of Change in Rate of Return and Risk," *Management Science,* **22,** No. 10 (June 1976), pp. 1064–1073.
18. Hill, Rowland. "An Algorithm for Counting the Number of Possible Port-

folios Given Linear Restrictions on the Weights," *Journal of Financial Economics,* **XI,** No. 3 (Sept. 1976), pp. 479–487.

19. Jacob, Nancy. "A Limited-Diversification Portfolio Selection Model for the Small Investor," *Journal of Finance,* **XXIX,** No. 3 (June 1974), pp. 847–856.

20. Jones-Lee, M.W. "Some Portfolio Adjustment Theorems for the Case of Non-Negativity Conditions on Security Holdings," *Journal of Finance,* **XXVI,** No. 3 (June 1971), pp. 763–775.

21. Lintner, John. "The Valuation of Risk Assets and the Selection of Risky Investments in Stock Portfolios and Capital Budgets," *Review of Economics and Statistics,* **XLVII,** (February, 1965), pp. 13–37.

22. Tucker, James, and Defaro, Clovis. "A Simple Algorithm for Stone's Version of the Portfolio Selection Problem," *Journal of Financial and Quantitative Analysis,* **X,** No. 5 (Dec. 1975), pp. 859–570.

23. Ziemba, William. "Solving Nonlinear Programming Problems with Stochastic Objective Functions," *Journal of Financial and Quantitative Analysis,* **VII,** No. 3 (June 1972), pp. 1809–1827.

SECTION 2

Simplifying the Portfolio Selection Process

Chapter 5

The Correlation Structure of Security Returns

The Single Index Model

In the first four chapters of this book we outlined the basics of modern portfolio theory. The core of the theory, as described in these chapters, is not new; in fact, it was presented as early as 1956 in Markowitz's pioneering article and subsequent book. The reader, noting that the theory is over 30 years old, might well ask what has happened since the theory was developed. Furthermore, if you had knowledge about the actual practices of financial institutions, you might well ask why the theory took so long to be used by financial institutions. The answers to both these questions are closely related. Most of the research on portfolio management in the last 30 years has concentrated on methods for *implementing* the basic theory. Many of the breakthroughs in implementation have been quite recent and it is only with these new contributions that portfolio theory becomes readily applicable to the management of actual portfolios.

In the next three chapters we are concerned with the implementation of portfolio theory. Breakthroughs in implementation fall into two categories: the first concerns a simplification of the amount and type of input data needed to perform portfolio analysis. The second involves a simplification of the computational procedure needed to calculate optimal portfolios. As will soon become clear, these issues are interdependent. Furthermore, their resolution vastly simplifies portfolio analysis. This results in the ability to describe the problem and its solution in relatively simple terms — terms that have intuitive as well as analytical meaning, and terms to which practicing security analysts and portfolio managers can relate.

In this chapter we begin the problem of simplifying the inputs to the portfolio problem. We start with a discussion of the amount and type of information needed to solve a portfolio problem. We then discuss the oldest and most widely used simplification of the portfolio structure: the single-index model. The nature of the model as well as some estimating techniques are examined.

In Chapter 6 we discuss alternative simplified representations of the portfolio problem. In particular, we will be concerned with other ways to represent and predict the correlation structure between returns. Finally, in the last chapter dealing with implementation we will show how each of the techniques that have been developed to simplify the input to portfolio analysis can be used to reduce and simplify the calculations needed to find optimal portfolios.

THE INPUTS TO PORTFOLIO ANALYSIS

Let us return to a consideration of the portfolio problem. From earlier chapters we know that to define the efficient frontier we must be able to determine the expected return and standard deviation of return on a portfolio. We can write the expected return on any portfolio as

$$\overline{R}_P = \sum_{i=1}^{N} X_i \overline{R}_i \tag{5.1}$$

while the standard deviation of return on any portfolio can be written as

$$\sigma_P = \left[\sum_{i=1}^{N} X_i^2 \sigma_i^2 + \sum_{i=1}^{N} \sum_{\substack{j=1; \\ j \neq i;}}^{N} X_i X_j \sigma_i \sigma_j \rho_{ij} \right]^{1/2} \tag{5.2}$$

These equations define the input data necessary to perform portfolio analysis. From Equation (5.1) we see that we need estimates of the expected return on each security that is a candidate for inclusion in our portfolio. From Equation (5.2) we see that we need estimates of the variance of each security, plus estimates of the correlation between each possible pair of securities for the stocks under consideration. The need for estimates of correlation coefficients differs both in magnitude and substance from the two previous requirements. Let's see why.

The principal job of the security analyst traditionally has been to estimate the future performance of stocks he follows. At a minimum this means producing estimates of expected returns on each stock he follows.[1]

With the increased attention that "risk" has received in recent years, more and more analysts are providing estimates of risk as well as return. The analyst who estimates the expected return of a stock should also be in a position to estimate the uncertainty of that return.

---

[1] Whether the analyst's estimates contain information or whether one is better off estimating returns from an equilibrium model (such as those to be presented in Chapters 11 and 12) is an open question. We have more to say about this later. However, the reader should note that portfolio selection models can help to answer this question.

Correlations are an entirely different matter. Portfolio analysis calls for estimates of the pairwise correlation between all stocks that are candidates for inclusion in a portfolio. Most firms organize their analysts along traditional industry lines. One analyst might follow steel stocks or, perhaps in a smaller firm, all metal stocks. A second analyst might follow chemical stocks. But portfolio analysis calls for these analysts not only to estimate how a particular steel stock will move in relationship to another steel stock, but also how a particular steel stock will move in relationship to a particular chemical stock or drug stock. There is no nonoverlapping organizational structure that allows such estimates to be directly produced.

The problem is made more complex by the number of estimates required. Most financial institutions follow between 150 and 250 stocks. To employ portfolio analysis, the institution needs estimates of between 150 and 250 expected returns and 150 and 250 variances. Let us see how many correlation coefficients it needs. If we let N stand for the number of stocks a firm follows, then it has to estimate ρ_{ij} for all pairs of securities i and j. The first index i can take on N values (one for each stock) the second can take on $(N - 1)$ values (remember $j \neq i$). This gives us $N(N - 1)$ correlation coefficients. However, since the correlation coefficient between stocks i and j is the same as that between stocks j and i, we have to estimate only $N(N - 1)/2$ correlations. The institution that follows between 150 and 250 stocks needs between 11,175 and 31,125 correlation coefficients. The sheer number of inputs is staggering.

It seems unlikely that analysts will be able to directly estimate correlation structures. Their ability to do so is severely limited by the nature of feasible organizational structures and the huge number of correlation coefficients that must be estimated. Recognition of this has motivated the search for the development of models to describe and predict the correlation structure between securities. In this chapter and in Chapter 6 we discuss some of these models and examine empirical tests of their performance.

The models developed for forecasting correlation structures fall into two categories: index models and averaging techniques. The most widely used technique assumes that the co-movement between stocks is due to a single common influence or index. This model is appropriately called the single-index model. The single-index model is used not only in estimating the correlation matrix, but also in efficient market tests discussed later and in equilibrium tests, where it is called a return-generating process. The rest of this chapter is devoted to a discussion of the properties of this model.

SINGLE-INDEX MODELS: AN OVERVIEW

Casual observation of stock prices reveals that when the market goes up (as measured by any of the widely available stock market indexes), most stocks tend to increase in price, and when the market goes down, most stocks tend to decrease in price. This suggests that one reason security returns might be correlated is because of a common response to market changes, and a useful measure of this correlation might be obtained by relating the return on a stock to the return on a stock market index. The return on a stock can be written as[2]

$$R_i = a_i + \beta_i R_m$$

where

a_i is the component of security i's return that is independent of the market's performance — a random variable.

R_m is the rate of return on the market index — a random variable.

β_i is a constant that measures the expected change in R_i given a change in R_m.

This equation simply breaks the return on a stock into two components, that part due to the market and that part independent of the market. β_i in the expression measures how sensitive a stock's return is to the return on the market. A β_i of 2 means that a stock's return is expected to increase (decrease) by 2% when the market increases (decreases) by 1%. Similarly, a β of 0.5 indicates that a stock's return is expected to increase (decrease) by ½ of 1% when the market increases (decreases) by 1%.[3]

The term a_i represents that component of return insensitive to (independent of) the return on the market. It is useful to break the term a_i into two components. Let α_i denote the expected value of a_i and let e_i represent the random (uncertain) element of a_i. Then

$$a_i = \alpha_i + e_i$$

where e_i has an expected value of zero. The equation for the return on a stock can now be written as

$$R_i = \alpha_i + \beta_i R_m + e_i \tag{5.3}$$

Once again, note that e_i and R_m both are random variables. They each have a probability distribution and a mean and standard deviation. Let us denote their standard deviations by σ_{ei} and σ_m, respectively. Up to this point we have made no simplifying assumptions. We have written return as the sum of several components but these components, when added together, must by definition be equal to total return.

---

[2]The return on the index is identical, in concept, to the return on a common stock. It is the return the investor would earn if he held a portfolio with a composition identical to the index. Thus, to compute this return, the dividends that would be received from holding the index should be calculated and combined with the price changes on the index.

[3]We are illustrating the single-index model with a stock market index. It is not necessary that the index used be a stock market index. The selection of the appropriate index is an empirical rather than a theoretical question. However, anticipating the results of future chapters, the results should be better when a broad-based market-weighted index is used, such as the S & P 500 index or the New York Stock Exchange Index.

It is convenient to have e_i uncorrelated with R_m. Formally, this means that

$$\text{cov}(e_i, R_m) = E[(e_i - 0)(R_m - \bar{R}_m)] = 0$$

If e_i is uncorrelated with R_m, it implies that how well Equation (5.3) describes the return on any security is independent of what the return on the market happens to be. Estimates of α_i, β_i, and σ_{ei}^2 are often obtained from time series-regression analysis.[4] Regression analysis is one technique that guarantees that e_i and R_m will be uncorrelated, at least over the period to which the equation has been fit. All of the characteristics of single-index models described to this point are definitions or can be made to hold by construction. There is one further characteristic of single-index models: it holds only by assumption. This assumption is the characteristic of single-index models that differentiates them from other models used to describe the covariance structure.

The key assumption of the single-index model is that e_i is independent of e_j for all values of i and j or, more formally, $E(e_i e_j) = 0$. This implies that the only reason stocks vary together, systematically, is because of a common co-movement with the market. There are no effects beyond the market (e.g., industry effects) that account for co-movement between securities. We will have more to say about this in our discussion of multi-index models in Chapter 6. However, at this time, note that, unlike the independence of e_i and R_m, there is nothing in the normal regression method used to estimate α_i, β_i, and σ_{ei}^2 that forces this to be true. It is a simplifying assumption that represents an approximation to reality. How well this model performs will depend, in part, on how good (or bad) this approximation is. Let us summarize the single-index model:

Basic Equation
$R_i = \alpha_i + \beta_i R_m + e_i$ for all stocks $i = 1, \cdots, N$

By Construction
1. Mean of $e_i = E(e_i) = 0$ for all stocks $i = 1, \cdots, N$

By Assumption
1. Index unrelated to unique return: for all stocks $i = 1, \cdots, N$
    $E[e_i(R_m - \bar{R}_m)] = 0$

2. Securities only related through common   for all pairs of stocks $i = 1,$
    response to market: $E(e_i e_j) = 0$ $\cdots, N$ and $j = 1, \cdots, N$
    $\hspace{10cm}$ but $i \neq j$

By Definition
1. Variance of $e_i = E(e_i)^2 = \sigma_{ei}^2$ for all stocks $i = i, \cdots, N$

2. Variance of $R_m = E(R_m - \bar{R}_m)^2 = \sigma_m^2$

---

[4]This will be discussed in more detail later in the chapter.

In the subsequent section we derive the expected return, standard deviation, and covariance when the single-index model is used to represent the joint movement of securities. The results are:

1. The mean return, $\overline{R}_i = \alpha_i + \beta_i\overline{R}_m$.
2. The variance of a security's return, $\sigma_i^2 = \beta_i^2\sigma_m^2 + \sigma_{ei}^2$.
3. The covariance of returns between securities i and j, $\sigma_{ij} = \beta_i\beta_j\sigma_m^2$.

Note that the expected return has two components: a unique part α_i and a market-related part $\beta_i\overline{R}_m$. Likewise, a security's variance has the same two parts, unique risk σ_{ei}^2 and market-related risk $\beta_i^2\sigma_m^2$. In contrast, the covariance depends only on market risk. This is what we meant earlier when we said that the single-index model implied that the only reason securities move together is a common response to market movements. In this section of the text delineated by the solid line we derive these results. The reader uninterested in the derivation can note the results and then skip to the end of the section.

The expected return on a security is:

$$E(R_i) = E[\alpha_i + \beta_iR_m + e_i]$$

Since the expected value of the sum of random variables is the sum of the expected values, we have

$$E(R_i) = E(\alpha_i) + E(\beta_iR_m) + E(e_i)$$

α_i and β_i are constants and by construction the expected value of e_i is zero. Thus,

$$E(R_i) = \alpha_i + \beta_i\overline{R}_m \qquad\qquad \textit{Result 1}$$

The variance of the return on any security is

$$\sigma_i^2 = E(R_i - \overline{R}_i)^2$$

Substituting for R_i and $\overline{R}_i$ from the expression above yields

$$\sigma_i^2 = E[(\alpha_i + \beta_iR_m + e_i) - (\alpha_i + \beta_i\overline{R}_m)]^2$$

Rearranging and noting that the α's cancel yields

$$\sigma_i^2 = E[\beta_i(R_m - \overline{R}_m) + e_i]^2$$

Squaring the terms in the brackets yields

$$\sigma_i^2 = \beta_i^2E(R_m - \overline{R}_m)^2 + 2\beta_iE[e_i(R_m - \overline{R}_m)] + E(e_i)^2$$

Recall that by assumption (or in some cases by construction) $E[e_i(R_m - \overline{R}_m)] = 0$. Thus,

$$\sigma_i^2 = \beta_i^2 E(R_m - \overline{R}_m)^2 + E(e_i)^2$$

$$\sigma_i^2 = \beta_i^2 \sigma_m^2 + \sigma_{ei}^2 \qquad\qquad \textit{Result 2}$$

The covariance between any two securities can be written as

$$\sigma_{ij} = E[(R_i - \overline{R}_i)(R_j - \overline{R}_j)]$$

Substituting for R_i, $\overline{R}_i$, R_j, and $\overline{R}_j$ yields

$$\sigma_{ij} = E\{[(\alpha_i + \beta_i R_m + e_i) - (\alpha_i + \beta_i \overline{R}_m)]$$
$$\cdot [(\alpha_j + \beta_j R_m + e_j) - (\alpha_j + \beta_j \overline{R}_m)]\}$$

Simplifying by canceling the α's and combining the terms involving β's yields

$$\sigma_{ij} = E[(\beta_i(R_m - \overline{R}_m) + e_i)(\beta_j(R_m - \overline{R}_m) + e_j)]$$

Carrying out the multiplication

$$\sigma_{ij} = \beta_i \beta_j E(R_m - \overline{R}_m)^2 + \beta_j E[e_i(R_m - \overline{R}_m)] + \beta_i E[e_j(R_m - \overline{R}_m)]$$
$$+ E(e_i e_j)$$

Since the last three terms are zero, by assumption

$$\sigma_{ij} = \beta_i \beta_j \sigma_m^2 \qquad\qquad \textit{Result 3}$$

These results can be illustrated with a simple example. Consider the returns on a stock and a market index shown in the first two columns of Table 5.1. These returns are what an investor might have observed over the prior five months. Now consider the values for the single-index model shown in the remaining columns of the table. Column three just reproduced column one and is the return on the security. Accept for the moment that $\beta_i = 1.5$. The fifth column is just the second column times 1.5 or the market return times a Beta of 1.5. Where does e_i come from? Recall that the average value of e_i is zero. If the average value of e_i is zero, then the sum of e_i is also zero. The single-index model is an equality. The return over the 5 periods for the stock is 40; 30 of the 40 is market-related return, hence 10 must be nonmarket-related or unique. If e_i sums to zero, then for the single-index model to be an equality, α_i must sum to 10. Since α_i is a constant and there are 5 periods, α_i is $^{10}/_5$ or 2 per period.

Table 5.1   Decomposition of Returns for the Single Index Model

Month	1 Return on Stock	2 Return on Market	3	4	5	6
			R_i =	α_i +	$\beta_i R_m$ +	e_i
1	10	4	10 =	2 +	6	+ 2
2	3	2	3 =	2 +	3	− 2
3	15	8	15 =	2 +	12	+ 1
4	9	6	9 =	2 +	9	− 2
5	3	0	3 =	2 +	0	+ 1
	40	20	40	10	30	0

Given the values for α_i and for $\beta_i R_m$, and since the single-index model is an equality, e_i is whatever is necessary to make the left- and right-hand sides the same. For example, in the first period the sum of α_i and $\beta_i R_m$ is 8. Since the return on the security in the first period is 10, e_i is +2.

The reader should now understand where all the values of the single-index model come from except β_i. β_i divides return into market-related and unique return. When β_i is set equal to 1.5, the market return is independent of the residual return e_i. A lower value of e_i leaves some market return in e_i and the covariance of e_i with the market is positive. A β_i greater than 1.5 removes too much market return and results in a negative covariance between e_i and the market. Thus the value of β_i is unique and is the value that exactly separates market from unique return, making the covariance between R_m and e_i zero.

Before leaving the simple example, let's apply the formulas presented earlier. The mean return on the security is

$$\overline{R}_i = 40/5 = 8$$

using the formula from the single-index model.

$$\overline{R}_i = \alpha_i + \beta_i \overline{R}_m = 2 + 1.5(4) = 8$$

The variance of security i is calculating from the formula derived for the single-index model.

$$\sigma_i^2 = \beta_i^2 \sigma_m^2 + \sigma_{ei}^2$$

$$= (1.5)^2 (8) + 2.8$$

$$= 20.8$$

Having explained the simple example, we can turn to the calculation of the expected return and variance of any portfolio if the single-index model holds. The expected return on any portfolio is given by

$$\overline{R}_P = \sum_{i=1}^{N} X_i \overline{R}_i$$

Substituting for $\overline{R}_i$ we obtain

$$\overline{R}_P = \sum_{i=1}^{N} X_i\alpha_i + \sum_{i=1}^{N} X_i\beta_i\overline{R}_m \tag{5.4}$$

We know that the variance of a portfolio of stocks is given by

$$\sigma_P^2 = \sum_{i=1}^{N} X_i^2\sigma_i^2 + \sum_{i=1}^{N} \sum_{\substack{j=1;\\ j\neq i}}^{N} X_iX_j\sigma_{ij}$$

Substituting in the results stated above for σ_i^2 and σ_{ij}, we obtain

$$\sigma_P^2 = \sum_{i=1}^{N} X_i^2\beta_i^2\sigma_m^2 + \sum_{i=1}^{N} \sum_{\substack{j=1;\\ j\neq i}}^{N} X_iX_j\beta_i\beta_j\sigma_m^2 + \sum_{i=1}^{N} X_i^2\sigma_{ei}^2 \tag{5.5}$$

There are many alternative ways of estimating the parameters of the single-index model. From Equations (5.4) and (5.5) it is clear that expected return and risk can be estimated for any portfolio if we have an estimate of α_i for each stock, an estimate of β_i for each stock, an estimate of σ_{ei}^2 for each stock, and, finally, an estimate of both the expected return $(\overline{R}_m)$ and variance (σ_m^2) for the market. This is a total of $3N + 2$ estimates. For an institution following between 150 and 250 stocks, the single-index model required between 452 and 752 estimates. Compare this with the 11,175 to 31,125 correlation estimates or 11,475 to 31,625 total estimates required when no simplifying structure was assumed. Furthermore, note that there is no requirement for direct estimates of the joint movement of securities, only estimates of the way each security moves with the market. A nonoverlapping organizational structure can produce all the required estimates.

The model can also be employed if analysts supply estimates of expected return for each stock, the variance of the return on each stock, the Beta (β_i) for each stock, and estimates of the expected return for the market, and the variance of the market return.[5] This is the same number of estimates $3N + 2$, as discussed

---

[5]The fact that these inputs are equivalent to those discussed earlier is easy to show. The expected returns can be used directly to estimate the expected return on a portfolio

$$\overline{R}_P = \sum_{i=1}^{N} X_i\overline{R}_i$$

The estimates of the variance of return on a stock, the variance of the market, and the beta on each stock can be used to derive estimates of its residual risk by noting that

$$\sigma_i^2 = \beta_i^2\sigma_m^2 + \sigma_{ei}^2$$

In addition, this structure is natural for those institutions that want analysts' estimates of means and variances and model estimates of correlations or covariances.

before. However, this alternative set of estimates has the advantage that they are in more familiar terms.

We have discussed means and variances before. The only new variable is Beta. The Beta is simply a measure of the sensitivity of a stock to market movements.

Before we discuss alternative ways of estimating Betas, let us examine some of the characteristics of the single-index model.

CHARACTERISTICS OF THE SINGLE-INDEX MODEL

Define the Beta on a portfolio β_P as a weighted average of the individual β_i's on each stock in the portfolio where the weights are the fraction of the portfolio invested in each stock. Then

$$\beta_P = \sum_{i=1}^{N} X_i \beta_i$$

Similarly define the Alpha on the portfolio α_P as

$$\alpha_P = \sum_{i=1}^{N} X_i \alpha_i$$

Then Equation (5.4) can be written as

$$\overline{R}_P = \alpha_P + \beta_P \overline{R}_m$$

If the portfolio P is taken to be the market portfolio (all stocks held in the same proportions as they were in constructing R_m), then the expected return on P must be $\overline{R}_m$. From the above equation the only values of β_P and α_P that guarantee $\overline{R}_P = \overline{R}_m$ for any choice of $\overline{R}_m$ is α_P equal to 0 and β_P equal to 1. Thus, the Beta on the market is 1 and stocks are thought of as being more or less risky than the market, according to whether their Beta is larger or smaller than 1.

Let us look further into the risk of an individual security. Equation (5.5) is

$$\sigma_P{}^2 = \sum_{i=1}^{N} X_i{}^2 \beta_i{}^2 \sigma_m{}^2 + \sum_{i=1}^{N} X_i{}^2 \sigma_{ei}{}^2 + \sum_{i=1}^{N} \sum_{\substack{j=1 \\ j \neq i}}^{N} X_i X_j \beta_i \beta_j \sigma_m{}^2$$

In the double summation $i \neq j$, if $i = j$ then the terms would be $X_i X_i \beta_i{}^2 \sigma_m{}^2$. But these are exactly the terms in the first summation. Thus, the variance on the portfolio can be written as

$$\sigma_P{}^2 = \sum_{i=1}^{N} \sum_{j=1}^{N} X_i X_j \beta_i \beta_j \sigma_m{}^2 + \sum_{i=1}^{N} X_i{}^2 \sigma_{ei}{}^2$$

Or by rearranging terms

$$\sigma_P^2 = \left(\sum_{i=1}^{N} X_i\beta_i\right)\left(\sum_{j=1}^{N} X_j\beta_j\right)\sigma_m^2 + \sum_{i=1}^{N} X_i^2\sigma_{ei}^2$$

Thus, the risk of the investor's portfolio could be represented as

$$\sigma_P^2 = \beta_P^2\sigma_m^2 + \sum_{i=1}^{N} X_i^2\sigma_{ei}^2$$

Assume for a moment that an investor forms a portfolio by placing equal amounts of his money into each of N stocks. The risk of this portfolio can be written as[6]

$$\sigma_P^2 = \beta_P^2\sigma_m^2 + \frac{1}{N}\left(\sum_{i=1}^{N} \frac{1}{N}\sigma_{ei}^2\right)$$

Look at the last term. This can be expressed as $1/N$ times the average residual risk in the portfolio. As the number of stocks in the portfolio gets large, the importance of the average residual risk,

$$\sum_{i=1}^{N} \frac{\sigma_{ei}^2}{N}$$

diminishes drastically. In fact, as Table 5.2 shows, the residual risk falls so rapidly that most of it is effectively eliminated on even moderately sized portfolios.[7]

The risk that is not eliminated as we hold larger and larger portfolios is the risk associated with the term β_P. If we assume that residual risk approaches zero, the risk of the portfolio approaches

$$\sigma_P = [\beta_P^2\sigma_m^2]^{1/2} = \beta_P\sigma_m = \sigma_m\left[\sum_{i=1}^{N} X_i\beta_i\right]$$

Since σ_m is the same, regardless of which stock we examine, the measure of the contribution of a security to the risk of a large portfolio is β_i.

The risk of an individual security is $\beta_i^2\sigma_m^2 + \sigma_{ei}^2$. Since the effect of σ_{ei}^2 on

---

[6]Examining the expression for the variance of portfolio P shows that the assumptions of the single-index model are inconsistent with $\sigma_P^2 = \sigma_m^2$. However, the approximation is very close. See Fama [33] for a detailed discussion of this issue.

[7]To the extent that the single-index model is not a perfect description of reality and residuals from the market model are correlated across securities, residual risk does not fall this rapidly. However, for most portfolios the amount of positive correlation present in the residuals is quite small and residual risk declines rapidly as the number of securities in the portfolio increases.

Table 5.2   Residual Risk and Portfolio Size

Number of Securities	Residual Risk (Variance) Expressed as a Percent of the Residual Risk Present in a One-stock Portfolio with σ_{ei}^2 a Constant
1	100
2	50
3	33
4	25
5	20
10	10
20	5
100	1
1000	0.1

portfolio risk can be made to approach zero as the portfolio gets larger, it is common to refer to σ_{ei}^2 as diversifiable risk.[8] However, the effect of $\beta_i^2 \sigma_m^2$ on portfolio risk does not diminish as N gets larger. Since σ_m^2 is a constant with respect to all securities, β_i is the measure of a security's nondiversifiable risk.[9] Since diversifiable risk can be eliminated by holding a large enough portfolio, β_i is often used as the measure of a security's risk.

ESTIMATING BETA

The use of the single-index model calls for estimates of the Beta of each stock that is a potential candidate for inclusion in a portfolio. Analysts could be asked to provide subjective estimates of Beta for a security or a portfolio. On the other hand, estimates of future Beta could be arrived at by estimating Beta from past data and using this historical Beta as an estimate of the future Beta. There is evidence that historical Betas provide useful information about future Betas. Futhermore, some interesting forecasting techniques have been developed to increase the information that can be extracted from historical data. Because of this, even the firm that wishes to use analysts' subjective estimates of future Betas should start with (supply analysts with) the best estimates of Beta available from historical data. The analyst can then concentrate on the examination of influences that are expected to change Beta in the future. In the rest of this chapter we examine some of the techniques that have been proposed for estimating Beta. These techniques can be classified as measuring historical Betas, correcting historical Betas for the tendnecy of historical Betas to be closer to the mean when estimated in a future period, and correcting historical estimates by incorporating fundamental firm data.

---

[8]An alternative nomenclature calls this nonmarket or unsystematic risk.

[9]An alternative nomenclature calls this market risk or systematic risk.

Estimating Historical Betas

In Equation (5.3) we represented the return on a stock as

$$R_i = \alpha_i + \beta_i R_m + e_i$$

This equation is expected to hold at each moment in time, although the values of α_i, β_i, or σ_{ei}^2 might differ over time. When looking at historical data, one cannot directly observe α_i, β_i, or σ_{ei}^2. Rather, one observes the past returns on the security and the market. If α_i, β_i, and σ_{ei}^2 are assumed to be constant through time, then the same equation is expected to hold at each point in time. In this case, a straightforward procedure exists for estimating α_i, β_i, and σ_{ei}^2.

Notice that Equation (5.3) is an equation of a straight line. If σ_{ei}^2 were equal to zero, then we could estimate α_i and β_i with just two observations. However, the presence of the random variable e_i means that the actual return will form a scatter around the straight line. Figure (5.1) illustrates this pattern. The vertical axis is the return on security i and the horizontal axis is the return on the market. Each point on the diagram is the return on stock i over a particular time interval, for example one month (t) plotted against the return on the market for the same time interval. The actual observed returns lie on and around the true relationship (shown as a solid line). The greater σ_{ei}^2, the greater the scatter around the line, and since we do not actually observe the line, the more uncertain we are about where it is. There are a number of ways of estimating where the line might be, given the observed scatter of points. Usually, we estimate the location of the line using regression analysis.

This procedure could be thought of as first plotting R_{it} versus R_{mt} to obtain a scatter of points such as that shown in Figure 5.1. Each point represents the return on a particular stock and the return on the market in one month. Additional

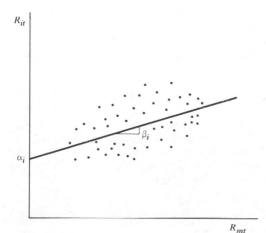

Figure 5.1

points are obtained by plotting the two returns in successive months. The next step is to fit that straight line to the data that minimized the sum of the squared deviation from the line in the vertical (R_{it}) direction. The slope of this straight line would be our best estimate of Beta over the period to which the line was fit, and intercept would be our best estimate of Alpha (α_i).[10]

More formally, to estimate the Beta for a firm for the period from $t = 1$ to $t = 60$ via regression analysis use

$$\beta_i = \frac{\sigma_{im}}{\sigma_m^{\,2}} = \frac{\displaystyle\sum_{t=1}^{60} [(R_{it} - \overline{R}_{it})(R_{mt} - \overline{R}_{mt})]}{\displaystyle\sum_{t=1}^{60} (R_{mt} - \overline{R}_{mt})^2}$$

and to estimate Alpha use[11]

$$\alpha_i = \overline{R}_{it} - \beta_i \overline{R}_{mt}$$

The values of α_i and β_i produced by regression analysis are estimates of the true α_i and β_i that exist for a stock. The estimates are subject to error. As such, the estimate of α_i and β_i may not be equal to the true α_i and β_i that existed in the period.[12] Furthermore, the process is complicated by the fact that α_i and β_i are not perfectly stationary over time. We would expect changes as the fundamental characteristics of the firm change. For example, β_i as a risk measure should be related to the capital structure of the firm and, thus, should change as the capital structure changes.

Despite error in measuring the true β_i and the possibility of real shifts in β_i

---

[10]If R_{it} and R_{mt} come from a bivariate normal distribution, the unbiased and most efficient estimates of α_i and β_i are those that come from regressing R_{it} against R_{mt}, the procedure described above.

[11]Two other statistics of interest can be produced by this analysis. First, the size of σ_{ei}^2 over the estimation period can be found by looking at the variance of the deviations of the actual return from that predicted by the model:

$$\sigma_{ei}^2 = \frac{1}{60} \sum_{t=1}^{60} [R_{it} - (\alpha_i + \beta_i R_{mt})]^2$$

Remember that, in performing regression analysis, one often computes a coefficient of determination. The coefficient of determination is a measure of association between two variables. In this case, it would measure how much of the variation in the return on the individual stock is associated with variation in the return on the market. The coefficient of determination is simply the correlation coefficient squared, and the correlation coefficient is equal to

$$\rho_{im} = \frac{\sigma_{im}}{\sigma_i \sigma_m} = \frac{\beta_i \sigma_m^2}{\sigma_i \sigma_m} = \beta_i \frac{\sigma_m}{\sigma_i}$$

[12]In fact, the analysis will produce an estimate of the standard error in both α_i and β_i. This can be used to make interval estimates of future Alphas and Betas under the assumption of stationarity.

over time, the most straightforward way to forecast β_i for a future period is to use an estimate of β_i obtained via regression analysis from a past period. Let us take a look at how well this works.

Accuracy of Historical Betas

The first logical step in looking at Betas is to see how much association there is between the Betas in one period and the Betas in an adjacent period. Both Blume [12] and Levy [57] have done extensive testing of the relationship between Betas over time. Let us look at some representative results from Blume's [12] study. Blume computed Betas using time series regressions on monthly data for nonoverlapping seven-year periods. He generated Betas on single stock portfolios, 2 stock portfolios, 4 stock portfolios, and so forth up to 50 stock portfolios and for each size portfolio examined how highly correlated the Betas from one period were with the Betas for a second period. Table 5.3 presents a typical result showing how highly correlated the Betas are for the period 7/54–6/61 and 7/61–6/68.

Table 5.3 Association of Betas Over Time

Number of Securities in the Portfolio	Correlation Coefficient	Coefficient of Determination
1	0.60	0.36
2	0.73	0.53
4	0.84	0.71
7	0.88	0.77
10	0.92	0.85
20	0.97	0.95
35	0.97	0.95
50	0.98	0.96

It is apparent from this table that, while Betas on very large portfolios contain a great deal of information about future Betas on these portfolios, Betas on individual securities contain much less information about the future Betas on securities. Why might observed Betas in one period differ from Betas in a second period? One reason is that the risk (Beta) of the security or portfolio might change. A second reason is that the Beta in each period is measured with a random error, and the larger the random error, the less predictive power Betas from one period will have for Betas in the next period.

Changes in security Betas will differ from security to security. Some will go up, some will go down. These changes will tend to cancel out in a portfolio and we observe less change in the actual Beta on portfolios than on securities.

Likewise, one would expect that the errors in estimating Beta for individual securities would tend to cancel out when securities are combined, and therefore, there would be less error in measuring a portfolio's Beta.[13] Since portfolio Betas are measured with less error, and since Betas on portfolios change less than Betas on securities, historical Betas on portfolios are better predictors of future Betas than are historical Betas on securities.

Adjusting Historical Estimates

Can we further improve the predictive ability of Betas on securities and portfolios? To aid in answering this question, let us examine a simple hypothetical distribution of Betas. Assume the true Betas on all stocks are really one. If we estimate Betas for all stocks, some of our estimated Betas will be one, but some will be above or below one due to sampling error in the estimate. Estimated Betas above one would be above one simply due to positive sampling errors. Estimated Betas below one would be below one due to negative sampling errors. Furthermore, since there is no reason to suspect that a positive sampling error for a stock will be followed by a positive sampling error for the same stock, we would find that historical Beta did a worse job of predicting future Beta than did a Beta of one for all stocks. Now, assume we have different Betas for different stocks. The Beta we calculate for any stock will be, in part, a function of the true underlying Beta and, in part, a function of sampling error. If we compute a very high estimate of Beta for a stock, we have an increased probability that we have a positive sampling error, while if we compute a very low estimate of Beta, we have an increased chance that we have a negative sampling error. If this scenario is correct, we should find that Betas, on the average, tend to converge to one in successive time periods. Estimated Betas that are a lot larger than one should tend to be followed by estimated Betas that are closer to one (lower), and estimated Betas below one should tend to be followed by higher Betas. Evidence that this does, in fact, happen has been presented by Blume [12] and Levy [57]. Blume's results are reproduced in Table 5.4. The reader should ex-

---

[13]Assuming that the relationship between R_{jt} and R_{mt} is described by a stationary bivariate normal distribution, then the standard error in the measurement of Beta for a security is given by

$$\sigma_{\beta i} = \sigma_{ei}/\sigma_m$$

The standard error for the β on a portfolio is given by

$$\sigma_{\beta p} = \sigma_{ep}/\sigma_m$$

where

$$\sigma_{ep}^2 = \frac{1}{T}\sum_{t=1}^{T}(e_{pt})^2 = \frac{1}{T}\sum_{t=1}^{T}\left(\sum_{i=1}^{N} X_i e_{it}\right)^2$$

where N is the number of securities in the portfolio and T is the number of time periods.

To the extent that the residuals for different stocks are not perfectly correlated, averaging them across stocks will lower the value of the residuals and, hence, the value of σ_{ep}^2 on the portfolio. In particular, if the assumptions of the single-index model are met and if stocks are held in equal proportions, the standard error of the Beta on the portfolio would equal the average standard error on all stocks times the reciprocal of the number of stocks in the portfolio.

amine the table and confirm the tendency of Betas in the forecast period to be closer to one than the estimates of these Betas obtained from historical data.[14]

Measuring the Tendency of Betas to Regress Toward One — Blume's Technique

Since Betas in the forecast period tend to be closer to one than the estimate obtained from historical data, the next obvious step is to try to modify past Betas to capture this tendency. Blume [12] was the first to propose a scheme for doing so. He corrected past Betas by directly measuring this adjustment toward one and assuming that the adjustment in one period is a good estimate of the adjustment in the next.

Table 5.4   Betas on Ranked Portfolios for Two Successive Periods

Portfolio	7/54–6/61	7/61–6/68
1	0.393	0.620
2	0.612	0.707
3	0.810	0.861
4	0.987	0.914
5	1.138	0.995
6	1.337	1.169

Source: Blume, Marshell. "On the Assessment of Risk," *Journal of Finance*, **VI**, No. 1 (March 1971).

Let us see how this could work. We could calculate the Betas for all stocks for the period 1948–54. We could then calculate the Betas for these same stocks for the period 1955–61. We could then regress the Betas for the later period against the Betas for the earlier period as shown in Figure 5.2. Note that each observation is the Beta on the same stock for the period 1948–54 and 1955–61. Following this procedure we would obtain a line that measures the tendency of the forecasted Betas to be closer to one than the estimates from historical data. When Blume did this for the period mentioned he obtained

$$\beta_{i2} = 0.343 + 0.677\beta_{i1}$$

where β_{i2} stands for the Beta on stock i in the later period (1955–61) and β_{i1} stands for the β for stock i for the earlier period (1948–54). The relationship implies that the Beta in the later period is $0.343 + 0.677$ times the Beta in the earlier period. Assume we wish to forecast the Beta for any stock for the period 1962–68. We then compute (via regression analysis) its Beta for the years 1955–61. To determine how this Beta should be modified, we substitute it for β_{i1} in the equation. We then compute β_{i2} from the foregoing equation and use it as our forecast.

---

[14]Through this section when we speak of Betas we are referring to estimates of Betas.

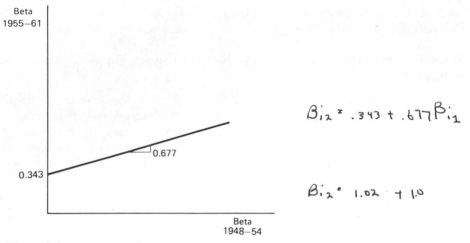

Figure 5.2

Notice the effect of this on the Beta for any stock. If β_{i1} were 2.0, then our forecast would be $0.343 + 0.677(2) = 1.697$, rather than 2.0. If β_{i1} were 0.5, our forecast would be $0.343 + 0.677(0.5) = 0.682$ rather than 0.5. The equation lowers high values of Beta and raises low values. One more characteristic of this equation should be noted. It modifies the average level of Betas for the population of stocks. Since it measures the relationship between Betas over two periods, if the average Beta increased over these two periods, it assumes that average Betas will increase over the next period. Unless there is reason to suspect a continuous drift in Beta, this will be an undesirable property. If there is no reason to expect this trend in the average Beta to continue, then the estimates can be improved by adjusting the forecasted Betas so that their mean is the same as the historical mean.

To make this point more concrete, let us examine an example. Assume that in estimating the equation Blume found the average Beta in 1948–54 was one and the average Beta in 1955–61 was 1.02. These numbers are consistent with his results, though there are other sets of numbers that would also be consistent with his results. Now, to determine what the average forecasted Beta should be for the period 1962–68, we simply substitute 1.02 in the right-hand side of the estimating equation. The answer is 1.033. As discussed above, Blume's technique results in a continued extrapolation of the upward trend in Betas observed in the earlier periods.

If there is no reason to believe that the next period's average Beta will be more than this period's, then the forecasts should be improved by adjusting the forecast Beta to have the same mean as the historical mean. This involves subtracting a constant from all Betas after adjusting them toward their mean. In our example, this is achieved by subtracting 1.033 from each forecast of Beta and adding 1.02.

Measuring the Tendency of Betas to Regress Toward One — Vasicek's Technique

Recall that the actual Beta in the forecast period tends to be closer to the average Beta than is the estimate obtained from historical data. A straightforward way to adjust for this tendency is to simply adjust each Beta toward the average Beta. For example, taking one-half of the historical Beta and adding it to one-half of the average Beta moves each historical Beta halfway toward the average. This technique is widely used.[15]

It would be desirable not to adjust all stocks the same amount toward the average but rather to have the adjustment depend on the size of the uncertainty (sampling error) about Beta. The larger the sampling error, the greater the chance of large differences from the average, being due to sampling error, and the greater the adjustment. Vasicek [87] has suggested the following scheme that incorporates these properties: If we let $\bar{\beta}_1$ equal the average Beta, across the sample of stocks, in the historical period, then the Vasicek procedure involves taking a weighted average of $\bar{\beta}_1$ and the historical Beta for security i. Let $\sigma_{\bar{\beta}1}^2$ stand for the variance of the distribution of the historical estimates of Beta over the sample of stocks. This is a measure of the variation of Beta across the sample of stocks under consideration. Let $\sigma_{\beta1i}^2$ stand for the square of the standard error of the estimate of Beta for security i measured in time period 1. This is a measure of the uncertainty associated with the measurement of the individual securities Beta. Vasicek [87] suggested weights of

$$\frac{\sigma_{\bar{\beta}1}^2}{\sigma_{\bar{\beta}1}^2 + \sigma_{\beta1i}^2} \text{ for } \beta_{1i} \quad \text{and} \quad \frac{\sigma_{\beta1i}^2}{\sigma_{\bar{\beta}1}^2 + \sigma_{\beta1i}^2} \text{ for } \bar{\beta}_1$$

Note that these weights add up to 1 and that the more the uncertainty about either estimate of Beta, the lower the weight that is placed on it. The forecast of Beta for security i is

$$\beta_{i2} = \frac{\sigma_{\beta1i}^2}{\sigma_{\bar{\beta}1}^2 + \sigma_{\beta1i}^2} \bar{\beta}_1 + \frac{\sigma_{\bar{\beta}1}^2}{\sigma_{\bar{\beta}1}^2 + \sigma_{\beta1i}^2} \beta_{1i}$$

This weighting procedure adjusts observations with large standard errors further toward the mean than it adjusts observations with small standard errors. As Vasicek has shown, this is a Bayesian estimation technique.[16]

While the Bayesian technique does not forecast a trend in Betas as does the Blume technique, it suffers from its own potential source of bias. In the Bayesian

---

[15]For example, Merrill Lynch has used a simple weighting technique like this to adjust their Betas.

[16]The reader should note that this is just one of an infinite number of ways of forming prior distributions. For example, priors could have been set equal to 1 (the average for all stocks market weighted) or to an average Beta for the industry to which the stock belongs, and so on.

technique, the weight placed on a stock's Beta, relative to the weight on the average Beta in the sample, is inversely related to the stock's standard error of Beta. High Beta stocks have larger standard errors associated with their Betas than do low Beta stocks. This means that high Beta stocks will have their Betas lowered by a bigger percentage of the distance from the average Beta for the sample than low Beta stocks will have their Betas raised. Hence, the estimate of the average future Beta will tend to be lower than the average Beta in the sample of stocks over which Betas are estimated.

Unless there is reason to believe that Betas will continually decrease, the estimate of Beta can be further improved by adjusting all Betas upward so that they have the same mean as they had in the historical period.

Accuracy of Adjusted Beta

Let us examine how well the Blume and the Bayesian adjustment techniques worked as forecasters, compared to unadjusted Betas. Klemkosky and Martin [54] tested the ability of these techniques to forecast over three five-year periods for both one-stock and 10-stock portfolios. As would be suspected, in all cases both the Blume and Bayesian adjustment techniques led to more accurate forecasts of future Betas than did the unadjusted Betas. The average squared error in forecasting Beta was often cut in half when one of the adjustment techniques was used. Klemkosky and Martin used an interesting decomposition technique to search for the source of the forecast error. Specifically, the source of error was decomposed into that part of the error due to a misestimate of the average level of Beta, that part due to the tendency to overestimate high Betas and underestimate low Betas, and that part that is unexplained by either of the first two influences. As might be expected, when the Blume and Bayesian techniques were compared with the unadjusted Betas, almost all of the decrease in error came from the reductions in the tendency to overestimate high Betas and underestimate low Betas. This is not surprising because this is exactly what the two techniques were designed to achieve. Klemkosky and Martin found that the Bayesian technique had a slight tendency to outperform the Blume technique. However, the differences were small and the ordering of the techniques varied across different periods of time.

Most of the literature dealing with Betas have evaluated Beta adjustment techniques by their ability to better forecast Betas. However, there is another, and perhaps more important criterion by which the performance of alternative Betas can be judged. At the beginning of this chapter we discussed the fact that the necessary inputs to portfolio analysis were expected returns, variances, and correlations. We believe that analysts can be asked to provide estimates of expected returns and variances, but that correlations will probably continue to be generated from some sort of historical model.[17] One way Betas can be used is to

---

[17]It is possible that analysts will be used to subjectively modify historical estimates of Beta to improve their accuracy. Wells Fargo Bank has been using analysts' modified estimates of Beta for several years.

generate estimates of the correlation between securities. The correlations between stocks (given the assumptions of the single-index model) can be expressed as a function of Beta.

$$\rho_{ij} = \frac{\sigma_{ij}}{\sigma_i \sigma_j} = \frac{\beta_i \beta_j \sigma_m^2}{\sigma_i \sigma_j}$$

Another way to test the usefulness of Betas, as well as the performance of alternative forecasts of Betas, is to see how well Betas forecast the correlation structure between securities.

Betas as Forecasters of Correlation Coefficients

Elton, Gruber, and Urich [30] have compared the ability of the following models to forecast the correlation structure between securities:

1. The historical correlation matrix itself
2. Forecasts of the correlation matrix prepared by estimating Betas from the prior historical period
3. Forecasts of the correlation matrix prepared by estimating Betas from the prior two periods and updating via the Blume technique
4. Forecasts prepared as in the third model but where the updating is done via the Vasicek Bayesian technique

One of the most striking results of the study was that the historical correlation matrix itself was the poorest of all techniques. In most cases it was outperformed by all of the Beta forecasting techniques at a statistically significant level. This indicates that a large part of the observed correlation structure between securities, not captured by the single-index model, represents random noise with respect to forecasting. The point to note is that the single-index model, developed to simplify the inputs to portfolio analysis and thought to lose information due to the sim- plification involved, actually does a better job of forecasting than the full set of historical data.

The comparison of the three Beta techniques is more ambiguous. In each of two five-year samples tested, the Blume adjustment technique outperformed both the unadjusted Betas and the Betas adjusted via the Bayesian technique. The difference in the techniques was statistically significant. However, the Bayesian adjustment technique performed better than the unadjusted Beta in one period and worse in a second. In both cases, the results were statistically significant. This calls for some further analysis. The performance of any forecasting technique is, in part, a function of its forecast of the average correlation between all stocks and, in part, a function of its forecast of previous differences from the mean. We might stop for a moment and see why each of the Beta techniques might produce forecasts of the average correlation coefficient between all stocks that is different from the average correlation coefficient in the data to which the technique is fitted.

Let us start with the unadjusted Betas. This model assumes that the only correlation between stocks is one due to common correlation with the market. It ignores all other sources of correlation such as industry effects. To the extent that there are other sources of correlation that are, on the whole, positive, this technique will underestimate the average correlation coefficient in the data to which it is fitted. This is exactly what Elton, Gruber, and Urich [30] showed happened in both periods over which the model was fitted.

The Blume technique suffers from the same bias, but it has two additional sources of bias. One is that the Blume technique adjusts all Betas toward one. This tends to raise the average correlation coefficient estimated from the Blume technique. The correlation coefficient is the product of two Betas. To the extent that Betas are reduced to one symmetrically (with no change in mean), the cross products between them will tend to be larger. For example, the product of 1.1 and 0.9 is larger than the product of 1.2 and 0.8. There is another source of potential problems in the Blume technique. Remember that the Blume technique adjusts the Betas in period two for the changes in Betas between period one and two. If the average change in Beta between periods one and two is positive (negative), the Blume technique will adjust the average Beta for period two up (down).[18] In the Elton, Gruber, and Urich study there was an upward drift in Betas over the period studied and this, combined with the tendency of the Blume technique to shrink all Betas toward one, resulted in forecasts of an average correlation coefficient well above the average correlation coefficient for the sample to which the model was fitted.

The Bayesian adjustment to Betas, like the Blume adjustment, has some upward forecast bias because of its tendency to shrink Betas toward one, but it does not continue to project a trend in Betas and, hence, correlation coefficients as the Blume technique does. However, as pointed out earlier, it has a new source of bias: one that tends to pull Betas and correlation coefficients in a downward direction. This occurs because high Beta stocks are adjusted more toward the mean than low Beta stocks.

Short of empirical tests, it is difficult to say whether, given any set of data, the alternative sources of bias, which work in different directions, will increase or decrease the forecast accuracy of the result. We do know that unless there are predictable trends in average correlation coefficients, the effect of these biases on forecast accuracy will be random from period to period. This source of randomness can be eliminated. One way to do it is to force the average correlation coefficient, estimated by each technique, to be the same and to be equal to the average correlation coefficient that existed in the period over which the model was fitted. If correlation coefficients do not have stable trends, this will be an efficient forecast procedure. It uses only available data and is also easy to do.

When the adjustments were made, the Bayesian adjustment produced the most accurate forecasts of the future correlation matrix. Its difference from the Blume

---

[18]This would be a desirable property if trends in average correlation coefficients were expected to persist over time, but we see no reason to expect them to do so.

technique, the unadjusted Beta, and the historical matrix was statistically significant in all periods tested. The second-ranked technique varied through time with
the Blume adjustment, outperforming the unadjusted Beta in one period and the
unadjusted Beta outperforming Blume in one period.[19]

The forecasts from the three Beta techniques were compared with the forecasts
from a fourth Beta estimate, Beta equals one for all stocks, as well as with the
historical correlation matrix, as a forecast of the future. The mean forecast was
adjusted to be the same for all techniques. The performance of the historical
correlation matrix and the Beta-equals-one model was inferior to the performance
of all other models at a statistically significant level.

Let us stop a minute and review the work on estimating Betas. There are two
reasons for estimating Betas: The first is in order to forecast future Betas. The
second is to generate correlation coefficients as input to the portfolio problem.
Empirical evidence strongly suggests that to forecast future Betas one should use
either the Bayesian adjustment or the Blume adjustment rather than unadjusted
Betas. The evidence on the choice between the Blume and Bayesian adjustment
is mixed, but the Bayesian adjustment seems to work slightly better.

If the goal is estimating the future correlation matrix as an input to the portfolio
problems, things get more complex. Unadjusted Betas and adjusted Betas, both
by the Bayesian and the Blume techniques, all contain potential bias as forecasters
of future correlation matrices.[20] The forecasts from all of these techniques can
be examined directly or the forecasts can be adjusted to remove bias in the forecast
of the average correlation coefficient. The first fact to note is that each of these
three estimates of Beta outperforms the historical correlation matrix as a forecast
of the future correlation matrix. Second, note that when compared to a Beta of
one, all produce better forecasts. The ranking among these three techniques is
a function of whether we make the adjustment to the average forecast. Since we
believe it is appropriate to do so, we find that the Bayesian adjustment technique
performs best.

Recently, attempts have been made to incorporate more data than past return
information into the forecasts of Betas. We will now take a brief look at some
of the work that has been done in this area.

Fundamental Betas

Beta is a risk measure that arises from the relationship between the return on
a stock and the return on the market. However, we know that the risk of a firm
should be determined by some combination of the firm's fundamentals and the
market characteristics of the firm's stock. If these relationships could be deter-

---

[19]In addition, tests were made that forced the average correlation coefficient from each technique to
be the same and equal to the average correlation coefficient that occurred in the forecast period.
This is equivalent to perfect foresight with respect to the average correlation coefficient. The rankings
were the same as those discussed above when this was done.

[20]As discussed earlier, a smaller set of potential biases is present when Betas are estimated.

mined, they would help us both to better understand Betas and to better forecast Betas.

One of the earliest attempts to relate the Beta of a stock to fundamental firm variables was performed by Beaver, Kettler, and Scholes [7]. They examined the relationship between seven firm variables and the Beta on a company's stock. The seven variables they used were:

1. Dividend payout (dividends divided by earnings)
2. Asset growth (annual change in total assets)
3. Leverage (senior securities divided by total assets)
4. Liquidity (current assets divided by current liabilities)
5. Asset size (total assets)
6. Earning variability (standard deviation of the earnings price ratio)
7. Accounting Beta (the Beta that arises from a time series regression of the earnings of the firm against average earnings for the economy, often called the earnings Beta)

An examination of these variables would lead us to expect a negative relationship between dividend payout and Beta under one of two arguments.

1. Since management is more reluctant to cut dividends than raise them, high payout is indicative of confidence on the part of management concerning the level of future earnings.
2. Dividend payments are less risky than capital gains; hence, the company that pays out more of its earnings in dividends is less risky.

Growth is usually thought of as positively associated with Beta. High-growth firms are thought of as more risky than low-growth firms.

Leverage tends to increase the volatility of the earnings stream, hence to increase risk and Beta.

A firm with high liquidity is thought to be less risky than one with low liquidity and, hence, liquidity should be negatively related to market Beta.

Large firms are often thought to be less risky than small firms, if for no other reason than that they have better access to the capital markets. Hence, they should have lower Betas.

Finally, the more variable a company's earning stream and the more highly correlated it is with the market, the higher its Beta should be.

Table 5.5 reports some of the results from the Beaver et al. [7] study. Note all variables had the sign that we expected.

The next logical step in developing fundamental Betas is to incorporate the effects of relevant fundamental variables simultaneously into the analysis. This

Table 5.5 Correlation between Accounting Measures of Risk and Market Beta

Variable	Period 1 1947–56		Period 2 1957–1965	
	1-Stock Portfolio	5-Stock Portfolio	1-Stock Portfolio	5-Stock Portfolio
Payout	−0.50	−0.77	−0.24	−0.45
Growth	0.23	0.51	0.03	0.07
Leverage	0.23	0.45	0.25	0.56
Liquidity	−0.13	−0.44	−0.01	−0.01
Size	−0.07	−0.13	−0.16	−0.30
Earnings variability	0.58	0.77	0.36	0.62
Earnings Beta	0.39	0.67	0.23	0.46

is usually done by relating Beta to several fundamental variables via multiple regression analysis. An equation of the following form is estimated:

$$\beta_i = a_0 + a_1 X_1 + a_2 X_2 + \cdots + a_N X_N + e_i \qquad (5.6)$$

where each X_i is one of the N variables hypothesized as affecting Beta. Several studies have been performed that link Beta to a set of fundamental variables, such as that studied by Beaver et al. [7].[21] The list of variables that has been studied and linked to Betas is too long to review here. For example, Thompson [86] reviews 43 variables while Rosenberg [75] reviews 101. Rather than discuss the long list of variables that have been used to generate fundamental Betas, let us review the relative strengths and weaknesses of fundamental and historical Betas as well as one system, that proposed by Barr Rosenberg [72–75], which has been put forth to combine both types of Betas.

The advantage of Betas based on historical return data is that they measure the response of each stock to market movements. The disadvantage of this type of Beta is that it reflects changes in the size or importance of company characteristics only after a long period of time has passed. For example, assume a company increased its debt-to-equity ratio. We would expect its Beta to increase. However, if we are using 60 months of return data to estimate Beta, one month after the company increased its debt-to-equity ratio, only one of the 60 data points will reflect the new information. Thus, the change in debt-to-equity ratio would have only a very minor impact on the Beta computed from historical return data. Similarly, one full year after the event only 12 of the 60 data points used to measure Beta will reflect the event.

---

[21]For examples of the use of fundamental data to estimate Betas, see [15], [39], [59], [63], [74], [75], and [86]. The ability of fundamental data to aid in the prediction of future Betas has been mixed. Some studies find large improvements in forecasting ability while others do not.

On the other hand, fundamental Betas respond quickly to a change in the companies' characteristics since they are computed directly from these characteristics. However, the weakness of fundamental Betas is that they are computed under the assumption that the responsiveness of all Betas to an underlying fundamental variable is the same. For example, they assume that the Beta for IBM will change in exactly the same way with a given change in its debt-to-equity ratio as will the Beta of GM.[22]

By combining the techniques of historical Betas and fundamental Betas into one system, Barr Rosenberg hopes to gain the advantages of each without being subject to the disadvantages of either. In addition, because Rosenberg and McKibben [74] found that there were persistent differences between the Betas of different industries, Rosenberg and Marathe [75] introduced a set of industry dummy variables into the analysis to capture these differences. Rosenberg's system can be described as follows.[23]

$$\beta_i = a_0 + a_1x_1 + a_2x_2 + a_3x_3 + \cdots + a_7x_7 + a_8x_8 + \cdots + a_{46}x_{46} \quad (5.7)$$

where

x_1 represents 14 descriptions of market variability. These 14 descriptions include historical values of Beta as well as other market characteristics of the stock such as share trading, volume, and stock price range.

x_2 represents 7 descriptors of earnings variability. These descriptors include measures of earnings variability, earnings Betas, and measures of the unpredictability of earnings such as the amount of extraordinary earnings reported.

x_3 represents 8 descriptors of unsuccess and low valuation. These descriptors include growth in earnings, the ratio of book value to stock price, relative strength, and other indicators of perceived success.

x_4 represents 9 descriptors of immaturity and smallness. These descriptors include total assets, market share, and other indicators of size and age.

x_5 represents 9 descriptors of growth orientation. These descriptors include dividend yield, earnings price ratios, and other measures of historical and perceived growth.

---

[22]Each of the regression coefficients of Equation (5.6) (e.g., a_1) has only one value for all firms. This means that a change of 1 unit in X_1 will change the Beta of every firm by a_1 units.

[23]Rosenberg changes the variables in his system over time. This description is based on his system as it existed at a point in time as described in [75].

x_6 represents 9 descriptors of financial risk. These include measures of leverage, interest coverage, and liquidity.

x_7 represents 6 descriptors of firm characteristics. These include indicators of stock listings and broad types of business.

x_8 through x_{46} are industry dummy variables. These variables allow the fact that different industries tend to have different Betas, all other variables held constant, to be taken into account.

While conceptually the Rosenberg technique is easy to grasp, the multitude of variables (101) makes it difficult to grasp the meaning of the parameterized model. The reason for moving to this complex model is to improve forecasting ability. While the model is too new for extensive testing to have been performed, Rosenberg and Marathe's [75] initial testing indicates that the model involving both fundamental data and historical Betas leads to better estimates of future Betas than the use of either type of estimate in isolation.

Before ending this chapter, we should mention one more type of model that is beginning to attract attention. The Rosenberg system quickly reflects changes in Beta that have occurred because it uses data that reflect present conditions (fundamental firm variables) to modify historical Betas as forecasts of the future. A more ideal system would employ forecasts of future fundamental firm variables to modify historical estimates of Beta — in other words, substitute estimates of future values on the right-hand side of Equation (5.7) rather than concurrent values. Now it seems unlikely that analysts can do this for the 101 variables used in Rosenberg's system. However, simpler systems employing a much smaller number of variables are being used in this way. For example, Wells Fargo is experimenting with such a system using fewer than seven variables and has claimed better than a 25% improvement in forecasting Beta. However, these systems are so new that rigorous analysis of their performance and comparison with Rosenberg's results cannot yet be made.

QUESTIONS AND PROBLEMS

1. Monthly return data are presented below for each of three stocks and the S&P index (corrected for dividends) for a 12-month period.
   Calculate the following quantities:

   A.   alpha for each stock

   B.   beta for each stock

   C.   the standard deviation of the residuals from each regression

   D.   the correlation coefficient between each security and the market

   E.   the average return on the market

   F.   the variance of the market

Month	Security			
	A	B	C	S&P
1	12.05	25.20	31.67	12.28
2	15.27	2.86	15.82	5.99
3	−4.12	5.45	10.58	2.41
4	1.57	4.56	−14.43	4.48
5	3.16	3.72	31.98	4.41
6	−2.79	10.79	−0.72	4.43
7	−8.97	5.38	−19.64	−6.77
8	−1.18	−2.97	−10.00	−2.11
9	1.07	1.52	−11.51	3.46
10	12.75	10.75	5.63	6.16
11	7.48	3.79	−4.67	2.47
12	−0.94	1.32	7.94	−1.15

2. **A.** Compute the mean return and variance of return for each stock in Problem 1 using:

  (1)   the single-index model

  (2)   the historical data

  B. Compute the covariance between each possible pair of stocks using:

  (1)   the single-index model

  (2)   the historical data

  C. Compute the return and standard deviation of a portfolio constructed by placing one-third of your funds in each stock, using:

  (1)   the single-index model

  (2)   the historical data

  D. Explain why the answers to parts A.1 and A.2 were the same, while the answers to parts B.1, B.2 and C.1, C.2 were different.

3. Show that the Vasicek technique leads to a simple proportional weighting of the market Beta and the stock's Beta if the standard error of all Betas is the same.

4. **A.** If the Blume adjustment equation is fit and the appropriate equation is

$$\beta_{it+1} = 0.41 + 0.60\beta_{i,t}$$

what is your best forecast of Beta for each of the stocks in Question 1?

  B. If the parameters of the Vasicek technique are fit, and they are

$$\beta_1 = 1.00 \qquad \begin{array}{ll} \sigma_{\bar{\beta}1}^2 = 0.25, & \sigma_{\bar{\beta}1a}^2 = 0.22, \\ \sigma_{\bar{\beta}1b}^2 = 0.36, & \sigma_{\bar{\beta}1c}^2 = 0.41 \end{array}$$

What is your best forecast of Beta for each of the stocks in Question 1?

BIBLIOGRAPHY

1. Alexander, Gordon J., and Benston, P. George. "More on Beta as a Random Coefficient," *Journal of Financial and Quantitative Analysis*, **XVII**, No. 1 (March 1982), pp. 27–36.
2. Alexander, Gordon J., and Chervany, Norman L. "On the Estimation and Stability of Beta," *Journal of Financial and Quantitative Analysis*, **XV**, No. 1 (March 1980), pp. 123–138.
3. Ali, Mukhtar M., and Giaccotto, Carmelo. "Optimum Distribution-Free Tests and Further Evidence of Heteroscedasticity in the Market Model," *Journal of Finance*, **37**, No. 5 (Dec. 1982), pp. 1247–1258.
4. Altman, Edward, Jacquillat, Bertram, and Levasseur, Michael. "Comparative Analysis of Risk Measures: France and the United States," *Journal of Finance*, **IX**, No. 5 (Dec. 1974), pp. 1495–1511.
5. Baesel, Jerome. "On the Assessment of Risk: Some Further Considerations," *Journal of Finance*, **IX**, No. 5 (Dec. 1976), pp. 1491–1494.
6. Barry, Christopher, and Winkler, Robert. "Nonstationarity and Portfolio Choice," *Journal of Financial and Quantitative Analysis*, **XI**, No. 2 (June 1976), pp. 217–235.
7. Beaver, W., Kettler, P., and Scholes, M. "The Association Between Market Determined and Accounting Determined Risk Measures," *The Accounting Review*, **45** (Oct. 1970), pp. 654–682.
8. Beja, Avraham. "On Systematic and Unsystematic Components of Financial Risk," *Journal of Finance*, **VII**, No. 1 (March 1972), pp. 37–45.
9. Bey, Roger P., and Pinches, George E. "Additional Evidence of Heteroscedasticity in the Market Model," *Journal of Financial and Quantitative Analysis*, **XV**, No. 2 (June 1980), pp. 299–322.
10. Bickler, J.L. "Comment: on [51]" *Journal of Financial and Quantitative Analysis*, **IX**, No. 2 (March 1974), pp. 227–230.
11. Bildersee, John S., and Roberts, Gordon S. "Beta Instability When Interest Rate Levels Change," *Journal of Financial and Quantitative Analysis*, **XVI**, No. 3 (Sept. 1981), pp. 375–380.
12. Blume, Marchall. "Betas and Their Regression Tendencies," *Journal of Finance*, **X**, No. 3 (June 1975), pp. 785–795.
13. ———. "On the Assessment of Risk," *Journal of Finance*, **VI**, No. 1 (March 1971), pp. 1–10.
14. ———. "Portfolio Theory: A Step Toward Its Practical Application," *Journal of Business*, **43**, No. 2 (April 1970), pp. 152–173.
15. Breen, William, and Lerner, Eugene. "Corporate Financial Strategies and Market Measures of Risk and Return," *The Journal of Finance*, **28** (May 1973), pp. 339–351.
16. Breen, William. "Homogeneous Risk Measures and the Construction of Composite Assets," *Journal of Financial and Quantitative Analysis*, **III**, No. 4 (Dec. 1968), pp. 405–413.
17. Brenner, Menachem, and Smidt, Seymour. "A Simple Model of Non-Sta-

tionarity of Systematic Risk," *Journal of Finance,* **XII,** No. 4 (Sept. 1977), pp. 1081–1092.

18. Brenner, Menachem. "On the Stability of the Distribution of the Market Component in Stock Price Changes," *Journal of Financial and Quantitative Analysis,* **IX,** No. 6 (Dec. 1974), pp. 945–961.

19. Brown, Steve. "Heteroscedasticity in the Market Model: A Comment on [61]," *Journal of Business,* **50,** No. 1 (Jan. 1977), pp. 80–83.

20. Chen, Son-Nan. "Beta Nonstationarity, Portfolio Residual Risk and Diversification," *Journal of Financial and Quantitative Analysis,* **XVI,** No. 1 (March 1981), pp. 95–112.

21. ————. "An Examination of Risk-Return Relationship in Bull and Bear Markets Using Time-Varying Betas," *Journal of Financial and Quantitative Analysis,* **XVII,** No. 2 (June 1982), pp. 265–286.

22. Cheng, Pao, and Deets, King. "Systematic Risk and the Horizon Problem," *Journal of Financial and Quantitative Analysis,* **VIII,** No. 2 (March 1973), pp. 299–316.

23. Cohen, K., Maier, S., Schwartz, R., and Whitcomb, D. "The Returns Generation Process, Returns Variance, and the Effect of Thinness in Security Markets," *Journal of Finance,* **XIII,** No. 1 (March 1978), pp. 149–167.

24. ————. "Limit Orders, Market Structure, and the Returns Generation Process," *Journal of Finance,* **XIII,** No. 3 (June 1978), pp. 723–736.

25. Cohen, Kalman, Ness, Walter, Okuda, Hitashi, Schwartz, Robert, and Whitcomb, David. "The Determinants of Common Stock Returns Volatility: An International Comparison," *Journal of Finance,* **XI,** No. 2 (May 1976), pp. 733–740.

26. Cooley, P., Roenfeldt, R., and Modani, N. "Interdependence of Market Risk Measures," *Journal of Business,* **50,** No. 3 (July 1977), pp. 356–363.

27. Cornell, Bradford, and Dietrich, Kimball, "Mean-Absolute-Deviation versus Least-Squares Regression Estimation of Beta Coefficients," *Journal of Financial and Quantitative Analysis,* **XIII,** No. 1 (March 1978), pp. 123–131.

28. Dickinson, J.P. "The Reliability of Estimation Procedures in Portfolio Analysis," *Journal of Financial and Quantitative Analysis,* **IX,** No. 3 (June 1974), pp. 447–462.

29. Dimson, Elroy, and Marsh, P. "The Stability of UK Risk Measures and the Problem in Thin Trading," *Journal of Finance,* **38,** No. 3 (June 1983), pp. 753–784.

30. Elton, Edwin J., Gruber, Martin J., and Urich, Thomas. "Are Betas Best?," *Journal of Finance,* **XIII,** No. 5 (Dec. 1978), pp. 1375–1384.

31. Fabozzi, Frank, and Francis, Clark. "Beta as a Random Coefficient," *Journal of Financial and Quantitative Analysis,* **XIII,** No. 1 (March 1978), pp. 101–116.

32. ————. "Stability Tests for Alphas and Betas over Bull and Bear Market Conditions," *Journal of Finance,* **XII,** No. 4 (Sept. 1977), pp. 1093–1099.

33. Fama, Eugene. "Risk, Return, and Equilibrium: Some Clarifying Comments," *Journal of Finance,* **23** (March 1968), pp. 29–40.

34. Fielitz, Bruce. "Stationarity of Random Data: Some Implications for the Distribution of Stock Price Changes," *Journal of Financial and Quantitative Analysis,* **VI,** No. 3 (June 1971), pp. 1025–1034.
35. Fouse, W., Jahnke, W., Rosenberg, B. "Is Beta Phlogiston?," *Financial Analysts Journal,* **30,** No. 1 (Jan.–Feb. 1974), pp. 70–80.
36. Frankfurter, G., and Phillips, H. "Alpha-Beta Theory: A Word of Caution," *Journal of Financial Management,* **3,** No. 4 (Summer 1977), pp. 35–40.
37. Frankfurter, George, Phillips, Hervert, and Seagle, John. "Performance of the Sharpe Portfolio Selection Model: A Comparison," *Journal of Financial and Quantitative Analysis,* **XI,** No. 2 (June 1976), pp. 195–204.
38. Francis, Jack Clark. "Intertemporal Differences in Systematic Stock Price Movements," *Journal of Financial and Quantitative Analysis,* **X,** No. 2 (June 1975), pp. 205–219.
39. Gonedes, Nicholas J. "Evidence on the Information Content of Accounting Numbers: Accounting-based and Market-based Estimates of Systematic Risk," *Journal of Financial and Quantitative Analysis,* **8** (June 1973), pp. 407–443.
40. Gooding, Arthur, and O'Malley, Terence. "Market Phase and the Stationarity of Beta," *Journal of Financial and Quantitative Analysis,* **XII,** No. 4 (Dec. 1977), pp. 833–857.
41. Gordon, Edward. "Comment: on [63]," *Journal of Financial and Quantitative Analysis,* **IX,** No. 2 (March 1974) pp. 234–245.
42. Hamada, S. Robert. "The Effect of the Firm's Capital Structure on the Systematic Risk of Common Stocks," *Journal of Finance,* **VII,** No. 2 (May 1971), pp. 435–452.
43. Hasty, John, and Fielitz, Bruce. "Systematic Risk for Heterogeneous Time Horizons," *Journal of Finance,* **X,** No. 2 (May 1975), pp. 659–673.
44. Haugen, Robert, and Wichern, Dean. "The Intricate Relationship Between Financial Leverage and the Stability of Stock Prices," *Journal of Finance,* **X,** No. 5 (Dec. 1975), pp. 1283–1292.
45. Hawawini, Gabriel A. "Intertemporal Cross-Dependence in Securities Daily Returns and the Short-Run Intervaling Effect on Systematic Risk," *Journal of Financial and Quantitative Analysis,* **XV,** No. 1 (March 1980), pp. 139–150.
46. ———. "An Analytical Examination of the Intervaling Effect on Skewness and Other Moments," *Journal of Financial and Quantitative Analysis,* **XV,** No. 5 (Dec. 1980), pp. 1121–1128.
47. Hawawini, Gabriel A., and Vora, Ashok. "Evidence of Intertemporal Systematic Risks in the Daily Price Movements of NYSE and AMEX Common Stocks," *Journal of Financial and Quantitative Analysis,* **XV,** No. 2 (June 1980), pp. 331–340.
48. Hill, Ned C., and Stone, Bernell K. "Accounting Betas, Systematic Operating Risk, and Financial Leverage: A Risk-Composition Approach to the Determinants of Systematic Risk," *Journal of Financial and Quantitative Analysis,* **XV,** No. 3 (Sept. 1980), pp. 595–638.
49. Jacob, Nancy. "The Measurement of Systematic Risk for Securities and

Portfolios: Some Empirical Results," *Journal of Financial and Quantitative Analysis,* **VI,** No. 2 (March 1971), pp. 815–833.

50. ———. "Comment on [22]," *Journal of Financial and Quantitative Analysis,* **VIII,** No. 2 (March 1973), pp. 351–354.
51. Joehnk, Michael, and Nielsen, James. "The Effects of Conglomerate Merger Activity on Systematic Risk," *Journal of Financial and Quantitative Analysis,* **IX,** No. 2 (March 1974), pp. 215–225.
52. Johnson, James, and Baesel, Jerome. "The Nature and Significance of Trend Betas," *Journal of Financial Management,* **4,** No. 3 (Spring 1978), pp. 36–40.
53. Klemkosky, Robert, and Martin, John. "The Effect of Market Risk on Portfolio Diversification," *Journal of Finance,* **X,** No. 1 (March 1975), pp. 147–153.
54. ———. "The Adjustment of Beta Forecasts," *Journal of Finance,* **X,** No. 4 (Sept. 1975), pp. 1123–1128.
55. Latane, Henry, Tuttle, Don, and Young, Allan. "How to Choose a Market Index," *Financial Analysts Journal,* **27,** No. 4 (Sept.–Oct. 1971), pp. 75–85.
56. Lee, Cheng. "On the Relationship Between the Systematic Risk and the Investment Horizon," *Journal of Financial and Quantitative Analysis,* **XI,** No. 5 (Dec. 1976), pp. 803–815.
57. Levy, Robert. "On the Short-Term Stationarity of Beta Coefficients," *Financial Analysts Journal,* **27,** No. 5 (Dec. 1971), pp. 55–62.
58. ———. "Beta Coefficients as Predictors of Return," *Financial Analysts Journal,* **30,** No. 1 (Jan.–Feb. 1974), pp. 61–69.
59. Logue, Dennis, and Merville, Larry. "Financial Policy and Market Expectations," *Financial Management,* **1** (Summer 1972), pp. 37–44.
60. Martin, John, and Keown, Arthur. "A Misleading Feature of Beta for Risk Measurement," *Journal of Financial Management,* **3,** No. 4 (Summer 1977), pp. 31–34.
61. Martin, J., and Klemkosky, R. "Evidence of Heteroscedasticity in the Market Model," *Journal of Business,* **48,** No. 1 (Jan. 1975), pp. 81–86.
62. McDonald, Bill. "Beta Nonstationarity and the Use of the Chen and Lee Estimator: A Note," *The Journal of Finance,* **38,** No. 3 (June 1983), pp. 1005–1010.
63. Melicher, Ronald. "Financial Factors which Influence Beta Variations within an Homogeneous Industry Environment," *Journal of Financial and Quantitative Analysis,* **IX,** No. 2 (March 1974), pp. 231–241.
64. Officer, R.R. "The Variability of the Market Factor of the New York Stock Exchange," *Journal of Business,* **46,** No. 3 (July 1973), p. 434.
65. Owen, Joel, and Rabinovitch, Ramon. "The Cost of Information and Equilibrium in the Capital Asset Market," *Journal of Financial and Quantitative Analysis,* **XV,** No. 3 (Sept. 1980), pp. 497–508.
66. Pinches, E. George, and Kinney, R. William, Jr. "The Measurement of the Volatility of Common Stock Prices," *Journal of Finance,* **VI,** No. 1 (March 1971), pp. 119–125.

67. Pogue, Gerald, and Solnik, Bruno. "The Market Model Applied to European Common Stocks: Some Empirical Results," *Journal of Financial and Quantitative Analysis,* **IX,** No. 6 (Dec. 1974), pp. 917–944.
68. Rentz, William, and Vandenberg, Pieteo. "The Impact of Changes in Trading Location on a Security's Systematic Risk," *Journal of Financial and Quantitative Analysis,* **X,** No. 5 (Dec. 1975), pp. 881–890.
69. Robichek, Alexander, and Cohn, Richard. "The Economic Determinants of Systematic Risk," *Journal of Finance,* **XXIX,** No. 2 (May 1974), pp. 439–447.
70. Roenfeldt, R., Griepentrog, G., and Pflaum, C. "Further Evidence on the Stationarity of Beta Coefficients," *Journal of Financial and Quantitative Analysis,* **XIII,** No. 1 (March 1978), pp. 117–121.
71. Roll, Richard. "Bias in Fitting the Sharpe Model to Time Series Data," *Journal of Financial and Quantitative Analysis,* **IV,** No. 3 (Sept. 1969), pp. 271–289.
72. Rosenberg, Barr, and Guy, James. "Prediction of Beta from Investment Fundamentals," *Financial Analysts Journal,* **32,** No. 3 (May–June 1976), pp. 60–72.
73. ———. "Prediction of . . . : Part II," *Financial Analysts Journal,* **32,** No. 3 (July–Aug. 1976), pp. 62–70.
74. Rosenberg, Barr, and Mickibben, Walt. "The Prediction of Systematic and Specific Risk in Common Stocks," *Journal of Financial and Quantitative Analysis,* **VIII,** No. 2 (March 1973), pp. 317–333.
75. Rosenberg, Barr, and Marathe, Vinay. "The Prediction of Investment Risk: Systematic and Residual Risk," Reprint 21, Berkeley Working Paper Series.
76. Rudd, Andrew, and Rosenberg, Barr. "The 'Market Model' in Investment Management," *The Journal of Finance,* **35,** No. 2 (May 1980), pp. 597–606.
77. Schaefer, Stephen, Brealey, Richard, and Hodges, Steward. "Alternative Models of Systematic Risk," in Elton and Gruber, *International Capital Markets* (Amsterdam: North Holland, 1976).
78. Schmalensee, Richard, and Trippi, Robert. "Common Stock Volatility Expectations Implied by Option Premi," *Journal of Finance,* **XIII,** No. 1 (March 1978), pp. 129–147.
79. Schneller, Meir. "Regression Analysis for Multiplicative Phenomenon and Its Implications for the Measurement of Investment Risk," *Management Science,* **2,** No. 4 (Dec. 1975), pp. 422–426.
80. Scholes, M., and Williams, J. "Estimating Betas from Non-Synchronous Data," *Journal of Financial Economies,* **5,** No. 3 (Dec. 1977), pp. 309–328.
81. Scott, Elton, and Brown, Stewart. "Biased Estimators and Unstable Betas," *The Journal of Finance,* **35,** No. 1 (March 1980), pp. 49–56.
82. Sharpe, William. "Mean-Absolute-Deviation Characteristic Lines for Securities and Portfolios," *Management Science,* **18,** No. 2 (Oct. 1971), pp. B1–B13.
83. Smith, Keith. "Stock Price and Economic Indexes for Generating Efficient Portfolios," *Journal of Business,* **42,** No. 3 (July 1969), pp. 226–326.

84. Sunder, Shyam. "Stationarity of Market Risk: Random Coefficients Tests for Individual Stocks," *Journal of Finance,* **35,** No. 4 (Sept. 1980), pp. 883–896.
85. Theobald, Michael. "Beta Stationarity and Estimation Period: Some Analytical Results," *Journal of Financial and Quantitative Analysis,* **XVI,** No. 5 (Dec. 1981), pp. 747–758.
86. Thompson II, Donald. "Sources of Systematic Risk in Common Stocks," *Journal of Business,* **40,** No. 2 (April 1978), pp. 173–188.
87. Vasicek, Oldrich. "A Note on Using Cross-Sectional Information in Bayesian Estimation of Security Betas," *Journal of Finance,* **VIII,** No. 5 (Dec. 1973), pp. 1233–1239.

Chapter 6

The Correlation Structure of Security Returns

Multi-index Models and Grouping Technique

In Chapter 5 we argued that because of both the huge number of forecasts required and the necessary restrictions on the organizational structure of security analysts, it was not feasible for anlaysts to directly estimate correlation coefficients. Instead, some structural or behavioral model of how stocks move together should be developed. The parameters of this model can be estimated either from historical data or by attempting to get subjective estimates from security analysts. We have already examined one such model, the single-index model, which assumes that stocks move together only because of a common co-movement with the market. There are two other approaches that have been widely used to explain and estimate the correlation structure of security returns: multi-index models and averaging techniques.

Multi-index models are an attempt to capture some of the nonmarket influences that cause securities to move together. The search for nonmarket influences is a search for a set of economic factors or structural groups (industries) that account for common movement in stock prices beyond that accounted for by the market index itself. While it is easy to find a set of indices that are associated with nonmarket effects over any period of time, as we shall see, it is quite another matter to find a set that is successful in predicting covariances that are not market related.

Averaging techniques are at the opposite end of the spectrum from multi-index models. Multi-index models introduce extra indices in the hope of capturing additional information. The cost of introducing additional indices is the chance that they are picking up random noise rather than real influences. Averaging techniques smooth the entries in the historical correlation matrix in an attempt to "damp out" random noise and so produce better forecasts. The potential disadvantage of averaging models is that real information may be lost in the averaging process.

In this chapter we examine both multi-index models and averaging models. Several of the models put forth in the finance literature are discussed as well as some of the empirical evidence on their relative merits.

MULTI-INDEX MODELS

The assumption underlying the single-index model is that stock prices move together only because of common movement with the market. Many researchers have found that there are influences beyond the market that cause stocks to move together. For example, as early as 1966, King [18] presented evidence on the existence of industry influences. Two different types of schemes have been put forth for handling additional influences. We have called them the general multi-index model and the industry index model.

General Multi-index Models

Any additional sources of covariance between securities can be introduced into the equations for risk and return, simply by adding these additional influences to the general return equation. Let us hypothesize that the return on any stock is a function of the return on the market, the level of interest rates, and a set of industry indexes. If R_i is the return on stock i, then the return on stock i can be related to the influences that affect its return in the following way:

$$R_i = a_i{}^* + b_{i1}{}^*I_1{}^* + b_{i2}{}^*I_2{}^* + \cdots + b_{iL}{}^*I_L{}^* + c_i$$

In this equation $I_j{}^*$ is the actual level of index j, $b_{ij}{}^*$ is a measure of the responsiveness of the return on stock i to changes in the index j. Thus, $b_{ij}{}^*$ has the same meaning as β_i in the case of the single-index model. A $b_{ij}{}^*$ of 2 would mean that if the index increased (decreased) by 1%, the stock's return is expected to increase (decrease) by 2%. As in the case of the single-index model, the return of the security not related to indices is split into two parts; $a_i{}^*$ and c_i. $a_i{}^*$ is the expected value of the unique return. This is the same meaning it had in the single-index model. c_i is the random component of the unique return. It has a mean of zero and a variance we will designate as $\sigma_{ci}{}^2$.

While a multi-index model of this type can be employed directly, the model would have some very convenient mathematical properties if the indices were uncorrelated (orthogonal). This would allow us to simplify both the computation of risk and the selection of optimal portfolios. Fortunately, this presents no theoretical problems because it is always possible to take any set of correlated indices and convert them into a set of uncorrelated indices. The method for doing so is outlined in Appendix A. Using this methodology, the equation can be rewitten as[1]

$$R_i = a_i + b_{i1}I_1 + b_{i2}I_2 + b_{i3}I_3 + \cdots + b_{iL}I_L + c_i$$

where all I_j are uncorrelated with each other. The new indices still have an economic interpretation. Assume I_1^* was a stock market index and I_2^* an index of interest rates. I_2 is now an index of the difference between actual interest rates and the level of interest rates that would be expected given the rate of return on the stock market (I_1). Similarly, b_{i2} becomes a measure of the sensitivity of the return on stock i to this difference. We can think of b_{i2} as the sensitivity of stock i's return to a change in interest rates when the rate of return on the market is fixed.

Not only is it convenient to make the indices uncorrelated, it is also convenient to have the residual uncorrelated with each index. Formally, this implies that $E[c_i(I_j - \bar{I}_j)] = 0$ for all j. The implication of this construction is that the ability of Equation (6.1) to describe the return on any security is independent of the value any index happens to assume. When the parameters of this model are estimated via regression analysis, as is usually done, this will hold over the period of time to which the model is fitted.

The standard form of the multi-index model can be written as follows:
Basic equation:

$$R_i = a_i + b_{i1}I_1 + b_{i2}I_2 + b_{i3}I_3 + \cdots + b_{iL}I_L + c_i$$
$$\text{for all stocks } i = 1, \ldots, N \quad (6.1)$$

By definition:

1. residual variance of stock i equals σ_{ci}^2 where $i = 1, \ldots, N$
2. variance of index j equals σ_{Ij}^2 where $j = 1, \ldots, L$

By construction:

1. mean of c_i equals $E(c_i) = 0$ for all stocks, where $i = 1, \ldots, N$
2. covariance between indices j and k equals $E[(I_j - \bar{I}_j)(I_k - \bar{I}_k)] = 0$ for all indices, where $j = 1, \ldots, L$ and $k = 1, \ldots, L$ $(j \neq k)$
3. covariance between the residual for stock i and index j equals $E[c_i(I_j - \bar{I}_j)] = 0$ for all stocks and indices, where $i = 1, \ldots, N$ and $j = 1, \ldots, L$

---

[1]The asterisks have been removed to indicate that the indices and coefficients are now different. Actually, if the procedure in Appendix A at the end of this chapter is followed $I_1 = I_1^*$, but all others are different. In applications it may be easier for analysts to estimate the model with correlated indexes. This model can then be transformed into one with uncorrelated indexes for purposes of portfolio selection.

By assumption:

1. covariance between c_i and c_j is zero ($E(c_i c_j) = 0$) for all stocks where $i = 1, \ldots, N$ and $j = 1, \ldots, N$ ($j \neq i$)

The assumption of the multi-index model is that $E(c_i c_j) = 0$. This assumption implies that the only reason stocks vary together is because of common co-movement with the set of indexes that have been specified in the model. There are no factors beyond these indices that account for co-movement between any two securities. There is nothing in the estimation of the model that forces this to be true. This is a simplification that represents an approximation to reality. The performance of the model will be determined by how good this approximation is. This, in turn, will be determined by how well the indices that we have chosen to represent co-movement really capture the pattern of co-movement between securities.

The expected return, variance, and covariance between securities when the multi-index model describes the return structure is derived in Appendix B and is equal to:

1. Expected return is

$$\overline{R}_i = a_i + b_{i1}\overline{I}_1 + b_{i2}\overline{I}_2 + \cdots + b_{iL}\overline{I}_L \tag{6.2}$$

2. Variance of return is

$$\sigma_i^2 = b_{i1}^2\sigma_{I1}^2 + b_{i2}^2\sigma_{I2}^2 + \cdots + b_{iL}^2\sigma_{IL}^2 + \sigma_{ci}^2 \tag{6.3}$$

3. Covariance between security i and j is

$$\sigma_{ij} = b_{i1}b_{j1}\sigma_{I1}^2 + b_{i2}b_{j2}\sigma_{I2}^2 + \cdots + b_{iL}b_{jL}\sigma_{IL}^2 \tag{6.4}$$

From equations (6.2), (6.3), and (6.4) it is clear that the expected return and risk can be estimated for any portfolio if we have estimates of a_i for each stock, and estimates of b_{ik} for each stock with each index, an estimate of σ_{ci}^2 for each stock and, finally, an estimate of the mean ($\overline{I}_j$) and variance σ_{Ij}^2 of each index. This is a total of $2N + 2L + LN$ estimates. For an institution following between 150 and 250 stocks and employing 10 indexes, this calls for between 1,820 and 3,020 inputs. This is larger than the number of inputs required for the single-index model but considerably less than the inputs needed when no simplifying structure was assumed. Notice that now the analyst must be able to estimate the responsiveness of each stock he follows to several economic and industry influences.

This model can also be used if analysts supply estimates of the expected return for each stock, the variance of each stock's returns, each index loading (b_{ik} between each stock i and each index k), and the means and variances of each index. This is the same number of inputs ($2N + 2L + LN$). However, the inputs are in more familiar terms. As discussed at several points in this book, the inputs needed to perform portfolio analysis are expected returns, variances, and correlation coefficients. By having the analysts estimate means and variances directly, it is clear that the only input derived from the estimates of the multi-index models are correlation coefficients. We stress this point because later in this chapter we evaluate the ability of a multi-index model to aid in the selection of securities by examining its ability to forecast correlation coefficients.

There is a certain type of multi-index model that has received a large amount of attention. This class of models restricts attention to market and industry influences. Alternative industry index models result from different assumptions about the behavior of returns and, hence, differ in the type and amount of input data needed. We now examine these models.

Industry Index Models

Several authors have dealt with multi-index models that start with the basic single-index model and add indices to capture industry effects. The early precedent for this work can be found in King [18], who measured effects of common movement between securities beyond market effects and found this extra market covariance was associated with industries. For example, two steel stocks had positive correlation between their returns, even after the effects of the market had been removed.[2]

If we hypothesize that the correlation between securities is caused by a market effect and industry effects, our general multi-index model could be written as:

$$R_i = a_i + b_{im}I_m + b_{i1}I_1 + b_{i2}I_2 + \cdots + b_{iL}I_L + c_i$$

where

I_m is the market index

I_j are industry indices that are constrained to be uncorrelated with the market and uncorrelated with each other

The assumption behind this model is that a firm's return can be affected by the market plus several industries. For some companies this seems appropriate as their lines of business span several traditional industries. However, some companies gain the bulk of their return from activities in one industry and, perhaps of more importance, are viewed by investors as members of a particular industry. In this case the effects on the firm's return of indices for industries to which they do not belong are likely to be small and their inclusion may introduce more random noise into the process than the information they supply. This has prompted some authors to advocate a simpler form of the multi-index model: one that assumes that returns of each firm are affected only by a market index and one industry index. Furthermore, the model assumes that each industry index has been constructed to be uncorrelated with the market and with all other industry

---

[2]King [18] found that over the entire period studied, 1927–60, about half of the total variation in a stock's price was accounted for by a market index while an average of another 10% was accounted for by industry factors. In the latter part of the period he studied, the importance of the market factor dropped to 30%, while the industry factors continued to explain 10% of price movement.

indexes. For firm i in industry j, the return equation can be written as

$$R_i = a_i + b_{im}I_m + b_{ij}I_j + c_i$$

The covariance between securities i and k can be written as

$$b_{im}b_{km}\sigma_m^2 + b_{ij}b_{kj}\sigma_{Ij}^2$$

for firms in the same industry and

$$b_{im}b_{km}\sigma_m^2$$

for firms in different industries. Notice that the number of inputs needed for portfolio selection has been cut to $4N + 2L + 2$.

The data needed are the expected return and variance for each stock, the loading of each stock on the market and industry index, and, finally, the mean and variance of each industry index and the market index.[3]

How Well do Multi-index Models Work?

At this point it is worth examining how well these multi-index models have performed when the parameters are estimated from historical data.[4] Remember, multi-index models lie in an intermediate position between the full historical correlation matrix itself and the single-index model in ability to reproduce the historical correlation matrix. The more indices added, the more complex things become and the more accurately the historical correlation matrix is reproduced. However, this does not imply that future correlation matrices will be forecast more accurately. Since there are an infinite number of multi-index models that can be tried, one cannot unequivocally say that multi-index models are better or worse than single-index models. However, we can examine some typical resutls on several multi-index models to see how well they work.

---

[3]As the reader can imagine, there is more than one way to write any model. This particular type of multi-index model has been popularized in another form by Cohen and Pogue [5].

It can be shown that the model Cohen and Pogue call the diagonal form of the multi-index model is identical to the form we have been discussing. The advantage of expressing the input data as suggested by Cohen and Pogue is that the analyst can deal directly with responsiveness of industries to the market. This may be easier than dealing with the responsiveness of stocks to industry indexes with market influences removed.

[4]All of the tests of the various models we've discussed have estimated the models using historical data. There is no reason that the estimates could not come from analysts. The ability of analysts to make these estimates and their value is still an open question.

Let us start with the most general form of the multi-index model:

$$R_i = a_i + b_{i1}I_1 + b_{i2}I_2 + b_{i3}I_3 + \cdots + b_{iL}I_L + c_i$$

This model explains firm returns in terms of a set of uncorrelated indexes.[5]

Before discussing the results, it is worth digressing for a moment to see how we might judge the performance of these models. Remember that all index models lead to the same estimates of expected returns and a stock's own variance (as opposed to covariances) when estimated from historical returns and variances. Furthermore, if analysts are used to estimate expected return and variance, the only estimate from a model is an estimate of the covariance. However, the covariance is the product of standard deviations and correlation coefficients. If analysts are used to estimate standard deviations, any differences in performance that exist must arise from differences in estimating the correlation structure of security returns. The most direct test of alternative models is to examine how well they estimate the future correlation matrix of security returns. Differences between forecasts and actual results can be measured and the statistical significance of these differences can be judged. While tests of statistical significance are useful for judging the superiority of forecasting techniques, tests of economic significance are often of more interest. Tests of economic significance examine the difference in return or profit that results from basing forecasts on one technique rather than on another. In this case the future returns (at alternative specified risk levels) that would result from selecting portfolios based on each forecasting model can be examined.

Now let us discuss the results of both the statistical tests and tests of economic significance. In general, Elton and Gruber [8] found (that on both statistical

---

[5]A mathematical technique exists that allows a set of indices that meet the criteria for this model to be constructed from a set of returns. The technique is called principal components analysis. Principal components analysis will extract from a historical variance-covariance matrix of returns that index (weighting of the individual returns) that best explains (reproduces) the variance of the original data. This index is called the first principal component. Principal components analysis then proceeds to extract the index that explains as much as possible of the variance of the original data unexplained by the first principal component, given that this second index is constrained to be uncorrelated with the first index. It proceeds to sequentially form additional indices, ensuring that each index formed explains as much as possible of the variation in the data that has not been explained by previous indices, given that each index extracted is uncorrelated with each index previously extracted. This technique can be used until the number of indices extracted equals the number of stocks whose variance-covariance matrix is being examined. At this point the principal components can exactly reproduce the historical variance-covariance matrix. However, since the first principal component explains as much as possible of the historical variance-covariance matrix, the second explains as much as possible of the remaining variance, and so on, we would expect the last few principal components to have almost no explanatory power. In fact, to the extent that there is any real underlying structure to the data, most of the correlation matrix should be explained by the first few principal components.

Elton and Gruber [9] used principal component analysis on 76 firms and found that the percentage of the variance in the original data explained with 1, 3, 8, and 17 principal components was 36%, 45%, 61%, and 75%, respectively.

grounds and economic grounds) adding additional indices to the single-index model led to a decrease in performance. Although adding more indices led to a better explanation of the historical correlation matrix, it led both to a poorer prediction of the future correlation matrix and to the selection of portfolios that, at each risk level, tended to have lower returns. In short, these added indices introduced more random noise than real information into the forecasting process.

The evidence that a generalized multi-index model, where the indexes are extracted according to explanatory power from past data, does not perform as well as a single-index model is very strong. This does not imply that a different form of a multi-index model might not work better than a single-index model. Indices based on interest rates or oil prices or other fundamental factors affecting different companies in different ways may lead to better performance. One would expect that other influences exist that should have a major and lasting influence on the correlation structure of stock prices. Whether they do or not is a matter for empirical research.

Another test of the multi-index model was performed by Cohen and Pogue [5]. They examined the use of a specialized multi-index model to select portfolios (test of economic significance).[6] Standard industrial classifications were used to divide the stocks in their sample into industries. Standard industrial classifications group firms by end product such as steel or chemical. Single-index models and a multi-index model, with a market and industry index, were then run. While Cohen and Pogue tested results, both over the period to which the models were fit and over the forecast period, only the latter set of tests are of interest to a person considering the adoption of these models. Cohen and Pogue conclude that with respect to these tests, the single-index model has more desirable properties. The single-index model led to lower expected risks and is much simpler to use.[7]

While Cohen and Pogue accepted standard industrial classifications in their analysis, other authors have sought to employ industry index models where industries were defined, not in terms of a standard classification but in terms of the tendency of firms to act alike. Procedures for forming homogeneous groups of firms or psuedo-industries were first examined in Elton and Gruber [7] and later again in Elton and Gruber [9] and [10]. Farrell [12] was the first to use the concepts and procedures of psuedo-industries to form indexes as input to a multi-index model.

The following question may occur to the reader. Why bother with a statistical

---

[6]The specialized form of the model they tested was their diagonal form of the multi-index model.

[7]Cohen and Pogue [5] also tested a more elaborate form of the multi-index industry model. In this form the entire covariance structure between industry indices was employed. However, the performance of this model was inferior to the simpler diagonal form of the industry multi-index model and, hence, inferior to the single-index model.

alternative to traditional industry classification? After all, the traditional grouping partitions firms into sets according to end product or service produced or sold. There are at least two problems with the use of these codes. One is that the increase in the number of multiproduct firms and the prevalence of company diversification have made classification by product difficult and, sometimes, arbitrary. Second, and even more important, classification by product or service may be useful for some purposes but it is far from a universal classification for all purposes. For example, General Motors and American Motors are in the same industry but there are major differences in their performance and the risk to which they are subject.

Given the problems with traditional industry classifications, it is useful to develop an alternative or group of alternative classifications. In fact, it is logical to have techniques for grouping that allow groups to be formed according to the objective in mind and the nature of the process under investigation. In the case of the multi-index model, the purpose is clear: develop groups such that the indices for them predict as much as possible of the correlation between securities that is not predicted (explained) by the market index. One logical way to do this is to remove the market index from stock returns and then to examine the correlation structure of residuals. Stocks that have highly correlated residuals are combined into a pseudo-industry. Indices for each pseudo-industry can be developed and these indices used in a multi-index model. This is similar to the procedure that was followed by Farrell [12, 13]. He found that the large sample of stocks he analyzed could be classified into four pseudo-industries. Furthermore, because of the nature of the stocks in each group, he could associate characteristics with each group. He labeled the four groups growth stocks, cyclical stocks, stable stocks, and oil stocks. Note that, in his sample, only one traditional industry was sufficiently homogeneous to show up in his groupings. The significance of these pseudo-industry indices over the period studied can be seen by the fact that, while the market index accounted for 30% of the variance in stock prices, the use of an appropriate pseudo-industry index with each stock accounted for an additional 15%. As would be expected, when mulit-index models were used, the models were able to account for a larger percentage of historical correlation than the single-index model. This is not surprising. Extracting more indices from this historical correlation matrix, according to their ability to explain it, has to mean that a model that includes these additional indices reproduces the correlation matrix from which they were extracted better than a model that excludes them. Remember that both Elton and Gruber [9] and Cohen and Pogue [5] found that their multi-index model did a better job of reproducing the historical correlation matrix, but it did not do a better job of forecasting than the single-index model.

The relevant question is how well a model employing pseudo-industries performs when it is used to predict future correlation matrices or to select portfolios. Perhaps the first question to ask is whether pseudo-industries are stable over time. To have any predictive ability, the composition of pseudo-industries must show a high degree of stability. Farrell tests for stability and concludes it is quite high. He next uses both the single-index model and a four-index model (based on his four groups) to select portfolios based on data from the period 1961–69 and observes how well these portfolios perform for the period 1970–74. Farrell concludes that his multi-index model based on homogeneous groups outperformed the single-index model.[8] Some caution is warranted in generalizing Farrell's results. An examination of them shows that, while on average the multi-index model does perform slightly better, it leads to inferior performance at some risk levels and superior performance at others. The dominance is not complete. Furthermore, the conclusions are based on one sample over one time period. Before his conclusion can be accepted, more testing is needed. Nevertheless, Farrell's work holds out hope for the development of multi-index models based on security groupings that can outperform single-index models.[9]

Up to this point we have discussed the use of multi-index models as a way of forecasting the future correlation structure between security returns. While this use holds great promise for the future, the results, to date, have been mixed. A natural question arises: If the addition of more indices to a single-index model can, at times, introduce more random noise than real information into the forecasting process, might not a technique that smoothes more of the historical data lead to better results?

Recently there has been a renewed interest in multi-index models. The testing has been to see how many indices best explain the historical variance-covariance or correlation matrix. Roll and Ross [26] report that at least three indices are needed to explain the historical variance-covariance matrix. Drymes, Friend, and Gultekin [6] show that the number of indices that are needed is very dependent on the number of firms that are being analyzed. Depending on the sample size, they find that many more than three are needed. Finally Gibbons [17], analyzing bond and stock data, finds that six or seven indices are needed. Unfortunately, none of these studies or other similar recent studies make an attempt to examine whether multi-index models are better as forecasters than single-index models of the future variance-covariance matrix. It would not be at all surprising if multi-index models better explained the historical variance-covariance matrix or correlation matrix but led to poorer forecasting due to a change in the structure over time. Thus although the recent research should encourage future work in this area, it does not provide very strong evidence in favor of the use of multi-index models in portfolio anlaysis.

---

[8]Leonard Fertuck [14] followed a procedure similar to Farrell's to form pseudo-industries. He then compared the ability of multi-index models based on pseudo-industries with multi-index models based on traditional industries to explain the variance of returns over a subsequent period. He found that the traditional industry grouping outperformed the pseudo-industry indices in most cases.

[9]In selecting all portfolios, Farrell forces his intercept for both the single-index and multi-index models to be zero. In Chapter 11 we show that the theoretical values of these intercepts is not zero and so this could bias his results.

AVERAGE CORRELATION MODELS

The idea of averaging (smoothing) some of the data in the historical correlation matrix as a forecast of the future has been tested by Elton and Gruber [9] and Elton, Gruber, and Urich [10].

The most aggregate type of averaging that can be done is to use the average of all pairwise correlation coefficients over some past period as a forecast of each pairwise correlation coefficient for the future. This is equivalent to the assumption that the past correlation matrix contains information about what the average correlation will be in the future but no information about individual differences from this average. This model can be thought of as a naive model against which more elaborate models should be judged. We refer to this model as the overall mean model.

A more disaggregate averaging model would be to assume that there was a common mean correlation within and between groups of stocks. For example, if we employ the idea of traditional industries as a method of grouping, we would assume that the correlation between any two steel stocks was the same as the correlation between any other two steel stocks and was equal to the average historical correlation between steel stocks. The averaging is done across all pairwise correlations between steel stocks in a historical period. Similarly, the correlation between any steel stocks and any chemical stocks is assumed to be equal to the correlation between any other steel stock and any other chemical stock and is set equal to the average of the correlations between each chemical and each steel stock. When this is done, with respect to traditional industry classifications, it will be referred to as the traditional mean model. The same technique has been used [9] with respect to pseudo-industries.

The overall mean has been extensively tested against single-index models, general multi-index models, and the historical correlation matrix itself. Tests have been performed using three different samples of stocks over a total of four different time periods. In every case, the use of the overall mean model outperformed the single-index model, the multi-index model, and the historical correlation matrix. The differences in forecasting future correlation coefficients were almost always statistically significant at the 0.05 level. Furthermore, for most risk levels, the differences in portfolio performance were large enough to have real economic significance. Using the overall mean technique, as opposed to the best of the single-index model, the multi-index model, or the historical correlation model, often led to a 25% increase in return (holding risk constant).

The next logical question is what happens when we introduce some disaggregation into the results by using the traditional mean or pseudo-mean model. Here the results are much more ambiguous. Averaging models based on either traditional industries or pseudo-industries outperformed single-index models, multiple-index models, and the historical correlation matrix both on statistical and economic criteria. However, their differences from each other and from the overall mean were much less clear. The ordering of these three techniques was different over different time periods and at different risk levels in the same time period. At this point all we can say is that, while it is worth continuing to investigate the performance of traditional mean and pseudo-mean averaging models, their superiority over the overall mean model has not yet been demonstrated.

MIXED MODELS

Before ending this discussion, there is one more type of model that should be discussed. This type is a combination of the models discussed in Chapter 5 and those introduced in this chapter. We call them mixed models. In a mixed model, the single-index model is used as the basic starting point. However, rather than assume that the extramarket covariance is zero, a second model is constructed to explain extramarket covariance. This concept should not be new to the reader. If we consider a general multi-index model, where the first index is the market, then we can consider all other indices as indices of extramarket covariance. What is new is the way that extramarket covariance is predicted. The most widely known model of this type is that described by Rosenberg [27]. In Chapter 5 we discussed Rosenberg's methods of relating Beta to a set of fundamental and technical data. Rosenberg has used the same method for predicting extramarket covariance. He relates extramarket covariance to the same type of fundamental variables and industry membership coefficients that were discussed in Chapter 5. After removing the market index, he regresses the extramarket covariance on 114 variables. These variables include traditional industry classification as well as firm variables such as debt-equity ratios and dividend payout measures. Initial results with this type of analysis appear quite promising, although extensive tests of the forecast ability have not been performed.

Another approach worth exploring is to apply the same type of averaging techniques discussed earlier directly to the extramarket covariance. That is, instead of performing the averaging on the correlation coefficients themselves, perform the averaging on the correlations of the residuals from the single-index model. For example, a traditional industry averaging scheme might be used. In this case, after removing the market influence, the residuals for each stock could be averaged within and between industries. Then the correlation between any two stocks would be predicted by combining their predicted correlation from the single-index model with the extramarket correlation predicted from the averaging model.

CONCLUSIONS

In this chapter we have discussed alternatives to the single-index model for predicting future correlation coefficients. There are an infinite number of such models. Thus, we cannot give definitive answers concerning their performance relative to single-index models. Many of the results are promising. This probably does not surprise the reader. What surprises most students is the ability of simple models such as the single-index model and overall mean to outperform more complex models in many tests. Although complex models better describe the historical correlation, they often contain more noise than information with respect to prediction. There is still a great deal of work to be done before complicated models consistently outperform simpler ones.

APPENDIX A

Procedure for Reducing Any Multi-index Model to a Multi-index Model with Orthogonal Indices

We illustrate the procedure with a two-index model. Let

$$R_i = a_i^* + b_{i1}^* I_1^* + b_{i2}^* I_2^* + c_i$$

For example, I_1^* might be a market index and I_2^* a sector index (e.g., aggregate index for companies producing capital goods). If two indices are correlated, the correlation may be removed from either index.

Define I_1 as equal to I_1^*. Now to remove the impact of the market from the sector index, we can establish the parameters of the following equation via regression analysis:

$$I_2^* = \gamma_0 + \gamma_1 I_1 + d_i$$

where γ_0 and γ_1 are regression coefficients and d_i is the random error term. By the techniques of estimation used in regression analysis, d_i is uncorrelated with I_1. Thus

$$d_i = I_2^* - (\gamma_0 + \gamma_1 I_1)$$

is an index of the performance of the sector index with the effect of I_1 (the market) removed.

If we define

$$I_2 = d_i = I_2^* - \gamma_0 - \gamma_1 I_1$$

we have defined an index of sector performance that is uncorrelated with the market. Solving for I_2^* and substituting into the return equation yields

$$R_i = a_i^* + b_{i1}^* I_1 + b_{i2}^* I_2 + b_{i2}^* \gamma_0 + b_{i2}^* \gamma_1 I_1 + c_i$$

Rearranging terms gives

$$R_i = (a_i^* + b_{i2}^* \gamma_0) + (b_{i1}^* + b_{i2}^* \gamma_1) I_1 + b_{i2}^* I_2 + c_i$$

The first term is a constant we define as a_i. The coefficient on the second term is a constant we define as b_{i1}. Now let $b_{i2} = b_{i2}^*$. Then this equation becomes

$$R_i = a_i + b_{i1}I_1 + b_{i2}I_2 + c_i$$

where I_1 and I_2 have been defined so that they are uncorrelated, and we have accomplished our task.

If the model contained a third index, for example, an industry index, then this index could be made orthogonal to the other two indexes by running the following regression:

$$I_3^* = \theta_1 + \theta_2 I_1 + \theta_3 I_2 + e_i$$

The index I_3 could be defined as

$$I_3 = I_3^* - (\theta_1 + \theta_2 I_1 + \theta_3 I_2)$$

The proof that this leads to a three-index model with uncorrelated indexes of the form

$$R_i = a_i + b_{i1}I_1 + b_{i2}I_2 + b_{i3}I_3 + c_i$$

is left as an exercise to the reader.

APPENDIX B

Mean Return, Variance, and Covariance of a Multi-index Model

In this appendix we derive the mean return variance and covariance of return when the multi-index model is assumed to describe the return structure in the market.

Expected Return

The expected return on a security with the multi-index model is

$$E(R_i) = E(a_i + b_{i1}I_1 + b_{i2}I_2 + \cdots + b_{iL}I_L + c_i)$$

Since the expected value of the sum of random variables is the sum of the expected values, we have

$$E(R_i) = E(a_i) + E(b_{i1}I_1) + E(b_{i2}I_2) + \cdots + E(b_{iL}I_L) + E(c_i)$$

Recognizing that a and b are constants and that by construction $E(c_i) = 0$, we have

$$E(R_i) = a_i + b_{i1}\bar{I}_1 + b_{i2}\bar{I}_2 + \cdots + b_{iL}\bar{I}_L$$

This is the result stated in the text.

Variance of Return

The variance of the return on a security is

$$\sigma_i^2 = E(R_i - \overline{R}_i)^2$$

Substituting for R_i and $\overline{R}_i$, we have

$$\sigma_i^2 = E[(a_i + b_{i1}I_1 + b_{i2}I_2 + \cdots + b_{iL}I_L + c_i)$$
$$- (a_i + b_{i1}\overline{I}_1 + b_{i2}\overline{I}_2 + \cdots + b_{iL}\overline{I}_L)]^2$$

Canceling the a_i's and rearranging yields

$$\sigma_i^2 = E[b_{i1}(I_1 - \overline{I}_1) + b_{i2}(I_2 - \overline{I}_2) + \cdots + b_{iL}(I_L - \overline{I}_L) + c_i]^2$$

The next step is to square the terms in the brackets. The results of this can be seen if we examine all terms involving the first index. The first index times itself and each of the other terms is

$$E[b_{i1}^2(I_1 - \overline{I}_1)^2 + b_{i1}b_{i2}(I_1 - \overline{I}_1)(I_2 - \overline{I}_2) + \cdots$$
$$|\ b_{i1}b_{iL}(I_1 - \overline{I}_1)(I_L - \overline{I}_L) + b_{i1}(I_1 - \overline{I}_1)(c_i)]$$

The expected value of the sum of random variables is the sum of the expected values and, since the b_i's are constants, we have

$$b_{i1}^2 E(I_1 - \overline{I}_1)^2 + b_{i1}b_{i2}E[(I_1 - \overline{I}_1)(I_2 - \overline{I}_2)] + \cdots$$
$$+ b_{i1}b_{iL}E[(I_1 - \overline{I}_1)(I_L - \overline{I}_L)] + b_{i1}E[(I_1 - \overline{I}_1)(c_i)]$$

By construction

$$E[(I_i - \overline{I}_i)(I_j - \overline{I}_j)] = 0$$

and

$$E[(I_1 - \overline{I}_1)(c_i)] = 0$$

thus, the only nonzero term involving index one is

$$b_{i1}^2 E(I_1 - \overline{I}_1)^2 = b_{i1}^2 \sigma_{I1}^2$$

When we examine terms involving the c_i, we get the c_i with each index that has an expected value of zero. We also get $E(c_i)^2 = \sigma_{ci}^2$; thus,

$$\sigma_i^2 = b_{i1}^2 \sigma_{I1}^2 + b_{i2}^2 \sigma_{I2}^2 + \cdots + b_{iL}^2 \sigma_{IL}^2 + \sigma_{ci}^2$$

The Covariance

The covariance between securities i and j is

$$\sigma_{ij} = E[(R_i - \overline{R}_i)(R_j - \overline{R}_j)]$$

Substituting in the expressions for R_i and R_j yields

$$\begin{aligned}
\sigma_{ij} = E\{ & [(a_i + b_{i1}I_1 + b_{i2}I_2 + \cdots + b_{iL}I_L + c_i) \\
& - (a_i + b_{i1}\overline{I}_1 + b_{i2}\overline{I}_2 + \cdots + b_{iL}\overline{I}_L)] \\
& \cdot [(a_j + b_{j1}I_1 + b_{j2}I_2 + \cdots + b_{jL}I_L + c_j) \\
& - (a_j + b_{j1}\overline{I}_1 + b_{j2}\overline{I}_2 + \cdots b_{jL}\overline{I}_L)]\}
\end{aligned}$$

Noting that the a's cancel, and combining the terms involving the same b's yields

$$\begin{aligned}
\sigma_{ij} = E\{ & [b_{i1}(I_1 - \overline{I}_1) + b_{i2}(I_2 - \overline{I}_2) + \cdots + b_{iL}(I_L - \overline{I}_L) + c_i)] \\
& \cdot [b_{j1}(I_1 - \overline{I}_1) + b_{j2}(I_2 - \overline{I}_2) + \cdots + b_{jL}(I_L - \overline{I}_L) + c_j]\}
\end{aligned}$$

The next step is to multiply out the terms. The results of this multiplication can be seen by considering the terms involving b_{i1}. They are

$$\begin{aligned}
E[& b_{i1}b_{j1}(I_1 - \overline{I}_1)^2 + b_{i1}b_{j2}(I_1 - \overline{I}_1)(I_2 - \overline{I}_2) \\
+ \; & b_{i1}b_{j3}(I_1 - \overline{I}_1)(I_3 - \overline{I}_3) + \cdots + b_{i1}b_{jL}(I_1 - \overline{I}_1)(I_L - \overline{I}_L) + b_{i1}(I_1 - \overline{I}_1)c_j]
\end{aligned}$$

The expected value of all terms involving different indices, for example, $(I_1 - \overline{I}_1)$ $(I_k - \overline{I}_k)$ is zero by construction. Furthermore, the expected value of $b_{i1}(I_1 - \overline{I}_1)c_j$ is zero by construction. Thus, the only nonzero term is

$$b_{i1}b_{j1}E(I_1 - \overline{I}_1)^2 = b_{i1}b_{j1}\sigma_{I1}^2$$

There are two types of terms involving the c's. First, there are terms like $b_{ik}(I_k - \overline{I}_k)c_j$, which is zero by construction. Second, there is the term c_ic_j. This is zero by assumption. Thus

$$\sigma_{ij} = b_{i1}b_{j1}\sigma_{I1}^2 + b_{i2}b_{j2}\sigma_{I2}^2 + b_{i3}b_{j3}\sigma_{I3}^2 + \cdots + b_{iL}b_{jL}\sigma_{IL}^2$$

QUESTIONS AND PROBLEMS

1. Given that the correlation coefficient between all securities is the same, call it ρ^*, and the assumption of the single-index model are accepted, derive an expression for the Beta on any stock in terms of ρ^*.

2. Complete the procedure in Appendix A for reducing a general three-index model to a three-index model with orthogonal indexes.

3. Assume that all assumptions of the single-index model hold, except that the covariance between residuals is a constant K instead of zero. Derive the covariance between the two securities and the variance on a portfolio.

4. Given a three-index model such that all indexes are orthogonal, derive the formulas for the expected return, variance, and covariance of any stock.

BIBLIOGRAPHY

1. Aber, John. "Industry Effects and Multivariate Stock Price Behavior," *Journal of Financial and Quantitative Analysis,* **XI,** No. 4 (Nov. 1976), pp. 617–624.
2. Altman, Edward, and Schwartz, Robert. "Common Stock Price Volatility Measures and Patterns," *Journal of Financial and Quantitative Analysis,* **IV,** No. 5 (Jan. 1970), pp. 603–625.
3. Bell, Frederick. "The Relation of the Structure of Common Stock Prices to Historical, Exceptional and Industrial Variables," *Journal of Finance,* **IX,** No. 1 (March 1976), pp. 187–197.
4. Chung, Peter. "An Investigation of the Firm Effects Influence in the Analysis of Earnings to Price Ratios of Industrial Common Stocks," *Journal of Financial and Quantitative Analysis,* **IX,** No. 6 (Dec. 1974), pp. 1009–1031.
5. Cohen, Kalman, and Pogue, Jerry, "An Empirical Evaluation of Alternative Portfolio Selection Models," *Journal of Business,* **46** (April 1967), pp. 166–193.
6. Dhrymes, Phoebus, Friend, Irwin, and Gultekin, Bulent. "A Critical Reexamination of the Empirical Evidence on the Arbitrage Pricing Theory," *The Journal of Finance,* **39** (June 1984), pp. 323–346.
7. Elton, Edwin J., and Gruber, Martin J. "Homogeneous Groups and the Testing of Economic Hypotheses," *Journal of Financial and Quantitative Analysis,* **IV,** No. 5 (Jan. 1970), pp. 581–602.
8. ———. "Improved Forecasting Through the Design of Homogeneous Groups," *Journal of Business,* **44,** No. 4 (Oct. 1971).
9. ———. "Estimating the Dependence Structure of Share Prices — Implications for Portfolio Selection," *Journal of Finance,* **VIII,** No. 5 (Dec. 1973), pp. 1203–1232.
10. Elton, Edwin J., Gruber, Martin J., and Urich, Thomas. "Are Betas Best?," *Journal of Finance,* **23,** No. 5 (Dec. 1978), pp. 1375–1384.
11. Eun, Cheol S., and Resnick, Bruce G. "Estimating the Correlation Structure of International Share Prices," *The Journal of Finance,* **39,** No. 5 (Dec. 1984), pp. 1311–1324.
12. Farrell, James. "Analyzing Covariation of Returns to Determine Homogeneous Stock Groupings," *Journal of Business,* **47,** No. 2 (April 1974), pp. 186–207.
13. ———. *The Multi-Index Model* and *Practical Portfolio Analysis,* The Financial Analysts Research Foundation Occasional Paper No. 4 (1976).
14. Fertuck, Leonard. "A Test of Industry Indices Based on SIC Codes," *Journal of Financial and Quantitative Analysis,* **X,** No. 5 (Dec. 1975), pp. 837–848.

15. Frankfurter, George, Phillips, Herbert, and Seagle, John. "Portfolio Selection: The Effects of Uncertain Means, Variances and Covariances," *Journal of Financial and Quantitative Analysis,* **VI,** No. 5 (Dec. 1971), pp. 1251–1262.
16. Friend, Irwin, and Vickers, Douglas. "Re-Evaluation of Alternative Portfolio-Selection Models," *Journal of Business,* **41,** No. 2 (April 1968), pp. 174–179.
17. Gibbons, Michael R. "Multivariate Tests of Financial Models, A New Approach," *Journal of Financial Economics,* **10** (March 1982), pp. 3–27.
18. King, Benjamine. "Market and Industry Factors in Stock Price Behavior," *Journal of Business,* **39** (Jan. 1966), pp. 139–140.
19. Lee, Cheng. "A Note on the Interdependent Structure of Security Returns," *Journal of Financial and Quantitative Analysis,* **XI,** No. 1 (March 1976), pp. 73–86.
20. Livingston, Miles. "Industry Movements of Common Stocks," *Journal of Finance,* **XII,** No. 3 (June 1977), pp. 861–874.
21. Lloyd, William, and Shick, Richard. "A Test of Stone's Two-Index Model of Returns," *Journal of Financial and Quantitative Analysis,* **XII,** No. 3 (Sept. 1977) pp. 363–376.
22. Martin, John, and Klemkosky, Robert. "The Effect of Homogeneous Stock Groupings on Portfolio Risk," *Journal of Business,* **49,** No. 3 (July 1976) pp. 339–349.
23. Meyers, Stephen. "A Re-examination of Market and Industry Factors in Stock Price Behavior," *Journal of Finance,* **VIII,** No. 3 (June 1973), pp. 695–705.
24. Morgan, I.G. "Grouping Procedures for Portfolio Formation," *Journal of Finance,* **XI,** No. 5 (Dec. 1977), pp. 1759–1765.
25. Reilly, Frank, and Drzycimski, Eugene. "Alternative Industry Performance and Risk," *Journal of Financial and Quantitative Analysis,* **IX,** No. 3 (June 1974), pp. 423–446.
26. Roll, Richard, and Ross, Stephen. "An Empirical Investigation of the Arbitrage Pricing Theory," *The Journal of Finance,* **35** (Dec. 1980), pp. 1073–1103.
27. Rosenberg, Barr. "Extra-Market Components of Covariance in Security Returns," *Journal of Financial and Quantitative Analysis,* **IX,** No. 2 (March 1974), pp. 263–274.
28. Rush, David. "Comment: The Interdependent Structure of Security Returns," *Journal of Financial and Quantitative Analysis,* **VIII,** No. 2 (March 1973), pp. 289–291.
29. Schwartz, Robert, and Altman, Edward. "Volatility Behavior of Industrial Stock Price Indices," *Journal of Finance,* **VIII,** No. 4 (Sept. 1973), pp. 957–970.
30. Simkowitz, Michael, and Logue, Dennis. "The Interdependent Structure of Security Returns," *Journal of Financial and Quantitative Analysis,* **VIII,** No. 2 (March 1973), pp. 259–272.

Chapter 7

Simple Techniques for Determining the Efficient Frontier

In Chapters 5 and 6 we examined several models that were developed to simplify the inputs to the portfolio selection problem. Each of these models makes an assumption about why stocks co-vary together. Each leads to a simplified structure for the correlation matrix or covariance matrix between securities. These models were developed to cut down on the number of inputs and simplify the nature of the inputs needed to forecast correlations between securities. The use of these models was expected to lead to some loss of accuracy in forecasting correlations, but the ease of using the models was expected to compensate for this loss of accuracy. However, we have seen in Chapters 5 and 6 that when fitted to historical data, these simplifying models result in an increase, not a decrease, in forecasting accuracy. The models are of major interest because they both reduce and simplify the inputs needed to perform portfolio analysis *and* increase the accuracy with which correlations and covariances can be forecast.

In this chapter we see that there is yet another advantage of these models. Each allows the development of a system for computing the composition of optimum portfolios that is so simple it can often be performed without the use of a computer. Perhaps even more important than the ease of computation is the fact that the methods of portfolio selection described in this chapter make it very clear why a stock does or does not enter into an optimal portfolio. Each model of the correlation structure discussed in Chapters 5 and 6 leads to a unique ranking of stocks, such that if a stock enters an optimal portfolio, any higher ranked stock must also enter the optimal portfolio. Similarly, if a stock does not enter an optimal portfolio, any lower ranked stock does not enter the optimal portfolio. This allows the analyst to judge the relative desirability of stocks even before the portfolio selection process is begun. Furthermore, as we shall see, the optimum ranking of stocks depends on variables that are already familiar to security analysts and portfolio managers, as well as to readers of this book. This should minimize the institutional barriers to their adoption.

In this chapter we describe, in detail, the methods for selecting optimal portfolios that are appropriate when the single-index model and the constant-correlation model are accepted as descriptions of the covariance structure between securities. In the text of this chapter we present the rules for optimal portfolio selection and show how to use them. This may appear as magic to the reader because, while we declare that the rules lead to the selection of optimal portfolios, the text does not contain a proof that this is so. For the reader who prefers science to magic, the appendices at the end of this chapter present the derivations of all of the rules described in the text. These derivations also act as proof of the optimality of the rules. We have separated the material in this way because the mathematical sophistication needed to understand the derivation of the rules is so much greater than the mathematical sophistication needed to use the rules.

We close this chapter with a brief discussion of the types of rules that some of the other models of correlation structure (presented in Chapter 6) lead to. The discussion here is quite concise, but, for the reader interested in learning more about these rules, the appropriate references are noted.

THE SINGLE-INDEX MODEL

In this section we present and demonstrate the optimum procedure for selecting portfolios when the single-index model is accepted as the best way to forecast the covariance structure of returns.

First we present the ranking criteria that can be used to order stocks for selection for the optimal portfolio. We next present the technique for employing this ranking device to form an optimum portfolio, along with a logical explanation for why it works. While the technique for forming optimum portfolios is easy to understand, the formal proof that it leads to the same portfolio that would be produced by the optimum procedure, presented in Chapter 4, is complex and is presented in Appendix A at the end of this chapter.

After presenting the criteria for the composition of an optimal portfolio, we demonstrate its use with some simple examples. In the first part of the section we assume that short sales are forbidden. In the later part we allow short sales. In addition, we start by assuming unlimited borrowing and lending at the riskless rate. This assumption is dropped later in the chapter.

The Formation of Optimal Portfolios

The calculation of optimal portfolios would be greatly facilitated, and the ability of practicing security analysts and portfolio managers to relate to the construction of optimal portfolios greatly enhanced, if there were a single number that measured the desirability of including a stock in the optimal portfolio. If one is willing to accept the standard form of the single-index model as describing the co-movement between securities, such a number exists. In this case, the desirability of any stock is directly related to its excess return to Beta ratio. Excess return is the difference between the expected return on the stock and the riskless rate of interest such as the rate on a treasury bill. The excess return to Beta ratio measures the additional return on a security (beyond that offered by a riskless asset) per unit of nondiversifiable risk. The form of this ratio should lead to its easy interpretation and acceptance by security analysts and portfolio managers for they are used to thinking in terms of the relationship between potential rewards and risk.[1] The numerator of this ranking device is the extra return over the riskless asset that we earn from holding a security other than the riskless asset. The denominator is the nondiversifiable risk (the risk we cannot get rid of) that we are subject to by holding a risky security rather than the riskless asset.

More formally, the index we use to rank stocks is "excess return to Beta," or

$$\frac{\overline{R}_i - R_F}{\beta_i}$$

where
$\overline{R}_i$ = the expected return on stock i
R_F = the return on a riskless asset
β_i = the expected change in the rate of return on stock i associated with a 1% change in the market return

If stocks are ranked by excess return to Beta (from highest to lowest), the ranking represents the desirability of any stock's inclusion in a portfolio. In other words, if a stock with a particular ratio of $(\overline{R}_i - R_F)/\beta_i$ is included in an optimal portfolio, all stocks with a higher ratio will also be included. On the other hand, if a stock with a particular $(\overline{R}_i - R_F)/\beta_i$ is excluded from an optimal portfolio, all stocks with lower ratios will be excluded (or if short selling is allowed, sold short). When the single-index model is assumed to represent the covariance structure of security returns, then a stock is included or excluded, depending only on the size of its excess return to Beta ratio. How many stocks are selected depends on a unique cut-off rate such that all stocks with higher ratios of $(\overline{R}_i - R_F)/\beta_i$ will be included and all stocks with lower ratios excluded. We call this cut-off ratio C^*.

The rules for determining which stocks are included in the optimum portfolio are as follows:

1. Find the "excess return to Beta" ratio for each stock under consideration, and rank from highest to lowest.

2. The optimum portfolio consists of investing in all stocks for which $(\overline{R}_i - R_F)/\beta_i$ is greater than a particular cut-off point C^*. Shortly, we will define C^* and interpret its economic significance.

---

[1] In Chapter 16 we see that one commonly used measure to rank portfolio performance is the portfolio's excess return to Beta ratio with the best portfolio being the one with the highest ratio. It is intuitively appealing to rank stocks by the same criteria as one uses to rank portfolios and, in fact, it is shown in the appendix that it is optimal to do so.

.The above procedure is extremely simple. Once C^* has been determined, the securities to be included can be selected by inspection. Furthermore, the amount to invest in each security is equally simple to determine, as will be discussed shortly.

Ranking Securities

In Tables 7.1 and 7.2 we present an example that illustrates this procedure. Table 7.1 contains the data necessary to apply our simple ranking device to determine an optimal portfolio. It is the normal output generated from a single-index or Beta model, plus the ratio of excess return to Beta. This same data could alternatively be generated by analysts' subjective estimates. There are 10 securities in the tables. For the readers' covenience, we have already ranked the securities according to $(\overline{R}_i - R_F)/\beta_i$ and have used numbers that make the calculations easy to follow. The application of rule 2 involves the comparison of $(\overline{R}_i - R_F)/\beta_i$ with C^*. Accept that $C^* = 5.45$ for the moment; we will shortly present a procedure for its calculation. Examining Table 7.1 shows that for securities 1 to 5 $(\overline{R}_i - R_F)/\beta_i$ is greater than C^* while for security 6 it is less than C^*. Hence, an optimal portfolio consists of securities 1 to 5.

Table 7.1   Data Required to Determine Optimal Portfolio $R_F = 5\%$

1	2	3	4	5	6
					Excess Return over Beta
	Mean	Excess		Unsystematic	$(\overline{R}_i - R_F)$
Security No.	Return	Return	Beta	Risk	
i	$\overline{R}_i$	$\overline{R}_i - R_F$	β_i	σ_{ei}^2	β_i
1	15	10	1	50	10
2	17	12	1.5	40	8
3	12	7	1	20	7
4	17	12	2	10	6
5	11	6	1	40	6
6	11	6	1.5	30	4
7	11	6	2	40	3
8	7	2	0.8	16	2.5
9	7	2	1	20	2
10	5.6	0.6	0.6	6	1.0

Setting the Cut-off Rate (C^*)

As discussed earlier, C^* is the cut-off rate. All securities whose excess-return-to-risk ratio are above the cut-off rate are selected and all whose ratios are below are rejected. The value of C^* is computed from the characteristics of all of the securities that belong in the optimum portfolio. To determine C^* it is necessary to calculate its value as if there were different numbers of securities in the optimum portfolio. Designate C_i as a candidate for C^*. The value of C_i is calculated when i securities are assumed to belong to the optimal portfolio.

Since securities are ranked from highest excess return to Beta to lowest, we know that if a particular security belongs in the optimal portfolio, all higher ranked securities also belong in the optimal portfolio. We proceed to calculate values of a variable C_i (the procedure is outlined below) as if the first ranked security was in the optimal portfolio ($i = 1$), then the first and second ranked securities were in the optimal portfolio ($i = 2$), then the first, second, and third ranked security were in the optimal portfolio ($i = 3$), and so forth. These C_i are candidates for C^*. We know we have found the optimum C_i, that is C^*, when all securities used in the calculation of C_i have excess returns to Beta above C_i and all securities not used to calculate C_i have excess returns to Beta below C_i. For example, column 7 of Table 7.2 shows the C_i for alternative values of i. Examining the table shows that C_5 is the only value of C_i for which all securities used in the calculation of i (1 through 5 in the table) have a ratio of excess return to Beta above C_i and all securities not used in the calculation of C_i (6 through 10 in the table) have an excess return to Beta ratio below C_i. C_5 serves the role of a cut-off rate in the way a cut-off rate was defined earlier. In particular, C_5 is the only C_i that when used as a cut-off rate selects only the stocks used to construct it. There will always be one and only one C_i with this property and it is C^*.

Table 7.2 Calculations for Determining Cut-off Rate with $\sigma_m^2 = 10$

1	2	3	4	5	6	7
Security No. i	$\dfrac{(\overline{R}_i - R_F)}{\beta_i}$	$\dfrac{(\overline{R}_i - R_F)\beta_i}{\sigma_{ei}^2}$	$\dfrac{\beta_i^2}{\sigma_{ei}^2}$	$\sum\limits_{j=1}^{i} \dfrac{(\overline{R}_i - R_F)\beta_j}{\sigma_{ej}^2}$	$\sum\limits_{j=1}^{i} \dfrac{\beta_i^2}{\sigma_{ej}^2}$	C_i
1	10	2/10	2/100	2/10	2/100	1.67
2	8	4.5/10	5.625/100	6.5/10	7.625/100	3.69
3	7	3.5/10	5/100	10/10	12.625/100	4.42
4	6	24/10	40/100	34/10	52.625/100	5.43
5	6	1.5/10	2.5/100	35.5/10	55.125/100	5.45
6	4	3/10	7.5/100	38.5/10	62.625/100	5.30
7	3	3/10	10/100	41.5/10	72.625/100	5.02
8	2.5	1/10	4/100	42.5/10	76.625/100	4.91
9	2.0	1/10	5/100	43.5/10	81.625/100	4.75
10	1.0	0.6/10	6/100	44.1/10	87.625/100	4.52

Calculating the Cut-off Rate C^*

Recall that stocks are ranked by excess return to risk from highest to lowest. For a portfolio of i stocks C_i is given by

$$C_i = \frac{\sigma_m^2 \sum\limits_{j=1}^{i} \dfrac{(\overline{R}_j - R_F)\beta_j}{\sigma_{ej}^2}}{1 + \sigma_m^2 \sum\limits_{j=1}^{i} \left(\dfrac{\beta_i^2}{\sigma_{ej}^2}\right)} \qquad (7.1)$$

where

$\sigma_m{}^2$ = the variance in the market index

$\sigma_{ej}{}^2$ = the variance of a stock's movement that is not associated with the movement of the market index. This is usually referred to as a stock's unsystematic risk.

This looks horrible. But a moment's reflection combined with a peek at the example below will show that it is not as hard to compute as it appears. While Equation (7.1) is the form that should actually be used to compute C_i, this expression can be stated in a mathematically equivalent way that clarifies the meaning of C_i.[2]

$$C_i = \frac{\beta_{iP}(\overline{R}_P - R_F)}{\beta_i} \tag{7.2}$$

where

β_{iP} = the expected change in the rate of return on stock i associated with a 1% change in the return on the optimal portfolio

$\overline{R}_P$ = the expected return on the optimal portfolio
all other terms as before

β_{iP} and $\overline{R}_P$ are, or course, not known until the optimal portfolio is determined. Hence, Equation (7.2) could not be used to actually determine the optimum portfolio; rather, Equation (7.1) must be used. However, this expression for C_i is useful in interpreting the economic significance of our procedure. Recall that securities are added to the portfolio as long as

$$\frac{\overline{R}_i - R_F}{\beta_i} > C_i$$

Rearranging and substituting in Equation (7.2) yields

$$(\overline{R}_i - R_F) > \beta_{iP}(\overline{R}_P - R_F)$$

The right-hand side is nothing more than the expected excess return on a particular stock based solely on the expected performance of the optimum portfolio. The term on the left-hand side is the security analyst's estimate of the expected excess return on the individual stock. Thus, if the analysis of a particular stock leads the portfolio manager to believe that it will perform better than would be expected, based on its relationship to the optimal portfolio, it should be added to the portfolio.

Now let us look at how Equation (7.1) can be used to determine the value of C_i for our example. While Equation (7.1) might look complex, the ease with which it can be calculated is demonstrated by Table 7.2. This table presents the intermediate calculations necessary to determine Equation (7.1).

---

[2]See Appendix A at the end of this chapter for a derivation of this expression.

Let's work through the intermediate calculations shown in Table 7.2 and find the value for C_i for the first security in our list of securities. The numerator of Equation (7.1) is

$$\sigma_m^2 \sum_{j=1}^{i} \frac{(\bar{R}_j - R_F)\beta_j}{\sigma_{ej}^2}$$

Column 3 of Table 7.2 presents the value of

$$\frac{(\bar{R}_i - R_F)\beta_i}{\sigma_{ej}^2}$$

for each security. This is necessary in order to determine the summation. For example, for the first security using the values shown in Table 7.1, it is

$$\frac{(15 - 5)1}{50} = \frac{2}{10}$$

Column 5 gives the value of the summation, or the running cumulative total of column 3. For the first security $i = 1$ and

$$\sum_{j=1}^{1} \frac{(\bar{R}_j - R_F)\beta_j}{\sigma_{ej}^2} = \frac{(\bar{R}_1 - R_F)\beta_1}{\sigma_{e1}^2}$$

Thus column 5 of Table 7.2 is the same as column 3 for security 1. The last term in the denominator of expression 7.1 is

$$\sum_{j=1}^{i} \frac{\beta_j^2}{\sigma_{ej}^2}$$

Since $i = 1$ for the first security, it is simply

$$\frac{\beta_1^2}{\sigma_{e1}^2} = \frac{(1)^2}{50} = \frac{2}{100}$$

This result is shown in column 4 and cumulated in column 6. We can now put these terms together to find C_i. Remembering that $\sigma_m^2 = 10$,

$$C_i = \frac{\sigma_m^2 \sum_{j=1}^{i} \frac{(\bar{R}_j - R_F)\beta_j}{\sigma_{ej}^2}}{1 + \sigma_m^2 \sum_{j=1}^{i} \frac{\beta_j^2}{\sigma_{ej}^2}}$$

$$= \frac{\sigma_m^2 \text{ (column 5)}}{1 + \sigma_m^2 \text{ (column 6)}} = \frac{10 \left(\dfrac{2}{10}\right)}{1 + 10 \left(\dfrac{2}{100}\right)} = 1.67 \qquad \frac{2}{1.2}$$

We now follow through the calculations for security 2 ($i = 2$). Column 3 is found to be

$$\frac{(17 - 5)1.5}{40} = \frac{4.5}{10}$$

Now column 5 is the sum of column 3 for security 1 and security 2 or

$$\frac{2}{10} + \frac{4.5}{10} = \frac{6.5}{10}$$

Column 4 is

$$\frac{(1.5)^2}{40} = \frac{5.625}{100}$$

Column 6 is the sum of column 4 for security 1 and 2, or

$$\frac{2}{100} + \frac{5.625}{100} = \frac{7.625}{100}$$

We can now find C_2 as

$$C_2 = \frac{\sigma_m^2 \,(\text{column 5})}{1 + \sigma_m^2 \,(\text{column 6})} = \frac{10 \dfrac{6.5}{10}}{1 + 10 \dfrac{7.625}{100}} = 3.68$$

Proceeding in the same fashion we can find all the C_i's.

Constructing the Optimal Portfolio

Once the securities that are contained in the optimum portfolio are determined, it remains to show how to calculate the percent invested in each security. The percentage invested in each security is

$$X_i = \frac{Z_i}{\displaystyle\sum_{j=1}^{N} Z_j}$$

where

$$Z_i = \frac{\beta_i}{\sigma_{ei}^2}\left(\frac{\overline{R}_i - R_F}{\beta_i} - C^*\right) \qquad (7.3)$$

The second expression determines the relative investment in each security while the first expression simply scales the weights on each security so they sum to one and, thus, ensure full investment. Note that the residual variance on each security σ_{ei}^2 plays an important role in determining how much to invest in each security. Applying this formula to our example we have

$$Z_1 = \frac{2}{100} (10 - 5.45) = 0.091$$

$$Z_2 = \frac{3.75}{100} (8 - 5.45) = 0.095625$$

$$Z_3 = \frac{5}{100} (7 - 5.45) = 0.0775$$

$$Z_4 = \frac{20}{100} (6 - 5.45) = 0.110$$

$$Z_5 = \frac{2.5}{100} (6 - 5.45) = 0.01375$$

$$\sum_{i-1}^{5} Z_i = 0.387875$$

Dividing each Z_i by the sum of the Z_i, we find that we should invest 23.5% of our funds in security 1, 24.6% in security 2, 20% in security 3, 28.4% in security 4, and 3.5% in security 5.

Let us stress that this is identical to the result that would be achieved had the problem been solved using the established quadratic programming codes. However, the solution has been reached in a fraction of the time with a set of relatively simple calculations.

Notice that the characteristics of a stock that make it desirable and the relative attractiveness of stocks can be determined before the calculations of an optimal portfolio is begun. The desirability of any stock is solely a function of its excess return to Beta ratio. Thus, a security analyst following a set of stocks can determine the relative desirability of each stock before the information from all analysts is combined and the portfolio selection process begun.

Up to this point we have assumed that all stocks have positive Betas. We believe that there are sound economic reasons to expect all stocks to have positive Betas and that the few negative Beta stocks that are found in large samples are due to measurement errors. However, as pointed out in [6], negative Beta stocks (and zero Beta stocks) are easily incorporated in the analysis.

Another Example

We have included a second example to illustrate the use of these formulas. This example is presented in Tables 7.3 and 7.4. Once again, securities are ranked by excess return to Beta. Examining Table 7.4 shows that the C_i associated with security 4 is the only C_i consistent with our definition of C^*. That is, it is the only value of C_i such that stocks ranked i or higher all have excess returns to

Table 7.3   Data Required to Determine Optimal Portfolio; $R_F = 5$

1	2	3	4	5	6
Security Number	Mean Return $\overline{R}_i$	Excess Return $\overline{R}_i - R_F$	Beta β_i	Unsystematic Risk σ_{ei}^2	Excess Return over Beta $\dfrac{(\overline{R}_i - R_F)}{\beta_i}$
1	19	14	1.0	20	14
2	23	18	1.5	30	12
3	11	6	0.5	10	12
4	25	20	2.0	40	10
5	13	8	1.0	20	8
6	9	4	0.5	50	8
7	14	9	1.5	30	6
8	10	5	1.0	50	5
9	9.5	4.5	1.0	50	4.5
10	13	8	2.0	20	4
11	11	6	1.5	30	4
12	8	3	1.0	20	3
13	10	5	2.0	40	2.5
14	7	2	1.0	20	2

Beta above C_i and all stocks ranked below i have excess returns to Beta below C_i. Thus the cut-off rate

$$C^* = C_4 = \frac{58}{7} = 8.29$$

The optimum amount to invest is determined using Equation (7.3). For this example, it is

$$Z_1 = \frac{1}{20}\left(14 - \frac{58}{7}\right) = \frac{40}{140} = \frac{240}{840}$$

$$Z_2 = \frac{1.5}{30}\left(12 - \frac{58}{7}\right) = \frac{39}{210} = \frac{156}{840}$$

$$Z_3 = \frac{.5}{10}\left(12 - \frac{58}{7}\right) = \frac{13}{70} = \frac{156}{840}$$

$$Z_4 = \frac{2}{40}\left(10 - \frac{58}{7}\right) = \frac{24}{280} = \frac{72}{840}$$

Scaling the Z's so that they add to one we have

$$X_1 = \frac{240}{240 + 156 + 156 + 72} = \frac{240}{624} = 0.38$$

$$X_2 = \frac{156}{240 + 156 + 156 + 72} = \frac{156}{624} = 0.25$$

$$X_3 = \frac{156}{240 + 156 + 156 + 72} = \frac{156}{624} = 0.25$$

$$X_4 = \frac{72}{240 + 156 + 156 + 72} = \frac{72}{624} = 0.12$$

Thus, in this example the optimum portfolio consists of four securities with the largest investment in security 1 and the smallest in security 4.

In solving this problem there is no need to fill in all the entries in Table 7.4. Clearly, all the intermediate calculations associated with the lower ranked securities are not needed. One could start by ranking all securities by excess return to Beta. Then proceed to calculate C_i for larger values of i (higher ranked stocks) until a value of i is found so that the ith + 1 stock is excluded. At that point we can ignore stocks ranked below the ith stock. Notice that, though excess return to Beta had to be computed for all stocks, the calculation of C_i and Z_i need only be done for i stocks or, in the case of this example, four stocks.

Short Sales Allowed

The procedures used to calculate the optimal portfolio when short sales are allowed are closely related to the procedures in the no short sales case. As a first step all stocks are ranked by excess return to Beta just as they were in the previous case. However, the cut-off point for stocks, C^*, now has a different meaning, as well as a different procedure for calculation. When short sales are allowed, all stocks will either be held long or sold short.[3] Thus, all stocks enter into the optimum portfolio and all stocks affect the cut-off point. Equation (7.1) still represents the cut-off point, but now the numerator and denominator of this equation are summed over all stocks. In addition, although Equations (7.1) and (7.3) still hold (with respect to the new C^*), the meaning of Z_i is now changed. We now have to calculate a value for Z_i for each stock. A positive value of Z_i indicates the stock will be held long, and a negative value indicates it will be sold short. Thus, the impact of C^* has changed. Stocks that have an excess return to Beta above C^* are held long (as before), but stocks with an excess return to Beta below C^* are now sold short.

Let us illustrate this by returning to the first example presented earlier in Table 7.2. Remember in order to calculate C^* we must employ Equation (7.1) with i

---

[3]Actually, it is possible for one or more stocks to have return and risk characteristics so that they are held in exactly zero proportions. This does not affect the procedure described in this section.

Table 7.4 Calculations for Determining Cut-off Rate with $\sigma_m^2 = 10$

Security Number i	$\dfrac{\bar{R}_i - R_F}{\beta_i}$	$\dfrac{(\bar{R}_i - R_F)\beta_i}{\sigma_{ei}^2}$	$\dfrac{\beta_i^2}{\sigma_{ei}^2}$	$\sum\limits_{j=1}^{i} \dfrac{(\bar{R}_j - R_F)\beta_j}{\sigma_{ej}^2}$	$\sum\limits_{j=1}^{i} \dfrac{\beta_j^2}{\sigma_{ej}^2}$	C_i
1	14	$\dfrac{70}{100}$	$\dfrac{5}{100}$	$\dfrac{70}{100}$	$\dfrac{5}{100}$	4.67
2	12	$\dfrac{90}{100}$	$\dfrac{7.5}{100}$	$\dfrac{160}{100}$	$\dfrac{12.5}{100}$	7.11
3	12	$\dfrac{30}{100}$	$\dfrac{2.5}{100}$	$\dfrac{190}{100}$	$\dfrac{15}{100}$	7.6
4	10	$\dfrac{100}{100}$	$\dfrac{10}{100}$	$\dfrac{290}{100}$	$\dfrac{25}{100}$	8.29
5	8	$\dfrac{40}{100}$	$\dfrac{5}{100}$	$\dfrac{330}{100}$	$\dfrac{30}{100}$	8.25
6	8	$\dfrac{4}{100}$	$\dfrac{0.5}{100}$	$\dfrac{334}{100}$	$\dfrac{30.5}{100}$	8.25
7	6	$\dfrac{45}{100}$	$\dfrac{7.5}{100}$	$\dfrac{379}{100}$	$\dfrac{38}{100}$	7.9
8	5	$\dfrac{10}{100}$	$\dfrac{2}{100}$	$\dfrac{389}{100}$	$\dfrac{40}{100}$	7.78
9	4.5	$\dfrac{9}{100}$	$\dfrac{2}{100}$	$\dfrac{398}{100}$	$\dfrac{42}{100}$	7.65
10	4	$\dfrac{80}{100}$	$\dfrac{20}{100}$	$\dfrac{478}{100}$	$\dfrac{62}{100}$	6.64
11	4	$\dfrac{30}{100}$	$\dfrac{7.5}{100}$	$\dfrac{508}{100}$	$\dfrac{69.5}{100}$	6.39
12	3	$\dfrac{15}{100}$	$\dfrac{5}{100}$	$\dfrac{523}{100}$	$\dfrac{74.5}{100}$	6.19
13	2.5	$\dfrac{25}{100}$	$\dfrac{10}{100}$	$\dfrac{548}{100}$	$\dfrac{84.5}{100}$	5.8
14	2	$\dfrac{10}{100}$	$\dfrac{5}{100}$	$\dfrac{558}{100}$	$\dfrac{89.5}{100}$	5.61

set equal to the number of stocks under consideration. In this case we have a population of 10 stocks so that

$$C^* = C_{10} = 4.52$$

Employing Equation (7.3) for each security we find

$$Z_1 = \frac{1}{50}[10 - 4.52] = 0.110 \qquad Z_7 = \frac{2}{40}[3 - 4.52] = -0.076$$

$$Z_2 = \frac{1.5}{40}[8 - 4.52] = 0.131 \qquad Z_8 = \frac{0.8}{16}[2.5 - 4.52] = -0.101$$

$$Z_3 = \frac{1}{20}[7 - 4.52] = 0.124 \qquad Z_9 = \frac{1}{20}[2 - 4.52] = -0.126$$

$$Z_4 = \frac{2}{10}[6 - 4.52] = 0.296 \qquad Z_{10} = \frac{0.6}{6}[1.0 - 4.52] = -0.352$$

$$Z_5 = \frac{1}{40}[6 - 4.52] = 0.037$$

$$Z_6 = \frac{1.5}{30}[4 - 4.52] = -0.026 \qquad \sum_{i=1}^{10} Z_i = 0.017$$

The last step in the procedure involves the scaling of the Z_i's so they represent the optimum proportions to invest in each stock (X_i's). There are actually two ways to do this scaling. These methods exactly parallel the two definitions of short sales we examined in earlier chapters. Under the standard definition of short sales, which presumes that a short sale of a stock is a source of funds to the investor, the appropriate scaling factor is given by

$$X_i = \frac{Z_i}{\displaystyle\sum_{j=1}^{N} Z_j}$$

where Z_i can be positive or negative. This scaling factor is arrived at by realizing that under this definition of short sales the constraint on the X_i's is that

$$\sum_{i=1}^{N} X_i = 1$$

The second definition of short sales we referred to earlier is Lintner's definition. Under this definition short sales are a use of the investor's funds; however, the investor receives the riskless rate of the funds involved in the short sale.[4] We have seen that this translates into the constraint

$$\sum_{i=1}^{N} |X_i| = 1$$

---

[4]To be precise the Lintner definition assumes that the proceeds of the short sale are not available for investment. Furthermore, the investor must put up an amount of funds equal to the proceeds of the short sale as collateral to protect against adverse price movements. The return on the short sale is the opposite of a long purchase. A negative value for X is required in determining the return on a portfolio. However, in analyzing the constraint on the amount invested, the additional funds invested must be considered — hence the absolute value sign in the constraint of the sum of X's. See footnote 1 in Chapter 4 for a further explanation.

The analogous scaling factor is

$$X_i = \frac{Z_i}{\sum_{j=1}^{N} |Z_j|} \tag{7.4}$$

In Table 7.5 we have presented the fraction of funds that the investor should place in each security when short sales are not allowed, when the standard definition of short sales is employed, and when Lintner's definition of short sales is used.

Note that under the two alternative definitions of short sales, not only are the same stocks always held long and sold short, but any two stocks are always held in the same ratio to each other. This is true because the two solutions differ by only a scale factor. From the foregoing analysis it is obvious that this scale factor is simply

One point of interest this example makes clear is that employing the normal definition of short sales can really change the scale of the optimal solution. While the proportions invested under the Lintner definition seem reasonable, for example, place 8% of your money in security 1 and use 25.5% of your funds to short sell security 10, the solution that can be reached under the standard definition of short sales can seem extreme. In this example the standard definition of short sales would involve investing in stock 1 a sum of money equal to 6.47 times the amount originally available for investment and selling short an amount of security 10 equal to 20.7 times the amount originally available for investment.

If we now compare either of the short sales examples with the short sales disallowed examples, we can see some interesting differences. First note that the proportion placed in any stock relative to a second stock need bear no relationship between the two cases. As an example examine security 1 and security 4 in the short sales allowed and short sales not allowed examples. Both call for security 1 and security 4 to be held long. When short sales are not allowed we hold 1.21 as much of security 4 as we hold of security 1. When short sales are allowed, we hold 2.69 as much of security 4 as we hold of security 1. This demonstrates that the proportions held of securities under short sales allowed need bear no particular relationship to the proportions held of the securities when short sales are not allowed.

In fact, although this particular example does not demonstrate it, the set of securities that is held long can be different according to whether short sales are allowed or not. This can be seen by reexamining example 2. When short sales were not allowed, we have seen that the first four securities are held long. If short sales are allowed, the appropriate value for C (all securities included) is 5.61 from Table 7.4. Examining Table 7.4 we now see that the first seven rather than the first four securities should be held long in the optimal portfolio.

The fact that allowing short sales changes the nature of the optimal solution should not come as a surprise to the reader. Allowing short sales is equivalent to adding new securities to the set from which the optimal portfolio will be selected. It is equivalent to adding a set of securities with the opposite characteristics from those included in the set when short sales are not allowed.

Table 7.5 Optimum Percentages

Security	Short Sales Disallowed	Lintner Definition of Short Sales	Standard Definition of Short Sales
1	23.5	8.0	647.1
2	24.6	9.5	770.6
3	20.0	9.0	729.4
4	28.4	21.5	1741.2
5	3.5	2.7	217.6
6	0	−1.9	−152.9
7	0	−5.5	447.1
8	0	−7.3	−594.1
9	0	−9.1	−741.2
10	0	−25.5	−2070.6

Constructing an Efficient Frontier

The procedure just described assumes the existence of a riskless lending and borrowing rate. It produces the composition of the optimal portfolio that lies at the point where a ray passing through the riskless asset is tangent to the efficient frontier in expected return standard deviation space. If the investor does not wish to assume the existence of a riskless asset, then it is necessary to derive the full efficient frontier.

Two cases need to be analyzed: when short sales are allowed and when they are forbidden. If short sales are allowed, then, as was shown in Chapter 4, the full efficient frontier can be constructed from combinations of any two portfolios that lie on the efficient frontier. The composition of two portfolios on the efficient frontier can be found easily by assuming two different values for R_F and repeating the procedure just described for each. From these two efficient portfolios, the full frontier can be traced. The efficient frontier is a little more difficult to determine when short sales are not allowed.

The brute force solution is to solve the portfolio composition problem for a large number of values of R_F and, thus, approximate the full efficient frontier. An alternative procedure that solves directly for the R_F associated with each corner portfolio is described in [6].[5] Since the frontier between corner portfolios can be found as combinations of corner portfolios, this procedure allows the full efficient frontier to be easily traced out.

THE CONSTANT CORRELATION MODEL

We now present and demonstrate the use of simple procedures for selecting optimum portfolios when the constant correlation model is accepted as the best way to forecast correlation coefficients. The reader will recall from earlier chapters that the constant correlation model assumes the correlation between all pairs of securities is the same. The procedures assuming a constant correlation coefficient exactly parallel those presented for the case of the single-index model. Once again, the derivation of these procedures and the proof that they are, indeed, optimum is left for Appendix B at the end of this chapter.

If the constant correlation model is accepted as describing the co-movement between securities, then all securities can be ranked by their excess return to standard deviation. To be precise, if σ_i is the standard deviation of the return on security i, then a security's desirability is determined by

$$\frac{(\overline{R}_i - R_F)}{\sigma_i}$$

Notice that we are still ranking on the basis of excess return to risk; but standard deviation has taken the place of Beta as the relevant risk measure.[6] This ratio provides an ordering of securities for which the top ranked securities are purchased and the lower ranked securities are not held in the case of short sales prohibited or are sold short if such sales are allowed. Once again, there is a unique cut-off rate.

Ranking and Selecting from Among Securities — Short Sales Not Allowed

We illustrate the manner in which an optimal portfolio can be designed with a simple example presented in Table 7.6. First, as has been done in Table 7.6, all stocks are ranked by excess return to standard deviation. Then, the optimal value of C_i, called C^*, is calculated and all stocks with higher excess returns to standard deviation are included in the optimal portfolio. All stocks with lower excess returns to standard deviation are excluded. For the moment accept that

---

[5]Recall that a corner portfolio is one in which a security either enters the efficient set or is deleted from the efficient set as we move along the efficient frontier.

[6]In Chapter 16 we see that excess return to standard deviation like excess return to Beta has been used as a technique for ranking portfolios.

C^* equals 5.25. In a moment we will discuss how to calculate it. Since securities 1 through 3 have higher excess returns to standard deviations, they are included in the optimum portfolio. Securities 4 through 12 have excess returns to standard deviation below 5.25 and, hence, are not included in the optimal portfolio.

Setting the Cut-off Rate

The procedure for setting the cut-off rate is directly analogous to that presented for the case of the single-index model. First, we need a general expression for C_i, where i represents the fact that the first i securities are included in the computation of C_i. As shown in Appendix B at the end of this chapter, C_i can be found from

$$C_i = \frac{\rho}{1 - \rho + i\rho} \sum_{j=1}^{i} \frac{\overline{R}_j - R_F}{\sigma_j}$$

where ρ is the correlation coefficient — assumed constant for all securities. The subscript i indicates that C_i is calculated, using data on the first i securities.

Just as in the single-index model case, we have determined the appropriate level of the cut-off rate C^* when we have found a C_i such that:

1. All stocks ranked 1 through i have an excess return to standard deviation above C_i
2. All stocks ranked $i + 1$ through N have a value of excess return to standard deviation lower than C_i

Tables 7.6 and 7.7 present an example and some of the intermediate calculations needed to design an optimal portfolio. Examine the two columns at the extreme right of Table 7.7. Note that only for a value of $C_i = C_3$ do all stocks 1 to i have higher excess returns to standard deviation and all stocks $i + 1$ to 12 have lower excess return to standard deviation. Thus, $C^* = C_3 = 5.25$.

As we show in Appendix B at the end of this chapter, the optimum amount to invest in any security is

$$X_i = \frac{Z}{\sum\limits_{j=1}^{N} Z_j}$$

where

$$Z_i = \frac{1}{(1 - \rho)\sigma_i} \left[\frac{\overline{R}_i - R_F}{\sigma_i} - C^* \right]$$

Table 7.6   Data to Determine Ranking $R_F = 5\%$

Security No. i	Expected Return $\overline{R}_i$	Excess Return $\overline{R}_i - R_F$	Standard Deviation σ_i	Excess Return to Standard Deviation $\dfrac{(\overline{R}_i - R_F)}{\sigma_i}$
1	29	24	3	8.0
2	19	14	2	7.0
3	29	24	4	6.0
4	35	30	6	5.0
5	14	9	2	4.5
6	21	16	4	4.0
7	26	21	6	3.5
8	14	9	3	3.0
9	15	10	5	2.0
10	9	4	2	2.0
11	11	6	4	1.5
12	8	3	3	1.0

Table 7.7   Determining the Cut-off Rate $\rho = 0.5$

Security No. i	$\dfrac{\rho}{1 - \rho + i\rho}$	$\sum\limits_{j=1}^{i} \dfrac{\overline{R}_j - R_F}{\sigma_j}$	C_i	$\dfrac{\overline{R}_i - R_F}{\sigma_i}$
1	$\dfrac{1}{2}$	8	$\dfrac{8}{2} = 4$	8
2	$\dfrac{1}{3}$	15	$\dfrac{15}{3} = 5$	7
3	$\dfrac{1}{4}$	21	$\dfrac{21}{4} = 5.25$	6
4	$\dfrac{1}{5}$	26	$\dfrac{26}{5} = 5.2$	5
5	$\dfrac{1}{6}$	30.5	$\dfrac{30.5}{6} = 5.08$	4.5
6	$\dfrac{1}{7}$	34.5	$\dfrac{34.5}{7} = 4.93$	4
7	$\dfrac{1}{8}$	38	$\dfrac{38}{8} = 4.75$	3.5
8	$\dfrac{1}{9}$	41	$\dfrac{41}{9} = 4.56$	3
9	$\dfrac{1}{10}$	43	$\dfrac{43}{10} = 4.3$	2
10	$\dfrac{1}{11}$	45	$\dfrac{45}{11} = 4.09$	2
11	$\dfrac{1}{12}$	46.5	$\dfrac{46.5}{12} = 3.88$	1.5
12	$\dfrac{1}{13}$	47.5	$\dfrac{47.5}{13} = 3.65$	1

For our example we have

$$Z_i = \frac{1}{(1-\rho)\sigma_i}\left[\frac{\bar{R}_i - R_F}{\sigma_i} - C^*\right]$$

$$Z_1 = \frac{1}{1.5}\left[8 - \frac{21}{4}\right] = \frac{11}{6} = \frac{44}{24} \quad \frac{1}{(1-.5)(3)}\left[8 - 5.25\right]$$

$$Z_2 = \frac{1}{1}\left[7 - \frac{21}{4}\right] = \frac{7}{4} = \frac{42}{24} \quad \frac{1}{1.5}\left[2.75\right]$$

$$Z_3 = \frac{1}{2}\left[6 - \frac{21}{4}\right] = \frac{3}{8} = \frac{9}{24} \quad Z_1 = 1.833 \ or \ \frac{44}{24}$$

Dividing each Z_i by the sum of the Z_i's gives the optimum amount to invest in each security. This calculation results in

$$X_1 = \frac{44}{44 + 42 + 9} = \frac{44}{95} \text{ or } 46.3\%$$

$$X_2 = \frac{42}{95} \text{ or } 44.2\%$$

$$X_3 = \frac{9}{95} \text{ or } 9.5\%$$

Short Sales Allowed

If short sales are allowed, then, as in the single-index case, all stocks will either be held long or sold short. This suggests, once again, that C^* should include all stocks, and this is correct. The C^* when all stocks are included is $C^* = C_{12} = 3.65$. Once again, C^* is the cut-off rate that separates securities that are purchased long from those that are sold short. In this example $C^* = 3.65$ implies that the first six securities are purchased long and securities 7 to 12 are sold short. The optimum amount to invest in any security is given by the same formula Equation (7.4) with C^* defined to incorporate all securities.

OTHER RETURN STRUCTURES

We have presented two simple ranking devices based on different correlation structures. As discussed in the last two chapters, there are a number of other models for estimating the covariance structure. For each of these other structures a simple ranking device exists. The references listed at the end of the chapter show where. However, a few comments are in order. There are two types of models for estimating correlation structure: index models and group models. The single- and multi-index models are examples of the former, while constant correlation and multi-group models are examples of the latter.

For index models the ranking is done by excess return to Beta. This is true for both single- and multi-index models. However, the cut-off rate for multi-index models is different than the cut-off rate for single-index models. For example, assume a multi-index model where securities are related to a general market index and an industry index. In this model the cut-off rate is different for each industry but depends on the members of all industries.

If a multi-group model is employed, then the ranking is always in terms of excess return to standard deviation. The cut-off rate varies from group to group and depends on which securities are included and in which groups.

Beta is important in index models because it is a measure of the securities' contribution to the risk of the portfolio. In multi-group or constant correlation models, the contribution to portfolio risk depends on the standard deviation and, hence, standard deviation is the risk measure in the portfolios.

CONCLUSIONS

In this chapter we have discussed several simple rules for optimal portfolio selection. These simple ranking devices allow the portfolio manager to quickly and easily determine the optimum portfolio. Furthermore, the manager uncertain about some of the estimates can easily manipulate them in order to determine if reasonable changes in the estimates lead to a different selection decision. The existence of a cut-off rate allows the manager to quickly determine if a new security should or should not be included in the portfolio.

Finally, the existence of simple ranking devices makes clear the characteristics of a security that are important and why a security is included, or excluded, from a portfolio.

APPENDIX A

Single-index Model — Short Sales Allowed

In this appendix we derive the simple ranking device when the investor is allowed to short sell securities and where he wishes to act as if the single-index model adequately reflects the correlation structure between securities. As we showed in Chapter 4, if the investor wishes to assume a riskless lending and borrowing rate, then he can obtain an optimum portfolio by solving a system of simultaneous equations. If, on the other hand, he desires to trace out the full efficient frontier, then he must solve this same system of simultaneous equations for two risk-free rates. This allows him to determine the characteristics of any two efficient portfolios and allows him to trace out the efficient frontier. The system of simultaneous equations he solves is

$$\overline{R}_i - R_F = Z_i\sigma_i^2 + \sum_{\substack{j=1 \\ j \neq i}}^{N} Z_j\sigma_{ij} \qquad i = 1, \ldots, N \qquad \text{(A.1)}$$

where

$\overline{R}_i$ is the expected return of security i

R_F is the return on the riskless asset

σ_i^2 is the variance of security i

σ_{ij} is the covariance between securities i and j

Z_i is proportional to the amount invested in security i

From Chapter 5 we know that if the single-index model is used to describe the structure of security returns, then the covariance between securities i and j is $\beta_i\beta_j\sigma_m^2$ and the variance of security i is $\beta_i^2\sigma_m^2 + \sigma_{ei}^2$. Substituting these relationships that hold for the single-index model into the general system of simultaneous equations (A.1) yields

$$\overline{R}_i - R_F = Z_i(\beta_i^2\sigma_m^2 + \sigma_{ei}^2) + \sum_{\substack{j=1 \\ j\neq i}}^{N} Z_j\beta_i\beta_j\sigma_m^2 \quad i = 1, \ldots, N$$

Look at the summation term. If $j = i$, it would be $Z_i\beta_i\beta_j\sigma_m^2$. But, this is exactly the first term on the right-hand side of the equality sign. Eliminating the $j \neq i$ underneath the summation sign by incorporating the term $Z_i\beta_i\beta_i\sigma_m^2$ within it yields

$$\overline{R}_i - R_F = Z_i\sigma_{ei}^2 + \sum_{j=1}^{N} Z_j\beta_i\beta_j\sigma_m^2 \quad i = 1, \ldots, N$$

Solving for Z_i and taking the constants outside the summation yields

$$Z_i = \frac{\overline{R}_i - R_F}{\sigma_{ei}^2} - \frac{\beta_i\sigma_m^2}{\sigma_{ei}^2} \sum_{j=1}^{N} Z_j\beta_j \quad i = 1, \ldots, N \tag{A.2}$$

This can be written as

$$Z_i = \frac{\beta_i}{\sigma_{ei}^2} \left[\frac{\overline{R}_i - R_F}{\beta_i} - C^* \right] \quad i = 1, \ldots, N$$

where

$$C^* = \sigma_m^2 \sum_{j=1}^{N} Z_j\beta_j \tag{A.3}$$

This is the equation presented in the text. To get the C^* in terms of known variables, we must express (A.2) and (A.3) in terms that do not invoke

$$\sum_{j=1}^{N} Z_j\beta_j$$

To do so, first multiply Equation (A.2) by β_i and sum over all values of $i = 1, \ldots, N$. This yields

$$\sum_{j=1}^{N} Z_j \beta_j = \sum_{j=1}^{N} \frac{(\overline{R}_j - R_F)\beta_j}{\sigma_{ej}^2} - \sigma_m^2 \sum_{j=1}^{N} \frac{\beta_j^2}{\sigma_{ej}^2} \sum_{j=1}^{N} Z_j \beta_j$$

Notice that the term

$$\sum_{j=1}^{N} Z_j \beta_j$$

is found on both the left-hand and right-hand sides of the equation. Solving for this yields

$$\sum_{j=1}^{N} Z_j \beta_j = \frac{\displaystyle\sum_{j=1}^{N} \frac{(\overline{R}_j - R_F)\beta_j}{\sigma_{ej}^2}}{1 + \sigma_m^2 \displaystyle\sum_{j=1}^{N} \frac{\beta_j^2}{\sigma_{ej}^2}}$$

From Equation (A.3) we see that

$$C^* = \frac{\sigma_m^2 \displaystyle\sum_{j=1}^{N} \frac{(\overline{R}_j - R_F)\beta_j}{\sigma_{ej}^2}}{1 + \sigma_m^2 \displaystyle\sum_{j=1}^{N} \frac{\beta_j^2}{\sigma_{ej}^2}}$$

The alternative form for C_i (Equation 7.2) employed in the text can be derived from Equation (A.3). From Equation (A.3) we see that

$$C^* = \sigma_m^2 \sum_{j=1}^{N} Z_j \beta_j$$

We also note from Chapter 4 that Z_j is proportional to the optimal fraction of the portfolio the investor should hold in each stock X_j. The constant is equal to the ratio of the excess return on the optimal portfolio to the variance of its return. Thus,

$$C^* = \sigma_m^2 \sum_{j=1}^{N} \frac{\overline{R}_P - R_F}{\sigma_P^2} X_j \beta_j$$

Recognizing

$$\sum_{j=1}^{N} X_j \beta_j$$

as the Beta on the investor's portfolio

$$C^* = (\overline{R}_P - R_F)\beta_P \frac{\sigma_m^2}{\sigma_P^2}$$

Dividing and multiplying the equation by β_i and recognizing that $\beta_i\beta_p\sigma_m^2$ is $cov(ip)$ under the assumption of the single-index model we have

$$C^* = (\overline{R}_P - R_F) \frac{cov(ip)}{\sigma_P^2} \frac{1}{\beta_i} = \frac{\beta_{ip}}{\beta_i}(\overline{R}_P - R_F)$$

where β_{ip} is the regression coefficient of the return on security i to the return on portfolio p.

APPENDIX B

Constant Correlation Coefficient — Short Sales Allowed

In this appendix we derive the simple ranking devices discussed in the text when the investor believes that the constant correlation coefficient adequately describes the structure of security returns. Once again, we utilize the result shown in Chapter 4 that the efficient frontier can be determined by solving a system of simultaneous equations. The system of simultaneous equations is

$$\overline{R}_i - R_F = Z_i\sigma_i^2 + \sum_{\substack{j=1 \\ j \neq i}}^{N} Z_j\sigma_{ij} \qquad i = 1, \cdots, N \qquad (B.1)$$

If the constant correlation model holds, then $\sigma_{ij} = \rho\sigma_i\sigma_j$. Note that the correlation coefficient between stocks i and j is by assumption the same for all i and j. Making the substitution into (B.1) yields

$$\overline{R}_i - R_F = Z_i\sigma_i^2 + \sum_{\substack{j=1 \\ j \neq i}}^{N} Z_j\rho\sigma_i\sigma_j \qquad i = 1, \ldots, N$$

If $j = i$, then the term in the summation is $Z_i\rho\sigma_i\sigma_i$. Adding this to the summation and subtracting the same term yields

$$\overline{R}_i - R_F = Z_i\sigma_i^2 - Z_i\rho\sigma_i\sigma_i + \sum_{j=1}^{N} Z_j\rho\sigma_i\sigma_j \qquad i = 1, \ldots, N$$

Solving for Z_i yields

$$Z_i(1 - \rho)\sigma_i^2 = \overline{R}_i - R_F - \rho\sigma_i \sum_{j=1}^{N} Z_j\sigma_j \qquad i = 1, \ldots, N$$

or

$$Z_i = \frac{1}{(1 - \rho)\sigma_i}\left[\frac{\overline{R}_i - R_F}{\sigma_i} - C^*\right] \qquad i = 1, \ldots, N \qquad (B.2)$$

where

$$C^* = \rho \sum_{j=1}^{N} Z_j\sigma_j$$

This is the equation used in the text. To express C^* in known terms, multiply (B.2) by σ_i and ρ and add up the N equations. This yields

$$C^* = \rho \sum_{j=1}^{N} Z_j\sigma_j = \frac{\rho}{1 - \rho} \sum_{j=1}^{N} \frac{\overline{R}_j - R_F}{\sigma_j} - \frac{N\rho C^*}{1 - \rho}$$

Solving for C^*

$$C^*\left(1 + \frac{N\rho}{1 - \rho}\right) = \frac{\rho}{1 - \rho} \sum_{j=1}^{N} \frac{\overline{R}_j - R_F}{\sigma_j}$$

or

$$C^* = \left(\frac{\rho}{1 - \rho}\right)\left(\frac{1 - \rho}{1 - \rho + N\rho}\right) \sum_{j=1}^{N} \frac{\overline{R}_j - R_F}{\sigma_j} = \frac{\rho}{1 - \rho + N\rho} \sum_{j=1}^{N} \frac{\overline{R}_j - R_F}{\sigma_j}$$

This is the expression shown in the text.

APPENDIX C

Single-index Model with Short Sales Not Allowed

In this appendix we derive simple ranking rules when the investor wishes to act as if the single-index model is a reasonable method of describing the structure of security returns. In Chapter 4 we showed that if we could find a solution that met the Kuhn–Tucker conditions, then we could be certain we had the optimum portfolio. In this appendix we show that our simple ranking procedure does, in fact, lead to a solution that meets the Kuhn–Tucker conditions.

The Kuhn–Tucker conditions were

1. $\overline{R}_i - R_F = Z_i\sigma_i^2 + \sum_{\substack{j=1 \\ j\neq i}}^{N} Z_j\sigma_{ij} - M_i \qquad i = 1, \ldots, N$

2. $Z_iM_i = 0 \qquad i = 1, \ldots, N$

3. $Z_i \geqslant 0$ and $M_i \geqslant 0 \qquad i = 1, \ldots, N$ \qquad (C.1)

where M_i is a variable added to make Equation (C.1) an equality.

If the single-index model is assumed to adequately describe the return structure, then

$$\sigma_{ij} = \beta_i \beta_j \sigma_m^2 \quad \text{and} \quad \sigma_i^2 = \beta_i^2 \sigma_m^2 + \sigma_{ei}^2$$

Substituting this into the first Kuhn–Tucker condition yields

$$\bar{R}_i - R_F = Z_i(\beta_i^2 \sigma_m^2 + \sigma_{ei}^2) + \sum_{\substack{j=1 \\ j \neq i}}^{N} Z_j \beta_i \beta_j \sigma_m^2 - M_i \quad i = 1, \ldots, N$$

Once again, noting that when $j = i$, the term in the summation would be $Z_i \beta_i \beta_i \sigma_m^2$, and this is the first term on the right-hand side of the equality. Incorporating this term into the summation we have

$$\bar{R}_i - R_F = Z_i \sigma_{ei}^2 + \beta_i \sigma_m^2 \sum_{j=1}^{N} Z_j \beta_j - M_i \quad i = 1, \ldots, N$$

If the security is not in the optimum portfolio, then $Z_j = 0$. Thus, the summation only has to include the Z_i and β_i for those securities in the optimum portfolio. We will call the set of securities in the optimum set k. Further, we will use the symbol

$$\sum_{j \in k}$$

to indicate that the summation is to include all securities in the optimum. Rewriting the equation yields

$$\bar{R}_i - R_F = Z_i \sigma_{ei}^2 + \beta_i \sigma_m^2 \sum_{j \in k} Z_j \beta_j - M_i \quad i = 1, \ldots, N \quad \text{(C.2)}$$

Examine conditions 2 and 3. Condition 3 says that Z_i and M_i must each be either zero or positive. Condition 2 states that their product must be zero. Thus, if Z_i is positive, M_i must be zero. For any security included in the optimum, Z_i is positive. Hence, we can drop the M_i for included securities (those in set k). Setting $M_i = 0$ in Equation (C.2) yields

$$\bar{R}_i - R_F = Z_i \sigma_{ei}^2 + \beta_i \sigma_m^2 \sum_{j \in k} Z_j \beta_j \quad \text{for } i \in k$$

or

$$Z_i = \frac{\beta_i}{\sigma_{ei}^2} \left[\frac{\bar{R}_i - R_F}{\beta_i} - \sigma_m^2 \sum_{j \in k} Z_j \beta_j \right] \quad \text{for } i \in k \quad \text{(C.3)}$$

We can eliminate

$$\sum_{j\epsilon k} Z_j\beta_j$$

by multiplying (C.3) by β_j and summing over set k

$$\sum_{j\epsilon k} Z_j\beta_j = \sum_{j\epsilon k} \frac{(\bar{R}_j - R_F)\beta_j}{\sigma_{ej}^2} - \sigma_m^2 \sum_{j\epsilon k} \frac{\beta_j^2}{\sigma_{ej}^2} \sum_{j\epsilon k} Z_j\beta_j$$

Rearranging

$$\sum_{j\epsilon k} Z_j\beta_j = \frac{\displaystyle\sum_{j\epsilon k} \frac{(\bar{R}_j - R_F)\beta_j}{\sigma_{ej}^2}}{1 + \sigma_m^2 \displaystyle\sum_{j\epsilon k} \frac{\beta_j^2}{\sigma_{ei}^2}}$$

(C.3) can be written as

$$Z_i = \frac{\beta_i}{\sigma_{ei}^2}\left[\frac{\bar{R}_i - R_F}{\beta_i} - C^*\right] \qquad i\epsilon k \qquad\qquad (C.4)$$

where

$$C^* = \sigma_m^2 \sum_{j\epsilon k} Z_j\beta_j = \frac{\sigma_m^2 \displaystyle\sum_{j\epsilon k} \frac{(\bar{R}_j - R_F)\beta_j}{\sigma_{ej}^2}}{1 + \sigma_m^2 \displaystyle\sum_{j\epsilon k} \frac{\beta_j^2}{\sigma_{ej}^2}}$$

Let us see how to determine a portfolio that meets the Kuhn–Tucker conditions. First condition 2 ($Z_iM_i = 0$) is met by construction. M_i was set to zero for all securities included in the optimum portfolio, those with $Z_i > 0$. For those not included in the optimum, $Z_i = 0$ guaranteeing $Z_iM_i = 0$.

Now consider the first and third conditions. Assume we have found a set of securities for which Z_i as determined by (C.4) is greater than zero for securities in the set and less than zero for securities not in the set.

For securities in the set Equation (C.4) is equivalent to condition 1 if $M_i = 0$. $Z_i > 0$ and $M_i = 0$ meets condition 3. Thus, conditions 1 and 3 are met.

For securities not in this set, (C.4) is not equivalent to condition 1. However, comparing these two shows that $M_i > 0$ will make condition 1 hold, and also Z_i is equal to zero so that condition 3 holds.

Thus, the Kuhn–Tucker conditions will be met if a set k can be determined for which (C.4) is positive for members of the set and negative for securities not in the set.

Examine (C.4). C^* is a constant. Assume for the moment that $\beta_i > 0$. Then the term outside the brackets is positive. The term in the brackets is positive if $(\overline{R}_i - R_F)/\beta_i > C^*$ and is negative if $(\overline{R}_i - R_F)/\beta_i < C^*$. The procedure discussed in the text assures that this will occur.

APPENDIX D

Constant Correlation Coefficient — Short Sales Not Allowed

The analysis in this section closely parallels the analysis of the last section. Once again, if the Kuhn–Tucker conditions are met, then the solution is an optimum. The Kuhn–Tucker conditions are as shown in (C.1). If an investor wishes to act as if the return structure is adequately described by the assumption of a constant correlation coefficient, then the covariance terms are $\sigma_{ij} = \rho\sigma_i\sigma_j$. Making this substitution into the first Kuhn–Tucker condition and adding and subtracting $\rho\sigma_i\sigma_i Z_i$ to eliminate $j \neq i$ under the summation sign yields

1. $\displaystyle \overline{R}_i - R_F = Z_i\sigma_i^2(1 - \rho) + \sum_{j=1}^{N} Z_j\rho\sigma_i\sigma_j - M_i \qquad i = 1, \ldots, N$

2. $Z_iM_i = 0, \qquad i = 1, \ldots, N$

3. $Z_i \geqslant 0$ and $M_i \geqslant 0 \qquad i = 1, \ldots, N$ (D.1)

The same considerations hold here as did in Appendix C. If set k is the set of included securities, then $Z_i = 0$ for securities not in set k and, thus,

$$\sum_{j\epsilon k} Z_j\sigma_j = \sum_{j=1}^{N} Z_j\sigma_j$$

Furthermore, if $Z_i > 0$, then $M_i = 0$ so that $M_i = 0$ for set k. Using these two observations, equation D.1 becomes

$$\overline{R}_i - R_F = Z_i\sigma_i^2(1 - \rho) + \rho\sigma_i \sum_{j\epsilon k} Z_j\sigma_j \qquad i\epsilon k \tag{D.2}$$

Rearranging and solving for Z_i

$$Z_i = \frac{1}{(1 - \rho)\sigma_i} \left[\frac{\overline{R}_i - R_F}{\sigma_i} - \rho \sum_{j\epsilon k} Z_j\sigma_j \right] \tag{D.3}$$

We can eliminate

$$\sum_{j\epsilon k} Z_j\sigma_j$$

by multiplying each equation by σ_i and then adding together all the equations in set k. This yields

$$\sum_{jek} Z_j \sigma_j = \frac{1}{1 - \rho} \left[\sum_{jek} \frac{\overline{R}_j - R_F}{\sigma_j} - \rho N_k \sum_{jek} Z_j \sigma_j \right]$$

where N_K is the number of securities in k. Rearranging

$$\sum_{jek} Z_j \sigma_j = \frac{1}{1 - \rho} \left(\frac{1 - \rho}{1 - \rho + \rho N_k} \right) \sum_{jek} \frac{\overline{R}_j - R_F}{\sigma_j}$$

Thus, (D.3) becomes

$$Z_i = \frac{1}{(1 - \rho)\sigma_i} \left[\frac{\overline{R}_i - R_F}{\sigma_i} - \phi_k \right] \qquad iek$$

$$\phi_k = \rho \sum_{jek} Z_j \sigma_j = \frac{\rho}{1 - \rho + \rho N_k} \sum_{jek} \frac{\overline{R}_j - R_F}{\sigma_j} \qquad (D.4)$$

The same considerations hold here as did in Appendix C. Namely, if (D.4) is positive for members of set k and negative for all other securities, the Kuhn–Tucker conditions are met. The procedures discussed in the text lead to this solution.

QUESTIONS AND PROBLEMS

1. Given the following data: $\sigma_m^2 = 10$

Security Number	Expected Return	Beta	σ_{ei}^2
1	15	1.0	30
2	12	1.5	20
3	11	2.0	40
4	8	.8	10
5	9	1.0	20
6	14	1.5	10

What is the optimum portfolio assuming no short sales if $R_F = 5\%$

2. What is the optimum portfolio assuming short sales if $R_F = 5\%$ and the data from Problem 1 used?

3. Using the data from Problem 1, what is the optimum portfolio assuming short sales are allowed but riskless lending and borrowing are forbidden?

4. Given the following data

Security Number	Expected Return	Standard Deviation
1	15	10
2	20	15
3	18	20
4	12	10
5	10	5
6	14	10
7	16	20

What is the optimum portfolio assuming no short sales if $R_F = 5\%$?

5. What is the optimum portfolio assuming short sales if $R_F = 5\%$ and $\rho = .5$?

6. What is the optimum portfolio assuming short sales but no riskless lending and borrowing with $\rho = .5$? Use the data in Problem 4.

BIBLIOGRAPHY

1. Alexander, Gordon J., and Resnick, Bruce G. "More on Estimation Risk and Simple Rules for Optimal Portfolio Selection," *The Journal of Finance,* **40,** No. 1 (March 1985), pp. 125–134.

2. Bawa, Vijay, Elton, Edwin J., and Gruber, Martin J. "Simple Rules for Optimal Portfolio Selection in a Stable Paretian Market," *Journal of Finance,* **34,** No. 2 (June 1979).

3. Chen, Son-Nan, and Brown, Stephen J. "Estimation Risk and Simple Rules for Optimal Portfolio Selection," *The Journal of Finance,* **38,** No. 4 (Sept. 1983), pp. 1087–1094.

4. Elton, Edwin J., Gruber, Martin J., and Padberg, Manfred W. "Optimal Portfolios from Simple Ranking Devices," *Journal of Portfolio Management,* **4,** No. 3 (Spring 1978), pp. 15–19.

5. ———. "Simple Criteria for Optimal Portfolio Selection: Tracing Out the Efficient Frontier," *Journal of Finance,* **XIII,** No. 1 (March 1978), pp. 296–302.

6. ———. "Simple Criteria for Optimal Portfolio Selection," *Journal of Finance,* **XI,** No. 5 (Dec. 1976), pp. 1341–1357.

7. ———. "Simple Rules for Optimal Portfolio Selection: The Multi Group Case," *Journal of Financial and Quantitative Analysis,* **XII,** No. 3 (Sept. 1977), pp. 329–345.

8. ———. "Simple Criteria for Optimal Portfolio Selection: The Multi-Index Case," in Elton and Gruber, *Portfolio Theory: 25 Years Later* (Amsterdam: North Holland, 1979).

9. ———. "Simple Criteria for Optimal Portfolio Selection with Upper Bonds," *Operation Research* (Nov.–Dec. 1978).

10. Kwan, Clarence C.Y. "Portfolio Analysis Using Single Index, Multi-Index, and Constant Correlation Models: A Unified Treatment," *The Journal of Finance,* **39,** No. 5 (Dec. 1984), pp. 1469–1484.
11. Lee, Sang, and Lerro, A.J. "Optimizing the Portfolio Selection for Mutual Funds," *Journal of Finance,* **VIII,** No. 5 (Dec. 1973), pp. 1087–1101.
12. Mao, C.T. James. "Essentials of Portfolio Diversification Strategy," *Journal of Finance,* **V,** No. 5 (Dec. 1970), pp. 1109–1121.
13. Porter, Burr, and Bey, Roger. "An Evaluation of the Empirical Significance of Optimal Seeking Algorithms in Portfolio Selection," *Journal of Finance,* **IX,** No. 5 (Dec. 1974), pp. 1479–1490.
14. Sharpe, W.F. "Simple Strategies for Portfolio Diversification: Comment," *Journal of Finance,* **VII,** No. 1 (March 1972), pp. 127–129.
15. ———. "Simple Strategies for Portfolio Diversification: Comment, A Correction," *Journal of Finance,* **VII,** No. 3 (June 1972), p. 733.
16. Sharpe, William. "A Linear Programming Formulation of the General Portfolio Selection Model," *Journal of Financial and Quantitative Analysis,* **VIII,** No. 4 (Sept. 1973), pp. 621–636.
17. Stone, Bernell. "A Linear Programming Formulation of the General Portfolio Selection Model," *Journal of Financial and Quantitative Analysis,* **VIII,** No. 4 (Sept. 1973), pp. 621–636.

SECTION 3
Selecting the Optimum Portfolio

Chapter 8

Utility Analysis

In Chapter 1 we pointed out that to solve any decision problem one had to define an opportunity set and define a preference function. In the preceding chapters we have discussed how an investor could construct this opportunity set and how, with some very general assumptions about preferences, he could limit this set to the efficient frontier.[1] The subject of this chapter is how to choose among the investor's opportunity set or, alternatively, how to specify a preference function.

Although the previous chapters dealt with the definition of the investor's opportunity set, we quite often made use of assumptions about the attributes of investor's preference functions in order to limit the opportunity set. For example, we have shown that, if the investor prefers more to less and is a risk avoider, the opportunity set can be reduced to the efficient frontier. We have also shown that if riskless lending and borrowing can take place at the same rate in unlimited quantities, then there is only one preferred portfolio of risky assets for each investor. That is, there is one portfolio of risky assets that will be preferred by a risk-avoiding investor, regardless of the investor's preference function. This means that the manager of a portfolio of risky assets can select the optimal portfolio of risky assets for an investor without regard to the investor's preference function. Does this mean that the investor's preference function plays no role in the decision process when riskless lending and borrowing is allowed? The answer

---

[1]This analysis assumed that means and variances constituted the relevant information for any decision problem. The analysis in this chapter is applicable whether the relevant decision space is formulated in terms of means and variances or higher movements of the probability distribution of returns are used.

is no. In this case, the investor's preference function determines what combination of the optimum risky portfolio and riskless asset the investor will hold, and how much he will consume and invest.

Thus, whatever the opportunity set facing the investor, his preference function will play a key role in his optimal decision. We devote the remainder of this chapter to a discussion of preference functions. We start off with a general description of the characteristics of choice functions. Appendix A at the end of this chapter contains a more rigorous axiomatic treatment of the material contained in the text. Then we explore the desirable economic features of preference functions and the types of preference functions that possess these characteristics. Finally, we explore the limited evidence on the types and characteristics of utility functions that are consistent with investor behavior.

AN INTRODUCTION TO PREFERENCE FUNCTIONS

We start our discussion of the choice between risky assets with a simple example. Consider the two alternatives shown in Table 8.1. Investment A and investment B each have three possible outcomes, each equally likely. Investment A has less variability in its outcomes but has a lower average outcome.

Table 8.1

	Investment A		Investment B	
Outcome	Probability of Outcome	Outcome	Probability of Outcome
15	1/3	20	1/3
10	1/3	12	1/3
5	1/3	4	1/3

There are several ways to decide between A and B. First, we could simply ask the decision maker which he prefers or whether he is indifferent between them. With the simple problem presented in Table 8.1, this probably is sufficient. Even for the more complicated problems, the direct analysis of the options may be the most sensible alternative.

Another approach is to specify how much more valuable the large outcomes are relative to the small outcomes and then to weight the outcomes by their value and find the expected value of these weighted outcomes. The idea of adding up or averaging weighted outcomes is very common. Consider, for example, how the winning team is selected in hockey. Table 8.2 shows the hypothetical records

Table 8.2

	Islanders	Flyers
Wins	40	45
Ties	20	5
Losses	10	20

for two hockey teams. Current practice weights wins by two, ties by one, and losses by zero. With this weighting scheme, the Islanders would be leading the Flyers 100 to 95. But there is nothing special about this weighting scheme. A league interested in deemphasizing the incentive for ties might weight wins by four, ties by one, and losses by zero. In this case, the Flyers would be considered the dominant team 185 to 180. If we denote W as the result (win, tie, lose), $U(W)$ as the value of this result, and $N(W)$ as the number of times (games) that W occurs, then to determine the better team we calculate[2]

$$\sum_W U(W)N(W)$$

The team with the higher U is considered the better team. For example, utilizing current practice $U(\text{win}) = 2$, $U(\text{tie}) = 1$, and $U(\text{loss}) = 0$. Applying the formula to the Islanders yields[3]

$$U = 2(40) + 1(20) + 0(10) = 100$$

This is the 100 we referred to earlier. While the particular function $U(W)$ differs between situations, the principle is the same. Traditionally, instead of using the number of outcomes of a particular type, the proportion is used. There were 70 hockey games in our example. If $P(W)$ is the proportion of the total games that resulted in outcome W, then $P(W) = N(W)/70$. Dividing through by 70 will not affect our choice. Weighting a function by the proportion of each outcome is equivalent to calculating an average or expected value. Letting $E(U)$ designate the expected value of U yields

$$E(U) = \sum_W U(W)P(W)$$

When we apply this principle to the decision problem shown in Table 8.1, we have special names for the principle. The weighting function is called a utility function and the principle is called the expected utility theorem. Consider the example shown in Table 8.1. The weighting function could look like this:

Outcome	Weight	Value of Outcome
20	0.9	18
15	1.0	15
12	1.1	13.2
10	1.2	12
5	1.4	7
4	1.5	6

---

[2]$\sum_W$ should read as the sum over all results.

[3]These numbers are hypothetical.

We have called the last column in the table the value of the outcome. Alternatively, it could be called the utility of an outcome. If this was the weighting function the investor felt was appropriate, then he would compare the expected utility of investments A and B, using this function. For example, the expected utility of A is

$$U(15)(1/3) + U(10)(1/3) + U(5)(1/3)$$

Referring to the weighting function, we have

$$15(1/3) + 12(1/3) + 7(1/3) = 34/3$$

and the expected utility of investment B is

$$U(20)\left(\frac{1}{3}\right) + U(12)\left(\frac{1}{3}\right) + U(4)\left(\frac{1}{3}\right) = 18\left(\frac{1}{3}\right) + 13.2\left(\frac{1}{3}\right) + 6\left(\frac{1}{3}\right) = \frac{37.2}{3}$$

In this situation the investor would select investment B because it offers the higher average or expected utility. In general we can say that the investor will choose among alternatives by maximizing expected utility or maximizing

$$E(U) = \sum_{W} U(W)P(W)$$

Consider a second example. Table 8.3 lists three separate investments. Assume the investor has the following utility function:

$$U(W) = 4W - (1/10)W^2$$

Then the utility of 20 is $80 - (1/10)(400) = 40$; the utility of 18 is $72 - (1/10)(324) = 39.6$; and the utility of 14 is $56 - (1/10)(196) = 36.4$.

Table 8.3

Investment A		Investment B		Investment C	
Outcome	Probability	Outcome	Probability	Outcome	Probability
20	3/15	19	1/5	18	1/4
18	5/15	10	2/5	16	1/4
14	4/15	5	2/5	12	1/4
10	2/15			8	1/4
6	1/15				

The rest of the values are shown in Table 8.4. The expected utility of the three investments is found by multiplying the probability of each outcome times the value of the outcome.

Table 8.4

	Investment A			Investment B			Investment C	
Outcome	Utility of Outcome	Probability	Outcome	Utility of Outcome	Probability	Outcome	Utility of Outcome	Probability
20	40	3/15	19	39.9	1/5	18	39.6	1/4
18	39.6	5/15	10	30	2/5	16	38.4	1/4
14	36.4	4/15	5	17.5	2/5	12	33.6	1/4
10	30	2/15				8	25.6	1/4
6	20.4	1/15						

Expected utility A = $(40)(3/15) + (39.6)(5/15) + (36.4)(4/15)$

$+ (30)(2/15) + (20.4)(1/15)$

$= \dfrac{544}{15} = 36.3$

Expected utility B = $(39.9)(1/5) + (30)(2/5) + (17.5)(2/5)$

$= \dfrac{134.9}{5} = 26.98$

Expected utility C = $(39.6)(1/4) + (38.4)(1/4) + (33.6)(1/4) + (25.6)(1/4)$

$= \dfrac{137.2}{4} = 34.4$

Thus, an investor with the utility function discussed earlier would select investment A.

An important attribute of utility analysis is that utility functions are unique up to a positive linear transformation. This means that $A + bv(W)$ will lead to the same investments being selected as $v(W)$. To see this, assume in the last example that the utility function was $2 + 4W - (1/10)W^2$ rather than $4W - (1/10)W^2$. The only difference between the two functions is the addition of the number 2. Thus, the value of each outcome would be increased by two times the probability of the outcome. Furthermore, expected utility would be increased by two times the sum of the probabilities of each outcome. But the probabilities must sum to 1. Thus, the expected utility of each investment increases by 2. If the expected utility of each investment increases by 2, the ranking is unchanged. A similar argument can be made for the effect of multiplication by a positive constant. In this case the expected utility is also multiplied by a positive constant. But such a multiplication does not change the order, and the same investment would be selected.

If the investor acts in certain ways (obeys certain postulates of behavior), then the choice of preferred investment, using the expected utility theorem, is identical to the choice made by examining the investment directly. For the reader interested in a formal statement and demonstration of these postulates, see Appendix A at the end of this chapter. It follows that, having an investor make choices between a series of simple investments, we can attempt to determine the weighting (utility) function that the investor is implicitly using. Applying this weighting function to more complicated investments, we should be able to determine which one the investor would choose.

A number of brokerage firms and banks have developed programs to extract the utility function of investors by confronting them with a choice between a series of simple investments. These have not been particularly successful. Many investors do not obey all the rationality postulates when faced with a series of choice situations, even though they may find the underlying principles perfectly reasonable. Also, many investors, when faced with more complicated choice situations, encounter aspects of the problem that were not of concern to them in the simple choice situations.

Even if the investor, or manager, does not believe in formally deriving utility functions, there is still a lot to be learned from utility analysis. An understanding of the properties of alternative utility functions can lead to insight into the process of rational choice. This will allow the investor to eliminate some portfolios from further consideration and will reduce the chances of making a really bad decision.

In the next section we examine more formally the characteristics of utility functions.

THE ECONOMIC PROPERTIES OF UTILITY FUNCTIONS

The first restriction placed on a utility function is that it be consistent with more being preferred to less. This attribute, known in the economic literature as nonsatiation, simply says that the utility of more $(X + 1)$ dollars is always higher than the utility of less (X) dollars. Thus, if we want to choose between two certain investments, we always take the one with the largest outcome. In this section we will formulate utility functions in terms of end of period wealth. This property then states that more wealth is always preferred to less wealth. If utility increases as wealth increases, then the first derivative of utility, with respect to wealth, is positive.[4] Thus, the first restriction placed on the utility function is a positive first derivative.

The second property of a utility function is an assumption about an investor's taste for risk. Three assumptions are possible: the investor is averse to risk, the investor is neutral toward risk, and the investor seeks risk. Risk aversion, risk neutrality, and risk seeking can all be defined in terms of a fair gamble. Consider the gambles (options) shown in Table 8.5.

Table 8.5

	Invest		Do Not Invest	
Outcome	Probability		Outcome	Probability
2	1/2		1	1
0	1/2			

The option "invest" has an expected value of $(1/2)(2) + (1/2)(0) = \$1$. Assume that an investor would have to pay $1 to undertake this investment and obtain

---

[4]The reader might note that in this chapter we discuss utility functions of end of period wealth. Earlier chapters discussed opportunity sets in terms of returns rather than wealth. This should present no conceptual problems as end of period wealth is simply beginning wealth times 1 plus the appropriate rate of return. Therefore, all the properties discussed with respect to wealth also hold with respect to returns.

these outcomes. Thus, if the investor chooses not to invest, the \$1 is kept. This is the alternative: do not invest. The expected value of the gamble is exactly equal to the cost. The position of the investor may be improved or hurt by undertaking the investment, but the expectation is that there will be no change in position. Because the expected value of the gamble shown in Table 8.5 is equal to its cost, it is called a fair gamble.

Risk aversion means that an investor will reject a fair gamble. In terms of Table 8.5, it means \$1 for certain will be preferred to an equal chance of \$2 or \$0. Risk aversion implies that the second derivative of utility, with respect to wealth, is negative. If $U(W)$ is the utility function and $U''(W)$ is the second derivative, then risk aversion is usually equated with an assumption that $U''(W) < 0$. Let us examine why this is true.

If an investor prefers not to invest, then the expected utility of not investing must be higher than the expected utility of investing or

$$U(1) > (1/2)U(2) + (1/2)U(0)$$

Multiplying both sides by 2 and rearranging, we have

$$U(1) - U(0) > U(2) - U(1)$$

Examine the above expression. The expression means that a one-unit change from 0 to 1 is more valuable than a one-unit change from 1 to 2. This latter change involves larger values of outcomes. A function where an additional unit increase is less valuable than the last unit increase is a function with a negative second derivative.

The assumption of risk aversion means an investor will reject a fair gamble because the disutility of the loss is greater than the utility of an equivalent gain. Functions that exhibit this property must have a negative second derivative. Therefore, the rejection of a fair gamble implies a negative second derivative.

Risk neutrality means that an investor is indifferent to whether or not a fair gamble is undertaken. In the context of Table 8.5, a risk-neutral investor would be indifferent to whether or not an investment was made. Risk neutrality implies a zero second derivative. Let us examine why. For the investor to be indifferent between investing and not investing, the expected utility of investing, or not investing, must be the same, or

$$U(1) = (1/2)U(2) + (1/2)U(0)$$

Multiplying by 2 and rearranging yields

$$U(1) - U(0) = U(2) - U(1)$$

This expression implies that the change in utility from a one-unit change in wealth is independent of whether we are moving from 0 to 1 or 1 to 2. This characteristic is associated with functions that exhibit a zero second derivative. Thus, indifference to a fair gamble implies a zero second derivative, and utility functions of risk-neutral investors should have zero second derivatives.

Risk seeking means that an investor would select a fair gamble. In the context of Table 8.5, the risk-seeking investor would choose to invest. Risk-seeking investors have utility functions with positive second derivatives. The reason why exactly parallels previous discussion. Since the risk-seeking investor chooses the investment, the expected utility of investment must be higher than the expected utility of not investing, or

$$(1/2)U(2) + (1/2)U(0) > U(1)$$

Once again, multiplying by 2 and rearranging yields

$$U(2) - U(1) > U(1) - U(0)$$

This expression indicates that the utility of a one-unit change from 1 to 2 is greater than the utility of a one-unit change from 0 to 1. Functions that exhibit the property of greater change in value for larger unit changes in the argument are functions with positive second derivatives. Thus, the acceptance of a fair gamble implies a positive second derivative. These conditions are summarized in Table 8.6.

Table 8.6

Condition	Definition	Implication
1. Risk aversion	Reject fair gamble	$U''(0) < 0$
2. Risk neutrality	Indifferent to fair gamble	$U''(0) = 0$
3. Risk preference	Select a fair gamble	$U''(0) > 0$

Figures 8.1a and 8.1b show preference functions exhibiting alternative properties with respect to risk aversion. Figure 8.1a presents the shape of utility functions in utility of wealth space that exhibit risk aversion, risk neutrality, and risk preference. Figure 8.1b presents the shape of the indifference curves in expected return standard deviation space that would be associated with each of these three types of utility functions.

As discussed in earlier chapters, investors who can state their feelings toward a fair gamble can significantly reduce the set of risky investments they must consider. For example, risk-averse investors must consider only the efficient frontier when choosing among alternative portfolios. Thus, an understanding of utility theory can simplify the selection problem of investors even if they are unwilling to more formally specify their utility function.

The third property of utility functions is an assumption about how the investor's preferences change with a change in wealth. If the investor's wealth increases, will more or less of that wealth be invested in risky assets? For example, assume that an investor with $10,000 to invest puts $5,000 into risky assets. Now assume the same investor's wealth increases to $20,000. Will the investor invest more than $5,000, less than $5,000 or $5,000 in risky assets? If the investor increases the amount invested in risky assets as wealth increases, then the investor is said to exhibit decreasing absolute risk aversion. If the investor's investment in risky assets is unchanged as wealth changes, then the investor is said to exhibit constant absolute risk aversion. Finally, if the investor invests fewer dollars in risky assets as wealth increases, then the investor is said to exhibit increasing absolute risk aversion. When we discussed risk aversion, we showed that different degrees of risk aversion were associated with different derivatives of the utility function. A similar result is true for absolute risk aversion. If $U'(W)$ and $U''(W)$ are the first

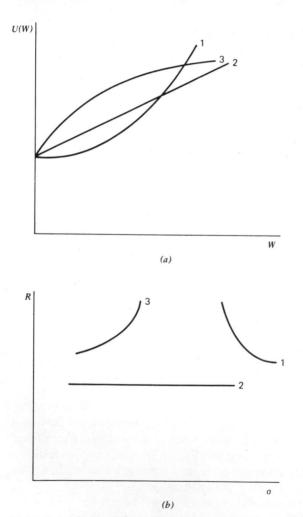

(a)

(b)

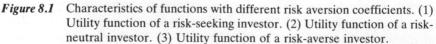

Figure 8.1 Characteristics of functions with different risk aversion coefficients. (1) Utility function of a risk-seeking investor. (2) Utility function of a risk-neutral investor. (3) Utility function of a risk-averse investor.

and second derivatives of the utility function at wealth level W, then we show in Appendix B, at the end of this chapter that

$$A(W) = \frac{-U''(W)}{U'(W)}$$

can be used to measure an investor's absolute risk aversion. Then $A'(W)$, the derivative of $A(W)$ with respect to wealth, is an appropriate measure of how absolute risk aversion behaves with respect to changes in wealth. Table 8.7 summarizes the important relationship between $A'(W)$ and changes in risk aversion and presents an example of a utility function exhibiting each type of behavior described in the table.

Table 8.7

Condition	Definition	Property of $A(W)$[a]	Example[b]
Increasing absolute risk aversion	As wealth increases hold fewer dollars in risky assets	$A'(W) > 0$	W^{-cW^2}
Constant absolute risk aversion	As wealth increases hold same dollar amount in risky assets	$A'(W) = 0$	$-e^{-cW}$
Decreasing absolute risk aversion	As wealth increases hold more dollars in risky assets	$A'(W) < 0$	$\ln W$

[a]$A'(W)$ is the first derivative of $A(W)$ with respect to wealth.
[b]The proof is left to the reader

Most evidence would indicate that, as wealth increases, the dollar amount invested in risky assets should increase, or that investors exhibit decreasing absolute risk aversion. Regardless of which condition of absolute risk aversion best describes investors' behavior, if they can specify their feelings regarding absolute risk aversion, then the number of possible options they need consider can be reduced. Furthermore, this assumption restricts the possible utility functions that could describe their preferences.

The final characteristic that is used to restrict the investor's utility function is how the percentage of wealth invested in risky assets changes as wealth changes. For example, if the investor puts 50% of her wealth in risky investments when her wealth is $10,000, does she still put 50% of her wealth in risky assets when her wealth increases to $20,000? If she does, then the investor's behavior is said to be characterized by constant *relative* risk aversion. If she invests a greater percentage of her wealth in risky investments, she is said to exhibit decreasing relative risk aversion, and if she invests a smaller percentage, she is said to exhibit increasing relative risk aversion. Relative risk aversion is closely related to absolute risk aversion. Relative risk aversion refers to the change in the percentage investment in risky assets as wealth changes. In contrast, absolute risk aversion refers to the change in dollar amount invested in risky assets as wealth changes. The measure of relative risk aversion is

$$R(W) = \frac{-WU''(W)}{U'(W)} = WA(W)$$

If $R'(W)$ is the first derivative of W, then $R'(W) < 0$ indicates that the utility function exhibits decreasing relative risk aversion. If $R'(W) = 0$, then the utility function is said to exhibit constant relative risk aversion. Finally, if $R'(W) > 0$, then the function is said to exhibit increasing relative risk aversion. This is summarized in Table 8.8.

Table 8.8

Condition	Definition	Property of $R'(W)$	Examples of Utility Functions
Increasing relative risk aversion	Percentage invested in risky assets declines as wealth increases	$R'(W) > 0$	$W - bW^2$
Constant relative risk aversion	Percentage invested in risky assets is unchanged as wealth increases	$R'(W) = 0$	$\ln W$
Decreasing relative risk aversion	Percentage invested in risky assets increases as wealth increases	$R'(W) < 0$	$-e^{2W-1/2}$

While there is general agreement that most investors exhibit decreasing absolute risk aversion, there is much less agreement concerning relative risk aversion. Often people assume constant relative risk aversion. The justification for this, however, is often one of convenience rather than belief about descriptive accuracy. In any case, if investors can articulate their feelings about the percentage they would invest in risky assets as wealth changes, then they can reduce the number of portfolios they must consider or further restrict the utility functions that might describe their behavior.

Let us examine some utility functions that have been used in the economics and finance literature to describe investor behavior and explore the characteristics of each. The most frequently used function is probably the quadratic. It is

$$U(W) = W - bW^2$$

Its derivatives are:

$$U'(W) = 1 - 2bW$$
$$U''(W) = -2b$$

If the investor displays a utility function that exhibits risk aversion, then the second derivative must be negative or b must be positive. If the investor is assumed to prefer more to less, then the first derivative must be positive. No matter how small b is, as long as it is positive there is always some value of W that will make the first derivative negative. Thus, for investors who prefer more to less, the quadratic utility could represent their desires over only a restricted range of wealth. To be consistent with nonsatiation, the following restriction must be placed on W: $1 - 2bW > 0$ or $W < 1/2b$. The absolute and relative risk aversion measures are

$$A(W) = \frac{-U''(W)}{U'(W)} = \frac{+2b}{(1 - 2bW)}$$

$$A'(W) = \frac{4b^2}{(1 - 2bW)^2} > 0$$

$$R(W) = \frac{-Wu''(W)}{u'(W)} = \frac{2bW}{1 - 2bW}$$

$$R'(W) = \frac{4b^2W}{(1 - 2bW)^2} + \frac{2b(1 - 2bW)}{(1 - 2bW)^2} = \frac{2b}{(1 - 2bW)^2} > 0$$

Examining the absolute risk aversion function shows that the quadratic utility function exhibits increasing absolute risk aversion. Thus, the quadratic function is consistent with investors who reduce the dollar amount invested in risky assets as wealth increases. Since they decrease the dollar amount invested, it is clear the percentage amount also decreases. Thus, the quadratic utility function must exhibit increasing relative risk aversion, also. A glance at the relative risk aversion function confirms that this is so.

The quadratic utility function has always had a special place in mean variance analysis because the assumption of a quadratic utility function leads to mean variance analysis being optimum.[5] As we have just discussed, the quadratic utility

---

[5]The variance of a random variable is defined as $\sigma_w^2 = E[W - E(W)]^2$. Performing the squaring yields $\sigma_w^2 = E\{W^2 - 2W \cdot E(W) + [E(W)]^2\}$. Since the expected value of the sum of random variables is the sum of the expected values, we have

$$\sigma_w^2 = E(W^2) - E[2W \cdot E(W)] + [E(W)]^2$$

Since the expected value of a constant times a random variable is the constant times the expected value of the random variable, σ_w^2 can be written as

$$\sigma_w^2 = E(W^2) - 2E(W) \cdot E(W) + E(W)^2 \quad \text{or} \quad \sigma_w^2 = E(W^2) - [E(W)]^2$$

Taking the expected value of a quadratic utility function yields

$$E[U(W)] = E(W) - bE(W^2)$$

Rearranging the previously derived relationship to solve for $E(W^2)$ yields $E(W^2) = \sigma_w^2 + [E(W)]^2$. Substituting this for $E(W^2)$ in the utility equation shows

$$E[U(W)] = E(W) - b\{\sigma_w^2 + [E(W)]^2\}$$

Thus, expected utility can be defined in terms of means and variances when utility is quadratic.

function has some characteristics that are undesirable. However, a number of authors (e.g., [13]) have shown that a quadratic function can be found that approximates very closely a function with more desirable properties. This approximation may well depend on the wealth of the investor. However, by changing the parameters of the quadratic function as wealth changes, one can obtain a function that closely resembles a function with more desirable characteristics and that still satisfies mean variance analysis.

As a second example of a utility function, consider the following log function:

$$U(W) = \ln W$$

The first and second derivatives of this function are

$$U'(W) = W^{-1}$$
$$U''(W) = -W^{-2}$$

An examination of the first derivative shows that the derivative is positive over all values of W. An examination of the second derivative shows that it is negative over all values. Thus, the log function is a candidate for an investor who prefers more to less and is risk averse. The absolute and relative risk aversion coefficients are

$$A(W) = \frac{-(-W^{-2})}{W^{-1}} = W^{-1}$$

$$A'(W) = -W^{-2} < 0$$

$$R(W) = \frac{-W(-W^{-2})}{W^{-1}} = 1$$

$$R'(W) = 0$$

Thus, the log function exhibits decreasing absolute risk aversion and constant relative risk aversion. The log function is consistent with the behavior of a risk-averse investor who prefers more to less and whose percentage invested in risky assets remains constant as wealth increases.

EMPIRICAL EVIDENCE ON THE SUITABILITY OF ALTERNATIVE PREFERENCE FUNCTIONS

In the earlier sections we continuously discussed the consistency of assumptions about investor behavior with observations of actual behavior. In this section, we elaborate on these statements.

Empirical evidence as to the form of a utility function that might reasonably represent behavior is of two types:

1. Experimental evidence from simple choice situations;
2. Survey data on investor's asset choices.

The assumption that investors prefer more to less is consistent with most evidence. Few investors, faced with a choice of securities with identical properties, except for expected return, select the one with the lowest expected return unless there are differences in transaction costs or control.

The assumption of risk aversion is also generally consistent with empirical evidence. Most investors purchase insurance on homes and cars. Since the insurance premiums are always larger than the expected loss (to cover insurance company profit and costs), the purchase of insurance is risk-averse behavior. In experimental situations, if return is held constant, most individuals choose the gamble with the least risky alternatives. A number of people have been disturbed by the observation that people buy lottery tickets or gamble. These activities are the opposite of insurance. The expected return on the gamble is negative and a gamble is risk-seeking behavior. In order to accommodate both gambling and insurance in an individual's utility function, Friedman and Savage suggested a function that exhibited risk aversion for some levels of wealth and risk-seeking behavior for others. This is one alternative. The other alternative is to argue that gambling provides entertainment value as well as risky outcomes. Accounting for the entertainment value means that a risk-averse individual might still gamble.

There are two major studies that attempt to determine investors' relative and absolute risk-aversion behavior. Both studies used survey data of individuals' asset holdings and wealth to draw inferences concerning investors' relative and absolute risk aversion. Ideally, to draw this type of inference, one would prefer to have observations concerning each investor's portfolio behavior over time as his wealth changes. Unfortunately, these data do not exist. Thus, one must resort to drawing inferences from different investors at different wealth levels.

One set of studies by Blume and Friend [4] examined the Federal Reserve Board survey of the financial characteristics of consumers. They found that the percentage invested in risky assets remained virtually unchanged when they examined asset holdings of investors with very different wealth. They concluded that their evidence was supportive of an assumption of constant relative risk aversion and this, of course, implies decreasing absolute risk aversion. The second major study was by Cohn, Lewellen, Lease, and Schlarbaum [5]. This study examined survey data obtained from questionnaires mailed by a brokerage firm to its customers. They examined the amount held in risky assets for investors with different wealth. They conclude that investors exhibit decreasing relative risk aversion, which also implies decreasing absolute risk aversion.

As mentioned earlier, some caution must be exercised with regard to these studies since they examined different investors with different levels of wealth, rather than the same investor at different wealth levels. However, these imaginative studies are very suggestive of the types of absolute or relative risk-aversion behavior that are consistent with actual behavior.

APPENDIX A

An Axiomatic Derivation of the Expected Utility Theorem

The expected utility theorem can be developed from a set of axioms or postulates concerning investor behavior. If an investor acts in accordance with these postulates, then the investor's behavior is indistinguishable from one who makes decisions on the basis of the expected utility theorem. The first two axioms concern the preference ordering of certain outcomes. The remaining two axioms concern rationality when ordering random prospects. The axioms are:

1.   *Comparability*. An investor can state a preference among all alternative certain outcomes. Thus, if the investor has a choice of outcome A or B, a preference for A to B or B to A can be stated or indifference between them can be expressed. An assumption that investors can make comparisons between outcomes (that are certain) is a standard assumption of economic theory.

2.   *Transitivity*. If an investor prefers A to B and B to C, then A is preferred to C. This is an assumption that investors are consistent in their ranking of outcomes. Although it would seem reasonable that most investors would behave in this manner in experimental situations, this is not always so. The difficulty occurs because some situations are sufficiently complex that the investor is unable to understand all of the implications of the choice. In experimental situations when the intransitivities are pointed out and the implication of the choice explored, most individuals want to revise their decisions in a way that is consistent with this axiom.

3.   *Independence*. Consider two certain prospects X and Y and assume the investor is indifferent between them. Designate a third prospect by Z. Independence implies that the investor is indifferent between the following two gambles:

    X with probability P and Z with probability $1 - P$, and

    Y with probability P and Z with probability $1 - P$.

The investor may like both or neither, but the point is she will feel equally good or bad about each.

    For example, if a person were indifferent between having a Chevrolet or a Ford, then that person would be indifferent to buying a raffle ticket for $10 that gave a 1 in 500 chance of winning a Ford or a raffle ticket for $10 that gave a 1 in 500 chance of winning a Chevrolet. This person might prefer to buy neither ticket, but if the decision to buy a ticket was made, then the person would not care which one was bought.

4. *Certainty Equivalent.* For every gamble there is a value (called certainty equivalent) such that the investor is indifferent between the gamble and the certainty equivalent. This assumption simply states that everything has a price.

Using these axioms, we can derive the expected utility theorem. What follows is an intuitive explanation. For a more rigorous derivation, see Fama and Miller [8]. Consider a security G with two possible outcomes:

$$G = \begin{bmatrix} b \text{ with probability } h \\ 0 \text{ with probability } 1 - h \end{bmatrix}$$

Let C be the amount of money that would make the investor indifferent between taking gamble G and receiving the money C, which is the certainty equivalent. Clearly C depends on the probability of receiving b (i.e., the value of h). However, from axiom 4, C must exist. If we vary h, then a different value of C would be appropriate. If we varied h over a large number of values and then plotted all values of h versus C, we might have a diagram such as Figure 8.2. The curve in this figure is the investor's preference curve. It separates combinations of C and h for which the investor prefers the security from points where the investor prefers the certain amount. Consider the point X', which represents the same gamble as X but a higher certainty equivalent. The investor has stated he is indifferent between X' and C', where C is a lower certainty equivalent than C'. Most investors prefer more to less, thus they would prefer the security X to the certainty equivalent C. This would imply that points above the curve are points where the gamble is preferred and points below the curve are points where the certainty equivalent is preferred.[6] Now consider a portfolio of securities S_1 with N possible outcomes defined as

$$S_1 = \begin{bmatrix} W_1 \text{ with probability } P_1 \\ W_2 \text{ with probability } P_2 \\ \vdots \\ W_N \text{ with probability } P_N \end{bmatrix}$$

Since each W_i is a known payoff and since C_i's of all sizes exist, we can replace each W_i with a C_i of the same size. Thus, portfolio S_1 can be represented as

$$S_1 = \begin{bmatrix} C_1 \text{ with probability } P_1 \\ C_2 \text{ with probability } P_2 \\ \vdots \\ C_N \text{ with probability } P_N \end{bmatrix}$$

---

[6]Strictly speaking, all we know is that the preference curve separates the area where the investor prefers the security from the area where he prefers the certain amount. It would be possible that above the curve he selects the certain amount. In this case he prefers less to more.

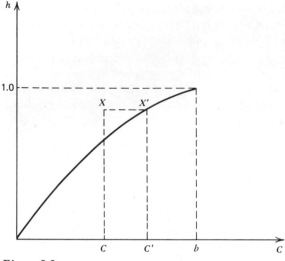

Figure 8.2

Since for every C_i there exists an equivalent lottery, we can represent an equivalent portfolio as

$$
S_2 = \begin{bmatrix}
\begin{bmatrix} b \text{ with probability } h_1 \\ 0 \text{ with probability } 1 - h_1 \end{bmatrix} & \text{with probability } P_1 \\
\begin{bmatrix} b \text{ with probability } h_2 \\ 0 \text{ with probability } 1 - h_2 \end{bmatrix} & \text{with probability } P_2 \\
\vdots & \\
\begin{bmatrix} b \text{ with probability } h_N \\ 0 \text{ with probability } 1 - h_N \end{bmatrix} & \text{with probability } P_N
\end{bmatrix}
$$

The investor declared indifference between each C_i and the lottery. Thus, it is reasonable that S_1 and S_2 should be equivalent.

Let us explore this in more detail. Assume that outcome i occurs. Then, if the investor selects S_1, C_i is received. If the investor selects S_2, then b with probability h_i and 0 with probability $1 - h_i$ is received. However, the investor has indicated in the construction of the preference curve an indifference between C_i and this lottery. Further, W_i is equal to C_i. Thus the investor is indifferent between W_i and this lottery. Thus, security 2 is equivalent to security 1. Note that from axiom 3 the investor does not change preference simply because the alternatives are part of a lottery.

A tree diagram might clarify this choice further. Figure 8.3 represents the portfolio S_1 and Figure 8.4 the portfolio S_2. Note that while S_2 is equivalent to S_1, S_2 has only two possible outcomes: b and 0. We could equivalently write S_2 as b with probability $\Sigma_i P_i h_i$ and 0 with probability $1 - \Sigma_i P_i h_i$. Utilizing the technique just discussed, we can do the same with any portfolio. Thus, any portfolio can be reduced to two outcomes, b and 0, with known probabilities.

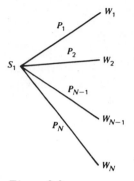

Figure 8.3

How do we choose between these portfolios? To decide, the individual need consider only the probability of receiving b, and the one with the higher probability is to be preferred. Define $H_i = \Sigma P_i h_i$, where the P and h are the values appropriate for the security under question. Then if $H_K > H_L$, security K is to be preferred to security L. This leads directly to the expected utility theorem. Earlier, we replaced every W_i with a C_i; associated with the C_i was an h_i. Thus, for each W_i there corresponds an h_i. Let us call the function that relates W_i to h_i a utility function and denote it by $U(\quad)$. Then, noting that h_i is a function of W_i is equivalent to writing $h_i = U(W_i)$. Furthermore, our feelings about a gamble

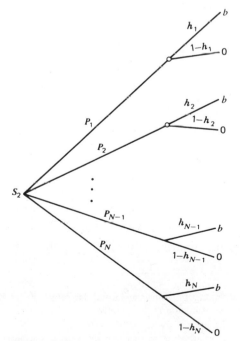

Figure 8.4

can be expressed as

$$H_i = \Sigma_i P_i h_i = \Sigma_i P_i U(W_i)$$

But $\Sigma_i P_i U(W_i)$ is simply expected utility. Thus, expressing the feelings about an investment in terms of H_i is equivalent to expressing them in terms of expected utility. Further ranking by H_i is equivalent to ranking by expected utility.

APPENDIX B

Absolute and Relative Risk Aversion

Assume an investor has wealth W and a security with outcomes represented by the random variable Z. Let Z be a fair gamble so that $E(Z) = 0$. Let σ_z^2 equal the variance of Z and $U(\ )$ the investor's utility function. Let W_c be the level of wealth such that the investor is indifferent between having W_c and having wealth W plus the gamble Z. Thus, the two choices are

Choice A   Choice B

$W + Z$ W_c

By assumption, the investor is indifferent between these positions, thus

$$E[(U(W + Z)] = EU(W_c) = U(W_c) \tag{B.1}$$

The last equality holds because W_c is received with certainty. The difference between W and W_c is the dollars the investor is willing to give up not to have to face the gamble. If the investor could take out an insurance policy, $W - W_c$ would be the maximum the investor would be willing to pay to avoid the risk of the investment. The greater this difference, the greater the amount of dollars the investor is willing to give up to avoid the gamble. Thus, it is natural to think of $\pi = W - W_c$ as a measure of the investor's absolute risk aversion.

Expanding $U(W + Z)$ in a Taylor series around W, we have[7]

$$U(W + Z) = U(W) + U'(W)[(W + Z) - W] + (1/2)U''(W)$$
$$[(W + Z) - W]^2 + \cdots$$

Taking the expected value of both sides and ignoring terms involving the third

---

[7]A Taylor series is a method of approximating a function using its derivatives. Let primes indicate derivatives. For example, $U'(\ )$ is the first derivative and $U''(\ )$ is the second derivative. Let $\simeq$ mean "approximately equal to." Then, the Taylor approximation in the vicinity of a is

$$U(X) \simeq U(a) + \frac{U'(a)}{1}[X - a] + \frac{U''(a)}{2 \cdot 1}[X - a]^2 + \frac{U'''(a)}{3 \cdot 2 \cdot 1}[X - a]^3 + \cdots$$

and higher order derivatives, we have

$$E[U(W + Z) \simeq E[U(W)] + U'(W)E(Z) + (1/2)U''(W)E(Z - 0)^2$$

Recalling that $U(W)$ is a constant and that

$$E(Z - 0)^2 = E[Z - E(Z)]^2$$

is the variance of Z yields

$$E[U(W + Z)] \simeq U(W) + (1/2)U''(W)\sigma_Z^2 \qquad (B.2)$$

Recall that W_c is equal to $W - \pi$. Expanding $U(W - \pi)$ in a Taylor series around W, we have

$$U(W_c) = U(W - \pi) \simeq U(W) + U'(W)[(W - \pi) - W] + \cdots$$

Ignoring terms above the first derivative, we have

$$U(W_c) \simeq U(W) + U'(W)(-\pi) \qquad (B.3)$$

From Equation (B.1) $E[U(W + Z)] = U(W_c)$ and Equation (B.2) equals Equation (B.3), or

$$U(W) + (1/2)U''(W)\sigma_Z^2 = U(W) + U'(W)(-\pi)$$

Rearranging

$$\pi = -(1/2)\sigma_Z^2 \frac{U''(W)}{U'(W)}$$

Since $(1/2)\sigma_Z^2$ is a constant, $A(W) = -U''(W)/U'(W)$ measures the amount of risk aversion.

Note that $A(W)$ has some special properties. First, if $U'(W) > 0$, then the sign of $A(W)$ depends on the sign of $U''(W)$. If $A(W)$ has the same sign for all values of W, then the investor has the same risk preference for all values of W and we refer to the investor as "globally" risk averse or globally risk neutral, or as a global risk seeker. Second, note that $A(W)$ is equivalent for investors with similar utility functions. Earlier we noted utility functions are unique only up to a linear transform. Thus, $U(W)$ and $V(W) = a + bU(W)$ lead to identical choices. Note that $V'(W) = bU'(W)$ and that $V''(W) = bU''(W)$. Computing $A(W)$ for function $V(W)$ yields

$$A(W) = \frac{-bU''(W)}{bU'(W)} = \frac{-U''(W)}{U'(W)}$$

Thus, both functions $U(W)$ and $V(W)$ not only rank investment identically but have the same absolute risk-aversion coefficient.

The relative risk-aversion coefficient is derived as follows. The percentage insurance premium one would pay is $\pi = (W - W_c)/W$, where π is the fraction of wealth an investor is giving up in order to avoid the gamble. With π defined in this manner, $W_c = W(1 - \pi)$. Change the definition of Z so that it represents outcome per dollar invested. Let $E(Z) = 1$ and variance of $Z = \sigma_z^2$. Thus, if we invest Z dollars, we obtain WZ as a dollar return. Expanding WZ in a Taylor series around W yields

$$U(WZ) = U(W) + U'(W)E(WZ - W) + \frac{U''(W)}{2} E(ZW - W)^2 + \cdots$$

Taking the expected value of both sides and simplifying yields

$$EU(WZ) = U(W) + 0 + \frac{U''(W)}{2} W^2 \sigma_z^2$$

Expanding W_c in a Taylor expansion around W yields

$$U(W_c) = U[W(1 - \pi)]$$

$$= U(W) + U'(W)[W(1 - \pi) - W] + \cdots$$

Ignoring higher order terms,

$$U(W_c) = U(W) + U'(W)(-\pi W)$$

Equating $E[U(WZ)]$ with $U(W_c)$ yields

$$U(W) + (1/2)U''(W)\sigma_z^2 W^2 = U(W) - \pi W U'(W)$$

Simplifying,

$$\pi = -\frac{\sigma_z^2}{2} \frac{W U''(W)}{U'(W)}$$

π is a measure of the percentage change in the risk premium. Define

$$R(W) = \frac{-W U''(W)}{U'(W)}$$

Then $R(W)$ is a measure of proportional or relative risk aversion.

In the derivation shown above, we dropped some higher order terms. In this sense, it is an approximation. It is possible to derive the absolute and relative risk coefficients directly without using the Taylor expansion. (See, for example, Mossin [13].) However, this derivation, while mathematically correct, conveys less economic intuition behind the meaning of relative and absolute risk aversion. Because of this, we have chosen to present the derivation using the approximation. It might also bother the reader that we dropped terms involving different derivatives in our expansion. However, note that the coefficients of the terms involved are π in one case and moments of Z in the other. Thus, the magnitude of the terms dropped are roughly the same.

QUESTIONS AND PROBLEMS

1. Consider the following three investments. Which are preferred if $U(W) = W - (1/2)W^2$?

Investment A		Investment B		Investment C	
$ Outcome	Probability	$ Outcome	Probability	$ Outcome	Probability
5	1/3	4	1/4	1	1/5
6	1/3	7	1/2	9	3/5
9	1/3	10	1/4	18	1/5

2. Assume the utility function is $U(W) = -W^{-1/2}$. What is the preferred investment in Problem 1?

3. Consider the following two investments:

Investment A		Investment B	
$ Outcome	Probability	$ Outcome	Probability
7	2/5	5	1/2
10	1/5	12	1/4
14	2/5	20	1/4

Which is preferred if the utility function is $U(W) = 2W - .04W^2$?

4. Consider the choice shown in Problem 3. The probability of a $5 return is ½ and $12 return is ¼. How much would these probabilities have to change so that the investor is indifferent between investments A and B?

5. Consider the utility function $U(W) = W^{-1/2}$. What are the characteristics of this function with respect to absolute and relative risk aversion?

6. Consider the function $U(W) = ae^{-bW}$, where a and b are constants. What are the signs of a and b if the investor is assumed to prefer more to less and to exhibit risk aversion?

7. Assume that an investor's utility function is $U(W) = a + be^{cW}$ where (a) a, b, c, are constants, and (b) W is wealth. Assuming that the investor prefers more to less and is risk averse, what can be said about the sign of a, b, c? What are the properties of this utility function in terms of absolute and relative risk aversion?

8. What are the properties of the utility function $U(W) = -W^{-1/2}$?

9. What are the properties of the function $U(W) = -e^{-w}$?

BIBLIOGRAPHY

1. Baker, Kent, Hargrove, Michael, and Haslem, John. "An Empirical Analysis of the Risk-Return Preferences of Individual Investors," *Journal of Financial and Quantitative Analysis,* **XII,** No. 3 (Sept. 1977), pp. 377–389.
2. Baron, David. "On the Utility Theoretic Foundations of Mean-Variance Analysis," *Journal of Finance,* **XII,** No. 5 (Dec. 1977), pp. 1683–1697.
3. Bernoulli, Daniel. "Exposition of a New Theory on the Measurement of Risk," *Econometrica,* **32** (Jan. 1954), pp. 23–26.
4. Blume, Marshall, and Friend, Irwin. "The Asset Structure of Individual Portfolios and Some Implications for Utility Functions," *Journal of Finance,* **X,** No. 2 (May 1975), pp. 585–603.
5. Cohn, Richard, Lewellen, Wilbur, Lease, Ronald, and Schlarbaum, Gary. "Individual Investor Risk Aversion and Investment Portfolio Composition," *Journal of Finance,* **X,** No. 2 (May 1975), pp. 605–620.
6. Diamond, Peter, and Stiglitz, Joseph. "Increases in Risk and in Risk Aversion," *Journal of Economic Theory,* **8,** No. 3 (July 1974), pp. 337–360.
7. Engelbrecht, Richard. "A Note on Multivariate Risk and Separable Utility Functions," *Management Science,* **23,** No. 10 (June 1977), pp. 1143–1144.
8. Fama, Eugene, and Miller, Merton. *Theory of Finance* (New York: Holt, Rinehart and Winston, 1972).
9. Friedman, Milton, and Savage, Leonard, J. "The Utility Analysis of Choices Involving Risk," *Journal of Political Economy* (Aug. 1948), pp. 279–304.
10. Lease, Ronald, Lewellen, Wilbur, and Schlarbaum, Gary. "The Individual Investor: Attributes and Attitudes," *Journal of Finance,* **IX,** No. 2 (May 1974), pp. 413–433.
11. Levy, Haim, and Sarnat, Marshall. "A Note on Portfolio Selection and Investor's Wealth," *Journal of Financial and Quantitative Analysis,* **VI,** No. 1 (Jan. 1971), pp. 639–642.
12. Markowitz, Harry. *Portfolio Selection: Efficient Diversification of Investments* (New York: John Wiley & Sons, 1959).
13. Mossin, Jan. *Theory of Financial Markets* (Englewood Cliffs, N.J.: Prentice Hall, 1973).
14. Pratt, J. "Risk Aversion in the Small and in the Large," *Econometrica* (Jan.– April 1964), pp. 122–136.

15. Remaley, William. "Suboptimization in Mean-Variance Efficient Set Analysis," *Journal of Finance,* **VIII,** No. 2 (May 1973), pp. 397–403.
16. Richard, Scott. "Multivariate Risk Aversion, Utility Independence, and Separable Utility Functions," *Management Science,* **22,** No. 1 (Sept. 1975), pp. 12–21.
17. Sarnat, Marshall. "A Note on the Implications of Quadratic Utility for Portfolio Theory," *Journal of Financial and Quantitative Analysis,* **IX,** No. 4 (Sept. 1974), pp. 687–689.
18. Sennetti, John. "On Bernoulli, Sharpe Financial Risk and the Petersburg Paradox," *Journal of Finance,* **XI,** No. 3 (June 1976), pp. 960–962.
19. Von Neumann, J. and Morgenstern, O. *Theory of Games and Economic Behavior,* 2nd ed. (Princeton, N.J.: Princeton University Press, 1947).
20. Williams, Joseph. "A Note on Indifference Curves in the Mean-Variance Model," *Journal of Financial and Quantitative Analysis,* **XII,** No. 1 (March 1977), pp. 121–126.
21. Wippern, Ronald. "Utility Implications of Portfolio Selection and Performance Appraisal Models," *Journal of Financial and Quantitative Analysis,* **VI,** No. 3 (June 1977), pp. 913–924.
22. Zeckhauser, R., and Keeler, E. "Another Type of Risk Aversion," *Econometrica,* **38,** No. 4 (Sept. 1970), pp. 661–665.

Chapter 9

Other Portfolio Selection Models

In all previous chapters and, in fact, in most of those that follow, we have assumed that investors are attempting to maximize the expected utility of the returns from an investment portfolio. Usually we have assumed that the expected utility of any opportunity could be meaningfully measured in terms of means and variances. This is the traditional and widely accepted mean-variance approach to portfolio management. While this is the central approach of this book, we would be remiss if we did not mention some of the other approaches that have been advocated in the finance and economic literature.

First, let us note that the mean-variance approach as we have presented it holds exactly when investors are expected utility maximizers, prefer more to less, are risk averse, and either (1) security returns are normally distributed or (2) utility functions are quadratic. Furthermore, the analysis is robust in that, as Markowitz [62] has shown, it frequently holds approximately even when assumptions (1) or (2) are violated. For example, quadratic approximations are almost always good local approximations to nonquadratic utility functions.

Other approaches to the portfolio problem make less stringent assumptions about the investor's choice framework, the form of the utility function, and/or the form of the distribution of security returns. In this chapter we examine four other criteria for portfolio selection: the geometric mean return, safety first, stochastic dominance, and analysis in terms of characteristics of the return distribution.

The geometric mean criterion is a choice framework that purports to select optimum portfolios without the need to consider the form of investor's utility functions or the distribution of security returns. The geometric mean return criterion was developed to represent what its proponents felt was common sense behavior on the part of investors (rather than because it was consistent with maximization of expected utility). This criterion can be viewed as maximizing the expected value of terminal wealth. It is not surprising that this criterion can lead to the selection of different portfolios than the expected utility framework. What is surprising is that, under several alternative assumptions, this criterion leads to the selection of a portfolio that is on the efficient set. Thus, under broad sets of assumptions, the advocate of maximum geometric mean criterion will find useful most of the analysis in the preceding chapters.

The alternative forms of safety first imply that investors cannot, or will not, go through the expected utility calculations, but rather will employ a simpler decision criterion concentrating on the avoidance of "bad" outcomes. As in the case of the geometric mean, we will find that the portfolio that optimizes a safety first · criterion will often lie on the efficient set and so most of the analysis presented to this point is still useful.

While the first two criteria discussed in this chapter do not utilize the idea of expected utility, the last two criteria, like mean variance analysis, utilize this idea.

Stochastic dominance defines efficient sets of investments under alternative (progressively more stringent) conditions on the behavior of utility functions. While stochastic dominance rules are more general than mean variance analysis, they are, under certain assumptions, consistent with mean variance analysis and lead to the same efficient set.

The final criterion we examine in this chapter is portfolio selection in terms of three moments. The introduction of skewness into the portfolio problem, in addition to mean and variance, complicates the analysis and requires an extension of the analysis needed to perform mean variance analysis.

MAXIMIZING THE GEOMETRIC MEAN RETURN

One alternative to mean variance analysis is simply to select that portfolio that has the highest expected geometric mean return. Many researchers have put this forth as a universal criterion. That is, they advocate its use without qualifications as to the form of utility function or the characteristics of the probability distribution of security returns. The proponents of the geometric mean usually proceed with one of the following arguments. Consider an investor saving for some purpose in the future, for example, retirement in 20 years. One reasonable portfolio criterion for such an investor would be to select that portfolio that has the highest expected value of terminal wealth. Latané [50] has shown that this is the portfolio with the highest geometric mean return. The proponents have also argued that the maximum geometric mean[1]:

1. Has the highest probability of reaching, or exceeding, any given wealth level in the shortest possible time[2];

---

[1]The accuracy of these statements is not universally accepted.

[2]See Brieman [17] for a discussion of this property. Roll [76] argues that this is true only in the limit.

2. Has the highest probability of exceeding any given wealth level over any given period of time.[3]

These characteristics of the maximum geometric mean portfolio are extremely appealing and have attracted many advocates.

Opponents quickly point out that, in general, maximizing the expected value of terminal wealth (or either of the other benefits discussed above) is not identical to maximizing the utility of terminal wealth.[4] Since opponents accept the tenets of utility theory, and, in particular, the idea that investors should maximize the expected utility of terminal wealth, they reject the geometric mean return criteria.

In short, some researchers find the characteristics of the geometric mean return so appealing they accept it as a universal criterion. Others find any criterion that is inconsistent with expected utility maximization unacceptable. Readers must judge for themselves which of these approaches is more appealing.

Having discussed the arguments in favor of and against the use of the geometric mean as a portfolio selection criterion, let us examine the definition of the geometric mean and some properties of portfolios that maximize the geometric mean criterion.

The geometric mean is easy to define. Instead of adding together the observations to obtain the mean, you multiply them. If R_{ij} is the ith possible return on the jth portfolio and each outcome is equally likely, then the geometric mean return on the portfolio $(\overline{R}_{Gj})$ is

$$\overline{R}_{Gj} = [(1 + R_{1j})^{1/N}(1 + R_{2j})^{1/N} \cdots (1 + R_{Nj})^{(1/N)} - 1.0]$$

If the likelihood of each observation is different and P_{ij} is the probability of the ith outcome for portfolio j, then the geometric mean return is

$$\overline{R}_{Gj} = (1 + R_{1j})^{P_{1j}}(1 + R_{2j})^{P_{2j}} \cdots (1 + R_{N-1j})^{P_{N-1j}}(1 + R_{Nj})^{P_{Nj}} - 1.0$$

This is sometimes written in compact form. The symbol Π means product. Thus, the above series can be written as

$$\overline{R}_{Gj} = \prod_{i=1}^{N} (1 + R_{ij})^{P_{ij}} - 1.0$$

The portfolio that has the maximum geometric mean is usually a diversified portfolio. This can be illustrated with an example. Table 9.1 shows three possible investments listed as securities A, B, and C. Each of these investments has two possible outcomes, each equally likely. The portfolio shown consists of equal proportions of each of the three securities. As can be seen from the table, the

---

[3]See Brieman [17] for a discussion of this property. Roll [76] and Hakansson [32] make a similar argument.

[4]It has been shown that the portfolio that maximizes the expected value of a logarithmic utility function is identical to the portfolio that maximizes the geometric mean return. This is not, in general, true for other utility functions.

portfolio has a higher geometric mean return than any of the individual securities. This result is easily explained. The geometric mean return penalizes extreme observations. In fact, a strategy with any probability of bankruptcy would never be selected as it would have a zero geometric mean.[5] As we've seen in other chapters, portfolios have less extreme observations than individual securities. Thus, the geometric mean strategy usually leads to a diversified strategy.

Table 9.1

		Securities		
Outcome	A	B	C	Portfolio
1	0.80	-0.10	-0.20	0.16 2/3
2	-0.30	0.30	0.60	0.20
Geometric mean	0.12	0.08	0.13	0.18

While that portfolio that maximizes the geometric mean is likely to be highly diversified, it will not (except in special circumstances) be mean-variance efficient. Furthermore, portfolios that are mean-variance efficient may have very low geometric mean returns. However, there are two cases where mean-variance analysis is meaningful for locating the portfolio with the highest geometric mean return.

First, maximizing the geometric mean return is equivalent to maximizing the expected value of a log utility function.[6] We know from earlier chapters that if

---

[5] If one possible outcome is a return of -1, then for that outcome $(1 + R_{ij}) = (1 - 1) = 0$. The geometric mean is the product of the $(1 + R_{ij})$. The whole product becomes zero if one element is zero. Thus, the geometric mean criteria would never select an investment with any probability of bankruptcy.

[6] The log utility function can be written as

$$\max E \ln W_1$$

where W_1 is end of period wealth, a random variable. Since utility functions are unchanged up to a linear transformation, if we let W_0 stand for the funds the investor can invest, then we can write the problem as

$$\max E(\ln W_1 - \ln W_0) = \max E \ln \left(\frac{W_1}{W_0}\right)$$

$$= \max E \ln(1 + R_i)$$

$$= \max \sum_i P_i \ln(1 + R_i)$$

$$= \max \sum_i \ln(1 + R_i)^{P_i}$$

Since the sum of the logs of a set of variables is the same as the log of the products, this problem can be written as

$$\max \ln \prod_i (1 + R_i)^{P_i}$$

But this is just the log of 1 plus the geometric mean return. Since taking the log of a set of numbers maintains the rank order, then that portfolio with the highest geometric mean return will also be the preferred portfolio if the investor has a log utility function.

returns are normally distributed, then mean-variance portfolio analysis is appropriate for investors interested in maximizing expected utility. Investors with log utility functions are such investors. Thus, investors interested in maximizing the geometric mean return could use mean-variance analysis if returns were normally distributed.

It has also been shown that the portfolio that maximizes the geometric mean return is mean-variance efficient if returns are log-normally distributed. In this case, a very simple formula exists that indicates which portfolio in the mean-variance efficient set is to be preferred.[7] With the exception of these two cases, the portfolio with the maximum geometric mean return need not be mean-variance efficient.

When returns are not normally, or log-normally, distributed, more general procedures are needed in order to determine the optimum portfolio. Ziemba [87] discusses one possible approach. Maier, Peterson, and Vanderweide [60] discuss a second approach.

The geometric mean return is more often advocated than any other alternative to mean variance analysis. While we leave the choice of these two criteria up to the reader, our preference for the tenets of expected utility theory and mean-variance analysis is unavoidably revealed by the amount of material we devote to each in this book. Note, also, that if returns are either normally or log-normally distributed, then mean-variance analysis can aid in finding that portfolio that has the highest geometric mean return.

SAFETY FIRST

A second alternative to the expected utility theorem that is advocated by many is a group of criteria called safety first models. The origin of these models stems from a belief that decision makers are unable, or unwilling, to go through the mathematics of the expected utility theorem, but rather will use a simpler decision model that concentrates on bad outcomes. The name "safety first" comes about because of the emphasis each of the criteria places on limiting the risk of bad outcomes. Three different safety first criteria have been put forth. The first, developed by Roy, states that the best portfolio is the one that has the smallest probability of producing a return below some specified level. If R_P is the return on the portfolio and R_L is the level below which the investor does not wish returns to fall, Roy's criterion is

$$(1) \quad \text{minimize Prob}(R_P < R_L)$$

If returns are *normally* distributed, then the optimum portfolio would be the one

---

[7]See Elton and Gruber [19]. The mathematics is sufficiently complex that we have not included the proofs, but rather refer the interested reader to the original source.

where R_L was the maximum number of standard deviations away from the mean.[8] For example, consider the three portfolios shown in Table 9.2. Assume 5% is the minimum return the investor desires. The investor wishes to minimize the chance of getting a return below 5%. If the investor selects portfolio A, then 5% is 1 standard deviation below the mean. The chance of getting a return below 5% is the probability of obtaining a return more than 1 standard deviation below the mean. If the investor selects investment B, then 5% is 2¼ standard deviations below the mean. The probability of obtaining a return below 5% is the probability of obtaining a return more than 2¼ standard deviations below the mean. If he selects investment C, the probability of obtaining a return below 5% is the probability of obtaining a return more than 1.5 standard deviations below the mean. Since the odds of obtaining a return more than 2¼ standard deviations below the mean are less than the odds of obtaining a return more than 1.5 or 1 standard deviation less than the mean, investment B is to be preferred. In order to determine how many standard deviations R_L lies below the mean, we calculated R_L minus the mean return divided by the standard deviation. To satisfy Roy's criterion if returns are normally distributed, we

$$\text{minimize } \frac{R_L - \overline{R}_P}{\sigma_P}$$

This is equivalent to maximizing minus this ratio or

$$\text{maximize } \frac{\overline{R}_P - R_L}{\sigma_P}$$

Table 9.2

	Portfolio		
	A	B	C
Mean return	10	14	17
Standard deviation (σ)	5	4	8
Difference from 5%	-1σ	-2.25σ	-1.5σ

This criterion should look familiar. If R_L were replaced by R_F, the riskless rate of interest, this would be the criterion we used throughout much of the book. All portfolios that are equally desirable under Roy's criterion would have the same value for this ratio. That is, they could be described by the following expression:

$$\frac{\overline{R}_P - R_L}{\sigma_P} = K$$

---

[8]Assuming the mean return is above R_L.

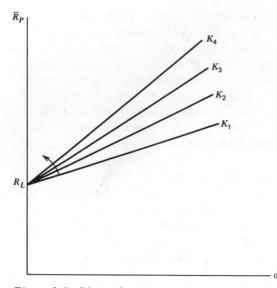

Figure 9.1   Lines of constant preference — Roy's
criterion.

Furthermore, if K was larger, the portfolio would be more desirable under Roy's
criterion. Rearranging this expression yields

$$\overline{R}_P = R_L + K\sigma_P$$

This is the equation of a straight line with an intercept of R_L and a slope of K.
Thus, all points of equal desirability (i.e., constant K) plot on a straight line and
the preferred line is one with the highest slope. This is shown in Figure 9.1 where
the K's are ordered such that $K_4 > K_3 > K_2 > K_1$. The Roy criterion with normally distributed returns produces a decision problem of exactly the same form
as the portfolio problem with riskless lending and borrowing. In this case, R_L
serves the role of the riskless rate, R_F. The desired portfolio is the feasible
portfolio lying on the line in the most counterclockwise direction and is easy to
find, utilizing the standard techniques discussed earlier. Notice that the portfolio
that maximizes Roy's criterion must lie along the efficient frontier in mean standard deviation space.[9]

Although the analysis was performed assuming normally distributed returns,
a similar result holds for any distribution that has first and second moments. The
very same maximization problem follows from the use of Tchebyshev's
inequality.[10]

---

[9]The location of portfolios that satisfy Roy's criterion when lending and borrowing are allowed is
discussed in Appendix A at the end of this chapter. This conclusion assumes $R_P > R_L$.

[10]One of the ways to determine the probability of some outcome is the use of Tchebyshev's inequality.
Tchebyshev's inequality allows one to determine the maximum probability of obtaining an outcome
less than some value. It does not assume any distribution for returns. If a distribution was assumed,

The Tchebyshev inequality makes very weak assumptions about the underlying distribution. It gives an expression that allows the determination of the maximum odds of obtaining a return less than some number. The use of this inequality leads to the same maximization problem and the same analysis as previously discussed. Thus, mean-variance analysis follows from the Roy safety first criterion.

The second safety first criterion was developed by Kataoka. Kataoka suggests the following criterion: maximize the lower limit subject to the constraint that the probability of a return less than, or equal to, the lower limit is not greater than some predetermined value. For example, maximize R_L subject to the constraint that the chance of a return below R_L is less than or equal to 5%. If α is the probability (in the example 5%), then in symbols this is

$$\text{maximize} \quad R_L$$

$$\text{subject to} \quad (1) \text{ Prob}(R_P < R_L) \leq \alpha$$

---

a more precise statement about probability could be made. Rather, it is a general statement applicable for all distributions.

The Tchebyshev inequality is

$$\text{Prob}\left(\left|\frac{R - \overline{R}_P}{\sigma_P}\right| > K\right) \leq \frac{1}{K^2}$$

where

R is the outcome
$\overline{R}_P$ is the mean return
σ_P is the standard deviation
K is a constant

Since we are interested in the case where the lower limit is less than $\overline{R}_P$, the returns we are interested in are those less than $\overline{R}_P$. Therefore, the term in the absolute value sign is negative. Noting this, we can write the term in the parenthesis as

$$\left(\frac{R - \overline{R}_P}{\sigma_P} < -K\right)$$

and the expression as

$$\text{Prob}\left(\frac{R - \overline{R}_P}{\sigma_P} < -K\right) \leq \frac{1}{k^2} \tag{9.1}$$

We can express the lower limit in Roy's criterion as the number of standard deviations K lies below the mean, or

$$K = \frac{\overline{R}_P - R_L}{\sigma_P} \tag{9.2}$$

Since Tchebyshev's inequality holds for any value of K, we can substitute the expression for K shown in Equation (9.2) into the left hand side of Equation (9.1). Doing so, and simplifying, yields

$$\text{Prob}\ (R < R_L) \leq \frac{1}{K^2}$$

Since this is precisely Roy's criterion, we want to maximize K or maximize Equation (9.2). But this is exactly what we did in the case of the normal distribution.

If returns are normally distributed, we can analyze this criterion in mean standard deviation space. Earlier, we noted that if returns are normally distributed, then the probability of obtaining returns below some number depends on the number of standard deviations below the mean that the number lies. Thus the odds of obtaining a return more than 3 standard deviations below the mean is 0.13% while the odds of obtaining a return more than 2 standard deviations below the mean is 2.28%. As an example set $\alpha = 0.05$. From the table of the normal distribution, we see that this is met as long as the lower limit is at least 1.65 standard deviations below the mean. With $\alpha = 0.05$, the constraint becomes

$$R_L \leq \overline{R}_P - 1.65\sigma_P$$

Since we want to make R_L as large as possible, this inequality can be written as an equality. Writing it as an equality and rearranging, we obtain for a constant R_L

$$\overline{R}_P = R_L + 1.65\sigma_P$$

This is the equation of a straight line. Since the intercept is R_L as R_L changes, the line shifts in a parallel fashion. Figure 9.2 illustrates this for various values of R_L. The objective is to maximize R_L or to move as far up as possible (in the direction of the arrow). If there is no lending or borrowing, then a unique maximum exists and it is the tangency point on the highest R_L line (R_{L_5} in the example). Note that, as in the case of Roy's criterion, the optimum portfolio must be on the efficient frontier in mean standard deviation space. Once again, the same analysis follows if one chooses to use the Tchebyshev inequality, rather than assuming normally distributed returns.

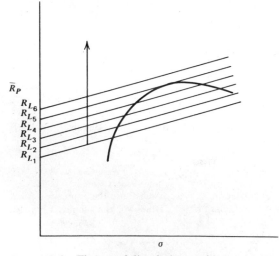

Figure 9.2   The portfolio choice problem with Kataoka's safety first rule.

The final safety first criterion was put forth by Telser. He suggested that a reasonable criterion would be for an investor to maximize expected return, subject to the constraint that the probability of a return less than, or equal to, some predetermined limit was not greater than some predetermined number. In symbols, we have

$$\text{maximize} \quad \overline{R}_P$$

$$\text{subject to} \quad (1) \; \text{Prob}(R_P \leqslant R_L) \leqslant \alpha$$

Once again, it is convenient to rearrange the constraint. In the discussion of the Kataoka criterion, it was shown that if returns are normally distributed, this constraint becomes

$$R_L \leqslant \overline{R}_P - (\text{constant})\sigma$$

Rearranging yields

$$\overline{R}_P \geqslant R_L + (\text{constant})\sigma$$

In the last section, the constant was set equal to 1.65 for the example. In general, it depends on the value of α. As discussed earlier, when the equality holds, this expression is the equation of a straight line. Consider Figure 9.3. The efficient frontier and the constraint are plotted in that figure. All points above the line meet the constraint. In Figure 9.3 the feasible set is bounded by the straight line and the efficient frontier (the shaded area). In this case the optimum is point A.

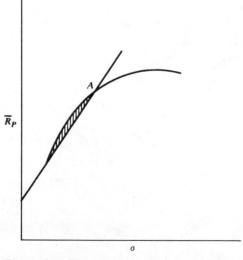

$\overline{R}_P$

σ

Figure 9.3   The investor's choice problem —
Telser's criterion.

If the portfolio with the overall highest return lies above the line, it will be selected. If it does not, the constraint line excludes part of the efficient set. In this case, the feasible portfolio with the highest mean return will lie at the highest intersection of the efficient frontier and the constraint. In either case, the point selected will be on the efficient set. It is possible that there are no feasible points that meet the constraint. For example, in Figure 9.4 the constraint lies above the efficient set. In this case, there is no feasible portfolio lying above the constraint and the criterion fails to select any portfolios.

Note that with the Telser criterion, the optimum portfolio either lies on the efficient frontier in mean standard deviation space or it does not exist.

As with the other two criteria, the same analysis follows if we use the Tchebyshev inequality rather than assuming normal returns.

The safety first criteria were originally suggested as appealing decision making and an alternative to the expected utility framework of traditional analysis. We see in this section that, under reasonable sets of assumptions, they lead to mean-variance analysis and to the selection of a particular portfolio in the efficient set. As shown in Appendix A, at the end of this chapter, with unlimited lending and borrowing at a riskless rate, the analysis may lead to infinite borrowing, an unreasonable prescription for managers. However, the difficulties lie, not with the criteria, but with the original assumption that investors can borrow unlimited amounts at a riskless rate of interest. Whether the safety first criteria are reasonable criteria can be answered only by the readers themselves. To some, they seem sensible as a description of reality. To others, the fact that they may be inconsistent with expected utility maximization leads to their rejection. If one accepts one of the safety first criteria and believes that the probability distribution of returns is normal or sufficiently well behaved that the Tchebyshev inequality holds, then the discussion in all previous chapters concerning the generation of the efficient frontier is useful in finding the optimal portfolio.

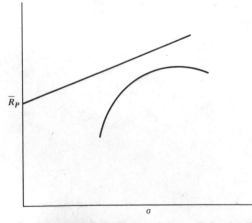

Figure 9.4   No feasible portfolio — Telser's criterion.

STOCHASTIC DOMINANCE

A third set of alternatives to mean variance analysis that has been advocated in the literature is stochastic dominance. The most general form of stochastic dominance makes no assumptions about the form of the probability distribution of returns. Furthermore, when we employ stochastic dominance we do not have to assume the specific form of investor's utility functions. Rather, we can define efficient sets under alternative assumptions about the general characteristics of investor's utility functions. These characteristics are consistent with whole families of utility functions. There are three progressively stronger assumptions about investor behavior that are employed in the stochastic dominance literature. They lead directly to first-, second-, and third-order stochastic dominance. First-order stochastic dominance assumes an investor prefers more to less. Second-order stochastic dominance assumes that, in addition to investors preferring more to less, they are risk averse. Finally, third-order stochastic dominance adds to the two assumptions of second-order dominance the assumption that investors have decreasing absolute risk aversion.[11]

Associated with each level of stochastic dominance is a theorem that allows the investor to eliminate many portfolios from consideration. Appendix B at the end of this chapter contains a proof of each of the theorems. In the chapter proper we intend to state the theorem and illustrate its use with a simple example.

Consider the example shown in Table 9.3. If an investor preferred more to less, then investment in asset A is preferable to investment in asset B because no matter which outcome occurs, A will always yield a higher return than B. For example, if market conditions are good, then A will return 10% and B will return 9%. The theorem of first-order stochastic dominance would, in fact, show that A dominated B. Now, consider the choices shown in Table 9.4. Investment A has the better outcomes. However, it is no longer certain that an investor will do worse by investing in B. For example, it is possible the return will be 11% if B is invested in and 10% or 8% if A is invested in. However, the chances are the investor will do worse with B. Let us rearrange this example (See Table 9.5). Note that no matter what the return is, the probability of obtaining less than that

Table 9.3

	Outcome	
Market Condition	A	B
Very good	11	10
Good	10	9
Average	9	8
Poor	8	7
Very poor	7	6

---

[11]Third-order stochastic dominance assumes the third derivative of utility is positive. A positive third derivative is a necessary condition for decreasing absolute risk aversion.

Table 9.4

Investment *A*		Investment *B*	
Outcome	Probability	Outcome	Probability
12	1/3	11	1/3
10	1/3	9	1/3
8	1/3	7	1/3

return (worse outcomes) are always as high with *B* as with *A*, or higher. Since we are assuming that the investor prefers more to less, *A* is preferred to *B*. Once again, *A* is preferred to *B*, not because the investor will always obtain a higher return, but rather because for all returns the odds of obtaining that return or less (doing worse) are as high with *B* as with *A*, or higher.

Table 9.5 shows the cumulative probability of any particular return. The cumulative probability is the likelihood of obtaining a given return or less. The example shown in Table 9.5 is plotted in Figure 9.5. Note that *B* coincides with *A* or lies above *A* at all levels of return. This implies that the odds of obtaining any return or less are as high with *B* as *A*, or higher.

The examples we have been discussing illustrate the ideas behind first-order stochastic dominance. The formal theorem is: if investors prefer more to less, and if the cumulative probability of *A* is never greater than the cumulative probability of *B* and sometimes less, then *A* is preferred to *B*.

The cumulative probability of *A* is never greater than the cumulative probability of *B* if, in diagrams such as Figure 9.5, the two curves do not cross and *A* does not lie above *B*. If the two curves cross, it is not possible to make a choice between *A* and *B* based on first-order stochastic dominance. To make a choice, we must make a stronger assumption about the characteristics of utility functions. To illustrate this, consider Table 9.6, which shows two possible investments, each with four equally likely outcomes. The cumulative probability for these two investments is shown in Table 9.7. At a return of 5%, *B* has a higher probability

Table 9.5

		Odds of Obtaining a Return Equal to or Less than That Shown in Column 1	
	Return	*A*	*B*
	7	0	1/3
	8	1/3	1/3
	9	1/3	2/3
	10	2/3	2/3
	11	2/3	1
	12	1	1

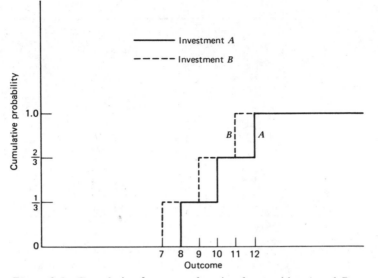

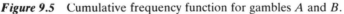

Figure 9.5 Cumulative frequency function for gambles *A* and *B*.

of a poor return than *A*, while at 8% *A* has a higher probability of a poorer return. Thus, we cannot select between *A* and *B* using first-order stochastic dominance. In order to be able to choose between these two investments, we have to be able to decide whether the higher probability of low returns in the range between 5 and 6% for *B* is more important than the higher probability of a low return from *A* in the range of 8 to 9%. If we assume risk aversion, in addition to preferring more to less, we can answer this question. Risk aversion means that the investor must be compensated for bearing risk. It arises when each increment in return is less valuable to the investor than the last. We still prefer obtaining 9% to 8%. However, the 1% increment in return from 8 to 9% is less valuable than the 1% increment from 5 to 6%. Examine Table 9.6. *A* differs from *B* in the lowest two returns. If both investments turn out as badly as possible, the investor obtains 6% from *A* and only 5% from *B*. The investor gets an extra 1% from *A* if the worst occurs. The cost of selecting *A* rather than *B* is that, if the second worst return occurs, the investor obtains 8% from *A* rather than 9% from *B*. He loses the extra 1%. If he is risk-averse, then he should be willing to lose 1% in return at a higher level of return in order to

Table 9.6

	A		B	
Outcome	Probability		Outcome	Probability
6	1/4		5	1/4
8	1/4		9	1/4
10	1/4		10	1/4
12	1/4		12	1/4

Table 9.7

Return	Cumulative Probability		Sum of Cumulative Probability		Sum of Cumulative Probabilities	
	A	*B*	*A*	*B*	*A*	*B*
4	0	0	0	0	0	0
5	0	1/4	0	1/4	0	1/4
6	1/4	1/4	1/4	1/2	1/4	3/4
7	1/4	1/4	1/2	3/4	3/4	1 1/2
8	1/2	1/4	1	1	1 3/4	2 1/2
9	1/2	1/2	1 1/2	1 1/2	3 1/4	4
10	3/4	3/4	2 1/4	2 1/4	5 1/2	6 1/4
11	3/4	3/4	3	3	8 1/2	9 1/4
12	1	1	4	4	12 1/2	13 1/4

obtain an extra 1% at a lower return level. This is exactly the idea behind second-order stochastic dominance, and second-order stochastic dominance implies *A* dominates *B*.

The same result can be seen by examining the cumulative probability distributions. Figure 9.6 is a plot of Table 9.6. The area between 5 and 6% is identical to the area between 8 and 9%. Since risk aversion is being assumed, it is pref-

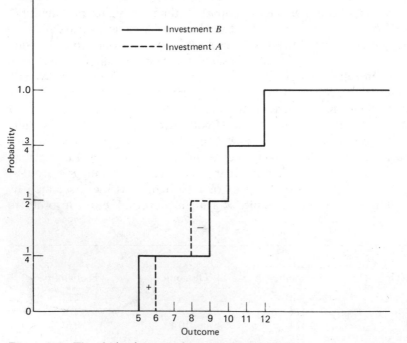

Figure 9.6   The choice between investments *A* and *B*.

erable to have a lower probability of a low return in the 5 to 6% range than the 8 to 9% range. Thus, A is preferred to B. The areas have been designated by $+$ and $-$. If, for all returns, the $+$ area below that return is no smaller than the $-$ area and for some returns it is larger, then A dominates B by second-order stochastic dominance.

These ideas can be formalized in the following theorem: If

1. Investors prefer more to less, and

2. Investors are risk-averse, and

3. The sum of the cumulative probabilities for all returns are never more with A than B and sometimes less,

then A dominates B with second-order stochastic dominance.

The application of this theorem is shown in Table 9.7. We have already seen that A dominates B by examining the cumulative probability distribution. We can see it more easily simply by applying point 3 above to the sum of the cumulative probability distribution shown in columns 4 and 5 of Table 9.7 entitled Sum of Cumulative Probability. Applying point 3 shows clearly that A dominates B.

The reader might be curious how this analysis relates to mean-variance analysis. If returns are normally distributed, then the answer is clear. First-order stochastic dominance assumes investors prefer more to less. The first part of the efficient set theorem utilizes this same assumption and leads to the result that, at any level of standard deviation, the investor preferred a higher mean return. Thus, first-order stochastic dominance implies the first part of the efficient set theorem if returns are normally distributed. When short sales are allowed, preferring a higher mean for any standard deviation leads to the efficient frontier. When short sales are disallowed, first-order stochastic dominance produces a set of portfolios that lie on the upper half of the outer boundary of the feasible set. These portfolios include the efficient set produced by mean variance analysis, plus all portfolios that have the highest return possible for each level of risk. In Figure 9.7, portfolios along the boundary segment BC are not in the efficient set AB but satisfy the first-order stochastic dominance condition.

Second-order stochastic dominance assumes investors are risk averse, as well as prefer more to less. These are the same assumptions that lead to the efficient set theorem. Thus, it should not surprise the reader that with normally distributed returns the only set of portfolios that is not dominated, using second-order stochastic dominance, is the mean-variance efficient set.

We have just seen that, when returns are normally distributed, second-order stochastic dominance (and, with short sales, first-order stochastic dominance) leads to a definition of an optimal set of portfolios that is consistent with the efficient set produced by mean-variance analysis. The advantage of stochastic dominance is that it can be used to derive sets of desirable portfolios when returns follow other distributions, or when one is unwilling to assume specific utility functions.

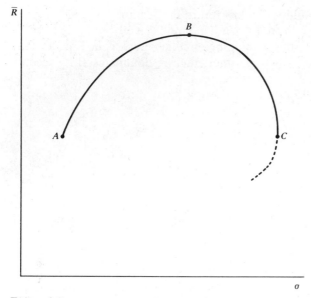

Figure 9.7

One should be careful not to overemphasize the importance of this advantage. In general, stochastic dominance involves pairwise comparisons of all alternatives. Since there is an infinite set of alternatives to consider in portfolio selection, the direct use of stochastic dominance becomes infeasible.[12] However, if returns follow any of a variety of well-behaved distributions, then the use of stochastic dominance shows that portfolios can be selected in simpler ways. We have already seen that, when returns are normally distributed, stochastic dominance leads to the familiar mean-variance analysis. Bawa [12] has shown that when returns follow any two-parameter distribution, stochastic dominance can be used to derive simple two-parameter rules for portfolio selection.

Before leaving this section, it is useful to examine third-order stochastic dominance.

Figure 9.8 plots the sum of the cumulative distribution function for the example presented in Table 9.7. The sum of the cumulative frequency function can be thought of as the cumulative of the cumulative frequency function. Note that A never lies to the left of B or above B. This allows us to choose among the alternatives using second-order stochastic dominance. If the curves cross, then neither A nor B can be eliminated by second-order stochastic dominance and third-order is necessary.

Third-order stochastic dominance assumes investors exhibit decreasing absolute risk aversion. One of the properties of a function exhibiting decreasing absolute

---

[12]This drawback is not as important in other areas. For example, in looking at the selection of investment alternatives by the firm we are dealing with, a limited set of alternatives and stochastic dominance would seem to be a very useful tool.

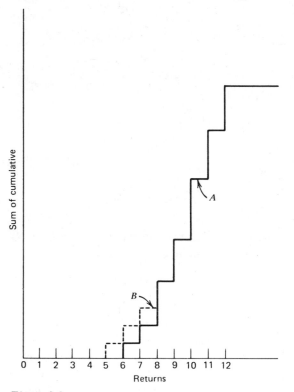

Figure 9.8

risk aversion is a positive third derivative.[13] The theorem for third-order stochastic dominance utilizes this fact. Since there are other characteristics of decreasing absolute risk aversion, a more powerful theorem awaits development.[14]

A dominates B using third-order stochastic dominance if:

1. Investors prefer more to less,

2. Investors are risk averse,

3. The third derivative of the investors utility function is positive,

4. The mean of A is greater than the mean of B, and

---

[13]A utility function exhibits decreasing absolute risk aversion. If $A'(W) < 0$ where $U'(W)$ and $U''(W)$ are the first and second derivatives of the utility function respectively, then

$$A(W) = -\frac{U''(W)}{U'(W)}$$

$$A'(W) = +\left(\frac{U''(W)}{U'(W)}\right)^2 - \frac{U'''(W)}{U'(W)}$$

The first term is positive since it is a ratio of squared terms. $U'(W) > 0$ by assumption. Therefore, for the second term to be negative, it is necessary for $U'''(W) > 0$. Note that $U'''(W)$ is a necessary, but not sufficient, condition for $A'(W) < 0$.

[14]For some distributions, such as theorem exists.

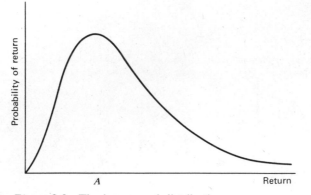

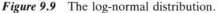

Figure 9.9   The log-normal distribution.

5. The sum of the sum of the cumulative probability distribution for all
returns is never more with A than B and sometimes less.

Columns 4 and 5 of Table 9.7 are the sums of the cumulative distributions.
Columns 6 and 7 are the sums of the sum of the cumulative distribution.

As can be seen from this table, A dominates B using third-order stochastic
dominance. This is to be expected since A dominates B under second-order
stochastic dominance and third-order is more restrictive.

The stochastic dominance analysis may seem to the reader to be a lot of analysis
with few results. Many of the results in portfolio analysis that can be obtained
from using stochastic dominance are well known and more easily obtainable in
other ways. However, stochastic dominance is a set of tools that is likely to lead
to substantial additional breakthroughs. Knowledge of these tools should help
the reader understand future research in this area.

SKEWNESS AND PORTFOLIO ANALYSIS

A number of authors have proposed selecting portfolios on the basis of the
first three moments of return distributions, rather than the first two (mean and
variance). The third moment is called skewness. Skewness is a measure of the
asymmetry of a distribution. The normal distribution has zero skewness since the
shape of the distribution above the mode is a mirror image of the shape below
the mode. The log-normal distribution shown in Figure 9.9 has positive skewness.
Point A indicates the mode or most likely value. The log-normal has more observations above this value than below. It is said to be skewed toward high values
or exhibit positive skewness. Researchers interested in skewness believe investors
should prefer positive skewness. All else constant, they should prefer portfolios
with a larger probability of very large payoffs. This is not only logical, but is also
consistent with some empirical evidence that investors exhibit this preference.[15]

---

[15]See Arditti [4] for evidence concerning investors' preferences for positive skewness. Kraus and
Litzenberger [48] have criticized Arditti for not differentiating between diversifiable and nondiversifiable skewness.

If three moments are important to the investor, then the portfolio problem is best represented in three-dimensional space with mean on one axis, variance on the second, and skewness on the third. The efficient set would be the outer shell of the feasible set with maximum mean return, minimum variance, and maximum skewness.

The skewness of a portfolio of securities is not simply a weighted average of the skewness of the component securities. Like variance, it depends on the joint movement of securities. This means that to measure the skewness on a portfolio, a great number of estimates of joint movement must be made. For these estimates to be feasible, it requires the type of model development discussed in Chapters 5 and 6 and the development of simple rules such as those discussed in Chapter 7. This developmental work has not been done. Thus, practical portfolio analysis in three moments must await development of a set of analytical techniques for estimating and solving problems involving skewness measures.[16]

CONCLUSION

In this chapter we have analyzed several alternatives to the traditional mean-variance portfolio model. Perhaps the most noteworthy point is that, if returns follow a normal distribution, many of these criteria produce optimal portfolios that lie on the mean-variance efficient frontier. This is true though some techniques like maximizing the geometric mean would, without analysis, seem to lead to very different results. Thus, if returns follow a normal distribution, the analysis performed in earlier chapters is still relevant to portfolio decision making even when the alternative decision criteria discussed in this chapter are utilized.

APPENDIX A

Safety First with Riskless Lending and Borrowing

In the text we discuss the choice of portfolios that satisfies each of the three standard formulations of the safety first criteria, assuming choices are to be made from among risky assets. In this appendix we extend the analysis to include riskless lending and borrowing.

Roy Criteria

If a riskless lending and borrowing rate exists and returns are normally distributed, then the Roy criteria leads to infinite borrowing or only investment in the riskless asset depending on the relationship between R_L and R_F.[17] Figures 9.10 and 9.11 illustrate two possible patterns.

---

[16]There are two justifications for three-moment portfolio theory. First, it is appropriate if investors have cubic utility functions. However, the cubic utility function does not always exhibit risk aversion and exhibits increasing absolute risk aversion over part of its domain. The other argument for three-moment portfolio theory is that distributions are nonnormal and the introduction of skewness better approximates the distribution. See Samuelson [78].

[17]There are an infinite number of solutions if $R_L = R_F$.

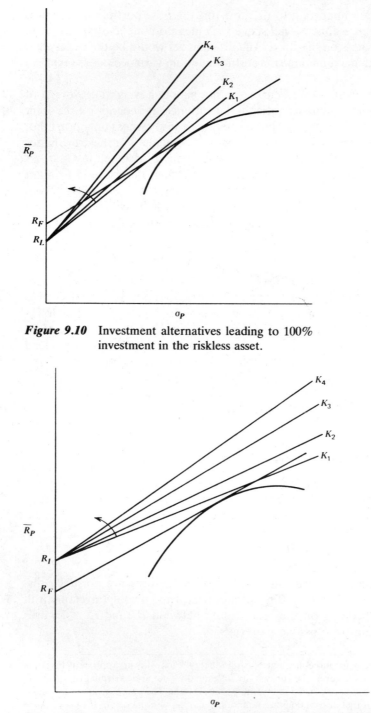

Figure 9.10   Investment alternatives leading to 100% investment in the riskless asset.

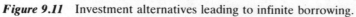

Figure 9.11   Investment alternatives leading to infinite borrowing.

In both cases the investor wishes to rotate the line passing through R_L as much as possible in the counterclockwise direction. In Figure 9.10 this leads to investing in the riskless portfolio. This makes intuitive sense. If the riskless asset yields more than R_L (as it does in Figure 9.10), then by investing in the riskless asset the investor has zero chance of obtaining a return below R_L. Since returns are assumed normally distributed, any policy involving a risky asset has some probability of a return below R_L; thus 100% investment in the riskless asset is optimal.

If R_F is below R_L, then investment in R_F guarantees a return below R_L. Examining the figure shows that borrowing an infinite amount at R_F and investing in a risky asset is optimal.

Kataoka Criteria

If lending and borrowing at the riskless rate of interest exists, then using Kataoka's criteria, the optimum policy is to invest 100% in the riskless asset or borrow an infinite amount, depending on the slope of the R_L lines in relation to the slope of the R_F line.[18] Figure 9.12 shows a situation where the optimum policy is to invest 100% in the riskless asset. (Slope of R_L lines greater than slope of lending–borrowing line.) Figure 9.13 shows a case where the optimum policy is infinite borrowing (slope of lending–borrowing line greater than slope of R_L line).

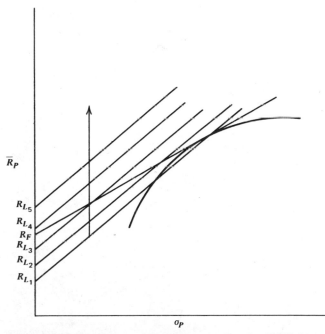

Figure 9.12 Investment alternative leading to 100% investment in riskless asset.

---

[18]There are an infinite number of solutions if the slope of the R_L lines is the same as the slope of the lending-borrowing line.

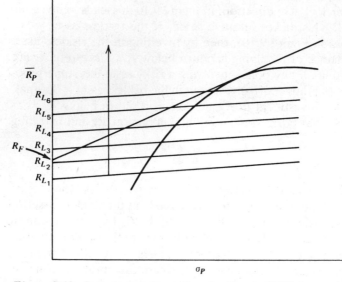

Figure 9.13   Investment alternatives leading to 100% borrowing.

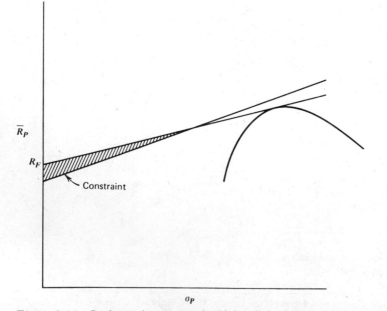

Figure 9.14   Optimum investment involving finite borrowing.

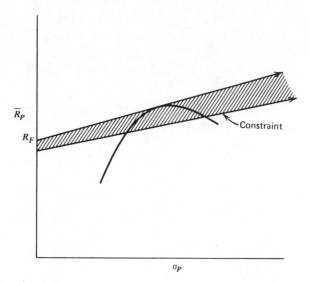

Figure 9.15   Optimum investment involving infinite
borrowing.

Telser Criteria

With riskless lending and borrowing, employing Telser's criteria leads to three possible solutions:

1. The optimum occurs at the intersection of the constraint with the lending and borrowing line.
2. The optimum occurs at infinite borrowing.
3. There is no portfolio that meets the constraint and thus no feasible solution.

Figure 9.14 shows the situation where the optimum is the intersection of the constraint with the lending and borrowing line. Figure 9.15 shows the situation where the optimum is infinite borrowing. The case where there was no feasible solution was demonstrated in Figure 9.4. The same analysis would follow with lending and borrowing at a riskless rate of interest. Once again, the optimum depends on the slope of the lending–borrowing line and the constraint.

APPENDIX B

Proof of the Sufficiency of the Stochastic Dominance Theorems.[19]

Theorem   First-order stochastic dominance. F dominates G if:

1. The investor prefers more to less $U'(X) > 0$, and

---

[19]These proofs follow Bawa [12]. For a proof of sufficiency and necessity, see Bawa [12].

2. $F(X) \leq G(X)$ for all X and $F(X) < G(X)$ for at least one value, where $F(X)$ and $G(X)$ are cumulative distribution functions of F and G, respectively.

Proof

F is preferred to G if the expected utility of distribution F is greater than the expected utility of G. The expected utility of

$$F = \int_a^b U(X) \, dF(X)$$

and the expected utility of

$$G = \int_a^b U(X) \, dG(X)$$

a and b are simply the smallest and largest values F and G can take on. Thus, for F to be preferred to G,

$$\int_a^b U(X) \, dF(X) > \int_a^b U(X) \, dG(X)$$

or

$$\int_a^b U(X) \, dF(X) - \int_a^b U(X) \, dG(X) > 0$$

Recall that $d(uw) = u \, dw + w \, du$. Integrating both sides and rearranging shows that $\int_a^b u \, dw = uw]_a^b - \int_a^b w \, du$. This expression is integration by parts. Defining u as $U(x)$ and dw as $d[F(X) - G(X)]$ and integration by parts yields

$$\int_a^b U(X) \, d[F(x) - G(x)]$$

$$= U(x)[F(x) - G(x)] \Big]_a^b - \int_a^b U'(x)[F(x) - G(x)] dx$$

$F(b) = G(b) = 1$ and $F(a) = G(a) = 0$ by definition. Thus, F dominates G if the last term is positive (i.e., the integral negative). By assumption, $U'(x)$ is positive. The integral adds up values of $U'(x)$ and $F(x) - G(x)$. For this integral to be negative no matter what pattern $U'(x)$ takes on (and, thus, for the last term to be positive), $F(x)$ must be less than or equal to $G(x)$ for all x. For it to have a value different from zero, the strict inequality must hold for some value. This completes the proof.

Theorem   Second-order stochastic dominance. F is preferred to G if:

1.   Investors prefer more to less $U'(x) > 0$,
2.   Investors are risk averse $U''(x) < 0$, and

3. $\displaystyle \int_a^b F(x) \, dx \leq \int_a^b G(x) \, dx$

for all x with the strict inequality holding for some value.

F is preferred to G if the expected utility of F is greater than the expected utility of G. In the last section we showed this is equivalent to

$$- \int_a^b U'(x)[F(x) - G(x)] \, dx < 0$$

Integrating once more by parts yields

$$- U'(x) \int_a^x [F(y) - G(y)] \, dy \Big]_a^b$$

$$+ \int_a^b U''(x) \int_a^x [F(y) - G(y)] \, dy \, dx$$

or

$$- U'(b) \int_a^b [F(y) - G(y)] \, dy$$

$$+ \int_a^b U''(x) \int_a^x [F(y) - G(y)] \, dy \, dx$$

$U'(b) > 0$ by definition. Therefore, the first term is positive if the integral is negative. $U''(x) < 0$ by definition. Thus the second term is positive if the integral is negative or zero for all values of X. For the terms to be nonzero, the integral must be strictly negative for at least one value of X. The theorem is proven.

Theorem   The theorem for third-order stochastic dominance is F dominates G if:

1.   Investors prefer more to less $U'(x) > 0$,
2.   Investors are risk averse $U''(x) < 0$,
3.   The third derivative of the utility function is positive $U'''(x) > 0$,
4.   The mean of F is greater than the mean of G, and

5. $\displaystyle \int_a^b \int_a^x [F(y) - G(y)] \, dx \, dy \leq 0$

for all x and the strict inequality holds for some value.

Proof

F dominates G if the expected utility of F is greater than the expected utility of G. In the last section this required that

$$- U'(b) \int_a^b [F(y) - G(y)] \, dy + \int_a^b U''(x) \int_a^x [F(y) - G(y)] \, dy \, dx > 0$$

Integrating the second term by parts yields

$$- U'(b) \int_a^b [F(y) - G(y)] \, dy + U''(b) \int_a^b \int_a^b [F(y) - G(y)] \, dy \, dx$$

$$- \int_a^b U'''(x) \int_a^b \int_a^x [F(y) - G(y)] \, dy \, dx$$

Note that

$$\int_a^b [F(y) - G(y)] \, dy$$

is the difference in means between G and F. Since, by assumption, the mean of G is less than the mean of F, this is negative. $U'(x) > 0$ by assumption; thus the first term is positive. Similarly, $U''(x) < 0$ and $U''' > 0$; thus the last two terms are positive if the double integral is negative. This completes the proof.

QUESTIONS AND PROBLEMS

1. Consider the following investments. What can be said about their desirability using first- or second-order stochastic dominance?

A		B		C	
Probability	Outcome	Probability	Outcome	Probability	Outcome
0.2	4	0.1	5	0.4	6
0.3	6	0.3	6	0.3	7
0.4	8	0.2	7	0.2	8
0.1	10	0.3	8	0.1	10
		0.1	9		

2. If R_L equals 5%, what is the preferred investment shown in Problem 1 using Roy's safety first criterion?

3. If α equals 10%, what is the preferred investment shown in Problem 1 using Kataoka's safety first criterion?

4. If $R_L = 5\%$ and $\alpha = 10\%$, what is the preferred investment shown in Problem 1 using Telser's safety first criterion?

5. Using geometric mean return as a criterion, which investment is to be preferred in Problem 1?

BIBLIOGRAPHY

1. Alderfer, Clayton, and Bierman, Harold. "Choices with Risk: Beyond the Mean and Variance," *Journal of Business,* **43,** No. 3 (July 1970), pp. 341–353.
2. Ali, Mukhtar. "Stochastic Dominance and Portfolio Analysis," *Journal of Financial Economics,* **2,** No. 2 (June 1975), pp. 205–230.
3. Ang, James. "A Note on the E, SL Portfolio Selection Model," *Journal of Finance and Quantitative Analysis,* **X,** No. 5 (Dec. 1975), pp. 849–857.
4. Arditti, Fred. "Risk and the Required Return on Equity," *Journal of Finance,* **XXII,** No. 1 (March 1967), pp. 19–36.
5. ———. "Skewness and Investors' Decisions: A Reply," *Journal of Financial and Quantitative Analysis,* **X,** No. 1 (March 1975), pp. 173–176.
6. Arditti, Fred, and Levy, Haim. "Distribution Moments and Equilibrium: A Comment," *Journal of Financial and Quantitative Analysis,* **VII,** No. 1 (Jan. 1972), pp. 1429–1433.
7. ———. "Portfolio Efficiency Analysis in Three Moments: The Multiperiod Case," *Journal of Finance,* **XXX,** No. 3 (June 1975), pp. 797–809.
8. Arzac, Enrique. "Utility Analysis of Change-Constrained Portfolio Selection," *Journal of Financial and Quantitative Analysis,* **IX,** No. 6 (Dec. 1974), pp. 993–1007.
9. ———. "Utility Analysis of Chance-Constrained Portfolio Selection: A Correction," *Journal of Financial and Quantitative Analysis,* **XII,** No. 2 (June 1977), pp. 321–323.
10. Aucamp, Donald. "A Comment on Geometric Mean Portfolios," *Management Science,* **24,** No. 8 (April 1978), pp. 859–868.
11. Banz, Rolf, and Miller, Merton. "Prices for State-Contingent Claims: Some Estimates and Applications," *Journal of Business,* **51,** No. 4 (Oct. 1978), pp. 653–672.
12. Bawa, Vijay. "Optimal Rules for Ordering Uncertain Prospects," *Journal of Financial Economics,* **2,** (1975), pp. 95–121.
13. ———. "Safety-First, Stochastic Dominance, and Optimal Portfolio Choice," *Journal of Financial and Quantitative Analysis,* **XIII,** No. 2 (June 1978), pp. 255–271.
14. Bawa, Vijay B., Bodurtha, James N., Jr., Rao, M.R., and Suri, Hira L. "On Determination of Stochastic Dominance Optimal Sets," *The Journal of Finance,* **40,** No. 2 (June 1985), pp. 417–432.
15. Bey, Roger P., and Howe, Keith M. "Gini's Mean Difference and Portfolio Selection: An Empirical Evaluation," *Journal of Financial and Quantitative Analysis,* **XIX,** No. 3 (Sept. 1984), pp. 329–338.

16. Brennan, Michael J., and Schwartz, Eduardo S. "On the Geometric Mean Index: A Note," *Journal of Financial and Quantitative Analysis*, **XX,** No. 1 (March 1985), pp. 119–122.
17. Brieman, Leon. "Investment Policies for Expanding Businesses Optimal in A Long Run Sense," *Naval Research Logistics Quarterly*, **7,** (Dec. 1960), pp. 647–651.
18. Cheng, Lee. "Functional Form, Skewness Effect, and the Risk-Return Relationship," *Journal of Financial and Quantitative Analysis*, **XII,** No. 1 (March 1977), pp. 55–72.
19. Cheng, Pao, and Deets, King. "Test of Portfolio Building Rules: Comment" *Journal of Finance*, **XXVI,** No. 4 (Sept. 1971), pp. 965–972.
20. Conine, Thomas E., Jr., and Tamarkin, Maurry J. "On Diversification Given Asymmetry in Returns," *The Journal of Finance*, **36,** No. 5 (Dec. 1981), pp. 1143–1156.
21. Ekern, Steinar. "Time Dominance Efficiency Analysis," *The Journal of Finance*, **36,** No. 5 (Dec. 1981), pp. 1023–1034.
22. Elton, Edwin J., and Gruber, Martin J. "On the Optimality of Some Multiperiod Portfolio Selection Criteria," *Journal of Business*, **47,** No. 2 (April 1974), pp. 231–243.
23. ———. "An Algorithm for Maximizing the Geometric Mean." *Management Science* (Dec. 1974), pp. 483–488.
24. Fama, Eugene, and Macbeth, James. "Long-Term Growth in a Short Term Market," *Journal of Finance*, **XXIX,** No. 3 (June 1974), pp. 857–885.
25. Fishburn, Peter. "Mean-Risk Analysis with Risk Associated with Below-Target Returns," *American Economic Review*, **67,** No. 2 (March 1977), pp. 116–126.
26. Francis, Jack Clark. "Skewness and Investors' Decisions," *Journal of Financial and Quantitative Analysis*, **X,** No. 1 (March 1975), pp. 163–172.
27. Frankfurther, George, and Phillips, Herbert. "Efficient . . . : Comment," *Journal of Financial and Quantitative Analysis*, **X,** No. 1 (March 1975), pp. 177–179.
28. Granito, Michael, and Walsh, Patrick. "Portfolio Efficiency Analysis in Three Moments — The Multiperiod Case: Comment," *Journal of Finance*, **XXXIII,** No. 1 (March 1978), pp. 345–361.
29. Grauer, Robert R. "A Comparison of Growth Optimal and Mean Variance Investment Policies," *Journal of Financial and Quantitative Analysis*, **XVI,** No. 1 (March 1981), pp. 1–22.
30. Hadar, Josef, and Russel, William. "Stochastic Dominance and Diversification," *Journal of Economic Theory*, **3,** No. 3 (Sept. 1971), pp. 288–305.
31. Hakansson, Nils. "Comment on Merton and Samuelson," *Journal of Financial Economics*, **1,** No. 1 (May 1974), pp. 950–970.
32. ———. "Capital Growth and the Mean-Variance Approach to Portfolio Selection," *Journal of Financial and Quantitative Analysis*, **VI,** No. 1 (Jan. 1971), pp. 517–557.
33. Hakansson, Nils, and Ching Liu Tien. "Optimal Growth Portfolios When

Yields Are Serially Correlated," *Review of Economics and Statistics*, **LII,** No. 4 (Nov. 1970), pp. 385–394.

34. Hakansson, Nils, and Miller, Bruce. "Compound-Return Mean-Variance Portfolios Never Risk Ruin," *Management Science,* **22,** No. 4 (Dec. 1975), pp. 391–400.

35. Hanoch, Giora, and Levy, Haim. "Efficient Portfolio Selection with Quadratic and Cubic Utility," *Journal of Business,* **43,** No. 2 (April 1970), pp. 191–198.

36. Hanssmann, Fred. "Probability of Survival as an Investment Criterion," *Management Science,* **15,** No. 1 (Sept. 1968), pp. 33–48.

37. Hogan, William, and Warren, James. "Computation of the Efficient Boundary in the E–S Portfolio Selection Model," *Journal of Financial and Quantitative Analysis,* **VII,** No. 4 (Sept. 1972), pp. 1881–1896.

38. Jahankhani, Ali. "E–V and E–S Capital Asset Pricing Models: Some Empirical Tests," *Journal of Financial and Quantitative Analysis,* **XI,** No. 4 (Nov. 1976), pp. 513–528.

39. Jean, William. "The Extension of Portfolio Analysis to Three or More Parameters," *Journal of Financial and Quantitative Analysis,* **VI,** No. 1 (Jan. 1971), pp. 505–515.

40. ———. "Distribution Moments and Equilibrium: Reply," *Journal of Financial and Quantitative Analysis,* **VII,** No. 1 (Jan. 1972), pp. 1435–1437.

41. ———. "More on Multidimensional Portfolio Analysis," *Journal of Financial and Quantitative Analysis,* **VIII,** No. 3 (June 1973), pp. 475–490.

42. ———. "A General Class of Three-Parameter Risk Measures: Comment," *Journal of Finance,* **XXX,** No. 1 (March 1975), pp. 224–225.

43. Jean, William H. "The Geometric Mean and Stochastic Dominance," *The Journal of Finance,* **35,** No. 1 (March 1980), pp. 151–158.

44. Jean, William H. and Helms, Billy P. "Geometric Mean Approximations," *Journal of Financial and Quantitative Analysis,* **XVIII,** No. 3 (Sept. 1983), pp. 287–294.

45. Johnson, Keith, and Burgess, Richard. "The Effects of Sample Sizes on the Accuracy of EV and SSD Efficiency Criteria," *Journal of Financial and Quantitative Analysis,* **X,** No. 5 (Dec. 1975), pp. 813–830.

46. Jones, E. Irwin. "Test of Portfolio Building Rules: Comment," *Journal of Finance,* **XXVI,** No. 4 (Sept. 1971), pp. 973–975.

47. Kane, Alex. "Skewness Preference and Portfolio Choice," *Journal of Financial and Quantitative Analysis,* **XVII,** No. 1 (March 1982), pp. 15–26.

48. Kraus, Alan, and Litzenburger, Robert. "Skewness Preference and the Valuation of Risky Assets," *Journal of Finance,* **21,** No. 4 (Sept. 1976), pp. 1085–1094.

49. Kumar, P., Philippatos, G., and Ezzell, J. "Goal Programming and the Selection of Portfolios by Dual-Purpose Funds," *Journal of Finance,* **XXXIII,** No. 1, (March 1978), pp. 303–310.

50. Latane, Henry. "Criteria for Choice Among Risky Ventures," *Journal of Political Economy* (April 1959), pp. 144–155.

51. Latane, Henry, and Young, E. Williams, "Test of Portfolio Building Rules," *Journal of Finance,* **XXIV,** No. 4 (Sept. 1969), pp. 595–612.

52. ———. "A Reply," *Journal of Finance,* **XXVI,** No. 4 (Sept. 1971), pp. 976–981.

53. Levy, Haim. "Stochastic Dominance, Efficiency Criteria, and Efficient Portfolios: The Multi-Period Case," *American Economic Review,* **LXIII,** No. 5 (Dec. 1973), pp. 986–994.

54. Levy, Haim. "Stochastic Dominance Rules for Truncated Normal Distributions: A Note," *The Journal of Finance,* **37,** No. 4 (Sept. 1982), pp. 1299–1304.

55. Levy, Haim, and Hanoch, Giora. "Relative Effectiveness of Efficiency Criteria for Portfolio Selection," *Journal of Financial and Quantitative Analysis,* **V,** No. 1 (March 1970), pp. 63–76.

56. Levy, Haim, and Kroll, Yoram. "Stochastic Dominance with Riskless Assets," *Journal of Financial and Quantitative Analysis,* **XI,** No. 5 (Dec. 1976), pp. 743–777.

57. Levy, Haim, and Sarnat, Marshall. "Alternative Efficiency Criteria: An Empirical Analysis," *Journal of Finance,* **XXV,** No. 5 (Dec. 1970), pp. 1153–1158.

58. ———. "Two-Period Portfolio Selection and Investors' Discount Rates," *Journal of Finance,* **XXVI,** No. 3 (June 1971), pp. 757–761.

59. Litzenberger, Robert, and Budd, A.P. "A Note on Geometric Mean Portfolio Selection and the Market Prices of Equities," *Journal of Financial and Quantitative Analysis,* **VI,** No. 5 (Dec. 1971), pp. 1277–1282.

60. Maier, Steven, Peterson, David, and Vanderweide, James. "A Monte Carlo Investigation of Characteristics of Optimal Geometric Mean Portfolios," *Journal of Financial and Quantitative Analysis,* **XII,** No. 2 (June 1977), pp. 215–233.

61. Markowitz, Harry. "Investment for the Long-Run: New Evidence for an Old Rule," *Journal of Finance,* **XXXI,** No. 5 (Dec. 1976), pp. 1273–1286.

62. ———. Portfolio Selection Efficient Diversification of Investments (New York: John Wiley & Sons, 1959).

63. Merton, Robert. "Lifetime Portfolio Selection Under Uncertainty: The Continuous Time Case," *Review of Economics and Statistics,* **LI,** No. 3 (Aug. 1969), pp. 247–257.

64. ———. "Optimum Consumption and Portfolio Rules in a Continuous-Time Model," *Journal of Economic Theory,* **3,** No. 4 (Dec. 1971), pp. 373–413.

65. Ohlson, James. "Quadratic Approximations of the Portfolio Selection Problem When the Means and Variances Are Infinite." *Management Science,* **23,** No. 6 (Feb. 1977), pp. 576–584.

66. Owen, Joel, and Ravinovitch, Ramon. "On the Class of Elliptical Distributions and Their Applications to the Theory of Portfolio Choice," *The Journal of Finance,* **38,** No. 3 (June 1983), pp. 745–752.

67. Perrakis, Stylianos, and Zerbinis, John. "Identifying the SSD Portion of the EV Frontier: A Note," *Journal of Financial and Quantitative Analysis,* **XIII,** No. 1 (March 1978), pp. 167–171.

68. Philippatos, Goerge, and Gressis, Nicolas. "Conditions of Equivalence Among E-V, SSD, and E-H Portfolio Selection Criteria; The Case for Uniform, Normal, and Lognormal Distributions," *Management Science*, **21,** No. 6 (Feb. 1975), pp. 617–625.

69. Porter, Burr. "An Empirical Comparison of Stochastic Dominance and Mean-Variance Portfolio Choice Criteria," *Journal of Financial and Quantitative Analysis*, **VIII,** No. 4 (Sept. 1973), pp. 587–608.

70. ———. "Semivariance and Stochastic Dominance: A Comparison," *American Economic Review*, **LXIV,** No. 1 (March 1974), pp. 200–204.

71. Price, Kelly, Price, Barbara, and Nantell, Timothy J. "Variance and Lower Partial Moment Measures of Systematic Risk: Some Analytical and Empirical Results," *The Journal of Finance*, **37,** No. 3 (June 1982), pp. 843–906.

72. Pye, Gordon. "Minimax Portfolio Policies," *Financial Analysts Journal*, **28,** No. 2 (March–April 1972), pp. 56–60.

73. Pyle, David, and Turnovsky, Stephen. "Risk Aversion in Chance Constrained Portfolio Selection," *Management Science*, **18,** No. 3 (Nov. 1971), pp. 218–225.

74. ———. "Safety-First and Expected Utility Maximization in Mean-Standard Deviation Portfolio Analysis," *Review of Economics and Statistics*, **LII,** No. 1 (Feb. 1970), pp. 75–81.

75. Rentz, William, and Westin, Richard. "A Note on First-Degree Stochastic Dominance and Portfolio Composition," *Management Science*, **22,** No. 4 (Dec. 1975), pp. 501–504.

76. Roll, Richard. "Evidence on the 'Growth-Optimum' Model," *Journal of Finance*, **XXVIII,** No. 3 (June 1973), pp. 551–556.

77. Roy, A.D. "Safety-First and the Holding of Assets," *Econometrics*, **20** (July 1952), pp. 431–449.

78. Samuelson, Paul. "The Fundamental Approximation Theorem of Portfolio Analysis in Terms of Means Variances and Higher Moments," *Review of Economic Studies*, **25** (Feb. 1958), pp. 65–86.

79. Saunders, Anthony, Ward, Charles, and Woodward, Richard. "Stochastic Dominance and the Performance of U.K. Unit Trusts," *Journal of Financial and Quantitative Analysis*, **XV,** No. 2 (June 1980), pp. 323–330.

80. Shalit, Haim, and Yitzhaki, Shlomo. "Mean-Gine, Portfolio Theory and the Pricing of Risky Assets," *The Journal of Finance*, **39,** No. 5 (Dec. 1984), pp. 1449–1468.

81. Stein, William, Pfaffenberg, Roger, and Kumar, P.C. "On the Estimation Risk in First-Order Stochastic Dominance: A Note," *Journal of Financial and Quantitative Analysis*, **XVIII,** No. 4 (Dec. 1983), pp. 471–476.

82. Tehranian, Hassan, and Helms, Billy P. "An Empirical Comparison of Stochastic Dominance among Lognormal Prospects," *Journal of Financial and Quantitative Analysis*, **XVII,** No. 2 (June 1982), pp. 217–226.

83. Vanderweide, James, Peterson, David, and Maier, Steven. "A Strategy Which Maximizes the Geometric Mean Return on Portfolio Investments," *Management Science*, **23,** No. 10 (June 1977), pp. 1117–1123.

84. ———. "Reply to Aucamp," *Management Science.* **24,** No. 8 (April 1978), p. 860.
85. Vickson, R.G. "Stochastic Dominance for Decreasing Absolute Risk Aversion," *Journal of Financial and Quantitative Analysis,* **X,** No. 5, (Dec. 1975), pp. 799–811.
86. Young, Williams, and Trent, Roberts. "Geometric Mean Approximations of Individual Securities and Portfolio Performance," *Journal of Financial and Quantitative Analysis,* **IV,** No. 2 (June 1969), pp. 179–199.
87. Ziemba, William. "Note on 'Optimal Growth Portfolios When Yields Are Serially Correlated'," *Journal of Financial and Quantitative Analysis,* **VII,** No. 4 (Sept. 1972), pp. 1995–2000.

SECTION 4

Widening the Selection Universe

Chapter 10

International Diversification

Portfolio managers in France, Germany, and England routinely include securities from other countries in their portfolios. Foreign securities are infrequently found in the portfolios of U.S. investors. Is this provincialism on the part of U.S. managers or are there sound economic reasons? In this chapter we try to present enough information so that readers can decide for themselves.

In the first section we examine the correlation between U.S. and foreign securities. It turns out that the correlation between securities from different countries is much less than the correlation between securities from the same country. This suggests that portfolios that include securities from several countries should have less risk than those containing securities from a single country. Given that risk can be lowered, what happens to return? This is the subject of the second section. In the third section we examine the impact of exchange risk on the rewards from international diversification. Changes in currency exchange rates make the return and risk characteristics of English securities different for the French investor than they are for the U.S. investor. Changes in exchange rates are an added element of risk and return. Having looked at risk and return from holding foreign securities, it is useful to examine the actual performance of portfolios with large components of foreign securities. Do these outperform portfolios that contain only domestic securities?

THE RISK OF FOREIGN SECURITIES

Table 10.1 presents the correlation between the equity markets of several countries for the period 1963–72. These correlation coefficients have been computed using weekly returns on market indexes. For example, the U.S. is represented by the Dow Jones Industrial Index. All returns have been converted to U.S. dollars at prevailing exchange rates before correlations were calculated. Thus, the table presents the correlation from the point of view of a U.S. investor. These are remarkably low correlation coefficients. The average correlation coefficient between a pair of U.S. securities is about 0.40, and the correlation between indices is even higher. For example, the correlation between an index of the New York Stock Exchange and the American Stock Exchange is well above 0.90. The correlation coefficient between two 100-security portfolios drawn at random from the New York Stock Exchange is on the order of 0.95. The numbers in the table are much smaller than this, with the average correlation being 0.133. The results shown in Table 10.1 are typical of dozens of other similar studies. This type of evidence strongly suggests that international diversification can lead to lower risk portfolios for the investor.

Table 10.1

	Australia	Austria	Belgium	Canada	France	Italy	Japan	Netherlands	Switzerland	U.K.	W. Germany	U.S.
Australia												
Austria	.013											
Belgium	.117	.044										
Canada	.167	.058	.179									
France	.082	.069	.177	.163								
Italy	.022	.011	.079	.060	.012							
Japan	.086	.071	.086	.192	.106	.102						
Netherlands	.134	.038	.232	.361	.158	.098	.167					
Switzerland	.173	.045	.164	.289	.148	.174	.192	.283				
U.K.	.171	.034	.093	.146	.039	.078	.110	.131	.002			
W. Germany	.106	.072	.186	.201	.153	.050	.113	.357	.207	.030		
U.S.	.137	.027	.205	.634	.107	.002	.092	.344	.242	.096	.163	

Correlations between various markets

Source: O. Maurice Joy, Don B. Panton, Frank K. Reilly, and Stanley A. Martin [17].

A second way to analyze the question of risk is to compare the risk of portfolios of different size selected from an international group of stocks with the risk when the selection is from domestic stocks. Is there less risk with a portfolio of internationally diversified securities? How do the risks on the two types of portfolios change as the number of securities in each portfolio is increased? Figure 10.1 from Solnik [37] provides some evidence on these issues. The horizontal axis lists the number of stocks in the portfolio. The vertical axis shows the risk of the portfolio expressed as a percentage of the average risk of an individual stock.[1]

---

[1]The average is taken over the full sample of both U.S. and foreign stocks and is the same for both portfolios.

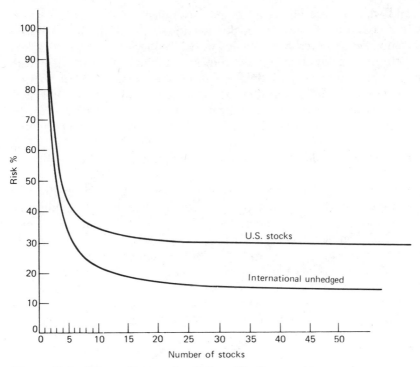

Figure 10.1 Effect of international diversification on risk.

A number of 20% implies that the portfolios is 20% as risky as an individual security. Two curves are shown, one for purchase of a portfolio of U.S. stocks and one for a portfolio of internationally diversified securities. All returns are converted into dollars. Thus, the figure is from the point of view of a U.S. investor. These are average results. Thus, the figure shown for a portfolio of 20 securities is the average of a large number of 20-security portfolios, each selected at random from the relevant population. The curve for U.S. stocks assumes equal investment in a randomly selected set of U.S. stocks. The curve for internationally diversified portfolios assumes equal investment in each stock and an equal likelihood of selecting any country's stock. The results are dramatic.

Diversification across countries produces a less risky portfolio than intra-country diversification. Note that this is true for any size portfolio. As portfolio size increases, risk asymptotically approaches a particular value. This is the risk on a fully diversified portfolio. From the graph the risk of a fully diversified domestic portfolio is 27% of the risk on a typical stock. The risk on an internationally fully diversified portfolio is 11.7% of the risk on a typical stock.

The countries included in this study, other than the U.S., are the United Kingdom, France, Germany, Italy, Belgium, Netherlands, and Switzerland. If countries from other areas of the world, such as Japan and South America, were included, the results would be even more dramatic.

One possible explanation for these results is that countries are a proxy for industries and what we are observing is the advantages of diversifying across industries, not countries. For example, this would be true if all German firms were steel companies and French companies were all wineries. In this case Solnik could be confusing the lowering of risk from international diversification with the lowering of risk from industry diversification. An examination of Solnik's data shows that the firms in one country are not primarily all from one industry. In addition, he checked whether diversification across industries affected the comparison. This was accomplished by forcing selection across industries in both the samples of U.S. stocks and the internationally diversified sample. Solnik found both curves shifted down, but the relative ranking remained roughly the same.

A third way to examine the reduction in risk from international diversification is to examine the importance of national security markets in determining the variability of security returns. To understand this viewpoint consider, for a moment, an investor confined to the U.S. market. Initially, assume that security returns are determined by economy-wide movements, industry movements, and the prospects of the company. For example, assume that the return on a steel stock depends on what happens in the economy, in the steel industry, and the unique prospects of the company. Likewise, assume that the return from a chemical stock depends on what happens in the economy, the chemical industry, and the unique prospects of the company.

If an investor confined his portfolio to steel stocks, then the risk on his portfolio would be related to both market risk and the risk of the steel industry. In a large enough portfolio the unique risk would be essentially zero. However, the risk due to market movements and the risk due to changes in the steel industry would remain.

In contrast, the investor could hold stocks from a number of different industries. In this case in a large portfolio not only would the unique risk be very small but so would the industry risk. The only remaining risk would be the market risk.

Insofar as industry risk is very small, relative to market risk, specialization in an industry and being subject to industry risk increases total risk very little. If, however, the industry risk is very large relative to the market risk, then the investor who specializes in one industry has a portfolio with substantially more risk. Thus, to understand the risk reduction caused by diversifying across industries, it is helpful to examine the importance of industry effects compared to market effects in determining the variability of security returns.

The same considerations follow when analyzing the effect of concentrating in domestic securities rather than diversifying internationally. Investors who restrict their purchases to domestic securities would bear additional risk versus those who held an internationally diversified portfolio. The greater the importance of the country factor relative to the world factor, the greater the additional risk resulting from specializing in domestic securities. Table 10.2, taken from Lessard [21], gives some indication of how much of the variance of the return on stocks is explained by a world index and how much is explained by a country's index. More specifically, he examined the proportion of the variance of the return for stocks in each of several countries explained by a world index. He also examined the proportion of the variance explained by each national index after the effects of the world index had been removed.

Table 10.2 World and Country Contributions to Variance of Individual Securities

Stocks Grouped by Country	Average Proportion of Variance Explained by		Average Proportion of Variance Explained by	
	Market Value — Weighted World Index	Country Index[a]	Equally Weighted World Index	Country Index[a]
Australia	0.107	0.250	0.168	0.197
Austria	0.013	0.097	0.131	0.264
Belgium	0.055	0.444	0.320	0.180
Denmark	0.051	0.280	0.148	0.191
France	0.028	0.437	0.256	0.211
Germany	0.086	0.366	0.275	0.169
Italy	0.012	0.427	0.062	0.356
Japan	0.088	0.190	0.129	0.156
Netherlands	0.188	0.221	0.344	0.079
Norway	0.008	0.457	0.188	0.294
Spain	0.011	0.393	0.110	0.311
Sweden	0.069	0.356	0.165	0.260
Switzerland	0.161	0.363	0.387	0.141
U.K.	0.084	0.297	0.100	0.287

[a]After removing the effect of the world index.

Lessard used two definitions of the world index in his analysis. The first weights the return on a country's stocks by the ratio of the market value of that country's stock to the total market value of all stocks. Because of the huge size of the stock market in the U.S. relative to its size in other countries, this index might overstate the importance of U.S. returns. Certainly, if the U.S. stocks were weighted by some other measure of economic activity, for example, GNP or trade, the U.S. would have less of an impact on the index. To compensate for this, Lessard examined an equally weighted world index, along with the market weighted world index. The former probably underestimates the importance of U.S. stocks while the latter overestimates its importance.

Lessard's [21] results are summarized in Table 10.2. For either definition of the world index, a large fraction of the variance of an individual security is related to its country index. For example, we see that when a market-weighted world index is used, the world index accounts for 10.7% of the variance of a typical Australian stock, while an additional 25% is explained by the index of Australian stocks. When the equally weighted world index is used, these numbers are 16.8% for the market index and 19.7% for the Australian index.[2]

The evidence suggests strongly that while a world index is important in ac-

---

[2]As suggested before, these numbers change because of a change in the definition of the world index. A market-weighted index overstates the importance of the U.S. market while an equally weighted average underestimates it.

counting for risk, country factors are also of great importance. Thus, investors who concentrate on the securities of one country bear substantial additional risk.

The evidence discussed in this section has led most observers to believe that the risk of internationally diversified portfolios is much lower than the risk of portfolios diversified within national boundaries.[3] The question still remains whether an investor will be rewarded for bearing this greater risk of holding a domestic portfolio by greater expected returns. This is examined in the subsequent section of this chapter.

RETURNS FROM INTERNATIONALLY DIVERSIFIED PORTFOLIOS

Most studies attempt to show the advantages of international diversification by forming an optimal portfolio of international securities using historical data and comparing the return to a domestically held portfolio over the same time period. An example of this is shown in Figure 10.2. Note that the portfolio of U.S. stocks is not on the efficient frontier. This analysis suggests that if one had perfect forecasts of return and variance, one would have held an international portfolio. While this is interesting, it does not provide evidence that, short of perfect forecasting ability, we should hold an internationally diversified portfolio.[4]

To gain a better understanding of the returns from international diversification, we should examine the structure of returns themselves and relate this to risk. We will make the logical assumption that expected returns are related to risk.[5]

We analyze two extremes. First, we assume that the expected returns on individual securities are determined by their risk in the domestic market. Second, we assume the expected returns are set by risks in the world market. Although these assumptions are extreme, they allow us to understand what happens in less extreme circumstances. Assume that each security's expected return is determined in its domestic market. This could describe reality if investors could not or did not diversify internationally. If investors were restricted to the domestic market, then the relevant measure of risk arises from the domestic market. The reader can envision a model where a security's return depends on its risk and where risk is determined by the relationship of the security to its national index[6] (the familiar Beta of Chapter 5). If this describes the determination of expected returns, then

---

[3]Recently, there has been great concern about the relationship between an investor's consumption choices and returns on securities. For example, all the tables converted returns to U.S. dollars. If an investor had an international consumption basket, this might be an inappropriate conversion. Likewise, if returns on U.S. securities are positively correlated with U.S. prices, the evidence just discussed might overstate the risk reduction of international diversification in real terms.

[4]In fact, if one had perfect forecasting ability of stock market indexes, one would not hold an internationally diversified portfolio: one would simply buy the stocks from the country that will have the highest rate of return.

[5]We introduced the relationship between return and risk in Chapter 5. We study this relationship more formally in Chapters 11, 12, and 13.

[6]The security market line discussed in Chapter 11 is consistent with this assumption.

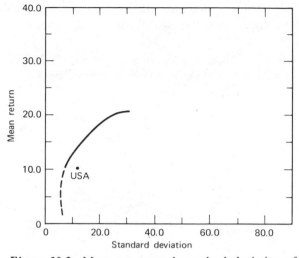

Figure 10.2   Mean return and standard deviation of
return of a portfolio of U.S. stocks and a
set of U.S. and international stocks.

by diversifying internationally, the investor can eliminate much of the risk inherent in the domestic market. To understand what happens to the return, consider first the investors in two countries. If the expected returns in the two
countries were the same, then investors in both countries would gain by diversifying internationally because the risk would be lower without affecting expected
return. If the returns were different, then it would still be possible for both to
gain but clearly one investor gains more. Table 10.3 illustrates this idea. This
table, derived from Lessard [21], shows the minimum expected return necessary
on a foreign stock to make it attractive to U.S. investors, under the assumption
that markets are totally segmented.[7] Two different returns on U.S. securities are
assumed, 10% and 15%. For example, as shown in the table, if Australian stocks
have an expected return of more than 7.776%, they are attractive to U.S. investors, even though the expected return on U.S. securities is 10%. As can be seen
from examining the table, because of low correlation between markets, the expected return in a foreign market can be less than the expected return in the
U.S. market and foreign securities still can be attractive to U.S. investors.[8] The
size of these numbers depends on the method of computing correlation coefficients. However, the correlation coefficients are generally small and these numbers are representative of expected returns. If markets are segmented, the ex-

---

[7]The figures in this table are based on correlation estimates from a single-index model using the
market-weighted world index. If a different index or model had been used, the numbers would be
different.

[8]These results assume portfolios of securities of two countries at a time. If we considered larger
portfolios, the numbers would be reduced.

pected return on foreign securities must be much lower than the expected return on domestic securities or international diversification will pay.

Table 10.3 Return on Foreign Securities Necessary to Justify Investment if the Return on U.S. Securities is 10% or 15% and the Riskless Rate of Interest is 6%

	Return on U.S. Securities	
	10%	15%
Australia	7.776	9.996
Austria	6.832	7.872
Belgium	6.552	9.942
Canada	9.020	12.795
Denmark	6.320	6.720
France	7.600	9.600
Germany	8.756	12.201
Italy	7.612	9.627
Japan	7.560	9.510
Netherlands	9.004	12.759
Norway	6.676	7.521
Spain	6.240	6.540
Sweden	7.480	9.330
Switzerland	9.048.	12.858
U.K.	7.960	10.410

Now let us consider the other extreme: capital markets are fully integrated and a security's return is determined by a world index. For example, the expected return on a security could be related to its risk where risk is determined by its sensitivity to a world index. In this case investors specializing in domestic securities would be subjecting themselves to high risk without corresponding return simply because they are bearing diversifiable risk. Table 10.4, from Lessard [21], shows the extra return an investor would gain by investing in an international portfolio of equivalent risk to the domestic. As Lessard recognizes, the 31 cents shown for U.S. investors should be accepted with a caution. The author, who calculated this table, used an international index dominated by U.S. securities and probably overstated the importance of the U.S. market in the the world economy. Much more representative of the additional return from international diversification are the entries next to the other countries.

While there appear to be extra returns from international diversification whether markets are fully integrated or totally segmented based on both theory and empirical evidence, the gains would be greater if markets were fully segmented. While it is difficult to measure the extent of segmentation, recent empirical work strongly suggests that the extent of integration lies somewhere between the two extremes we have discussed.[9]

The reader should be cautioned about drawing too strong a conclusion from

[9]See Stehle [43].

Tables 10.3 and 10.4. They represent one sample from one time period, although they are probably representative. Much more work is necessary to establish this.

Table 10.4

Country	Loss in Return from Holding Domestic Portfolio
Australia	4.06
Austria	3.88
Belgium	2.08
Canada	0.85
Denmark	3.96
France	4.47
Germany	3.87
Italy	6.14
Japan	5.01
Netherlands	1.83
Norway	5.19
Spain	4.50
Sweden	3.27
Switzerland	3.22
U.K.	3.30
U.S.A.	0.31

We argued in the first section that international diversification lowers risk. In this section we have shown that returns in foreign markets have to be much lower than returns in the domestic market or international diversification pays. However, what is foreign to one investor is domestic to another. Are there any circumstances where international diversification does not pay for investors of all countries?

To understand this issue, consider the U.S. and U.K. markets and refer to Table 10.3. This table assumes returns are set in the domestic market and shows that if the return in the U.K. market was not less than 7.96% when returns in the U.S. market are 10%, a U.S. investor should purchase some U.K. securities. Furthermore, it is easy to show that if a U.K. investor expected returns in the U.K. to be less than the U.S., then the U.K. investor should purchase U.S. stocks. If investors in the two markets agree on expected returns, we have one of three situations: both gain from diversification, the U.S. investor gains, or the U.K. investor gains. However, in all three cases some investor should diversify internationally. If the investors do not agree on returns in the two markets, then it is possible for international diversification not to pay for both U.S. and U.K. investors. For example, assume U.S. investors believed U.K. markets would yield 5% while U.S. markets would yield 10%. Further assume U.K. investors believe U.K. markets will yield 10% while U.S. markets will yield 5%. Are there any circumstances in which this is sensible? The answer is *yes*.

If governments tax foreign investments at very different rates than domestic investments, then the pattern just discussed would be possible. Differential taxation has occurred in the past and will likely occur again. A second situation that could produce the return pattern discussed before is if there were differential transaction costs for domestic and foreign purchases. This could occur if there was difficulty in purchasing foreign securities or currency controls. For example, there may be restrictions in converting domestic to foreign currency that could affect returns. The exchange rate of currency A for B might be at an official rate higher than the free market rate and there might be an expectation of a later reversal. A third influence that can result in investors in all countries having an expectation of higher returns from domestic investments relative to foreign is a danger of governments restricting the ability of foreigners to withdraw funds. Governments can and do place such restrictions on foreigners. This can reduce returns to foreigners. These are real considerations and affect the returns from international diversification.

Before leaving this section, one more point should be mentioned. It has often been suggested that investors could confine themselves to a national market and get most of the benefits of international diversification by purchasing stocks in multinational corporations. Jacquillat and Solnik [16] have tested this for the American investor. They find that stock prices of multinational firms do not seem to be affected by foreign factors and behave much like the stocks of domestic firms. The American investor cannot gain very much of the advantage of international diversification by investing in the securities of the multinational firm.

THE EFFECT OF EXCHANGE RATE RISK

One influence that affects the attractiveness of international diversification is changes in exchange rates. In this section we examine the affects of exchange rate changes on risk and return. Let us start with a simple example. Assume U.S. stocks and German stocks both appreciate 10%. Further, assume that at the beginning of the year $1.00 equaled 3 marks and at the end of the year $1.00 equaled 2.7 marks. The U.S. investor investing in German stocks would have the following flows:

1. An investment of $1.00 at the beginning of the year that buys 3 marks of German stock.
2. At the end of the year the German stock is worth $3(1.10) = 3.3$ marks.
3. Converting into dollars, the American investor has stock worth 3.3/ 2.7 = $1.22.

The American investor has gained from both the increase in the stock and the favorable movement in the currency market. The German investor is not in such a favored position. For every 3 marks he buys $1.00 of U.S. stocks, which is worth $1.10 at the end of the period. However, in German currency this is worth only $1.10 × 2.7 or 2.97 marks. The German investor has lost money on his U.S. investment.

In recent years exchange rate fluctuations have occurred sufficiently often and have been of a large enough magnitude that they frequently dominate returns earned on the investment. The charts and tables discussed in previous sections took into account exchange rate fluctuations. However, many of them were estimated during periods when exchange rate fluctuations were not as important as they are currently. Thus, they underestimated their impact. The example just discussed makes clear how the country of domicile of the investor is important. The earlier tables were calculated from the viewpoint of the American investor. In other words, at the beginning of the period dollars were turned into the currency of the country whose securities were being purchased at the prevailing exchange rates and at the end of the period they were reconverted back into dollars. As the example presented above makes clear, the numbers would have been different if we assumed the investor was German and converted everything to marks.

As another example consider Table 10.5, taken from Levy and Sarnat [27]. The mean returns and standard deviations of returns were calculated from a U.S.

Table 10.5

	U.S. Viewpoint		Israeli Viewpoint	
Country	Mean Rate of Return	Standard Deviation	Mean Rate of Return	Standard Deviation
Australia	4.8	13.2	19.0	31.7
Austria	16.3	24.4	34.6	57.2
Belgium	6.2	13.9	22.5	44.5
Canada	9.0	13.5	25.1	43.0
Denmark	8.9	23.6	24.6	43.3
Finland	14.1	25.6	29.2	39.5
France	10.3	20.1	28.9	58.3
Germany	17.0	25.0	34.1	53.7
India	0.6	12.9	15.1	35.4
Israel	4.7	33.9	13.4	28.1
Italy	9.0	20.8	26.7	54.8
Japan	20.6	29.7	44.5	86.5
Mexico	2.5	18.6	17.9	43.1
Netherlands	10.5	17.7	25.9	37.7
New Zealand	6.1	15.8	20.2	32.0
Norway	4.7	14.5	19.3	36.8
Peru	−2.5	12.9	12.2	41.3
Philippines	−2.2	21.3	11.7	43.1
Portugal	18.0	43.0	35.6	61.4
South Africa	7.1	21.0	22.2	39.7
Spain	7.4	20.8	23.7	45.4
Sweden	8.7	14.2	23.9	36.5
Switzerland	8.6	19.1	24.3	42.7
United Kingdom	8.2	16.0	23.4	37.3
United States	10.2	11.5	26.4	41.9
Venezuela	5.5	13.0	22.6	48.6

and Israeli viewpoint. The same study showed that the correlation coefficient between Japanese and U.S. securities from a U.S. viewpoint was -0.06. However, the correlation coefficient between the Japanese and U.S. securities from an Israeli viewpoint was 0.91. Thus, exchange risk affects all parameters of the distribution. Figures 10.3 and 10.4 show why the correlation is affected. Figure 10.3 is from the U.S. viewpoint; Figure 10.4 is from the Israeli. Obviously, which currency was utilized made a substantial difference.

It is possible to partially protect against exchange rate fluctuations. An investor can enter into a contract for future delivery of a currency. For example, an American investor purchasing German securities could simultaneously agree to exchange marks into dollars at a future date and at a known rate. If the investor knew exactly what the security would be worth at the end of the period, the investor would be completely protected against exchange rate fluctuations by agreeing to switch an amount of marks exactly equal to the value of the investment. However, given that, in general, the outcome of the investment is random, the best the investor can do is to protect against a particular outcome.

Exchange rate fluctuations are not necessarily bad for the investor. The American investor in the previous example gained from the fluctuations. Even if they are not always in the investor's favor, they need not be harmful. If exchange rate

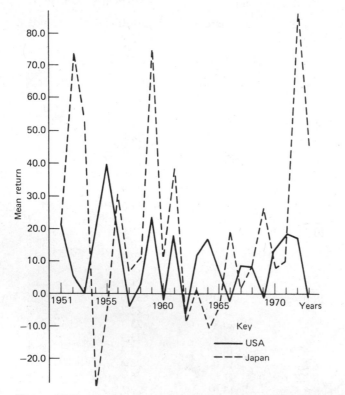

Figure 10.3

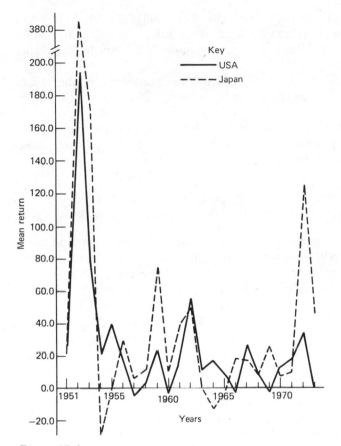

Figure 10.4

fluctuations are independent, then they can be diversified away and have neg-ligible impact on the risk of the portfolio. Similarly, if exchange rate fluctuations tend to move opposite to domestic conditions, then they favorably impact the risk of an internationally diversified portfolio relative to a domestic portfolio. As a hypothetical example, assume that when the domestic economy is doing well the currency is moving up relative to foreign currencies, and vice versa. This movement would reduce the correlation of foreign portfolios with domestic port-folios. From earlier chapters we know that lowering correlation reduces portfolio risk.

Exchange rate fluctuations introduce an unfavorable element into international diversification insofar as one currency tends to fluctuate uniformly compared to all other currencies. For example, if the dollar is doing poorly relative to all currencies, then exchange rate fluctuations increase risk because they lead to all foreign investments doing more poorly and lower the risk reduction aspects of holding multiple foreign investments. To elaborate, without exchange rate fluc-tuations, French and Japanese securities are reasonably independent. Thus, inclusion of both securities lowers risk. However, if the dollar is likely to move in the same direction against both and the fluctuations are likely to be large, then to an American investor investment in securities of the two countries are highly correlated with each other.

In the studies mentioned earlier, exchange risk did not have a major impact on results. Recent increases in the instability of exchange rates could modify these results.

We discussed rather thoroughly the reasons for or against international diversification. It is time to examine evidence on how well internationally diversified portfolios have actually performed.

THE PERFORMANCE OF INTERNATIONALLY DIVERSIFIED PORTFOLIOS

Earlier we discussed the performance of domestic portfolios compared to internationally diversified portfolios when perfect forecasting ability was assumed. The real test, however, is the performance of actual portfolios.

In a later chapter we see that mutual fund performance has been poorer than random selection. Outside the U.S. there are funds that specialize in an international portfolio. How does the performance of these funds compare to funds who limit their investments to domestic securities? The evidence we can quote is very limited and not conclusive.

McDonald [29] examined the performance of French mutual funds. French funds, in general, hold a substantial part of their portfolio in foreign securities, primarily U.S. securities. Of the eight funds he examined, seven of them held foreign securities. The risk of the seven internationally diversified funds relative to an index of the French stock market is shown in Table 10.6. All of the funds are less risky than the French market. There are two possible explanations for this low risk. First, there are substantial restrictions on the investments selected by French funds. French funds are required to invest at least 30% of their assets in bank deposits or marketable debt. This leads to a lower risk portfolio than their U.S. counterparts. Second, the French and U.S. stock markets are reasonably uncorrelated. Thus, investment in both markets should produce less risk

Table 10.6

Fund	Standard Deviations	Standard Deviation as Percent of Market
1	0.0222	60.2
2	0.0302	81.8
3	0.0269	72.9
4	0.0221	59.9
5	0.0244	66.1
6	0.0229	62.1
7	0.0253	68.6
Index	0.0369	

Table 10.7 Proportion of Variance Explained by Market Movements

Fund	Variance Explained by Movements in the Market
1	62%
2	51%
3	36%
4	34%
5	51%
6	58%
7	17%
Average	44.1%

than exclusive investment in one market. Either of these explanations could account for the results and, hence, we cannot state with certainty that the results were due to international diversification.

One would expect that a large part of the variability of the mutual fund returns would be unrelated to movements of the French stock market and this is, in fact, the case. Table 10.7 shows the results for the same sample of seven funds. These are low numbers. Large diversified portfolios such as mutual funds usually have 90% or more of their variance explained by movements in the market index. This is true whether the funds are primarily equity funds or whether the funds have a substantial portion of their assets in bonds. Even if the funds have large bond holdings, the bulk of the variability comes from the equity portion and this variability is usually related to the market. Thus, the low relationship of these funds to the index cannot be explained by their bond holdings. Rather, the low relationship has to be a result of international diversification. The promise of an internationally diversified portfolio having a low relationship to the domestic market seems to hold.

The period of McDonald's study was a period where the U.S. market outperformed the French market. Thus, it should not be surprising that the internationally diversified mutual funds also outperformed the French market. In this period they did about 30% better. U.S. markets did not have to outperform French markets for the internationally diversified funds to be superior. Even if the U.S. market had a lower return and securities were selected randomly, the funds would have been good purchases given their low risk.[10] Thus, while the evidence we can quote can be described as suggestive, at best, it does give support to international diversification.

CONCLUSION

In this chapter we have discussed the evidence in support of international diversification. The evidence that international diversification reduces risk is uniform and extensive. The studies were done during periods when exchange rate

---

[10]McDonald attributes the higher return to superior selection of French securities. It is impossible to say why it occurred.

fluctuations were less extensive than recently. Nevertheless, they would probably not be different if they were done with recent data. Given the lower risk, international diversification is justified even if expected returns are less. Unless there are mechanisms such as taxes or currency restrictions that substantially reduce the return on foreign investment relative to domestic investment, international diversification has to be profitable for investors of some countries and possibly all.

QUESTIONS AND PROBLEMS

1. Assume that you expect that the average return on a security in various markets is as shown in the following table. Assume further that the historical correlation coefficients shown in Table 10.1 are a reasonable estimate of future correlation coefficients. Finally, assume that securities expected return is related to risk in the domestic market. Which markets are attractive investments for an American investor if the riskless lending and borrowing rate if 6%?

	Market	Expected Return
1.	Austria	14%
2.	France	16%
3.	Japan	14%
4.	U.K.	15%
5.	U.S.A.	20%

2. Assume all information is the same as in Question 1, except that the securities expected return is related to risk in the world market; assume the expected return on the world index is 12.5% while its standard deviation is 15%. What countries are attractive investments?

3. Consider the following returns:

Period	U.S.	U.K.	Exchange Rate[a]
1	10%	5%	$3
2	15%	-5%	2.5
3	-5%	15%	2.5
4	12%	8%	2.0
5	6%	10%	1.5
6			2.5

[a]Beginning of period dollars for pounds

What is the average return in each market from the point of view of a U.S. investor and of a U.K. investor?

4. What is the standard deviation of return from the point of view of a U.S. investor and of a U.K. investor?

5. What is the correlation of return between the two markets from the point of view of a U.S. investor and of a U.K. investor?

6. If the riskless lending and borrowing rate is 5% to both investors and neither can borrow or lend in the others market, what is the optimum portfolio?

BIBLIOGRAPHY

1. Adler, Michael. "The Cost of Capital and Valuation of a Two-Country Firm," *Journal of Finance*, **XXIX**, No. 1 (March 1974), pp. 119–132.
2. Adler, Michael, and Horesh, Reuven. "The Relationship Among Equity Markets: Comment on [3]," *Journal of Finance*, **XXIX**, No. 4, (Sept. 1974), pp. 1131–1317.
3. Agmon, Tamir. "The Relations Among Equity Markets: A Study of Share Price Co-Movements in the United States, United Kingdom, Germany and Japan," *Journal of Finance*, **XXVII**, No. 3 (June 1972), pp. 839–855.
4. ———. "Country Risk: The Significance of the Country Factor for Share-Price Movements in the United Kingdom, Germany, and Japan," *Journal of Business*, **46**, No. 1 (Jan. 1973), pp. 24–32.
5. ———. "Reply to [2]," *Journal of Finance*, **XXIX**, No. 4 (Sept. 1974), pp. 1318–1319.
6. Agmon, Tamir, and Lessard, Donald. "Investor Recognition of Corporate International Diversification," *Journal of Finance*, **XXXII**, No. 4 (Sept. 1977), pp. 1049–1055.
7. Black, F. "International Capital Market Equilibrium with Investment Barriers," *Journal of Financial Economics*, **1**, No. 4 (Dec. 1974), pp. 337–352.
8. Branch, Ben. "Common Stock Performance and Inflation: An International Comparison," *Journal of Business*, **47**, No. 1 (Jan. 1973), pp. 48–52.
9. Cohn, A. Richard, and Pringle, J. John. "Imperfections in International Financial Markets: Implications for Risk Premia and the Cost of Capital to Firms," *Journal of Finance*, **XXVIII**, No. 1 (March 1973), pp. 59–66.
10. Farber, Andre L. "Performance of Internationally Diversified Mutual Funds," in Elton and Gruber, *International Captial Markets* (Amsterdam: North-Holland, 1975).
11. Fatemi, Ali M. "Shareholder Benefits from Corporate International Diversification," *The Journal of Finance*, **39**, No. 5 (Dec. 1984), pp. 1325–1344.
12. Grauer, F., Litzenberger, R., and Stehle, R. "Sharing Rules and Equilibrium in an International Capital Market Under Uncertainty," *Journal of Financial Economics*, **3**, No. 3 (June 1976), pp. 233–256.
13. Grubel, Herbert, "Internally Diversified Portfolios: Welfare Gains and Capital Flows," *American Economic Review*, **LVIII**, No. 5, Part 1 (Dec. 1968), pp. 1299–1314.
14. Grubel, G. Herbert, and Fadner, Kenneth. "The Interdependence of International Equity Markets," *Journal of Finance*, **XXVI**, No. 1 (March 1971), pp. 89–94.

15. Gultekin, N. Bulent. "Stock Market Returns and Inflation: Evidence from Other Countries," *The Journal of Finance*, **38**, No. 1 (March 1983), pp. 49–68.

16. Jacquillat, Bertrand, and Solnik, Bruno. "Multi-Nationals Are Poor .Tools for Diversification," *Journal of Portfolio Management* (Winter 1978), pp. 8–12.

17. Joy, Maurice, Panton, Don, Reilly, Frank, and Martin, Stanley. "Co-Movements of International Equity Markets," *The Financial Review* (1976), pp. 1–20.

18. Lessard, Donald. "World, Country, and Industry Relationships in Equity Returns: Implications for Risk Reduction Through International Diversification," *Financial Analysts Journal*, **32**, No. 1 (Jan./Feb. 1976), pp. 32–38.

19. ———— . "International Portfolio Diversification: A Multivariate Analysis for a Group of Latin American Countries," *Journal of Finance*, **XXVIII**, No. 3 (June 1973), pp. 619–633.

20. ———— . "World, National and Industry Factors in Equity Returns," *Journal of Finance*, **XXIV**, No. 2 (May 1974), pp. 379–391.

21. ———— ."The Structure of Returns and Gains from International Diversification: A Multivariate Approach," in Elton and Gruber, *International Capital Markets* (Amsterdam: North-Holland, 1975).

22. Levich, Richard, and Frenkel, Jacob. "Covered Interest Arbitrage: Unexplored Profits?" *Journal of Political Economy* (April, 1975), pp. 325–338.

23. ———— . "Transaction Costs and Interest Arbitrage: Tranquil versus Turbulent Periods," *Journal of Political Economy* (Dec. 1977), pp. 1209–1286.

24. Levich, Richard. "On the Efficiency of Markets for Foreign Exchange," in Frenkel and Dornbusch, *International Economic Policy: Theory and Evidence* (Baltimore, Md.: Johns Hopkins Press, 1970).

25. ———— . "The Efficiency of Markets for Foreign Exchange: A Review and Extension," in Lessard, *International Financial Management: Theory and Application* (New York: Warren, Gorhan and Lamont, 1979).

26. Levy, Haim, and Sarnat, Marshall, "International Diversification of Investment Portfolios," *American Economic Review*, **LX**, No. 4 (Sept. 1970), pp. 668–675.

27. ———— . "Devaluation Risk and the Portfolio Analysis of International Investment," in Elton and Gruber, *International Capital Markets* (Amsterdam: North-Holland, 1975).

28. Makin, John. "Portfolio Theory and the Problem of Foreign Exchange Risk," *Journal of Finance*, **XXXIII**, No. 2 (May 1978), pp. 517–534.

29. McDonald, John. "French Mutual Fund Performance: Evaluation of Internationally-Diversified Portfolios," *Journal of Finance*, **XXVIII**, No. 5 (Dec. 1973), pp. 1161–1180.

30. Panton, Don, Lessig, Parker, and Joy, Maurice. "Co-Movement of International Equity Markets: A Taxonomic Approach," *Journal of Financial and Quantitative Analysis*, **XI**, No. 3 (Sept. 1976), pp. 415–432.

31. Ripley, Duncan. "Systematic Elements in the Linkage of National Stock

Market Indices," *Review of Economics and Statistics,* **LV,** No. 3 (Aug. 1973), pp. 356–361.

32. Robicher, Alexander, and Eaker, Mark. "Foreign Exchange Hedging and the Captial Asset Pricing Model," *Journal of Finance,* **XXXIII,** No. 3 (June 1978), pp. 1011–1018.

33. Severn, Alan. "Investor Evaluation of Foreign and Domestic Risk," *Journal of Finance,* **XXIX,** No. 2 (May 1974), pp. 545–550.

34. Sharma, J. L., and Kennedy, Robert. "A Comparative Analysis of Stock Price Behavior on the Bombay, London, and New York Stock Exchanges," *Journal of Financial and Quantitative Analysis,* **XII,** No. 3 (Sept. 1977), pp. 391–413.

35. Solnick, Bruno. "The Advantages of Domestic and International Diversification," in Elton and Gruber, *International Capital Markets* (Amsterdam: North-Holland, 1975).

36. Solnik, Bruno. "Why Not Diversify Internationally?" *Financial Analysts Journal,* **20,** No. 4 (July/Aug. 1974), pp. 48–54.

37. ———— . "The International Pricing of Risk: An Empirical Investigation of the World Capital Market Structure," *Journal of Finance,* **XXIX,** No. 2 (May 1974), pp. 365–378.

38. ———— . "An Equilibrium Model of the International Capital Market," *Journal of Economic Theory,* **8,** No. 4 (Aug. 1974), pp. 500–524.

39. ———— . "An International Market Model of Security Price Behavior." *Journal of Financial and Quantitative Analysis,* **IX,** No. 4 (Sept. 1974), pp. 537–554.

40. ———— . "Testing International Asset Pricing: Some Pessimistic Views," *Journal of Finance,* **XXXII,** No. 2 (May 1977), pp. 503–512.

41. Stehle, Richard. "An Empirical Test of the Alternative Hypotheses of National and International Pricing of Risky Assets," *Journal of Finance,* **XII,** No. 2 (May 1977), pp. 493–502.

42. Subrahmanyam, Marti. "On the Optimality of International Capital Market Integration," *Journal of Financial Economics,* **2,** No. 1 (March 1975), pp. 3–28.

43. Subrahmanyam, Marti. "International Captial Markets, Equilibrium, and Investor Welfare with Unequal Interest Rates," in Elton and Gruber, *International Capital Markets* (Amsterdam: North-Holland, 1975).

PART 2
MODELS OF EQUILIBRIUM IN THE CAPITAL MARKETS

Chapter 11

The Standard Capital Asset Pricing Model

All of the preceding chapters have been concerned with how an individual or institution, acting upon a set of estimates, could select an optimum portfolio, or set of portfolios. If investors act as we have prescribed, then we should be able to draw on the analysis to determine how the aggregate of investors will behave, and how prices and returns at which markets will clear are set. The construction of general equilibrium models will allow us to determine the relevant measure of risk for any asset and the relationship between expected return and risk for any asset when markets are in equilibrium. Furthermore, though the equilibrium models are derived from models of how portfolios should be constructed, the models, themselves, have major implications for the characteristics of optimum portfolios.

The subject of equilibrium models is so important that we have devoted four chapters to it. In this chapter we develop the simplest form of an equilibrium model, called the standard capital asset pricing model, or the one-factor capital asset pricing model. This was the first general equilibrium model developed, and it is based on the most stringent set of assumptions. The second chapter on general equilibrium models deals with models that have been developed under more realistic sets of assumptions. The third chapter in this sequence deals with tests of general equilibrium models. The final chapter deals with a new theory of asset pricing: arbitrage pricing theory.

It is worthwhile pointing out, at this time, that the final test of a model is not how reasonable the assumptions behind it appear but how well the model describes reality. As the reader proceeds with this chapter he will, no doubt, find many of its assumptions objectionable. Furthermore, the final model is so simple the reader may well wonder about its validity. As we shall see, despite the stringent assumptions and the simplicity of the model, it does an amazingly good job of describing prices in the capital markets.

THE ASSUMPTIONS UNDERLYING THE STANDARD CAPITAL ASSET PRICING MODEL (CAPM)

The real world is sufficiently complex that to understand it and construct models of how it works, one must asume away those complexities that, hopefully, have only a small (or no) effect on its behavior. As the physicist builds models of the movement of matter in a frictionless environment, the economist builds models where there are no institutional frictions to the movement of stock prices.

The first assumption we make is that there are no transaction costs. There is no cost (friction) of buying or selling any asset. If transaction costs were present, the return from any asset would be a function of whether or not the investor owned it before the decision period. Thus, to include transaction costs in the model adds a great deal of complexity. Whether it is worthwhile introducing this complexity depends on the importance of transaction costs to investors' decisions. Given the size of transaction costs, they are probably of minor importance.

The second assumption behind the CAPM is that assets are infinitely divisible. This means that investors could take any position in an investment, regardless of the size of their wealth. For example, they can buy one dollar's worth of IBM stock.

The third assumption is the absence of personal income tax.[1] This means, for example, that the individual is indifferent to the form (dividends or capital gains) in which the return on the investment is received.

The fourth assumption is that an individual cannot affect the price of a stock by his buying or selling action. This is analogous to the assumption of perfect competition. While no single investor can affect prices by an individual action, investors in total determine prices by their actions.

The fifth assumption is that investors are expected to make decisions solely in terms of expected values and standard deviations of the returns on their portfolios. In other words, they make their portfolio decision, utilizing the framework discussed in other chapters.

The sixth assumption is that unlimited short sales are allowed. The individual investor can sell short any amount of any shares.[2]

The seventh assumption is unlimited lending and borrowing at the riskless rate. The investor can lend or borrow any amount of funds desired at a rate of interest equal to the rate for riskless securities.

The eighth and ninth assumptions deal with the homogeneity of expectations. First, investors are assumed to be concerned with the mean and variance of returns (or prices over a single period), and all investors are assumed to define the relevant period in exactly the same manner. Second, all investors are assumed

---

[1]The major results of the model would hold if income tax and capital gains taxes were of equal size.

[2]This model can be derived under either of the descriptions of short sales discussed in Chapter 3.

to have identical expectations with respect to the necessary inputs to the portfolio decision. As we have said many times, these inputs are expected returns, the variance of returns, and the correlation matrix representing the correlation structure between all pairs of stocks.

The tenth assumption is that all assets are marketable. All assets, including human capital, can be sold and bought on the market.

Readers can now see the reason for the earlier warning that they might find many of the assumptions behind the CAPM untenable. It is clear that these assumptions do not hold in the real world just as it is clear that the physicist's frictionless environment does not really exist. The relevant questions are: How much is reality distorted by making these assumptions? What conclusions about capital markets do they lead to? Do these conclusions seem to describe the actual performance of the capital market?

THE CAPITAL ASSET PRICING MODEL

The standard form of the general equilibrium relationship for asset returns was developed independently by Sharpe, Lintner, and Mossin. Hence, it is often referred to as the Sharpe-Lintner-Mossin form of the capital asset pricing model. This model has been derived in several forms involving different degrees of rigor and mathematical complexity. There is a trade-off between these derivations. The more complex forms are more rigorous and provide a framework within which alternative sets of assumptions can be examined. However, because of their complexity, they do not convey as readily as some of the simpler forms the economic intuition behind the capital asset pricing model. Because of this, we approach the derivation of the model at two distinct levels. The first derivation consists of a simple intuitively appealing derivation of the CAPM. This is followed by a more rigorous derivation.

Deriving the CAPM — A Simple Approach

Recall that in the presence of short sales, but without riskless lending and borrowing, each investor faced an efficient frontier such as that shown in Figure 11.1. In this figure BC represents the efficient frontier while ABC represents the set of minimum variance portfolios. In general the efficient frontier will differ among investors because of differences in expectations.

When we introduced riskless lending and borrowing, we showed that the portfolio of risky assets that any investor would hold could be identified without regard to the investor's risk preferences. This portfolio lies at the tangency point between the original efficient frontier of risky assets and a ray passing through the riskless return (on the vertical axis). This is depicted in Figure 11.2 where P_i denotes investor i's portfolio of risky assets.[3] The investors satisfy their risk preferences by combining portfolio P_i with lending or borrowing.

---

[3]We have subscripted P because each individual can face a different efficient frontier and, thus select a different P_i. This is true, though the composition of P_i does not depend on investor i's risk preference.

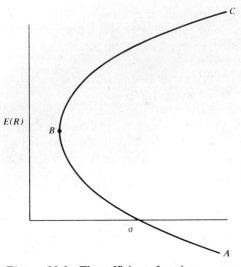

Figure 11.1 The efficient frontier — no lending and borrowing.

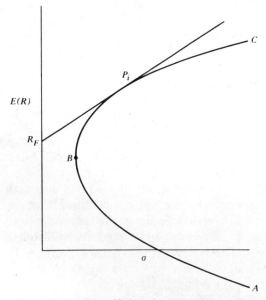

Figure 11.2 The efficient frontier with lending and borrowing.

If all investors have homogeneous expectations and they all face the same lending and borrowing rate, then they will each face a diagram such as in Figure 11.2 and, furthermore, all of the diagrams will be identical. The portfolio of risky assets P_i held by any investor will be identical to the portfolio of risky assets held by any other investor. If all investors hold the same risky portfolio, then, in equilibrium, it must be the market portfolio. The market portfolio is a portfolio comprised of all risky assets. Each asset is held in the proportion that the market value of that asset represents of the total market value of all risky assets. For example, if IBM stock represents 3% of all risky assets, then the market portfolio contains 3% IBM stock and each investor will take 3% of the money that will be invested in all risky assets and place it in IBM stock.

Notice that we have already learned something important. All investors will hold combinations of only two portfolios: the market portfolio (M) and a riskless security. This is sometimes referred to as the two mutual fund theorem because all investors would be satisfied with a market fund, plus the ability to lend or borrow a riskless security.

The straight line depicted in Figure 11.2 is usually referred to as the capital market line. All investors will end up with portfolios somewhere along the capital market line and all *efficient portfolios* would lie along the capital market line. However, not all securities or portfolios lie along the capital market line. In fact, from the derivation of the efficient frontier, we know that all portfolios of risky and riskless assets, except those that are efficient, lie below the capital market line. By looking at the capital market line we can learn something about the market price of risk. In Chapter 3 we showed that the equation of a line connecting a riskless asset and a risky portfolio (the line we now call the capital market line) is

$$\overline{R}_e = R_F + \frac{\overline{R}_M - R_F}{\sigma_M} \sigma_e$$

where the subscript e denotes an efficient portfolio.

The term $[(\overline{R}_M - R_F)/\sigma_M]$ can be thought of as the market price of risk for all efficient portfolios.[4] It is the extra return that can be gained by increasing the level of risk (standard deviation) on an efficient portfolio by one unit. The second term on the right-hand side of this equation is simply the market price of risk times the amount of risk in a portfolio. The second term represents that element of required return that is due to risk. The first term is simply the price of time or the return that is required for delaying potential consumption, one period given perfect certainty about the future cash flow. Thus, the expected return on an efficient portfolio is

(Expected return) = (Price of time) + (Price of risk) × (Amount of risk)

---

[4]The reader should be alerted to the fact that many authors have defined $(\overline{R}_M - R_F)/\sigma_M^2$ as the market price of risk. The reason we have selected $(\overline{R}_M - R_F)/\sigma_M$ will become clear as you proceed with this chapter.

Although this equation establishes the return on an efficient portfolio, it does not describe equilibrium returns on nonefficient portfolios or on individual securities. We now turn to the development of a relationship that does so.

Earlier (in Chapter 5) we argued that, for very well-diversified portfolios, Beta was the correct measure of a security's risk. For *very* well-diversified portfolios, nonsystematic risk tends to go to zero and the only relevant risk is systematic risk measured by Beta. As we have just explained, given the assumptions of homogeneous expectations and unlimited riskless lending and borrowing, all investors will hold the market portfolio. Thus the investor will hold a *very* well-diversified portfolio. Since we assume that the investor is concerned only with expected return and risk, the only dimensions of a security that need be of concern are expected return and Beta.

Let us hypothesize two portfolios with the characteristics shown below:

Investment	Expected Return	Beta
A	10	1.0
B	12	1.4

We have already seen (Chapter 3) that the expected return from portfolio A is simply the sum of the products of the proportion invested in each stock and the expected return on each stock. We have also seen that the Beta on a portfolio is simply the sum of the product of the proportion invested in each stock times the Beta on each stock. Now consider a portfolio C made up of one half of portfolio A and one half of portfolio B. From the facts stated above, the expected return on this portfolio is 11 and its Beta is 1.2. These three potential investments are plotted in Figure 11.3. Notice they lie on a straight line. This is no accident. All portfolios composed of different fractions of investments A and B will lie along a straight line in expected return Beta space.[5]

Now hypothesize a new investment D that has a return of 13% and a Beta of 1.2. Such an investment cannot exist for very long. All decisions are made in terms of risk and return. This portfolio offers a higher return and the same risk as portfolio C. Hence, it would pay all investors to sell C short and buy D. Similarly, if a security were to exist with a return of 8% and a Beta of 1.2

---

[5] If we let X stand for the fraction of funds invested in portfolio A, then the equation for return is

$$\overline{R}_P = X\overline{R}_A + (1 - X)\overline{R}_B$$

The equation for Beta is

$$\beta_P = X\beta_A + (1 - X)\beta_B$$

Solving the second equation for X and substituting in the first equation, we see that we are left with an equation of the form

$$\overline{R}_P = a + b\beta_P$$

or the equation of a straight line.

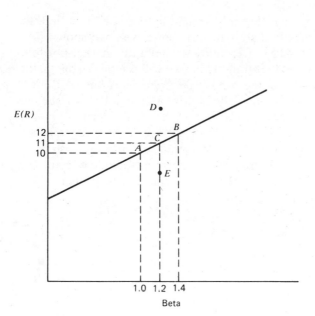

Figure 11.3 Combinations of portfolios.

(designated by E), it would pay arbitragers to step in and buy portfolio C while selling security E short. Such arbitrage would take place until C, D, and E all yielded the same return. This is just another illustration of the adage that two things that are equivalent cannot sell at different prices. We can demonstrate the arbitrage discussed above in a slightly more formal manner. Let us return to the arbitrage between portfolio's C and D. An investor could sell $100 worth of portfolio C short and with the $100 buy portfolio D. If the investor were to do so, the characteristics of this arbitraged portfolio would be as follows:

	Cash Invested	Expected Return	Beta
Portfolio C	$-$100	$-$11	-1.2
Security D	$+$100	$13	1.2
Arbitrage portfolio	0	$ 2	0

From this example it is clear that as long as a security lies above the straight line, there is a portfolio involving zero risk and zero net investment that has a positive expected profit. An investor will engage in this arbitrage as long as any security or portfolio lies above the straight line depicted in Figure 11.3. A similar arbitrage will exist if any amount lies below the straight line in Figure 11.3.

We have now established that all investments and all portfolios of investments must lie along a straight line in return-Beta space. If any investment were to lie above or below that straight line, then an opportunity would exist for riskless arbitrage. This arbitrage would continue until all investments converged to the line. There are many different ways that this straight line can be identified, for it takes only two points to identify a straight line. Since we have shown that, under the assumptions of the CAPM, everybody will hold the market portfolio and since all portfolios must lie on the straight line, we will use this as one point. Recall in Chapter 5 we showed that the market portfolio must have a Beta of one. Thus, in Figure 11.4 the market portfolio is point M with a Beta of one and an expected return of $\bar{R}_M$. It is often convenient to choose the second point to identify a straight line as the intercept. The intercept occurs when Beta equals zero, or when the asset has zero systematic risk. One asset with zero systematic risk is the riskless asset. Thus, we can treat the intercept as the rate of return on a riskless asset. These two points identify the straight line shown in Figure 11.4. The equation of a straight line has the form

$$\bar{R}_i = a + b\beta_i \qquad (11.1)$$

One point on the line is the riskless asset with a Beta of zero. Thus,

$$R_F = a + b(0)$$

or

$$R_F = a$$

A second point on the line is the market portfolio with a Beta of one. Thus,

$$\bar{R}_M = a + b(1)$$

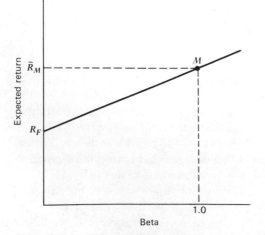

Figure 11.4 The security market line.

or

$$(\overline{R}_M - a) = b$$

Putting these together and substituting into Equation (11.1) yields

$$\overline{R}_i = R_F + \beta_i(\overline{R}_M - R_F) \qquad (11.2)$$

Think about this relationship for a moment. It represents one of the most important discoveries in the field of finance. Here is a simple equation, called the security market line, that describes the expected return for all assets and portfolios of assets in the economy. The expected return on any asset, or portfolio, whether it is efficient or not, can be determined from this relationship. Notice that $\overline{R}_M$ and R_F are not functions of the assets we examine. Thus, the relationship between the expected return on any two assets can be related simply to their difference in Beta. The higher Beta is for any security, the higher must be its equilibrium return. Furthermore, the relationship between Beta and expected return is linear. One of the greatest insights that comes from this equation arises from what it states is unimportant in determining return. Recall that in Chapter 5 we saw that the risk of any stock could be divided into systematic and unsystematic risk. Beta was the index of systematic risk. This equation validates the conclusion that systematic risk is the only important ingredient in determining expected returns and that nonsystematic risk plays no role.[6] Put another way, the investor gets rewarded for bearing systematic risk. It is not total variance of returns that affects expected returns, but only that part of the variance in returns that cannot be diversified away. This result has great economic intuition for, if investors can eliminate all nonsystematic risk through diversification, there is no reason they should be rewarded, in terms of higher return, for bearing it. All of these implications of the CAPM are empirically testable. Indeed, in Chapter 13 we examine the results of these tests. Provided the tests hold, we have, with a simple model, gained great insight in the behavior of the capital markets.

We digress for a moment and point out one seeming fallacy in the potential use of the CAPM. Invariably, when a group of investors is first exposed to the CAPM, one or more investors will find a high Beta stock that last year produced a smaller return than low Beta stocks. The CAPM is an equilibrium relationship. High Beta stocks are expected to give a higher return than low Beta stocks because they are more risky. This does not mean that they will give a higher return over all intervals of time. In fact, if they always gave a higher return, they would be less risky, not more risky, than low Beta stocks. Rather, because they are more risky, they will sometimes produce lower returns. However, over long periods of time, they should on the average produce higher returns.

---

[6]This result is somewhat circular for, in this proof, we assumed that Beta was the relevant risk measure. In the more rigorous proof that follows, we make no such assumption, yet we end up with the same equation for the security market line.

We have written the CAPM model in the form

$$\overline{R}_i = R_F + \beta_i(\overline{R}_M - R_F)$$

This is the form in which it is most often written and the form most amenable to empirical testing. However, there are alternative forms that give added insight into its meaning. Recall that

$$\beta_i = \frac{\sigma_{iM}}{\sigma_M^2}$$

We could then write the security market line as

$$\overline{R}_i = R_F + \left(\frac{\overline{R}_M - R_F}{\sigma_M}\right)\frac{\sigma_{iM}}{\sigma_M} \qquad (11.3)$$

This, in fact, is the equation of a straight line located in expected return σ_{iM}/σ_M space. Recall that earlier in our discussion of the capital market, line $(\overline{R}_M - R_F)/\sigma_M$ was described as the market price of risk. Since σ_{iM}/σ_M is a definition of the risk of any security, or portfolio, we would see that the security market line, like the capital market line, states that the expected return on any security is the riskless rate of interest plus the market price of risk times the amount of risk in the security or portfolio.[7]

---

[7]Below we offer theoretical justification that σ_{iM}/σ_M is the relevant measure of the risk of any security in equilibrium. Recall that the standard deviation of the market portfolio is given by

$$\sigma_M = \left[\sum_{i=1}^{N} X_i^2 \sigma_i^2 + \sum_{i=1}^{N}\sum_{\substack{j=1 \\ j\neq i}}^{N} X_i X_j \sigma_{ij}\right]^{1/2}$$

where all X_i's are market proportions. Since all investors hold the market portfolio, the relevant definition of the risk of a security is the change in the risk of the market portfolio, as the holdings of that security are varied. This can be found as follows:

$$\frac{d\sigma_M}{dX_i} = d\frac{\left[\sum_{i=1}^{N} X_i^2 \sigma_i^2 + \sum_{i=1}^{N}\sum_{\substack{j=1 \\ j\neq i}}^{N} X_i X_j \sigma_{ij}\right]^{1/2}}{dX_i}$$

$$= \frac{\left(\frac{1}{2}\right)\left[2X_i\sigma_i^2 + (2)\sum_{\substack{j=1 \\ j\neq i}}^{N} X_j\sigma_{ij}\right]}{\left[\sum_{i=1}^{N} X_i^2\sigma_i^2 + \sum_{j=1}^{N}\sum_{\substack{j=1 \\ j\neq i}}^{N} X_i X_j\sigma_{ij}\right]^{1/2}} = \frac{X_i^2\sigma_i^2 + \sum_{\substack{j=1 \\ j\neq i}}^{N} X_j\sigma_{ij}}{\sigma_M} = \frac{\sigma_{iM}}{\sigma_M}$$

Therefore, the relevant risk of security is equal to σ_{iM}/σ_M.

Many authors write the CAPM equation as

$$\overline{R}_i = R_F + \left(\frac{\overline{R}_M - R_F}{\sigma_M{}^2}\right)\sigma_{iM}$$

They define $(\overline{R}_M - R_F)/\sigma_M{}^2$ as the market price of risk and σ_{iM} as the measure of the risk of security i. We have chosen the form we used because σ_{iM}/σ_M is the measure of how the risk on a security affects the risk of the market portfolio. It seems to us that this is the appropriate way to discuss the risk of a security.

We have now completed our intuitive proof of the CAPM. We are about to present a more complex mathematical proof. There are two reasons for presenting this mathematical proof. The first is that it is more rigorous. The second, and more important, reason is that one needs a richer framework to incorporate modifications of the assumptions of the standard CAPM. The method of proof used before is too restrictive to allow forms of general equilibrium equations that make more realistic assumptions about the world to be derived. The framework presented subsequently can be used to derive equilibrium models under alternative assumptions and, indeed, will be used to do so in the next chapter. The reader who finds both these reasons unappealing can skip the next section and the derivations in the next chapter with no loss of continuity.

Deriving the CAPM — A More Rigorous Approach

To derive the CAPM more rigorously, we return to the analysis presented in Chapter 4. Recall that in the first section of Chapter 4 we solved for the optimal portfolio when short sales were allowed and the investor could lend and borrow unlimited amounts of money at the riskless rate of interest. The solution involved finding the composition of the portfolio that maximized the slope of a straight line passing through the riskless rate of interest on the vertical axes and the portfolio itself. As shown in Chapter 4, this involved maximizing the function

$$\theta = \frac{\overline{R}_P - R_F}{\sigma_P}$$

When the derivative of θ was taken with respect to all securities in the portfolio and each equation was set equal to zero, a set of simultaneous equations of the following form was derived:

$$\lambda(X_1\sigma_{1k} + X_2\sigma_{2k} + \cdots + X_k\sigma_k{}^2 + \cdots + X_N\sigma_{kN}) = \overline{R}_k - R_F \quad (11.4)$$

This equation held for each security and there is one such equation for each security in the market. If there are homogeneous expectations, then all investors must select the same optimum portfolio. If all investors select the same portfolio, then, in equilibrium, that portfolio must be a portfolio in which all securities are held in the same percentage that they represent of the market. In other words, in equilibrium, the proportion invested in security 1 must be that fraction of the total market value of all securities that security 1 represents. To get from Equation (11.4) to the CAPM involves simply recognizing that the left-hand side of Equation (11.4) is $\lambda \, \text{cov}(R_k R_M)$. To see this, first note that

$$R_M = \sum_{i=1}^{N} R_i X'_i$$

where the prime indicates market proportions. Thus

$$\text{cov}(R_k R_M) = E\left[(R_k - \overline{R}_k) \left(\sum_{i=1}^{N} R_i X'_i - \sum_{i=1}^{N} \overline{R}_i X'_i \right) \right] \qquad (11.5)$$

Rearranging the second term

$$\text{cov}(R_k R_M) = E\left[(R_k - \overline{R}_k) \left(\sum_{i=1}^{N} X'_i (R_i - \overline{R}_i) \right) \right]$$

Multiplying out the terms

$$\begin{aligned}
\text{cov}(R_k R_M) = E[& X'_1 (R_k - \overline{R}_k)(R_1 - \overline{R}_1) \\
& + X'_2 (R_k - \overline{R}_k)(R_2 - \overline{R}_2) + \cdots \\
& + X'_k (R_k - \overline{R}_k)(R_k - \overline{R}_k) + \cdots + X'_N (R_k - \overline{R}_k)(R_N - \overline{R}_N)]
\end{aligned}$$

Since the expected value of the sum of random variables is the sum of the expected values, factoring out the X's yields

$$\begin{aligned}
\text{cov}(R_k R_M) = \ & X'_1 E(R_k - \overline{R}_k)(R_1 - \overline{R}_1) + X'_2 E(R_k - \overline{R}_k)(R_2 - \overline{R}_2) + \cdots \\
& + X'_k E(R_k - \overline{R}_k)^2 + \cdots + X'_N E(R_k - \overline{R}_k)(R_N - \overline{R}_N)
\end{aligned}$$

Earlier we argued that the X's in Equation (11.4) were market proportions. Comparing Equation (11.5) with the left-hand side of Equation (11.4) shows that they are, indeed, equal. Thus, Equation (11.4) can be written as

$$\lambda \, \text{cov}(R_k R_M) = \overline{R}_k - R_F \qquad (11.6)$$

Since this must hold for all securities (all possible values of k), it must hold for all portfolios of securities. One possible portfolio is the market portfolio. Writing Equation (11.6) for the market portfolio involves recognizing that $\text{cov}(R_M R_M) = \sigma_M^2$.

$$\lambda \sigma_M^2 = \overline{R}_M - R_F$$

or

$$\lambda = \frac{\overline{R}_M - R_F}{\sigma_M{}^2}$$

Substituting this value for λ in Equation (11.6) and rearranging yields

$$\overline{R}_k = R_F + \frac{\overline{R}_M - R_F}{\sigma_M{}^2} \text{cov}(R_k R_M) = R_F + \beta_k(\overline{R}_M - R_F)$$

This completes the more rigorous derivation of the security market line.

The advantages of this proof over that presented earlier are that we have not had to assume that Beta is the relevant measure of risk and we have established a framework that, as we see in the next chapter, can be used to derive general equilibrium solutions when some of the present assumptions are relaxed.

PRICES AND THE CAPM

Up to now we have discussed equilibrium in terms of rate of return. In the introduction to this chapter we mentioned that the CAPM could be used to describe equilibrium in terms of either return or prices. The latter is of importance in certain situations, for example, the pricing of new assets It is very easy to move from the equilibrium relationship in terms of rates of return to one expressed in terms of prices. All that is involved is a little algebra.

Let us define:

P_i as the present price of asset i.

P_M as the present price of the market portfolio (all assets).

Y_i as the dollar value of the asset one period hence. It is market value plus any dividends.

Y_M as the dollar value of the market portfolio one period hence including dividends.

$\text{cov}(Y_i Y_M)$ as the covariance between Y_i and Y_M.

$\text{var}(Y_M)$ as the variance in Y_M.

r_F as $(1 + R_F)$.

The return on asset i is

$$R_i = \frac{\text{Ending value} - \text{Beginning value}}{\text{Beginning value}}$$

In symbols,

$$R_i = \frac{Y_i - P_i}{P_i} = \frac{Y_i}{P_i} - 1$$

Similarly,

$$R_M = \frac{Y_M - P_M}{P_M} = \frac{Y_M}{P_M} - 1$$

Substituting these expressions into Equation (11.3) yields

$$\frac{\overline{Y}_i}{P_i} - 1 = R_F + \left(\frac{\overline{Y}_M}{P_M} - 1 - R_F\right) \frac{\text{cov}(R_i R_M)}{\sigma_M{}^2} \tag{11.7}$$

Now we can rewrite $\text{cov}(R_i R_M)$ as

$$\text{cov}(R_i R_M) = E\left[\left(\frac{Y_i - P_i}{P_i} - \frac{\overline{Y}_i - P_i}{P_i}\right)\left(\frac{Y_M - P_M}{P_M} - \frac{\overline{Y}_M - P_M}{P_M}\right)\right]$$

$$= E\left[\left(\frac{Y_i}{P_i} - \frac{\overline{Y}_i}{P_i}\right)\left(\frac{Y_M}{P_M} - \frac{\overline{Y}_M}{P_M}\right)\right] = \frac{1}{P_i P_M} \text{cov}(Y_i Y_M)$$

Similarly,

$$\sigma_m{}^2 = \frac{1}{P_M{}^2} \text{var}(Y_M)$$

Substituting these into Equation (11.7) adding 1 to both sides of the equation and recalling that $r_F = 1 + R_F$,

$$\frac{\overline{Y}_i}{P_i} = r_F + \left(\frac{\overline{Y}_M}{P_M} - r_F\right) \frac{\dfrac{1}{P_i}\dfrac{1}{P_M} \text{cov}(Y_i Y_M)}{\dfrac{1}{P_M{}^2} \text{var}(Y_M)}$$

Multiplying both sides of the equation by P_i and simplifying the last term on the right-hand side,

$$\overline{Y}_i = r_F P_i + (\overline{Y}_M - r_F P_M) \frac{\text{cov}(Y_i Y_M)}{\text{var}(Y_M)}$$

Solving this expression for P_i,

$$P_i = \frac{1}{r_F}\left[\overline{Y}_i - (\overline{Y}_M - r_F P_M) \frac{\text{cov}(Y_i Y_M)}{\text{var}(Y_M)}\right]$$

Valuation formulas of this type have often been suggested in the security analysis literature. The equation involves taking the expected dollar return next year, $(\overline{Y}_i)$, subtracting off some payment as compensation for risk-taking, and then taking the present value of the net result. The term in square brackets can be thought of as the certainty equivalent of the horizon cash payment, and to find the present value of the certainty equivalent, we simply discount it at the riskless rate of interest. While this general idea is not new, the explicit definition of how to find the certainty equivalent is one of the fundamental contributions of the CAPM. It can be shown that

$$\frac{\overline{Y}_M - r_F P_M}{[\text{var}(Y_M)]^{1/2}}$$

is equal to a measure of the market price of risk and that

$$\frac{\text{cov}(Y_i Y_M)}{[\text{var}(Y_M)]^{1/2}}$$

is the relevant measure of risk for any asset.

CONCLUSION

In this chapter we have discussed the Sharpe-Lintner-Mossin form of a general equilibrium relationship in the capital markets. This model, usually referred to as the capital asset pricing model or standard CAPM, is a fundamental contribution to understanding the manner in which capital markets function. It is worthwhile highlighting some of the implications of this model.

First, we have shown that, under the assumptions of the CAPM, the only portfolio of risky assets that any investor will own is the market portfolio. Recall that the market portfolio is a portfolio in which the fraction invested in any asset is equal to the market value of that asset divided by the market value of all risky assets. Each investor will adjust the risk of the market portfolio to his or her preferred risk-return combination by combining the market portfolio with lending or borrowing at the riskless rate. This leads directly to the two mutual fund theorem. The two mutual fund theorem states that all investors can construct an optimum portfolio by combining a market fund with the riskless asset. Thus, all investors will hold a portfolio along the line connecting R_F with $\overline{R}_M$ in expected return, standard deviation of return space. See Figure 11.5.

This line, usually called the capital market line, which describes all efficient portfolios, is a pictorial representation of the equation

$$\overline{R}_e = R_F + \frac{\overline{R}_M - R_F}{\sigma_M} \sigma_e$$

Thus, we can say that the return on an efficient portfolio is given by the market price of time plus the market price of risk times the amount of risk on an efficient

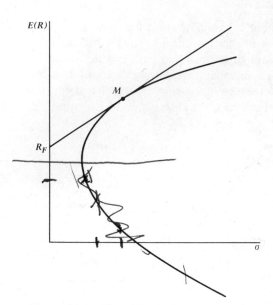

Figure 11.5   The efficient frontier.

portfolio. Note that risk is defined as the standard deviation of return on any efficient portfolio.

From the equilibrium relationship for efficient portfolios we were able to derive the equilibrium relationship for any security or portfolio (efficient or inefficient). This relationship, presented in Figure 11.6, is given by

$$\overline{R}_i = R_F + \left(\frac{\overline{R}_M - R_F}{\sigma_M} \right) \frac{\sigma_{iM}}{\sigma_M}$$

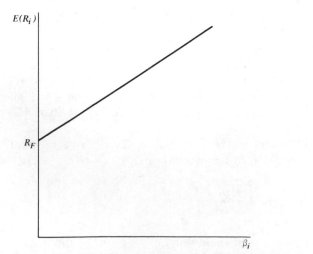

Figure 11.6   The security market line.

or

$$\bar{R}_i = R_F + \beta_i(\bar{R}_M - R_F)$$

This relationship is usually called the security market line. Notice that it might have been called the security-portfolio market line for it describes the equilibrium return on all portfolios, as well as all securities.

Examination of the first form of the security market line shows that it is analogous in many ways to the capital market line. As we have shown, the impact of a security on the risk of the market portfolio is given by σ_{iM}/σ_M. Thus, we can state that the equilibrium return on any security is equal to the price of time plus the market price of risk times the relevant definition of risk for the security.

The security market line clearly shows that return is an increasing function, in fact, a linearly increasing function, of risk. Furthermore, it is only market risk that affects return. The investor receives no added return for bearing diversifiable risk.

The capital asset pricing model has been derived under a set of very restrictive assumptions. The test of a model is how well it describes reality. The key test is: Does it describe the behavior of returns in the capital markets? These tests will be taken up in Chapter 13. However, before we turn to these tests, it is logical to examine forms of the general equilibrium relationship that exist under less restrictive assumptions. Even if the standard CAPM model explains the behavior of security returns, it obviously does not explain the behavior of individual investors. Individual investors hold nonmarket and, in fact, quite often, very small portfolios. Furthermore, by developing alternative forms of the general equilibrium relationship, we can test whether observed returns are more consistent with one of these than they are with the standard CAPM.

QUESTIONS AND PROBLEMS

1. Assume that the following assets are correctly priced according to the security market line. Derive the security market line. What is the expected return on an asset with a Beta of two?

$$\bar{R}_1 = 6\% \qquad \beta_1 = 0.5$$
$$\bar{R}_2 = 12\% \qquad \beta_2 = 1.5$$

2. Assume the security market line given below. Assume that analysts have estimated the Beta on two stocks as follows: $\beta_x = 0.5$ and $\beta_y = 2$. What must the expected return on the two securities be in order for them to be a good purchase?

$$\bar{R}_i = 0.04 + 0.08\beta_i.$$

3. Assume that over some period a CAPM was estimated. The results are shown below. Assume that over the same period two mutual funds had the following results:

Fund A　　　Actual return = 10%　Beta = 0.8
Fund B　　　Actual return = 15%　Beta = 1.2

What can be said about the fund performance?

$$\overline{R}_i = 0.06 + 0.19\beta_i$$

4. Consider the CAPM line shown below. What is the excess return of the market over the risk-free rate? What is the risk-free rate?

$$\overline{R}_i = 0.04 + 0.10\beta_i$$

5. Write the CAPM shown in Problem 4 in price form.

6. Show that the standard CAPM should hold even if short sales are not allowed.

7. Assume that an asset exists with $\overline{R}_3 = 15\%$ and $\beta_3 = 1.2$. Further assume the security market line discussed in Problem 1. Design the arbitrage opportunity.

BIBLIOGRAPHY

1. Aivazian, Varouj. "The Demand for Assets under Conditions of Risk: Comment," *Journal of Finance,* **XXXII,** No. 3 (June 1976), pp. 927–929.
2. Bernstein, Peter L. "What Rate of Return Can You 'Reasonably' Expect?" *Journal of Finance,* **XXVIII,** No. 2 (May 1973), pp. 273–282.
3. Fama, Eugene. "Risk, Return and Equilibrium: Some Clarifying Comments," *Journal of Finance,* **XXIII,** No. 1 (March 1968), pp. 29–40.
4. ———. "Risk, Return and Equilibrium," *Journal of Political Economy,* **79,** No. 1 (Jan./Feb. 1971), pp. 30–55.
5. ———. "Risk, Return and Portfolio Analysis: Reply to [20]," *Journal of Political Economy,* **81,** No. 3 (May/June 1973), pp. 753–755.
6. Levy, Haim. "The Demand for Assets under Conditions of Risk," *Journal of Finance,* **XXVIII,** No. 1 (March 1973), pp. 79–96.
7. ———. "The Demand for Assets under Conditions of Risk: Reply to [1]," *Journal of Finance,* **XXXII,** No. 3 (June 1976), pp. 930–932.
8. Lintner, John. "Security Prices, Risk, and Maximal Gains from Diversification," *Journal of Finance* (Dec. 1965), pp. 587–615.
9. ———. "The Aggregation of Investor's Diverse Judgments and Preferences in Purely Competitive Security Markets," *Journal of Financial and Quantitative Analysis,* **IV,** No. 4 (Dec. 1969), pp. 347–400.
10. ———. "The Market Price of Risk, Size of Market and Investor's Risk Aversion," *Review of Economics and Statistics,* **LII,** No. 1 (Feb. 1970), pp. 87–99.

11. Markowitz, Harry M. "Nonnegative or not Nonnegative: A Question about CAPM's," *The Journal of Finance,* **38,** No. 2 (May 1983), pp. 283–296.
12. Modigliani, Franco, and Pogue, Jerry. "An Introduction to Risk and Return," *Financial Analysts Journal,* **30,** No. 2 (March/April 1974), pp. 68–80.
13. ———. "An Introduction to Risk and Return: Part II," *Financial Analysts Journal,* **30,** No. 3 (May/June 1974), pp. 69–86.
14. Ross, Stephen. "A Simple Approach to the Valuation of Risky Streams," *Journal of Business,* **51,** No. 3 (July 1978), pp. 453–475.
15. Rubinstein, Mark. "An Aggregation Theorem for Securities Markets," *Journal of Financial Economy,* **1,** No. 3 (Sept. 1974), pp. 225–244.
16. Rubinstein, Mark E. "A Mean-Variance Synthesis of Corporate Financial Theory," *Journal of Finance,* **XXXVIII,** No. 1 (March 1973), pp. 167–181.
17. Sharpe, W.F. "Capital Asset Prices: A Theory of Market Equilibrium Under Conditions of Risk," *Journal of Finance* (Sept. 1964), pp. 425–442.
18. Sharpe, William. "Bonds Versus Stocks: Some Lessons from Capital Market Theory," *Financial Analysts Journal,* **29,** No. 6 (Nov./Dec. 1973), pp. 74–80.
19. Stapleton, C. Richard. "Portfolio Analysis, Stock Valuation and Capital Budgeting Decision Rules for Risky Projects," *Journal of Finance,* **XXVI,** No. 1 (March 1971), pp. 95–117.
20. Tsiang, S.C. "Risk, Return and Portfolio Analysis: Comment on [4]," *Journal of Political Economy,* **81,** No. 81, No. 3 (May/June 1973), pp. 748–752.
21. Turnbull, Stuart. "Market Value and Systematic Risk," *Journal of Finance,* **XXXII,** No. 4 (Sept. 1977), pp. 1125–1142.

Chapter 12

Nonstandard Forms of Capital Asset Pricing Models

The CAPM model developed in the previous chapter would provide a complete description of the behavior of capital markets if each of the assumptions set forth held. The test of the CAPM model is how well it describes reality. But even before we examine these tests, it is useful to develop equilibrium models based on more realistic assumptions. Most of the assumptions underlying the CAPM violate conditions in the real world. This does not mean that we should disregard the CAPM model, for the differences from reality may be sufficiently unimportant that they do not materially affect the explanatory power of the model. On the other hand, the incorporation of alternative, more realistic assumptions into the model has several important benefits. While the CAPM may describe equilibrium returns on the macro level, it certainly is not descriptive of micro (individual investor) behavior. For example, most individuals and many institutions hold portfolios of risky assets that do not resemble the market portfolio. We might get better insight into investor behavior by examining models developed under alternative and more realistic assumptions. Another reason for examining other equilibrium models is that it allows us to formulate and test alternative explanations of equilibrium returns. The CAPM may work well; but do other models work better and explain discrepancies from the CAPM? Finally, and perhaps most important, because the CAPM assumes several real-world influences away, it does not provide us with a mechanism for studying the impact of those influences on capital market equilibrium or on individual decision making. Only by recognizing the presence of these influences can their impact be investigated. For example, if we assume personal taxes do not exist, there is no way the equilibrium model can be used to study the effects of taxes. By constructing a model that includes taxes, we can study the impact of taxes on individual investor behavior and on equilibrium returns in the capital market.

The effects of modifying most of the assumptions of the CAPM model have been examined in the economics and finance literature. We review much of this work in this chapter. We place special emphasis on two assumptions: the ability to lend and borrow infinite sums of money at the riskless rate and the absence of personal taxes. The reason we do so is not only because these are important influences, but also because they lead to the development of full-fledged general equilibrium models of a form that are amenable to testing.

In the remainder of this chapter we discuss general equilibrium models derived under more realistic assumptions about each of the following influences:

Short sales

Riskless lending and borrowing

Personal taxes

Nonmarketable assets

Heterogeneous expectations

Non-price-taking behavior

Multiperiod analysis

SHORT SALES DISALLOWED

One of the assumptions made in deriving the capital asset pricing model is that the investor can engage in unlimited short sales. Furthermore, short sales were defined in the broadest sense of the term in that the investor was allowed to sell any security (whether owned or not) and to use the proceeds to buy any other security.[1] This was a convenient assumption and it simplified the mathematics of the derivation, but it was *not* a necessary assumption. Exactly the same result would have been obtained had short sales been disallowed. The economic intuition behind this is quite simple.[2] In the CAPM framework all investors hold the market portfolio in equilibrium. Since in equilibrium no investor sells any security short, prohibiting short selling cannot change the equilibrium.[3] Thus, the same CAPM relationship would be derived irrespective of whether short sales are allowed or prohibited.

MODIFICATIONS OF RISKLESS LENDING AND BORROWING

A second assumption of the CAPM is that investors can lend and borrow unlimited sums of money at the riskless rate of interest. Such an assumption is clearly not descriptive of the real world. It seems much more realistic to assume

---

[1]The allowance of short sales was reflected in the constraint on our basic problem in Chapter 4, that $\Sigma X_i = 1$ while simultaneously not constraining X_i to be positive.

[2]For a formal proof, see Lintner [45].

[3]The more mathematically inclined reader can reach this same conclusion by using the Kuhn–Tucker conditions on the basic problem outlined in the previous chapter. The derivative of the Lagrangian with respect to each security will have a Kuhn–Tucker multiplier added to it; but since each security is contained in the market portfolio, the value of each Kuhn–Tucker multiplier will be zero. Hence, the solution will be unchanged.

that investors can lend unlimited sums of money at the riskless rate but cannot borrow at a riskless rate. The lending assumption is equivalent to investors being able to buy government securities equal in maturity to their single-period horizon. Such securities exist and they are, for all intents and purposes, riskless. Furthermore, the rate on such securities is virtually the same for all investors. On the other hand, it is not possible for investors to borrow unlimited amounts at a riskless rate. It is convenient to examine the case where investors can neither borrow nor lend at the riskless rate first, and then to extend the analysis to the case where they can lend but not borrow at the riskless rate.

No Riskless Lending or Borrowing

This model is the second most widely used general equilibrium model. The simple capital asset pricing model developed in the last chapter is the most widely used. Because of the importance of this model, we derive it twice. The first derivation stresses economic rationale, the second is more rigorous.

Simple Proof   In the last chapter we argued that systematic risk was the appropriate measure of risk and that two assets with the same systematic risk could not offer different rates of return. The essence of the argument was that the unsystematic risk of large diversified portfolios was essentially zero. Thus, even if an individual asset had a great deal of unsystematic risk, it would have little impact on portfolio risk and, therefore, unsystematic risk would not require a higher return. This was formalized in Figure 11.3, and an analogous diagram Figure 12.1 will be used here.

Let us recall why all assets are plotted on a straight line. First, we showed that combinations of two risky portfolios lie on a straight line connecting them in expected return Beta space. For example, positive combinations of portfolios A

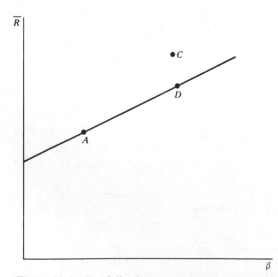

Figure 12.1   Portfolios in expected return Beta space.

and D lie on the line segment A–D. Thus, if securities or portfolios happened to lie on a straight line in expected return Beta space, all combinations of securities (e.g., portfolios) would lie on the same line.

Now consider securities C and D in Figure 12.1. They both have the same systematic risk, but C has a higher return. Clearly, an investor would purchase C rather than D until the prices adjusted so that they offered the same return. In fact, an investor could purchase C and sell D short and have an asset with positive expected return and no systematic risk. Such an opportunity cannot exist in equilibrium. In short, all portfolios and securities must plot along a straight line.

One portfolio that lies along the straight line is the market portfolio. This can be seen in either of two ways. If it did not lie along the straight line, two assets would exist with the same systematic risk and different return, and in equilibrium, equivalent assets must offer the same return. In addition, note that all combinations of securities lie on the line and the market portfolio is a weighted average of the securities.

A straight line can be described by any two points. One convenient point is the market portfolio. A second convenient portfolio is where the straight line cuts the vertical axis (where Beta equals zero).[4]

The equation of a straight line is

$$\text{Expected return} = a + b(\text{Beta})$$

This must hold for a portfolio with zero Beta. Letting $\overline{R}_z$ be the expected return on this portfolio, we have

$$\overline{R}_z = a + b(0) \quad \text{or} \quad a = \overline{R}_z$$

The equation must also hold for the market portfolio. If $\overline{R}_M$ is the expected return on the market and, recalling that the Beta for the market portfolio is one, we have

$$\overline{R}_M = \overline{R}_z + b(1) \quad \text{or} \quad b = \overline{R}_M - \overline{R}_Z$$

Putting this together and letting $\overline{R}_i$ and β_i be the expected return and Beta on an asset or portfolio, the equation for the expected return on any security or portfolio becomes

$$\overline{R}_i = \overline{R}_Z + (\overline{R}_M - \overline{R}_Z)\beta_i \tag{12.1}$$

This is the so-called zero Beta version of the capital asset pricing model and is

---

[4]To see that such a point exists, note that the straight line must go indefinitely in both directions. All positive combinations of A and D lie on the line segment between A and D. However, if we purchase D and sell A short, we move above D, and vice versa. Thus, the line continues indefinitely and, in particular, cuts the vertical axis.

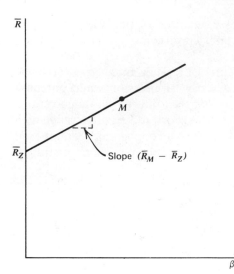

Figure 12.2 The zero Beta capital asset pricing line.

plotted in Figure 12.2. This form of the general equilibrium relationship is often referred to alternatively as a two-factor model.

Rigorous Derivation Assume for the moment that the market portfolio lies on the efficient frontier in expected return standard deviation space. Later in this chapter we show that it must, indeed, do so. In Chapter 4 we showed that the entire efficient frontier can be traced out by allowing the riskless rate of interest to vary and finding the tangency point between the efficient frontier and a ray passing through the riskless rate (on the vertical axis). Corresponding to every "risk-free rate" there was one point on the efficient frontier, and vice versa. There is, of course, one unique riskless rate in the market (if any). Thus, the procedure of varying the riskless rate was simply a method of obtaining the full efficient frontier. In all cases but one what we called the riskless rate was an artificial construct we used to obtain one point on the efficient frontier. Define R'_F as the riskless rate such that if investors could lend and borrow unlimited amounts of funds at the rate R'_F, they would hold the market portfolio.

The investor who could lend and borrow at the riskless rate R'_F would face an investment opportunity set as depicted in Figure 12.3. To solve for optimal proportions, he or she would face a set of simultaneous equations directly analogous to Equation (11.4). One such equation is[5]

$$\lambda \left(X_1 \sigma_{1j} + X_2 \sigma_{2j} + \cdots + X_j \sigma_j^2 + \cdots + X_N \sigma_{Nj} \right) = \overline{R}_j - R'_F \qquad (12.2)$$

---

[5]These equations are first-order conditions and must hold for the tangency point of any line drawn from the vertical axis and the efficient frontier.

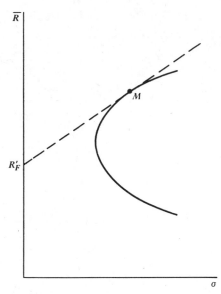

Figure 12.3   The opportunity set with rate R_F.

Note that in the equation the X_i's are market proportions because R'_F is defined as that value of the riskless rate that causes investors to hold the market portfolio.

In the previous chapter we showed that the term in parenthesis in the left-hand side of Equation (12.2) was simply the covariance between the return on security j and the return on the market portfolio. Thus, Equation (12.2) can be written as

$$\lambda \, \text{cov}(R_J R_M) = \overline{R}_j - R'_F$$

or

$$\overline{R}_j = R'_F + \lambda \, \text{cov}(R_J R_M) \tag{12.3}$$

The expected return on the market portfolio is a weighted average of the expected return on individual securities. Since Equation (12.3) holds for each security, it must also hold for the market. Thus,

$$\overline{R}_M = R'_F + \lambda \, \text{cov}(R_M R_M).$$

But $\text{cov}(R_M R_M)$ is the variance of M so that

$$\overline{R}_M = R'_F + \lambda \sigma_M^2 \qquad \text{or} \qquad \lambda = \frac{\overline{R}_M - R'_F}{\sigma_M^2}$$

Substituting the expression for λ into equation (12.3) and rearranging yields

$$\overline{R}_j = R'_F + \frac{\overline{R}_M - R'_F}{\sigma_M^2} \text{cov}(R_j R_M)$$

or

$$\overline{R}_j = R'_F + \beta_j(\overline{R}_M - R'_F) \qquad (12.4)$$

Note that a riskless asset with a return of R'_F does not really exist. However, there are an infinite number of assets and portfolios giving a return of R'_F. They are located along the solid portion of the line segment $R'_F - C$ shown in Figure 12.4. Examine Equation (12.4). For R_j to be equal to R'_F the last term must be zero. Thus, any security or portfolio that has an expected return of R'_F must have a Beta (covariance with the market portfolio) equal to zero.

While equilibrium can be expressed in terms of any of the zero Beta portfolios on the solid portion of the line segment $R'_F - C$, it makes sense to utilize the least risky zero Beta portfolio. This is equivalent to the zero Beta portfolio that has the least total risk. We designate the minimum variance zero Beta portfolio as Z and its expected return as $\overline{R}_Z$.

Then, since $\overline{R}_Z = R'_F$, the security market line can be written as

$$\overline{R}_j = \overline{R}_Z + (\overline{R}_M - \overline{R}_Z)\beta_j$$

This is exactly the expression [Equation (12.1)] we found for the security market line earlier in this chapter.

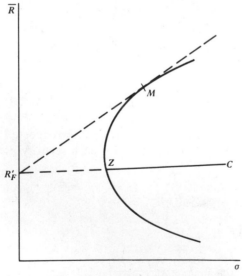

Figure 12.4 The location of portfolios with return R'_F.

Let us see if we can learn anything about the location of this minimum variance zero Beta portfolio. First, we know that the expected return on the zero Beta portfolio must be lower than the expected return on the market portfolio. The market portfolio is on the efficient segment of the minimum variance frontier, and the slope at this point must be positive. Thus, as we move along the line tangent to $\overline{R}_M$ toward the vertical axis, we lower return. Since $\overline{R}_Z$ is the intercept of the tangency line and the vertical axis, it has a return less than $\overline{R}_M$. Second, as we prove below, the minimum variance zero Beta portfolio cannot be efficient.

Proof

Denote by s the portfolio that has the smallest possible variance. This portfolio can be formed as a combination of the market portfolio and the zero Beta portfolio.

$$\sigma_s^2 = X_Z^2 \sigma_Z^2 + (1 - X_Z)^2 \sigma_M^2$$

There is no covariance term since the covariance between these two assets is zero. To find the weights in each portfolio that minimize variance, take the derivative with respect to X_Z and set it equal to zero, or

$$\frac{d\sigma_s^2}{dX_Z} = 2X_Z\sigma_Z^2 - 2\sigma_M^2 + 2X_Z\sigma_M^2 = 0$$

Solving for X_Z,

$$X_Z = \frac{\sigma_M^2}{\sigma_M^2 + \sigma_Z^2}$$

Since both σ_M^2 and σ_Z^2 must be positive numbers, that portfolio with the smallest possible variance must involve positive weights on both the zero Beta and market portfolio. Since $\overline{R}_Z < \overline{R}_M$, portfolios of Z and M with positive weights must have higher expected returns than Z. Since the minimum variance portfolio has higher return and smaller variance than Z, Z cannot be on the efficient portion of the minimum variance frontier.

We can locate portfolios Z, M, and s on the minimum variance frontier of all portfolios in expected return standard deviation space.[6] This is done in Figure 12.5. This figure presents the location of all efficient portfolios in expected return standard deviation space. All investors will hold some portfolio that lies along the efficient frontier (*SMC*). Investors who hold portfolios offering returns be-

---

[6]The minimum variance curve or minimum variance frontier contains the set of portfolios that offers the lowest risk at any obtainable level of return. The efficient set (frontier) is a subset of these minimum variance portfolios.

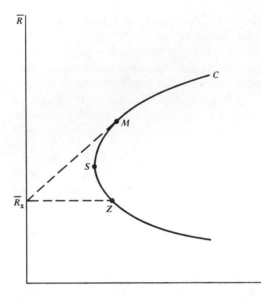

Figure 12.5   The minimum variance frontier.

tween s and $\overline{R}_M$ will hold combinations of the zero Beta portfolio and the market portfolio.[7] Investors who choose to hold portfolios to the right of M (choose returns above $\overline{R}_M$) will hold a portfolio constructed by selling portfolio Z short and buying the market portfolio. No investor will choose to hold only portfolio Z for this is an inefficient portfolio. Furthermore, since investors in the aggregate hold the market portfolio, the aggregate holding of portfolio Z (long positions minus short positions) must be exactly zero. Note also that we still have a two mutual fund theorem. All investors can be satisfied by transactions in two mutual funds: the market portfolio and the minimum variance zero Beta portfolio.

We started out this section by assuming that the market portfolio is efficient. While we do not intend to provide a rigorous proof of its efficiency, a few comments should convince the reader of its truth. Those interested in a rigorous proof are referred to Fama [17].

With homogeneous expectations, all investors face the same efficient frontier. Recall that with short sales allowed all combinations of any two minimum variance portfolios are minimum variance. Thus, if we combine any two investors' portfolios we have a minimum variance portfolio. The market portfolio is a weighted average or portfolio of each investor's portfolio where the weights are the proportion each investor owns of the total of all risky assets. Thus, it is minimum variance. Since each investor's portfolio is efficient and since the return on the market is an average of the return on the portfolios of individual investors, the return on the market portfolio is the return of a portfolio on the efficient segment

---

[7]Recall that from Chapter 4 that the entire efficient frontier can be generated as portfolios of any two portfolios on the efficient frontier.

of the minimum variance frontier. Thus, the market portfolio is not only minimum variance but efficient.

Riskless Lending But no Riskless Borrowing

We have gone too far in changing our assumptions. As we agreed earlier, while it is unrealistic to assume that individuals can borrow at the riskless rate, it is realistic to assume that they can lend at a rate that is riskless. Individuals can place funds in government securities that have a maturity equal to their time horizon and, thus, be guaranteed of a riskless payoff at the horizon.

If we allow riskless lending, then the investor's choice can be pictured as in Figure 12.6[8] As we argued in earlier chapters, all combinations of a riskless asset and a risky portfolio lie on the straight line connecting the asset and the portfolio. The preferred combination lies on the straight line passing through the risk-free asset and tangent to the efficient frontier. This is the line $R_F T$ in Figure 12.6.

Notice that we have drawn T below and to the left of the market portfolio M and, hence, $\overline{R}_Z > R_F$. This was not an accident. Let us examine why this must hold. Before we introduced the ability to lend at the riskless rate, all investors held portfolios along the efficient frontier SMC (portfolios along the line $\overline{R}_Z M$ do not exist). With riskless lending the investor can hold portfolios of riskless and risky assets along the line $R_F T$. If the investor chooses to hold an investment on the line $R_F T$, he would be placing some of his funds in the portfolio of risky assets denoted by T and some in the riskless asset. The choice to hold any portfolio of risky assets other than T would never be made. Now, why can't T and M be

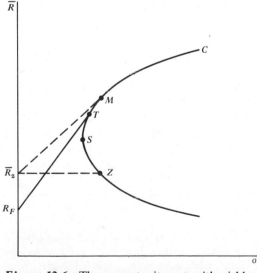

Figure 12.6 The opportunity set with riskless lending.

---

[8]Once again we are assuming short sales are allowed. This is a necessary assumption.

the same portfolio? As long as any investor has a risk–return trade-off such that he or she chooses to hold a portfolio of investments to the right of T, the market must lie to the right of T. For example, assume that all investors but one choose to lend money and hold portfolio T. Now this one investor who does not choose T must hold a portfolio to the right of T on the efficient frontier STC. If the investor did not, then he or she would be better off holding a portfolio on the line R_FT and, hence, holding portfolio T. Since the market portfolio is an average of the portfolios held by all investors, the market portfolio must be a combination of the investor's portfolio and T. Thus, it lies to the right of T.

M, being to the right of T, leads directly to $\overline{R}_z$ being larger than R_F. R_F is the intersection of the vertical axis and a line tangent to the efficient frontier at T. Similarly, $\overline{R}_z$ is the intersection of the vertical axis and a line tangent at M. Since the slope of the efficient frontier at M is less than at T and since M lies above T, the line tangent at M must intersect the vertical axis above the line tangent at T.[9] Thus, $\overline{R}_Z$ must be greater than R_F.

The efficient frontier is given by the straight line segment R_FT and curve TMC.[10] Notice that, in the case of no lending and borrowing, combinations of all efficient portfolios were efficient. In the case where riskless lending is allowed, not all combinations of efficient portfolios are efficient. It should be obvious to the reader that combinations of a portfolio from the line segment R_FT and a portfolio from the curve TMC are dominated by a portfolio lying along the curve TMC.

Portfolio T can be obtained by combining portfolios Z and M. Examining the efficient frontier we see that investors who select a portfolio along the line segment R_FT are placing some of their money in portfolio T (which is constructed from the market portfolio plus portfolio Z) and some in the riskless asset. Those that select a portfolio on the segment TM are placing some of their money in portfolio M and some in Z. Those that select a portfolio on MC are selling portfolio Z short and investing all of the proceeds in M. Notice that our two mutual fund theorem has been replaced with a three mutual fund theorem. All investors can be satisfied by holding (long or short) some combination of the market portfolio, the minimum variance zero Beta portfolio, and the riskless asset.[11]

Having examined all efficient portfolios in expected return standard deviation space, let us turn our attention to the location of securities and portfolios in expected return Beta space. Let us develop the security market line.

The market portfolio M is still an efficient portfolio. Thus, the analysis of the

---

[9] The property of the two slopes follows directly from the concavity of the efficient frontier proved in Chapter 3.

[10] The reader might note that portfolio T is a corner portfolio, a portfolio whose composition is different from those immediately adjacent to it. All portfolios to the right of T on the efficient frontier are made up of combinations of portfolios M and Z, while those to the left of T are made up of portfolios M and Z plus the riskless security.

[11] Note that while we continually speak of using the market portfolio and the minimum variance zero Beta portfolio to obtain the efficient frontier, any other two minimum variance portfolios would serve equally well.

last section holds. All securities contained in M have an expected return given by

$$\overline{R}_j = \overline{R}_Z + \beta_j(\overline{R}_M - \overline{R}_Z) \tag{12.5}$$

Similarly, all portfolios composed solely of risky assets have their return given by Equation (12.5). This plots as a straight line in expected return Beta space and is the line $\overline{R}_Z TMC$ in Figure 12.7. This equation holds only for risky assets and for portfolios of risky assets. It does not describe the return on the riskless asset or the return on portfolios that contain the riskless asset.

In the previous chapter we examined combinations of the riskless asset and a risky portfolio and found that they lie on the straight line connecting the two points in expected return Beta space. Since investors who lend all hold risky portfolio T, the relevant line segment is $R_F T$ in Figure 12.7.

Thus, while the straight line $\overline{R}_Z M$ can be thought of as the security market line for all risky assets and for all portfolios composed entirely of risk assets, it does not describe the return on portfolios (and, of particular note, on those efficient portfolios) that contain the riskless asset. Efficient portfolios have their return given by the two line segments $R_F T$ and TC in Figure 12.7. The fact that efficient portfolios have lower return for a given level of Beta than individual assets may seem startling. But remember that securities or portfolios on $\overline{R}_Z T$ have a higher standard deviation than portfolios with the same return on segment $R_F T$. In order to understand this, remember that the return on portfolio Z is uncertain, even though it has a zero Beta, while the return on the riskless asset is certain.

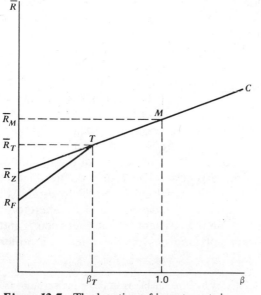

Figure 12.7 The location of investments in expected return Beta space.

Before moving on to other models, it is well worth reviewing certain characteristics of those we have been discussing, particularly insofar as they resemble or are different from the characteristics of the simple capital asset pricing model.

First, note that, under either of these models, all investors no longer hold the same portfolio in equilibrium. This is comforting for it is more consistent with observed behavior. Of less comfort is that investors still hold most securities (either long or short) and hold many securities short. In the case where neither lending nor borrowing is allowed, we have a two mutual fund theorem. In the case where riskless lending is allowed, we have a three mutual fund theorem.

As in the case of the simple CAPM, we still get a security market line. In addition, many of the implications of this relationship are the same. For risky assets or portfolios expected return is still a linearly increasing function of risk as measured by Beta. It is only market risk that affects the return on individual risky securities and portfolios of risky securities. On these securities the investor gains no extra return from bearing diversifiable risk. In fact, the only difference lies in the intercept and slope of the security market line.[12]

Other Lending and Borrowing Assumptions

Brennan [5] has analyzed the situation where riskless lending and borrowing is available, but at different rates. The efficient frontier for the individual when riskless borrowing and lending at different rates is possible was analyzed in Chapter 3. If all investors face the same efficient frontier, this efficient frontier must appear as in Figure 12.8.

In this diagram L stands for the portfolio of risky securities that will be held by all investors who lend money and B stands for the portfolio of all securities that will be held by investors who borrow money. The market portfolio must lie on the efficient frontier and it must lie between L and B.

Let us examine why. The only portfolios of risky securities held by investors are L and B and intermediate portfolios on the curve LB. Earlier we showed that combinations of efficient portfolios were efficient. In the earlier section lending and borrowing was not allowed so that the proof was that combinations of portfolios on the efficient portion of the minimum variance frontier were also on the efficient portion. The market portfolio is a weighted average of all portfolios held by individuals. Since these are efficient, we know from the earlier discussion that the market portfolio lies on the efficient portion of the minimum variance curve. But we can be even more precise. The return on the market portfolio is a weighted average of the return of portfolio L, portfolio B, and all intermediate portfolios. Thus, its return must be between L and B. Therefore, the market portfolio must lie somewhere on the efficient frontier between L and B. Having established that the market portfolio lies on the efficient frontier

---

[12]In all models the efficient frontier itself is affected by diversifiable risk. Since the shape of the frontier affects the location of the tangency portfolio, diversifiable risk has some effect on security returns.

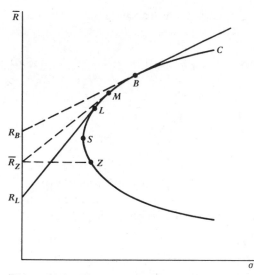

Figure 12.8   The opportunity set with a differential lending and borrowing rate.

between L and B, we derive, in the same manner, the same security market line
as we derived in the last section of this chapter. Equation (12.1) still holds.
However, remember that this equation only describes the return on securities
and portfolios that do not have any investment in the riskless asset (long or short).
Thus, the equation will not describe the return on portfolios between L and R_L
or with return more than R_B.

Brennan [5] has also examined the case where the borrowing rate differed from
the lending rate and where these rates were different for each investor. Once
again, because the market portfolio lies on the efficient frontier, an equation
identical in form to Equation (12.1) describes the return on all risky assets and
on all portfolios composed entirely of risky assets.

PERSONAL TAXES

The simple form of the capital asset pricing model ignores the presence of
taxes in arriving at an equilibrium solution. The implication of this assumption
is that investors are indifferent between receiving income in the form of capital
gains or dividends and that all investors hold the same portfolio of risky assets.
If we recognize the existence of taxes and, in particular, the fact that capital gains
are taxed, in general, at a lower rate than dividends, the equilibrium prices should
change. Investors should judge the return and risk on their portfolio after taxes.
This implies that, even with homogeneous expectations about the before-tax
return on a portfolio, the relevant (after tax) efficient frontier faced by each
investor will be different. However, a general equilibrium relationship should
still exist since, in the aggregate, markets must clear. In the appendix at the end
of this chapter we derive the general equilibrium pricing equation for all assets

and portfolios, given differential taxes on income and capital gains. The return on any asset or portfolio is given by

$$E(R_i) = R_F + \beta_i[(E(R_M) - R_F) - \tau(\delta_M - R_F)] + \tau(\delta_i - R_F) \quad (12.6)$$

where

δ_M = the dividend yield (dividends divided by price) of the market portfolio

δ_i = the dividend yield for stock i

τ = a tax factor that measures the relevant market tax rates on capital gains and income. τ is a complex function of investors' tax rates and wealth. However, it should be a positive number. See the appendix for further discussion.

The equilibrium relationship for expected returns has now become very complex. When dividends are on average taxed at a higher rate than capital gains (as they are in the U.S. economy), τ is positive and expected return is an increasing function of dividend yield. This is intuitively appealing since the larger the fraction of return paid in the form of dividends the more taxes the investor will have to pay and the larger the pretax return required. The reader may wonder why the last term contains R_F as well as the dividend yield. The reason for this is the tax treatment of interest on lending and borrowing. Since interest payments are for all intents and purposes taxed at the same rate as dividends, they enter the relationship in a parallel manner although with an opposite sign.[13] The fact that the term in square brackets has the correct form can be seen by letting security i be the market portfolio and noting that (since Beta equals one for the market portfolio) the equation reduces to $E(R_M) = E(R_M)$.

Examination of Equation (12.6) reveals that a security market line is no longer sufficient to describe the equilibrium relationship. In previous versions of general equilibrium relationships the only variable associated with the individual security that affected expected return was its Beta. Now we see from Equation (12.6) that both the securities Beta and its dividend yield affect expected return. This means that equilibrium must be described in three-dimensional spaces (R_i, β_i, δ_i) rather than two-dimensional space. The resultant equilibrium relationship [Equation (12.6)] will be a plane rather than a straight line. The plane will be located such that for any value of Beta expected return goes up as dividend yield goes up, and for any value of dividend yield expected return goes up as Beta goes up. We will have more to say about the location of the plane (the parametrization of this equation) in the next chapter.

---

[13]The implications of this for investor behavior are interesting. For example, an investor could convert a dividend-paying stock into one with only a capital gains return by borrowing a sum of money such that when the sum borrowed plus the initial planned investment in a stock is invested in the stock, interest payments exactly equal the dividend payments on the stock.

If returns are determined by an equilibrium model like that presented in Equation (12.6), it should be possible to derive optimal portfolios for any investor as a function of the tax rates paid on capital gains and dividends. While the mathematics of the solution are rather complex, the economic intuition behind the results is strong.[14] All investors will hold widely diversified portfolios that resemble the market portfolio, except they will be tilted in favor of those stocks in which the investor has a competitive advantage. For example, investors whose tax bracket is below the average effective rate in the market should hold more of high-dividend stocks in their portfolio than the percentage these stocks constitute of the market portfolio, while they should hold less (and in extreme cases even short sell) stocks with very low dividends. Low-tax-bracket investors have a comparative advantage in holding high-dividend stocks for the tax disadvantage of these stocks is less disadvantageous to them than it is to the average stockholder. Individual investors in the market seem to behave as the analysis suggests they should.[15] The optimization rules described in Elton and Gruber [12] ensure that markets will clear at the returns established in Equation (12.6).

NONMARKETABLE ASSETS

Up to now we have assumed that all assets are readily marketable so that each investor was free to adjust his or her portfolio to an optimum. In truth, every investor has nonmarketable assets or assets that he or she will not consider marketing. Human capital is an example of a nonmarketable asset. People are forbidden by law from selling themselves into slavery in the United States. There is no direct way that an investor can market his or her claims to future labor income. Similarly, the investor has other future monetary claims such as social security payments or the future payments from a private retirement program that cannot be marketed. There are categories of marketable assets that, although the investor might be able to market them, he or she considers them a fixed part of the portfolio. For example, investors who own their own home can market it, but they will often not consider switching houses as part of changes in their "optimum investment portfolio." This is due, in part, to large transaction costs but also because of nonmonetary factors.

If we divide the world up into marketable and nonmarketable assets, then a simple equation exists for the equilibrium return on all assets. Let

R_H equal the one period rate of return on nonmarketable assets
P_H equal the total value of all nonmarketable assets
P_M equal the total value of all marketable assets

---

[14]See Elton and Gruber [12] for the derivation of the composition of optimal portfolios under taxation.

[15]Pettit and Stanley [57] have found that investors tend to behave as this model suggests they should behave.

All other terms are defined as before. Then, it can be shown that [16]

$$E(R_j) = R_F + \frac{E(R_M) - R_F}{\sigma_M^2 + P_H/P_M \, \text{cov}(R_M R_H)} \left[\text{cov}(R_j R_M) + \frac{P_H}{P_M} \text{cov}(R_j R_H) \right]$$

To contrast this with the simple capital asset pricing model we can write the simple model as

$$E(R_j) = R_F + \frac{E(R_M) - R_F}{\sigma_M^2} [\text{cov}(R_j R_M)]$$

Notice that the inclusion of nonmarketable assets leads to a general equilibrium relationship of the same form as the simple model that excluded nonmarketable assets. However, the market trade-off between return and risk is different, as is the measure of risk for any asset. Including nonmarketable assets, the market risk-return trade-off becomes

$$\frac{E(R_M) - R_F}{\sigma_M^2 + \dfrac{P_H}{P_M} \text{cov}(R_M R_H)}$$

rather than

$$\frac{E(R_M) - R_F}{\sigma_M^2}$$

It seems reasonable to assume that the return on the total of nonmarketable assets is positively correlated with the return on the market, which would suggest that the market return-risk trade-off is lower than that suggested by the simple form of the model. How much lower is a function of both the covariance between the return on the nonmarketable assets and the marketable assets and the total value of nonmarketable assets relative to marketable assets. If nonmarketable assets had a very small value relative to marketable assets or if there was an extremely low correlation between the return on marketable and nonmarketable assets, there would be little harm done in using the standard CAPM. However, it seems likely that, since nonmarketable assets include at a minimum human capital and since wage rates as well as market performance are correlated with the performance of the economy, there will be important differences between these models.

---

[16]For a derivation see Mayers. Although this equation does not appear in Mayers [49], it can be derived from his Equation (19) with a little algebra. The reader may be bothered by the fact that P_H appears in our equation while the Mayers equations make use of the income (actually income plus value) of the asset one period hence. However, there is no inconsistency as Mayers's Equation (15) allows for the determination of P_H.

In addition, the definition of the risk of any asset has been changed. With nonmarketable assets it is a function of the covariance of an asset with the total stock of nonmarketable assets, as well as with the total stock of marketable assets. The weight this additional term receives in determining risk depends on the total size of nonmarketable assets relative to marketable assets. The risk on any asset that is positively correlated with the total of nonmarketable assets will be higher than the risk implied by the simple form of the CAPM.

Considering the difference in both the reward-risk ratio and the size of risk itself, we can see that the equilibrium return for an asset can be either higher or lower than it is under the standard form of the CAPM. If the asset is negatively correlated with the total of nonmarketable assets, its equilibrium return will be lower for its risk and the price of risk will be lower. However, if its return is positively correlated with the return on marketable assets, its equilibrium return could be higher or lower, depending on whether the increased risk is high enough to offset the decreased market price of risk.

Mayer [49] explores the implications of his model for the optimal portfolio holdings of individuals. As you would suspect, investors tilt their portfolio, holding a smaller percentage of those stocks (than found in the market) with which their nonmarketable securities are most highly correlated.

Brito [8, 9] has examined, in more detail, the optimum portfolio holdings of individuals in equilibrium when nonmarketable assets are present. He finds that each individual can select an optimal portfolio from among three mutual funds. The first mutual fund is a portfolio that has a covariance with each marketable asset equal in magnitude but opposite in sign to the covariance between the investor's nonmarketable portfolio and each marketable asset. Note two things about this fund: First, it will have a different composition for different investors, according to the nonmarketable assets they hold. Second, the reason for its optimality has an intuitive explanation. It is that portfolio that diversifies away as much of the nonmarketable risk as it is possible to diversify away. In short, it allows the investor to "market" as much of his or her nonmarketable assets as is possible. Brito then shows that each individual will allocate the remainder of his or her wealth between the riskless security (the second fund) and a third fund that is the market portfolio minus the *aggregate* of all investments made in the first type of fund by all investors. Note that, while the second and third funds are the same for all investors, the first fund has a different composition for each investor, according to the composition of his or her nonmarketable assets.

While Mayers's analysis is important for the insight it provides into the pricing of nonmarketable assets, it is at least as important for the insight it gives us into the missing asset problem. Empirical tests of general equilibrium models will always have to be conducted with the market defined as including something less than the full set of assets in the economy. The equilibrium equations described previously are perfectly valid for examining the missing asset problem, where R_M is now defined as the return on the collection of assets selected to represent the market and R_H is the return on the assets that were left out. In a manner exactly parallel to that presented, they allow us to think through the infuence of missing assets on both the markets risk-return trade-off and the equilibrium return from missing assets.

HETEROGENEOUS EXPECTATIONS

Several researchers have examined the existence and characteristics of a general equilibrium solution when investors have heterogeneous expectations.[17] Although all of these models lead to forms of an equilibrium pricing equation that have some similarity to those presented earlier in this chapter and in the last chapter, there are important differences. Equilibrium can still be expressed in terms of expected returns, covariances, and variance, but now these returns, covariances, and variances are complex weighted averages of the estimates held by different individuals. The weightings are very complex because they involve information about investor utility functions. In particular, they involve information about investors' trade-offs (marginal rate of substitution) between expected return and variance. But this trade-off for most utility functions is a function of wealth and, hence, prices. This means that prices are required to determine the risk-return trade-offs that we need to determine prices. Thus, in general, an explicit solution to the heterogeneous expectation problem cannot be reached. The problem can be made simpler by placing additional restrictions either on investor utility functions or on the characteristics of opportunities facing the investor.

The first approach was taken by Lintner [46]. He could not derive a simple capital asset pricing model under heterogeneous expectations because the marginal rate of substitution between expected return and variances was, itself, a function of equilibrium prices. If we assume a utility function such that the marginal rate of substitution is not a function of wealth, then we will not face this problem. We have already studied such a class of utility functions in Chapter 8. They were the functions exhibiting constant absolute risk aversion. Lintner assumed this type of function (to be precise, he assumed a negative exponential utility function).[18] Utilizing this function, he showed that the Sharpe–Lintner–Mossin form of the CAPM model holds and that the term $(\overline{R}_M - R_F)/\sigma_M^2$ in Equation (11.2) is proportional to the harmonic mean of the risk avoidance coefficient, and all expected values, variances, and covariances are complicated averages of the probability beliefs and risk preferences of all individuals.

A second way to arrive at more testable models of equilibrium under heterogeneous assumptions is to place restrictions on the form that the heterogeneity can assume. Gonedes [23] assumes that a set of basic economic activities exist such that any firm can be viewed as some combination of these basic economic activities and the heterogeneous expectations arise because of disagreement about the exact combination (weighting) of those basic economic activities that represent

---

[17]See Lintner [46], Sharpe [70], Fama [17], and Gonedes [23].

[18]Lintner assumes the negative exponential utility function given by $u(w) = e^{-a_i w_i}$. The measure of risk aversion is given by a_i.

a firm. Gonedes analyzes the case where this is the one source of heterogeneous expectations. He shows that, under this assumption, the minimum variance frontier is the same for all investors, even though they have heterogeneous expectations about the returns from different securities. Furthermore, the market portfolio is a minimum variance portfolio for each and every investor. Gonedes then proceeds to show that Beta is a sufficient measure of risk and that the equilibrium models lead to a linear relationship between expected return and Beta parallel to that found under simpler forms of the CAPM.

NON-PRICE-TAKING BEHAVIOR

Up to now we have assumed that individuals act as price takers in that they ignore the impact of their buying or selling behavior on the equilibrium price of securities and, hence, on their optimal portfolio holdings. The obvious question to ask is what happens if there are one or more investors, such as mutual funds or large pension funds, who believe that their behavior impacts price. The method of analysis used by Lindenberg [43, 44] derives equilibrium conditions under all possible demands by the price affector. The price affector selects his or her portfolio to maximize utility given the equilibrium prices that will result from his or her action. Assuming that the price affector operates so as to maximize utility, we can then arrive at equilibrium conditions. Lindenberg finds that all investors, including the price taker, hold some combination of the market portfolio and the riskless asset. However, the price affector will hold less of the riskless asset (will be less of a risk avoider) than would be the case if the price affector did not recognize the fact that his or her actions affected price. By doing so the price affector increases utility. Because the price affector still holds a combination of the riskless asset and the market portfolio, we still get the simple form of the CAPM, but the market price of risk is lower than it would be if all investors were price takers.

Lindenberg [44] goes on to analyze collective portfolio selection and efficient allocation among groups of investors. He finds that by colluding or merging, individuals or institutions can increase their utility. This analysis provides us with one reason for the existence of large financial institutions.

MULTIPERIOD CAPM

Up to now we have assumed that all investors make investment decisions based on a single-period horizon. In fact, the portfolio an investor selects, at any point in time, is really one step in a series of portfolios that he or she intends to hold over time to maximize his or her utility of lifetime consumption. Two questions immediately become apparent:

1. What are the conditions under which the simple CAPM adequately describes market equilibrium?
2. Is there a fully general multiperiod equilibrium model?

Fama [18] and Elton and Gruber [13, 14] have explored the conditions under which the multiperiod investment consumption decision can be reduced to the problem of maximizing a one-period utility function. These conditions are:

1. The consumer's tastes for particular consumption goods and services are independent of future events (any future sets of conditions).

2. The consumer acts as if consumption opportunities in terms of goods and their prices are known at the beginning of the decision period (are not state dependent).[19]

3. The consumer acts as if the distribution of one-period returns on all assets are known at the beginning of the decision period (are not state dependent).

Furthermore, Fama [18] has shown that if the investor's multiperiod utility function, expressed in terms of multiperiod consumption, exhibits both a preference of more to less and risk aversion with respect to each period's consumption, then the derived one-period utility has the same properties with respect to that period's consumption.

Recall earlier that risk aversion and preferring more to less were two assumptions necessary to obtain an efficient frontier. If we make the additional assumptions of the standard CAPM, we obtain the standard CAPM even for investors with a multiperiod horizon. If we make the additional assumptions underlying the zero Beta version of the CAPM, the zero Beta model is appropriate for investors with a multiperiod horizon. In short, the Fama multiperiod assumptions make single-period capital asset pricing models appropriate for investors with multiperiod horizons. The particular single-period model that results depends on the additional assumptions that are being made.

It is comforting to know that there are conditions under which the standard CAPM is appropriate when investors treat the portfolio selection problem in a multiperiod framework. However, we would expect that future utilities, returns, and prices are state dependent. For an excellent treatment of multiperiod equilibrium, under some general assumptions, the reader is referred to Stapleton and Subrahymanyam [72]. The reader should be warned that the mathematics involved are beyond any attempted in this book.

One specific case of a multiperiod general equilibrium model that has received special attention is the case where all of Fama's assumptions are met except that there is uncertain inflation. Friend, Lanskroner, and Losq [21] derive a general equilibrium relationship for the expected return on any asset under uncertain inflation, assuming that all utility functions exhibit constant proportional risk aversion. Their equilibrium appears similar to the simple form of the CAPM, but both the definition of the market price of risk and the risk on an asset are modified. In particular, they show that as long as the correlation between the

---

[19]A process is not state dependent if its outcomes do not depend on which one of a set of events occurs.

rate of return on the market and the rate of inflation is positive, the market price of risk is higher than that depicted in the standard CAPM. Furthermore, they show that the risk of any asset is not just a function of its covariance with the market; it is also a function of its covariance with the rate of inflation. If an asset's rate of return is positively correlated with the rate of inflation, the standard CAPM formulation overstates the risk of the asset. Finally, they show that the traditional CAPM will understate (overstate) the equilibrium rate of return on any asset if the correlation of the return on that asset with the rate of inflation is less than (greater than) the product of the correlation of the rate of return on the asset with the market return and the correlation between the market return and the rate of inflation.

SUMMARY

In this chapter we have shown that the simple form of the CAPM is remarkably robust. Modifying some of its assumptions leaves the general model unchanged, whereas modifying other assumptions leads to the appearance of new terms in the equilibrium relationship or, in some cases, to the modification of old terms. That the CAPM changes with changes in the assumptions is not unusual. What is unusual is (1) the robustness of the methodology in that it allows us to incorporate these changes, and (2) the fact that many of the conclusions of the original model hold, even with changes in assumptions.

The reader should be warned, however, that these results may seem stronger than they are. We have modified the assumptions one at a time. When assumptions are modified, simultaneously, the departure from the standard CAPM may be much more serious. For example, when short sales were disallowed but lending and borrowing were allowed, the standard CAPM held. When riskless lending and borrowing were disallowed but short sales were allowed, we got a model that very much resembled the standard CAPM, except that the slope and intercept were changed. Ross [62] has shown that when both riskless lending and borrowing and short sales are disallowed, one cannot derive a simple general equilibrium relationship.

There is no doubt that the general equilibrium models we now have are imperfect. The question is how well they describe conditions in the capital markets. We shall turn to this subject in the next chapter.

APPENDIX

Derivation of the General Equilibrium with Taxes

Earlier in this chapter we saw that any security or portfolio has an equilibrium return given by

$$\overline{R}_j = \overline{R}_Z + (\overline{R}_M - \overline{R}_Z)\frac{\sigma_{jM}}{\sigma_M^{\,2}}$$

We derived this expression by maximizing

$$\theta = \frac{\overline{R}_P - R'_F}{\sigma_P}$$

for the investor's portfolio (P) equal to the market portfolio M and the riskless rate defined as the intercept of a line tangent to point M. $\overline{R}_Z$ in the foregoing solution is the return on the minimum variance portfolio that is uncorrelated with the portfolio M.

We could have repeated this analysis for any portfolio P different from M, and for assets included in portfolio P we would get the following equilibrium relationship:

$$\overline{R}_j = \overline{R}_{0P} + (\overline{R}_P - \overline{R}_{0P}) \frac{\sigma_{jP}}{\sigma_P{}^2}$$

Where $\overline{R}_{0P}$ is the expected return on the minimum variance portfolio that is uncorrelated with portfolio P.

We will now make several changes in this expression. In a world of taxes, investors will reach equilibrium in terms of after-tax returns. The superscript A will be added to each variable to show that it holds in after-tax terms. In addition, the portfolio selected by each investor may be different because homogeneous before-tax expectations will produce heterogeneous after-tax expectations. Thus, we will use the subscript i to stand for investor i. Finally, since we are assuming unlimited lending and borrowing, an asset exists (the riskless asset) that is uncorrelated with all portfolios. Thus we can replace $\overline{R}_{0P}$ with R_F. With these changes, the equation above can be written as

$$\overline{R}_{ji}{}^A = R_{Fi}{}^A + (\overline{R}_{Pi}{}^A - R_{Fi}{}^A) \frac{\mathrm{cov}(R_{ji}{}^A R_{Pi}{}^A)}{(\sigma_{Pi}{}^A)^2} \tag{A.1}$$

While expectations of after-tax returns are heterogeneous, expectations of before-tax returns are homogeneous. We can write this expression in terms of before-tax returns.

Let

δ_j = the dividend yield on stock j
t_{di} = stockholder i's marginal tax rate on interest and dividends
t_{gi} = stockholder i's marginal tax rate on capital gains
w_i = the amount of stockholder i's wealth invested in risky assets
W = the sum of all wealth invested in risky assets

$$W = \sum_i w_i$$

Then,

$$\bar{R}_{ji}{}^A = (\bar{R}_j - \delta_j)(1 - t_{gi}) + \delta_j(1 - t_{di})$$
$$= \bar{R}_j(1 - t_{gi}) - \delta_j(t_{di} - t_{gi})$$
$$R_{Fi}{}^A = R_F(1 - t_{di})$$

If we assume that next period's dividend is sufficiently predictable, then we can treat it as a certain stream and,

$$\text{cov}(R_{ji}{}^A R_{Pi}{}^A) = \text{cov}(R_j R_{Pi})(1 - t_{gi})^2$$
$$(\sigma_{Pi}{}^A)^2 = \sigma_{Pi}{}^2(1 - t_{gi})^2$$

Substituting in Equation (A.1),

$$(\bar{R}_j - R_F)(1 - t_{gi}) - (\delta_j - R_F)(t_{di} - t_{gi}) = \frac{\bar{R}_{Pi}{}^A - R_{Fi}{}^A}{\sigma_{Pi}{}^2} \text{cov}(R_j R_{Pi})$$

Dividing through by $1 - t_{gi}$ and multiplying through by w_i and dividing through by λ_i where λ_i is defined as

$$\frac{\bar{R}_{Pi}{}^A - R_{Fi}{}^A}{\sigma_{Pi}{}^2} \frac{1}{(1 - t_{gi})}$$

we get

$$\frac{w_i}{\lambda_i}(\bar{R}_j - R_F) - (\delta_j - R_F)\frac{(t_{di} - t_{gi})}{(1 - t_{gi})}\frac{w_i}{\lambda_i} = w_i \text{cov}(R_j R_{Pi}) \qquad \text{(A.2)}$$

Summing this equation across all investors and dividing by Σw_i,

$$(\bar{R}_j - R_F)\frac{\displaystyle\sum_i (w_i/\lambda_i)}{\displaystyle\sum_i w_i} - (\delta_j - R_F)$$

$$\times \left[\sum_i \frac{(t_{di} - t_{gi})w_i}{(1 - t_{gi})\lambda_i} \Big/ \sum_i w_i\right] = \frac{\displaystyle\sum_i w_i \text{cov}(R_j R_{Pi})}{\displaystyle\sum_i w_i}$$

But note that since

$$\frac{\displaystyle\sum_i w_i R_{Pi}}{\displaystyle\sum_i w_i} = R_M$$

the right-hand side of this equation is equal to $\text{cov}(R_j R_M)$. Define the following symbols,

$$H = \left(\sum_i w_i \right) \bigg/ \left(\sum_i w_i / \lambda_i \right)$$

$$\tau = H \left(\sum_i \frac{(t_{di} - t_{gi}) w_i}{(1 - t_{gi}) \lambda_i} \right) \bigg/ \sum_i w_i$$

We can see that the tax factor τ is a complex weighted average of the investors' tax rates where the weights on each investor's tax rate is a function of the wealth he places in risky securities and his degree of risk avoidance as expressed by the ratio of excess return to variance on the portfolio he chooses to hold. Equation (A.2) can now be written as

$$(\overline{R}_j - R_F) - (\delta_j - R_F)\tau = H \, \text{cov}(R_j R_M) \tag{A.3}$$

Since expression (A.3) must hold for any asset or portfolio, it must hold for the market portfolio. Thus,

$$(\overline{R}_M - R_F) - (\delta_M - R_F)\tau = H\sigma_M^2$$

or

$$H = \frac{(\overline{R}_M - R_F) - (\delta_M - R_F)\tau}{\sigma_M^2}$$

Substituting the expression for H into the equation and rearranging yields

$$\overline{R}_j = R_F + \frac{(\overline{R}_M - R_F) - (\delta_M - R_F)\tau}{\sigma_M^2} \, \text{cov}(R_j R_M) + (\delta_j - R_F)\tau$$

or

$$\overline{R}_j = R_F + \beta_j[(\overline{R}_M - R_F) - (\delta_M - R_F)\tau] + (\delta_j - R_F)\tau$$

QUESTIONS AND PROBLEMS

1. Assume the equilibrium equation shown below. What is the return on the zero Beta portfolio and the return on the market assuming the zero Beta model holds?

$$\overline{R}_i = 0.04 + 0.10\beta_i$$

2. In the previous chapter we showed that the standard CAPM model could be written in price form. What is the zero Beta model in price form?

3. Given the model shown below, what is the risk-free rate if the post-tax equilibrium model describes returns?

$$\overline{R}_i = 0.05 + 0.10\beta_i + 0.24\delta_i$$

4. Given the following situation:

$$\overline{R}_M = 15 \qquad \sigma_M = 22$$
$$\overline{R}_Z = 5 \qquad \sigma_Z = 8$$
$$R_F = 3$$

Draw the minimum variance curve and efficient frontier in expected return standard deviation space. Be sure to give the coordinates of all key points. Draw the security market line.

5. You have just lectured two tax-free institutions on the necessity of including taxes in the general equilibrium relationship. One believed you and one did not. Demonstrate that if the model holds, the one that did could engage in risk-free arbitrage with the one that did not in a manner such that:

    A. Both parties believed they were making an arbitrage profit in the transaction.

    B. The one who believed in the post-tax model actually made a profit; the other institution incurred a loss.

6. Assume that returns are generated as follows:

$$R_i = \overline{R}_i + a_i(R_M - \overline{R}_M) + b_i(C - \overline{C})$$

where C is the rate of change in interest rates. Derive a general equilibrium relationship for security returns.

7. If $\overline{R}_M = 15\%$ and $R_F = 5\%$ and risk-free lending is allowed but riskless borrowing is not, sketch what the efficient frontier might look like in expected return standard deviation space. Sketch the security market line and the location of all portfolios in expected return Beta space. Label all points and explain why you have drawn them as you have.

8. Assume you paid a higher tax on income than on capital gains. Furthermore, assume that you believed that prices were determined by the post-tax CAPM. Now another investor comes along who believes that prices are determined by the pre-tax CAPM. Demonstrate that you can make an excess return by engaging in a two-security swap with him.

9. As we will see in the next chapter, most tests of the CAPM involve tests on common stock data and perform the tests using thc S&P index. You have just had a revelation that bonds are also marketable assets and thus should belong in the market return. Show what effect leaving them out might have on stocks with different characteristics.

BIBLIOGRAPHY

1. Alexander, Gordon. "An Algorithmic Approach to Deriving the Minimum-Variance Zero-Beta Portfolio," *Journal of Financial Economics,* **4,** No. 2 (March 1977), pp. 231–236.
2. Arzac, Enrique, and Bawa, Vijay. "Portfolio Choice and Equilibrium in Capital Markets with Safety-First Investors," *Journal of Financial Economics,* **4,** No. 3 (May 1977), pp. 277–288.
3. Black, Fischer. "Capital Market Equilibrium with Restricted Borrowing," *Journal of Business,* **45,** No. 3 (July 1972), pp. 444–455.
4. Borch, Karl. "Equilibrium, Optimum and Prejustices in Capital Markets," *Journal of Financial and Quantitative Analysis,* **IV,** No. 1 (March 1969), pp. 4–14.
5. Brennan, Michael J. "Capital Market Equilibrium with Divergent Borrowing and Lending Rates," *Journal of Financial and Quantitative Analysis,* **VI,** No. 5 (Dec. 1971), pp. 1197–1205.
6. ———. "Taxes, Market Valuation, and Corporate Financial Policy," *National Tax Journal,* **25** (1970), pp. 417–427.
7. Brenner, Menachem, and Subrahmanyam, Marti. "Intra-Equilibrium and Inter-Equilibrium Analysis in Capital Market Theory: A Clarification," *Journal of Finance,* **XXII,** No. 4 (Sept. 1977), pp. 1313–1319.
8. Brito, O. Ney. "Marketability Restrictions and the Valuation of Capital Assets under Uncertainty," *Journal of Finance,* **XXXII,** No. 4 (Sept. 1977), pp. 1109–1123.
9. ———. "Portfolio Selection in an Economy with Marketability and Short Sales Restrictions," *Journal of Finance,* **XXXIII,** No. 2 (May 1978), pp. 589–601.
10. Constantinides, George M. "Admissible Uncertainty in the Intertemporal Asset Pricing Model," *Journal of Financial Economics,* **8,** No. 1 (March 1980), pp. 71–87.
11. Easley, David, and Jarrow, Robert A. "Consensus Beliefs Equilibrium and Market Efficiency," *The Journal of Finance,* **38,** No. 3 (June 1983), pp. 903–912.
12. Elton, Edwin J., and Gruber, Martin J. "Taxes and Portfolio Composition, *Journal of Financial Economics,* **6** (1978), pp. 399–410.
13. ———. *Finance as a Dynamic Process* (Englewood Cliffs, N.J.: Prentice-Hall, 1975).
14. ———. "The Multi-Period Consumption Investment Decision and Single Period Analysis," *Oxford Economic Papers* (Sept. 1974).

15. Errunza, Vihang, and Losq, Etienne. "International Asset Pricing Under Mild Segmentation: Theory and Test," *The Journal of Finance,* **40,** No. 1 (March 1985), pp. 105–124.
16. Fama, Eugene. "A Note on the Market Model and the Two-Parameter Model," *Journal of Finance,* **XXVIII,** No. 5 (Dec. 1973), pp. 1181–1185.
17. ———. *Foundations of Finance* (New York: Basic Books, 1976).
18. ———. "Multi-Period Consumption-Investment Decision," *American Economic Review,* **60** (March 1970), pp. 163–174.
19. ———. "Risk, Return and Equilibrium," *Journal of Political Economy,* **79,** No. 1 (Jan.–Feb. 1971), pp. 30–55.
20. Figlewski, Stephen. "Information Diversity and Market Behavior," *The Journal of Finance,* **37,** No. 1 (March 1982), pp. 87–102.
21. Friend, Irwin, Landskroner, Yoram, and Losq, Etienne. "The Demand for Risky Assets and Uncertain Inflation," *Journal of Finance,* **XXXI,** No. 5 (Dec. 1976), pp. 1287–1297.
22. Friend, Irwin, and Westerfield, Randolph. "Co-Skewness and Capital Assets Pricing," *The Journal of Finance,* **35,** No. 4 (Sept. 1980), pp. 897–914.
23. Gonedes, Nicholas. "Capital Market Equilibrium for a Class of Heterogeneous Expectations in a Two-Parameter World," *Journal of Finance,* **XXXI,** No. 1 (March 1976), pp. 1–15.
24. Hagerman, Robert, and Kim, Han. "Capital Asset Pricing with Price Level Changes," *Journal of Financial and Quantitative Analysis,* **XI,** No. 3 (Sept. 1976), pp. 381–391.
25. Hart, Oliver. "On the Existence of Equilibrium in a Securities Model," *Journal of Economic Theory,* **9,** No. 3 (Nov. 1974), pp. 293–311.
26. Heckerman, Donald. "Portfolio Selection and the Structure of Capital Asset Prices When Relative Prices of Consumption Goods May Change," *Journal of Finance,* **XXVII,** No. 1 (March 1972), pp. 47–60.
27. ———. "Reply to [30]," *Journal of Finance,* **XXVIII,** No. 5 (Dec. 1973), p. 1361.
28. Hilliard, Jimmy E. "Asset Pricing under a Subset of Linear Risk Tolerance Functions and Log-Normal Market Returns," *Journal of Financial and Quantitative Analysis,* **XV,** No. 5 (Dec. 1980), pp. 1041–1062.
29. Hogan, William, and Warren, James. "Toward the Development of an Equilibrium Capital-Market Model Based on Semi-Variance," *Journal of Financial and Quantitative Analysis,* **IX,** No. 1 (Jan. 1974), pp. 1–11.
30. Hopewell, Michael. "Comment on [56]: A Model of Capital Asset Risk," *Journal of Financial and Quantitative Analysis,* **VII,** No. 2 (March 1972), pp. 1673–1677.
31. Jarrow, Robert. "Heterogeneous Expectations, Restrictions on Short Sales, and Equilibrium Asset Prices," *The Journal of Finance,* **35,** No. 5 (Dec. 1980), pp. 1105–1114.
32. Kamoike, Osamu. "Portfolio Selection When Future Prices of Consumption Goods May Change: Comment on [26]," *Journal of Finance,* **XXVIII,** No. 5 (Dec. 1973), pp. 1357–1360.

33. Korkie, Bob. "Comment: on [73]," *Journal of Financial and Quantitative Analysis,* **IX,** No. 5 (Nov. 1974), pp. 723–725.
34. Kraus, Alan, and Litzenberger, Robert. "Market Equilibrium in a Multi-Period State Preference Model with Logarithmic Utility," *Journal of Finance,* **XXX,** No. 5 (Dec. 1975), pp. 1213–1227.
35. ———. "Skewness Preference and the Valuation of Risk Assets," *Journal of Finance,* **XXXI,** No. 4 (Sept. 1976), pp. 1085–1100.
36. Kryzanowski, Lawrence, and Chau, To Hinh. "Asset Pricing Models When the Number of Securities Held is Constrained: A Comparison and Reconciliation of the Mao and Levy Models," *Journal of Financial and Quantitative Analysis,* **XVII,** No. 1 (March 1982), pp. 63–74.
37. Kumar, Prem. "Market Equilibrium and Corporation Finance: Some Issues," *Journal of Finance,* **XXIX,** No. 4 (Sept. 1974), pp. 1175–1188.
38. Landskroner, Yoram. "Nonmarketable Assets and the Determinants of the Market Price of Risk," *Review of Economics and Statistics,* **LIX,** No. 4 (Nov. 1977), pp. 482–514.
39. ———. "Intertemporal Determination of the Market Price of Risk," *Journal of Finance,* **XXXII,** No. 5 (Dec. 1977), pp. 1671–1681.
40. Lee, Chang. "Investment Horizon and the Functional Form of the Capital Asset Pricing Model," *Review of Economics and Statistics,* **LVIII,** No. 3 (Aug. 1976), pp. 356–363.
41. Lehari, David, and Levy, Haim. "The Capital Asset Pricing Model and the Investment Horizon," *Review of Economics and Statistics,* **LIX,** No. 1 (Feb. 1977), pp. 92–104.
42. Levy, Haim. "The Capital Asset Pricing Model, Inflation, and the Investment Horizon: The Israeli Experience," *Journal of Financial and Quantitative Analysis,* **XV,** No. 3 (Sept. 1980), pp. 561–594.
43. Lindenberg, Eric. "Capital Market Equilibrium with Price Affecting Institutional Investors," in Elton and Gruber. *Portfolio Theory 25 Years Later* (Amsterdam: North Holland, 1979).
44. ———. "Imperfect Competition Among Investors in Security Markets," Ph.D. Dissertation, New York University, 1976.
45. Lintner, John. "The Effect of Short Selling and Margin Requirements in Perfect Capital Markets," *Journal of Financial and Quantitative Analysis,* **VI,** No. 5 (Dec. 1971), pp. 1173–1195.
46. ———. "The Aggregation of Investors Diverse Judgments and Preferences in Purely Competitive Security Markets," *Journal of Financial and Quantitative Analysis,* **4,** No. 4 (Dec. 1969), pp. 347–400.
47. Long, John. "Stock Prices, Inflation, and the Term Structure of Interest Rates," *Journal of Financial Economics,* **1,** No. 2 (July 1974), pp. 131–170.
48. Losq, Etienne, and Chateau, John Peter D. "A Generalization of the CAPM Based on a Property of the Covariance Operator," *Journal of Financial and Quantitative Analysis,* **XVII,** No. 5 (Dec. 1982), pp. 783–798.
49. Mayers, D. "Nonmarketable Assets and Capital Market Equilibrium under

Uncertainty," in Jensen, M.C. (ed.). *Studies in Theory of Capital Markets* (New York: Praeger, 1972).

50. Mayers, David. "Nonmarketable Assets, Market Segmentation and the Level of Asset Prices," *Journal of Financial and Quantitative Analysis,* **XI,** No. 1 (March 1976), pp. 1–37.

51. ———. "Nonmarketable Assets and the Determination of Capital Asset Prices in the Absence of a Riskless Asset," *Journal of Business,* **46,** No. 2 (April 1973), pp. 258–267.

52. Merton, Robert. "An Intertemporal Capital Asset Pricing Model," *Econometrica,* **41,** No. 5 (Sept. 1973), pp. 867–888.

53. Milne, Frank, and Smith, Clifford, Jr. "Capital Asset Pricing with Proportional Transaction Cost," *Journal of Financial and Quantitative Analysis,* **XV,** No. 2 (June 1980), pp. 253–266.

54. Ohlson, James. "Equilibrium in Stable Markets," *Journal of Political Economy,* **85,** No. 4 (Aug. 1977), pp. 859–864.

55. Peles, Yoram. "A Note on Risk and the Theory of Asset Value," *Journal of Financial and Quantitative Analysis,* **VI,** No. 1 (Jan. 1971), pp. 643–647.

56. Pettit, R. Richardson, and Westerfield, Randolph. "A Model of Capital Asset Risk," *Journal of Financial and Quantitative Analysis,* **VII,** No. 2 (March 1972), pp. 1649–1668.

57. Pettit, R. Richardson, and Stanley, L. "Consumption-Investment Decisions with Transaction Costs and Taxes: A Study of the Clientele Effect of Dividends," *Journal of Financial Economics,* **5,** No. 3 (1979).

58. Rabinovitch, Ramon, and Owen, Joel. "Non-Homogeneous Expectations and Information in the Capital Asset Market," *Journal of Finance,* **XXXIII,** No. 2 (May 1978), pp. 575–587.

59. Reinganum, Marc R. "A New Empirical Perspective on the CAPM," *Journal of Financial and Quantitative Analysis,* **XVI,** No. 4 (Nov. 1981), pp. 439–462.

60. Roberts, Gordon. "Endogenous Endowments and Capital Asset Prices," *Journal of Finance,* **XXX,** No. 1 (March 1975), pp. 155–162.

61. Roll, Richard, and Ross, Stephen. "An Emperical Investigation of Arbitrage Pricing Theory," *Journal of Finance* (Dec. 1980), pp. 1073–1105.

62. Ross, Stephen. "Return, Risk, and Arbitrage," in Friend and Bickster. *Risks and Return in Finance* (Cambridge, Mass.: Ballinger, 1977).

63. ———. "The Capital Asset Pricing Model (CAPM), Short-Sale Restrictions and Related Issues," *Journal of Finance,* **XXXII,** No. 1 (March 1977), pp. 177–183.

64. ———. "Mutual Fund Separation in Financial Theory—The Separating Distributions," *Journal of Economic Theory,* **17,** No. 2 (April 1978), pp. 254–286.

65. ———. "The Current Status of the Capital Asset Pricing Model (CAPM)," *Journal of Finance,* **XXXIII,** No. 3 (June 1978), pp. 885–901.

66. Rubinstein, Mark. "The Strong Case for the Generalized Logarithmic Utility

Model as the Premier Model of Financial Markets," *Journal of Finance,* **XXXI,** No. 2 (May 1976), pp. 551–571.

67. Samuelson, Paul. "Lifetime Portfolio Selection by Dynamic Stochastic Programming," *Review of Economics and Statistics,* **LI,** No. 3 (Aug. 1969), pp. 239–246.

68. Samuelson, Paul, and Merton, Robert. "Generalized Mean-Variance Trade-offs for Best Perturbation Corrections to Approximate Portfolio Decisions," *Journal of Finance,* **XXIX,** No. 1 (March 1974), pp. 27–40.

69. Sandmo, Agnar. "Capital Risk, Consumption and Portfolio Choice," *Econometrica,* **37,** No. 4 (Oct. 1969), pp. 586–599.

70. Sharpe, William. *Portfolio Theory and Capital Markets* (New York: McGraw-Hill, 1970).

71. Siegel, Jeremy, and Warner, Jarold. "Indexation, The Risk-Free Asset, and Capital Market Equilibrium," *Journal of Finance,* **XXXII,** No. 4 (Sept. 1977), pp. 1101–1107.

72. Stapleton, Richard, and Subrahmanyam, Marti. "Multi-Period Equilibrium Asset Pricing Model," *Econometrica,* **46** (1977).

73. Stone, Bernell. "Systematic Interest-Rate Risk in a Two-Index Model of Returns," *Journal of Financial and Quantitative Analysis,* **IX,** No. 5 (Nov. 1974), pp. 709–721.

74. Williams, Joseph. "Risk, Human Capital, and the Investor's Portfolio," *Journal of Business,* **51,** No. 1 (Jan. 1978), pp. 65–89.

Chapter 13

Empirical Tests of Equilibrium Models

In the previous two chapters we stressed the fact that the construction of a theory necessitates a simplification of the phenomena under study. To understand and model any process, elements in the real world are simplified or assumed away. While a model based on simple assumptions can always be called into question because of these assumptions, the relevant test of how much damage has been done by the simplification is to examine the relationship between the predictions of the model and observed real-world phenomena. In our case the relevant test is how well the simple CAPM, or perhaps some other general equilibrium model, describes the behavior of actual capital markets.

The principle is easily stated and intuitively appealing. However, it opens up a new series of problems. Namely, how does one design meaningful empirical tests of a theory? In particular, how can one test the CAPM or any of its numerous variants? In this chapter we review several of the tests of the general equilibrium models that have been presented in the literature. In doing so, we discuss many of the problems encountered in designing these tests. Finally, we discuss recent work by Roll [29] that suggests certain problems with all of the tests of general equilibrium models and opens up the area to further questions.

THE MODELS — EX-ANTE EXPECTATIONS AND EX-POST TESTS

Most tests of general equilibrium models deal with either the standard CAPM or the zero Beta (two-factor) form of a general equilibrium model. The basic CAPM can be written as

$$E(R_i) = R_F + \beta_i[E(R_M) - R_F]$$

The no lending or borrowing version, often called the two-factor model, can be written as

$$E(R_i) = E(R_Z) + \beta_i[E(R_M) - E(R_Z)]$$

Recall that $E(R_Z)$ is the expected return on the minimum variance portfolio that is uncorrelated with the market portfolio.

Notice that these models are formulated in terms of expectations. All variables are expressed in terms of future values. The relevant Beta is the future Beta on the security. Furthermore, both the return on the market and the return on the minimum variance zero Beta portfolio are expected future returns.

Since large-scale systematic data on expectations does not exist, almost all tests of the CAPM have been performed using ex-post or observed values for the variables. This raises the logical question of how one justifies testing an expectational model in terms of realizations.

There are two lines of defense that have commonly been used by researchers. The simpler defense is to argue that expectations are on average and, on the whole, correct. Therefore, over long periods of time, actual events can be taken as proxies for expectations.

The more complex defense starts by assuming that security returns are linearly related to the return on a market portfolio (a version of the single-index model of Chapter 5). This model, called the market model, can be written as

$$\tilde{R}_{it} = \alpha_i + \beta_i \tilde{R}_{Mt} + \tilde{e}_{it} \tag{13.1}$$

The squiggle over a variable indicates that the variable is random.

The expected value of the return on security i is

$$E(R_i) = \alpha_i + \beta_i E(R_M)$$

Thus,

$$E(R_i) - \alpha_i - \beta_i E(R_M) = 0$$

Adding this equation to the right-hand side of Equation (13.1) and rearranging yields

$$\tilde{R}_{it} = E(R_i) + \beta_i[\tilde{R}_{Mt} - E(R_M)] + \tilde{e}_{it}$$

The simple form of the CAPM model is

$$E(R_i) = R_F + \beta_i[E(R_M) - R_F]$$

Substituting the expression for $E(R_i)$ into the previous equation and simplifying,

$$\tilde{R}_{it} = R_F + \beta_i(\tilde{R}_{Mt} - R_F) + \tilde{e}_{it} \tag{13.2}$$

Testing a model of this form with ex-post data seems appropriate. However, notice that there are three assumptions behind this model:

1. The market model holds in every period.
2. The CAPM model holds in every period.
3. The Beta is stable over time.

A test of this model on ex-post data is really a simultaneous test of all three of these hypotheses.

The reader should note that, if one had used the two-factor model instead of the Sharpe-Lintner-Mossin form, we would have found

$$\bar{R}_{it} = \bar{R}_{Zt} + \beta_i(\bar{R}_{Mt} - \bar{R}_{Zt}) + \bar{e}_{it} \tag{13.3}$$

rather than Equation (13.2). As in the previous case, a test of this model is really a simultaneous test of three hypotheses: the zero Beta version of the CAPM model holds in every period, the market model holds in every period, and Beta is stable over time. However, making these assumptions does express the model in terms of realized returns.

EMPIRICAL TESTS OF THE CAPM

There has been a huge amount of empirical testing of the standard form and the two-factor form of the CAPM model. A discussion of all empirical work would take a volume by itself. The approach we have adopted is to review the hypotheses that should be tested, to review some of the early work on testing the CAPM, then to discuss briefly a few of the problems inherent in any test of the CAPM. Finally, we review, in more detail, some of the more rigorous tests.

Some Hypotheses of the CAPM

Certain hypotheses can be formulated that should hold whether one believes in the simple CAPM or the two-factor general equilibrium model.

The first is that higher risk (Beta) should be associated with a higher level of return.

The second is that return is linearly related to Beta; that is, for every unit increase in Beta, there is the same increase in return.

The third is that there should be no added return for bearing nonmarket risk.

In addition, if some form of general equilibrium model holds, then investing should constitute a fair game with respect to it. That is, deviations of a security or portfolio from equilibrium should be purely random and there should be no way to use these deviations to earn an excess profit.

In addition to the hypotheses common to both the standard and the two-factor form of the CAPM, we can formulate hypotheses that attempt to differentiate between these general equilibrium models. In particular, the standard version implies that the security market line, drawn in return Beta space, should have an intercept of R_F and a slope of $(\overline{R}_M - R_F)$, while the two-factor version requires that it should have an intercept of $\overline{R}_Z$ and a slope of $(\overline{R}_M - \overline{R}_Z)$.

A Simple Test of the CAPM

Before we become involved in a discussion of the history and methodology of tests of the CAPM model, it seems worthwhile examining the results of a simple test of the CAPM to see if, over long periods of time, higher return has been associated with higher risk (as measured by Beta). Sharpe and Cooper [32] examined whether following alternative strategies, with respect to risk over long periods of time, would produce returns consistent with modern capital theory. In order to get portfolios with different Betas they divided stocks into deciles once a year on the basis of the Beta of each security.[1] To be more precise, Beta at a point in time was measured using 60 months of previous data. Once a year, for each year 1931–67, all New York Stock Exchange stocks were divided into deciles based on their rank by Beta. An equally weighted portfolio was formed of the stocks that comprised each decile. A strategy consisted of holding the stocks of a particular decile over the entire period. The stocks one holds change both because of the reinvestment of dividends and because the stocks that make up a particular decile change as the decile's composition is revised once a year. Notice that the strategy outlined by Sharpe and Cooper could actually be followed by an investor. Each year the investor divides stocks into deciles by Beta based on the previous five years' (60 months) returns. If investors want to pursue the high Beta strategy, they simply divide their funds equally among the stocks in the highest Beta decile. They do this every year and observe the outcomes. Table 13.1 shows what would have happened, on average, if an investor had done this each year from 1931 to 1967.

Table 13.1

Strategy	Average Return	Portfolio Beta
10	22.67	1.42
9	20.45	1.18
8	20.26	1.14
7	21.77	1.24
6	18.49	1.06
5	19.13	0.98
4	18.88	1.00
3	14.99	0.76
2	14.63	0.65
1	11.58	0.58

[1]The measure of Beta they used was analogous to the standard Beta computed by regressing the returns from any security against the market. The difference was that dividends were excluded both from the market and the stocks' return. The authors found the coefficient of determination between standard Beta and their measure was 0.996.

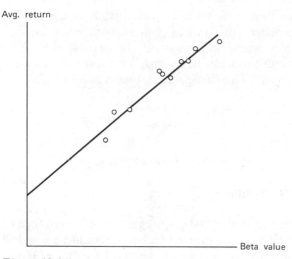

Figure 13.1

While the relationship between strategy and return is not perfect, it is very close. In general, stocks with higher Betas have produced higher future returns. In fact, the rank correlation coefficient between strategy and return is over 0.93, which is statistically significant at the 0.01 level. Similarly, buying stocks with higher forecast Beta would lead to holding portfolios with higher realized Betas. The rank correlation between strategy and Beta is 95%, which is significant at the 0.01 level.

The next logical step is to examine the relationship between the return that would have been earned and the risk (Beta) from following alternative strategies. Figure 13.1 from Sharpe and Cooper [32] shows this relationship. The equation of this graph is

$$\overline{R}_i = 5.54 + 12.75\beta_i$$

Over 95% of the variation in expected return is explained by differences in Beta. Thus, Beta has explained a very significant portion of the difference in return between these portfolios (strategies).

Sharpe and Cooper's work presents rather clear and easily interpreted evidence that, as general equilibrium theory suggests, there is a positive relationship between return and Beta. Furthermore, an examination of Figure 13.1 provides confidence that the relationship is both strong and linear. Let us now turn to some more sophisticated tests of the CAPM.

Some Early Empirical Tests

Most of the early empirical tests of the CAPM involved the use of a time series (first pass) regression to estimate Betas and the use of a cross-sectional (second pass) regression to test the hypotheses we derived from the CAPM model. To make this more concrete, let us turn to an early empirical study of the CAPM performed by Lintner and reproduced in Douglas [13]. Lintner first estimated Beta for each of the 301 common stocks in his sample. He estimated Beta by regressing each stock's yearly return against the average return for all stocks in the sample using data from 1954–63. The first-pass regression had the form

$$R_{it} = \alpha_i + b_i R_{Mt} + e_{it}$$

where b_i (the regression coefficient) was the estimate of the true Beta for stock i. Lintner then performed the second-pass cross-sectional regression

$$\overline{R}_i = a_1 + a_2 b_i + a_3 S_{ei}^2 + \eta_i$$

where S_{ei}^2 is the residual variance from the first-pass regression (the variance of e_i). Each parameter of this model has a theoretical value. a_3 should be equal to zero, a_1 should be equal to either R_F or $\overline{R}_Z$, and a_2 should be equal to either $\overline{R}_M - R_F$ or $\overline{R}_M - \overline{R}_Z$, according to the form of the CAPM that is being tested.[2] The values he obtained were

$$a_1 = 0.108$$

$$a_2 = 0.063$$

$$a_3 = 0.237$$

These results seem to violate the CAPM.[3] The term representing residual risk was statistically significant and positive. The intercept term a_1 would seem to be larger than any reasonable estimate of either R_F or $\overline{R}_Z$ and a_2, although statistically significant, has a value slightly lower than we could reasonably expect. Douglas [13] employed a similar methodology and found results that were similar to Lintner's.

Some Problems in Methodology

Miller and Scholes [27] in a classic article provide an analysis of the statistical problems inherent in all empirical tests of the CAPM. In addition to discussing the various theoretical problems associated with these tests, they also conducted a series of carefully constructed simulations designed to measure the extent to which certain previous studies have produced results that were biased by these statistical problems.

Miller and Scholes start with a discussion of possible biases due to misspecification of the basic estimation equations. One of the first considerations here is

---

[2] These theoretical values arise from Equations (13.2) and (13.3).

[3] Both a_2 and a_3 are statistically different from zero at the 0.01 level. The t values for these coefficients are 6.9 and 6.8, respectively.

that, if returns are really generated by the simple form of the CAPM, then the time series equation used to estimate Beta should be consistent with the CAPM. The CAPM in time series form is

$$\tilde{R}_{it} = R_{Ft} + \beta_i(\tilde{R}_{Mt} - R_{Ft})$$

or

$$\tilde{R}_{it} = (1 - \beta_i)R_{Ft} + \beta_i\tilde{R}_{Mt}$$

But the equation used by both Lintner and Douglas was the market model

$$\tilde{R}_{it} = \alpha_i + \beta_i\tilde{R}_{Mt}$$

Now, if R_F is a constant over the estimation period, no damage is done. The estimate of α_i should be equal to $(1 - \beta_i)R_{Ft}$. However, if R_{Ft} fluctuates over time and, if it is correlated with R_{Mt}, we have a classic case of missing variable bias and β_i will be a biased estimate of the true β_i. Furthermore, Miller and Scholes prove that if R_{Ft} and R_{Mt} are negatively correlated, then this will have the effect of biasing the intercept of the second-pass regression upward and its slope downward and this could, in part, explain the inconsistencies found by Lintner and Douglas. Miller and Scholes examine historical data and find a negative correlation. This is not surprising, for the stock market usually declines when interest rates go up. They test for the importance of this in explaining the Lintner findings. Although they find the influence is in the direction discussed herein, the order of magnitude of the bias is so small that it had almost no effect on Lintner's results.

Another possible source of equation misspecification that could account for finding an intercept too high and a slope too low is if the relationship between expected return and Beta was, in reality, nonlinear. Miller and Scholes test for nonlinearity and conclude that any nonlinearity that was present did not lead to the increased intercept and decreased slope.

A third possible source of distortion is the presence of heteroscedasticity. Heteroscedasticity is an often encountered problem in econometric tests. It occurs when the variance of the error is larger for higher values of the independent variable than it is for smaller values. In this case, it would imply that higher Beta stocks have a higher variance of return, unexplained by the market (nonmarket risk), than lower Beta stocks. Although Miller and Scholes found evidence of heteroscedasticity, they did not find that heteroscedasticity accounted for the high intercept and low slope. In fact, if anything, it biased the results in the other direction.[4]

---

[4]The reader should note that heteroscedasticity does reduce the estimate of the errors in the regression coefficients and so may lead you to conclude that a relationship is statistically significant when it, in fact, is not.

Having demonstrated that errors in estimating the basic equations did not account for the differences between the Lintner results and those predicted by some form of the CAPM, Miller and Scholes next consider the effect of possible errors in the definition of the variables.

One form of bias that we know is present is due to the error in measuring Beta for the second-pass regression. The β_i we arrive at in the first-pass regression is an estimate of the "true" Beta for stock i. Even if a true and stable Beta exists for stock i, all we have is an estimate of it, an estimate that may be unbiased but subject to sampling error. Any error in the estimate of Beta will cause the coefficient of β_i in the second-pass regression to be downward biased and the intercept to be upward biased.[5] Miller and Scholes show that this has an important effect on the results they estimate, that this resulted in the second-pass regression coefficient on Beta being only 64% of its true value, and that it caused a commensurate increase in the intercept.

There is a second effect of the Betas being measured with error that is also extremely important. To the extent that the true value of Beta is positively correlated with a compnay's residual variance, residual variance will serve as a proxy for the true Beta and return will be positively correlated with residual risk. Miller and Scholes conclude that this is, in fact, the case in the Lintner tests. Thus, although return is not dependent on residual variance, residual variance may show up as being statistically related to return in cross-sectional regression analysis because residual risk acts as a proxy variable for the true, but unobserved, Beta.

Miller and Scholes finally demonstrate that return distributions appear to be positively skewed and, if there is skewness, that the cross-sectional regression will show an association between residual risk and return, even though there is no such association.[6]

Having been able, thanks to Miller and Scholes, to catalog the potential problems present in any test of the CAPM, let us turn to an examination of two of the best sets of tests that have been performed.

Tests of Black, Jensen, and Scholes

Black, Jensen, and Scholes [6] were the first to conduct an in-depth time series test of the CAPM. They took as their basic time series model

$$R_{it} - R_{Ft} = \alpha_i + \beta_i(R_{Mt} - R_{Ft}) + e_{it}$$

When this equation is estimated on time series data, the regression coefficient α_i should be equal to zero if the simple CAPM describes returns.

---

[5] A proof of this is contained in the appendix at the end of this chapter.

[6] In addition to these considerations, Miller and Scholes also examine the sensitivity of the results to the index Lintner chooses for the market. They find that the results are reasonably insensitive to the choice of the stock market index. Roll [29], as discussed later, questions this result.

In order to test the CAPM, it is desirable to use a large number of securities. The obvious method is to estimate the equation for each of a series of securities and then examine the distribution of α_i. However, this is inappropriate because tests of the distribution of α's assume that the residuals (e_{it}, e_{jt}) are independent, and they are not.

One way to alleviate the problem is to run the time series regression on portfolios. Now $\bar{R}_{it}$ is the return on portfolio i and β_i is the Beta on portfolio i. Since portfolios utilized data on more than one security and, since the residual variance from the regression using portfolios will incorporate the effect of any cross-sectional interdependencies, the standard error of the intercept can be used to test the difference of α_i from zero.

When they form portfolios, Black, Jensen, and Scholes want to maximize the spread in Betas across portfolios so they can examine the effect of Beta on return. The most obvious way to do this is to rank stocks into portfolios by true Beta. But all we have is observed Beta. To rank into portfolios by observed Beta would introduce selection bias. Stocks with high observed Beta (in the highest group) would be more likely to have a positive measurement error in estimating Beta. This would introduce a positive bias into the Beta for high Beta portfolios and would introduce a negative bias into an estimate of the intercept α_i. In an attempt to avoid this problem, an instrumental variable was used to rank stocks into portfolios. An instrumental variable is one that ideally is highly correlated with the true Beta but can be observed independently. The instrumental variable used in this study and, indeed in most studies of the CAPM, is the Beta for each security in the previous time period.

The exact procedure Black, Jensen, and Scholes used was to employ five years of monthly data to estimate Betas and rank stocks into deciles (from highest to lowest). Each decile was then considered the portfolio in the next (e.g., sixth) year. Then data for the second through sixth year was used to rank stocks and

Table 13.2

	β	Excess Return[a]	α_i Intercept	ρ[b]
1	1.561	0.0213	−0.0829	0.963
2	1.384	0.0177	−0.1938	0.988
3	1.248	0.0171	−0.0649	0.988
4	1.163	0.0163	−0.0167	0.991
5	1.057	0.0145	−0.0543	0.992
6	0.923	0.0137	0.0593	0.983
7	0.853	0.0126	0.0462	0.985
8	0.753	0.0115	0.0812	0.979
9	0.629	0.0109	0.1968	0.956
10	0.490	0.0091	0.2012	0.898
Market	1.000	0.0142		

[a]On monthly terms 0.0213 should be read as 2.13% return per month. Excess return is average return on the portfolio minus the risk-free rate.
[b]Correlation coefficient.

form deciles that were considered portfolios for the seventh year. This was done until deciles and the return for each decile was computed for 35 years. Then the return for decile one in each year was considered a series of returns from a portfolio, the return for decile two in each year considered a series of returns on a portfolio, and so forth. Each of the 10 portfolios could then be regressed against the market and an intercept, a Beta, and a correlation coefficient for the equation computed.

Table 13.2 shows the Beta, excess return, intercept, and correlation coefficient for each decile reported by Black, Jensen, and Scholes. Note, first, how well the model explains excess return (the high value of correlation coefficients). This would tend to support the structure of the linear equation as a good explanation of security returns. Note, however, that the intercepts vary quite a bit from zero. In fact, when $\beta > 1$ the intercepts tend to be negative and when $\beta < 1$ the intercepts tend to be positive. This, as explained below, is consistent with the two-factor capital asset pricing model rather than the standard CAPM. The implications of the zero Beta form of the CAPM are that

$$R_{it} = \overline{R}_Z(1 - \beta_i) + \beta_i R_{Mt}$$

The model tested is

$$R_{it} = \alpha_i + R_F(1 - \beta_i) + \beta_i R_{Mt}$$

If the zero Beta model really explains security prices, then rearranging these equations to eliminate $B_i R_{Mt}$ and solving for α_i yields

$$\alpha_i = (\overline{R}_Z - R_F)(1 - \beta_i)$$

As shown in Chapter 12 $\overline{R}_Z$ should be larger than R_F. Thus, $(\overline{R}_Z - R_F)$ should be positive. Therefore, if β_i is less than 1, α_i should be positive; and if β_i is greater than 1, α_i should be negative. This is exactly what the empirical results show. Black, Jensen, and Scholes repeat these tests for four subperiods and find, by and large, the same type of behavior we have described for the overall period.

To this point we have described the time series tests of the CAPM performed by Black, Jensen, and Scholes. We now very briefly describe their cross-sectional tests. Recall that one of the major problems in cross-sectional tests (second-pass regressions) was an inability to identify the true Beta. This biased the intercept of the second-pass regression upward, biased its slope downward, and caused residual risk to serve as a proxy variable for Beta risk. One way to decrease substantially the error in estimating Beta is to measure Betas for portfolios rather than for securities. To the extent that errors in measuring each stock's Betas are random, they will cancel out and the aggregate error will be very small when Betas are estimated for portfolios.[7] The grouping procedures we have already

---

[7]See the appendix in Black, Jensen, and Scholes [6] for a formal proof of this statement.

described are an excellent way of forming portfolios to estimate Betas for second-pass regressions. When the excess returns for the 10 portfolios described in Table 13.2 are regressed against the Betas for each portfolio, the results are

$$\overline{R}_i - R_F = 0.00359 + 0.01080\beta_i, \qquad \rho^2 = 0.98$$

The results are shown diagrammatically in Figure 13.2.

The positive value of the intercept that emerges from this analysis is powerful evidence in support of the two-factor model.[8] Let us now turn to an examination of the Fama and MacBeth tests of the CAPM.

Tests of Fama and MacBeth

Fama and MacBeth [18] used an interesting methodology to test the CAPM. They formed 20 portfolios of securities to estimate Betas from a first-pass regression, using the same procedure as Black et al. However, they then performed one second-pass regression for each month over the time period 1935 to 1968. The equation they tested was

$$\tilde{R}_{it} = \hat{\gamma}_{0t} + \hat{\gamma}_{1t}\beta_i + \hat{\gamma}_{2t}\beta_i^2 + \hat{\gamma}_{3t}S_{ei} + \eta_{it} \qquad (13.4)$$

By estimating this equation (in cross section) for each month, it is possible to study how the parameters change over time.

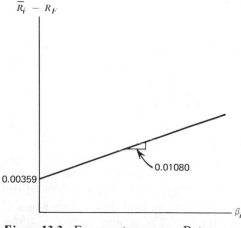

Figure 13.2 Excess return versus Beta.

---

[8]Black et al. analyze the intercept of the second-pass regression over several subperiods. This analysis provides further evidence that the two-factor model is a better description of security returns than the one-factor model.

This form of the equation allows the test of a series of hypotheses regarding the CAPM. The tests are:

1. $E(\hat{\gamma}_{3t}) = 0$ or residual risk does not affect return.

2. $E(\hat{\gamma}_{2t}) = 0$ or there are no nonlinearities in the security market line.

3. $E(\hat{\gamma}_{1t}) > 0$ that is, there is a positive price of risk in the capital markets.

If both $E(\hat{\gamma}_{2t})$ and $E(\hat{\gamma}_{3t})$ are not different from zero, we can also examine both $E(\hat{\gamma}_{0t})$ and $E(\hat{\gamma}_{1t})$ to see whether the standard CAPM or zero Beta model is a better description of market returns.

Finally, we can examine all of the coefficients and the residual term to see if the market operates as a fair game. If the market is a fair game, then there is no way that one should be able to use knowledge about the value of the parameters in previous periods to make an excess return. For example, if the standard CAPM or the zero Beta model holds, then, regardless of the prior values of γ_{2t} and γ_{3t}, each of their expected values at time $t + 1$ should be zero. Furthermore, if the zero Beta model is the best description of general equilibrium, then deviations of $\hat{\gamma}_{0t}$ from its mean $E(R_Z)$ and $\hat{\gamma}_{1t}$ from its mean $E(R_M) - E(R_Z)$ are random, regardless of what happened at time period $t - 1$ or any earlier time period. If the simple form of the CAPM holds the same, statements should be true with R_F substituted for $\overline{R}_Z$.

Fama and MacBeth have estimates of $\hat{\gamma}_{0t}$, $\hat{\gamma}_{1t}$, $\hat{\gamma}_{2t}$, and $\hat{\gamma}_{3t}$ and η_{it} for each month over the period January 1935–June 1968. The average value of any $\hat{\gamma}_{it}$ (denoted by $\bar{\hat{\gamma}}_i$) can be found simply by averaging the individual values, and this mean can be tested to see if it is different from zero.[9]

Table 13.3 from [18] presents the results of estimating Equation (13.4) and several variations of it over the full time period of 1935–68, as well as for several subperiods. Notice that Fama and MacBeth have estimated the full Equation (13.4), as well as forms of the equation with all values of $\hat{\gamma}_{2t}$ and $\hat{\gamma}_{3t}$ both separately and simultaneously forced to zero. If both theory and empirical evidence indicate that one or more variables have no influence on an equation, better estimates of the remaining coefficients can be made when these influences do not enter the estimating equation. For example, theory and the initial empirical results (as we shall see) indicate that neither β^2 nor residual risk affect return. Therefore, better estimates of the effect of Beta on return can be made when these variables are excluded because the coefficient on Beta will not be affected by the multicollinearity between Beta and Beta square and between Beta and residual risk.

Examining panels C and D of Table 13.3 reveals that, when measured over the entire period, $\bar{\hat{\gamma}}_3$ is small and is not statistically different from zero. Furthermore, when we examine it over several subperiods, we find that it remains small in each subperiod, is not significantly different from zero, and, in fact, exhibits different signs in different subperiods. We can safely conclude that residual risk

---

[9]The statistical significance of each parameter can be found by calculating the standard deviation of the mean and testing to see if the mean is a significant number of standard deviations from zero. From the central limit theorem the mean is normally distributed with standard deviation equal to the standard deviation of the $\hat{\gamma}_{it}$'s divided by the square root of the number of observations on $\hat{\gamma}_{it}$.

has no affect on the expected return of a security. However, it is still possible that the market does not constitute a fair game with respect to any information contained in $\hat{\gamma}_{3t}$. That is, it is possible that the fact that $\hat{\gamma}_{3t}$ differs from zero in any period gives us insight into what its value (and, therefore, returns) will be next period. The easiest way to test this is to examine the correlation of $\hat{\gamma}_{3t}$ in one period with its value in the prior period where the mean of all periods is assumed to be zero.[10] Panels C and D show that the value of this correlation coefficient $[\rho_0(\gamma_3)]$ is close to zero and not statistically significant.[11] Fama and MacBeth also compute the correlation between $\hat{\gamma}_{3t}$ and its prior value for lags of more than one period. They find, once again, that there is no usable information contained in $\hat{\gamma}_{3t}$.

The results of Fama and MacBeth are opposite to those of Lintner and Douglas regarding the importance of residual risk. The earlier discussion provides a clue. Recall that Miller and Scholes showed that if Beta had large sampling error, then residual risk served as a proxy for true Beta. Fama and MacBeth have much less sampling error than Lintner and Douglas because of their use of portfolios. When Beta is estimated more accurately, residual risk no longer shows up as important.

The results, with respect to $\bar{\hat{\gamma}}_{2t}$, are very similar. Examining panels B and D we see that $\bar{\hat{\gamma}}_2$ is small, is not statistically significant, and changes sign over alternative subperiods. Furthermore, an examination of the correlation of $\hat{\gamma}_{2t}$ with its previous value (with means assumed to be zero) shows that there is no information contained in individual values of $\hat{\gamma}_{2t}$. Thus, the Beta squared term neither affects the expected return on securities, nor does its coefficient contain information with respect to an investment strategy.

Having concluded that neither Beta squared nor residual risk has an influence on returns, the correct form of the equation to examine for further tests is that displayed in panel A.

Fama and MacBeth examine the performance of $\bar{\hat{\gamma}}_1$ for the entire period and conclude that there is evidence that the relationship between expected return and Beta is positive as well as linear. Furthermore, by testing the correlation of the difference between $\hat{\gamma}_{1t}$ and its mean with prior values of the same variable, they show that difference in $\hat{\gamma}_{1t}$ from its mean cannot be employed to produce a better forecast of a future value of $\hat{\gamma}_{1t}$ than simply using the mean.

Fama and MacBeth find that $\bar{\hat{\gamma}}_0$ is generally greater than R_F and over the entire period $\bar{\hat{\gamma}}_1$ is statistically significantly greater than zero. In addition, they find that $\bar{\hat{\gamma}}_1$ is generally less than $\overline{R}_M - R_F$. The fact that $\bar{\hat{\gamma}}_0$ is substantially greater than R_F and $\bar{\hat{\gamma}}_1$ is substantially less than $\overline{R}_M - R_F$ would seem to indicate that the zero Beta model is more consistent with equilibrium conditions than is the simple CAPM.[12]

---

[10]This is often called the autocorrelation around zero.

[11]Fama and MacBeth point out that the standard deviation of the correlation coefficient can be approximated by one divided by the square root of the number of observations or 0.05 for the overall period, 0.09 for the 10-year subperiod, and 0.13 for the 5-year subperiod.

[12]A warning is in order. Roll [29] demonstrates that this difference could be due to the choice of a market index and Fama [18] also indicates that this might be true.

Table 13.3 Tests of the Two-parameter Model

Period	$\bar{\gamma}_0$	$\bar{\gamma}_1$	$\bar{\gamma}_2$	$\hat{\gamma}_3$	$\bar{\gamma}_0 - \bar{R}_F$	$s(\hat{\gamma}_0)$	$s(\hat{\gamma}_1)$	$s(\hat{\gamma}_2)$	$s(\hat{\gamma}_3)$	$\hat{\rho}_0(\hat{\gamma}_0 - R_f)$	$\hat{\rho}_0(\hat{\gamma}_1)$	$\hat{\rho}_0(\hat{\gamma}_2)$	$\hat{\rho}_0(\hat{\gamma}_3)$	$t(\bar{\gamma}_0)$	$t(\hat{\gamma}_1)$	$t(\hat{\gamma}_2)$	$t(\hat{\gamma}_3)$	$t(\overline{\bar{\gamma}_0 - R_F})$	$\bar{\rho}^2$	$s(\rho^2)$
Panel A:																				
									$R_{it} = \hat{\gamma}_{0t} + \hat{\gamma}_{it}\beta_i + \eta_{it}$											
1935–6/68	0.0061	0.0085			0.0048	0.038	0.066			0.15	0.02			3.24	2.57			2.55	0.29	0.30
1935–45	0.0039	0.0163			0.0037	0.052	0.098			0.10	−0.03			0.86	1.92			0.82	0.29	0.29
1946–55	0.0087	0.0027			0.0078	0.026	0.041			0.18	0.07			3.71	0.70			3.31	0.31	0.32
1956–6/68	0.0060	0.0062			0.0034	0.030	0.044			0.27	0.15			2.45	1.73			1.39	0.28	0.29
1935–40	0.0024	0.0109			0.0023	0.064	0.116			0.07	−0.09			0.32	0.79			0.31	0.23	0.30
1941–45	0.0056	0.0229			0.0054	0.034	0.069			0.23	0.15			1.27	2.55			1.22	0.37	0.28
1946–50	0.0050	0.0029			0.0044	0.031	0.047			0.20	0.04			1.27	0.48			1.10	0.39	0.33
1951–55	0.0123	0.0024			0.0111	0.019	0.035			0.20	0.08			5.06	0.53			4.56	0.24	0.29
1956–60	0.0148	−0.0059			0.0128	0.020	0.034			0.37	0.18			5.68	−1.37			4.89	0.22	0.31
1961–6/68	0.0001	0.0143			−0.0029	0.034	0.048			0.22	0.09			0.03	2.81			−.80	0.32	0.27
Panel B:																				
									$R_{it} = \hat{\gamma}_{0t} + \hat{\gamma}_{it}\beta_i + \hat{\gamma}_{2t}\beta_i^2 + \eta_{it}$											
1935–6/68	0.0049	0.0105	−0.0008		0.0036	0.052	0.118	0.056		0.03	−0.11	−0.11		1.92	1.79	−0.29		1.42	0.32	0.31
1935–45	0.0074	0.0079	0.0040		0.0073	0.061	0.139	0.074		−0.10	−0.31	−0.21		1.39	0.65	0.61		1.36	0.32	0.30
1946–55	−0.0002	0.0217	−0.0087		−0.0012	0.036	0.095	0.034		0.04	0.00	0.00		−0.07	2.51	−2.83		−0.38	0.36	0.32
1956–6/68	0.0069	0.0040	0.0013		0.0043	0.054	0.116	0.053		0.17	0.07	0.03		1.56	0.42	0.29		0.97	0.30	0.30
1935–40	0.0013	0.0141	−0.0017		0.0012	0.069	0.160	0.075		−0.13	−0.36	−0.35		0.16	0.75	−0.19		0.14	0.24	0.30
1941–45	0.0148	0.0004	0.0108		0.0146	0.050	0.111	0.073		−0.04	−0.19	−0.04		2.28	0.03	1.15		2.24	0.39	0.29
1946–50	−0.0008	0.0152	−0.0051		−0.0015	0.037	0.104	0.032		0.14	0.04	0.00		−0.18	1.14	−1.24		−0.32	0.44	0.32
1951–55	0.0004	0.0281	−0.0122		−0.0008	0.030	0.085	0.035		−0.17	−0.14	−0.01		0.10	2.55	−2.72		−0.20	0.28	0.29
1956–60	0.0128	−0.0015	−0.0020		0.0108	0.030	0.072	0.029		0.35	0.11	0.26		3.38	−0.16	−0.54		2.84	0.25	0.31
1961–6/68	0.0029	0.0077	0.0034		−0.0000	0.066	0.138	0.064		0.14	0.06	−0.01		0.42	0.53	0.51		−0.01	0.34	0.29

$$R_{it} = \hat{\gamma}_{0t} + \hat{\gamma}_{1t}\beta_i + \hat{\gamma}_{3t}s_{ei} + \eta_{it}$$

Panel C:

Period																
1935–6/68	0.0054	0.0072	0.0198	0.0041	0.052	0.065	0.868	0.04	-0.12	-0.04	2.10	2.20	0.46	1.59	0.32	0.31
1935–45	0.0017	0.0104	0.0841	0.0015	0.373	0.083	0.921	-0.00	-0.26	-0.08	0.26	1.41	1.05	0.24	0.32	0.31
1946–55	0.0110	0.0075	-0.1052	0.0100	0.332	0.056	0.509	0.08	0.02	-0.20	3.78	1.47	-1.89	3.46	0.34	0.32
1956–6/68	0.0042	0.0041	0.0633	0.0016	0.040	0.052	0.984	0.12	0.08	0.03	1.28	0.96	0.79	0.50	0.30	0.29
1935–40	0.0036	0.0119	-0.0170	0.0035	0.082	0.105	0.744	-0.03	-0.26	-0.18	0.37	0.97	-0.19	0.36	0.25	0.30
1941–45	-0.0006	0.0085	0.2053	-0.0005	0.061	0.052	1.091	0.07	-0.29	-0.02	-0.08	1.25	1.46	-0.11	0.41	0.30
1946–50	0.0069	0.0081	-0.0920	0.0062	0.034	0.066	0.504	0.14	0.06	-0.02	1.56	0.95	-1.41	1.40	0.42	0.33
1951–55	0.0150	0.0069	-0.1185	0.0138	0.029	0.043	0.702	0.06	-0.18	-0.32	4.05	1.24	-1.31	3.72	0.42	0.29
1956–60	0.0127	-0.0081	0.0728	0.0107	0.037	0.045	1.164	0.15	0.15	0.21	2.68	-1.40	0.48	2.26	0.27	0.30
1961–6/68	-0.0014	0.0122	0.0570	-0.0044	0.042	0.055	0.850	0.10	0.00	-0.19	-0.32	2.12	0.64	-0.98	0.33	0.27

$$R_{it} = \hat{\gamma}_{0t} + \hat{\gamma}_{1t}\beta_i + \hat{\gamma}_{2t}\beta_e^2 + \hat{\gamma}_{3t}s_{ei} + \eta_{it}$$

Panel D:

Period																			
1935–6/68	0.0020	0.0114	-0.0026	0.0516	0.0008	0.075	0.123	0.060	0.929	-0.09	-0.12	-0.10	0.55	1.85	-0.86	1.11	0.20	0.34	0.31
1935–45	0.0011	0.0118	-0.0009	0.0817	0.0010	0.103	0.146	0.079	1.003	-0.20	-0.24	-0.15	0.13	0.94	-0.14	0.94	0.11	0.34	0.31
1946–55	0.0017	0.0209	-0.0076	-0.0378	0.0008	0.042	0.096	0.038	0.619	-0.10	-0.01	-0.20	0.44	2.39	-2.16	-0.67	0.20	0.36	0.32
1956–6/68	0.0031	0.0034	-0.0000	0.0966	0.0005	0.065	0.122	0.055	1.061	0.12	0.01	-0.05	0.59	0.34	-0.00	1.11	0.10	0.32	0.29
1934–40	0.0009	0.0156	-0.0029	0.0025	0.0008	0.112	0.171	0.085	0.826	-0.16	-0.26	-0.12	0.07	0.78	-0.29	0.03	0.06	0.26	0.30
1941–45	0.0015	0.0073	0.0014	0.1767	0.0012	0.092	0.109	0.072	1.181	-0.28	-0.22	-0.18	0.12	0.52	0.15	1.16	0.10	0.43	0.31
1946–50	0.0011	0.0141	-0.0040	-0.0313	0.0004	0.047	0.106	0.042	0.590	-0.10	-0.01	-0.12	0.18	1.03	-0.73	-0.41	0.07	0.44	0.33
1951–55	0.0023	0.0277	-0.0112	-0.0443	0.0011	0.037	0.085	0.034	0.651	-0.11	-0.01	-0.28	0.48	2.53	-2.54	-0.53	0.23	0.29	0.30
1956–60	0.0103	-0.0047	-0.0020	0.0979	0.0083	0.049	0.078	0.032	1.286	-0.16	-0.01	0.02	1.63	-0.47	-0.49	0.59	1.31	0.28	0.30
1961–6/68	-0.0017	0.0088	0.0013	0.0957	-0.0046	0.073	0.144	0.066	0.887	0.20	0.01	-0.15	-0.21	0.58	0.19	1.02	-0.60	0.35	0.29

Source: Eugene F. Fama and James D. MacBeth. "Risk, Return, and Equilibrium: Empirical Tests," *Journal of Political Economy,* **71** (May–June 1973), pp. 622–623.

Before finishing our discussion of these tests one more point is worth mentioning. If the equilibrium model describes market conditions, then an individual security's deviation from the model should contain no information. That is, a positive residual value for any one stock at any moment in time should convey no information about the differential performance of that stock (from the expected value produced by the model) in future periods. For this to be true, there should be no correlation (with any lag) between the residuals in Equation (13.4). This is, in fact, what Fama and MacBeth found.

Two Recent Tests of the CAPM

Two recent articles have developed new methodologies for testing whether the simple CAPM adequately describes returns. Gibbons [21] employs the fact that the CAPM places a non-linear restriction on a set of N regression equations, one for each security. More specifically, we know that the market model requires

$$R_{it} = \alpha_i + \beta_i(R_{mt}) + e_{it} \tag{13.5}$$

If the market model and the CAPM hold simultaneously, then

$$R_{it} = \gamma_1(1 - \beta_i) + \beta_i(R_{mt}) + e_{it}$$

or

$$\alpha_i = \gamma_1(1 - \beta_i) \tag{13.6}$$

where γ_1 is a constant for all securities. For the standard form of the CAPM, γ_1 should equal R_F, for the zero-Beta form, γ_1 should equal $\overline{R}_Z$, which should be larger than R_F. Now a set of N equations (one for each security) like (13.5) can be estimated simultaneously.

The same set of equations can be estimated under the constraint that all α_i's equal a constant times the sum of one minus β_i. Obviously the constrained equation cannot have more explanatory power than the unconstrained equation. However, if it has less at a statistically significant level, it would be strong evidence for rejecting both the standard and zero-Beta form of the CAPM. Gibbons performs this test using the methodology of seemingly unrelated regression and does a likelihood ratio test on the difference in explanatory power between the constrained and unconstrained regression. Defining the market as an equally weighted portfolio of New York Stock Exchange stocks, Gibbons rejects both the standard form and the zero-Beta form of the CAPM.

Stambaugh [36] takes a similar approach to Gibbons in examining the CAPM. However, he uses a different statistical test (a Lagrangian Multiplier test rather than a likelihood ratio test). Stambaugh claims that his test is more powerful for samples of the size studied by both authors, and based on his tests he reaches very different conclusions than does Gibbons. Stambaugh finds strong support for the zero-Beta form of the CAPM and evidence against the standard form. Furthermore, Stambaugh performs these tests using several alternative defini-

of the market portfolio, including corporate bonds, government bonds, treasury bills, home furnishings, residential real estate, and automobiles as well as common stocks. His major conclusions appear robust over alternative definitions of the market portfolio.

TESTING THE POST-TAX FORM OF THE CAPM MODEL

While a great deal of attention has been paid to tests of the zero Beta (two-factor) CAPM model, almost no testing has been done on the other forms of general equilibrium models described in the previous chapter. The one exception to this in tax-adjusted versions of the general equilibrium model. Black and Scholes [5] have tested a form of the CAPM that includes a dividend term and concluded that dividends do not affect the equilibrium relationship. Since a dividend term is present in the post-tax CAPM, this would seem to indicate that a pre-tax CAPM is more descriptive of equilibrium returns. However, more recently Litzenberger and Ramaswamy [26] have found strong, positive support for dividends affecting equilibrium prices. Their results differ from Black and Scholes at least in part because while Black and Scholes assumed that dividends were received in equal amounts each month, Litzenberger and Ramaswamy formulated their tests so that dividends were assumed to be received in the month in which they could reasonably be expected to occur.[13] They tested a model of the form

$$R_{it} - R_{Ft} = \gamma_0 + \gamma_1 \beta_{it} + \gamma_2(\delta_{it} - R_{Ft}) + e_{it}$$

where δ_{it} is the dividend divided by price for stock i in month t. This model appears like a test of the two-factor model with the addition of a new term involving dividend yields. The form of this new term is consistent with the post-tax model presented in Chapter 12 with γ_2 interpreted as τ.[14]

When Litzenberger and Ramaswamy tested this model using maximum likelihood estimates on monthly data, they found the following results for the period 1936–77.[15]

$$R_{it} - R_{Ft} = 0.0063 + 0.0421\beta_{it} + 0.236(\delta_{it} - R_{Ft})$$
$$(2.63) \qquad (1.86) \qquad (8.62)$$
$$t\text{-statistics in parenthesis}$$

---

[13]Other differences are that Litzenberger and Ramaswamy based the form of their dividend term on the general equilibrium equation. Black and Scholes simply added a dividend term to the standard CAPM. In addition, Litzenberger and Ramaswamy used maximum likelihood methods for estimating their equation, rather than relying on the portfolio grouping techniques of Black and Scholes.

[14]τ is related to tax rates as explained below.

[15]Litzenberger and Ramaswamy estimate this equation for six subperiods during the 1936–77 time span. In each subperiod the dividend yield term has positive signs. It is statistically significant in five of the six periods. This is the best behaved of the three coefficients as each of the other coefficients have the wrong sign in two subperiods and are statistically significant in only one or two of the subperiods.

The key point to note from this analysis is that the dividend term is positive and statistically significant. Furthermore, it is obvious that the dividend term is of economic significance. This term indicates that for every \$1 of dividends paid, stock investors require 23.6¢ in extra return. The model also allows us to infer the effective tax rates for determining equilibrium in the market. Recall that γ_2 is equal to τ.

In Chapter 12 we demonstrated that τ was equal to an average of τ_i

$$\tau_i = \frac{t_{di} - t_{gi}}{1 - t_{gi}}$$

where

t_{di} = tax rate paid on dividend income
t_{gi} = tax rate paid on capital gain income

The assumption behind this derivation was that capital gains taxes as well as ordinary income taxes were paid at the end of each period (e.g., year). Litzenberger and Ramaswamy developed an analogous model under the assumption that capital gains taxes are postponed indefinitely and are essentially equal to zero. Under this assumption t_{gi} equals zero and τ equals an average of t_{di}. The truth probably lies somewhere between these two extremes. Using their estimate of τ, the effective income tax rate lies in the following range:[16]

$$0.236 \leq t_{di} \leq 0.382$$

They also tested for and found evidence supporting the presence of a clientele effect. That is, stockholders in high tax brackets tended to hold stocks with low dividend yields, while investors in low tax brackets tended to hold stocks with high dividend yields. These results are consistent with the findings of Elton and Gruber [14].

SOME RESERVATIONS ABOUT TRADITIONAL TESTS OF GENERAL EQUILIBRIUM RELATIONSHIPS AND SOME NEW RESEARCH

In this chapter we have reviewed some of the more important tests of general equilibrium relationships. These tests represent the state of the art of testing the theories we have described in the previous two chapters. Recently, Roll [29] published an article in which he argues that general equilibrium models of the form of the CAPM are not amenable to testing or, at least, that the tests performed so far provide little evidence in support of, or against, CAPM. Roll raised some legitimate questions and his arguments are well worth reviewing.

---

[16]The lower estimate is of course their coefficient on the dividend term. The higher estimate is obtained by setting

$$\frac{t_{di} - t_{gi}}{1 - t_{gi}} = 0.236 \quad \text{and} \quad t_{gi} = (1/2)t_{di}$$

Perhaps the easiest way to understand Roll's case is to start with his proof that if *any* ex-post mean variance efficient portfolio is selected as the market portfolio and Betas are computed using this as the market proxy, then the equation

$$\overline{R}_i = \overline{R}_{ZP} + \beta_{iP}(\overline{R}_P - \overline{R}_{ZP})$$

must hold.[17] In fact, it is a tautology that has nothing to do with the way equilibrium is set in the capital markets or with investor's attitude toward risk.

Proof

Return to Equation (11.4). Assume a riskless asset exists with a return R_F. Then

$$\lambda(X_1\sigma_{1k} + X_2\sigma_{2k} + \cdots + X_k\sigma_k^2 + \cdots + X_N\sigma_{kN}) = \overline{R}_k - R_F$$

If all X_i's stand for the proportion of stock i in portfolio P we can write this expression as

$$\lambda\sigma_{kP} = \overline{R}_k - R_F \tag{13.7}$$

Since this expression must hold for each security in portfolio P, it must also hold for portfolio P itself or

$$\lambda\sigma_P^2 = \overline{R}_P - R_F$$

Solving for λ, substituting in Equation (13.5) and rearranging,

$$\overline{R}_k = R_F + \frac{\sigma_{kP}}{\sigma_P^2}(\overline{R}_P - R_F)$$

Recognizing the $(\sigma_{kP}/\sigma_P^2) = \beta_{kP}$, we can write this as

$$\overline{R}_k = R_F + \beta_{kP}(\overline{R}_P - R_F) \tag{13.8}$$

Now, as we did in Chapter 12, assume that lending and borrowing cannot take place at the riskless rate R_F. However, as we have seen, an infinite number of portfolios will exist that have the return R_F. From Equation (13.8) they all must be uncorrelated with portfolio P. Let $\overline{R}_{ZP}$ stand for the minimum variance portfolio that is uncorrelated with portfolio P. Then, since $\overline{R}_{ZP} = R_F$, Equation (13.8) can be written as

$$\overline{R}_k = \overline{R}_{ZP} + \beta_{kP}(\overline{R}_P - \overline{R}_{ZP})$$

---

[17]In this expression P is the proxy for the market portfolio, $\overline{R}_P$ is the expected return on the proxy for the market portfolio, β_{iP} is the Beta for security i with the proxy market portfolio, and R_{ZP} is the minimum variance portfolio that has a zero Beta with the market proxy portfolio.

From the proof it follows that the return on an asset or portfolio is an *exact* linear function of Beta if Betas are computed using any efficient portfolio. Conversely, if the portfolio used to compute Betas is not efficient, then return is not an exact linear function of Beta.

From this proof it follows that the two-factor form of the CAPM must always hold with respect to ex-post data if the proxy chosen for the market portfolio is ex-post efficient. Furthermore, Roll argues that tests performed with any portfolio other than the true market portfolio are not tests of the CAPM. They are simply tests of whether the portfolio chosen as a proxy for the market is efficient or not. Since over an interval of time efficient portfolios exist, a market proxy may be chosen that satisfies all the implications of the CAPM model, even when the market portfolio is inefficient. On the other hand, an inefficient portfolio may be chosen as a proxy for the market and the CAPM rejected when the market itself is efficient. Roll demonstrates that the high correlation that exists among most reasonable proxies for the market does not mean that the choice of a proxy is unimportant. Though they are highly correlated, some may be efficient while others are inefficient.

Roll proceeds to show that the choice between alternative forms of the CAPM model is extremely sensitive to the choice of a market proxy. For example, while the Black, Jensen, and Scholes results did not support the Sharpe–Lintner–Mossin form of the CAPM, Roll shows there was a mean variance efficient market proxy that had a correlation of 0.895 with the market proxy used by Black et al., which supported the Sharpe–Lintner–Mossin form of the model perfectly.

The logical conclusion of Roll's work is that equilibrium theory is not testable unless the exact composition of the true market portfolio is known and used in the tests. The true test of the generalized two-parameter CAPM is whether the market portfolio is mean-variance efficient. Alternative forms of the CAPM can be judged only against one another if the true market portfolio is used in these tests.

Perhaps Roll's feelings about the state of testing of the capital asset pricing theory can best be summarized by a quote from his work: "Unfortunately, it [capital asset pricing theory] has never been subjected to an unambiguous empirical test. There is considerable doubt, moreover, at least by me, that it ever will."

CONCLUSION

This is, perhaps, the most difficult chapter in this book to conclude. On the one hand, we have a host of evidence that purports to support the CAPM. On the other hand, we have Roll's very cogent arguments questioning this evidence. Can we conclude anything positive from all this?

First, we should be careful to note that Roll has not cast aspersions on any specific form of the CAPM; he has not said that they do not hold. What he has simply said is that we have not tested whether they do or do not hold, nor, in his opinion, are we likely to be able to do so.

If we reexamine the tests in this chapter, not as tests of the CAPM but as inputs to the portfolio process, do we gain useful information? We would argue that we do. The fact that return and risk appear to be linearly related for securities and portfolios over long periods of time, when risk is defined as systematic risk, is important. The same can be said for the fact that return is not related to residual risk. Even if these statements do not constitute tests of the CAPM, they have important implications for behavior. Investors are not rewarded for taking nonmarket risk and they are rewarded for bearing added market risk. These statements seem to hold under alternative methods of calculating systematic risk. Furthermore, they seem to hold even more firmly when systematic risk is calculated using a value-weighted, rather than equally weighted, market proxy.[18] The fair game nature of the model is also important. Not only does the model seem to hold over long periods of time, but intertemporal deviations from the model cannot be used to make an extra return.

In summary, while the empirical work is not fully a satisfactory test of the CAPM, it produces results that are consistent with what one would expect from a test of the CAPM. Furthermore, these results are produced with respect to observable variables (market proxies). While we should continue to search for true tests of the CAPM, we can, with some care, proceed on the basis of the results produced by tests of observable, but not optimum, phenomena.

APPENDIX

Random Errors in Beta and Bias in the Parameters of the CAPM

This appendix contains a proof that a random (unbiased) error in identifying Beta leads to a downward bias slope and upward biased intercept in the second-pass (cross-sectional) regression used to test the CAPM.

Define the correct model for the second-pass regression as

$$R_i - R_F = \gamma_1 \beta_i + e_i \qquad (A.1)$$

where β_i is the true, but unobserved, value of Beta for security i. Furthermore, note that β_i has a cross-sectional mean of 1 and a variance of $\sigma^2(\beta_i)$.

Now assume that the estimate of β_i from the first-pass regression has an error that is independent of β_i and e_i (unbiased), and is drawn from the same distribution for all stocks. Let b_i equal the observed value of β_i; then we can write

$$b_i = \beta_i + v_i \qquad (A.2)$$

where $E(v_i) = 0$ and variance $(v_i) = \sigma^2(v_i)$,

$$\text{cov}(v_i, e_i) = 0 \qquad \text{cov}(v_i, \beta_i) = 0$$

[18]See, for a comparison, Foster [19]. CAPM tests have usually been performed utilizing an equally weighted index for all NYSE stocks. Foster compares tests employing an equally weighted index with those employing a market-weighted index.

The second-pass regression that is actually run is

$$R_i - R_F = \gamma_0 + \gamma_1 b_i + e_i$$

For very large sample sizes, the limit of

$$\operatorname*{plim}_{n \to \infty} \hat{\gamma}_1 = \frac{\operatorname{cov}(R_i - R_F, b_i)}{\sigma^2(b_i)}$$

Substituting (A.1) for $R_i - R_F$ and (A.2) for b_i,

$$\operatorname*{plim}_{n \to \infty} \hat{\gamma}_1 = \frac{\operatorname{cov}(\gamma_1 \beta_i + e_i, \beta_i + v_i)}{\sigma^2(\beta_i + v_i)}$$

Recalling that $\operatorname{cov}(e_i, v_i) = 0$, $\operatorname{cov}(e_i, \beta_i) = 0$, and $\operatorname{cov}(v_i, \beta_i) = 0$,

$$\operatorname*{plim}_{n \to \infty} \hat{\gamma}_1 = \gamma_1 \frac{\sigma^2(\beta_i)}{\sigma^2(\beta_i) + \sigma^2(v_i)} \tag{A.3}$$

As long as there is a measurement error, $\sigma^2(v_i)$ is positive and $\hat{\gamma}_1$ is a downward biased estimate of the true γ_1.

To examine the bias in the intercept, recall that the regression must pass through the mean of both the dependent and independent variable, or

$$\frac{1}{N} \sum_{i=1}^{N} (R_i - R_F) = \hat{\gamma}_0 + \hat{\gamma}_1 \frac{1}{N} \sum_{i=1}^{N} \beta_i$$

By summing (A.1) across securities and dividing by N,

$$\frac{1}{N} \sum_{i=1}^{N} (R_i - R_F) = \gamma_1 \frac{1}{N} \sum_{i=1}^{N} \beta_i$$

But,[19]

$$\frac{1}{N} \sum_{i=1}^{N} \beta_i = 1$$

therefore,

$$\frac{1}{N} \sum_{i=1}^{N} (R_i - R_F) = \gamma_1 = \hat{\gamma}_0 + \hat{\gamma}_1 \qquad \text{or} \qquad \hat{\gamma}_0 = \gamma_1 - \hat{\gamma}_1$$

---

[19]The average Beta equals one only for equally weighted market portfolios. Otherwise the following equation is an approximation.

If $\hat{\gamma}_1$ was equal to γ_1, then $\hat{\gamma}_0$ would, indeed, be zero. Substituting in Equation (A.3),

$$\operatorname*{plim}_{n\to\infty} \hat{\gamma}_0 = \gamma_1 \left[1 - \frac{\sigma^2(\beta_i)}{\sigma^2(\beta_i) + \sigma^2(v_i)} \right]$$

Thus, $\hat{\gamma}_0$ is an upward biased estimate of the true intercept.

Based on the cross-sectional variance of b_i [as a proxy for $\sigma(\beta_i)$] and the square of the standard error of b_i [as a proxy for $\sigma(v_i)$], Miller and Scholes conclude $\operatorname*{plim}_{n\to\infty} \hat{\gamma}_1 = 0.64\gamma_1$.

QUESTIONS AND PROBLEMS

1. We have sometimes heard investment managers say: "I followed that (expletive deleted) theory and bought high Beta stocks last year and they did worse than low Beta stocks. That theory is 'expletive deleted'." Is this a valid test and is this empirical evidence inconsistent with the theory?

2. A new theory has been proposed. The expected percentage increase in alcoholism in each city is equal to the rate of change in the price of gold plus the product of two terms. The first is the covariance of the percentage change in alcoholism in the city with the percentage change in professors' salaries divided by the variance of the percentage change in professors' salaries. The second term is the percentage change in professors' salaries minus the percentage increase in gold. How would you test this proposition?

3. Show that if the market portfolio is not an efficient portfolio, then

$$\overline{R}_i = \overline{R}_Z + \beta_i(\overline{R}_M - \overline{R}_Z)$$

    cannot in general hold.

4. Explain how you might use general equilibrium theory to evaluate the performance of one or more common stocks managers.

5. Assume the post-tax CAPM holds but the Sharpe–Lintner model is tested. What would you expect the empirical results to look like?

BIBLIOGRAPHY

1. Adler, Michael. "On the Risk-Return Trade-Off in the Valuation of Assets," *Journal of Financial and Quantitative Analysis,* **IV,** No. 4 (Dec. 1969), pp. 492–512.

2. Bar-Yosef, Sasson, and Koldny, Richard. "Dividend Policy and Capital Market Theory," *Review of Economics and Statistics,* **LVIII,** No. 2 (May 1976), pp. 181–190.

3. Belkaoui, Ahmed. "Canadian Evidence of Heteroscedasticity in the Market Model," *Journal of Finance,* **XII,** No. 4 (Sept. 1977), pp. 1320–1324.
4. Best, Michael J., and Grauer, Robert R. "Capital Asset Pricing Compatible with Observed Market Value Weights," *The Journal of Finance,* **40,** No. 1 (March 1985), pp. 85–104.
5. Black, F., and Scholes, M. "The Effects of Dividend Yield and Dividend Policy on Common Stock Prices and Returns," *Journal of Financial Economics,* **1,** 1974 pp. 1–22.
6. Black, F., Jensen, M.C., and Scholes, M. "The Capital Asset Pricing Model: Some Empirical Tests," in Jensen (ed.), *Studies in the Theory of Capital Markets* (New York: Praeger, 1972).
7. Blume, Marshall, and Husic, Frank. "Price, Beta, and Exchange Listings," *Journal of Finance,* **VIII,** No. 2 (May 1973), pp. 283–299.
8. Blume, Marshall, and Friend, Irwin. "A New Look at the Capital Asset Pricing Model," *Journal of Finance,* **VIII,** No. 1 (March 1973), pp. 19–33.
9. Blume, Marshall, and Friend, Irwin. "Risk, Investment Strategy, and the Long-Run Rates of Return," *Review of Economics and Statistics,* **LVI,** No. 3 (Aug. 1974), pp. 259–269.
10. Brown, David P., and Gibbons, Michael R. "A Simple Econometric Approach for Utility-Based Asset Pricing Models," *The Journal of Finance,* **40,** No. 2 (June 1985), pp. 359–382.
11. Brown, Stephen J., and Weinstein, Mark I. "A New Approach to Testing Asset Pricing Models: The Bilinear Paradigm," *The Journal of Finance,* **38,** No. 3 (June 1983), pp. 711–744.
12. Chen, Nai-Fu, Roll, Richard, and Ross, Stephen. "Economic Forces and the Stock Market: Testing the APT and Alternative Asset Pricing Theories," Working Paper No. 119, University of Chicago, 1983.
13. Douglas, George. *Risk in the Equity Markets: An Empirical Appraisal of Market Efficiency* (Ann Arbor, Mich.: University Microfilms, Inc., 1968).
14. Elton, Edwin J., and Gruber, Martin J. "Marginal Stockholder Tax Rates and the Clientele Effect," *Review of Economics and Statistics,* **52** (1970), pp. 68–74.
15. Eubank, Arthur. "Risk-Return Contrasts: NYSE, AMEX, and OTL," *Journal of Portfolio Management,* **3,** No. 4 (Summer 1977), pp. 25–30.
16. Fama, Eugene. *Foundations of Finance* (New York: Basic Books, 1976).
17. Fama, Eugene, and MacBeth, J. "Tests of the Multiperiod Two-Parameter Model," *Journal of Financial Economics,* **1,** No. 1 (May 1974), pp. 43–66.
18. ———. "Risk, Return, and Equilibrium: Empirical Tests," *Journal of Political Economy,* **71,** (May/June 1973), pp. 607–636.
19. Foster, George. "Asset Pricing Models: Further Tests," *Journal of Financial and Quantitative Analysis,* **XIII,** No. 1 (March 1978), pp. 39–53.
20. Friend, Irwin, Westerfield, Randolf, and Granito, Michael. "New Evidence on the Capital Asset Pricing Model," *Journal of Finance,* **XII,** No. 3 (June 1978), pp. 903–917.
21. Gentry, James, and Pike, John. "An Empirical Study of the Risk-Return Hypothesis Using Common Stock Portfolios of Life Insurance Companies,"

Journal of Financial and Quantitative Analysis, **V,** No. 2 (May 1970), pp. 179–185.

22. Gibbons, Michael R. "Multivariate Tests of Financial Models: A New Approach," *Journal of Financial Economics,* **X,** No. 1 (March 1982), pp. 3–28.

23. Gibbons, Michael R., and Ferson, Wayne. "Testing Asset Pricing Models with Changing Expectations and an Unobservable Market Portfolio," *Journal of Financial Economics,* **XIV,** No. 2 (June 1985), pp. 217–236.

24. Lau, Sheila, Quay, Stuart, and Ramsey, Carl. "The Tokyo Stock Exchange and the Capital Asset Pricing Model," *Journal of Finance,* **IX,** No. 2 (May 1974), pp. 507–514.

25. Litzenberger, R.H., and Budd, A.P. "Secular Trends in Risk Premiums," *Journal of Finance,* **VII,** No. 3 (June 1972), pp. 857–864.

26. Litzenberger, R.H., and Ramaswamy, K. "The Effect of Personal Taxes and Dividends on Capital Asset Prices: Theory and Empirical Evidence," *Journal of Financial Economics* (June 1979), pp. 163–195.

27. Miller, M.H., and Scholes, M. "Rates of Return in Relation to Risk: A Re-Examination of Some Recent Findings," in Jensen (ed.), *Studies in the Theory of Capital Markets* (New York: Praeger, 1972).

28. Morgan, I.G. "Prediction of Return with the Minimum Variance Zero-Beta Portfolio," *Journal of Financial Economics,* **2,** No. 4 (Dec. 1975), pp. 361–376.

29. Roll, Richard, "A Critique of the Asset Pricing Theory's Tests; Part I: On Past and Potential Testability of the Theory," *Journal of Financial Economics,* **4,** No. 2 (March 1977), pp. 129–176.

30. Roll, Richard. "Orthogonal Portfolios," *Journal of Financial and Quantitative Analysis,* **XV,** No. 5 (Dec. 1980), pp. 1005–1024.

31. Roll, Richard, and Ross, Stephen. "An Empirical Investigation of the Arbitrage Pricing Theory," *Journal of Finance* (Dec. 1980), pp. 1073–1105.

32. Sharpe, W.F., and Cooper, G.M. "Risk-Return Class of New York Stock Exchange Common Stocks, 1931–1967," *Financial Analysts Journal,* **28,** (March–April 1972), pp. 46–52.

33. Sharpe, W.F., and Sosin, H. "Risk, Return, and Yield: New York Stock Exchange Common Stocks, 1928–1969," *Financial Analysts Journal,* **32,** No. 2 (March–April 1976), pp. 33–42.

34. Sharpe, W.F., "Risk, Market Sensitivity, and Diversification," *Financial Analysts Journal,* **28,** No. 1 (Jan.–Feb. 1972), pp. 74–79.

35. Smith, Keith. "The Effect of Intervaling on Estimating Parameters of the Capital Asset Pricing Model," *Journal of Financial and Quantitative Analysis,* **XIII,** No. 2 (June 1978), pp. 313–332.

36. Stambaugh, Robert F. "On the Exclusion of Assets from Tests of the Two-Parameter Model: A Sensitivity Analysis," *Journal of Financial Economics,* **X,** No. 3 (Nov. 1982), pp. 237–268.

37. Upson, Roger, and Jessup, Paul. "Risk-Return Relationships in Regional Securities Markets," *Journal of Financial and Quantitative Analysis,* **IV,** No. 5 (Jan. 1970), pp. 677–695.

Chapter **14**

The Arbitrage Pricing Model APT—A New Approach to Explaining Asset Prices

All of the equilibrium models discussed in Chapters 11, 12, and 13 have their basis in mean-variance analysis. All require that it is optimal for the investor to choose investments on the basis of expected return and variance. However, definitions of returns for which means the variances are calculated differ between models. For example, in the version of the CAPM involving taxes, investors examine means and variances of after-tax returns. As a second example, Elton and Gruber [16] have shown that the alternative version of CAPM under conditions of uncertain inflation can be derived by assuming that investors maximize a utility function defined in terms of the mean and variance of real as compared to nominal returns. As noted in the previous chapter, there are major obstacles to testing any of these equilibrum theories.

Recently, Ross [50, 51] has proposed a new and different approach to explaining the pricing of assets. Ross has developed a mechanism that, given the process that generates security returns, derives asset prices from arbitrage arguments analogous to (but more complex than) those used in the beginning of Chapters 11 and 12 to derive CAPMs. In this chapter we first present the mechanism of arbitrage pricing theory (APT). This is the derivation of equilibrium conditions given any prespecified return-generating process.

Following this we discuss implementation of the APT. APT theory provides interesting insight into the nature of equilibrium. However, the theory is far from easy to implement. Empirical research is just starting in this area. Furthermore, alternative approaches have been advocated for implementing the theory. After discussing some of those alternatives, we close with an examinaton of whether evidence supporting APT is necessarily inconsistent with the standard form or any alternative form of the CAPM as a model of equilibrium.

APT—WHAT IS IT?

Arbitrage pricing theory is a new and different approach to determining asset prices. It is based on the law of one price: two items which are the same can't sell at different prices. The strong assumptions made about utility theory in deriving the CAPM are not necessary. In fact, the APT description of equilibrium is more general than that provided by a CAPM-type model in that pricing can be affected by influences beyond simply means and variances. An assumption of homogeneous expectations is necessary. The assumption of investors utilizing a mean variance framework is replaced by an assumption of the process generating security returns. APT requires that the returns on any stock be linearly related to a set of indices as shown in Equation (14.1).[1]

$$R_i = a_i + b_{i1}I_1 + b_{i2}I_2 + \cdots + b_{ij}I_j + e_i \qquad (14.1)$$

where

a_i = the expected level of return for stock i if all indices have a value of zero

I_j = the value of the jth index that impacts the return on stock i

b_{ij} = the sensitivity of stock i's return to the jth index

e_i = a random error term with mean equal to zero and variance equal to σ_{ei}^2

For the model to fully describe the process-generating security returns:

$$E(e_i e_j) = 0 \qquad \text{for all } i \text{ and } j \text{ where } i \neq j$$

$$E[e_i(I_j - \bar{I}_j)] = 0 \qquad \text{for all stocks and indices}$$

If you are beginning to get the feeling that you have seen all this before, you are right. This representation is nothing more or less than the description of the multi-index model presented in Chapter 6. APT is the description of the expected returns that can be derived when returns are generated by a single- or multi-index model meeting the conditions defined before. The contribution of APT is in demonstrating how (and under what conditions) one can go from a multi-index model to a description of equilibrium.

In the following pages we will demonstrate the derivation of an APT equilib-

---

[1] The linearity assumption is not as restrictive as it might at first appear. Any of the indices can be a nonlinear function of a variable. It could be a variable squared, the log of a variable, or any other nonlinear transformation that seems appropriate.

rium in two different ways. The first proof stresses the economic rationale behind APT whereas the second proof is mathematically more rigorous.

A Simple Proof of APT

We will demonstrate the expected returns that must arise from the APT with a two-index model. Suppose that the following two-index model describes returns:

$$R_i = a_i + b_{i1}I_1 + b_{i2}I_2 + e_i \qquad (14.2)$$

If an investor holds a well-diversified portfolio, residual risk will tend to go to zero and only systematic risk will matter. The only terms in the above equation that affect the systematic risk in a portfolio are b_{i1} and b_{i2}. Since the investor is assumed to be concerned with expected return and risk he or she need be concerned only with three attributes of any portfolio (p): $\overline{R}_p$, b_{p1}, an b_{p2}.

Let us hypothesize the existence of the three widely diversified portfolios shown in the following table.

Portfolio	Expected Return	b_{i1}	b_{i2}
A	15	1.0	.6
B	14	5	1.0
C	10	.3	.2

We know from the concepts of geometry that three points determine a plane just as two points determine a line. The equation of the plane in $\overline{R}_p$, b_{p1}, and b_{p2} space defined by these three portfolios is[2]

$$\overline{R}_i = 7.75 + 5b_{i1} + 3.75b_{i2}$$

The expected return and risk measures of any portfolio of these three portfolios are given by

$$\overline{R}_p = \sum_{i=1}^{N} X_i \overline{R}_i$$

$$b_{p1} = \sum_{i=1}^{N} X_i b_{i1}$$

$$b_{p2} = \sum_{i=1}^{N} X_i b_{i2}$$

$$\sum_{i=1}^{N} X_i = 1$$

[2]The reader interested in verifying this can recall that the equation of a plane can be written as $R_i = \lambda_0 + \lambda_1 b_{i1} + \lambda_2 b_{i2}$. By substituting in the values of R_i, b_{i1}, and b_{i2} for portfolios A, B, and C, we obtain three equations with three unknowns: λ_0, λ_1, and λ_2. Solving the three equations gives the values for λ_0, λ_1 and λ_2 shown in the equation in the text.

Since a weighted combination of points on a plane (where the weights sum to one) also lies on the plane, all portfolios constructed from portfolios A, B, and C lie on the plane described by portfolios A, B, and C.[3]

What happens if we consider a new portfolio not on this plane. For example, assume a portfolio E exists with an expected return of 15%, a b_{i1} of .6 and a b_{i2} of .6.

Compare this with a portfolio (call it D) constructed by placing ⅓ of the funds in portfolio A, ⅓ in portfolio B, and ⅓ in portfolio C. The b_{pj}'s on this portfolio are

$$b_{p1} = \frac{1}{3}(1.0) + \frac{1}{3}(.5) + \frac{1}{3}(.3) = .6$$

$$b_{p2} = \frac{1}{3}(.6) + \frac{1}{3}(1.0) + \frac{1}{3}(.2) = .6$$

The risk for portfolio D is identical to the risk on portfolio E. The expected return on portfolio D is

$$\frac{1}{3}(15) + \frac{1}{3}(14) + \frac{1}{3}(10) = 13$$

Alternatively, since portfolio D must lie on the plane described above, we could have obtained its expected return from the equation of the plane:

$$\overline{R}_i = 7.75 + 5(.6) + 3.75(.6) = 13$$

By the law of one price, two portfolios that have the same risk cannot sell at a different expected return. In this situation it would pay arbitrageurs to step in and buy portfolio E while selling an equal amount of portfolio D short. Buying portfolio E and financing it by selling D short would guarantee a riskless profit with no investment and no risk. We can see this quite easily. Assume the investor sells $100 worth of portfolio D short and buys $100 worth of portfolio E. The results are shown in the following table.

	Initial Cash Flow	End of Period Cash Flow	b_{i1}	b_{i2}
Portfolio D	+$100	−$113.0	−.6	−.6
Portfolio E	−$100	$115.0	.6	.6
Arbitrage portfolio	0	2.0	0	0

[3]The reader is encouraged to form a portfolio of portfolios $A, B,$ and C with any set of X_i summing to one. One can then see that this portfolio lies on the plane given by $\overline{R}_i = 7.75 + 5 b_{i1} + 3.75 b_{i2}$. One example of this is portfolio D analyzed shortly in the text.

The artibrage portfolio involves zero investment, has no systematic risk (b_{i1} and b_{i2}), and earns \$2. Arbitrage would continue until portfolio E lies on the same plane as portfolio A, B, and C.

We have established that all investments and portfolios must be on a plane in expected return, b_{i1}, b_{i2} space. If an investment were to lie above or below the plane an opportunity would exist for riskless arbitrage. The arbitrage would continue until all investments converged to a plane.

The general equation of a plane in expected return, b_{i1}, b_{i2} space is

$$\overline{R}_i = \lambda_0 + \lambda_1 b_{i1} + \lambda_2 b_{i2} \tag{14.3}$$

This is the equilibrium model produced by the APT when returns are generated by a two-index model. Notice that λ_1 is the increase in expected return for a one-unit increase in b_{i1}. Thus λ_1 and λ_2 are returns for bearing the risks associated with I_1 and I_2, respectively.

More insight can be gained into the meaning of the λ_i's by using Equation (14.3) to examine a particular set of portfolios. Examine a portfolio with b_{i1} and b_{i2} both equal to zero. The expected return on this portfolio equals λ_0. This is a zero b_{ij} portfolio, and we denote its return by $\overline{R}_z$. If riskless lending and borrowing exist, $\overline{R}_z = R_F$.

Substituting $\overline{R}_z$ for λ_0 and examining a portfolio with a b_{i2} of zero and a b_{i1} of one, we see that

$$\lambda_1 = \overline{R}_1 - \overline{R}_z$$

where $\overline{R}_1$ is the return on a portfolio having a b_{i1} of one and a b_{i2} of zero. In general, $\lambda_i = \overline{R}_j - \overline{R}_z$ or λ_j is the expected excess return on a portfolio only subject to risk of index j and having a unit measure of this risk.

The analysis in this section can be generalized to the J index case

$$R_i = a_i + b_{i1} I_1 + b_{i2} I_2 + \cdots + b_{iJ} I_J + e_i$$

By analogous arguments it can be shown that all securities and portfolios have expected returns described by the J-dimensional hyperplane

$$\overline{R}_i = \lambda_0 + \lambda_1 b_{i1} + \lambda_2 b_{i2} + \cdots + \lambda_J b_{iJ} \tag{14.4}$$

with $\lambda_0 = \overline{R}_z$ and $\lambda_j = \overline{R}_j - \overline{R}_z$.

A More Rigorous Proof of APT

Once again we will derive APT assuming a two-index return-generating process. This derivation is sufficiently rich to allow generalization to any arbitrary number of indices. The two-index model we use is that presented in Equation (14.2).

Taking the expected value of Equation (14.2) and subtracting it from Equation (14.2), we have

$$R_i = \overline{R}_i + b_{i1}(I_1 - \overline{I}_1) + b_{i2}(I_2 - \overline{I}_2) + e_i \qquad (14.5)$$

Now a sufficient condition for an APT proof to hold is that there are enough securities in the market so that a portfolio with the following characteristics can be formed:

$$\sum_{i=1}^{N} X_i = 0$$

$$\sum_{i=1}^{N} X_i b_{i1} = 0$$

$$\sum_{i=1}^{N} X_i b_{i2} = 0$$

$$\sum_{i=1}^{N} X_i e_i \approx 0$$

The last condition is a requirement that residual risk be approximately zero. The first of these four equations states that this portfolio involves zero investment. The remaining equations imply that this portfolio has no risk. This portfolio involves no investment and no risk; therefore, it must produce an expected return of zero. In other words, the three equations plus the condition on residual risk just discussed imply that

$$\sum_{i=1}^{N} X_i \overline{R}_i - 0$$

Now there is another more mathematical interpretation of these equations. The equation

$$\sum_{i=1}^{N} X_i b_{i1} = 0$$

means that the vector of security proportions is orthogonal to the vector of b_{i1}'s. Similarly, the first equation

$$\sum_{i=1}^{N} X_i = 0$$

means that the vector of security proportions is orthogonal to a vector of ones.

We have just shown, in the previous paragraph, that if the vector of portfolio proportions is orthogonal to a vector of ones, a vector of b_{i1}'s, and a vector of b_{i2}'s, this implies that the vector of security proportions is orthogonal to the vector of expected returns. But there is a well-known theorem in linear algebra that states that if the fact that a vector is orthogonal to $N - 1$ vectors implies it is orthogonal to the Nth vector, then the Nth vector can be expressed as a linear combination of the $N - 1$ vectors. In this case, the vector of expected returns can be expressed as a linear combination of a vector of ones, a vector of b_{i1}'s, and a vector of b_{i2}'s. Thus we can write the expected value for any security as a constant times 1, plus a second constant times b_{i1}, plus a third constant times b_{i2} or

$$\overline{R}_i = \lambda_0 + \lambda_1 b_{i1} + \lambda_2 b_{i2}$$

This equation must hold for all securities and all portfolios. The λ's can be evaluated by following the procedure used in the previous section of this chapter, namely forming three portfolios with the following characteristics

$$
\begin{aligned}
&1. \quad b_{p1} = 0 \quad &&\text{and} \quad && b_{p2} = 0 \\
&2. \quad b_{p1} = 1 \quad &&\text{and} \quad && b_{p2} = 0 \\
&3. \quad b_{p1} = 0 \quad &&\text{and} \quad && b_{p2} = 1
\end{aligned}
$$

we find that

$$\overline{R}_i = \overline{R}_z + b_{i1}(\overline{R}_1 - \overline{R}_z) + b_{i2}(\overline{R}_2 - \overline{R}_z)$$

or for the general case

$$\overline{R}_i = \overline{R}_z + b_{i1}(\overline{R}_1 - \overline{R}_z) + \cdots + b_{iJ}(\overline{R}_J - \overline{R}_z)$$

Defining λ_0 as $\overline{R}_z$ and λ_j as $\overline{R}_j - \overline{R}_z$, we can write this equation as

$$\overline{R}_i = \lambda_0 + \lambda_1 b_{i1} + \lambda_2 b_{i2} + \cdots + \lambda_J b_{iJ}$$

The APT theory is extremely general. The generality of the theory is both its strength and its weakness. While it allows us to describe equilibrium in terms of any multi-index model, it gives us no evidence as to what might be an appropriate multi-index model. Furthermore, APT tells us nothing about the size or the signs of the λ_j's. This makes interpretation of tests difficult. We'll have more to say about this shortly.

ESTIMATING AND TESTING APT

The proof of any economic theory is how well it describes reality. Tests of APT are particularly difficult to formulate because all the theory specifies is a structure for asset pricing: the economic or firm characteristics that should affect expected return are not specified. Let us review the structure of APT that will enter any test procedure.

We can write the multifactor return-generating process as

$$R_i = a_i + \sum_{j=1}^{J} b_{ij}I_j + e_i \qquad (14.6)$$

The APT model that arises from this return-generating process can be written as

$$\overline{R}_i = \overline{R}_z + \sum_{j=1}^{J} b_{ij}\lambda_j \qquad (14.7)$$

It's worth spending a little time discussing the meaning of the variables b_{ij}, I_j, and λ_j.

Notice from Equation (14.6) that each security i has a unique sensitivity to each I_j but that any I_j has a value that is the same for all securities. Any I_j affects more than one security (if it did not, it would have been compounded in the residual term e_i). These I_j's have generally been given the name factors in the APT literature. They are identical to the influences we called indices in earlier chapters. The factors affect the returns on more than one security and are the sources of covariance between securities. The b_{ij}'s are unique to each security and represent an attribute of the security. This attribute may be simply the sensitivity of the security to a particular factor, or it can be a characteristic of the security such as dividend yield.

Finally, from Equation (14.7) we see that λ_j is the extra expected return required because of a security's sensitivity to the jth attribute of the security. At this point the reader might note that Equation (14.6) looks suspiciously like the type of relationship we used in first-pass regression tests of the CAPM in Chapter 13, whereas Equation (14.7) bears a close resemblance to the type of equation used in second-pass tests. This intuition is correct. The problem is that, whereas for the CAPM the correct I_j is defined (e.g., the excess return on the market portfolio for the simple CAPM), for the multifactor model and the APT the set of I_j's is not defined by the theory. In order to test the APT, one must test Equation (14.7), which means that one must have estimates of the b_{ij}'s. Most tests of APT use Equation (14.6) to estimate the b_{ij}'s. However, to estimate the b_{ij}'s we must have definitions of the relevant I_j's. The most general approach to this problem is to estimate simultaneously factors (I_j's) and firm attributes (b_{ij}'s) for Equation (14.6). Most tests of the APT have employed this methodology, and many of the most outspoken adherents of the APT believe this is the only appropriate way to test APT. We examine this type of simultaneous estimation technique shortly. However, before we do so, let us point out two alternative methods. One method is to hypothesize (we hope on the basis of economic theory) a set of influences that might affect return and use Equation (14.6) to estimate b_{ij}. These influences might include variables such as the rate of inflation and the rate of interest. A second method is to specify a set of attributes (firm characteristics) that might affect expected return. With the approach the b_{ij}'s are directly specified. The b_{ij}'s might include such characteristics as dividend yield and the firm's Beta with the market.[4] If either of these last two procedures is used to obtain the b_{ij}'s for testing APT, one is really conducting a joint test of the APT and the relevancy of the factors or characteristics that have been hypothesized as determining equilibrium. Each of these general approaches will now be discussed in more detail.

Simultaneous Determination of Factors and Characteristics

A complete specification of Equation (14.6) would call for all factors (I_j) and attributes (b_{ij}) to be defined, so that the covariance between any residual return (the e_i's not explained by the equation) was zero. While it is not possible to produce this exact result, there is a body of statistical methodology that is very well suited to approximating this result. These techniques are called *factor analysis*.

Factor analysis determines a specific set of I_j's and b_{ij}'s such that the covariance of residual returns (returns after the influence of these indices have been removed) is as small as possible.[5] In the terminology of factor analysis the I_j's are called factors and the b_{ij}'s are called factor loadings. A specific factor analysis is performed for a specific number of hypothesized factors. By repeating this process for alternative hypotheses about the number of factors, a solution for 2 factors, 3 factors, . . . , and j factors is obtained. One can stop when the probability that the next factor explains a statistically significant portion of the covariance matrix

---

[4]A simple example of the role played by b_{ij} can be seen by employing the notion of duration discussed in Chapter 19 on bond valuation. If change in interest rates is hypothesized as an index in Equation (14.6), the b_{ij} associated with it is a security's sensitivity to the change in interest rates. This empirically determined b_{ij} can be used to determine λ_j. An alternative approach might be to hypothesize from theory that a security's duration is the appropriate sensitivity of the security to changes in interest rates, and to use duration as the value of b_{ij} in Equation (14.7) to estimate λ_j.

[5]Principal component analysis is somewhat analogous to factor analysis. Recall from Chapter 6 that principal component analysis extracts from the data a set of indices that best explain the variance of the data. Indices are extracted in order of importance and as many indices are extracted as the smaller of the number of stocks or the number of observations. Factor analysis is covariance rather than variance driven. For a specified number of indices it finds the set of that many indices that best explains the covariance in the original data. There are alternative ways of performing factor analysis. Most empirical work in this area uses maximum likelihood factor analysis, and the techniques developed by Joreskog [30, 31, 32] are often used.

drops below some level—for example, 50%.[6] Using this technique, it is not possible to be sure that one has captured all relevant factors. At best, statements such as the following can be made: "There is less than a 50% probability that another factor is needed." Whether one chooses to stop extracting factors when there is a 50% chance that no more are needed, or a 10% chance, or some other level is a matter of taste rather than mathematical rigor. Without a theory of how many factors should be present, the decision as to how many to extract from the data has to be made subjectively.

Factor analysis produces estimates of the factor loadings (b_{ij})and the factors (I_j). Recall that the factor loadings b_{ij} are sensitivity measures and are like the β_i's of the simple CAPM. At this point a set of tests analogous to the first-pass regression tests discussed in Chapter 13 has been performed. The major difference is that one has not only identified the b_{ij}'s, but one has estimated how many factors (indices) there should be and has determined the definition of each I_j. Each I_j is an index consisting of a (different) weighted average of the securities on which the factor analysis is performed.

The next step in testing the APT is to form a set of tests directly analogous to the second-pass tests performed by Fama and McBeth [18] on the simple CAPM. By running a cross-sectional test, estimates of λ's can be computed for each time period and the average value of each λ_j and its variance over time computed. Roll and Ross [48] were the first to perform this type of test. The mathematics of factor analysis allow this to be done more easily than with regression techniques, but the results are analogous to those that would be obtained by using the generalized least squares regression procedure. However, there are some problems with the use of factor analysis of which the reader should be aware. First, we have the same error in variables problem that we had when testing the standard CAPM. The factor loading b_{ij}'s, like the Betas from the first-pass regression, are estimated with error. This means that significance tests of λ_j's are only asymptotically correct. There are three additional problems that are unique to factor analysis. First, there is no meaning to the signs of the factors produced by factor analysis, so the signs on the b_{ij}'s and on the λ_j's could be reversed. Second, the scaling of the b_{ij}'s and the λ_j's is arbitrary. For example, all b_{ij}'s could be doubled and the resultant λ_j's halved. Third, there is no guarantee that factors are produced in a particular order, so when analysis is performed on separate samples the first factor from one sample may be the third from another sample.

The procedure discussed above is that used by Roll and Ross [48] in their classic study of APT. They applied factor analysis to 42 groups of 30 stocks using daily data for the time period July 3, 1962, to December 1972. The results of their first-pass test are rather striking. These tests show that, in over 38% of the groups, there was less than a 10% chance that a sixth factor had explanatory

---

[6]See Lawley and Maxwell [37] for a discussion of the test procedure described. The reader should be aware that these tests are based on the assumption of multivariate normality. This is the procedure applied by Roll and Ross [48].

power and in over three-fourths of the groups there was a 50% chance that 5 factors were sufficient. While Roll and Ross try several different second-pass tests, their major results are that at least three factors are significant in explaining equilibrium prices but that it is unlikely that four are significant. On the surface it would appear that they find more factors significant than one would expect to find under the standard CAPM model or the zero Beta version of the CAPM.

It is logical to question whether there is any way these results could be consistent with the CAPM or whether there seem to be additional factors at work in the market. Although we cannot answer definitely, the analysis of Cho, Elton, and Gruber [12] would seem to indicate that there are additional influences at work. They repeat the Roll and Ross methodology for a later period and find more factors to be significant than do Roll and Ross. They then simulate a set of data using the zero Beta form of CAPM while enforcing the same means and variances on the returns for each stock that were present in the original data. In doing so, they allow the rate on the zero Beta portfolio and the Beta on each asset to change over time. When the Roll and Ross methodology is applied to these data, the number of factors that are found to be significant is consistent with the zero Beta form of the CAPM. The fact that many more factors were found to be significant when actual returns were analyzed lends support to Roll and Ross's argument that additional factors beyond those embodied by the zero Beta form of the CAP determine equilibrium prices. While this analysis would seem to suggest that more than one or two factors are important in determining both returns and equilibrium returns, there still remain some questions about the implementation of APT through the use of factor analysis.[7]

The usefulness of an APT model cannot be differentiated from the methodology used to estimate it. The theory may well be correct, but if it cannot be implemented or estimated in a meaningful sense, then, while it remains useful as a way of thinking about the world, it cannot be used as part of the investment process. A test of the APT is a joint test of the theory and the methodology used to implement the theory.

Factor analysis is the principal methodology used to estimate simultaneously the factors that affect equilibrium return and the sensitivity of firms to these factors. One problem with employing this methodology to estimate factors is that the mathematics of factor analysis is so complex that only a limited number of securities can be analyzed at one time.[8] A set of factors and factor loadings are extracted that can best describe the behavior of a small sample of risky assets

---

[7]In the last section of this chapter we discuss an alternative way in which the zero Beta form of the CAPM could be consistent with the Roll and Ross results.

[8]Chen [8] has described a procedure that allows APT to be estimated and tested across large numbers of securities. However, his procedure, which involves forming a small number of portfolios of securities based on an initial factor solution for use in further tests, has been questioned by Dhrymes, Friend, and Gultekin [15]. The resolution of the adequacy of this procedure, and in particular the value of estimates for some securities versus the loss of information involved in his portfolio aggregation technique, will have to await further study.

rather than all risky assets. Roll and Ross used groups of 30 assets. The reader may well ask, "So what? If the abritrage pricing theory is correct, why don't we obtain the true factors whether we use 30 securities or 2,000 securities?" Dhrymes, Friend, and Gultekin [15] present evidence that the number of factors that appear significant is an increasing function of the size of the group analyzed. In their samples the number of signifiant factors increased from 3 for groups of 15 securities to 7 for groups of 60 securities, the largest groups studied. The authors suggest that dividing the sample into subgroups may ignore important sources of covariance between the securities in different groups and, further, that the factors identified within any subgroup may not be the same as the factor identified in a second subgroup.

While the necessity of estimating the APT for small groups provides some major problems with respect to the applicability of the result, it does provide a unique oportunity for testing the theory and methodology jointly. According to the theory,

$$\overline{R}_i = \overline{R}_z + \sum_{j=1}^{J} b_{ij}\lambda_j$$

Now if the theory is correct and if through factor analysis we have identified the correct factors in the return-generating process, and thus the b_{ij}'s, then the value of the market price of all factor λ_j's and the intercept should be the same for each group. Testing this is not as easy as it may seem at first. Remember that the sign of the b_{ij}'s and λ_j's are not uniquely determined, nor is the order in which factors appear in different groups uniquely determined.

Methodology does exist for evaluating whether the intercept is constant across groups and whether the factor prices estimated are the same across groups. The methodology and test results have been described very well in an article by Brown and Weinstein [5]. They are able to test (1) whether the intercept term is the same for all groups, (2) whether the factor prices are the same for all groups given that the intercept is constrained to be the same, and (3) whether both the intercept and factor prices are the same for all groups, a joint hypothesis. Unfortunately their results are ambiguous. Although they cast some doubt on the use of the maximum likelihood factor analysis to explain equilibrium return succesfully, as Brown and Weinstein recognize, their "results cannot be viewed as compelling evidence against the APT." Dhrymes, Friend, and Gultckin [15] in another set of tests find that, depending on the method of grouping stocks employed, the intercept term may be significantly different or not significantly different across groups.

Other tests of the APT have failed to demonstrate its clear superiority over other models although results arc mixed. Dhrymes, Friend, and Gultekin find that a multifactor model of the APT has better explanatory power than a one-factor model. This tends to support the existence of more than one factor. However, they find that the explanatory power of either model is modest and that there is some doubt about whether the risk premia (prices) of the five risk factors employed by Roll and Ross are significantly different from zero.

Other tests of the Roll and Ross type APT have produced equally ambiguous results. For example, one test of the APT that would give us great confidence is if a stock's residual risk was not priced when added as another factor in the equilibrium pricing equation. Recall that the b_{ij}'s are supposed to capture the impact of all systematic components of risk. Any other attribute of a security, and in particular its residual risk, should be unique to each security and therefore diversifiable. Roll and Ross test for the impact of residual risk and find almost no evidence that it is priced. Dhrymes, Friend, and Gultekin also test and find that both a stock's own standard deviation and skewness generally yield insignificant coefficients. However, they find that these two influences are significant at least as frequently as the factors suggested by Roll and Ross.[9]

At this point the reader might well question where we are in our analysis. We have discussed results of the APT when statistical techniques are used to estimate both b_{ij}'s and I_j's. The technique used is maximum likelihood factor analysis and, in particular, the procedure developed by Roll and Ross. All of the tests are joint tests of the APT and the particular statistical methodology used to test it. The results are highly ambiguous. It appears likely that there are more than two factors affecting equilibrium returns, but it is uncertain whether they have been correctly identified. Adding to our uncertainty about this approach to APT is the fact that, while some attempts have been made to test the stability of factor prices across groups, no attempt has yet been made to test the stability of the factor structure over time. Recall that the factors developed from the factor analysis are a set of indices or a weighted average of a set of individual stock returns over time. Are these indices stable over time? Do the same set of indices explain stock prices at different points in time? If the answer to this is yes, the next logical problem to examine is the stability of the b_{ij}'s over time. Answers to these questions will have to await further empirical research.

An Alternative Approach to Testing the APT

Earlier we indicated that there was an alternative approach to testing APT. If we could specify a priori either the factors that affected stock returns or the characteristics of stocks that affected returns, we would then have a much easier estimation problem to solve. A debate exists among academics and practitioners about whether part of the model should be prespecified on the basis of theory

---

[9]One other type of test has been performed on Roll and Ross type of multifactor models. In applying the standard CAPM and zero Beta CAPM, certain anomalies have been noted. For example, small (low capitalization) firms tend consistently to produce returns in excess of those we would expect based on CAPM. This anomaly is either due to a market inefficiency or a deficiency in the CAPM as a model of equilibrium returns. If a Roll and Ross type of multifactor of equilibrium better explained anomalies, such as the small-firm effect, one would have added faith in such models. Reinganum [45] has investigated this issue and finds that a Roll and Ross multifactor model could not explain the size anomaly any better than the standard CAPM.

or whether all of the parameters should be determined empirically. This type of debate has gone on since the dawn of modern science. The issue is discussed by Roll and Ross [48]. They state that "we do consider the basic underlying causes of the generating process of returns to be a potentially important area of research but we think it is an area that can be investigated separately from testing asset pricing theories." The problem is that, without a theory, the empirical tools one uses are a lot weaker and the results of tests harder to interpret. For example, in the APT we have no idea of what the size or even the sign of factor prices should be. All we can say is that we expect some of them to be statistically different from zero. On the other hand, in the Sharpe–Lintner CAPM the price of Beta was supposed to be $\overline{R}_m - R_F$, a quantity that we expected to be positive and about which we have some rough idea of magnitude.

The controversy we are discussing would be easy to resolve if we had a theory of the appropriate factors or characteristics that determine security returns. Someday we hope we will have one. In the absence of such a theory all we can do is examine two attempts to prespecify one set of variables in the multifactor model. One attempt hypothesized a set of firm characteristics, while another hypothesized a set of indices.

Specifying Attributes of Securities In the preceding section of this chapter we examined the use of maximum likelihood factor analysis to determine simultaneously the characteristics that affect return and the extra return required because of a security's sensitivity to these characteristics. If a set of characteristics that affect return could be specified a priori, then the market price of these characteristics over any period of time could be measured fairly easily. The estimating equation would be the form

$$\overline{R}_i = \lambda_0 + \lambda_1 b_{i1} + \lambda_2 b_{i2} + \cdots + \lambda_J b_{iJ}$$

for the case of J characteristics. In this equation the b_{ij}'s would be the value each characteristic took on, and the λ_j's the average extra return required because of these characteristics. The values of the λ_j's would be estimated via regression analysis. This procedure is directly analogous to a second-pass test of the CAPM. In fact, we have already examined two models that could be viewed as this type of test. The first was the model tested by Fama and McBeth [18] and reviewed in Chapter 13; although they viewed the model as a test of the CAPM, it could be viewed as a test of APT. The model they tested was

$$\overline{R}_i = \lambda_0 + \lambda_1 \beta_i + \lambda_2 \beta_i^2 + \lambda_3 S_{ei}$$

The firm characteristics examined were the Beta for each firm, the Beta for each stock squared, and the residual risk of each stock. These tests clearly show that, at least with respect to the hypothesized set of characteristics, a multifactor model did not outperform the zero Beta form of the CAPM. None of the added characteristics were priced. Remember that tests of this type are a joint test of the

APT in general and the specific characteristics that were hypothesized as explaining equilibrium returns. Fama and McBeth tested characteristics that on the basis of economic theory should not explain equilibrium returns and concluded that they did not.

We examined a second model in Chapter 13 that hypothesized an additional firm characteristic as affecting equilibrium return. Recall that Litzenberger and Ramaswamy [40] included dividend yield as an added variable and found its impact was statistically significant. This should encourage the pursuit of models containing more characteristics.

One such model has been constructed and tested by Sharpe [55]. He starts with the hypothesis that equilibrium returns should be effected by the following characteristics: a stock's Beta with the S&P index, its dividend yield, the size of the firm (market value of equity), its Beta with long-term bonds, its past value of Alpha (the intercept of the regression of past excess return against excess returns on the S&P index), and eight sector membership variables. Sharpe does not attempt an elaborate economic rationale for these variables but rather states that he has selected them more or less "ex cathedra." We would expect both Beta and dividend yield to be related positively to expected returns based on the theory discussed in Chapters 11, 12, and 13. Size may well be, at least in part, a proxy for liquidity. If so, size should enter the model with a negative sign. If sensitivity to interest rates is an important variable, we would expect bond Beta to play a role in determining equilibrium returns. If the past value of Alpha proves significant, it would be evidence of autocorrelation of the residuals from the CAPM. This might indicate that there are some added variables explaining cross-sectional returns that were not captured in the model. The use of sector membership as an additional set of variables implies that membership in a particular sector of the economy has an important effect on equilibrium return.

The results of applying this model to 2,197 stocks on a monthly basis for all months between 1931 and 1979 are summarized in Table 14.1. Table 14.1 reports the average coefficients (on an annualized basis) over the entire period and the percent of months in which the coefficients were significantly different from zero at the 5% level. Note that for those variables where we had clear expectations about the sign of the relationship with return, our expectations are borne out. Furthermore, note that while on the basis of chance we would expect any firm characteristic to be significant about 5% of the time, each characteristic was significant a much higher percentage of the time.

Another way to judge the importance of including more than one characteristic in the description of equilibrium is by examining the explanatory power (coefficient of determination) of the model as more characteristics are employed. The average coefficient of determination for monthly data when Beta is used as the only characteristic to explain cross-sectional returns is .037. This might seem low relative to the results reported in Chapter 13, but recall that monthly data are being used and portfolio grouping is not being done. This is in fact consistent with other studies employing similar research designs. When the security characteristics of yield, size, bond Beta, and Alpha are added, the coefficient of determination adjusting for added variables more than doubles to .079. When

Table 14.1   Cross-sectional Data on Sharpe's Multifactor Model

Attribute	Annualized Value of Associated λ	Percent of Months in Which Associated λ Was Significantly Different from Zero
Beta	5.36	58.3
Yield	0.24	39.5
Size	−5.56	56.5
Bond Beta	−0.12	28.2
Alpha	−2.00	43.5
Sector Membership		
Basic industries	1.65	32.5
Capital goods	0.16	18.7
Construction	−1.59	15.3
Consumer goods	−0.18	39.3
Energy	6.28	36.9
Finance	−1.48	16.3
Transportation	−0.57	43.9
Utilities	−2.62	35.0

all the characteristics in Table 14.1 are used, it goes up to .104. The use of firm characteristics in addition to Beta has increased the explanatory power of the model. In addition, these factors seem to be significant a considerably higher percentage of the time than chance alone would explain.

Sharpe seems to have identified some additional characteristics, beyond a stock's Beta with a proxy for the market portfolio, that are useful for explaining cross-sectional returns over time. He recognizes that his model is rather ad hoc in nature, but it is an indication that increased research into significant economic characteristics of a stock should allow us to build better models of equilibrium.

Specifying the Influences Affecting the Return-generating Process   Another alternative to the joint determination of factor loadings and factors discussed in the earlier section of this chapter is the specification (one hopes on the basis of economic theory) of the set of influences or indices (I_j's) that should enter the return-generating process.

Chen, Roll, and Ross [10] have hypothesized and tested a set of economic variables. They reason that return on stocks should be affected by any influence that affects either future cash flows from holding a security or the value of these cash flows to the investor (e.g., changes in the appropriate discount rate on future cash flows). Chen, Roll, and Ross construct sets of alternative measures of unanticipated changes in the following influences:

1.   *Inflation.* Inflation impacts both the level of the discount rate and the size of the future cash flows.

2.   *The term structure of interest rates.* Differences between the rate on bonds with a long maturity and a short maturity affect the value of payments far in the future relative to near-term payments.

3. *Risk premia.* Differences between the return on safe bonds (Aaa) and more risky bonds (Baa) is used to measure the market's reaction to risk.

4. *Industrial production.* Changes in industrial production affect the opportunities facing investors and the real value of cash flows.

Chen, Roll, and Ross then examined these measures or indices:

1. To see if they were correlated with the set of indices extracted by the factor analysis used by Roll and Ross as described in a previous section of this chapter.

2. To see if they explained equilibrium returns.

When they examine the relationship between the macroeconomic variables and the factors (indices) over the period to which the factors were formed (fit), they find a strong relationship. Furthermore, when the relationship is tested over a hold-out period (a period following the fit period) the relationship continues to be strong. There appears to be a significant relationship between the hypothesized macroeconomic variables and the statistically identified systematic factors in stock market returns.

The second set of tests involves investigating whether returns are related to the sensitivity of a stock to their macroeconomic variables. The procedure is analogous to the two-step procedure used by Fama and Macbeth (and discussed in the previous chapter) to investigate the CAPM. In the first stage, time series regressions are run for each of a series of portfolios to estimate each portfolio's sensitivity to each macroeconomic variable [the b_{ij}'s of Equation (14.6)]. Then the market price of risk [the λ_j's of Equation (14.7)] is estimated by running a cross-sectional regression each month and looking at the average of the market price in each month. Chen, Roll, and Ross find that the macrovariables are significant explanatory influences on pricing. Furthermore, when the Beta of each portfolio with the market was introduced as an additional variable along with the sensitivity of each portfolio to the macroeconomic variables, it did not show up as significant in the second stage (cross-sectional) regression.

Chen, Roll, and Ross recognize that they cannot claim to have found the (correct) state variables for asset pricing. However, they certainly have made an important start in that direction.

APT AND CAPM

Before closing this chapter, we should discuss the fact that the APT model and, in fact, the existence of a multifactor model, including one where more than one factor is priced, is not necessarily inconsistent with the Sharpe–Lintner–Mossin form or one of the other forms of the CAPM.

The simplest case in which an APT model is consistent with the simple form of the CAPM is the case where the return-generating function is of the form

$$R_i = a_i + \beta_i R_m + e_i$$

If returns are generated by a single-index model, the single index is the return on the market portfolio, and a riskless rate exists, then the methodology at the beginning of the chapter can be used to show that

$$\overline{R}_i = R_F + \beta_i(\overline{R}_m - R_F)$$

If the return-generating function is more complex than this, does it imply that the simple CAPM cannot hold? The answer is no. Recall that the simple CAPM does not assume that the market is the only source of covariance between returns. Let us assume that the return-generating function is of the multi-index type.

$$R_i = a_i + b_{i1}I_1 + b_{i2}I_2 + e_i \tag{14.8}$$

The indices can be industry indices, sector indices, or indices of broad economic influences such as the rate of inflation. All we assume is that the set of indices used capture all the sources of covariance between securities: [e.g., $E(e_ie_j) = 0$].

The APT equilibrium model for this multifactor return-generating process with a riskless asset is

$$\overline{R}_i = R_F + b_{i1}\lambda_1 + b_{i2}\lambda_2 \tag{14.9}$$

Recall that if the CAPM is the equilibrium model, it holds for all securities, as well as all portfolios of securities. Assume the indices can be represented by portfolios of securities. Actually, we have seen that λ_j is the excess return on a portfolio with a b_{ij} of one on one index and a b_{ij} of zero on all other indices. If the CAPM holds, the equilibrium return on each λ_j is given by the CAPM or

$$\lambda_1 = \beta_{\lambda 1}(\overline{R}_m \quad R_F)$$

$$\lambda_2 = \beta_{\lambda 2}(\overline{R}_m - R_F)$$

Substituting into Equation (14.9) yields

$$\overline{R}_i = R_F + b_{i1}\beta_{\lambda 1}(\overline{R}_m - R_F) + b_{i2}\beta_{\lambda 2}(\overline{R}_m - R_F)$$

$$\overline{R}_i = R_F + (b_{i1}\beta_{\lambda 1} + b_{i2}\beta_{\lambda 2})(\overline{R}_m - R_F)$$

Defining β_i as $(b_{i1}\beta_{\lambda 1} + b_{i2}\beta_{\lambda 2})$ results in the expected return of $\overline{R}_i$ being priced by the CAPM.

$$\overline{R}_i = R_F + \beta_i(\overline{R}_m - R_F)$$

The APT solution with multiple factors appropriately priced is fully consistent with the Sharpe–Lintner–Mossin form of the CAPM.

We wish to stress this point. Employing the Roll and Ross procedure and finding that more than one λ_j is significantly different from zero is not sufficient proof to reject any CAPM. If the λ_j's are not significantly different from

$\beta_{\lambda j}(\overline{R}_m - R_F)$, the empirical results could be fully consistent with the Sharpe–Lintner–Mossin form of the CAPM. It is perfectly possible that more than one index explains the covariance between security returns but that the CAPM holds.

While we have demonstrated this with the simple CAPM, it should be apparent to the reader that other values of λ_j's can exist that are fully consistent with the more complex nonstandard forms of the CAPM reviewed in Chapter 12.

CONCLUSIONS

The APT promises to be a more important contribution to understanding the nature of asset prices. The theory has already given us great insight into asset prices. Empirical work on implementing APT is just beginning. While the promise is great, this promise has not yet been achieved.

QUESTIONS AND PROBLEMS

1. Assume that the following two-index model describes returns

$$R_i = a_i + b_{i1}I_1 + b_{i2}I_2 + e_i$$

Assume that the following three portfolios are observed.

Portfolio	Expected Return	b_{i1}	b_{i2}
A	12.0	1	0.5
B	13.4	3	0.2
C	12.0	3	-0.5

Find the equation of the plane that must describe equilibrium returns.

2. Referring to the results of Problem 1, illustrate the arbitrage opportunities that would exist if a portfolio called D with the following properties were observed.

$$\overline{R}_D = 10 \qquad b_{D1} = 2 \qquad b_{D2} = 0$$

3. Repeat Problem 1 if the three portfolios observed have the following characteristics.

Portfolio	Expected Return	b_{i1}	b_{i2}
A	12	1.0	1
B	13	1.5	2
C	17	0.5	-3

4. Referring to the results of Problem 3, illustrate the arbitrage opportunities that would exist if a portfolio called D with the following characteristics were observed.

$$\overline{R}_i = 15 \qquad b_{i1} = 1 \qquad b_{i2} = 0$$

5. If we accept the Sharpe model as a description of expected returns, using the data in Table 14.1 find the expected return on a stock in the construction industry with the following characteristics.

$$
\begin{array}{ll}
\text{Beta} & = 1.2 \\
\text{Yield} & = 6 \\
\text{Size} & = .4 \\
\text{Bond Beta} & = .2 \\
\text{Alpha} & = 1
\end{array}
$$

6. Return to Problem 1. If $(\overline{R}_m - R_F) = 4$, find the values for the following variables that would make the expected returns from Problem 1 consistent with equilibrium determined by the simple (Sharpe–Lintner–Mossin) CAPM.

   A. $\beta_{\lambda 1}$ and $\beta_{\lambda 2}$
   B. β_p for each of the three portfolios
   C. R_F

BIBLIOGRAPHY

1. Black, F. "Capital Market Equilibrium with Restricted Borrowing," *Journal of Business,* **45** (July 1972), pp. 444–454.
2. Bower, Dorothy H., Bower, Richard S., and Logue, Dennis E. "Arbitrage Pricing Theory and Utility Stock Returns," *The Journal of Finance,* **39,** No. 4 (Sept. 1984), pp. 1041–1054.
3. Brennan, M. "Capital Asset Pricing and the Structure of Security Returns," Working Paper, University of British Columbia, 1971.
4. Brennan, M. "Discussion," *Journal of Finance,* **36** (May 1981), pp. 352–357.
5. Brown, S.J., and Weinstein, M.I. "A New Approach to Testing Asset Pricing Models: The Bilinear Paradigm," *Journal of Finance* (June 1983).
6. Chamberlain, G., and Rothschild, M. "Arbitrage, Factor Structure, and Mean-Variance Analysis on Large Asset Markets," Working Paper, University of Wisconsin at Madison, 1981.
7. Chen, N. "The Arbitrage Pricing Theory: Estimation and Applications," Working Paper, Graduate School of Management, UCLA, 1981.
8. Chen, Nai-fu. "Some Empirical Tests of the Theory of Arbitrage Pricing," *The Journal of Finance,* **38,** No. 5 (Dec. 1983), pp. 1393–1414.
9. Chen, Nai-fu, Ingersoll, Jonathan E., Jr. "Exact Pricing in Linear Factor Models with Finitely Many Assets: A Note," *The Journal of Finance,* **38,** No. 3 (June 1983), pp. 985–988.

10. Cho, D. Chinhyung. "Some fundamental factors effecting asset prices" Working Paper University of Wisconsin.
11. Cho, D. Chinhyung. "On Testing the Arbitrage Pricing Theory: Inter-Battery Factor Analysis," *The Journal of Finance,* **39,** No. 5 (Dec. 1984), pp. 1485–1502.
12. Cho, D. Chinhyung, Elton, Edwin J., and Gruber, Martin J. "On the Robustness of the Roll and Ross Arbitrage Pricing Theory," *Journal of Financial and Quantitative Analysis,* **XIX,** No. 1 (March 1984), pp. 1–10.
13. Connor, G. "A Factor Pricing Theory for Capital Assets," Working Paper, Kellog Graduate School of Management, Northwestern University, 1981.
14. Connor, G. "A Unified Beta Pricing Theory," Working Paper, Kellog Graduate School of Management, Northwestern University, 1982.
15. Dhrymes, Pheobus J., Friend, Irwin, and Gultekin, N. Bulent. "A Critical Reexamination of the Empirical Evidence on the Arbitrage Pricing Theory," *The Journal of Finance,* **39,** No. 2 (June 1984), pp. 323–346.
16. Elton, E., and Gruber, M. "Non-Standard CAPMs and the Market Portfolio," Working Paper, New York University, Graduate School of Business, 1982.
17. Elton, Edwin J., Gruber, Martin J., and Rentzler, Joel. "The Arbitrage Pricing Model and Returns on Assets Under Uncertain Inflation," *The Journal of Finance,* **38,** No. 2 (May 1983), pp. 525–538.
18. Fama, E., and McBeth, J. "Risk, Return, and Equilibrium: Empirical Tests," *Journal of Political Economy,* **81,** No. 3 (May/June 1973), pp. 607–636.
19. Fogler, H. Russell, John, Kose, and Tipton, James. "Three Factors Interest Rate Differentials and Stock Groups," *The Journal of Finance,* **36,** No. 2 (May 1981), pp. 323–336.
20. Garman, Mark B., and Ohlson, James A. "A Dynamic Equilibrium for the Ross Arbitrage Model," *The Journal of Finance,* **35,** No. 3 (June 1980), pp. 675–684.
21. Gehr, A., Jr. "Some Tests of the Arbitrage Pricing Theory," *Journal of the Midwest Finance Association* (1975), pp. 91–105.
22. Gibbons, M.R. "Empirical Examination of the Return Generating Process of the Arbitrage Pricing Theory," Working Paper, Stanford University, 1981.
23. Gibbons, M. "Multivariate Tests of Financial Models: A New Approach," *Journal of Financial Economics,* **10,** No. 1 (March 1982), pp. 3–27.
24. Grinblatt, M., and Titman, S. "Factor-Pricing in a Finite Economy," Working Paper, UCLA, Graduate School of Management, 1983.
25. Harman, H. *Modern Factor Analysis,* third edition (Chicago: University of Chicago, 1976).
26. Huberman, G. "A Simple Approach to Arbitrage Pricing Theory," *Journal of Economic Theory,* **28,** No. 1 (Oct. 1982), pp. 183–193.
27. Hughes, P. "A Test of the Arbitrage Pricing Theory," Working Paper, University of British Columbia, 1981.
28. Ingersoll, Jonathan E., Jr. "Some Results in the Theory of Arbitrage Pricing," *The Journal of Finance,* **39,** No. 4 (Sept. 1984), pp. 1021–1054.

29. Jobson, J.D. "A Multivariate Linear Regression Test for the Arbitrage Pricing Theory," *The Journal of Finance,* **37,** No. 4 (Sept. 1982), pp. 1037–1042.
30. Joreskog, K.J. *Statistical Estimation in Factor Analysis* (Stockholm: Almqvist & Wiksell, 1963).
31. Joreskog, K.G. "Some Contributions to Maximum Likelihood Factor Analysis," *Psychometrika,* **32,** No. 4 (Dec. 1967), pp. 443–482.
32. Joreskog, K.G. "Factor Analysis by Least Squares and Maximum Likelihood Methods." In K. Enslein, A. Ralston, and H.S. Wilf (eds.), *Statistical Methods of Digital Computers* (New York: John Wiley & Sons, 1977).
33. King, B. "Market and Industry Factors in Stock Price Behavior," *Journal of Business,* **39** (Jan. 1966), pp. 139–190.
34. Kristof, W. "Orthogonal Inter-Battery Factor Analysis," *Psychometrika,* **32,** No. 2 (June 1967), pp. 199–227.
35. Kryzanowski, L., and To, M.C. "General Factor Models and the Structure of Security Returns," *Journal of Financial and Quantitative Analysis,* **18,** No. 1 (March 1983), pp. 31–37.
36. Lawley, D.N. "The Estimation of Factor Loadings by the Method of Maximum Likelihood," *Proceedings of the Royal Society of Edinburgh, Section A,* **60** (1940), pp. 64–82.
37. Lawley, D.N., and Maxwell, M.A. *Factor Analysis as a Statistical Method* (London, England: Butterworths, 1963).
38. Levine, M.S. *Canonical Analysis and Factor Comparison* (Beverly Hills: SAGE Publications, 1977).
39. Lintner, J. "The Valuation of Risk Assets and the Selection of Risky Investments in Stock Portfolios and Capital Budgets," *Review of Economics and Statistics,* **47** (February 1965), pp. 13–37.
40. Litzenberger, R.H., and Ramaswamy, K. "The Effect of Personal Taxes and Dividends on Capital Asset Prices: Theory and Empirical Evidence," *Journal of Financial Economics,* **7** (1979), pp. 163–196.
41. Morrison, D.F. *Multivariate Statistical Methods* (New York: McGraw-Hill, 1976).
42. Mossin, J. "Equilibrium in a Capital Asset Market," *Econometrika,* **34** (Oct. 1966), pp. 768–783.
43. Neyman, J., and Pearson, E.S. "On the Use and Interpretation of Certain Test Criteria for Purposes of Statistical Inference," *Biometrika,* **20A** (1928), pp. 175–240, 263–294.
44. Oldfield, George S., Jr., and Rogalski, Richard J. "Treasury Bill Factors and Common Stock Returns," *The Journal of Finance,* **36,** No. 2 (May 1981), pp. 337–349.
45. Reinganum, M. "The Arbitrage Pricing Theory: Some Empirical Results," *Journal of Finance,* **36** (May 1981), pp. 313–321.
46. Roll, R. "A Critique of the Asset Pricing Theory's Tests," *Journal of Financial Economics,* **4** (May 1977), pp. 129–176.
47. Roll, R. "Ambiguity When Performance Is Measured by the Securities Market Line," *Journal of Finance,* **33** (Sept. 1978), pp. 1051–1069.

48. Roll, R., and Ross, S.A. "An Empirical Investigation of the Arbitrage Pricing Theory," *Journal of Finance, 35,* No. 5 (Dec. 1980), pp. 1073–1103.
49. Roll, Richard, and Ross, Stephen A. "A Critical Reexamination of the Empirical Evidence on the Arbitrage Pricing Theory: A Reply," *The Journal of Finance, 39,* No. 2 (June 1984), pp. 347–350.
50. Ross, S.A. "The Arbitrage Theory of Capital Asset Pricing," *Journal of Economic Theory, 13* (Dec. 1976), pp. 341–360.
51. Ross, S.A. "Return Risk, and Arbitrage." In Irwin Friend and James L. Bicksler (eds.), *Risk and Return in Finance, I* (Cambridge, Mass.: Ballinger, 1977).
52. Rubinstein, M. "The Valuation of Uncertain Income Streams and the Pricing of Options," *Bell Journal of Economics, 7* (1976), pp. 407–425.
53. Shanken, J. "The Arbitrage Pricing Theory: Is It Testable?" *Journal of Finance, 37,* No. 5 (Dec. 1982), pp. 1129–1140.
54. Sharpe, W. "Capital Asset Prices: A Theory of Market Equilibrium under Conditions of Risk," *Journal of Finance, 19* (Sept. 1964), pp. 425–442.
55. Sharpe, W. "Factors in NYSE Security Returns, 1931–1979," *Journal of Portfolio Management, 8,* No. 2 (Summer 1982), pp. 5–19.
56. Sinclair, N.A. "Security Return Data and 'Blind' Factor Analysis," Working Paper, Australian Graduate School of Management, 1981.
57. Solnik, Bruno. "International Arbitrage Pricing Theory," *The Journal of Finance, 38,* No. 2 (May 1983), pp. 449–458.

PART 3
SECURITY ANALYSIS AND PORTFOLIO THEORY

Chapter 15

Efficient Markets

One of the dominant themes in the academic literature since the 1960s has been the concept of an efficient capital market. Although the reader may well be able to visualize several meanings of the term *efficient markets* and although it has, in fact, been used to denote different phenomena at different times, it has come to have a very specific meaning in finance. When someone refers to efficient capital markets, they mean that *security prices fully reflect all available information*.

For prices to reflect all available information is an extremely stringent requirement. Thus, the efficient market hypothesis has been subdivided into three categories, each dealing with a different type of information. In *weak form* tests of the efficient market hypothesis, the information tested is the past sequence of security price movements. Thus, weak form tests are tests of whether all information contained in historical prices is fully reflected in current prices. *Semistrong form* tests of the efficient market hypothesis are tests of whether publicly available information is fully reflected in current stock prices. Finally, *strong form* tests of the efficient market hypothesis are tests of whether all information, whether public or private, is fully reflected in security prices and whether any type of investor can make an excess profit.[1]

---

[1]Our definition of strong form tests is different from that contained in the literature. Most authors (e.g., Fama [57]) define strong form tests as tests of whether markets fully reflect nonpublic information. This is examined by analyzing whether any group of investors can earn excess returns. We believe that if excess returns were found, the tests cannot differentiate as to whether the excess returns arose from monopoly access to information or superior use of publicly available information. Thus, a more general definition of strong form efficiency is necessary.

Careful consideration will show that the efficient markets model is really concerned with the speed with which information is impounded into security prices. For example, assume a firm announces that earnings will be three times larger than expected next year with no additional investment on the part of the firm. Furthermore, suppose that there have been fundamental changes in the company that imply that this increase in the level of earnings is permanent. Finally, assume that investors believe this announcement. Clearly the company is worth considerably more than before. The share price should go up to reflect this increase in value. The efficient market hypothesis does not deny the usefulness of this information, nor does it deny that prices should increase. What the efficient market hypothesis is concerned with is under what conditions an investor can earn excess returns in this security. Consider several scenarios.

First, assume that after the announcement, the price gradually increases over the week in response to the announcement. Investors examining the price sequence would observe that the price was moving away from that level at which it had previously traded. If they purchased securities when the securities started to trade away from historical prices, they would purchase the security a day or two after the announcement (after they had observed this new price behavior). However, if it took a week for the price to fully reflect the announcement, investors purchasing securities on the basis of movements away from historical prices would benefit from part of the price increase and make excess returns. Tests of the weak form of the efficient market hypothesis are tests of whether this type of trading behavior can lead to excess profits. If the weak form of the efficient market hypothesis holds, then it implies that this new information is incorporated in the security price sufficiently fast that, by the time an investor could tell from the price movements themselves that there had been a fundamental change in company prospects, the fundamental change is already fully reflected in price. For example, if it takes two days to be sure by examining price changes that there is a fundamental change in the company's prospects, then the weak form of the efficient markets hypothesis implies that the price would have fully adjusted to the new level in two days.

Consider a second scenario. Assume the investor hears the announcement of the improved prospects and believes it. The investor immediately buys shares of the company in anticipation of a price rise. The semi-strong tests of the efficient markets hypothesis are tests of whether this strategy leads to excess profits. The semi-strong form of the efficient markets hypothesis assumes that investors who wish to sell the security, as well as those who wish to buy, hear the announcement and reassess the value of the security. This reassessment leads to an immediate increase in price. The new price need not be the new equilibrium price, but it is not systematically lower or higher than the equilibrium price.[2] Thus, an investor

---

[2] It may take several days or weeks before investors can fully assess the impact of the change in firm conditions. Thus, the price may be very volatile for a number of days. In efficient markets, the price after the announcement is an unbiased estimate of the equilibrium after investors have fully assessed the impact of the earnings increase.

who buys the security after the announcement may be paying too little or too much for the security. If the semi-strong form of the efficient markets hypothesis holds, then over a large number of similar situations the investor would be paying on average about what the securities are worth. The investor would be unable to earn an excess profit by purchasing securities on the basis of such announcements.

The strong form of the efficient market hypothesis is concerned with two different ideas. Both can be demonstrated in terms of our previous example. One idea concerns itself with whether anyone can earn money by acting on the basis of information such as the announcement discussed earlier. Tests of the semi-strong form of the efficient market hypothesis would examine all announcements like the one under discussion. Assume an investor immediately purchased after the announcement, and see if this leads to excess returns. There is nothing in this type of test that utilizes the information contained in the announcement to reevaluate the value of the company. Assume the investor hears the announcement and can fairly accurately reassess its effect on the value of the company. When the price after the announcement is below the reassessed value, the investor purchases; when it is above, the investor sells if the shares are owned or shorts the stock (or does nothing) if the shares are not owned. The strong form of the efficient market hypothesis states that there is no investor with this superior ability. Because it is impossible to determine exactly how investors might utilize the announcement to reassess the value of the firm, tests of the strong form of the efficient markets hypothesis are examinations of whether an investor or groups of investors have earned excess returns. Because of the lack of data on most types of investors, the group that is most frequently tested is managers of mutual funds.

The strong form of the efficient market hypothesis has a second facet that can also be illustrated with this example. Suppose the managers of the firm knew about the improved prospects ahead of the announcement. They had access to the information before it was publicly available. Could they purchase the security on the basis of the private information and make money? The most extreme form of the strong form of the efficient market hypothesis says "no."[3] It should not surprise the reader that the evidence does not support this extreme form of the efficient market hypothesis. What might surprise the reader, initially, is the strength of the evidence in favor of the less extreme forms. However, once the reader considers the ideas behind these hypotheses, it should not be as surprising. Information about securities is rapidly disseminated. There are thousands of people that follow securities professionally. Information should be rapidly incorporated in price.

The efficient market hypothesis has strong implications for security analysis. If, for example, the weak form is supported by empirical test, then trading rules based on an examination of the sequence of past prices are worthless. If the semi-

---

[3]The law in most countries also says "no," as this type of insider trading is illegal.

strong form of the hypothesis is supported by empirical evidence, then trading rules based on publicly available information are suspect. Finally, if the strong form tests show efficiency, then the value of security analysis itself would be suspect. Thus, an understanding of efficient market tests should provide guidance for the reader in determining what types of analysis are useful.

This chapter is divided into four sections. The first section provides some additional background on the efficient market hypothesis and the last three sections discuss efficient market tests.

SOME BACKGROUND

In order to test the efficient market hypothesis it is necessary to be a little more precise regarding terms such as excess return. The purpose of this section is to introduce some of the terminology of the efficient market literature.

The discussion in the last section is consistent with the process determining prices being a "fair game." "Fair game" is a very descriptive term. It says that there is no way to use "information" available at a point in time (t) to earn a return above normal. To clarify this further, let ϕ_t represent a set of information that is available to investors at a time t. Now, based on this information, the investor can make an estimate of what a stock's return will be between time t and time $t + 1$. The investor can then compare the estimated return with the equilibrium return. Perhaps the estimate of equilibrium return comes out of one of the models discussed in Chapters 11 and 12. Deviations of the investor's estimated return from the equilibrium return should contain no information about future returns. Whether the investor's estimate of return is above or below equilibrium should be unrelated to whether actual return is above or below equilibrium. There is no way the investor can use the information in the set ϕ_t to make a profit beyond that which is consistent with the risk inherent in the security.

This discussion may seem either intuitively obvious or completely unappealing. To further clarify it, let us specify some conditions under which it would not be correct. Let us assume the information set ϕ_t contains real information that is not incorporated in stock price at time t but that will be incorporated at time $t + 1$. For example, assume that a government employee in charge of military contracts is about to approve a large contract for a small and previously unused supplier of butter to the Army. This contract will result in a huge increase in profit for the company, but the market has assessed the probability of the company getting it as very small. Thus, only a fraction of the potential profits are incorporated in price. The procurement officer could make a much larger return than the equilibrium return for this company by purchasing its stock. The fair game model would not hold with respect to him. Thus, if the information set available to an investor is not incorporated in price, the fair game model does not hold with respect to that information set.

For the fair game model to hold, there must be no way in which the information set ϕ_t can be used to earn above equilibrium returns. For weak form tests ϕ_t is defined as the past history of stock prices. For semi-strong form tests, it is defined as one or more pieces of publicly available information. For strong form tests it is defined as all information, whether publicly available or not, that is at the disposal of some group of investors.

To test any fair game model we need to have an estimate of expected return in period $t + 1$. In tests of the efficient market, estimates of expected return usually come from two sources. In many tests, the average return earned in previous periods is used as an estimate of expected return in the next period. In other cases the expected return is implied from some model. The most commonly used models are the capital asset pricing models discussed in Chapters 11 and 12 or the single-index model without the assumption concerning uncorrelated residuals. This latter model is often called the market model. However, other models have been used. Roll [158], in examining the efficiency of the market for short-term government bonds (T bills), implied the expected return from the yield structure of interest rates. Throughout this chapter, when discussing empirical research, we try to be clear about how expected return is determined.

The reader should note that there is no implication in any of our discussion that the expected return on any security is zero. One would expect that, in general, it would not only be different from zero but, in fact, be positive. Further, one would expect that the return was related to risk with the more risky securities offering the higher return.

The reader might well wonder why we bother mentioning such an obvious point. However, this point has been a source of great confusion to many writers. One frequently reads that, if the weak form of the efficient market hypothesis holds, then the best estimate of tomorrow's price is today's price, or an expected return of zero. This is not a correct implication of the weak form of the efficient market model. Rather, the implication is that the past price series contains no information about the change from today's price to tomorrow's price.

Let us now examine weak form tests.

WEAK FORM TESTS

The efficient market hypothesis had a strange beginning. Generally, a theory is suggested and then extensive tests are undertaken to try to see if it better describes reality than previously accepted theories. The efficient market theory was developed in the opposite way. First, extensive tests were undertaken that demonstrated that, contrary to popular belief, certain types and ways of using information (usually past prices) did not lead to superior profits. When evidence along these lines accumulated, academics went in search of a theory to explain these findings and the efficient market theory was born.

Most of the tests discussed in this section were performed before the efficient market hypothesis was developed. Originally, they were simply tests of the usefulness of past security price movements in selecting securities. Later there were tests of the random walk model.

The random walk model is a restrictive version of the weak form of the efficient market hypothesis. The random walk model assumes that successive returns are independent and that the returns are identically distributed over time. To understand the random walk model, visualize a roulette wheel with various returns written on it. Each period the wheel is spun and the return for the next period is read from the wheel. The outcomes from spins of the wheel are unrelated through time so that past returns are unrelated to future returns. Furthermore, the same wheel is spun each period. This causes the returns to be identically distributed.

The random walk model is a restricted version of the fair game model discussed earlier. The fair game model does not require identical return distributions in the various periods. Furthermore, the fair game model does not imply that returns are independent through time. For example, a firm could be increasing its debt and risk over successive periods of time and show increasing expected and increasing actual returns. In this case we would observe a correlation in the sequence of returns and past returns that could be used to predict future returns. However, the weak form of the efficient market model would imply that this information could not be used to earn an excess return. If the random walk hypothesis holds, the weak form of the efficient market hypothesis must hold (though not vice versa). Thus, evidence supporting the random walk model is evidence supporting weak form efficiency.

Before examining weak form tests, it might be useful to say a little about why anyone might believe that the sequence of past price changes is useful in predicting future price changes.

Have you ever looked at a chart showing prices of a security or a market index over time? Most people who do start to see patterns. They look at a chart showing the S&P index over time. Suddenly, they notice that the prices were high every seven years. Then they notice that there is an exception to this pattern: in the third period the peak does not occur until the tenth year. They then notice that after each peak the index declines over 30%. With rising excitement, they realize that if they had sold their portfolio every seven years (except in the third cycle where it takes ten years) and bought when the index declines by at least 30%, they would make substantial money. A theory of stock market behavior is born. If the individual is a manager of a mutual fund and vocal, then the theory will likely be discussed in the financial press. The latest copy of *Business Week* will have an article on the seven-year cycle. A reader will learn that the third seven-year cycle takes ten years because the market is tired after its earlier thrusts.

The authors have visited mutual fund managers that managed billion dollar portfolios on the basis of these patterns. One was particularly memorable. The fund had a dozen clerks that plotted the prices through time of the securities the fund owned or were considering owning. In addition, they plotted the values of various market and economic indexes over time. The fund maintained a war room in the shape of a theater. In the war room was installed an extremely efficient procedure for flashing the charts of security prices on a screen in the front of the war room. The fund managers would meet every day and examine the charts of the securities in which they were considering investing. The discussion concerned patterns they saw. Had the price of a security broken through a price it had not

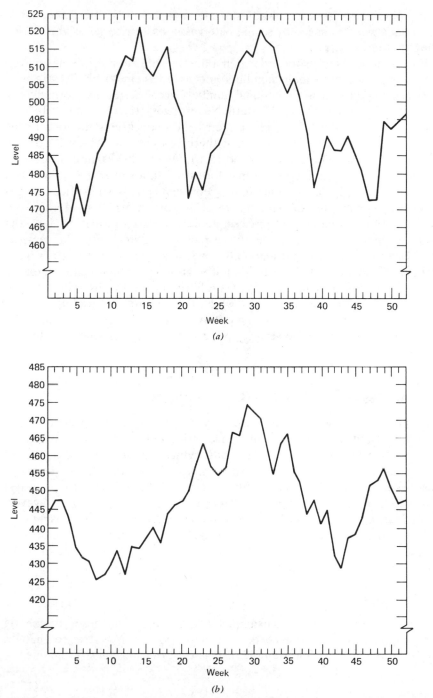

Figure 15.1 Random and actual market movements (from Cootner [35]). The upper figure (*a*) is the market.

previously obtained? Was the upward movement slowing? Was it at the end of a cycle? Funds were managed by seeing patterns in past price series and buying or selling on that basis.

The human mind searches for order. On a number of occasions we have given students a sequence of random numbers and asked them to predict the next number. The students receive additional numbers in the series that normally are inconsistent with any hypothesized pattern. Nevertheless, they continue to believe the sequence has a pattern. They revise their beliefs concerning the form of the pattern rather than rejecting the idea that there is a pattern. As an illustration of this we have included Figures 15.1a and 15.1b. One of these figures represents weekly closing levels from the Dow Jones Industrial Index over the period Dec. 30, 1955, to Dec. 25, 1956. The other figure represents prices when price changes are drawn from a table of random numbers. Can you tell which is which?

Those who believe that the past price sequence contains information about the future do so because they believe they see patterns in stock price movements and/or because they believe information is slowly incorporated in security prices. If information is incorporated slowly, then it might be possible to earn an excess return on the basis of spotting changes in equilibrium price by observing a movement away from the range of prices at which the security was trading. On the other hand, if information is rapidly incorporated in security prices, then by the time a change is observed, the security price has already responded to the information.

EMPIRICAL TESTS OF WEAK FORM EFFICIENCY

In the previous section we discussed why one would not expect to find a relationship between the past price or return series and future prices or returns. One can never prove the statement that past returns cannot be used to predict future returns since there are an infinite number of ways that the sequence of past prices can be used to forecast future prices. All that can be done is to test particular ways of combining past price data to predict future returns. However, a huge number of tests of alternative price patterns have been made, using data on both American and foreign security prices. The conclusion of the studies is that if there is information in the past price series, it is insufficient to make money. We examine the major types of studies in turn.

Linear Relationships

The original studies in this area examined whether price changes were linearly related over time. They examined the correlation between past price changes and future price changes. For example, if P_t is the price in t, they fit the line

$$P_t - P_{t-1} = a + b(P_{t-1-T} - P_{t-2-T}) + e_t \qquad (15.1)$$

The term a measures the expected change in price, unrelated to the previous price change. Since most securities give a positive return, a should be positive. The term b measures the relationship between the previous price change and the next price change. If $T = 0$, then it is the relationship between the next price change and the last price change. If $T = 1$, it is the relationship between the next price change and the price change two periods previously. e_t is a random number and incorporates the variability of the current price change not related to the previous price change. Equation (15.1) is clearly a linear equation. In any test, b could be no different from zero, suggesting no relationship between the previous price change and next price change, and yet there may be a nonlinear relationship between successive price changes. For cxample, $P_t - P_{t-1}$ might be related to complex combinations of $(P_{t-1} - P_{t-2})$ raised to various powers.

In the process of estimating Equation (15.1), the researcher obtains a measure called a correlation coefficient. The square of the correlation is the fraction of the variation of today's price change explained by the price change shown on the right-hand side of the equation. For example, a correlation coefficient of 0.5 means that $(0.5)^2 = 0.25$ of the variation of the term on the left-hand side of the equation is explained by the term on the right-hand side. Because of its importance as a measurc of explanatory power, most researchers report primarily the correlation coefficient in the random walk tests of Equation (15.1).

Not all researchers interested in examining linear relationships have utilized Equation (15.1). Some have taken the log of price relatives. The log of price ielatives is the log of ending price divided by beginning price and is the continuously compounded rate of return. Others have used the rate of return (change in price plus dividend divided by price) on both sides of thc cquation. It has been shown that for random walk tesls il makes little difference which is used.[4] For example, if a test utilizing price changes shows no relationship, then a test utilizing log pricc relatives would also show no relationship. A typical example of these tests is shown in Table 15.1.

The table shows the correlation coefficient between log daily price relatives for various lags. Recall that since the log of the price relatives is the continuously compounded return, the first column is a test of the relationship between today's return and yesterday's return. The second column is a test of the relationship between today's return and the return two days prior. As discussed earlier, the square of the number in the table is a measure of how much the equation explains. For example, the largest number (in absolute magnitude) in the first column is -0.123 associated with Goodyear. This implies that relating yesterday's log price relative to today's log price explains $(-0.123)^2$ or 1.51% of the variation in today's log price relative. This is extremely small. The negative number implies that today's return is affected negatively by yesterday's return.

Despite the small size of the numbers, looking at the table might provide some evidence in favor of a weak relationship between returns over time. Twenty-two of the 30 numbers are positive, which is fairly high if there is really no rclationship.

---

[4]See Granger [81].

Table 15.1   Daily Correlation Coefficients (from Fama [56])

Stock	Lag				
	1	2	3	4	5
Allied Chemical	0.017	−0.042	0.007	−0.001	0.027
Alcoa	0.118^a	0.038	−0.014	0.022	−0.022
American Can	−0.087^a	−0.024	0.034	−0.065^a	−0.017
A.T.&T.	−0.039	−0.097^a	0.000	0.026	0.005
American Tobacco	0.111^a	−0.109^a	−0.060^a	−0.065^a	0.007
Anaconda	0.067^a	−0.061^a	−0.047	−0.002	0.000
Bethlehem Steel	0.013	−0.065^a	0.009	0.021	−0.053
Chrysler	0.012	−0.066^a	−0.016	−0.007	−0.015
Du Pont	0.013	−0.033	0.060^a	0.027	−0.002
Eastman Kodak	0.025	0.014	−0.031	0.005	−0.022
General Electric	0.011	−0.038	−0.021	0.031	−0.001
General Foods	0.061^a	−0.003	0.045	0.002	−0.015
General Motors	−0.004	−0.056^a	−0.037	−0.008	−0.038
Goodyear	−0.123^a	0.017	−0.044	0.043	−0.002
International Harvester	−0.017	−0.029	−0.031	0.037	−0.052
International Nickel	0.096^a	−0.033	−0.019	0.020	0.027
International Paper	0.046	−0.011	−0.058^a	0.053^a	0.049
Johns Manville	0.006	−0.038	−0.027	−0.023	−0.029
Owens Illinois	−0.021	−0.084^a	−0.047	0.068^a	0.086^a
Procter & Gamble	0.099^a	−0.009	−0.008	0.009	−0.015
Sears	0.097^a	0.026	0.028	0.025	0.005
Standard Oil (Calif.)	0.025	−0.030	−0.051^a	−0.025	−0.047
Standard Oil (N.J.)	0.008	−0.116^a	0.016	0.014	−0.047
Swift & Co.	−0.004	−0.015	−0.010	0.012	0.057^a
Texaco	0.094^a	−0.049	−0.024	−0.018	−0.017
Union Carbide	0.107^a	−0.012	0.040	0.046	−0.036
United Aircraft	0.014	−0.033	−0.022	−0.047	−0.067^a
U.S. Steel	0.040	−0.074^a	0.014	0.011	−0.012
Westinghouse	−0.027	−0.022	−0.036	−0.003	0.000
Woolworth	0.028	−0.016	0.015	0.014	0.007

^{a}Coefficient is twice its computed standard error.

Furthermore, 11 of the numbers are significantly larger than would be expected by chance (although two of these are negative). Once again, this is more than one would expect. However, lest one get too excited by the relationship, the average absolute value of column 1 is 0.026. This implies that 0.057% of the variation in today's log price change is explained by yesterday's price change.

As a second example consider Table 15.2.[5] This table shows the average correlation coefficient from a number of random walk studies performed on both American and foreign stock exchanges. As the reader can see, none of the correlations is very strong.

---

[5]This table is based on Granger [81], but some additional data have been added.

Earlier we noted that a was the expected return in Equation (15.1). Investigators using correlation tests are, in essence, fitting Equation (15.1) to a body of data. The estimate of expected price change they arrive at for a security is the average unexplained by the past price change. In essence, this is very close to the average historical price change. Different results might be obtained if the term a was set equal to different estimates of expected return. In the next section we see that, in semi-strong tests of the efficient market hypothesis, expected price change is usually obtained by the single-index model discussed in Chapter 5. It is possible that there may be a different correlation in the price change series when average price change is defined using some other model, such as the single index model.

The possibility of this has been examined by a number of authors.

An interesting set of tests of this was performed by Fama and MacBeth [59]. While the details of the Fama and MacBeth study are discussed in Chapter 13, it is worthwhile to briefly review them here. Fama and MacBeth examined the return series rather than the price change series. They used the capital asset

Table 15.2

Author	Data	Variables	Time Interval	Average Correlation Coefficient
1. Kendall & Alexander [35]	19 indicies U.K.	Price	1 week	0.131
			2 weeks	0.134
			4 weeks	0.006
			8 weeks	−0.054
			16 weeks	0.156
2. Moore [35]	30 companies U.S.	Log prices	1 week	−0.056
3. Cootner [35]	45 companies U.S.	Log prices	1 week	−0.047
			14 weeks	0.131
4. Fama [56]	30 companies U.S.	Log prices	1 day	0.026
			4 days	−0.039
			9 days	−0.053
			16 days	−0.057
5. King [35]	63 companies U.S.	Log prices	1 month	0.018
6. Niarchos [137]	15 companies Greece	Log prices	1 month	0.036
7. Praetz [149]	16 indices	Log prices	1 week	0.000
	20 companies Australia		1 week	−0.118
8. Griffiths [83]	5 companies U.K.	Prices	9 days	−0.026
			1 month	0.011
9. Jennergren [103]	15 companies Norway	Log prices	1 day	0.068
			2 days	−0.070
			5 days	−0.004
10. Jennergren & Korsvold [104]	30 companies Sweden	Log prices	1 day	0.102
			3 days	−0.021
			5 days	−0.016

pricing model of Chapter 12 to estimate expected return on a security. They then examined the correlation of excess returns (actual return minus expected return) and found virtually no correlation.[6]

Other researchers have used more complicated models of expected return and then examined the correlation of excess returns. Galai [72] used a model developed by Black and Scholes to estimate expected returns on the option market and then examined the correlation of excess returns. Similarly, Roll used the term "structure" of interest rates to estimate expected return in the Treasury Bill market and then looked at the correlation of excess returns. In both cases the market was weak form efficient.

Most of these tests make use of correlation coefficients to examine weak form efficiency. The correlation coefficient tends to be heavily influenced by extreme observations. Thus, results can be due to one or two unusual observations. An alternative analysis, which eliminates the effect of extremely large observations, is to examine the sign of the price change. Designate a price increase by $+$ and a price decrease by $-$. Then, if price changes were positively related, it would be more likely that a $+$ was followed by a $+$ and a $-$ by a $-$, than to have a reversal in sign. This would mean that an investigator analyzing a sequence of correlated price changes would expect to find longer sequences of $+$'s and $-$'s than could be attributed to chance. A sequence of the same sign is called a run. Thus, $+ - - - + + + 0$ has four runs, a run of one $+$, a run of three $-$'s followed by a run of three $+$'s followed by a run of one no change. If there were a positive relationship between price changes, there should be more long sequences of $+$ and $-$ than could be attributed to chance and fewer runs. If there was a negative correlation, then there should be too many short sequences or too many runs. Since runs tests depend only on the sign, they are insensitive to whether price changes are being used or log price changes or rates of return.

Many of the authors who examined correlation also examined runs. Table 15.3 is a typical example taken from Fama [56]. For one-day intervals 760 runs were expected and 735 were obtained. Thus, there were fewer runs than were expected, which is evidence of a small positive relationship between the log of successive price relatives. The results for longer intervals are very striking. The actual number of runs in each case was almost exactly equal to the expected number.

In summary, correlation and runs tests seem to show some small positive relationship between successive price changes (or log price changes or returns), but it is very small, on average, and frequently negative for individual securities.

Another type of test used to examine the relationship of past price changes to future changes is to look for cycles. Granger and Morgenstern did the most work in this area. They found some evidence of slight monthly and seasonal cycles. They suggest that this might be caused by the mean return changing over time.

---

[6]If we let (1) $\bar{r}_t$ be expected return in t and (2) r_t be actual return in t, then Fama and MacBeth correlated $(r_t - \bar{r}_t)$ with previous values of this difference; for example, $(r_{t-1} - \bar{r}_{t-1})$.

Table 15.3 Total Actual and Expected Numbers of Runs for One-, Four-, Nine-, and Sixteen-day Differencing Intervals (from Fama [56]).

Stock	Daily		Four-day		Nine-day		Sixteen-day	
	Actual	Expected	Actual	Expected	Actual	Expected	Actual	Expected
Allied Chemical	683	715.4	160	162.1	71	71.3	39	38.6
Alcoa	601	670.7	151	153.7	61	66.9	41	39.0
American Can	730	755.5	169	172.4	71	73.2	48	43.9
A.T.&T.	657	688.4	165	155.9	66	70.3	34	37.1
American Tobacco	700	747.4	178	172.5	69	72.9	41	40.6
Anaconda	635	680.1	166	160.4	68	66.0	36	37.8
Bethlehem Steel	709	719.7	163	159.3	80	71.8	41	42.2
Chrysler	927	932.1	223	221.6	100	96.9	54	53.5
Du Pont	672	694.7	160	161.9	78	71.8	43	39.4
Eastman Kodak	678	679.0	154	150.1	70	70.1	43	40.3
General Electric	918	956.3	225	224.7	101	96.9	51	51.8
General Foods	799	825.1	185	191.4	81	75.8	43	40.5
General Motors	832	868.3	202	205.2	83	85.8	44	46.8
Goodyear	681	672.0	151	157.6	60	65.2	36	36.3
International Harvester	720	713.2	159	154.2	84	72.6	40	37.8
International Nickel	704	712.6	163	154.0	68	70.5	34	37.6
International Paper	762	826.0	190	193.9	80	82.8	51	46.9
Johns Manville	685	699.1	173	150.0	64	69.4	39	40.4
Owens Illinois	713	743.3	171	158.6	69	73.3	36	39.2
Procter & Gamble	826	858.9	180	190.6	66	81.2	40	42.9
Sears	700	748.1	167	172.8	66	70.6	40	34.8
Standard Oil (Calif.)	972	979.0	237	228.4	97	98.6	59	54.3
Standard Oil (N.J.)	688	704.0	159	159.2	69	68.7	29	37.0
Swift & Co.	878	877.6	209	197.2	85	83.8	50	47.8
Texaco	600	654.2	143	155.2	57	63.4	29	35.6
Union Carbide	595	620.9	142	150.5	67	66.7	36	35.1
United Aircraft	661	699.3	172	161.4	77	68.2	45	39.5
U.S. Steel	651	662.0	162	158.3	65	70.3	37	41.2
Westinghouse	829	825.5	198	193.3	87	84.4	41	45.8
Woolworth	847	863.4	193	198.9	78	80.9	48	47.7
Averages	735.1	759.8	175.7	175.8	74.6	75.3	41.6	41.7

In any case, the evidence suggests, at most, a very weak relationship — one too small to allow excess profits to be earned.

Some correlation could be observed and the market still be efficient. An investor must incur transaction costs to trade securities. Thus, if the correlation is very low, transaction costs should more than eliminate any potential profits from attempting to take advantage of correlated series. In fact, in an efficient market, transaction costs would set an upper limit to the amount of correlation. One indication that markets are efficient would be if we observed higher correlation in markets with higher transaction costs. This is exactly what Jennergren and Korsvold [104] found when they examined Norwegian stocks.[7]

Although this is an indication that the correlation is insufficient to cover transaction costs, more direct tests are necessary. It is to these tests and tests of more complicated patterns that we now turn.

Filter Rules

We have discussed tests of whether particular patterns exist in security returns, for example, linear patterns, or cyclical patterns. Even in the absence of such regular and simple patterns, it is possible that complex patterns exist that allow excess profits to be made. The simplest way to test for the existence of more complex patterns is to formulate a trading rule appropriate for a particular pattern of returns and to see what would have happened if one had actually traded on these rules.

One price pattern that has frequently been hypothesized for price movements is depicted in Figure 15.2. The argument behind this figure proceeds as follows.

As long as no new information enters the market, the price fluctuates randomly

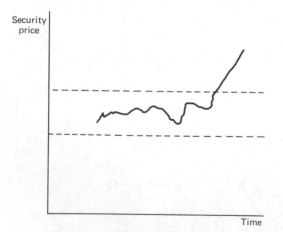

Figure 15.2   Price as a function of time.

---

[7]Jennergren and Korsvold [104] found 338.2 runs per stock over a period when uncorrelated returns would have led to 394.6.

within the two barriers around the "fair" price. If the actual price differs too much from the "fair" price, then "professionals" will step in and purchase or sell the security. This will keep the security price within the security price barriers. However, if new information comes into the market, then a new equilibrium price will be determined. If the news is very favorable, then the price should move up to a new equilibrium, well above the old price. Investors will know that this is occurring when the price breaks through the old barriers. If investors purchase at this point, they will benefit from the price increase to the new equilibrium level. Likewise, if bad news concerning the company is forthcoming, the stock will drop to a new equilibrium level. If investors sell the stock as it breaks the lower barrier, then they will avoid much of the decline. If they sell the stock short as it breaks through the barrier, they will benefit from the decline. This argument is intuitively appealing. It is closely analogous to the idea of control charts and is put forth as an appropriate investment strategy by many who believe price series can be used to make superior profits. The strategy is called a filter rule. The filter rule is usually stated in the following way: Purchase the stock when it rises by $X\%$ from the previous low and hold it until it declines by $Y\%$ from the subsequent high. At this point, sell the stock short or hold cash.

Filter rules are a timing strategy. They show investors when they should be long in a security and when they should sell it short. The alternative to timing is to buy and hold the security. Thus, filter rules are analyzed by comparing them to a buy and hold strategy. One further assumption is necessary for the buy and hold strategy to be relevant; namely, the expected return is positive. If the expected return is negative, then the relevant alternative is to hold cash.

A number of tests of filter rules have analyzed returns during periods of market decline. During these periods, any rule that randomly caused the investor to sell a security and hold cash or go short should, on average, outperform a buy and hold strategy at least before transaction costs are considered. The filter rule is purported to be a rule that utilizes past price behavior to lead to superior timing. It is important (if the rule is tested during periods of price decline) to determine that the rule outperforms a rule that randomly causes an investor to sell the security. If the filter rule leads to superior timing, then its return should be superior to the return on the opposite rule (sell when the filter would buy and buy when the filter rule leads to a sale). During periods of price decline, comparison with the opposite filter is one possible way to examine superior timing.[8]

The most extensive tests of filter rules were performed by Fama and Blume [61]. Table 15.4 reproduces their major results. The numbers under the letter F are the returns using the filter rule, the numbers under the letter B are returns from the buy and hold strategy. The only filter that showed a profit was a filter of 0.5%. However, Fama and Blume show elsewhere in their article that the long purchases were profitable for filters of 1% and 1.5%. The average profits on each trade were very small, but, over long periods of time, they substantially

---

[8]If the investor could anticipate the price decline, then a strategy of holding cash or selling short is the appropriate comparison to a filter rule.

Table 15.4 Comparison of Rates of Return, before Commissions, under the Filter Technique and under a Buy and Hold Policy

Security	Filter size															
	0.005		0.010		0.015		0.020		0.025		0.030		0.035		0.040	
	F	B	F	B	F	B	F	B	F	B	F	B	F	B	F	B
Allied Chemical	0.155	0.068	0.037	0.069	0.042	0.063	−0.030	0.066	−0.105	0.069	0.008	0.066	−0.002	0.064	−0.010	0.051
Alcoa	0.401	0.025	0.308	0.023	0.318	0.016	0.330	0.021	0.241	0.022	0.303	0.025	0.270	0.008	0.182	0.006
American Can	0.121	0.085	−0.065	0.075	−0.123	0.075	−0.088	0.078	−0.057	0.074	−0.129	0.072	−0.201	0.071	−0.226	0.070
A.T.&T.	0.150	0.189	0.146	0.189	0.158	0.189	0.133	0.185	0.135	0.182	0.131	0.180	0.143	0.176	0.076	0.182
Amer. Tobacco	0.165	0.170	0.019	0.168	0.018	0.172	0.012	0.168	−0.057	0.170	−0.080	0.168	0.002	0.163	0.048	0.162
Anaconda	0.288	0.047	0.101	0.049	−0.012	0.046	−0.048	0.042	−0.038	0.059	−0.005	0.057	−0.030	0.055	−0.019	0.055
Beth. Steel	0.082	0.032	0.051	0.033	0.030	0.036	−0.004	0.038	−0.038	0.054	−0.128	0.052	−0.250	0.049	−0.169	0.044
Chrysler	0.031	0.004	−0.090	−0.002	−0.090	0.002	−0.183	0.016	−0.234	0.015	−0.152	0.015	−0.082	0.012	0.029	0.012
Du Pont	0.152	0.107	0.125	0.106	0.087	0.108	0.100	0.105	0.032	0.097	0.054	0.097	0.084	0.098	0.058	0.103
Eastman Kodak	0.078	0.194	0.025	0.195	0.005	0.189	0.057	0.185	0.085	0.183	0.009	0.183	0.032	0.178	0.133	0.175
G.E.	0.080	0.078	0.046	0.075	−0.015	0.075	−0.016	0.069	0.013	0.069	−0.052	0.069	0.011	0.072	−0.010	0.070
General Foods	0.122	0.257	0.122	0.256	0.146	0.257	0.028	0.251	0.084	0.250	0.062	0.246	0.112	0.250	0.080	0.250
General Motors	0.107	0.088	0.108	0.091	0.065	0.091	0.048	0.094	−0.063	0.093	−0.101	0.098	−0.151	0.099	−0.171	0.095
Goodyear	−0.229	0.086	−0.195	0.083	−0.151	0.085	−0.109	0.076	−0.092	0.070	0.048	0.077	−0.013	0.077	0.076	0.112
Int. Harvester	−0.088	0.180	−0.082	0.177	−0.206	0.176	−0.112	0.174	−0.142	0.170	−0.113	0.178	−0.036	0.175	−0.018	0.178
Int. Nickel	0.218	0.148	0.170	0.136	0.118	0.136	0.077	0.137	0.005	0.155	0.088	0.148	0.105	0.147	0.041	0.160
Int. Paper	0.205	0.010	0.156	0.007	0.095	0.005	0.063	0.003	0.034	0.010	0.026	0.011	0.014	0.011	−0.013	0.015
Johns Manville	0.021	0.094	−0.016	0.093	−0.162	0.087	−0.159	0.085	−0.070	0.077	−0.194	0.072	−0.204	0.074	−0.157	0.074
Owens-Illinois	0.008	0.113	−0.036	0.116	−0.043	0.115	−0.130	0.119	−0.120	0.120	−0.112	0.120	−0.091	0.124	−0.037	0.106
Procter & Gamble	0.315	0.210	0.290	0.212	0.221	0.206	0.176	0.208	0.130	0.212	0.066	0.212	0.015	0.219	0.100	0.222
Sears	0.337	0.258	0.249	0.256	0.225	0.252	0.167	0.252	0.196	0.251	0.181	0.255	0.238	0.247	0.203	0.241
Std. Oil (Calif.)	0.076	0.093	0.052	0.090	−0.079	0.094	−0.106	0.099	−0.124	0.099	−0.123	0.094	−0.117	0.097	−0.158	0.098
Std. Oil (N.J.)	0.036	0.077	−0.072	0.067	−0.094	0.067	−0.093	0.070	−0.084	0.068	−0.083	0.064	−0.084	0.057	−0.086	0.056
Swift & Co.	0.010	0.047	0.002	0.042	−0.026	0.037	0.016	0.035	−0.044	0.037	−0.115	0.037	−0.052	0.034	−0.060	0.031
Texaco	0.172	0.188	0.165	0.192	0.105	0.189	0.095	0.188	0.109	0.186	0.166	0.184	0.144	0.183	0.115	0.178
Union Carbide	0.290	0.052	0.124	0.052	0.145	0.049	0.097	0.050	0.067	0.049	0.028	0.047	0.038	0.038	0.089	0.037
United Aircraft	−0.025	0.054	−0.020	0.052	−0.023	0.054	−0.110	0.059	−0.134	0.053	−0.189	0.048	−0.025	0.049	−0.026	0.046
U.S. Steel	0.101	0.014	−0.039	0.010	0.036	0.014	0.049	0.027	0.077	0.028	0.072	0.035	0.027	0.030	0.032	0.025
Westinghouse	0.008	0.038	−0.103	0.040	−0.047	0.038	−0.215	0.054	−0.216	0.048	−0.097	0.049	−0.083	0.051	−0.015	0.047
Woolworth	0.068	0.128	0.012	0.132	0.088	0.131	0.029	0.129	−0.058	0.131	−0.076	0.132	−0.052	0.141	−0.061	0.140
Average	0.115	0.104	0.055	0.103	0.028	0.102	0.002	0.103	−0.016	0.103	−0.017	0.103	−0.008	0.102	0.001	0.101

Source: From Fama and Blume [61].

outperformed buy and hold strategies. However, even with small transaction costs, these strategies are unprofitable. The profitability of these very small filter rules is consistent with a slight positive correlation of security price changes and is consistent with the evidence discussed earlier.

Jennergren and Korsvold [104] found some of the highest correlation coefficients of any investigators when they examined the lightly traded Norwegian and Swedish stocks. The relatively high correlations suggest that these securities are prime candidates for profitable filter rules. Jennergren examined filter rules for these securities. Norwegian and Swedish stocks cannot be held short so that the alternative to holding securities long was to invest in a savings account. Some of the filter rules outperformed a buy and hold strategy. However, when taxes and transaction costs were considered, only the Queen (the only tax-exempt investor) had any prospects of making a profit.

We have examined one type of filter rule that purports to aid in timing decisions. We could test other types that suggest trades on the basis of alternative price patterns. Indeed, technical analysts are fond of talking about such things as head-and-shoulder patterns and other esoteric perceived price phenomena. However, there is no evidence that trading on the basis of any of these patterns can lead to an excess profit. Rather than review other timing models that are based on historic price movements, let us review a system put forth to select stocks based on past price performance.

Relative Strength

One of the most popular ways of combining past price information about securities in order to select stocks is relative strength. An example of a relative strength rule is the one suggested by Levy [125]. Define $\overline{P}_{jt}$ as the average price over the last 27 weeks for stock j at time t. Further define P_{jt} as the price of the stock at time t. Then, the relative strength of the stock is its current price relative to its average price, or $P_{jt}/\overline{P}_{jt}$. According to Levy the securities to select are the $X\%$ with the highest ratio and they should be purchased in equal dollar amounts. In subsequent periods if the relative strength of a security drops below the relative strength of $K\%$ of securities, sell and invest the proceeds in the top $X\%$ of the securities. Levy tested a number of values for X and K, with the most profitable being $X = 5\%$ and $K = 70\%$.

Note that the relative strength rule causes funds to be invested in securities that have appreciated the most in the recent past. The most risky securities are usually those with the greatest mean return and variability of return. This suggests that the group of securities with greatest relative strength is likely to include a predominance of risky securities and the return earned from this investment must be adjusted for risk.

Also note that this rule does not involve the selection of a single security. Rather, it involves the selection of a set of securities. The relevant comparison is the rate of return on the securities that are selected by the relative strength rule adjusted for risk compared to the rate of return on the full population of securities from which the selection was made.

When Jensen and Bennington [105] tested several relative strength rules (including the one used by Levy and discussed previously), they found that the return after transaction costs for the relative strength rule was no more than the return on the full population. Furthermore, after adjustment for risk, it was inferior to purchasing the full set of securities.

We are continually shown various forms of relative strength rules along with the tests that purport to demonstrate their superiority. Even with the simple rule discussed before, there are many parameters that may be varied in the search for a rule that works. For example, should average price be calculated over 27 weeks, 20 weeks, or 30 weeks? Should one purchase the upper 5% or 7.2% of the securities? More complicated versions of relative strength rules make these decisions as a function of market conditions. Levy in his work tested some 68 variations of his basic rule. Given enough parameters to vary, one can find a mechanical trading rule that works on a set of random numbers. It is extremely important that the rules be tested on a fresh sample of data and over several market conditions. For example, a rule designed to work under certain market conditions (e.g., selects high growth stocks) will work in periods when growth stocks did well. Picking such a period to test this rule will, of course, "show the value of the rule," but is, of course, useless unless accompanied by a method of selecting such a period in the future. All of the times we have been involved in or seen tests of these rules, they have performed more poorly than buying the full population. This, of course, does not prove that a good relative strength rule does not exist.

The discussion up to this point has been concerned with price movements of days or weeks. Very short-term price changes have also been investigated and these results are different.

Short-term Correlation

Niederhoffer and Osborn [136] have examined the correlation between the price changes from transaction to transaction. They found a number of departures from randomness. Most interestingly, they found that reversals in price changes (a decline followed by an increase) was two to three times as likely as a continuation of the same price change.

The explanation of this is found in the structure of the New York Stock Exchange. Investors can place two types of orders: limit or market. A limit buy order is an order to buy a security if it falls below a certain price. A limit sell order is an order to sell if it rises above a particular price. Limit orders are kept on a specialist's books until they are executed. A market order is an order to purchase a stock at the lowest selling price or to sell at the highest buying price of another investor. It is executed by either matching with another market order for the opposite side of the transaction or by matching it with the most attractive limit order.

Unexecuted sell orders must lie above unexecuted buy orders or a trade would have taken place. For example, the unexecuted sell orders may be at 50 and the unexecuted buy orders at 49⅞. If a market purchase order is made, it would be matched with a sell and executed at 50 unless a market sell order was received at the same time. If a market sell order is made, it would be matched with the purchase and executed at 49⅞.

Suppose a market purchase order is made, the order is executed at 50 and this is an increase in price. If it is followed by a market sell order, the price will decline to 49⅞. Thus, an increase will be followed by a decrease, a negative correlation. If the purchase order is followed by another purchase order, the price may not change if there were a number of limit orders at 50. Only if the purchase is for sufficient shares, so that the number of shares at 50 is insufficient to fill the order, will it change. Thus, an increase is likely to be followed by a decrease or no change and negative correlation is obtained.

The reader can likely see a number of ways an investor who did not pay transaction costs might benefit from this. However, the bulk of us, who are not so fortunate, cannot gain.

Year-end Selling[9]

A popular suggestion of investment advisors, at year end, is to sell securities for which an investor has incurred substantial losses and purchase an equivalent security. This creates a tax loss for the investor. If the tax loss is substantial, it should more than cover transaction costs. This year-end tax selling could potentially cause inefficiencies in security returns over the year end and a profitable trading rule might exist. Notice that the transaction involves a swap. Thus, most investors will be purchasing as well as selling and one would not expect a general effect on the market. However, there might be an effect on individual securities.

Branch [20] analyzed a trading rule that involved the purchase of a security that reached its annual low in the last week of trading. He found that these securities rose faster in the first four weeks of the new year than the market as a whole, with very little difference in risk. He obtained average returns 8% above the market for a four-week holding period. During the period he examined, this just about covered transaction costs for an investor. Thus, it was questionable whether it was a sufficient excess return to represent an inefficiency. However, his results suggest that an investor considering purchasing a security near the end of the year might be advised to purchase it before year end if the price had declined at the end of the year.

The evidence that has been compiled to date strongly indicates that patterns in historical returns cannot be used to earn an excess return. Even if this is true, on average, other types of information may still not be instantaneously reflected in stock prices. This brings us to our examination of semi-strong form tests.

SEMI-STRONG FORM TESTS

Semi-strong form tests deal with whether or not security prices fully reflect all publicly available information. There is an enormous amount and variety of public information. Semi-strong form tests have been performed with respect to many

---

[9]For additional discussion of returns in January see the section entitled "Other Anomalies."

different types of information. There is little reason to believe that markets are efficient with respect to some information and not with other similar information. For example, one would expect that if markets were efficient with respect to earnings announcements, they would be efficient with respect to dividend announcements. Thus, each test is further evidence concerning the reasonableness of the semi-strong form of the efficient market hypothesis.

Tests of the semi-strong form of the efficient market hypothesis are very similar. In this section we discuss a couple in detail, and then briefly mention some others.

Much of the methodology that has been employed in the literature on semi-strong form tests was introduced by Fama, Fisher, Jensen, and Roll [60] (FFJR). They examined the effect of stock splits on security prices. A number of prior studies had suggested that stock splits increased the value of the firm. This was disturbing to many because stock splits simply involve changing the number of shares, per shareholder, without changing the percentage ownership of any shareholder or the assets or earnings of the company. FFJR argued that stock splits might be associated with other more fundamental changes and the effects that researchers were attributing to stock splits might be better attributed to these other phenomena.

FFJR estimated expected return by using the market model (the single-index model discussed in Chapter 5 without the assumption of uncorrelated residuals). The particular model they used was

$$R_i = a_i + b_i R_M + e_i \tag{15.2}$$

where R_i is the return on security i, R_M is the return on a market index, a_i and b_i are constants, and e_i is a random error. This relationship was estimated for each security, using all the data available from 1926 to 1960, with the exception of 15 months before the split and 15 months after the split for those stocks that had stock splits. FFJR then examined the difference between the actual return and the expected return obtained by utilizing Equation (15.2). Two types of numbers were examined. First, they examined the excess return itself for each month. This is the difference between actual return and expected return. Second, they cumulated the excess return for each month starting 30 months before the split. This can be interpreted as total excess return from 30 months prior to the split to the month under consideration.

Figure 15.3 shows the average pattern of the cumulative excess return that they observed. Month 0 is the month of the split, -10 is 10 months before the split, $+5$ is 5 months after the split, and so forth. As can be seen by examining the figures, the cumulative excess return increases dramatically before the split. In fact, the excess return is positive in every single month. It is unlikely that positive excess returns 30 months before a split are due to anticipation of a split. It is unlikely that even the management of a company would anticipate splitting its stock that far before they executed the split. Rather, early excess returns are an indication that stocks that are performing abnormally well tend to split their shares. After the split, the stocks on average perform just as expected. The average excess return is just about zero.

As mentioned earlier, FFJR hypothesized that other occurrences associated with a split might account for the effects found in previous studies. In particular, many firms raise their dividends when they split their shares. The evidence is fairly strong that firms are reluctant to decrease dividends. Dividend increases can be viewed as a statement by the firm that earnings prospects are sufficiently good to be able to maintain the increased level of dividends. Thus, dividend increases are indirect announcements by the firm of improved earnings prospects. To test this, FFJR divided their sample into those firms that increased dividends and those that did not. For those firms with subsequent dividend increases, the cumulative excess returns continue to increase after the date of the split. For those firms without dividend increases, the cumulative excess returns decline.

The lack of excess return for the firms, in total, and the distinct patterns for firms with different changes in dividend policy, indicates that the market makes an unbiased estimate of future performance and that individual security prices are then adjusted, depending on subsequent dividend changes.

The primary purpose of the study was to examine the semi-strong form of the efficient market hypothesis. To test this hypothesis, it is important to examine the performance of the securities after the announcement of the split. Since the announcement of the split occurred several months before the actual split, the investor still could make excess returns, even if the excess returns after the month of the split are zero. A cursory examination of Figure 15.3 might suggest that the investor could make excess returns since the cumulative excess returns are increasing in the months before the split but after the announcement. FFJR assure

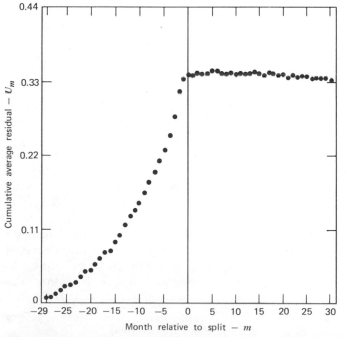

Figure 15.3 Cumulative residuals in months surrounding stock splits.

us that this is not so. They state that examining the performance after the month of the announcement of the split did not lead to excess returns.

FFJR was the first of the studies that were directly concerned with the testing of the semi-strong form of the efficient market hypothesis. Subsequent to their study, a number of refinements have been developed in the test procedure. Before examining several further tests, some discussion of the alternative methodologies of testing is useful.

First, if markets are reasonably efficient, then any effects of new information should be incorporated into the security price within a few days of the announcement. Thus, to effectively examine the potential for earning excess returns, some researchers utilize daily data. The difficulty with using monthly data is that even if there is an opportunity to earn an excess return, it may well be undetectable when the two or three days of excess return are mixed (averaged) with the 20 or more days of random differences between actual and expected return. Thus, real effects might be missed when using monthly returns.[10]

Since the efficient market hypothesis deals with the effect of information on security prices, most researchers choose to examine the price movement around the date that information is publicly released rather than the date the event takes place. For example, if dividend increases are announced, most researchers examine the excess returns after the announcement rather than after the date of the payment of the dividend. In most subsequent studies (and in our discussion below), time 0 is the date of the announcement and +5 is 5 periods after the announcement.

The method of obtaining expected return has the most variations. First, in Chapters 11 and 12 we discussed a number of equilibrium models that purport to explain how expected return is related to risk. Any of these models could be used as models for determining expected returns in tests of the efficient market hypothesis. Alternatively, in Chapter 5 we discussed index models. These also could be used to make estimates of expected return.

Whatever the choice of a model for expected return, we have problems of estimation. Many of these have been discussed elsewhere in this volume and the discussion will not be repeated here. However, it is useful to highlight one particular problem since it has strong implications for the likelihood of finding positive residuals. One of the most common methods researchers use to estimate expected return is the market model (single-index model). Often the slope of the market model is estimated over the period preceding the event under investigation. In earlier chapters we discussed the fact that the slope term in the single-index model, estimated from historical data, tended to be a biased estimate of its future value. Furthermore, the estimate could be improved by adjusting it toward 1. For example, an estimate of 2 for the slope, based on historical data, was likely to be too high and could be improved by use of one of the adjustment techniques discussed in Chapter 5. When studying the effect of some announce-

---

[10]The use of daily data has the difficulty that there is autocorrelation in the return series due to the lack of frequent trading for some securities. See Scholes and Williams [168].

ment on security price, the sample of firms being studied is unlikely to be a random cross section of firms. Rather, they are likely to be firms with slope coefficients substantially different from the average in the market. If the slope coefficients, estimated in the historical period, are, on average, below the market, then they should, on average, be higher in the subsequent period. Using the historically estimated slope coefficients to compute expected return will lead to positive residuals, even if there is no effect of the announcement on security price. The opposite would hold if the historically estimated slope coefficients were higher than the average in the market. This suggests that researchers estimating expected return from the single-index model and using historical data to estimate the slope coefficient would have more accurate tests if they adjusted the slope coefficient before examining the excess returns.

Another technique used to try to improve estimates of the parameters in tests of efficient markets is called a moving window. The moving window can best be explained by an example. Suppose we want to examine residuals over ten periods and we estimate expected return using the single-index model. Then, the data used to estimate the parameters of the single-index model is the actual returns in the months surrounding the month for which the excess return is being estimated. For example, in order to estimate the expected return in the first period, data from a year prior to the first period and the year after the first period might be used with the first period excluded. The excluded period is the "window." To estimate the excess return in the second period, data from a year prior to the second period and a year after the second period might be used. In this case, the second period is excluded. The second period is the window. Since the period being excluded changes, the "window" changes; hence, the name moving window.

The last aspect of testing that needs to be discussed is the cumulative excess return. FFJR cumulated excess returns by simply adding them up. Dividing these by the number of months in the sum would be the average monthly return. Other authors take the product of one plus the excess return. If the excess returns are 20%, -10%, and $+5\%$, they take (1.20), (0.90), and (1.05). This is a standard procedure to obtain a return over three periods. The product of these three numbers is the total excess return over the three periods.[11] Having discussed some issues concerned with testing, it is time to briefly examine several other studies.

A number of studies have examined whether markets are efficient with respect to the announcement of the purchase or sale of securities. (See Kraus and Stoll [116], Grier and Albin [83], Guthman and Bakay [89], Dodd and Ruback [41],

---

[11]There is one problem with intepreting this number. If the model used to obtain excess return is accurate, then deviations from the expected return should average zero. In this case, the average compounded return over several periods will be less than zero. For example, the following deviations average zero: $+0.20$, -0.20, $+0.20-0.20$. The average compounded return over the four periods is -7.84%. Thus, even if there is no effect of the announcement, one would expect a negative excess return over the four periods. More importantly, a negative compound excess return over a number of periods could occur, even when the impact of the information on the security price is positive.

and Carey [28].) In general, these studies find that markets are efficient. (See Grier and Albin for an exception.) One of the more interesting studies of this type was by Firth [68]. He examined the efficiency with respect to an announcement that an individual or firm had acquired 10% of a firm. In the U.K. (which Firth analyzed) as well as in the U.S., ownership of more than some percentage must be made public. Firth examined the market efficiency with respect to these announcements. One would expect that the purchase of a substantial percentage of a company might be an indication of a takeover or merger attempt, and Firth showed that this is an appropriate expectation. Empirical evidence indicates that mergers and takeovers normally involve premiums being paid to the stockholders of the company being taken over. Thus, the announcement of someone taking a large position in a security should be an indication of favorable prospects. Firth uses the single-index model to calculate expected return. He adjusts the slope coefficient of this model toward the market average using a procedure like those discussed in Chapter 5. Figure 15.4 shows the cumulative excess return from 30 days prior to the announcement.[12] The cumulative excess returns through the first day after the announcement are, in general, increasing. An investor with inside information that somebody was accumulating a large block could make excess profits possibly larger than transaction costs. There is a substantial increase in cumulative excess returns on the day of the announcement. However, Firth shows the bulk of this occurs between the last trade before the announcement and the next trade. Thus, an investor without prior information about the announcement could not benefit from the price increase. From the first trade after the announcement until 30 days after the announcement, there is a slight decline in the cumulative excess return. This is what one would expect when returns are being cumulated in the manner Firth used. Thus, this evidence is consistent with the semi-strong form of the efficient market hypothesis.

Another example of semi-strong form tests of efficiency was performed by Davies and Canes [38]. They analyzed whether analyst information could be used to earn excess returns or was already incorporated in share price. There is an enormous amount of information sold to investors. This includes stock recommendations as well as detailed information on individual securities. One would expect that recommendations that are purchased contain sufficient information to justify their cost. Davies and Canes [38] analyze this by examining the usefulness of the "Heard on the Street" column in *The Wall Street Journal*. This column usually consists of a number of opinions on a number of different stocks. The publication of the analysts' opinions in *The Wall Street Journal* usually occurs one or two weeks after the opinion was circulated to the firms' clients. However, *The Wall Street Journal* is usually the first large-scale dissemination of the opinions of several analysts.

The method of analysis was very similar to that discussed previously. The market model was used to estimate the relationship between each security's return

---

[12]This is the product of one plus the daily excess return, minus one.

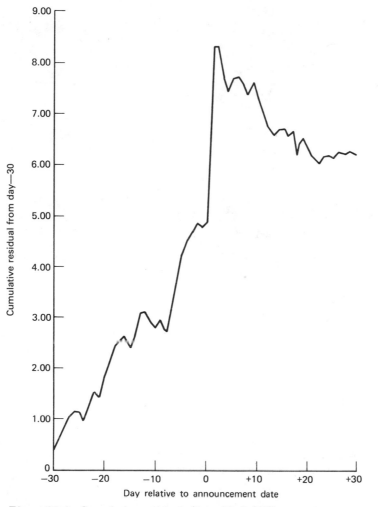

Figure 15.4   Cumulative residuals (from Firth [60]).

and the market.[13] This equation was then used to estimate the expected return on each day given the actual level of the market. The difference between actual return and expected return was then tabulated. Figure 15.5 shows the results. As can be seen by examining the figure, the publication of the information seems to have an impact on returns. Davies and Canes tested to see if the large differences were statistically significant. The standard procedure would be to calculate a standard deviation of each day's return and then to see how many standard deviations from zero the excess return lies. The difficulty with this is that the observations of different recommendations may not be independent or from the

---

[13]The market model is the single-index model of Chapter 5 without the assumption of uncorrelated residuals.

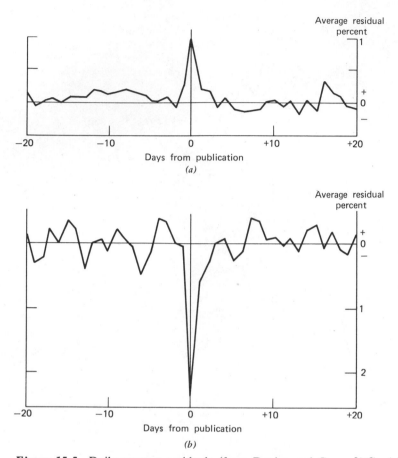

Figure 15.5   Daily average residuals (from Davies and Canes [38]). (*a*) Purchase recommendations. (*b*) Sell recommendations.

same distribution and this can bias the estimate of standard deviation. Davies
and Canes used the standard procedure as well as several modifications. In each
case, the difference at announcement day was significant.

The reader might note that the residuals were 1 to 2%. This study would
indicate an inefficient market only if transaction costs were less than 1 or 2%.
Otherwise, the results would be consistent with an efficient market.

As a final example of the semi-strong efficient market tests, consider the examination of dividend announcements by Pettit [144] or by Watts [185]. Two
aspects of these studies are different from those discussed previously. First, they
must carefully define the event relative to expectations. What should affect security prices is surprises, not events that are anticipated. It is reasonable to
assume that an announcement of a stock split, or the acquisition by one investor
of a large position in a security, is a surprise. However, changes in dividends
may well be anticipated. It has been shown that firms tend to follow a stable

dividend policy. Thus, when earnings increase, the firm may have a policy of increasing dividends. This implies that a dividend increase may have been anticipated.

To determine whether the dividend is good news (above anticipations), bad news (below anticipations), or no news (anticipated), both of these authors build a model of dividend policy. For example, Watts relates changes in dividends to the level of previous dividends and earnings. Firms are then dichotomized into two groups: those firms whose dividends are above those predicted by Watts, and those that are below. Examining the excess return for these two groups allows one to examine the effect of unanticipated dividend changes.

The second difference in these studies is the need to disentangle the dividend changes from other effects. In the study of stock splits, we discussed that many times stock splits and dividend increases occurred simultaneously. However, in some cases they did not. However, dividend announcements almost always occur simultaneously with earnings announcements and it is important to deal with contemporaneous earnings surprises. Pettit handles this by splitting his firms, not only by size of dividend surprise, but also by the earnings change.

Other than these two aspects, the studies use methodology similar to that discussed earlier. Furthermore, their conclusions are similar. The market seems to adjust to new information rapidly with much of the impact taking place in anticipation of the announcement.

STRONG FORM TESTS

So far we have seen that the market displays efficiency with respect to both weak form tests and semi-strong form tests. Let us now examine strong form tests. Strong form tests really involve two subclasses of tests. The first type of test attempts to isolate whether excess returns arise directly from inside (nonpublic) information. Since we cannot identify nonpublic information, these tests involve examining the investment performance of individuals or groups who can be identified as in a position to possess nonpublic information.[14] The second type of test looks at the performance of major market participants. These tests are really a combination test of whether these institutions possess superior ability to use public information to earn an excess profit and whether they possess nonpublic information through which they can earn an excess profit.

The strong form of the efficient market hypothesis is that all information, public or private, is so rapidly impounded in security prices that an investor cannot make excess returns. The most frequently examined institution for this type of test has been mutual funds because of the ready availability of mutual fund data. However, trust funds and individuals have also been examined. Because tests of

---

[14]The reader might note that a failure to earn an excess return by these groups could mean either that they could not use the nonpublic information to earn an excess return, or that they did not do so for legal or moral reasons.

portfolio performance are important, in themselves, a full chapter is devoted to them. This type of efficient market test is discussed in Chapter 22.

A second type of strong form test involves analyzing the recommendations of security analysts. Mutual fund performance depends on information "content" in analyst predictions supplied to the portfolio manager as well as the portfolio manager utilizing any information properly. It is possible that there is information in analyst forecasts and yet the mutual fund performs poorly because the information was incorrectly used by the fund manager.

Two of the most extensive studies of the ability of security analysts to forecast the returns that would be earned from holding individual stocks was performed by Dimson and Marsh [40] and Elton, Gruber, and Grossman [47].[15] Dimson and Marsh analyzed 4,000 return forecasts made for 200 of the largest United Kingdom common stocks provided by 35 different firms of analysts. The data were gathered by a large fund that requested their brokers to forecast excess return on shares given a zero return on the market. In terms of the standard CAPM, the analysts were asked to supply their estimate of the securities' return above or below the riskless rate when the return on the market was the riskless rate (e.g., deviations from the CAPM line). Dimson and Marsh correlated actual return with forecasted returns and found an average correlation coefficient of .08. This result is consistent with other research in the area. Recall that the square of the correlation coefficient is the percentage explained. Thus, $(.08)^2 = .0064$ of realized return is explained by analysts' forecasts of return. Forecasting ability differed across the 35 firms. The range of correlation coefficients for brokers recording over 50 forecasts was $-.19$ to $+.26$. Furthermore, past forecasting ability was not predictive of future forecasting ability. The best estimate of which firm forecasted best in the next period was that all firms were equal. However, combining the forecasts did lead to improvement. The correlation between realized return and the average analyst forecast was .12.

The forecasts of return were utilized by a fund for actual trades. Despite the small amount of information contained in the forecasts, as indicated by the size of the correlation presented before, the performance of the fund exceeded the market by 2.2%. Tests showed that over one-half of the information contained in the forecasts was incorporated in share price in the first month following the forecast. Thus a rapid reaction to analyst forecasts was necessary.

Elton, Gruber, and Grossman [47] employed a data base that was constructed by Bankers Trust and disseminated under the name of I/B/O/S/S. This data base contained the rankings of stocks into five groups: best buys, buys, holds, and two classes of sells. The data contained over 10,000 classifications per month prepared by over 720 analysts at 34 brokerage houses. An analysis of forecasts prepared in the form of discrete classifications is interesting because this is the form in which most decision makers in the financial community receive information. Elton, Gruber, and Grossman found that both a change in classification

---

[15]Dimson and Marsh [40] present an extensive bibliography and review of previous research on analysts' forecasts. The reader interested in further research in this area should consult their article.

(e.g., from a hold to a buy or from a best buy to a buy) and the classification itself contained information. Excess risk adjusted returns could be earned by buying upgraded stocks or stocks that were in a better classification and selling downgraded stocks or stocks that were in a lower classification. Excess returns were found in the forecast (classification) month and for two months following the classification. Acting on changes in classification produced larger excess returns than acting on the recommendations themselves. In addition, no superior forecasters could be identified. One was better off following the advice of the average or consensus forecaster than the advice of any set of forecasters who performed best over a previous period.

Both Dimson and Marsh and Elton, Gruber, and Grossman find information in analysts' forecasts. There does not seem to be much, if any, information in acting on the advice of single brokerage firms. However, by aggregating across brokerage firms, there appears to be real information that persists for short periods of time.

Nonpublic information is most often examined by looking at the profitability of insider trading. All investors who own more than a certain percentage of the outstanding shares or are at a sufficiently high management level are considered insiders. Insiders must list their purchases and sales with the S.E.C. If insiders trade on privileged information, then one would expect to see insiders purchase in months before the security price increases and sell in months before the security price declines. This pattern is, in fact, the pattern that Jaffe [97] and Lorie and Niederhoffer [128] found. Furthermore, they found, using methodology similar to that discussed earlier, that insiders earned returns in excess of expected return. Unless these insiders just happened to possess superior analytical ability, their excess return must be due to the illegal exploitation of insider information.

Another indication of the usefulness of insider trading is a legal action involving the man who set the type for the "Value Line" forecasts. "Value Line" is an investment advisory service. It divides firms into five groups, depending on its estimate of next period's performance. The typesetter knew what the recommendations of "Value Line" would be and sold these to two brokers at a large brokerage firm. The brokers, in turn, used it to manage money for their clients. As *The Wall Street Journal* [184] reports, the brokers made a fair amount of money before they were apprehended.

The studies by Jaffe and Lorie and Niederhoffer are indications that markets are probably not strong form efficient.

IMPLICATIONS OF EFFICIENCY

There are a number of implications of the previous analysis for security analysis.

First, the evidence indicates that public information, be it past prices or dividend announcements, are fairly rapidly incorporated in security prices. Attempts to earn excess returns on the basis of public information in standard ways are unlikely to be successful. Clearly, all techniques and all forms of public information have not been tested for excess returns. However, a sufficient number have been tested to indicate that an investor should be cautious about selecting stocks simply on the basis of new publicly available information.

Second, in the tests of the efficient market hypothesis, investors looked at price movements after good or bad news. Good and bad news was defined relative to expectations. When investigators found price movements, they found them when information differed from expectations. This implies a very different mode of behavior for an analyst. Most analysts examine earnings prospects, growth in earnings, the outlook for the industry, and recommend a security for purchase hold or sale, depending on how favorable the characteristics of the security appear. This discussion implies that this analysis is insufficient. The analyst's job is not to find securities with favorable characteristics, but rather to find securities with characteristics more favorable than is generally believed by the market. This idea is worth further amplification. Many mutual funds have a growth stock philosophy. They purchase securities that are expected to have high growth in earnings. The efficient market tests have found that the price movement occurs with securities that exhibit an unexpected change. This implies that the simple purchase of growth stocks is an unprofitable strategy. What is necessary is to find securities with growth prospects higher than those expected by the market. We will present additional evidence on this point in Chapter 17.

The third characteristic of efficient market tests is that they have been concerned with expected return. There is evidence that large security price changes tend to follow large security price changes. Further, there is evidence that the variability of stock prices tends to be high after the announcement of some new information. This evidence makes intuitive sense. When new information becomes public concerning a security, there is more uncertainty concerning the appropriate new equilibrium price. Although the original adjustment after the announcement may be an unbiased estimate of the new equilibrium price, and, hence, the excess expected return of this adjustment is zero, it may take a while for the price to fully adjust to the new equilibrium. This suggests that option strategies designed to take account of this increased variability may be profitable, although given efficient market evidence elsewhere, one should be cautious. It also suggests that estimates of security variability from historical data should take into account this abnormal behavior around announcement dates.

Finally, the implication of these tests is that any hope for earning abnormal returns lies in nonstandard ways of combining and analyzing information, or in obtaining information that is not generally available to other market participants, or in obtaining this information prior to other market participants.

MARKET ANOMALIES

As we have pointed out several times in this chapter, markets do seem to be efficient with respect to most types of publicly available information. However, recently certain apparent major irregularities have been detected in the capital markets. These irregularities have been persistent and of such a large order of magnitude that they have been called market anomalies. Perhaps the most widely studied of these anomalies is the "size effect." Firms with a low total market value of common stock seem to produce returns above those warranted by the CAPM (security market line). Among the other major anomalies that have been pointed out in the financial literature are these:

1. The high earnings price effect. Stocks that sell at a high earnings price ratio seem to produce extra returns.

2. The January effect. Stocks seem to produce an excess return in the month of January.

We discuss the size effect in some detail and then comment briefly on the other two anomalies.

The "Size Effect"

Banz [5] published one of the earliest and most often quoted empirical articles on the size effect. Employing a methodology similar to that used by Fama and MacBeth [59] (see Chapter 13), Banz documented that excess returns (Alphas) would have been earned over the period 1936–1977 by holding low capitalization companies. The striking aspects of Banz's analysis is that the size effect appeared to be important in terms of both statistical significance and empirical relevancy. The size term had roughly the same statistical significance in explaining returns as did Beta. Furthermore, the differential returns from buying very small firms versus very large firms was 19.8% per year. Two other points should be mentioned. The real payoff from holding small stocks came from holding the smallest 20% of firms in Banz's sample of New York Stock Exchange firms. The differential between other quintiles were quite small. While the return from holding the smallest firms was large and statistically significant, on average there were periods of time where large firms outperformed small firms.

The documentation of the size effect has motivated a great deal of research into a possible explanation for its existence. Research attempting to explain the size effect has been concerned with measurement and statistical problems and an economic explanation for the size effect.

Measurement and Statistical Problems

Several authors have questioned either the estimation of Beta used in calculating the size effect or the measurement of returns for different stocks. Christie and Hertzel [32] presented evidence that risk is understated for small-size firms and that this understatement causes a positive return. While their analysis is based on a hypothesized change in the economic characteristics of small firms, Roll [159] and Reinganum [152] have argued that the Beta for small firms will be biased downward because they trade less often than large firms and nonsynchronous trading leads to an underestimate of Beta. While these papers present evidence that the small firm effect is partly owing to errors in estimating the risk of small firms, they are at best a partial explanation for the small firm effect.

This effect is present even when the problems in risk measurement have been corrected.

An additional problem with some of the early papers documenting the size effect is that they assume daily rebalancing of the portfolio because of the method used to calculate return. Recently Roll [161] and Blume and Stambaugh [18] have estimated that the magnitude of the small firm effect is cut in half if annual rather than daily rebalancing is assumed. If the reader wonders why not simply buy small firms and rebalance daily, the answer is that large transaction costs would be incurred.

Rationale for the Small Firm Effect

One explanation for a small firm effect would be the existence of a rational reason for size to enter into the equilibrium relationship. We have already seen that, under APT, factors other than the market can account for differences in expected returns. If individuals and institutions faced different transaction costs on small size firms than on large size firms, this might account for why size enters the equilibrium relationship. Stoll and Whaley [179] have estimated that round-trip transaction costs average 6.8% for the smallest decile of New York Stock Exchange Stock while they average 2.7% for the largest decile. They find that a round-trip transaction cost every three months is enough to eliminate the small firm effect. This provides a partial explanation for the size effect. However, investors would have to turn over their portfolios four times a year for this to be a full explanation.

Other researchers have tried to explain the size effect by hypothesizing that size serves as a proxy variable for some other influence that is related to returns. Other variables examined include E/P ratios [11,152] dividend yield [34,112], standard deviation of return [118] and co-skewness [88]. None of this research supplies a satisfactory explanation of the size effect.

The size anomaly is a puzzle. We have explained part of the excess return by showing in some studies that (1) returns for small firms have been computed in a way that biases their returns upward, (2) the risk on small firms have been understated, (3) transaction costs can account for a significant portion of the excess return, and (4) size may be in part a proxy for some other economic influence. Although we can explain part of the excess return, we don't seem to be able to explain all of it. There does seem to be a size anomaly. Whether it is really an inefficiency in the capital markets or appears because we haven't measured risks or return correctly or because we don't have the appropriate equilibrium model against which to judge efficiency, only time will tell.

Other Anomalies

Another anomaly that has been cited in the literature is the tendency for firms with high E/P ratios to produce an excess return. While the folklore of Wall Street has advocated buying low P/E ratio stocks for years, Basu [10] was the first to study the E/P effect in a risk-adjusted-framework. He found that high E/P stock produced excess returns. There is a high degree of relationship between E/P and the size of the firm. The literature contains empirical articles representing two different views. Reinganum presents empirical evidence that the E/P effect is an imperfect proxy for the size effect, whereas Basu [10] presents evidence that the size effect is an imperfect proxy for the E/P effect. Since we do not have a satisfactory theory for either effect, resolution of this controversy will have to await further research.

The final anomaly we will discuss is the year-end effect. A great deal of literature has been produced that supplies evidence that securities yield high excess returns for the entire month of January. Recently this phenomenon has been tied in with the small firm effect. For example, Keim [113] presents evidence that about 25% of the size effect occurs during the first five trading days in January. A natural explanation for this might be tax loss selling. Roll [160] presents this position and suggests that the phenomenon is larger for small firms since these firms are unlikely to be held by large institutions. Reinganum [155] shows that small firms tend to produce larger returns for the first five days in January whether they showed capital loss or capital gains over the previous period. This would seem to invalidate the tax loss hypothesis. This view gets further support from Berges, McConnell, and Schlarbaum [13], who find a small firm January effect in Canada, but the effect is present both before and after the introduction of a capital gains tax.

It is difficult to conclude this section on market anomalies. We call them anomalies because we don't understand why they exist. We could view them as inefficiencies or as evidence that we don't as yet completely understand equilibrium. If they are truly anomalies with no economic basis, then one would expect the very research we have described to draw sufficient attention to them that they will cease to exist.

QUESTIONS AND PROBLEMS

1. Discuss a trading strategy to utilize information such as that analyzed by Davies and Canes. How low would transaction costs have to be for the rule to be profitable? How would risk affect the usefulness of the rule?

2. Filter rules are one way to use past price movements to predict future movements. Discuss an alternative way to use past data. How would you test this alternative?

3. One rule for selecting stocks that has been suggested is to buy high growth, low P/E stocks. How could this rule be tested?

4. It has been suggested that the efficient market hypothesis could be used to determine whether you have monopoly access to a type of information. Explain how this might be done.

5. If the market is semi-strong form efficient, must it be weak form efficient?

6. You have been hired as a consultant to a large brokerage firm. The firm thinks it has discovered an inefficiency in the market. At certain times large blocks of stocks that are held by individuals and institutions under restrictive agreements become available for trading. The dates on which this happens is a matter of public record. How would you test whether the market is efficient with respect to the potential increased supply in stock?

7. A number of different models can be used to estimate return. Derive the circumstances under which the use of the zero Beta model might lead to the market being considered inefficient when the standard CAPM indicated efficiency.

8. Is the betting market at roulette an efficient market?

9. You have just become convinced that whenever the president of a company retires, an excess return can be made by buying the stock. Design a study to test this hypothesis.

BIBLIOGRAPHY

1. Albin, Peter. "Information Exchange in Security Markets and the Assumption of 'Homogeneous Beliefs'," *Journal of Finance,* **XXIX,** No. 4 (Sept. 1974), pp. 1217–1227.
2. Aharony, Joseph, and Swary, Itzhak. "Quarterly Dividend and Earnings Announcements and Stockholders' Returns: An Empirical and Analysis," *The Journal of Finance,* **35,** No. 1 (March 1980), pp. 1–12.
3. Ball, Ray. "Risk, Return and Disequilibrium: An Application to Changes in Accounting Techniques," *Journal of Finance,* **XXVII,** No. 2 (May 1972), pp. 343–353.
4. ———. "Anomalies in Relationships Between Securities' Yields and Yield-Surrogates," *Journal of Financial Economics,* **6** (1978), p. 103.
5. Banz, Rolf W. "The Relationship Between Return and Market Value of Common Stock," *Journal of Financial Economics,* **9** (1981), pp. 3–18.
6. Baron, David. "Information, Investment Behavior, and Efficient Portfolios," *Journal of Financial and Quantitative Analysis,* **IX,** No. 4 (Sept. 1974), pp. 555–556.
7. Barry, Christopher B., and Brown, Stephen J. "Anomalies in Security Returns and the Specification of the Market Model," *The Journal of Finance,* **39,** No. 3 (July 1984), pp. 807–818.
8. ———. "Differential Information and the Small Firm Effect," *Journal of Financial Economics,* **13,** No. 2 (June 1983), pp. 283–294.
9. Bar-Yosef, Sasson, and Brown, Lawrence. "A Reexamination of Stock Splits Using Moving Betas," *Journal of Finance,* **XXXII,** No. 4 (Sept. 1977), pp. 1069–1080.
10. Basu, S. "Investment Performance of Common Stocks in Relation to Their Price-Earnings Ratios: A Test of the Efficient Market Hypothesis," *Journal of Finance,* **XXXII,** No. 2 (June 1977), p. 663.

11. ———. "The Relationship Between Earnings' Yield, Market Value and the Return for NYSE Common Stocks: Further Evidence," *Journal of Financial Economics,* **12,** No. 1 (1983).

12. Beja, Auraham, and Hakansson, Nils. "Dynamic Market Processes and the Rewards to Up-to-Date Information," *Journal of Finance,* **XXXII,** No. 2 (May 1977), pp. 291–304.

13. Berges, Angel, McConnell, John J., and Schlarbaum, Gary G. "An Investigation of the Turn-of-the-Year Effect, the Small Firm Effect, and the Tax-Loss-Selling-Pressure Hypothesis in Canadian Stock Returns," manuscript (West Lafayette, Ind.: Purdue University, 1982).

14. Bjerring, James H., Lakonishok, Josef, and Vermaelen, Theo. "Stock Prices and Financial Analysts' Recommendations," *The Journal of Finance,* **38,** No. 1 (March 1983), pp. 187–204.

15. Black, Fischer, and Scholes, Myron. "The Valuation of Option Contracts and a Test of Market Efficiency." *Journal of Finance,* **XXVII,** No. 2 (May 1972), pp. 399–417.

16. Blattberg, Robert, and Gonedes, Nicholas. "A Comparison of the Stable and Student Distributions as Statistical Models for Stock Prices," *Journal of Business,* **47,** No. 2 (April 1974), pp. 244–280.

17. ———. "A Comparison of the Stable and Student Distributions as Statistical Models of Share Price: Reply to [133]," *Journal of Business,* **50,** No. 1 (Jan. 1977), pp. 78–79.

18. Blume, Marshall E., and Stambaugh, Robert F. "Biases in Computed Returns: An Application to the Size Effect," manuscript (Philadelphia, Pa.: University of Pennsylvania, 1983).

19. Boness, James, and Jen, Frank. "A Model of Information Diffusion, Stock Market Behavior, and Equilibrium Price," *Journal of Financial and Quantitative Analysis,* **V,** No. 3 (Sept. 1970), pp. 274–296.

20. Branch, Ben. "A Tax Loss Trading Rule," *Journal of Business,* **50,** No. 2 (April 1977), pp. 198–207.

21. Brenner, Menachem. "A Note on [51]: Risk, Return and Equilibrium: Empirical Tests," *Journal of Political Economy,* **84,** No. 2 (April 1976), pp. 407–409.

22. ———. "The Effect of Model Misspecification on Tests of the Efficient Market Hypothesis," *Journal of Finance,* **XXXII,** No. 1 (March 1977), pp. 57–66.

23. Brown, Philip, Keim, Donald B., Kleidon, Allan W., and Marsh, Terry A. "Stock Return Seasonalities and the 'Tax-Loss Selling' Hypothesis: Analysis of the Arguments and Australian Evidence," *Journal of Financial Economics,* **12,** No. 1 (1983).

24. Brown, Philip, Kleidon, Allan W., and Marsh, Terry A. "New Evidence on the Nature of Size Related Anomalies in Stock Prices," *Journal of Financial Economics,* **12,** No. 1 (1983), pp. 33–56.

25. Brown, Stephen J., and Warner, Jerold B. "Using Daily Stock Returns: The Case of Event Studies," *Journal of Financial Economics,* **14,** No. 1 (March 1985), pp. 3–32.

26. Brown, Stewart. "Earnings Changes, Stock Prices, and Market Efficiency," *Journal of Finance,* **XXXIII,** No. 1 (March 1978), pp. 17–28.
27. Brown, Stewart L., and Nichols, William D. "Assimilating Earnings and Split Information: Is the Capital Market Becoming More Efficient?" *Journal of Financial Economics,* **9,** No. 3 (Sept. 1981), pp. 309–314.
28. Carey, Kenneth. "Non-Random Price Changes in Association with Trading in Large Blocks: Evidence of Market Efficiency in Behavior of Investor Returns," *Journal of Business,* **50,** No. 4 (Oct. 1977), pp. 407–414.
29. Cheng, L. Pao, and Deets, M. King. "Portfolio Returns and the Random Walk Theory," *Journal of Finance,* **XXVI,** No. 1 (March 1971), pp. 11–30.
30. ———. "Reply to [160]," *Journal of Finance,* **XXVIII,** No. 3 (June 1973), pp. 742–745.
31. ———. "Reply to [64]," *Journal of Finance,* **XXXI,** No. 1 (March 1976), pp. 157–161.
32. Christie, Andrew A., and Hertzel, Michael. "Capital Asset Pricing 'Anomalies': Size and Other Correlations," manuscript Rochester, N.Y.: University of Rochester, 1981).
33. Constantinides, George M. "Optimal Stock Trading with Personal Taxes: Implications for Prices and the Abnormal January Returns," *Journal of Financial Economics,* **X,** No. 4 (March 1984), pp. 65–90.
34. Cook, Thomas J., and Rozeff, Michael S. "Size, Dividend Yield and Co-Skewness Effects on Stock Returns: Some Empirical Tests," manuscript (University of Iowa, Iowa City, 1982).
35. Cootner, Paul. *The Random Character of Stock Market Prices* (Cambridge, Mass.: MIT Press, 1974).
36. Copeland, Thomas E., and Mayers, David. "The Value Line Enigma (1965–1978): A Case Study of Performance of Evaluation Issues," *Journal of Financial Economics,* **X,** No. 3 (Nov. 1982), pp. 289–322.
37. Dann, Larry, Mayers, David, and Raab, Robert. "Trading Rules, Large Blocks, and the Speed of Price Adjustment," *Journal of Financial Economics,* **4,** No. 1 (Jan. 1977), pp. 3–22.
38. Davies, Peter Lloyd, and Canes, Michael. "Stock Prices and the Publication of Second-Hand Information," *Journal of Business,* **51,** No. 1 (Jan. 1978), pp. 43–56.
39. Dennis, Charles. "Comment on [43]: The Information Content of Daily Market Indicators," *Journal of Financial and Quantitative Analysis,* **VIII,** No. 2 (March 1973), pp. 193–194.
40. Dimson, Elroy, and Marsh, Paul. "An Analysis of Brokers' and Analysts' Unpublished Forecasts of UK Stock Returns," *The Journal of Finance,* **39,** No. 5 (Dec. 1984), pp. 1257–1292.
41. Dodd, Peter, and Ruback, Richard. "Tender Offers and Stockholders Returns," *Journal of Financial Economics,* **5,** No. 3 (Dec. 1977), pp. 351–375.
42. Dowell, Dwayne, and Grube, Corwin. "Common Stock Return Distributions During Homogeneous Activity Periods," *Journal of Financial and Quantitative Analysis,* **XIII,** No. 1 (March 1978), pp. 79–92.

43. Dryden, M. Myles. "Share Prices Movements: A Markovian Approach," *Journal of Finance,* **XXIV,** No. 1 (March 1969), pp. 49–60.

44. Dryden, Myles. "A Source of Bias in Filter Tests on Share Prices," *Journal of Business,* **42,** No. 3 (July 1969), pp. 321–325.

45. Dyl, Edward. "Capital Gains Taxation and Year-End Stock Market Behavior," *Journal of Finance,* **XXXII,** No. 1 (March 1977), pp. 165–175.

46. Ellert, James. "Mergers, Anti-Trust Law Enforcement and Stockholder Returns," *Journal of Finance,* **XXXI,** No. 2 (May 1976), pp. 715–732.

47. Elton, Edwin J., Gruber, Martin J., and Grosman, Seth. "Discreet Expectational Data and Portfolio Performance," *Journal of Finance,* XXXXI, No. 3 (July 86) pp. 699–712.

48. Elton, E., Gruber, M., and Kleindorfer, P. "A Closer Look at the Implications of the Stable Paretian Hypotheses," *Review of Economics and Statistics,* **LVII,** No. 2 (May 1975), pp. 231–235.

49. Emery, John. "The Information Content of Daily Market Indicators," *Journal of Financial and Quantitative Analysis,* **VIII,** No. 2 (March 1973), pp. 183–190.

50. ———. "Efficient Capital Markets and the Information Content of Accounting Numbers," *Journal of Financial and Quantitative Analysis,* **IX,** No. 2 (March 1974), pp. 139–149.

51. Epps, Thomas. "Security Price Changes and Transaction Volumes: Some Additional Evidence," *Journal of Financial and Quantitative Analysis,* **XII,** No. 1 (March 1977), pp. 141–146.

52. ———. "Security Price Changes and Transaction Volumes: Theory and Evidence," *American Economic Review,* **LXV,** No. 4 (Sept. 1975), pp. 586–597.

53. ———. "Security Price Changes and Transaction Volumes: Additional Evidence: Reply to [144]," *American Economic Review,* **68,** No. 4 (Sept. 1978), pp. 698–700.

54. Eskew, Robert, and Wright, William. "An Empirical Analysis of Differential Capital Market Reactions to Extraordinary Accounting Items," *Journal of Finance,* **XXXI,** No. 2 (May 1976), pp. 631–674.

55. Evans, John. "The Random Walk Hypothesis, Portfolio Analysis and the Buy-and-Hold Criterion," *Journal of Financial and Quantitative Analysis,* **III,** No. 3 (Sept. 1968), pp. 327–342.

56. Fama, Eugene. "The Behavior of Stock Market Prices," *Journal of Business,* **38** (Jan. 1965), pp. 34–105.

57. ———. "Efficient Capital Markets: A Review of Theory and Empirical Work," *Journal of Finance,* **XXV,** No. 2 (March 1970), pp. 383–417.

58. ———. "Reply to [105]," *Journal of Finance,* **XXXI,** No. 1 (March 1976), pp. 143–145.

59. Fama, Eugene, and MacBeth, James. "Risk, Return and Equilibrium: Empirical Tests," *Journal of Political Economy,* **81,** No. 3 (May/June 1973), pp. 607–636.

60. Fama, E., Fisher, L., Jensen, M., and Roll, R. "The Adjustment of Stock

Prices to New Information," *International Economic Review*, **10,** No. 1 (Feb. 1969), pp. 1–21.

61. Fama, Eugene, and Blume, Marshall. "Filter Rules and Stock Market Trading," *Journal of Business*, **39,** (Jan. 1966), pp. 226–241.

62. Fama, Eugene, and Laffer, Arthur. "Information and Capital Markets," *Journal of Business*, **44,** No. 3 (July 1971), pp. 289–298.

63. Fielitz, Bruce. "On the Stationarity of Transition Probability Matrices of Common Stocks," *Journal of Financial and Quantitative Analysis*, **X,** No. 2 (June 1975), pp. 327–339.

64. ———. "Further Results on Asymmetric Stable Distribution of Stock Price Changes," *Journal of Financial and Quantitative Analysis*, **XI,** No. 1 (March 1976), pp. 39–55.

65. Finnerty, Joseph. "Insiders' Activity and Inside Information: A Multivariate Analysis," *Journal of Financial and Quantitative Analysis*, **XI,** No. 2 (June 1976), pp. 205–215.

66. ———. "Insiders and Market Efficiency," *Journal of Finance*, **XXXI,** No. 4 (Sept. 1976), pp. 1141–1148.

67. ———. "The Chicago Board Options Exchange and Market Efficiency," *Journal of Financial and Quantitative Analysis*, **XIII,** No. 1 (March 1978), pp. 29–38.

68. Firth, Michael. "The Information Content of Large Investment Holdings," *Journal of Finance*, **XXX,** No. 5 (Dec. 1975), pp. 1265–1281.

69. Folger, Russell, and Radcliffe, Robert. "A Note of Measurement of Skewness," *Journal of Financial and Quantitative Analysis*, **IX,** No. 3 (June 1974), pp. 485–489.

70. French, Kenneth R. "Stock Returns and the Weekend Effect," *Journal of Financial Economics*, **8** (1980), pp. 55–70.

71. Furst, Richard. "Does Listing Increase the Market Price of Common Stocks?" *Journal of Business*, **43,** No. 2 (April 1970), pp. 174–180.

72. Galai, Dan. "Tests of Market Efficiency of the Chicago Board Options Exchange," *Journal of Business*, **50,** No. 2 (April 1977b), pp. 421–442.

73. Gibbons, Michael R., and Hess, Patrick J. "Day of the Week Effects and Asset Returns," *Journal of Business*, **54** (1981), pp. 579–96.

74. Goldman, Barry. "Portfolio Returns and the Random Walk: Comment on [21]," *Journal of Finance*, **XXXI,** No. 1 (March 1976), pp. 153–156.

75. Gonedes, Nicholas. "Evidence on the Information Content of Accounting Numbers: Accounting-Based and Market-Based Estimates of Systematic Risk," *Journal of Financial and Quantitative Analysis*, **VIII,** No. 3 (June 1973), pp. 407–443.

76. ———. "Information-Production and Capital Market Equilibrium," *Journal of Finance*, **XXX,** No. 3 (June 1975), pp. 841–864.

77. ———. "A Note on Accounting-Based and Market-Based Estimates of Systematic Risk," *Journal of Financial and Quantitative Analysis*, **X,** No. 2 (June 1975), pp. 355–365.

78. ———. "The Capital Market, the Market for Information and External Accounting," *Journal of Finance*, **XXXI,** No. 2 (May 1976), pp. 611–630.

79. Granger, C.W. "Some Aspects of the Random Walk Model of Stock Market Prices," *International Economic Review,* **9,** No. 2 (June 1968), pp. 253–257.

80. ———. "What the Random Walk Model Does Not Say," *Financial Analyst Journal,* **26,** No. 3 (May/June, 1970), pp. 91–93.

81. ———. "A Survey of Empirical Studies on Capital Markets," in Elton and Gruber, *International Capital Markets* (Amsterdam: North-Holland, 1975).

82. Granger, C.W., and Morgenstern, O. *Predictability of Stock Market Prices* (Boston, Mass.: Heath, 1970).

83. Grier, Paul, and Albin, Peter. "Non-Random Price Changes in Association with Trading in Large Blocks," *Journal of Business,* **46,** No. 3 (July 1973), pp. 425–433.

84. Griffin, Paul. "Competitive Information in the Stock Market: An Empirical Study of Earnings, Dividends, and Analysts' Forecasts," *Journal of Finance,* **XXXI,** No. 2 (May 1976), pp. 631–650.

85. Griffiths, R.J. "Relative Strength — An Indicator for investment in the Equity Market," thesis (Department of Statistics, Cranfield College, Cambridge, England: 1970).

86. Grossman, Sanford. "On the Efficiency of Competitive Stock Markets Where Trades Have Diverse Information," *Journal of Finance,* **XXXI,** No. 2 (May 1976), pp. 573–585.

87. Grossman, S.J., and Hart, O.D. "Disclosure Law and Takeover Bids," *The Journal of Finance,* **35,** No. 2 (May 1980), pp. 323–334.

88. Gultekin, Mustafa N., and Gultekin, N. Bulent. "Stock Market Seasonality and the Turn of the Tax Year Effect: International Evidence," manuscript (Philadelphia, Pa.: University of Pennsylvania, 1982).

89. Guthman, H., and Bakay, A. "The Market Impact of the Sale of Large Blocks of Stock," *Journal of Finance,* **20** (Dec. 1966).

90. Hagerman, Robert, and Richmond, Richard. "Random Walks, Martingale and the OTC," *Journal of Finance,* **XXVIII,** No. 4 (Sept. 1973), pp. 897–909.

91. Hanna, Mark. "Security Price Changes and Transaction Volumes: Additional Evidence Comment on [41]," *American Economic Review,* **68,** No. 4 (Sept. 1978), pp. 692–695.

92. Hausman, W.H., West, R.R., and Largay, J.A. "Stock Splits, Price Changes, and Trading Profits: A Synthesis," *Journal of Business,* **44,** No. 1 (Jan. 1971), pp. 69–77.

93. Hayes, Douglas. "The Multi-Dimensional Aspects of Risks," *Journal of Portfolio Management,* **2,** No. 4 (Summer 1976), pp. 23–28.

94. Heathcotte, Bryan. "Comment: On Emery [44]," *Journal of Financial and Quantitative Analysis,* **IX,** No. 2 (March 1974), pp. 151–153.

95. Heathcotte, Bryan, and Apilado, Vincent. "The Predictive Content of Some Leading Economic Indicators for Future Stock Prices," *Journal of Financial and Quantitative Analysis,* **IX,** No. 2 (March 1974), pp. 247–258.

96. Ibbotson, Roger, and Jaffe, Jeffrey. "Hot Issue Markets," *Journal of Finance,* **XXX,** No. 2 (Sept. 1975), pp. 1027–1042.

97. Jaffe, Jeffrey. "Special Information and Insider Trading," *Journal of Business,* **47,** No. 3 (July 1974), pp. 410–428.

98. Jaffe, Jeffrey, and Mandelker, Gershon. "The Fisher Effect for Risky Assets: An Empirical Investigation," *Journal of Finance,* **XXXI,** No. 2 (May 1976), pp. 447–458.

99. Jaffe, Jeffrey, and Winkler, Robert. "Optimal Speculation Against an Efficient Market," *Journal of Finance,* **1** (March 1976), pp. 49–61.

100. Jaffe, Jeffrey, and Merville, Larry. "Stock Price Dependencies and the Valuation of Risky Assets with Discontinuous Temporal Returns," *Journal of Finance,* **XXXIX,** No. 5 (Dec. 1974), pp. 1437–1448.

101. Jaffe, Jeffrey, and Westerfield, Randolph. "The Week-end Effect in Common Stock Returns: The International Evidence," *The Journal of Finance,* **40,** No. 2 (June 1985), pp. 433–454.

102. Jaim, Prem C. "The Effect of Voluntary Sell-off Announcements on Shareholder Wealth," *The Journal of Finance,* **40,** No. 1 (March 1985), pp. 209–224.

103. Jennergren, Peter. "Filter Tests of Swedish Share Prices," in Elton and Gruber, *International Capital Markets* (Amsterdam: North-Holland, 1975).

104. Jennergren, Peter, and Korsvold, Paul. "The Non-Random Character of Norwegian and Swedish Stock Market Prices," in Elton and Gruber, *International Capital Markets* (Amsterdam: North-Holland, 1975).

105. Jensen, Michael, and Bennington, George. "Random Walks and Technical Theories: Some Additional Evidence," *Journal of Finance,* **XXV,** No. 2 (May 1970), pp. 469–482.

106. Jones, P. Charles, and Litzenberger, H. Robert. "Quarterly Earnings Reports and Intermediate Stock Price Trends," *Journal of Finance,* **XXV,** No. 1 (March 1970), pp. 143–148.

107. Jones, Charles P., Latane, Henry A., and Rendleman, Richard J. "Empirical Anomalies Based on Unexpected Earnings and the Importance of Risk Adjustments," *Journal of Financial Economics,* **X,** No. 3 (Nov. 1982), pp. 269–288.

108. Jordan, Ronald. "An Empirical Investigation of the Adjustment of Stock Prices to New Quarterly Earnings Information," *Journal of Financial and Quantitative Analysis,* **VIII,** No. 4 (Sept. 1973), pp. 609–620.

109. Kaplan, Robert, and Roll, Richard, "Investor Evaluation of Accounting Information: Some Empirical Evidence," *Journal of Business,* **45,** No. 2 (July 1972), pp. 225–257.

110. ———. "Accounting Changes and Stock Prices," *Financial Analysts, Journal,* **29,** No. 1 (Jan./Feb. 1973), pp. 48–53.

111. Katz, Steven. "The Price Adjustment Process of Bonds to Rating Reclassifications: A Test of Bond Market Efficiency," *Journal of Finance,* **XXIX,** No. 2 (May 1974), pp. 551–559.

112. Keim, Donald B. "Dividend Yield and Stock Returns: Implications of Abnormal January Returns," manuscript (Philadelphia, Pa.: University of Pennsylvania, 1982).

113. ———. "Size Related Anomalies and Stock Return Seasonality Further Empirical Evidence," *Journal of Financial Economics,* **12** (1983).
114. Keim, Donald B., and Stambaugh, Robert F. "A Further Investigation of the Weekend Effect in Stock Returns," *The Journal of Finance,* **39,** No. 3 (July 1984), pp. 819–840.
115. Kraus, Alan, and Sick, Gordon A. "Distinguishing Beliefs and Preferences in Equilibrium Prices," *The Journal of Finance,* **35,** No. 2 (May 1980), pp. 335–343.
116. Kraus, Alan, and Stoll, Hans. "Price Impacts of Block Trading on the New York Stock Exchange," *Journal of Finance,* **XXVII,** No. 3 (June 1972), pp. 569–588.
117. Kwan, Clarence C.Y. "Efficient Market Tests of the Informational Content of Dividend Announcements: Critique and Extension," *Journal of Financial and Quantitative Analysis,* **XVI,** No. 2 (June 1981), pp. 193–206.
118. Lakonishok, Josef, and Shapiro, Alan C. "Partial Diversification as an Explanation of the Small Firm Effect: An Empirical Analysis," manuscript (University of Southern California, Los Angeles, Ca., 1982).
119. Larcker, David F., Gordon, Lawrence A., and Pinches, George E. "Testing for Market Efficiency: A Comparison of the Cumulative Average Residual Methodology and Intervention Analysis," *Journal of Financial and Quantitative Analysis,* **XV,** No. 2 (June 1980), pp. 267–288.
120. Latane, H., Tuttle, D., and Jones, C. "E/P Ratios v. Changes in Earnings in Forecasting Future Price Changes," *Financial Analysts Journal,* **25,** No. 1 (Jan./Feb. 1969), pp. 117–120, 123.
121. Latane, Henry, and Jones, Charles. "Standardized Unexpected Earnings — A Progress Report," *Journal of Finance,* **XXXII,** No. 5 (Dec. 1977), pp. 1457–1465.
122. Laub, Michael. "On the Informational Content of Dividends," *Journal of Business,* **49,** No. 1 (Jan. 1976), pp. 73–80.
123. Leroy, Stephen. "Risk Aversion and the Martingale Property of Stock Prices," *International Economic Review,* **14,** No. 2 (June 1973), pp. 436–446.
124. ———. "Efficient Capital Markets: Comment on [49]," *Journal of Finance,* **XXXI,** No. 1 (March 1976), pp. 139–141.
125. Levy, Robert, "Relative Strength as a Criterion for Investment Selection," *Journal of Finance,* **22** (Dec. 1967), pp. 595–610.
126. Litzenberger, Robert, Joy, Maurice, and Jones, Charles. "Ordinal Predictions and the Selection of Common Stocks," *Journal of Financial and Quantitative Analysis,* **VI,** No. 9 (Sept. 1971), pp. 1059–1068.
127. Logue, Dennis. "On the Pricing of Unseasoned Equity Issues: 1965–1969," *Journal of Financial and Quantitative Analysis,* **VIII,** No. 1 (Jan. 1973), pp. 91–103.
128. Lorie, James, and Niederhoffer, Victor. "Predictive and Statistical Properties of Insider Trading," *Journal of Law and Economics,* **11** (April 1968), pp. 35–53.
129. Mandelbrot, Benoit. "Some Aspects of the Random Walk Model of Stock

Market Prices: Comment on [69]," *International Economic Review,* **9,** No. 2 (June 1968), pp. 258–259.

130. ———. "When Can Price Be Arbitraged Efficiently? A Limit to the Validity of the Random Walk and Martingale Models," *Review of Economics and Statistics,* **LIII,** No. 3 (Aug. 1971), pp. 225–236.

131. McCaly, Marvin. "The Penalties of Incurring Unsystematic Risk," *Journal of Portfolio Management,* **4,** No. 3 (Spring 1978), pp. 31–35.

132. McCulloch, Huston. "Continuous Time Processes with Stable Increments," *Journal of Business,* **51,** No. 4 (Oct. 1978), pp. 601–619.

133. McDonald, J.G., and Fisher, A.K. "New-Issue Stock Price Behavior," *Journal of Finance,* **XXVII,** No. 1 (March 1972), pp. 97–102.

134. McDonald, John, and Baron, Donald. "Risk and Return on Short Positions in Common Stocks," *Journal of Finance,* **XXVIII,** No. 1 (March 1973), pp. 97–107.

135. Niederhoffer, Victor. "The Analysis of World Events and Stock Prices," *Journal of Business,* **44,** No. 2 (April 1971), pp. 193–219.

136. Niederhoffer, V., and Osborn, M. "Market Making and Reversal on the Stock Exchange," *Journal of the American Statistical Association,* **61** (Dec. 1966), pp. 897–916.

137. Niarchos, N.A. "Statistical Analysis of Transactions on the Athens Stock Exchange," thesis (Nottingham England: Nottingham College), 1971.

138. Officer, Robert R. "Seasonality in the Australian Capital Markets: Market Efficiency and Empirical Issues," *Journal of Financial Economics,* **2** (1975), pp. 29–52.

139. Ohlson, James A., and Penman, Stephen H. "Volatility Increases Subsequent to Stock Splits: An Empirical Aberration," *Journal of Financial Economics,* **14,** No. 2 (June 1985), pp. 251–266.

140. Oldfield, G., Rogalski, R., and Jarrow, R., "An Autoregressive Jump Process for Common Stock Returns," *Journal of Financial Economics,* **5,** No. 3 (Dec. 1977), pp. 389–418.

141. Oppenheimer, Henry R., and Schlarbaum, Gary G. "Investing with Ben Graham: An Ex Ante Test of the Efficient Market Hypothesis," *Journal of Financial and Quantitative Analysis,* **XVI,** No. 3 (Sept. 1981), pp. 341–360.

142. Pankoff, Lyn. "Market Efficiency and Football Betting," *Journal of Business,* **41,** No. 2 (April 1968), pp. 203–214.

143. Patell, James M., and Wolfson, Mark A. "The Intraday Speed of Adjustment of Stock Prices to Earnings and Dividend Announcements," *Journal of Financial Economics,* **13,** No. 2 (June 1983), pp. 223–252.

144. Pettit, R. Richardson. "Dividend Announcements, Security Performance, and Capital Market Efficiency," *Journal of Finance,* **XXVII,** No. 5 (Dec. 1972), pp. 993–1007.

145. ———. "The Impact of Dividend and Earnings Announcements: A Reconciliation," *Journal of Business,* **49,** No. 1 (Jan. 1976), pp. 86–89.

146. Pettit, R. Richardson, and Westerfield, Randolph. "Using the Capital Asset

Pricing Model and the Market Model to Predict Security Returns," *Journal of Financial and Quantitative Analysis,* **IX,** No. 4 (Sept. 1974), pp. 579–605.

147. Pinches, George. "The Random Walk Hypothesis and Technical Analysis," *Financial Analysts Journal,* **26,** No. 2 (March/April 1970), pp. 104–110.

148. Pinches, George, and Simon, Gary. "An Analysis of Portfolio Accumulation Strategies Employing Low-Priced Common Stocks," *Journal of Financial and Quantitative Analysis,* **VII,** No. 3 (June 1972), pp. 1773–1796.

149. Praetz, Peter. "The Distribution of Share Price Changes," *Journal of Business,* **45,** No. 1 (Jan. 1972), pp. 49–55.

150. ———. "Rates of Return on Filter Tests," *Journal of Finance,* **XXXI,** No. 1 (March 1976), pp. 71–75.

151. ———. "A Comparison of the Stable and Student Distributions as Structural Models of Stock Prices: Comment on [12]," *Journal of Business,* **50,** No. 1 (Jan. 1977), pp. 76–77.

152. Reinganum, Marc R. "Misspecification of Capital Asset Pricing: Empirical Anomalies Based on Earnings Yields and Market Values," *Journal of Financial Economics,* **9** (1981), pp. 19–46.

153. ———. "The Arbitrage Pricing Theory: Some Empirical Results," *Journal of Finance,* **37** (1981), pp. 27–35.

154. ———. "A Direct Test of Roll's Conjecture on the Firm Size Effect," *The Journal of Finance,* **37,** No. 1 (March 1982), pp. 27–36.

155. ———. "The Anomalous Stock Market Behavior of Small Firms in January: Empirical Tests for Tax-Loss Selling Effect," *Journal of Financial Economics,* **12,** No. 1 (1983).

156. Renshaw, Edward F.V. "Simulating the Dow Jones Industrial Average: A Further Test of the Random Walk Hypothesis," *Financial Analysts Journal,* **26,** No. 4 (Sept./Oct. 1970), pp. 51–59.

157. Renwick, Fred. "Theory of Investment Behavior and Empirical Analysis of Stock Market Price Relatives," *Management Science,* **15,** No. 1 (Sept. 1968), pp. 57–71.

158. Roll, Richard. *The Behavior of Interest Rates: An Application of the Efficient Market Model to U.S. Treasury Bills* (New York: Basic Books, 1970).

159. ———. "A Possible Explanation of the Small Firm Effect," *Journal of Finance,* **36** (1981), pp. 879–88.

160. ———. "The Turn of the Year Effect and the Return Premium of Small Firms," *Journal of Portfolio Management* (1982).

161. ———. "On Computing Mean Returns and the Small Firm Premium," Working Paper No. 22–82 (Graduate School of Management, UCLA, Los Angeles, Ca. 1982).

162. Rosenberg, Barr. "Statistical Analysis of Price Series Obscured by Averaging Measures," *Journal of Financial and Quantitative Analysis,* **VI,** No. 4 (Sept. 1971), pp. 1083–1094.

163. Ross, Stephen A. "The Arbitrage Theory of Capital Asset Pricing," *Journal of Economic Theory,* **13** (1976), pp. 341–60.

164. Rozeff, Michael S., and Kinney, Jr., William R. "Capital Market Seasonality: The Case of Stock Returns," *Journal of Financial Economics,* **3** (1976), pp. 379–402.
165. Ryan, Terence. "Security Prices as Markov Processes," *Journal of Financial and Quantitative Analysis,* **VIII,** No. 1 (Jan. 1973), pp. 17–36.
166. Samuelson, Paul. "Limited Liability, Short Selling, Bounded Utility, and Infinite-Variance Stable Distributions," *Journal of Financial and Quantitative Analysis,* **XI,** No. 3 (Sept. 1976), pp. 485–503.
167. Schneller, Meir. "Security Price Changes and Transaction Volumes: Additional Evidence: Comment on [80]," *American Economic Review,* **68,** No. 4 (Sept. 1978), pp. 696–697.
168. Scholes, Myron, and Williams, Joseph. "Estimating Betas from Nonsynchronous Data," *Journal of Financial Economics,* **5,** No. 3 (Dec. 1977), pp. 309–329.
169. Schultz, Paul. "Transaction Costs and the Small Firm Effect: A Comment," *Journal of Financial Economics,* **12** (1983).
170. Schwartz, Robert, and Whitcomb, David. "Evidence on the Presence and Causes of Serial Correlation in Market Model Residuals," *Journal of Financial and Quantitative Analysis,* **XII,** No. 2 (June 1977), pp. 291–313.
171. Schwert, G. William. "The Adjustment of Stock Prices to Information about Inflation," *The Journal of Finance,* **36,** No. 1 (March 1981), pp. 15–30.
172. ———. "Size and Stock Returns, and Other Empirical Regularities," *Journal of Financial Economics,* **12,** No. 1 (1983).
173. Seelenfreund, Alan, Parker, George, and Van Horne, James. "Stock Price Behavior and Trading," *Journal of Financial and Quantitative Analysis,* **III,** No. 3 (Sept. 1968), pp. 263–281.
174. Sharpe, William. "Likely Gains from Market Timing," *Financial Analysts Journal,* **31,** No. 2 (March/April 1975), pp. 60–69.
175. ———. "Capital Asset Prices: A Theory of Market Equilibrium Under Conditions of Risk," *Journal of Finance,* **19,** (1964), pp. 425–442.
176. Simonson, Donald. "Comment on [83]," *Journal of Financial and Quantitative Analysis,* **IX,** No. 2 (March 1974), pp. 259–261.
177. Smidt, Seymour. "A New Look at the Random Walk Hypothesis," *Journal of Financial and Quantitative Analysis,* **III,** No. 3 (Sept. 1968), pp. 235–261.
178. Solnik, Bruno. "Note on the Validity of the Random Walk for European Stock Prices," *Journal of Finance,* **XXVIII,** No. 5 (Dec. 1973), pp. 1151–1159.
179. Stoll, Hans R., and Whaley, Robert E. "Transaction Costs and the Small Firm Effect," *Journal of Financial Economics,* **12,** No. 1 (1983).
180. Taylor, Stephen J. "Tests of the Random Walk Hypothesis against a Price-Trend Hypothesis," *Journal of Financial and Quantitative Analysis,* **XVII,** No. 1 (March 1982), pp. 37–62.
181. Umstead, David. "Forecasting Stock Market Prices," *Journal of Finance,* **XXXII,** No. 2 (May 1977), pp. 427–441.

182. Van Horne, James, and Parker, George. "Technical Trading Rules: A Comment," *Financial Analysts Journal,* **21,** No. 4 (July/Aug. 1968), pp. 128–132.
183. Vasicek, O., and McQuown, J.A. "The Efficient Market Model," *Financial Analysts Journal,* **28,** No. 4 (Sept./Oct. 1972), pp. 71–84.
184. *The Wall Street Journal.*
185. Watts, Ross. "The Information Content of Dividends," *Journal of Business,* **45,** No. 2 (April 1973), pp. 191–211.
186. ———. "Comment on [103] . . . On the Informational Content of Dividends," *Journal of Business,* **49,** No. 1 (Jan. 1976), pp. 81–85.
187. ———. "Comments on [127] . . . The Impact of Dividend and Earnings Announcements: A Reconciliation," *Journal of Business,* **49,** No. 1 (Jan. 1976), pp. 97–106.
188. West, Richard, and Tinic, Seha. "Portfolio Returns and the Random Walk Theory: Comment on [21]," *Journal of Finance,* **XXVIII,** No. 3 (June 1973), pp. 733–741.
189. Westerfield, Randolph. "The Distribution of Common Stock Price Changes: An Application of Transaction, Time and Subordinated Stochastic Models," *Journal of Financial and Quantitative Analysis,* **10,** No. 4 (Dec. 1977), pp. 743–765.
190. Winsen, J. "Investor Behavior and Changes in Accounting Methods," *Journal of Financial and Quantitative Analysis,* **XI,** No. 5 (Dec. 1976), pp. 873–881.
191. Ying, Louis, Lewellen, Wilbur, Schlarbaum, Gary, and Lease, Ronald. "Stock Exchange Listings and Securities Returns," *Journal of Financial and Quantitative Analysis,* **XII,** No. 3 (Sept. 1977), pp. 415–432.

Chapter 16
The Valuation Process

The search for the "correct" way to value common stocks, or even one that works, has occupied a huge amount of effort over a long period of time. Attempts have ranged from simple mechanical techniques for picking winners to hypotheses about the broad influences affecting stock prices. At one extreme, the attempt to find a simple rule for selecting stocks that will have above-average performance can be likened to the search for a perpetual motion machine. Just as the laws of thermodynamics tell us we cannot build a perpetual motion machine, the theory of efficient markets tells us there is no simple mechanical way to pick winners in the stock market, or at least none that will recover its cost of operation. Yet people continue to spend a disproportionate amount of time on both of these endeavors.

At the other extreme the determinants of common stock prices are quite easy to specify in general terms. The price of common stock is a function of the level of a company's earnings, dividends, risk, the cost of money, and future growth rate. While it is easy to specify these broad influences, the implementation of a system that uses these concepts to successfully value or select common stocks is a difficult task. This is the task that a valuation model purports to accomplish.

A valuation model is a mechanism that converts a set of forecasts of (or observations on) a series of company and economic variables into a forecast of market value for the company's stock. The input to a valuation model is in terms of economic variables, for example, future earnings, dividends, variability of earnings, and so forth. The output is in terms of expected market value or expected return from holding the stock or, at the very least, a buy, sell, hold recommendation. The valuation model can be considered a formalization of the relationship that is expected to exist between a set of corporate and economic factors and the market's valuation of these factors.

Every financial organization employs a valuation model. Often the valuation model is implicit in the way the organization makes decisions rather than an explicit model. For example, the organization that holds an index fund is implicitly accepting the simple form of the capital asset pricing model, though it may not explicitly invoke the model every time it makes a decision.[1] The company that buys low price earnings ratio stocks is implicitly stating that only the present price earnings ratios, and not predictions of future growth or risk, affect the return that can be earned on stocks. The advantages of employing an explicit valuation model are tremendous. An explicit model requires the definition of relevant inputs. Furthermore, it assures that these inputs will be systematically collected and used in a consistent manner over time. Finally, the use of a valuation model allows for feedback and control in the functioning of a financial institution. By breaking the process of portfolio analysis into forecasting inputs, valuing securities, and forming portfolios, the ability of the organization to perform in each of these areas can be measured and those areas where the organization has ability can be capitalized upon.

For example, it is feasible that an organization has a superior ability to forecast corporate variables but that the informational content of the forecasts is lost either in the valuation process or when securities are formed into portfolios. Only by breaking the process into logical steps can an institution see what it does well and what it does poorly. Only then can it capitalize on any special abilities it does have and improve its performance.[2]

In this chapter we review some of the more widely used approaches to security valuation. We have made no attempt to be exhaustive in the models we have selected. Rather we have attempted to present some typical models with perhaps some bias toward those that we find more appealing. We start this chapter with a review of the general discounted cash flow approach to security valuation.

DISCOUNTED CASH FLOW MODELS

Discounted cash flow models are based on the concept that the value of a share of stock is equal to the present value of the cash flow that the stockholder expects to receive from it.[3] We will argue that this is equivalent to the present value of all future dividends. To facilitate this argument, let us assume that a stockholder intends to hold a share of stock for one period. In this one period the stockholder

---

[1] An index fund is a portfolio designed to replicate the market portfolio.

[2] We will have more to say about evaluation and control in Chapters 22 and 23.

[3] There is a long history of discussion in the academic literature about what should be discounted. Some authors argued earnings, some dividends, and others earnings plus non-cash expenses such as depreciation. It turns out that, properly defined, these approaches are equivalent. See Miller and Modigliani [66].

will receive a dividend and the value of the stock when he or she sells it. If the dividend occurs at the end of the period, then the value of this share of stock should be given by

$$P_t = \frac{D_{t+1}}{(1 + k)} + \frac{P_{t+1}}{(1 + k)} \qquad (16.1)$$

where

$\quad P_t \quad$ = the price of a share at time t
$\quad D_{t+1}$ = the dividend received at time $t + 1$
$\quad P_{t+1}$ = the price at time period $t + 1$
$\quad k \quad$ = the appropriate discount rate

To value this share the stockholder must estimate the price at which the stock will sell one period hence. Using the method employed before,

$$P_{t+1} = \frac{D_{t+2}}{(1 + k)} + \frac{P_{t+2}}{(1 + k)} \qquad (16.2)$$

Substituting Equation (16.2) into Equation (16.1),

$$P_t = \frac{D_{t+1}}{(1 + k)} + \frac{D_{t+2}}{(1 + k)^2} + \frac{P_{t+2}}{(1 + k)^2} \qquad (16.3)$$

If we, in turn, solved for P_{t+2} and substituted in Equation (16.3), then solved for P_{t+3} and so on, we would find that

$$P_t = \frac{D_{t+1}}{(1 + k)} + \frac{D_{t+2}}{(1 + k)^2} + \frac{D_{t+3}}{(1 + k)^3} + \cdots + \frac{D_{t+n+1}}{(1 + k)^{n+1}} + \cdots \qquad (16.4)$$

or that the value of share of stock is equal to the present value of all future dividends. Stating the problem in terms of a stream of dividends plus a terminal price as in Equation (16.3) does not avoid the problem of forecasting how the future price will be set. It is not incorrect to state the problem in this way, but it may confuse the real issue that dividends have (at least in theory) to be forecast into the indefinite future.[4]

At this point a question invariably arises. What happened to earnings? The reader instinctively feels that earnings should be worth something, whether they are paid out as dividends or not, and wants to know why they do not appear in the valuation equation. In fact, they do appear in the equation but in the correct form. Earnings can be used for one of two purposes: they can be paid out to stockholders in the form of dividends or they can be reinvested in the firm. If they are reinvested in the firm, they should result in increased future earnings and increased future dividends. To the extent earnings at any time, say, time t,

---

[4]In practice, because of the discounting process, dividends that are expected to be received in the very distant future have very little impact on price.

are paid out to stockholders, they are measured by the term D_t, and to the extent they are retained in the firm and used productively they are reflected in future dividends and should result in future dividends being larger than D_t. To discount the future earnings stream of a share of stock would be double counting since we would count retained earnings both when they were earned and when they, or the earnings from their reinvestment, were later paid to stockholders.

It might be worth noting that Equation (16.4), like any of the discounted cash flow (DCF) models discussed in this chapter, can be employed in any of three ways. First, P_t can be treated as the unknown and a value of P_t computed based on estimates of future dividends and the appropriate discount rate. This should be an estimate of the value of the stock, and a market price very different from value should be an indication that price will move in the direction of value.

Second, the present market price can be used for P_t, estimates of future dividends substituted in the equation, and the equation solved for k. The value arrived at for k should be the rate of return the stockholder will earn on the stock.[5] If the value of k arrived at is higher than is warranted by the risk of the stock, then price should adjust upward and rates of return greater than k be earned.[6]

Finally, this equation can be converted to a price earnings ratio by simply dividing each side by earnings. The left-hand side of the equation would then represent the normal price earnings ratio at which the stock should sell.

To use an infinite dividend stream model in its purest form, it would be necessary to forecast the growth rate in dividends each year from now to infinity, use this infinite series of growth rates to derive a dividend stream, and then discount it back to the present. It is impractical to use the model in its purest form. No individual or institution can differentiate between short-term growth forecasts in the distant future. All users of infinite horizon DCF models make some simplifying assumptions about the pattern that growth will follow over time. A number of different assumptions about growth-rate patterns have been made and embodied in valuation models. We review a few of the more widely used ones here. In particular, we examine three sets of growth assumptions. They are:

1.   Constant growth over an infinite amount of time.[7]

2.   Growth for a finite number of years at a constant rate, then growth at the same rate as a typical firm in the economy from that point on.[8]

---

[5]It should be obvious that the appropriate level of k is related to the risk of a stock. One way to determine the appropriate level of k is to employ capital market theory and to determine k from the security market line and an estimate of the firm's risk.

[6]If a stock is incorrectly priced, the rate of return earned may be different from the computed value of k. For example, if the value of k arrived at is higher than that warranted by the risk of the stock, the price of the stock should adjust upward. If this adjustment takes place rapidly, the return earned by buying the stock may be much greater than that implied by the computed value of k.

[7]See Williams [73] or Gordon [40] for discussion of models of this type.

[8]See Malkiel [63] for the presentation of a model of this type.

3.   Growth for a finite number of years at a constant rate, followed by a period during which growth declines to a steady-state level over a second period of years.[9] Growth is then assumed to continue at the steady-state level into the indefinite future.

We can, for obvious reasons, refer to these three models respectively as one-period, two-period, and three-period growth models. It should be equally as obvious that we could have a four-period, five-period, or N-period growth model.

As we move down this list of models, we are assuming more complex growth patterns for a company. We may be gaining the potential to more accurately forecast what a company will do, but we are asking the analyst to supply not only more data, but data increasingly difficult to forecast. As the type of data we ask to have forecasted becomes more difficult and the amount of information grows, forecasts are likely to contain less information and more random noise. As models become more complex, a point of diminishing returns is reached. Where this point is cannot be answered in the abstract; it is a function of the forecasting skills of the organization employing the model. Thus, the question can be answered only by examining the forecast ability of the organization that is using, or proposes using, one or more valuation models. Let us now turn to an examination of some of the DCF models mentioned earlier.

Constant Growth Model

One of the best known and certainly the simplest DCF model assumes that dividends will grow at the same rate (g) into the indefinite future. Under this assumption the value of a share of stock is

$$P = \frac{D}{(1 + k)} + \frac{D(1 + g)}{(1 + k)^2} + \frac{D(1 + g)^2}{(1 + k)^3} + \cdots + \frac{D(1 + g)^{N-1}}{(1 + k)^N} + \cdots$$

Using the formula for the sum of a geometric progression,[10]

$$P(k-g) = D$$
$$k - g = \frac{D}{P} + g$$

$$P = \frac{D}{k - g} \tag{16.5}$$

---

[9]See Molodovsky, May, and Chottinger [67] for the presentation of a model of this type.

[10]The sum of a geometric progression is given by Sum = First term $[1 - (\text{common ratio})^N]/(1 - \text{common ratio})$, where N is the number of terms over which we are summing. For this model we have

$$P = \frac{\dfrac{D}{1 + k}\left[1 - \left(\dfrac{1 + g}{1 + k}\right)^N\right]}{1 - \dfrac{1 + g}{1 + k}}.$$

As N goes to infinity and

$$\left(\frac{1 + g}{1 + k}\right)^N$$

goes to zero, we obtain the formula in the text.

This model states that the price of a share of stock should be equal to next year's expected dividend divided by the difference between the appropriate discount rate for the stock and its expected long-term growth rate. Alternatively, this model can be stated in terms of the rate of return on a stock as

$$k = D/P + g \qquad (16.6)$$

The constant growth model is often defended as the model that arises from the following assumptions: The firm will maintain a stable dividend policy (keep its retention rate constant) and earn a stable return on new equity investment over time. If we let b stand for the fraction of earnings retained within the firm, r stand for the rate of return the firm will earn on all new investments, and I_t stand for investment at t, we get a very simple expression for growth. The formula requires an estimate of the growth in dividends over time. We can derive an expression for the growth in dividends by first examining the growth in earnings. Growth in earnings arises from the return on new investments. We can write earnings at any moment as

$$E_t = E_{t-1} + rI_{t-1}$$

If the firm's retention rate is constant, then

$$E_t = E_{t-1} + rbE_{t-1} = E_{t-1}(1 + rb)$$

Growth in earnings is the percentage change in earnings, or

$$g = \frac{E_t - E_{t-1}}{E_{t-1}} = \frac{E_{t-1}(1 + rb) - E_{t-1}}{E_{t-1}} = rb$$

Since a constant proportion of earnings is assumed to be paid out each year, the growth in earnings equals the growth in dividends, or

$$g_E = g_D = rb$$

Using this expression for growth, we can rewrite Equations (16.5) and (16.6) as[11]

$$P = \frac{D}{k - rb} \qquad k = \frac{D}{P} + rb \qquad (16.5b)$$

It is worthwhile examining the implications of this model for the growth in stock

---

[11]Analysts frequently like to work in terms of price earnings multiples. Since $D = (1 - b)E$, if we divide both sides of Equation (16.5b) by earnings, we have

$$\frac{P}{E} = \frac{1 - b}{k - br}$$

prices over time. The growth in stock price is

$$g_P = \frac{P_{t+1} - P_t}{P_t}$$

Recognizing that P_t can be defined by Equation (16.5b) and that P_{t+1} is also given by Equation (16.5b) except that D must be replaced by $D(1 + br)$, we find

$$g_P = br$$

Thus, under the one-period model dividends, earnings and prices are all expected to grow at the same rate. It might be worthwhile to point out the key role expectations about the future profitability of investment opportunities play in this model. The rate of return on new investments can be expressed as a fraction (perhaps larger than one) of the rate of return security holders require, or

$$r = ck$$

Substituting this in Equation (16.5b) noting that $D = (1 - b)E$ and rearranging yields

$$k = \frac{(1 - b)E}{(1 - cb)P}$$

Notice that if the firm has no extraordinary investment opportunities ($r = k$), then $c = 1$ and the rate of return that security holders require is simply the inverse of the stock's price earnings ratio. On the other hand, if the firm has investment opportunities that are expected to offer a return above that required by the firm's stockholders ($c > 1$), the earnings price ratio at which the firm sells will be below the rate of return required by investors.[12]

Let us spend a moment examining how the single-period model might be used to select stocks. One way is to predict next year's dividends, the firm's long-term growth rate, and the rate of return stockholders require for holding the stock. Equation (16.5) could then be solved for the theoretical price of the stock that could be compared with its present price. Stocks that have theoretical prices above their actual prices are candidates for purchase; those with theoretical prices below their actual price are candidates for sale. The same procedure could be followed using the equation in footnote 11 with respect to price earnings ratios.

Another way to use the DCF approach is to find the rate of return implicit in the price at which the stock is now selling. This can be done by substituting the current price, estimated dividend, and estimated growth rate into Equation (16.6)

---

[12]For a detailed analysis of the role that investment opportunities play in the valuation of securities, see Elton and Gruber [32].

and solving for the discount rate that equates the present price with the expected flow of future dividends. If this rate is higher than the rate of return considered appropriate for the stock, given its risk, it is a candidate for purchase.

We illustrate the use of the single-period model with a simple example. In the past, IBM's stock was selling for $65 a share. At that time IBM's earnings were $3.99 per share and it paid a $2.00 dividend. At that time a major brokerage firm was estimating IBM's long-term growth rate at 12% and its dividend payout rate at 50%. If we assume 13% is an appropriate discount rate for IBM, we would compute a theoretical price of

$$P = \frac{2.00}{0.13 - 0.12} = \$200$$

While IBM's stock would seem to be undervalued selling at $65 a share, notice the sensitivity of this valuation equation to both the estimate of the appropriate discount rate and the estimate of the long-term growth rate. For example, if IBM's growth rate was estimated to be 9% rather than 12%, its theoretical price would be one-fourth as large or $50.

It seems logical to assume that firms that have grown at a very high rate will not continue to do so into the infinite future. Likewise, firms with very poor growth might improve in the future. While a single growth rate can be found that will produce the same value as a more complex pattern, it is so hard to estimate this single number, and the resultant valuation is so sensitive to this number, that many investment firms have been reluctant to use the single-period growth model. As a result, they have turned to two- and three-period growth models.

The Two-period Growth Model

The simplest extension of the one-period model is to assume that a period of extraordinary growth (good or bad) will continue for a certain number of years, after which growth will change to a level at which it is expected to continue indefinitely.

Let us assume that the length of the first period is N years, that the growth rate in the first period is g_1, and that P_N is the price at the end of period N. We can write the value of the firm as[13]

$$P = \frac{D}{1 + k} + \frac{D(1 + g_1)}{(1 + k)^2} + \frac{D(1 + g_1)^2}{(1 + k)^3} + \cdots + \frac{D(1 + g_1)^{N-1}}{(1 + k)^N} + \frac{P_N}{(1 + k)^N}$$

This can, of course, be simplified using the formula for the sum of a geometric

---

[13]Many authors write the first term's dividend as $D(1 + g_1)$. In this case, the dividend is the current dividend rather than next period's dividend.

progression. The result is

$$P = D \left[\frac{1 - \left(\dfrac{1 + g_1}{1 + k} \right)^N}{k - g_1} \right] + \frac{P_N}{(1 + k)^N}$$

In the two-period model we are assuming that after N periods the firm exhibits a constant infinite growth. Thus, the model developed in the earlier section describes P_N. If g_2 is the growth in the second period and D_{N+1} is the dividend in the $N + 1$ period, we have

$$P_N = \frac{D_{N+1}}{k - g_2}$$

The dividend in the $N + 1$ period can be expressed in terms of the dividend in the first period

$$D_{N+1} = D(1 + g_1)^{N-1}(1 + g_2)$$

With these substitutions we have

$$P = D \left[\frac{1 - \left(\dfrac{1 + g_1}{1 + k} \right)^N}{k - g_1} \right] + \frac{D(1 + g_1)^{N-1}(1 + g_2)}{(1 + k)^N(k - g_2)}$$

This formula can easily be solved for the theoretical price of any stock. How-ever, the two-period model is often used in a slightly different form.

In one form of this model in year N the stock is assumed to change its characteristics so that it resembles the average stock in the economy. After year N the stock is expected to grow at the same rate, have the same dividend policy, and be subject to the same risk as the average stock in the economy. In this case the P/E ratio at which it sells in year N must be the same as the average P/E ratio for the economy. Let us define this as M_g.[14] The price in year N can be then defined as the expected earnings in year N times the appropriate P/E ratio or

$$P_N = \frac{P_N}{E_N}(E_N) = M_g E_N$$

If earnings grow at the same rate as dividends, then earnings in year N are next

---

[14]See Malkiel [63] for a formal derivation of this model.

period's earnings E times $(1 + g_1)^{N-1}$ and price can be expressed as

$$P = \frac{D}{k - g_1} \left[\frac{(1 + k)^N - (1 + g_1)^N}{(1 + k)^N} \right] + \frac{M_g E(1 + g_1)^{N-1}}{(1 + k)^N}$$

Notice that while we started with the value of a share of stock being equal to the present value of all future dividends, we could state the valuation in terms of the present value of a stream of dividends and terminal N year earnings plus a terminal P/E ratio. While this has no mathematical advantages over the sum of an infinite stream of dividends, it does have the advantage of being expressed in terms with which the security analyst feels more at home.

Like the constant growth model, this type of model can be used to arrive at a theoretical price that can then be compared with actual price, or alternatively the rate of return implicit in the present price can be solved for. To illustrate the first of these calculations, let us return to our IBM example. Let us assume that the analyst expects IBM's 12% growth rate to continue for 15 years, after which the analyst expects IBM to become an average company. Furthermore, assume that after 16 years the P/E ratio for the market is expected to be 9.5. Then the theoretical value of IBM's stock would be[15]

$$P = \frac{2.00}{0.13 - 0.12} \left[\frac{(1.13)^{15} - (1.12)^{15}}{(1.13)^{15}} \right] + \frac{(9.5)(3.99)(1.12)^{14}}{(1.13)^{15}} = \$54.59$$

By coincidence, this was close to the actual price of $65 at the time of the computation.

The Three-period Model

The two-period model assumed that during the initial period earnings would continue to grow at some constant rate. At year N the second period started and growth was assumed to instantly drop to some steady-state value. Normally, the change to a new long-term growth rate would not occur instantly; rather, it would occur over a period of time. Thus, a logical extension is to assume a third period. The resultant model would assume that in period one growth is expected to be constant at some level. The analyst must forecast both the level of growth and the duration of period one. During period two the growth changes from its value in period one to a long-run steady-state level. The analyst must forecast both the duration of period two and the pattern of change in growth. While some firms (e.g., Wells Fargo) allow the analyst to select from among a predetermined set of patterns, most firms employ one pattern (usually linear) for all firms. The third and final period is the period of steady-state growth. Many organizations

---

[15]In the example we assume that both the $2.00 dividend and the $3.99 earnings will arise one period after the time of the valuation.

assume that once a firm reaches steady-state growth, it will have the same characteristics as the average firm in the economy. When this happens, the contribution of the third period to value can be found in a manner directly analogous to the formulation of the second period in the two-period model. Other users of the three-period model have assumed zero growth in the third period, while still others allow the analyst to forecast whatever growth is deemed appropriate.

As we move from a constant growth model to a two-period growth model to a three-period growth model, and perhaps even beyond this, we have increased the number and the complexity of the inputs the analyst must provide while, hopefully, picking up some information. If growth patterns are overly simplified, insufficient information will be provided by the forecasts. If they are made too complex, the forecasts are likely to be inaccurate. This trade-off is most apparent in the two extreme models discussed earlier. Analysts cannot develop year-by-year growth estimates into the indefinite future. At the other extreme, asking the analysts to provide only a single average growth forecast means losing the chance for the analyst to provide information about the future pattern of the company's growth. The trade-off between complexity and manageability will have to be made on the basis of the forecasting skills of an organization. No matter how this is decided, one of the principal benefits of using a valuation model can be the preparation of a comparable and explicit set of forecasts over time. Only if forecasts are made explicit can an organization evaluate and improve its performance over time.

Before leaving DCF models, it is worth noting another type of DCF model that is sometimes used by security analysts.

Finite Horizon Models

We have just seen that a model based on discounting a finite stream of dividends and a terminal price can be consistent with discounting an infinite stream of dividends. In this case, the finite nature of the model arose from consideration of future growth. Let us now look at a finite horizon model that arises from the way many organizations work, rather than from discounting an infinite stream of dividends.

Many organizations make short-run earnings forecasts for stocks (one- and two-year forecasts) and intermediate (five-year) growth forecasts. Analysts frequently predict future prices or P/E ratios rather than patterns of growth into the indefinite future. These forecasts can be incorporated into a valuation model by discounting expected dividends for the five years and the terminal price (the product of the expected P/E ratio and expected earnings based on the forecasted growth rate). Keep in mind that the five-year horizon used in this approach is not a function of the economics of the firm, the period over which a steady growth is expected to continue; rather, it arises from the forecasting pattern of the organization analyzing the stock. While the model is mathematically equivalent to that discussed in the previous section, the rationale for the model is entirely different. Five years may not be an appropriate time horizon for the firm under study.

The major factor that separates this model from those we have previously discussed is the selection of a terminal P/E ratio without a specification of the economic rationale or assumptions behind either that P/E ratio or the five-year horizon. If the terminal P/E ratio is determined by assumptions about the future growth of the company, then the model reduces to one of those already discussed. If the terminal P/E ratio is simply asserted by the analyst, based on experience or sense of the market, the analyst has implicitly made an assumption about the future growth pattern for the company. Assumptions about future growth cannot be avoided. If they are not made explicitly, they will be made implicitly by the selection of a terminal P/E ratio.

It would seem to be better to make growth assumptions explicitly, rather than implicitly. If the analyst is going to use this type of model, he or she should at least explore the future growth rate implicit in the use of a terminal P/E ratio.

In fact, perhaps the most interesting aspect of this type of model is that it makes explicit the market expectations of future P/E ratios necessary to justify the price of a stock. That is, it can be used to answer the following question: Given my estimate of both growth rates and the appropriate discount rate, what P/E ratio five years in the future justifies the present price? Returning to our IBM example, we find that a P/E ratio of 16.50 would be necessary five years from now to justify the price of the stock today.[16]

The analyst could proceed to use one of the other growth models to discover the growth rate implicit in the expected future P/E ratio of 16.5. For example, using the constant growth rate assumption, we find that the implicit growth rate is close to 13% from year five into the indefinite future.

CROSS-SECTIONAL REGRESSION ANALYSIS

While DCF models are enjoying a rapidly increased popularity in the investment community, they have been adopted by only a small fraction of the practicing security analysts.[17] By far, the bulk of security analysts still value common stocks by applying some sort of earnings multiple (price earnings ratio) to either present earnings, normalized earnings, or forecasted earnings. Approaches to the establishment of this P/E ratio cover a huge range. Some firms use the historical P/E ratios for companies or the historical P/E ratio for a company relative to the market P/E ratio. Another approach, and one popular in many of the standard texts of security analysis, is to list and discuss large numbers of factors that should affect P/E ratios but leave the weighting and often the explicit definition of these factors up to the security analyst.[18] Still another approach is to take the broad

---

[16]This comes from an assumption of a constant payout ratio. The solution is

$$\$65 = P = \frac{2.00}{1.13} + \frac{2(1.12)}{(1.13)^2} + \frac{2(1.12)^2}{(1.13)^3} + \frac{2(1.12)^3}{(1.13)^4} + \frac{2(1.12)^4}{(1.13)^5} + \left(\frac{P}{E}\right)(3.99)\frac{(1.12)^4}{(1.13)^5}$$

[17]For one survey in this area, see Bing [12].

[18]Graham, Dodd, and Cottle [41], perhaps the best-known book on security analysis, takes this approach.

determinants of common stock prices, earnings, growth, risk, time value of money, and dividend policy and to measure these and weight them together in some manner to form an estimate of the P/E ratio. This section reviews one way to do this. We discuss the use of cross-sectional regression analysis to define the weights the market places on a set of hypothesized determinants of common stock prices. Attempts to use this technique to measure the influence of potential determinants of common stock prices were very popular in the 1960s, and there is an indication that interest in them has recently revived.

The realtionship that exists in the market at any point in time between price or price earnings ratios and a set of specified variables can be estimated using regression analysis. This is the same tool that was used to determine Betas back in Chapter 5. Figure 16.1 presents the relationship between P/E ratios and forecasted growth for a sample of stocks as of the end of 1971. Each point in the diagram represents the P/E ratio and forecasted growth rate for a company as of the end of 1971. The straight line is fitted via regression analysis and its equation is given by[19]

$$\text{Price/Earnings} = 4 + 2.3 \text{ (growth rate in earnings)}$$

The usual technique of relating price or price earnings ratios to more than one variable is directly analogous to this. Called multiple regression analysis, it finds that linear combination of a set of variables that best explains price earnings ratios.

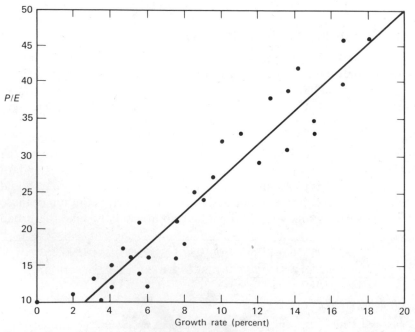

Figure 16.1 P/E ratios versus growth rates.

One of the earliest attempts to use multiple regression to explain price earnings ratios, which received wide attention, was the Whitbeck–Kisor model [72]. We indicated earlier that the price of a share of stock was related to earnings, dividend policy, growth, and risk. We could have said, equally well, that the price earnings ratio of a stock was related to dividend policy, growth, and risk. It was exactly this relationship that Whitbeck and Kisor set out to measure. In particular, they obtained estimates of earnings growth rates, dividend payouts, and the variation (standard deviation) of growth rates from a group of security analysts. Then, using multiple regression analysis to define the average relationship between each of these variables and price earnings ratios, they found (as of June 8, 1962) that

Price earnings ratio = 8.2
+ 1.50 (earnings growth rate)
+ 0.067 (dividend payout rate)
− 0.200 (standard deviation in growth rate)

This equation represents the estimate at a *point in time* of the simultaneous impact of the three variables on the price earnings ratios. The numbers represent the weight that the market placed on each variable at that point in time. The signs represent the direction of the impact of each variable on the price earnings ratio. We might take some comfort from the fact that the signs are consistent with what theory and common sense would lead us to expect: the higher growth, the higher the dividends (growth held constant), and the lower risk, the higher the price earnings ratio. The equations tell us that on average a 1% increase in earnings growth is associated with a 1.5-unit increase in the price earnings ratio, a 1% increase in the dividend payout ratio is associated with a 0.067-unit increase in the price earnings ratio, and a 1% increase in the standard deviation of growth is associated with a 0.2-unit decrease in the P/E ratio.

An equation such as this can be used to arrive at the theoretical P/E ratio for any stock. Simply by substituting the forecasted earnings growth rate, dividend payout ratio, and risk for the stock on the right-hand side of the equation, one arrives at a theoretical P/E ratio. We can illustrate this with the IBM example used previously.[20] When IBM's price was $65, IBM's growth was forecast at 12%, its dividend payout ratio was 50%, and its standard deviation in growth rate was about 5. Substituting these numbers in the expression for price earnings ratios presented before, we get a theoretical P/E ratio of 28.55. Many researchers have taken what seems like a small step from here and advocated buying stocks with theoretical price earnings ratios above their actual price earnings ratios, and selling short stocks with theoretical prices below their market price earnings ratio.

---

[19]This example comes from Cohen, Zinbarg, and Zeikel [25], p. 244.

[20]The reader should be warned that this example is intended solely to illustrate the use of the model. The parameters of the model were estimated in 1962, and we are using 1976 data. The parameters of the model should not be expected to be stable over this period of time. We have more to say later about the stability of the parameters of regression models.

Literally hundreds of models like the Whitbeck–Kisor model have appeared in print since the 1960s.

Every conceivable variable and combination of variables has been tried.[21] The common element of almost all of these models is that they are highly successful in explaining stock prices at a point in time, but they are much less successful in selecting the appropriate stocks to buy or sell short. It is not uncommon for these models to explain more than 80% of the difference in stock prices at a point in time. This gives us confidence that the models can be helpful in finding the variables and set of weights that determine price at a point in time. Why, then, haven't they been more successful in picking winners? The theory behind their use in finding under- and overvalued securities is that the market price will converge to the theoretical price before the theoretical price itself changes. There are at least three reasons why this might, in fact, not happen:[22]

1. Market tastes change. With changes in market tastes, the weight on each variable changes over time.

2. The values of the inputs, such as dividends and growth in earnings, change over time.

3. There are firm effects not captured by the model.

We discuss each of these in turn.

Market Tastes

One reason that price might not converge to theoretical price before theoretical price itself changes is that the parameters that determine theoretical price might change. Tastes, or the importance of certain variables in the market, change over time, and these changes are often rapid and drastic.

Let us return to the relationship between P/E ratios and growth examined earlier. The relationship found at the end of 1971 in a period of a bull market was

$$\text{Price earnings ratio} = 4 + 2.3 \text{ growth}$$

When the relationship was measured as of 1970 in a bear market using the same firms, it was

$$\text{Price earnings ratio} = 3 + 1.8 \text{ growth}$$

---

[21]Some of the more interesting models are Bower and Bower [17], Gordon [40], Gruber [43], and Malkiel and Cragg [64].

[22]A fourth reason should be briefly mentioned. The values in the equations are only estimates. Many researchers have tried large numbers of alternative definitions of variables or alternative variables in search of a "good" fit. Often what they are finding is spurious correlation (the variables happened to move together over the period). In this case there is no reason to believe the model will help select securities.

Notice that the importance of growth was higher in the bull market than it was in the bear market. For a stock with an expected growth rate of 20% per year, the estimated multiple rose from 39 in 1970 to 50 in 1971 or by more than 25%. The result is not surprising; it indicates the large magnitude of shift in market tastes that occurs over time. A similar shift with respect to a fuller set of determinants of common stock prices was reported by Gruber [43]. He examined the weight the market placed on dividends, growth, and three risk variables (earnings instability, financial leverage, and size) in each of 13 consecutive years. He found that the weights shifted drastically from year to year and were different at a statistically significant level.[23] Furthermore, the weights moved in a reasonable pattern, with growth becoming more important as the market moved up, and dividends less important. The opposite phenomenon occurred during downturns in the market. The shifts in the importance of the variables were more dramatic in those years when the market changed direction.

Input Data

Even if the market preference for variables remained stable over time, the theoretical value for a stock would change because the estimates of the variables like growth and dividends change. Input data are arrived at either by historical extrapolation or by the use of analysts' expectations. In any case, both the value of the inputs (earnings, growth, etc.) and expectations about these variables can and do change drastically over time. Every change in one of these variables — for example, expected growth — changes the theoretical value for a stock.

Firm Effects

Even when a model is constructed that explains a high fraction of the difference in stock prices, there are firms that have actual prices that lie above (or below) their theoretical prices and continue to do so period after period. Economists usually refer to this as firm effects. They are probably due to persistent influences that are not captured by the variables in the mode.[24] For example, in the early 1960s, tobacco stocks always had theoretical prices above their actual prices. This may well have been because theoretical prices did not take into consideration the threat of government intervention, while actual prices did.

Although cross-sectional regression models have been successfully used to examine the major determinants of common stock prices and the weight the market places on these determinants, the results from their use as a stock-selection tool has been mixed. Some authors, for example, Whitbeck and Kisor [72], have reported an ability to outperform random selection; others, for example, Bower and Bower [16] and Malkiel and Cragg [64], have reported the failure of their models to lead to superior selection. The differences may be caused by the test

---

[23]This means that it is inappropriate to pool cross-sectional samples in an attempt to define average weights.

[24]See Bower and Bower [16] for a discussion of firm effects.

periods used, the sample selected, or the authors' access to a better, or inferior, set of forecasts.

There is no doubt that cross-sectional regression models are helpful in understanding what has happened in the market over time. In addition, they may prove of some use in selecting stocks. However, the evidence at this time is not conclusive. It is clear that their usefulness is very dependent on the forecasting ability of the institution utilizing the model.

AN ONGOING SYSTEM

In this chapter we have considered several techniques for valuing common stock. The one with the strongest theoretical base involves the discounting of future dividends where the discount rate is appropriately formulated in terms of risk. In recent years several firms have attempted to implement stock valuation and selection systems that incorporate the DCF approach to stock selection and modern capital market theory. Perhaps the best known is the Wells Fargo stock evaluation system.

The first step in the Wells Fargo analysis is to estimate the rate of return implicit in the price at which a stock is selling. They do this by finding the discount rate that equates the present value of all future dividends with price. The growth model they use to predict dividends is similar to the three-period model discussed earlier in the chapter.

In the Wells Fargo system the analyst is required to estimate:

1. Dividends (and earnings per share) for each of the next five years.
2. The fifth-year normalized earnings per share, growth rate, and payout.
3. An eventual steady-state payout and growth rate [the assumption here is that after a large number of years (larger than the five mentioned earlier), there will be a growth rate and payout rate that adequately describes the future behavior of the firm].
4. The number of years that are expected to elapse before the steady-state condition is reached.
5. The pattern of growth expected between the fifth year and the time that steady-state growth is expected to begin. The analyst is free to select one from among several typical patterns that are presented to him.

This gives an expected flow of dividends from the time of the analysis to infinity. This is used to find the expected rate of return, that is, the rate that equates expected dividends with present price.

In addition to dividend flows, the analyst provides estimates of the risk (Beta) of each security. The analyst is given a measure of Beta developed using historical data and is allowed to modify these estimates according to his analysis of the fundamental characteristics of the firm.

This results in an expected return and an expected Beta for each stock. Now the expected return and expected Beta for each of the companies in Wells Fargo's sample is plotted and the straight line that fits these points is used as an estimated security market line.[25] Note that the Wells Fargo security market line is an expectational construct. Most security market lines (see Chapter 13) have been estimated on historical data (realizations) rather than expectations. The Wells Fargo security market line is a representation of a set of expectations. It represents the relationship between expected return and expected Betas.

If stock has a return (given its Beta) above the security market line, it should offer a superior risk-adjusted return; if below, an inferior risk-adjusted return.

Perhaps an alternative explanation of this methodology might help. Analysts, by forecasting dividends, provide an estimate of the return expected from each stock. To understand whether this return is sufficient to compensate for risk, we need to know what the risk of the security is and average expected rate of return the market requires for bearing that risk. The analyst estimates the risk (Beta) on the stock. The average relationship between expected return and expected risk (the security market line) is found by looking at all stocks that analysts follow. If the stock offers a return above the return that should be warranted, given its risk (from the security market line), the stock should be a good buy. If it has a lower return, it should not be a good buy.

This approach has much to commend it. It uses the concept of the value of a share of stock being equal to the present value of future dividends, as well as the concepts of modern capital market theory. That is, it provides a consistent and theoretically defensible framework for the collection and use of output from security analysts. These are qualities that we have described earlier as being highly desirable.

Does this guarantee that the system will work? No. To work, the estimates from security analysts must contain real information. That is, their estimates of future dividends, future Betas, and the security market line must, in combination, provide information about future returns.

Does the system work? An independent study done on the forecasting ability of the Wells Fargo Stock Advisory Service on the 250 stocks followed by TIAA CREF found that the service provided useful information on the relative value of stocks over a four-year period. Although this is not conclusive, it does suggest that systematic use of the data supplied by security analysts can lead to superior performance.

CONCLUSION

A valuation model can be considered as the black box that converts forecasts of fundamental data about companies and/or the economy into forecasts or evaluations of market price. In this chapter we have reviewed several approaches to valuation models. No valuation model can perform well if the forecasts on which it is based are of poor quality. On the other hand, good forecasts can be capitalized upon only if their effect on prices is evaluated in a sensible manner.

---

[25]Actually, Wells Fargo divides stocks into risk groups by Beta range and examines the return on a stock against the average Beta for its group.

QUESTIONS AND PROBLEMS

1. A firm has just paid (the moment before valuation) a dividend of 55¢ and is expected to exhibit a growth rate of 10% into the indefinite future. If the appropriate discount rate is 14%, what is the value of the stock?

2. Consider the one-period growth model shown in the Equation (16.5b). Assume that next period's dividend is $1, that stockholders require a 12% return, that new investment is expected to yield 14%, and that the retention rate is 50%. What is the implied fair price?

3. Assume that price of the security discussed in Problem 2 was $30. Assume that all other information is the same except for the stockholders' required return. What does a $30 price imply for return?

4. Assume the information in Problem 2 and a price of $60. Furthermore, assume that the stockholder was most unsure concerning the return on new investment. How much would return have to change before the security was fairly priced?

5. The analyst who supplied you with the information in Problem 1 has just revised her forecast. She now realizes that the growth rate of 10% can continue for only five years, after which the company will have a long-term growth rate of 6%. Furthermore, at the end of the five years she expects the company's payout rate to increase from its present 30% up to 50%. What value would you assign to the company?

6. Assume that the forecast for the company in Problem 5 was such that at the end of the fifth year its growth was to decline linearly for four years to reach the steady-state 6% growth rate. Assume that the payout ratio was constant at 30% until it is changed to 50% at the end of the ninth year. What is the value of the company?

7. In Problem 2, assume that the price of the stock was $9.00 and solve for the expected rate of return from buying the stock.

8. In Problem 1, assume that the price of the stock was $9 and solve for the expected rate of return from buying the stock.

9. Consider the two-period model. Assume the same information as Problem 2, except that after 10 years growth would change to 5%. What is the implied price?

10. Assume the security sold for $25, the two-period growth model is appropriate, and all other information is identical to Problem 9. What is the implied return?

11. Assume the same information as Problem 9. However, assume the length of time of the higher growth is uncertain. How long would it have to last to justify an $18 price?

12. Derive a three-period valuation model where the transitional period was N_2 years and involved a linear change from the first growth rate to a steady-state growth rate.

BIBLIOGRAPHY

1. Altman, Ed. "Bankrupt Firm's Equity Securities as an Investment Alternative," *Financial Analysts Journal,* **25,** No. 4 (July/Aug. 1969), pp. 129–133.
2. Ambachtsheer, Keith. "Portfolio Theory and the Security Analyst," *Financial Analysts Journal,* **28,** No. 5 (Nov./Dec. 1972), pp. 53–57.
3. Arditti, Fred, and Pinkerton, John. "The Valuation and Cost of Capital of the Levered Firm with Growth Opportunities," *Journal of Finance,* **XXXIII,** No. 1 (March 1978), pp. 54–73.
4. Baker, Kent, and Haslem, John. "Toward the Development of Client-Specified Valuation Models," *Journal of Finance,* **XXIX,** No. 4 (Sept. 1974), pp. 1255–1263.
5. Baron, David. "Firm Valuation, Corporate Taxes, and Default Risk," *Journal of Finance,* **XXX,** No. 5 (Dec. 1975), pp. 1251–1264.
6. Baylis, Robert, and Bhirud, Suresh. "Growth Stock Analysis: A New Approach," *Financial Analysts Journal,* **29,** No. 4 (July/Aug. 1973), pp. 63–70.
7. Beaver, W., and Morse, D. "What Determines Price-Earnings Ratios?" *Financial Analysts Journal,* **34,** No. 4 (July/Aug. 1978), pp. 65–76.
8. Beidelman, Carl. "Pitfalls of the Price-Earnings Ratio," *Financial Analysts Journal,* **27,** No. 4 (Sept./Oct. 1971), pp. 86–91.
9. Bierman, Harold, and Hass, Jerome. "Normative Stock Price Models," *Journal of Financial and Quantitative Analysis,* **VI,** No. 4 (Sept. 1971), pp. 1135–1144.
10. Bierman, Harold, Downes, David, and Hass, Jerome. "Closed-Form Price Models," *Journal of Financial and Quantitative Analysis,* **VII,** No. 3 (June 1972), pp. 1797–1808.
11. Bildersee, John. "Some Aspects of the Performance of Non-Convertible Preferred Stocks," *Journal of Finance,* **XXVIII,** No. 5 (Dec. 1973), pp. 1187–1201.
12. Bing, Ralph. "Survey of Practitioners' Stock Evaluation Methods," *Financial Analysts Journal,* **27,** No. 3 (May/June 1971), pp. 55–69.
13. Black, Fischer. "The Dividend Puzzle," *Journal of Portfolio Management,* **2,** No. 2 (Winter 1976), pp. 5–8.
14. Black, Fischer, and Scholes, M. "The Effects of Dividend Yield and Dividend Policy on Common Stock Prices and Returns," *Journal of Financial Economics,* **1,** No. 1 (May 1974), pp. 4–22.
15. Boness, James, Chen, Andrew, and Jatusipitak, Som. "On Relations among Stock Price Behavior and Changes in the Capital Structure of the Firm," *Journal of Financial and Quantitative Analysis,* **VII,** No. 4 (Sept. 1972), pp. 1967–1982.

16. Bower, Dorothy, and Bower, S. Richard. "Test of a Stock Valuation Model," *Journal of Finance,* **XXV,** No. 2 (May 1970), pp. 483–492.
17. Bower, Richard, and Bower, Dorothy. "Risk and the Valuation of Common Stock," *Journal of Political Economy,* **77,** No. 3 (May/June 1969), pp. 349–362.
18. Bower, Richard, and Wippern, Ronald. "Risk-Return Measurement in Portfolio Selection and Performance Appraisal Models: Progress Report," *Journal of Financial and Quantitative Analysis,* **IV,** No. 4 (Dec. 1969), pp. 417–447.
19. Breen, William, and Savage, James. "Portfolio Distributions and Tests of Security Selection Models," *Journal of Finance,* **XXIII,** No. 5 (Dec. 1968), pp. 805–819.
20. Breen, William, and Lerner, Eugene M. "Corporate Financial Strategies and Market Measures of Risk and Return," *Journal of Finance,* **XXVIII,** No. 2 (May 1973), pp. 339–351.
21. Brennan, Michael. "Valuation and the Cost of Capital for Regulated Industries: Comment on [30]," *Journal of Finance,* **XVII,** No. 5 (Dec. 1972), pp. 1147–1149.
22. Brennan, M.J. "An Approach to the Valuation of Uncertain Income Streams," *Journal of Finance,* **XXVIII,** No. 3 (June 1973), pp. 661–674.
23. Brigham, Eugene, and Pappas, James. "Rates of Return on Common Stock," *Journal of Business,* **42,** No. 3 (July 1969), pp. 302–316.
24. Budd, A.P., and Litzenberger, R.H. "Changes in the Supply of Money, the Firm's Market Value, and Cost of Capital," *Journal of Finance,* **XXVIII,** No. 1 (March 1973), pp. 49–57.
25. Cohen, J., Zinbarg, E., and Zeikel, A. *Investment Analysis and Portfolio Management* (Homeland, Ill.: Richard D. Irwin, 1973).
26. Dennis, Charles N. "An Investigation into the Effects of Independent Investor Relations Firms on Common Stock Prices," *Journal of Finance,* **XXVIII,** No. 2 (May 1973), pp. 373–380.
27. Elton, E., and Gruber, Martin. "Asset Selection with Changing Capital Structure," *Journal of Financial and Quantitative Analysis,* **VIII,** No. 3 (June 1973), pp. 459–474.
28. ———. "The Effect of Share Repurchases on the Value of the Firm," *Journal of Finance,* **XXIII,** No. 1 (March 1968), pp. 135–149.
29. ———. "Marginal Stockholder Tax Rates and the Clientele Effect," *Review of Economics and Statistics,* **LII,** No. 1 (Feb. 1970), pp. 68–74.
30. ———. "Valuation and the Cost of Capital for Regulated Industries," *Journal of Finance,* **XXVI,** No. 3 (June 1971), pp. 661–670.
31. ———. "Valuation and the Cost of Capital for Regulated Industries: Reply to [21]," *Journal of Finance,* **XXVII,** No. 5 (Dec. 1972), pp. 1150–1155.
32. ———. "Valuation and the Asset Selection Under Alternative Investment Opportunities," *Journal of Finance,* **XXXI,** No. 2 (May 1976), pp. 525–539.
33. ———. "Optimal Investment and Financing Patterns for a Firm Subject to

Regulation with a Lag," *Journal of Finance,* **XXXII,** No. 5 (Dec. 1977), pp. 1485–1500.

34. Elton, Edwin, Gruber, Martin, and Lieber, Zvi. "Valuation, Optimum Investment, and Financing for the Firm Subject to Regulation," *Journal of Finance,* **XXX,** No. 2 (March 1975), pp. 401–425.

35. Fewings, David. "The Impact of Corporate Growth on the Risk of Common Stocks," *Journal of Finance,* **XXX,** No. 2 (May 1975), pp. 525–531.

36. Foster, Earl. "Price-Earnings Ratio and Corporate Growth," *Financial Analysts Journal,* **26,** No. 1 (Jan.–Feb. 1970), pp. 96–99.

37. ———. "Price-Earnings and Corporate Growth: A Revision," *Financial Analysts Journal,* **26,** No. 3 (May–June 1970), pp. 115–118.

38. Fouse, W. "Risk and Liquidity: The Keys to Stock Price Behavior," *Financial Analysts Journal,* **32,** No. 3 (May–June 1976), pp. 35–45.

39. Good, Walter. "Valuation of Quality-Growth Stocks," *Financial Analysts Journal,* **28,** No. 4 (Sept.–Oct. 1972), pp. 47–59.

40. Gordon, Myron. *The Investment, Financing, and Valuation of the Corporation* (Homeland, Ill.: Richard D. Irwin, 1962).

41. Graham, B., Dodd, D., and Cottle, S. *Security Analysis Principles and Techniques,* 4th ed. (New York: McGraw-Hill, 1962).

42. Granger, Clive W.J. "Some Consequences of the Valuation Model When Expectations are Taken to Be Optimum Forecasts," *Journal of Finance,* **XXX,** No. 1 (March 1975), pp. 135–145.

43. Gruber, Martin J. *The Determinants of Common Stock Prices* (University Park, Pa.: Pennsylvania State Press, 1971).

44. Gupta, Manak. "Money Supply and Stock Prices: A Probabilistic Approach," *Journal of Financial and Quantitative Analysis,* **IX,** No. 1 (Jan. 1976), pp. 57–68.

45. Hakansson, Nils. "On the Dividend Capitalization Model Under Uncertainty," *Journal of Financial and Quantitative Analysis,* **IV,** No. 1 (March 1969), pp. 65–87.

46. Hamburger, Michael, and Kochin, Levis. "Money and Stock Prices: The Channels of Influence," *Journal of Finance,* **XXVII,** No. 2 (May 1972), pp. 231–249.

47. Haugen, Robert. "Expected Growth, Required Return, and the Variability of Stock Prices," *Journal of Financial and Quantitative Analysis,* **V,** No. 3 (Sept. 1970), pp. 297–307.

48. Haugen, Robert, and Kumar, Prem. "The Traditional Approach to Valuing Levered-Growth Stocks: A Clarification," *Journal of Financial and Quantitative Analysis,* **IX,** No. 6 (Dec. 1974), pp. 1031–1044.

49. Haugen, Robert, and Pappas, J.L. "Equilibrium in the Pricing of Capital Assets, Risk-Bearing Debt Instruments, and the Question of Optimal Capital Structure," *Journal of Financial and Quantitative Analysis,* **VI,** No. 3 (June 1971), pp. 943–953.

50. ———. "Equilibrium in the Pricing of Capital Assets, Risk-Bearing Debt

Instruments, and the Question of Optimal Capital Structure: A Reply," *Journal of Financial and Quantitiative Analysis,* **VII,** No. 4 (Sept. 1972), pp. 2005–2008.

51. Haugen, Robert, and Udell, John. "Rates of Return to Stockholders of Acquired Companies," *Journal of Financial and Quantitative Analysis,* **VII,** No. 1 (Jan. 1972), pp. 1387–1398.

52. Hawkins, D. "Toward an Old Theory of Equity Valuation," *Financial Analysts Journal,* **33,** No. 6 (Nov.–Dec. 1977), pp. 48–53.

53. Hunt, Lacy. "Determinants of the Dividend Yield," *Journal of Portfolio Management,* **3,** No. 3 (Spring 1977), pp. 43–48.

54. Imai, Yutaka, and Rubinstein, Mark. "Equilibrium in the Pricing of Capital Assets, Risk-Bearing Debt Instruments, and the Question of Optimal Capital Structure: Comment," *Journal of Financial and Quantitative Analysis,* **VII,** No. 4 (Sept. 1972), pp. 2001–2003.

55. Jaffee, Jeffrey, and Mandelker, Gershon. "The Value of the Firm Under Regulation," *Journal of Finance,* **XXXI,** No. 2 (May 1976), pp. 701–713.

56. Joy, Maurice, and Jones, Charles. "Another Look at the Value of P/E Ratios," *Financial Analysts Journal,* **26,** No. 4 (Sept.–Oct. 1970), pp. 61–64.

57. Keenan, Michael. "Models of Equity Valuation: The Great Bubble," *Journal of Finance,* **XXV,** No. 2 (May 1970), pp. 243–273.

58. Kraft, John, and Kraft, Arthur. "Determinants of Common Stock Prices: A Time Series Analysis," *Journal of Finance,* **XXXII,** No. 2 (May 1977), pp. 417–425.

59. Kummer, Donald, and Hoffmeister, Ronald. "Valuation Consequences of Cash Tender Offers," *Journal of Finance,* **XXXIII,** No. 2 (May 1978), pp. 505–515.

60. Latane, Henry, Joy, Maurice, and Jones, Charles. "Quarterly Data, Sort-Rank Routines, and Security Evaluation," *Journal of Business,* **43,** No. 3 (July 1970), pp. 427–438.

61. Litzenberger, Robert, and Budd, Alan. "Corporate Investment Criteria and the Valuation of Risk Assets," *Journal of Financial and Quantitative Analysis,* **V,** No. 4 (Dec. 1970), pp. 385–419.

62. Malkiel, Burton. "The Valuation of Closed-End Investment-Company Shares," *Journal of Finance,* **XXXII,** No. 3 (June 1977), pp. 847–859.

63. ———. "Equity Yields, Growth, and the Structure of Share Prices," *American Economic Review,* **53,** (Dec. 1963), pp. 1004–1031.

64. Malkiel, Burton, and Cragg, John. "Expectations and the Structure of Share Prices," *American Economic Review,* **LX,** No. 4 (Sept. 1970), pp. 601–617.

65. Mehta, Dileep. "The Impact of Outstanding Convertible Bonds on Corporate Dividend Policy," *Journal of Finance,* **XXXI,** No. 2 (May 1976), pp. 489–506.

66. Miller, M., and Modigliani, F. "Dividend Policy, Growth, and the Valuation of Shares," *Journal of Business,* **34** (Oct. 1961), pp. 411–433.

67. Molodovsky, N., May, C., and Chottinger, S. "Common Stock Valuation," *Financial Analysts Journal,* **21** (March–April 1965), pp. 104–123.

68. Myers, Stewart. "A Time-State Preference Model of Security Valuation," *Journal of Financial and Quantitative Analysis,* **III,** No. 1 (March 1968), pp. 1–33.
69. Nerlove, Marc. "Factors Affecting Differences among Rates of Return on Investments in Individual Common Stocks," *Review of Economics and Statistics,* **L,** No. 3 (Aug. 1968), pp. 312–331.
70. Sloane, William, and Reisman, Arnold. "Stock Evaluation Theory: Classification, Reconciliation, and General Model," *Journal of Financial and Quantitative Analysis,* **III,** No. 2 (June 1968), pp. 171–204.
71. Warren, James. "A Note on the Algebraic Equivalence of the Holt and Malkiel Models of Share Valuation," *Journal of Finance,* **XXIX,** No. 3 (June 1974), pp. 1007–1010.
72. Whitbeck, V., and Kisor, M. "A New Tool in Investment Decision Making," *Financial Analysts Journal* (May–June 1963), pp. 55–62.
73. Williams, J.B. *The Theory of Investment Value* (Cambridge, Mass.: Harvard University Press, 1938).

Chapter 17

Earnings Estimation

In the previous chapter we saw that both earnings and growth in earnings play a key role in valuation models. In this chapter we examine both the nature of earnings and some models for forecasting future earnings.

We start this chapter by briefly reviewing some of the ambiguities associated with the term "earnings." Different firms and even the same firm, at different times, can define earnings in alternative ways. A logical question is: If earnings can be defined differently, does the figure earnings per share, which shows up on the firm's income statement, have any impact on valuation? This question is examined in the second section of this chapter. As we shall see, despite the ambiguous meaning of reported earnings, there is a real payoff from being able to forecast it.

The final two sections of this chapter examine models for forecasting future earnings. The first of the two sections examines the time series behavior of earnings while the second discusses the relationship between earnings and other fundamental firm characteristics.

THE ELUSIVE NUMBER CALLED EARNINGS

The value of any asset is determined by its future earning power and not by what it cost at some time in the past. An economist would define earnings as cash flow plus the change in market value of an asset. Consider a bond originally purchased for $100 that carries a 10% interest rate. Assume the bond is worth $95 after one period. What has the earnings been on this investment over the period? The economist would say the earnings were $10 in interest plus the $5 decrease in value or a net of $5. An economist would apply the same principles to a physical investment. For example, if a manager purchases a machine, what are the earnings of the machine over the period? Clearly, one component of earnings is the profits earned from producing a product using the machine. An economist would argue that the change in the market value of the machine is also a part of earnings. The economist's concept of earnings is, of course, closely related to the idea of return we discussed in earlier chapters.

If an accountant reported the economist's definition of earnings and it was accurate, the analyst's job of valuing the asset or firm would be over. He or she could simply use the estimate of the change in the value of the asset or firm together with the old selling price to determine the new price. However, there is circularity. The best estimate of the change in the value of the asset is, of course, the actual change in the value of the asset. If the actual change is determined by the accountant's estimate, then how can the actual change be used as the estimate? The accountant can still look at the fundamental characteristics of the firm and try to estimate the change in value. Likewise, the accountant could just try to report the income earned in the single period and leave the estimating of the change in value to others. The accounting profession pursues a policy somewhere in between. The number the accountant calls earnings is a mixture of the income earned and an attempt to measure some part of the change in the value of the asset. The accountant's treatment of depreciation, research and development expenditures, and pension liabilities have elements associated with them that are related to change in value. However, these attempts to measure changes in value tend to be related more to the allocation or using up of historic costs than they are related to changes in market value. For example, depreciation reflects a somewhat arbitrary assumption about allocating the historical cost of an asset, as a change in value, over the life of an asset. The number the accountant uses for change in value (depreciation) is, at least in theory, related to the change in market value of an asset because the asset is used up. However, it makes no attempt to capture changes in the value of the asset due to either general or specific price changes. Thus, accounting earnings are a mixture of the within-period earnings and an easily replicated but somewhat arbitrary allocation of some of the change in value of the asset. This is not the end of the story. There are still more difficulties with accounting earnings.

The most often cited problem is the lack of consistency in defining the components of earnings for different firms. Leonard Spacek [25] has presented an interesting example in which he utilized generally accepted accounting principles and showed how he could obtain reported earnings ranging anywhere from $.80 to $1.79. This is highlighted in Table 17.1, reproduced from his tables. The first column shows the earnings of company A. Each subsequent column shows the effect of a change in accounting. For example, column three is a change in the method of depreciation. The last column shows the cumulative effect of several changes that results in earnings being increased from $.80 to $1.79. These various options make a major difference when making comparisons across firms. Two firms could be identical and yet have very different reported earnings per share. Let us consider a few of these changes in detail.

Table 17.1 Accounting Magic (All "In Conformity with Generally Accepted Accounting Principles")[a]

	Company A Col. 1	Company B's Profits Are Higher Because of:						Company B Col. 8
		Use of FIFO in Pricing Inventory Col. 2	Use of Straight-line Depreciation Col. 3	Deferring Research Costs Over 5 Years Col. 4	Funding Only the Pensions Vested Col. 5	Use of Stock Options for Incentives Col. 6	Including Capital Gains in Income Col. 7	
Sales in units	100,000 units $100 each							100,000 units $100 each
Sales in dollars	$10,000,000							$10,000,000
Costs and expenses								
Cost of goods sold	$ 6,000,000							$ 6,000,000
Selling, general and administrative	1,500,000							1,500,000
LIFO inventory reserve		$(400,000)[b]						—
Depreciation	400,000		$(100,000)					300,000
Research costs	100,000			(80,000)				20,000
Pension costs	200,000				$(150,000)			50,000
Officers' compensation								
Base salaries	200,000							200,000
Bonuses	200,000					$(200,000)		—
Total costs and expenses	$ 9,000,000	$(400,000)	$(100,000)	$(80,000)	$(150,000)	$(200,000)	$ —	$ 8,070,000

Profit before income taxes	$ 1,000,000	$ 400,000	$ 100,000	80,000	$ 150,000	$ 200,000	$ —	$ 1,930,000
Income taxes	520,000	208,000	52,000	42,000	78,000	104,000	—	1,004,000
	$ 480,000	$ 192,000	$ 48,000	$ 38,000	$ 72,000	$ 96,000	$ —	$ 926,000
Gain on sale of property (net of income tax)	—	—	—	—	—	—	$150,000	150,000
Net profit reported	$ 480,000	$ 192,000	$ 48,000	$ 38,000	$ 72,000	$ 96,000	$150,000	$ 1,076,000
Per share on 600,000 shares	$ .80	$ .32	$ .08	$.06	$ .12	$ .16	$ .25	$ 1.79
Market value at								
10 times earnings	$ 8.00	$3.20	$ .80	$.63	$1.20	$1.60	$2.50	$17.93
12 times earnings	$ 9.60	$3.84	$ .96	$.76	$1.44	$1.92	$3.00	$21.52
15 times earnings	$12.00	$4.80	$1.20	$.95	$1.80	$2.40	$3.75	$26.90

[a]Taken from Lorie and Hamilton [17].
[b]( ) denotes deduction.

Source: Spacek, "Business Success," p. 27.

When the economy experiences very high inflation rates, the differences in the treatment of the costs of material used from inventory becomes important for many firms. There are two generally accepted methods of determining the cost of material used from inventory LIFO and FIFO. LIFO (last in first out) uses as the cost of an item taken from inventory, the cost of the last identical item purchased for inventory. FIFO (first in first out) uses as the cost of an item taken from inventory, the cost of the oldest identical item in inventory. In periods of inflation the cost of the oldest item in inventory is often much lower than the cost of the most recent purchase of the same item. Using LIFO during periods of increasing inflation leads to lower reported earnings than the use of FIFO.

As a second case, consider pension liabilities. Pension liabilities are a source of increasing cost to firms. A firm makes a payment to the pension trustees to cover future liabilities. This payment is an expense to the firm and lowers earnings. The size of the payment a firm has to make depends, in part, on the assumed rate of return of the pension fund assets. Different rates of return can result in very different contributions and very different impacts on a firm's reported earnings.

There are no simple rules that allow an analyst to adjust the firm's earnings so that they are on a comparable basis. The impact of alternative accounting methods depends on the characteristics of the various firms. For example, the effect of differences in depreciation policies depends on the importance of fixed assets in the firm's costs, the age of the assets, and the life of the assets. The effect of differences in assumptions concerning the return on the pension assets depends on the size of the pension assets relative to the size of the firm's earnings. Thus, in comparing the earnings across firms, individual adjustments are necessary if they are to be put on a comparable basis.

The fact that different accounting methods can lead to different reported earnings, together with the belief held by many accountants and managers that earnings are important to the valuation process, has led to another problem. Accountants and management may attempt to manage the level and growth of earnings. There are a number of studies that have examined whether or not investors can see through attempts to manage earnings. While these studies support the hypothesis that they can, many firms believe the opposite strongly enough that they continue to incur costs in an attempt to manage reported earnings.

In the next part of this chapter we show that, despite the problems with accounting earnings, they still represent one of the important inputs in judging a firm's value.

THE IMPORTANCE OF EARNINGS

Several studies have shown that the ability to predict reported earnings, despite all the ambiguity in the meaning of "earnings," will lead to the investor earning superior returns.

An often quoted example is the study by Niederhoffer and Regan [21]. They determined the 50 best and worst performing stocks in 1970 and examined their characteristics. Compared to a random sample of 100 stocks, the 50 best performing stocks increased in value by between 37% and 125%. The 50 worst performing stocks declined in value by −49% to −78%. Table 17.2 shows the changes in earnings associated with each of these three groups of stocks.

The most striking difference between the best and worst performing securities is the actual change in earnings. The earnings for the worst performing securities declined dramatically while the earnings for the best performing firms increased substantially. This suggests strongly that stocks that perform well are stocks that have huge increases in earnings. Reported earnings would seem to be an important determinant of stock prices. The relationship between predicted earnings and price changes is much less clear. The worst performing firms had the higher predicted change in earnings.[1] However, in all cases where data were available, the actual change was less than predicted. In contrast, the best performing firms had a predicting earnings change only slightly higher than the random sample. However, in all but five cases examined, the actual change was higher than the predicted. This study suggests that stock price movements are associated with earnings changes and that differences between actual and predicted change lead to substantial price adjustments.

Elton, Gruber, and Gultekin [11] examined the effect of earnings estimates and price changes in greater detail. While Niederhoffer and Regan [21] examined the attributes of stocks that had high and low rates of return, Elton, Gruber, and Gultekin directly looked at the risk-adjusted excess return that could be earned by purchasing stocks on the basis of earnings and earnings forecast data. The first question they examined was, Do earnings affect prices? If reported earnings are important, then buying those stocks that will experience the largest growth in earnings should lead to an excess risk-adjusted return. To study this question, Elton, Gruber, and Gultekin divided stocks into deciles by the size of the next year's growth in earnings. Then they examined the excess risk-adjusted return that would be earned if each decile were purchased and held until after actual

Table 17.2

	Worst 50 Performers[a]	Best 50 Performers[a]	Random 100 Firms
Median actual change in earnings	−83%	+21.4%	−10.5%
Median predicted change in earnings	+15.3%	+ 7.7%	+ 5.8%
Median actual change in stock price	−56.7%	+48.4%	− 3.2%

[a]Some stocks were deleted in order to insure common fiscal year.

Source: Niederhoffer and Regan [21].

---

[1]Predictions were collected from a large number of security analysts as reported in Standard and Poor's earnings forecaster.

earnings were announced.[2] Stocks that had the highest future growth in earnings provided the highest excess return. The results were statistically significant at the 1% level. Furthermore, the results seem to be economically significant. For example, the 30% of firms that had the highest growth provided an excess risk-adjusted return of 7.48%, while the 30% of firms with the lowest growth (candidates for short sale) provided an excess risk-adjusted return of −4.93%. This provides strong evidence that reported earnings, despite their deficiencies, do impact stock prices.

The next logical subject to look at is the impact of expectational data on stock prices. Economists believe that expectations determine stock prices. If this is true, and the market is efficient, then expectations about future earnings should be incorporated into stock prices. It follows logically that the investor should not be able to make an excess return by either buying or selling stock on the basis of the average (consensus) expectations about future earnings.[3] On the other hand, if prices reflect the consensus estimate, then the investor should be able to earn large excess returns by acting on either the difference between consensus estimates and realizations or changes in the consensus estimates.

Elton, Gruber, and Gultekin examined whether an investor could make an excess return by buying and selling stocks on the basis of the consensus estimate of earnings growth. They divided stocks into deciles based on the consensus forecast of earnings growth. They found that there was no difference in excess return between the deciles. The investor who bought the stocks that were expected to have low growth would have done just as well as the one who bought the stocks with high expected growth. This is what one would expect if markets are reasonably efficient and expectations are reflected in security prices. Their second test involved dividing firms into deciles by the error in the forecast of earnings growth. Here the results were dramatically different. The firms for which the actual earnings growth was higher than the forecasted earnings growth had returns well above normal. The firms with actual earnings growth below estimated earnings growth had returns well below normal. An investor who could forecast earnings better than average could earn excess returns. Finally, Elton, Gruber, and Gultekin divided firms into deciles by the change in the forecast of earnings. This led to even higher returns. While it was profitable to forecast earnings, it was even more profitable to forecast the change in expectations about future earnings. A number of mutual funds have a strategy of buying high-growth firms. By itself this should not be a useful strategy. What is important is to find high-growth firms that the market believes will be low-growth firms. Even more valuable would be to forecast changes in the market's belief about the future growth of a firm.

---

[2]To define excess risk-adjusted return, Elton, Gruber, and Gultekin used the methodology outlined in "Efficient Markets," Chapter 15. Each portfolio had its return adjusted by subtracting from actual returns expected returns based on the market model $R_i = \alpha_i + \beta_i R_m$.

[3]The consensus estimate was defined as the average estimate of security analysts at major brokerage houses following a stock. Only stocks followed by three or more analysts were included in the study.

Table 17.3 Excess Returns by Eliminating from Portfolio Those Firms that Had Earnings Estimates the Most Above (or Least Below) Realizations

Percentage of Firms Eliminated	Excess Return if Completely Accurate	Excess Return if 50% Error	Excess Return if 90% Error
0%	0	0	0
10%	1.56	0.78	0.16
20%	2.88	1.44	0.29
30%	3.07	1.53	0.31
40%	4.32	2.16	0.43
50%	5.77	2.88	0.58
60%	7.35	3.67	0.74
70%	9.08	4.54	0.91
80%	9.90	4.95	0.99
90%	10.42	5.21	1.04

Source: Elton, Gruber, and Gultekin [11].

The studies just discussed provide strong evidence that earnings affect returns and that superior forecasts of earnings can lead to excess returns. The question is, How much better does the analyst have to be in order to earn excess returns? Table 17.3, taken from the Elton, Gruber, and Gultekin study, provides a partial answer to this question. The table shows the excess return that can be earned if analysts are able to identify the firms whose earnings will be less than the consensus forecast. For example, the second entry in the second column is 1.56%. If the analysts were able to eliminate the 10% of the stocks with the largest overestimate of growth, they would earn 1.56% more than normal, given the risk of the stocks. Likewise, if they were able to eliminate the 20% of stocks with the greatest overestimate of actual growth, an extra 2.88% return above normal would be earned. Columns 3 and 4 show the excess return if there is error in the analyst's ability to select firms with inaccuracies in the average estimate of earnings. The second column assumes that 50% of the time the analyst picks stocks, she picks one in the category shown (e.g., the 70% of the stocks with the least overestimate of average growth) and 50% of the time she picks stocks that have the average characteristics of the population of stocks. Column 4 is similar, except that it is assumed that the analyst can select from the best category only 10% of the time. As can be seen by examining these columns, even information with little accuracy can lead to excess returns.

This section illustrates the importance of earnings to the valuation process and the importance of being able to forecast earnings. In the next section we examine some time series characteristics of earnings and some methods for forecasting it.

CHARACTERISTICS OF EARNINGS AND EARNINGS FORECASTS

In this section we are going to analyze the characteristics of earnings. Are earnings changes highly related to the performance of the economy? Are future changes in earnings highly related to past earnings? Can analysts forecast earnings? In the last section we saw that good forecasts of earnings can lead to profitable returns. Hence, it is important to understand the characteristics of earnings and earnings changes.

The Influence of the Economy and Industry

In earlier chapters we showed that a stock's returns are strongly affected by market movements and by industry or sector returns. A similar phenomenon exists with respect to earnings. Earnings of a firm are strongly influenced by changes in aggregate earnings for the economy and there is some evidence that they are influenced by changes in the earnings of the industry to which the firm belongs. Table 17.4 illustrates the strength of these influences. The sample used in calculating this table was the earnings from 217 firms for the years 1948–1966. The earnings on the companies that comprise the S&P 425 index was used to represent the market index. The companies in the sample were divided into industries and the earnings averaged across each of the companies in the industry to obtain an industry index. The percentage of changes in each firm's earnings that could be attributed to the market and the industry was then determined. The results for individual firms were then averaged across an industry.

As can be seen by examining the table, on average 21% of the changes in firms' earnings can be accounted for by changes in the market's earnings, and an additional 21% of the changes in a firm's earnings can be accounted for by

Table 17.4 Proportion of Earnings Movement Attributable to Economy or Industry Influences

Industry	Economy Influence (%)	Industry Influence (%)
Aircraft	11	5
Autos	48	11
Beer	11	7
Cement	6	32
Chemicals	41	8
Cosmetics	5	6
Department Stores	30	37
Drugs	14	7
Electricals	24	8
Food	10	10
Machinery	19	16
Nonferrous Metals	26	25
Office Machinery	14	6
Oil	13	49
Paper	27	28
Rubber	26	48
Steel	32	21
Supermarkets	6	33
Textiles and Clothing	25	29
Tobacco	8	19
All Companies	21	21

Source: Brealey [2].

the changes in the industry earnings. The strength of these influences varied considerably. Earnings for companies in industries such as autos, chemicals, and steel seemed to be heavily influenced by market-wide changes. The earnings of firms in the oil industry and the rubber industry seemed to be strongly influenced by industry changes. Many of the differences shown in the table may well be unique to the period examined. However, the large effects of market and industry factors are probably indicative of real influences.[4] A forecast of economy-wide changes and industry-wide changes may be useful first steps in estimating the companies' earnings.

The important effect of the economy on a company's earnings can be illustrated in another way. A number of authors have divided earnings by the book value of the assets to obtain a return on assets. This is then correlated with a similar measure for the market. Gonedes [13] performed this correlation for 316 firms using data from 1946–1969. He found on average that 23% of the variation of return on book assets can be explained by variation in the market return on book assets.

Gonedes [14] also analyzed the correlation of total income (rather than earnings per share) and a similar measure for the economy and industry. His sample consisted of 99 firms in the years 1946–1968. Gonedes used the average of the total income for the firms in his sample as a measure of the economy's earnings. Similarly, he used the firms in his sample to obtain an average for each industry. Since the earnings of each industry are affected by the economy's earnings, he removed this influence before calculating the correlations. Gonedes found that the industry influence was insignificant once the effect of the economy was taken into account. However, he did find a strong influence of the economy. Over his full period he found that variations in aggregate income for the economy explained about 50% of the variation in the firm's total income.

All of these studies strongly suggest that changes in the economy's earnings influence the earnings of many firms. Furthermore, there is some evidence that industry earnings are also important.

In order to be able to utilize relationships such as those described above, it is necessary that the relationships be reasonably stable over time and that economy and industry earnings be more easily forecasted than the earnings for individual companies. There is no evidence concerning this. Thus, at this time, while we can say that economy-wide and industry-wide earnings are useful in explaining the earnings of individual companies, demonstration that this is useful in improving prediction must await further research.

Past Earnings and Future Earnings

Two separate issues have been examined with respect to the time series behavior of earnings. One is whether past growth is an indication of future growth. The second is whether the concept of normal earnings is meaningful. We discuss each of these in turn.

---

[4]There is some overstatement of the correlation since the firms themselves are part of the industry and economy.

One of the popular terms used in the financial literature is the term "growth stock." This term often refers to a stock that has had substantial growth in the past and is expected to in the future. Names like IBM and Xerox come to mind. From this, one would expect that stocks that have had high growth in the past would have high growth in the future. A number of studies have seriously questioned this assumption. Lintner and Glauber [16] examined the correlation of aggregate earnings and earnings per share for 323 companies during 1946–1965. The 20 years of data were divided in four five-year periods and two ten-year periods. Growth was estimated for each of these periods and correlations between the growth rates in adjacent periods was calculated.[5] The results give little comfort to anyone expecting past growth to predict the future. The highest association between successive growth rates implied that less than 2% of the variation in growth in the latter period was explained by growth in the earlier period. Lintner and Glauber introduced two modifications to try to improve the correlation in growth rates. First they deflated earnings by a measure of aggregate economic conditions. Second, they divided firms into groups by stability of growth rate and ran correlations within each group. This did lead to improvement. In one time period they were able to explain almost 50% of the variation in future growth rates by past growth rates. However, for most periods and most cases studied, less than 10% of the variation in future growth rates was explained by past growth.

Brealey [2] analyzed the same question in a slightly different way. He analyzed the growth of 610 industrial companies from 1950–1964. Each year he determined

Table 17.5

Length of Time in Same Group	No. of Consecutive Years of High Growth	No. of Consecutive Years of Low Growth	Expected No. of Consecutive Years of Low or High Growth if Odds are 50–50 Regardless of Past Performance
1	1,152	1,102	1,068
2	562	590	534
3	266	300	267
4	114	120	133
5	55	63	67
6	24	20	33
7	23	12	17
8	5	6	8
9	3	3	4
10	6	0	2
11	2	0	1
12	1	0	1
13	0	0	0
14	0	0	0

Source: Brealey [2].

[5]Growth was estimated using a logarithmic regression on time.

the 305 firms with the highest growth and the 305 firms with the lowest. If past growth is helpful in predicting future growth, then one would expect that firms would tend to have long periods when they were in the high-growth group and long periods when they were in the low-growth groups. The alternative is that the odds of being in either group is 50–50, independent of the firm's position in the previous period. Table 17.5 shows the results. The first column indicates the number of years the firms were in the same group. For example, the first entry in the second column is 1,152. This means 1,152 times firms were in the high-growth group one year and not in that group the next. The second entry, 562, means that 562 times firms were in the high-growth group two years in a row and in the low-growth group the next year. The first two columns look very similar to the last. In fact, the odds of long runs are, in general, higher for the last column than in the first two. The most striking place where the first two columns have higher odds than the last is for lengths of time one. But this implies that a good year follows a bad year more than expected by chance and vice versa.[6] This is the opposite of what one expects if past growth was a good predictor of the future.

These two studies are typical of the results found by a number of authors. These results have led them to speculate that earnings changes might be independent from period to period. The economic argument of why this might be so goes as follows: The economy is highly competitive. The earnings of a company are subject to a large number of uncertainties not under management control. These include strikes, mineral discoveries, regulatory changes, foreign competition, changing tastes, and so on. These kinds of uncertainties are the dominant influences on a company's fortunes on a year-to-year basis.

The counterargument is that there are a number of companies with monopoly control of the markets, with patent protection on unique products, or superior management, and these companies are able to sustain a high level of growth over a long period of time.

The argument for independence in earnings is much less persuasive than the argument for the independence of security prices presented in Chapter 15. Earnings are determined by a physical process while stock prices are determined by expectations. It is reasonable to assume that changes in expectations cannot be predicted from past data or they would already be incorporated in the expecta-

---

[6]There is a potential bias here. One plus growth from t to $t + 1$ is

$$\frac{\text{Earnings } t + 1}{\text{Earnings } t}$$

Likewise, one plus growth from $t - 1$ to t is

$$\frac{\text{Earnings } t}{\text{Earnings } t - 1}$$

Thus, earnings in t appear on both sides of the equation. Under certain circumstances (such as the reversion to the mean process of generating earnings discussed in the next section), this can cause a negative basis and could account for the results just discussed.

tions. It is a more stringent requirement to assume that past levels of a physical process do not convey information about the future. However, the empirical evidence reviewed above is a useful cautionary note to those who would place too heavy a reliance on past earnings to predict the future.

The second major issue concerning the time series of earnings is the concept of normal earnings. To understand this issue, it is easiest to ignore growth for the moment and to assume independence of earnings between time periods. One view of a firm's earnings is as follows: The firm's earnings are on average $1.00, but there is some variation. Table 17.6 shows a possible scenario. If this is the process that describes earnings, then one would expect, if earnings were at an extreme, they would be closer to the mean the next period. For example, if you observed earnings of $1.20 in one period, you would expect, on average, that they would be less the next period. Extremes followed by observations closer to the mean would tend to introduce a negative correlation in the time series.

The second alternative scenario is illustrated in Table 17.7. The distinctive element of this process is that there is no tendency to revert to some mean level of earnings. The change occurs from the last level of earnings. If earnings are $1.20, then 10% of the time they will increase by 10% to $1.32, 20% of the time they will increase by 5% to $1.26, and so forth. This period's earnings serve as a starting point for the change to next period's earnings. If we observe earnings of $1.20, we are just as likely to have an increase in the earnings as a decrease. With this view of earnings there is no such thing as extreme earnings and one would not expect the negative correlation discussed earlier.

The issue of which process describes earnings is important. If the first process is a better description, then the starting point for any forecast of future earnings is an estimate of the mean or "normal" earnings. If the second process is more descriptive, then the starting point of any forecast is the latest observed level of earnings.

Throughout the discussion we assumed zero growth. This just simplified the discussion. The same discussion holds with growth. If a process like that in Table 17.6 is descriptive of earnings patterns except for the presence of a growth rate, then the starting point for the estimate of earnings using historical earnings is normal earnings plus an estimate of growth. If the second model is more descriptive, then the starting point is this period's earnings plus an estimate of growth. We also assumed independence. If there is positive dependence, then this should mitigate the negative correlation in the first case and impart positive

Table 17.6   Possible Levels of Earnings

Earnings	Odds
1.20	10%
1.10	20%
1.00	40%
0.90	20%
0.80	10%

Table 17.7 Possible Changes in Earnings

Earnings Change	Odds
+10%	10%
+5%	20%
0%	40%
−5%	20%
−10%	10%

correlation in the second. There are two types of evidence on this issue. The first is correlation in successive earnings changes. Brealey examined this question and found slight negative correlation in the series. While this is supportive of the concept of normal earnings, it was so small that it is not very strong support. The second type of evidence is forecast evidence. Does this concept of normalized earnings lead to a better forecast of earnings or does using last period's earnings produce a better forecast?

Elton and Gruber [9] examined this question and found that allowing smoothing over a longer period of time led to better forecasts than did the simple use of last period's earnings. Ball and Watts, in contrast, found that last period's earnings worked best. There were two major differences in the studies. First, Elton and Gruber utilized much more complicated forecasting models than Ball and Watts.[7] Second, Ball and Watts required that the same forecasting model be used to forecast the earnings of all firms. Elton and Gruber allowed a different model for each firm and selected the one to use in making comparisons that had provided the most accurate forecasting of earnings in prior periods. For many firms this was, in fact, last period's earnings, but in other cases it was a smoothed value of past earnings. When Elton and Gruber allowed this variation, they achieved improved forecasts. Lieber and Ronen [15] repeated this for the Ball and Watts sample and found that allowing individual variation led to improved forecasting. Thus, reality probably includes both of the models of firm's earnings discussed in Tables 17.6 and 17.7. For many firms the concept of normal earnings is superior, while for other firms last period's earnings provide a better forecast of next period's earnings.

---

[7]Elton and Gruber [9] used an exponential smoothing model with an arithmetic change in growth. Their model is presented here:

Let E be earnings, g be growth, and subscripts indicate time periods. Let a and b be constants with a value between 0 and 1, and carets ($\cdot$) indicate smoothed values. Then:

1. Forecast of earnings $= \hat{E}_t + \hat{g}_t$
2. $\hat{E}_t = (\hat{E}_{t-1} + \hat{g}_{t-1}) + a[E_t - (\hat{E}_{t-1} + \hat{g}_{t-1})]$
3. $\hat{g}_t = (\hat{g}_{t-1}) + b[(\hat{E}_t - \hat{E}_{t-1}) - \hat{g}_{t-1}]$

In contrast, the Ball and Watts model [1] was:

1. Forecast of earnings $= \hat{E}_t$
2. $\hat{E}_t = a\hat{E}_{t-1} + (1 - a)E_t$

The research that has been done on using the time series of past earnings to predict future earnings is not very encouraging. The evidence seems to suggest that in many cases the naive model of next year's earnings equals this year's earnings seems to do as well as more sophisticated extrapolations. This should serve as a cautionary note to anyone predicting future earnings using the past levels.

Forecasting Earnings with Additional Types of Historical Data

Firms make available a great deal more information than past levels of earnings per share. Perhaps this information can be used to forecast future levels of earnings per share or future growth in earnings per share. For example, changes in sales or research and development expense or new investment might be related to future earnings. If such a relationship exists, then past values could be used to estimate the relationship and this relationship could be used to forecast the future.

How can this be done? Assume that a set of variables is important in estimating earnings per share for firms in the same industry. Then a forecasting equation could be determined by estimating across the firms in the industry the best relationship between this set of variables and future earnings. Elton and Gruber [10] tried this with 180 firm samples. They estimated for each industry in their sample a relationship between earnings and past values of other firm variables. They compared the forecasting equations derived for each industry with a method using past earnings alone. The method using past earnings alone was superior.

This does not necessarily mean that the basic idea is unsound. It is possible that the variables they selected were poor or the industry groupings they utilized were not homogeneous with respect to the variables affecting future earnings or the relationship between these variables and future earnings.

Elton and Gruber [10] explored this latter explanation. They divided firms into groups by similarity in the pattern of their previous growth. They argued that if firms had similar growth patterns they probably had responded to similar influences. Their procedure yielded a set of 10 groups or pseudo-industries. They then repeated the same analysis done previously, treating each of these 10 groups the same way they had treated traditional industries. This yielded a set of 10 forecast equations, one for each group. When they examined the accuracy of the forecasts generated in this way with the accuracy of a model utilizing only past earnings, they found that the forecasting equations utilizing other firm variables were superior. They repeated the analysis over several periods and several samples and the results were similar.

These results suggest that firm information, other than past earnings, may be useful in predicting future earnings.

Analysts' Forecasts

We have seen in earlier sections that accurate forecasts can lead to superior returns. Given this, it should not be surprising that security analysts spend a great

Table 17.8 Agreement among Growth-Rate Predictions

				Correlation Coefficients						
		1962						1963		
	A	*B*	*C*	*D*		*A*	*B*	*C*	*D*	*E*
A	1.000				*A*	1.000				
B	0.840	1.000			*B*	0.832	1.000			
C	0.889	0.819	1.000		*C*	0.854	0.764	1.000		
D	0.563	0.621	0.848	1.000	*D*	0.537	0.567	0.898	1.000	
					E	0.827	0.835	0.889	0.704	1.000

Source: Cragg and Malkiel [6].

deal of time forecasting earnings. In this section we intend to analyze the properties of these forecasts.

There seems to be a great deal of agreement among security analysts concerning
the future earnings of a company. Cragg and Malkiel [6] examined the correlation
between estimates of the growth in earnings forecasted by five different organizations in 1963 (labeled A to E) and four in 1962 (labeled A to D). Table 17.8
reproduces their results. An examination of the table shows that there is a high
degree of agreement among analysts concerning the future prospects of a company. They tested to see if this agreement came about because of a common
agreement concerning the prospects of particular industries and found that it was
not a major factor. Rather, the agreement comes about because of similar forecasts of individual companies.

Table 17.9 Predictions and Past Growth Rates[a] (Correlations of Predicted with Past
Growth Rates)

	1962				1963				
	A	*B*	*C*	*D*	*A*	*B*	*C*	*D*	*E*
g_{p1}	0.78	0.68	0.75	0.41	0.85	0.73	0.84	0.56	0.67
g_{p2}	0.75	0.67	0.72	0.51	0.79	0.69	0.80	0.58	0.76
g_{p3}	0.77	0.71	0.82	0.61	0.75	0.72	0.79	0.70	0.74
g_{p4}	0.34	0.37	0.59	0.44	0.33	0.45	0.70	0.75	0.58
g_{c1}	0.55	0.46	0.65	0.32	0.63	0.52	0.61	0.30	0.58
g_{c2}	0.67	0.60	0.68	0.18	0.72	0.58	0.73	0.20	0.56
g_{c3}	0.75	0.63	0.73	0.17	0.79	0.66	0.76	0.17	0.57
g_{c4}	0.82	0.68	0.79	0.24	0.83	0.69	0.79	0.29	0.60

[a] g_{p1} is 8–10 year historic growth rate supplied by A.
g_{p2} is 4–5 year historic growth rate supplied by A.
g_{p3} is 6 year historic growth rate supplied by D.
g_{p4} is preceding 1 year growth rate supplied by D.
g_{c1} is log-regression trend fitted to last 4 years.
g_{c2} is log-regression trend fitted to last 6 years.
g_{c3} is log-regression trend fitted to last 8 years.
g_{c4} is log-regression trend fitted to last 10 years.

Source: Cragg and Malkiel [6].

The second characteristic of analysts' estimates is that they are heavily influenced by past growth. Table 17.9 shows the correlations of the analysts' forecasts with a number of historical growth measures. Comparing this table with the previous one indicates that the correlation with past growth is just about as high as the correlation among the analysts. Analysts seem to place a heavy reliance on past growth rates in making their estimates of the future. Cragg and Malkiel went on to examine whether or not the correlation among analysts' estimates can be explained completely in terms of the correlation with past growth. Although the common reliance of analysts on past growth is an important reason for the similarity of forecasts, it is not the sole reason. After adjusting for the influence of past growth on analysts' forecasts, there is still a substantial amount of commonality in their forecasts.

In Chapter 23 we return to the question of the accuracy of analysts' forecasts. We place special emphasis on techniques for determining the accuracy of these forecasts.

CONCLUSION

In a later chapter we are going to analyze, in some detail, the accuracy of analysts' estimates. It is sufficient to state here that most studies have not found a great deal of predictive content in their estimates.

The studies discussed in this section do not provide a magic formula for predicting earnings. This should not be surprising, nor especially disturbing. Even if such a formula existed, its value would already be mitigated as investors utilized it to obtain superior predictions and this was reflected in security price. We view the studies discussed in this section as suggestive of the kinds of analysis that might be worthwhile as well as the types of behavior and research that are unlikely to be productive. Research is underway and should continue in this area.

QUESTIONS AND PROBLEMS

1. Write down the forecast of next period's earnings if:

    A. Earnings are a mean reverting process with no trend or cycle.

    B. Earnings are a mean reverting process with a trend but not a cycle.

    C. Earnings are a mean reverting process with a trend and a cycle.

2. How would earnings be forecast if there was a strong relationship between the firm's earnings and the industry's and economy's earnings?

3. Is a strong relationship between a firm's earnings and an economy's earnings consistent with a mean reversion process for earnings generation?

4. Is a strong relationship between a firm's earnings and an economy's earnings consistent with last period's earnings being a better estimate of next period's earnings than normal earnings?

5. If expectations determine share price, what is a valuable analyst?

BIBLIOGRAPHY

1. Ball, Ray, and Watts, Ross. "Some Time Series Properties of Accounting Numbers," *Journal of Finance,* **27** (June 1972), pp. 663–681.
2. Brealey, Richard. *An Introduction to Risk and Return from Common Stocks* (Cambridge, Mass.: M.I.T. Press, 1969).
3. Brown, Lawrence, and Rozeff, Michael. "The Superiority of Analyst Forecasts as Measures of Expectations: Evidence from Earnings," *Journal of Finance,* **XXXIII,** No. 1 (March 1978), pp. 1–16.
4. Chant, Peter D. "On the Predictability of Corporate Earnings per Share Behavior," *The Journal of Finance,* **35,** No. 1 (March 1980), pp. 13–22.
5. Copelåd, Ronald, and Marioni, Robert. "Executives' Forecasts of Earnings per Share Versus Forecasts of Naive Models," *Journal of Business,* **45,** No. 4 (Oct. 1972), pp. 497–512.
6. Cragg, J.G., and Malkiel, Burton. "The Consensus and Accuracy of Some Predictions of the Growth of Corporate Earnings," *Journal of Finance,* **XXIII,** No. 1 (March 1968), pp. 67–84.
7. Deschamps, Benoît, and Mchta, Dileep R. "Predictive Ability and Descriptive Validity of Earnings Forecasting Models," *The Journal of Finance,* **35,** No. 4 (Sept. 1980), pp. 933–950.
8. Edwards, Charles, and Hilton, James. "Some Comments on Short-Run Earnings Fluctuation Bias," *Journal of Financial and Quantitative Analysis,* **V,** No. 2 (May 1970), pp. 187–201.
9. Elton, Edwin J., and Gruber, Martin. "Earnings Estimation and the Accuracy of Expectational Data," *Management Science,* **18,** No. 2 (April 1972), pp. 409–424.
10. ———— . "Improved Forecasting Through the Design of Homogeneous Groups," *Journal of Business,* **44,** No. 4 (Oct. 1971), pp. 432–450.
11. Elton, Edwin, Gruber, Martin, and Gultekin, M. "The Usefulness of Analyst Estimates of Earnings," unpublished manuscript, 1978.
12. ———— . "Professional Expectations: Accuracy and Diagnosis of Errors," *Journal of Financial and Quantitative Analysis,* **19,** No. 4 (Dec. 1984), pp. 351–364.
13. Gonedes, Nicholas. "Evidence on the Information Content of Accounting Numbers: Accounting-Based and Market-Based Estimates of Systematic Risk," *Journal of Financial and Quantitative Analysis,* **VIII,** No. 3 (June 1973), pp. 407–443.
14. ———— . "A Note on Accounting-Based and Market-Based Estimates of Systematic Risk," *Journal of Financial and Quantitative Analysis,* **X,** No. 2 (June 1975), pp. 355–367.
15. Lieber, Zvi, and Ronen, Joshua. "Earnings Estimates and Historical Data," unpublished manuscript, Ross Center, New York University.
16. Lintner, John, and Glauber, Robert. "Higgeldy-Piggeldy Growth in America," unpublished manuscript, 1969.
17. Lorie, J., and Hamilton, M. *The Stock Market: Theories and Evidence* (Homeland, Ill.: Richard D. Irwin, 1973).

18. Mastrapasqua, Frank, and Bolten, Steven. "A Note on Financial Analyst Evaluation," *Journal of Finance,* **XXVIII,** No. 3 (June 1973), pp. 707–712.
19. McEnally, Richard. "An Investigation of the Extrapolative Determinants of Short-run Earnings Expectations," *Journal of Financial and Quantitative Analysis,* **VI,** No. 2 (March 1971), pp. 687–706.
20. Newell, Gale. "Revisions of Reported Quarterly Earnings," *Journal of Business,* **44,** No. 3 (July 1971), pp. 282–285.
21. Niederhoffer, V., and Regan, P. "Earnings Changes, Analysts' Forecasts, and Stock Prices," *Financial Analysts Journal,* **28,** No. 3 (May–June 1972), pp. 65–71.
22. Penman, Stephen H. "The Predictive Content of Earnings Forecasts and Dividends," *The Journal of Finance,* **38,** No. 4 (Sept. 1983), pp. 1181–1200.
23. ——— . "A Comparison of the Information Content of Insider Trading and Management Earnings Forecasts," *Journal of Financial and Quantitative Analysis,* **20,** No. 1 (March 1985), pp. 1–18.
24. Richards, Malcolm. "Analysts' Performance and the Accuracy of Corporate Earnings Forecasts," *Journal of Business,* **49,** No. 3 (July 1976), pp. 350–357.
25. Spacek, Leonard. In Lorie, J., and Hamilton, M. [17], p. 146.

Chapter 18

Interest Rate Theory and the Pricing of Bonds

Until recently, bond valuation was considered a rather dull subject. After all, a bond is easier to value than a stock because the issuer has agreed to a certain stream of payments (coupon and principal) and the bond has a maximum life (maturity). Of course, bonds can be made more complex by sinking fund provisions or by call features or by other special attributes; but most special features can be valued separately and added to the value of a basic bond. The basic bond should be valued as the present value of the promised cash flows over the life of the bond. Adjustments can be made for risk or other special considerations. When adjustments are made for risk, they are usually based on the risk of default.

When interest rates go up, bond prices fall so that outstanding bonds offer returns similar to those earned by new issues. Interest rates were volatile during the 1970s and early 1980s. Accompanying this increased volatility were huge swings in the market value of bond portfolios. This increased volatility in market values was viewed as an opportunity and as a risk. Active bond portfolio management began to receive a lot of attention.

Table 18.1 presents the yearly holding period return that would have been earned by holding four different portfolios of bonds from 1973 to 1982. The returns from holding long-term corporate bonds were extremely volatile over this period. For example, the return from this portfolio was −0.15% in 1981 and 44.52% in 1982. These returns bear little resemblance to the interest rate on long-term bonds during those years. Given the variability of bond returns, you might suspect that we are heading toward a consideration of a portfolio theory for bonds. In fact, that is the subject of the next chapter. But before we attempt to construct portfolio strategies, we must understand the pricing of bonds —

Table 18.1 Yearly Holding Period Return Earned by Four Diversified Bond Portfolios

Portfolio	1973	1974	1975	1976	1977	1978	1979	1980	1981	1982
Lehman Government Bond Index										
Intermediate	3.36	7.03	8.33	11.73	3.01	2.22	6.59	6.65	10.78	25.42
Long term	0.88	3.36	9.08	17.44	1.30	-1.11	-0.86	-2.96	0.48	42.08
Lehman Corporate Bond Index										
Intermediate	3.19	1.06	14.16	14.63	4.60	1.65	3.35	5.34	8.98	30.02
Long term	1.09	-7.61	17.56	21.03	2.67	-0.10	-4.08	-2.60	-0.15	44.52

discussed in this chapter. The first part of this chapter discusses the many meanings of interest rates and places special emphasis on the role of one of these rates, the spot rate, in determining bond prices. The second part of the chapter discusses the determination of bond prices. The third and longer part of the chapter deals with the factors that explain bond prices.

THE MANY DEFINITIONS OF RATES

An investor who examines the literature on bond valuation will find a confusing array of terms all seemingly related to interest rates — terms like spot rates, future rates, yield to maturity, and current yield. In the following we define and explain these alternative rates.

Three dates that are important in determining the rate of interest on a loan are the date on which the lender and borrower set the fixed rate on the loan (the commitment date), the date the money is to be lent, and the date the money is to be repaid.

Let

1. i be the rate of interest
2. t_0 be the date of the commitment
3. t_1 be the date of the loan
4. t_2 be the date the loan is to be repaid

Then we write an interest rate as

$$_{t_0}i_{t_1 t_2}$$

Throughout most of this chapter we will be concerned with a commitment date at time zero. Therefore $t_0 = 0$ and we suppress t_0 and write the interest rate as $i_{t_1 t_2}$.

There are alternative rates of interest each with its own name. For example, names can differ depending on the cash flow pattern of the bond. It is useful to understand what these different names mean. Spot interest rates are interest rates on loans or bonds that have only one cash flow to the investor. A bond with only one cash flow to the investor is called a pure discount bond or a zero coupon bond. Thus a bond that involves an investment of $797.19 and returns a principal of $1000 in two years is a two-year pure discount bond. The return on such a bond is the two-year spot rate. Recognizing i_{02} as the two-year spot rate expressed on an annualized basis

$$\$797.19 = \frac{1{,}000}{(1 + i_{02})^2}$$

and

$$i_{02} = 12\%$$

Rates are normally quoted as annual rates. Thus i_{02} is earned each year and one plus the two-year return is $(1 + i_{02})^2$.

Table 18.2 presents a number of other examples of spot rates. Each bond is assumed to cost the amount shown. The cash flows associated with each bond are as indicated. Note that these cash flows involve only a principal payment. The spot rates are calculated and displayed in Table 18.2. As we will see later in the chapter, spot rates play an important role in bond pricing. Until the early 1980s the only pure discount bonds were bonds issued by the U.S. government with maturities of one year or less. These instruments are called Treasury bills. As a result, more complex techniques involving the inference of spot rates from coupon paying bonds are necessary in order to estimate longer term spot rates. The techniques used in this calculation are discussed in the appendix. In the early 1980s, corporations started to issue pure discount instruments with longer maturities and brokerage firms put together packages of coupon bonds and sold off each year's payment separately, thereby creating pure discount bonds. These bonds were called "striped coupon" bonds. However, these bonds are sufficiently limited in number that the techniques of the appendix are still needed in order to calculate spot rates for maturities over one year.

A second category of interest rates is forward rates. Forward rates are interest rates on bonds where the date the commitment is made and the date the money is loaned are different. If a commitment is made now on a two-year loan to commence in one year, the annualized interest rates from year 1 to year 3 is a forward rate. For example, assume $797.19 is to be lent in year 1 and $1000 to be repaid in year 3. This is a two-year forward rate to begin in year 1. This rate is designated as

$$(1 + i_{13})^2 = \frac{1,000}{\$797.19}$$

Thus,

$$i_{13} = 12\%$$

Table 18.3 shows the calculation of forward rates for a series of bonds with different cash flow patterns. You should make certain that you understand these calculations. Forward rates are often estimated from spot rates. If 12% is the two-period spot rate and 11% is the one-period spot rate, then the one-period forward rate in the second period is

$$i_{23} = \frac{(1.12)^2}{1.11} - 1 = .13$$

Thus, the one-period forward rate on a loan to begin in one year is 13%.

A third type of rate is current yield. Current yield is simply the annual coupon

Table 18.2 Cash Flow Patterns with Pure Discount Bonds

| | | Cash Flows of Pure Discount Bond | | | | | | Determination of Spot Rate | |
| | | Cash Inflows | | | | | | | |
Maturity	Cost	1	2	3	4	5	Symbol	Calculation	Spot Rate
1	-$909.09	1,000					i_{01}	$(1 + i_{01})^2 = \dfrac{1,000}{909.09}$	$i_{01} = 10\%$
2	-$811.62	0	1,000				i_{02}	$(1 + i_{02})^2 = \dfrac{1,000}{811.62}$	$i_{02} = 11\%$
3	-$711.78	0	0	1,000			i_{03}	$(1 + i_{03})^3 = \dfrac{1,000}{711.78}$	$i_{03} = 12\%$
4	-$635.52	0	0	0	1,000		i_{04}	$(1 + i_{04})^4 = \dfrac{1,000}{635.52}$	$i_{04} = 12\%$
5	-$519.37	0	0	0	0	1,000	i_{05}	$(1 + i_{05})^5 = \dfrac{1,000}{519.37}$	$i_{05} = 14\%$

Table 18.3 Determination of Forward Rates

Date of Loan	Length of Loan in Years	Cash Flow Pattern (Minus Are Outlays)					Determination of Forward Interest Rates		
		1	2	3	4	5	Symbol	Calculation	Forward Rate
1	1	-909.09	1,000				i_{12}	$(1 + i_{12})^1 = \dfrac{1,000}{909.09}$	$i_{12} = 10\%$
1	2	-797.19	0	1,000			i_{13}	$(1 + i_{13})^2 = \dfrac{1,000}{797.19}$	$i_{13} = 12\%$
2	2		-797.19	0	1,000		i_{24}	$(1 + i_{24})^2 = \dfrac{1,000}{797.19}$	$i_{24} = 12\%$
3	2			-811.62	0	1,000	i_{35}	$(1 + i_{35})^2 = \dfrac{1,000}{811.62}$	$i_{35} = 11\%$
4	1				-884.96	1,000	i_{45}	$(1 + i_{45})^1 = \dfrac{1,000}{884.96}$	$i_{45} = 13\%$

payment divided by the price. If a bond pays $50 semi-annually and costs $800, its current yield is 12.5%. This is determined by 100/800 = 12.5%. Current yield is the "interest rate" normally quoted in the financial press. It has very limited usefulness. Current yield is not the expected return over the year, nor is it the return if the bond is held to maturity. For example, the current yield on a pure discount instrument is zero, since it has zero coupons. An investor who selects investments on the basis of current yield will reject bonds with low coupons but large return in the form of capital gains.

A fourth type of rate is yield to maturity. Yield to maturity is the interest figure quoted most often by the investment community. It is the internal rate of return earned from holding a bond to maturity. The yield to maturity on a three-year bond with annual interest payments of $100, a principal payment of $1,000, and a cost of $900 is that rate that equates the present value of the three cash flows on the bond with its present price of

$$900 = \frac{100}{(1 + i)} + \frac{100}{(1 + i)^2} + \frac{100 + 1,000}{(1 + i)^3}$$

Therefore,

$$i = 14.3\%$$

How do you solve $? besides plugging in numbers.

Most bonds pay semi-annual interest rates. This must be taken into account in calculating the yield to maturity. The yield to maturity on these bonds is calculated differently. Assume a three-year bond with semi-annual interest payments of $50, a principal payment of $1,000, and a cost of $900. The yield to maturity is calculated as follows.

$$900 = \frac{50}{\left(1 + \frac{i}{2}\right)} + \frac{50}{\left(1 + \frac{i}{2}\right)^2} + \frac{50}{\left(1 + \frac{i}{2}\right)^3}$$

$$+ \frac{50}{\left(1 + \frac{i}{2}\right)^4} + \frac{50}{\left(1 + \frac{i}{2}\right)^5} + \frac{1,050}{\left(1 + \frac{i}{2}\right)^6}$$

Thus,

$$i = 14.2\%$$

The yield to maturity is the return to the investor if he or she holds the bond to maturity and if coupons are reinvested at the yield to maturity. The yield to maturity is generally not the return that would be earned if the bond were sold before maturity. The yield to maturity on a pure discount bond is the spot rate.

In the next section we discuss which rates determine bond prices and returns.

BOND PRICES AND SPOT RATES

Table 18.4 shows the cash flows associated with three different bonds. The bonds have cash flows in two periods. The cash flows from bond A can be reproduced by taking $^{22}/_{21}$ of bond B and $^{1}/_{21}$ of bond C. Thus an investor who desires the cash flow pattern of bond A can either purchase bond A directly or $^{22}/_{21}$ of bond B and $^{1}/_{21}$ of bond C. Don't be disturbed that the weights don't add up to one. These are not portfolio weights representing the proportion of the money placed in each asset; rather, they represent how much of B and C must be purchased to duplicate the cash flows of bond A. If the fractions are bothersome, the equivalent transaction is the purchase of 22 bond B's and 1 bond C to duplicate the cash flow of 21 bond A's.

Assume that bond A is more expensive than the corresponding portfolio of bonds B and C. Then an investor wishing to hold bond A could purchase the equivalent more cheaply by buying a combination of bonds B and C. Similarly, an investor holding bond A could sell bond A and replace it with $^{22}/_{21}$ of bond B and $^{1}/_{21}$ of bond C. The portfolio would still have the same cash flow but the investor would obtain an immediate riskless profit equal to the difference in price of bond A and the price of the portfolio of bonds B and C less transaction costs.

A similar argument can be made if bond A is cheaper. In this case, any investor holding bonds B and C could replace an appropriate mixture of them with bond A, maintain the same cash flows, and obtain an immediate riskless profit. The belief that the price of A should be equal to the price of an appropriate mixture of B and C is an application of the law of one price.

Table 18.4   Cash Flows Associated with Three Different Bonds

		Cash Inflows	
Bond	Price	1	2
A	P_A	10	110
B	P_B	5	105
C	P_C	100	0

The law of one price states that two identical items should sell at the same price. In this case, the identical items are the cash flows of bond A and the cash flows from the portfolio of $^{22}/_{21}$ of bond B and $^{1}/_{21}$ of bond C. If these items do not sell at the same price, then everyone interested in the bonds will buy the cheaper, or anyone holding the more expensive bond will swap the more expensive for the cheaper, until they are the same price.

The law of one price has an important implication for bond pricing. It implies that if bonds A, B, and C are of identical risk, such as all government bonds, then alternative cash flows arising in the same period must be discounted at an identical rate. This does not imply that the same rate is used each period, just that all cash flows that occur in the same period must be discounted at an identical rate. We can demonstrate why this is true with an example: If

1. $i_{01} = 10\%$

2. $i_{02} = 12\%$

then

$$P_A = \frac{10}{(1.10)} + \frac{110}{(1.12)^2} = \$96.78$$

$$P_B = \frac{5}{1.10} + \frac{105}{(1.12)^2} = \$88.25$$

$$P_C = \frac{100}{1.10} = \$90.91$$

With these prices the price of bond A is equal to the sum of $^{22}\!/_{21}$ of the price of bond B and $^{1}\!/_{21}$ of the price of bond C: $^{22}\!/_{21}$ (88.25) + $^{1}\!/_{21}$ (90.91) = \$96.78. If the discount rate for the cash flows of any of the three bonds is different, then the price of bond A is not the same as the price of the portfolio and the law of one price is violated. For example, if the first-period cash flow for bond B is discounted at 11%, its price is \$88.21, and the price of the portfolio is less expensive than bond A. This general principle has to hold for all bonds including pure discount bonds. Thus, the rate used to discount the cash flows is the spot rate. In summary, either bonds are priced so that their price is equal to the present value of their cash flows discounted at the spot rates, or the law of one price is violated and swap opportunities that were described earlier in the chapter are available. As discussed previously, forward rates can be derived from spot rates; therefore, forward rates can be used equally well to determine bond prices.

THE DETERMINANTS OF BOND PRICES

Bonds can differ in a number of respects. These differences affect bond prices, spot rate, yields to maturity, the expected return in the next period, and the risk associated with next period's return. Standard bond theory deals with the determination of the yield to maturity or price. The yields to maturity on bonds differ for a number of reasons. Among the more important are the following.

1. The length of time before the bond matures.

2. The risk of not receiving coupon and principal payments.

3. The tax status of the cash flows.

4. The existence of provisions that allow the corporation or government to redeem the debt before maturity.

5. The amount of the coupon.

Term to Maturity and Term Structure Theory

In order to gain insight into the effect of maturity on the yield or price of a bond, it is necessary to understand the relationship between yield and time. This relationship is usually called the term structure. More precisely, the theory of the term structure of interest rates deals with why pure discount bonds of different maturities have different yields to maturity.[1] In the last section, it was pointed out that spot rates are equivalent to the yield to maturity on pure discount instruments. Thus, term structure theory could be described equally well as dealing with the determination of spot rates.

In analyzing the effect of maturity on yield, all other influences are held constant. Pure discount instruments are chosen to eliminate the effect of coupon payments. In addition, most analysis is done using government bonds without early redemption features. Therefore, bonds of different maturities are similar with respect to risk, tax liabilities, and redemption possibilities.

Figures 18.1 and 18.2 depict two different yield curves. Figure 18.1 shows a yield curve where the yield to maturity declines as maturity increases. In Figure 18.2 the yield curve has a more normal upward slope. Term structure theory deals with why we observe these different shapes. In the next sections we will discuss four different explanations.

Segmented Market Theory   Segmented market theory has its origin in the observation that many investors and issuers of debt seem to have a strong preference for debt of a certain maturity. Furthermore, they seem to be insensitive to differentials in yields between debt of this maturity and debt of a different maturity.

Consider first debt with a long maturity. Let us examine the problem of maturity selection from the viewpoint of an insurance company. Life insurance companies offer insurance policies that are unlikely to require any payment for a long time. An insurance policy issued to a 25-year-old individual may involve 25 or more years before the company anticipates having to make a payment. The size of the

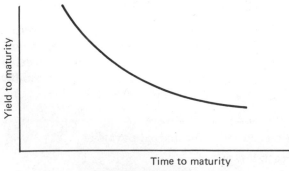

Figure 18.1.   Possible term structure.

---

[1] Term structure theory is often incorrectly defined as explaining why coupon paying bonds of different maturities have different yields to maturity.

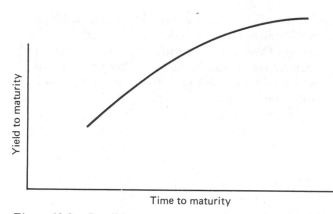

Time to maturity

Figure 18.2. Possible term structure.

premium payments is determined in part by the anticipated interest rate. If the insurance company invests in a long-term bond, the interest earned on the bond is known and if it exceeds what was promised on the insurance contract, it substantially reduces the insurance company's risk. There is still some risk because the coupon payments will have to be reinvested at some future unknown rate. However, the principal remains invested at a known rate, which substantially reduces the risk. Alternatively, the insurance company could meet its long-term obligation by buying a sequence of one-year bonds. However, in this case, all earnings beyond the first year are unknown. If interest rates decline below what was anticipated in the insurance contract, the company may have difficulty meeting its obligations. Not only is there uncertainty associated with the rate that will be earned on the investment of the coupon payments, there is also uncertainty about the rate earned on the principal. Consequently, many insurance companies invest in long-term bonds even when short-term rates are considerably higher than long-term rates.

Let us examine the maturity selection problem from the viewpoint of the issuers of long-term debt. The construction of a manufacturing plant or warehouse or other physical facility can involve a large expenditure of funds for a corporation. These structures are long-lived assets. Corporations normally wish to pay for them over a long period of time. They can achieve this payment pattern by issuing long-term debt. Alternatively, they can issue short-term debt and keep reissuing it for a long period of time. If they issue the long-term debt, their costs are known ahead of time and there is no interest rate risk associated with the investment. This suggests that corporations will generally issue long-term debt to meet these types of obligations.

Similar considerations apply to short-term debt. Corporations have a number of known short-term obligations that occur at fixed intervals: tax payments and wages are two examples. Money is normally put aside to meet these obligations. If the corporation buys pure discount securities maturing exactly on the date the payment is due, they have zero risk concerning the amount of money they will have available. If they buy a longer term security, the treasurer faces the risk that interest rates will increase, the price of the security will fall, and the amount that will be available to meet the obligations will be less than anticipated. Commercial banks hold a large number of short-term securities. For example, checking accounts comprise a large percentage of the liabilities of commercial banks. Commercial banks engage in short-term lending in order to match the maturity of their assets with the maturity of their debt.

Market segmentation theory argues that investors are sufficiently risk averse that they operate only in their desired maturity spectrum. No yield differential will induce them to change maturities. Thus, what determines long-term rates is solely the supply and demand of long-term funds. Similarly, short-term rates are determined only by supply and demand of short-term funds. People who believe in market segmentation theory examine flows of funds into these market segments in order to predict changes in the yield curve.

Market segmentation theory is very popular with practitioners. Statements in the popular press often display an implicit belief in the market segmentation theory. The theory is much less popular with academics, who maintain that while there are investors who have strong maturity preferences, there are others who are attracted by relative yields. The effects of segmentation on interest rates will be offset if there are enough such investors.

Pure Expectations Theory   The pure expectations theory explains the term structure in terms of expected one-period spot rates. Advocates of the expectations theory believe that the yield on a two-year bond is set so that the return on the two-year bond is the same as the return on a one-year bond plus the expected return on a one-year bond purchased one year hence.

If the expectations theory is correct, then an upward sloping yield curve is an indication that short-term rates are expected to increase. Similarly, a flat yield curve is an indication that short-term rates are likely to remain the same. Finally, a downward sloping yield curve indicates that short-term rates are expected to decline.

The easiest way to understand the expectations theory is to assume that the investors setting prices don't care about risk (are risk neutral). In this case, no matter what their time horizon, they will select the security or securities that give them the highest expected return. This is exactly the opposite of the market segmentation theory. Consider an investor with a two-year time horizon. Assume that the yield to maturity on a pure discount one-year bond is 10% and on a two-year pure discount bond is 12%. Furthermore, assume that the investor expects the one-year spot rate to be 16% in one year. The two-year investment can be accomplished by holding a two-year bond with earnings per dollar invested of

$$1(1.12)^2 - 1 = 1.254 - 1 = 25.4¢$$

Alternatively, the investor can hold two one-year bonds with expected earnings per dollar invested of

$$1(1.1)(1.16) - 1 = 1.276 - 1 = 27.6¢$$

The 16% is, of course, the expected one-period spot rate one year in the future. Given this combination of observed and expected rates, holding two one-year bonds gives the higher return, and all two-period investors will wish to hold one-period bonds.

The same choice will be made by investors with different horizons. To see this, consider an investor with a one-period horizon. This investor has a choice of buying the one-year bond or buying the two-year bond and selling it in one year. In one year, the two-year bond will have one year remaining in its life. At that point it will have to offer the same yield as a newly issued one-year bond. With annual payment of interest, the two-year bond will pay $1.12 at maturity for each dollar invested. For it to have a 16% return with a year left before it matures, its price per dollar invested must be

$$\frac{\$1.12}{\$1.16} = 0.966$$

This price offers the investor a 16% yield since multiplying it by 1.16 gives the ending value of 1.12. An investment in a one-year bond earns the investor 10¢. An investment in a two-year bond for one year earns the investor 12¢ in coupon payments. However, the sale of the two-year bond will result in a loss of $1 less 96.6¢ or 3.4¢. The net return is 12¢ − 3.4¢ or 8.6¢. Thus, the investor with a one-year horizon expects to earn a greater return from buying a one-year bond than from buying a two-year bond and selling it in one year.

We have analyzed the return for investors with one- and two-year horizons. The same results apply to investors with any other horizon. Thus, investors with three-year horizons will find investment in a one-year bond preferable to investment in the two-year bond. Given this universal preference, prices should adjust until the expected return from holding a two-year bond is exactly the same as the expected return from holding two one-year bonds.

Let us examine an example of what the ten-year rate must be, given actual and expected one-year rates. Assume one-year rates are 10% this period and are expected to be 16% one year hence. Recall that i_{02} is the yield to maturity on a two-year pure discount bond. We can determine i_{02} by equating final wealth from investment in a two-year bond with final wealth from investing in two one-year bonds.

Thus,

$$(1 + i_{02})^2 = (1.10)(1.16)$$

or

$$i_{02} = 13\%$$

Under the expectations theory the yield curve can be derived directly from a series of expected one-period spot rates. Table 18.5 shows two hypothesized

sequences of expected one-period rates. One of these sequences produces an
upward sloping yield curve while the other sequence produces a downward sloping
yield curve. All of the entries are calculated in the same manner as the prior
example. For example, the entry for period 3 for the upward sloping yield curve
is determined by

$$(1 + i_{03})^3 = (1.10)(1.11)(1.12)$$

$$i_{03} = .11$$

Table 18.5 Two Hypothesized Sequences of Expected One-period Rates

| | Upward Yield Curve | | Downward Yield Curve | |
Period	Expected One-period Spot Rates	Yield to Maturity	Expected One-period Spot Rates	Yield to Maturity
1	10	10.0	10	10.0
2	11	10.5	9	9.5
3	12	11.0	8	9.0
4	13	11.5	7	8.5
5	14	12.0	6	8.0
6	15	12.5	5	7.5
7	16	13.0	5	7.1
8	16	13.4	5	6.9
9	16	13.6	5	6.7
10	16	13.9	5	6.5

Similarly, under the expectations theory the market's belief about future one-
period rates can easily be derived from an observed yield curve.

It is important to keep in mind the distinction between the one-year rate
expected to prevail one year from now ($_1\bar{i}_{12}$) and the one-year forward rate, $_0i_{12}$.
The expectations theory simply states that the two must be equal.[1] In the next
two sections we examine alternative theories under which they are no longer
equal.

Liquidity Premium Theory Liquidity premium theory is also based on investors
analyzing the returns from holding bonds of varying maturities. However, unlike
expectations theory, liquidity premium theory assumes investors must be offered
a higher expected return to hold a bond with a horizon different from their
preferred horizon. Furthermore, it is assumed that there is a shortage of longer
term investors so that extra return must be offered on long-term bonds to induce
investors to hold them.

In the prior example, we considered investors with one- and two-period time
horizons. We assumed the one-period rate was 10% and the one-period rate that
was expected to prevail one period hence was 16%. Under the expectations

---

[1] $_1\bar{i}_{12}$ is the spot rate that is expected to prevail at time 1. The expectation is as of time 0.

theory, the two-period rate would be 13%. With the liquidity premium theory, this rate would have to be higher. The assumption is that there is an excess of investors with short-term horizons. These investors have a choice of holding a one-year bond or of holding a two-year bond and selling it in one year. The investment in the two-year bond involves risk to the one-year investor. In order to induce some one-year investors to hold two-year bonds a premium will have to be offered. Thus the return from holding a two-year bond will be above the expected return from holding two one-year bonds.

For an investor with a one-year horizon, a bond with a maturity longer than two years is even riskier than a two-year bond. Thus, an even larger premium would be required on three- and four-year bonds. If the market is dominated by short-term investors, then the longer-term bonds will require larger premiums. This is the basic idea behind liquidity premium theory.

An investor with a long-term horizon can hold a bond matching his or her horizon and earn the liquidity premium. Thus, such an investor earns an extra return without any extra risk.

In Table 18.6 we have taken the returns from Table 18.5 and added a liquidity premium to each. These are then used to construct a term structure. For example, for period 3 the yield to maturity was calculated by solving for i_{03} where

$$(1 + i_{03})^3 = (1.10)(1.11 + 0.002)(1.12 + 0.004)$$

or

$$i_{03} = 11.2\%$$

Even though Yield curve declining, liquidity premium increases.

Table 18.6   Yield Curve with a Liquidity Premium

Period	Upward Sloping Yield Curve			Downward Sloping Yield Curve		
	Expected One-period Spot Rate	Liquidity Premium	Yield to Maturity	Expected One-period Spot Rates	Liquidity Premium	Yield to Maturity
1	10	0	10.00	10	0	10.00
2	11	0.2	10.60	9	0.2	9.60
3	12	0.4	11.20	8	0.4	9.20
4	13	0.6	11.79	7	0.6	8.80
5	14	0.8	12.39	6	0.8	8.39
6	15	1.0	12.98	5	1.0	7.99
7	16	1.2	13.57	5	1.2	7.73
8	16	1.4	14.05	5	1.6	7.59
9	16	1.6	14.44	5	2.0	7.53
10	16	1.8	14.77	5	2.4	7.51

Liquidity premium theory modifies the conclusions drawn in the prior section concerning the shape of the yield curve and the implied one-period rates in future periods. If expectations are for an unchanged one-period rate, then the presence

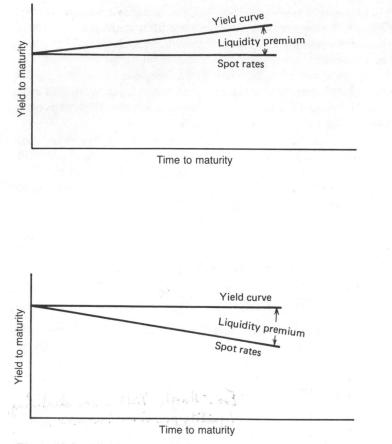

Figure 18.3.   Yield curves with liquidity premiums.

of a liquidity premium imparts an upward sloping shape to the yield curve. Even if expectations are for a declining series of one-period rates, it is still possible to observe an upward sloping yield curve. This would occur if the risk premiums were sufficiently large to overcome the expectations of a decline in one-period rates. Thus an upward sloping yield curve would be consistent with any pattern of expectations concerning one-period rates. A flat or downward sloping yield curve is only consistent with a decrease in one-period rates.

Figure 18.3 depicts two yield curves and the associated liquidity premiums.

Preferred Habitat   Preferred habitat theory rests on the premise that investors who match the life of their assets with the life of their liabilities are in the lowest risk position. Matching the life of the assets and liabilities is their preferred position. If their is sufficient extra return to be earned on assets of other lives, they will adjust their position to include more of these higher yielding assets.

If this theory is correct, premiums will exist for maturities where there is insufficient demand. These premiums are necessary in order to induce investors to leave their preferred habitat. If there are a large number of firms issuing long-term debt relative to the number of investors interested in long-term debt, a premium will have to be offered on long-term debt. If many firms and institutions wish to issue short-term debt and there are few investors who wish to invest short terms, a premium will have to be offered on short-term debt.

What is meant by a premium? For simplicity consider two periods. Let i_{01} be the spot interest rate in the first period and $_1\bar{i}_{12}$ be the expected one-period spot rate in the second. If the expectations theory holds, the two-period rate expressed as a rate per period is

$$(1 + i_{02})^2 = (1 + i_{01})(1 + {_1\bar{i}_{12}})$$

Assume that there is a surplus of short-term investors and therefore an extra return is necessary to induce investors to hold the two-year bond. If P is the size of the premium then

$$(1 + i_{02})^2 = (1 + i_{01})(1 + {_1\bar{i}_{12}} + P)$$

$$P > 0$$

In this case, preferred habitat theory would result in a set of spot rates that could have been derived equally well from the liquidity premium theory. If, on the other hand, there is a need to move investors to the short term, holding the two-year bond will be less profitable than holding two one-year bonds or

$$(1 + i_{02})^2 = (1 + i_{01})(1 + {_1\bar{i}_{12}} + P)$$

with

$$P < 0$$

With the preferred habitat theory, the premiums can be positive or negative. Without an idea of the sign and size of the premiums, nothing can be concluded about future one-period rates from observing the yield curve.

Term Structure and Coupon Bonds In the last section we examined the term structure for pure discount bonds. We will now examine the term structure for coupon paying bonds. A coupon paying bond can be considered a portfolio of pure discount bonds. Consider a three-period bond with a coupon of $75 and a principal repayment of $1,000. Its price is calculated as follows.

$$\text{Price} = \frac{75}{(1 + i_{01})} + \frac{75}{(1 + i_{02})^2} + \frac{1{,}075}{(1 + i_{03})^3} \tag{18.1}$$

This bond can be viewed as one bond or as a portfolio of three bonds — one-period, two-period, and three-period pure discount bonds paying $75, $75, and $1,075, respectively. The price on this portfolio is given by Equation (18.1).

The price of the portfolio is, of course, the same as the price of the bond. The yield to maturity on the bond lies between the spot rates. Let us examine what this implies for yield curves of coupon bonds relative to yield curves of pure discount bonds. Consider a downward sloping yield curve. The spot rates associated with the earlier coupon payments are higher than the spot rate associated with the final maturity. Since the yield to maturity lies between these rates, the yield to maturity on the coupon bond lies above the spot rate associated with the final payment (see Figure 18.4). The higher the coupon payments, the greater the importance of earlier payments relative to the last payment and the more important the influence of earlier spot rates on the yield to maturity. Thus the higher the coupon payment, the greater the difference between the yield to maturity on the coupon paying bond and the spot rate on the final payment.

Figure 18.4 shows the plot of yield to maturity on coupon bonds compared to pure discount bonds. As just discussed, the greater the coupon, the greater the difference between yields to maturity and the spot rate of the final payment.

If the yield curve is upward sloping, then the yield to maturity on coupon bonds lies below the yield to maturity on discount bonds. The larger the coupon, the greater the difference between the yield on the coupon and noncoupon debt. Figure 18.5 plots the yield to maturity on bonds with various coupons with upward sloping yield curves.

A number of organizations examine yield curves on coupon paying debt. Pure discount debt for government bonds did not exist at all for bonds with maturities over one year until the 1980s. When pure discount debt for longer maturities was first offered, it was created by brokerage firms removing coupons from coupon bonds and selling them off separately. These instruments are not quite equivalent to pure discount government bonds since they may be less marketable

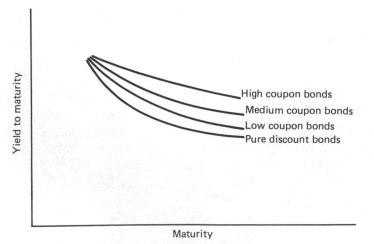

Figure 18.4. Possible term structure curves.

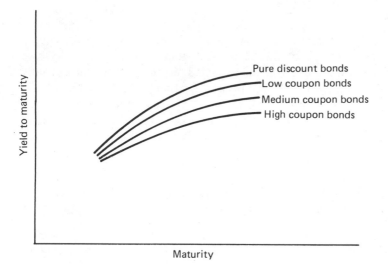

Figure 18.5.   Possible term structure curves.

than when the government originally issued them, and there is some risk of the brokerage firm defaulting. Furthermore, even now there are not enough of them to allow accurate estimation of the yield curve. Most firms plot yield curves of coupon paying debt rather than go through the process of estimating the yield curve for pure discount debt using techniques discussed in the appendix at the end of the chapter. Examining Figures 18.4 and 18.5 shows that the general shape of the yield curve is preserved if the coupon rate on bonds of varying maturities is the same. The problem is that they are not the same. Most bonds with inter-mediate maturity are long-term bonds that were issued several years before. For example, a bond with a 7-year maturity might be a 30-year bond issued 23 years ago. Interest rates change dramatically over time. Thus the coupon rate on bonds of different maturities are likely to be very different. A yield curve drawn from coupon paying bonds is likely to be a mixture of the yield curves shown in Figures 18.4 and 18.5. In this case, even the shape need not be preserved.

Organizations examine yield curves for investment decisions and for deter-mining interest rates to be offered their customers. Using coupon bonds can lead to very misleading yield curves and incorrect decisions.

Summary of the Term Structure of Interest Rates   We have shown how spot rates can be used to arrive at the correct price of any bond. To estimate spot rates beyond the maturity spectrum where pure discount bonds are available, one should use the methodology outlined in the appendix at the end of this chapter. Spot rates are determined by current one-period rates, expectations about future one-period rates, theories of institutional behavior, and risk preferences. While we have not attempted to reach a categorical answer to which of these term structures is correct, we have provided you with enough information about the contrasting theories to give insight into the term structure of interest rates.

Default Risk

Unlike government bonds, for corporate bonds there is a risk that the coupon or principal payments will not be met. For these bonds it is necessary to make a distinction between promised return and expected return. A bond could promise a return of 17%, but if there were some probability that the principal or coupon might not be paid, its expected return could be 15%. In addition, since there is risk associated with these bonds, investors should require that the expected return be greater than the return on a similar bond that is default free. These concepts are illustrated in Table 18.7.

Table 18.7 Components of Interest Rates on Corporate Bonds

2%	Default premium	
1%	Risk premium	17% Total return
14%	Return on default-free bonds	

We have referred to the difference between the promised return and the expected return as the default premium. The difference between the expected return and the return on a default-free instrument is the risk premium. The investor requires this extra return because of the chance that a particular bond selected may default, resulting in a very poor and probably negative return.

There are three large investment services that estimate the likelihood of default for most corporate bonds: Moody's, Standard and Poor's, and Fitch. The estimates from Moody's and from Standard and Poor's are widely available. Their services are similar in that they classify bonds by likelihood of loss. Likelihood of loss includes both the probability of a missed, delayed, or partial payment and the size of the loss if a loss occurs. For example, consider two bonds with the same probability of a missed principal payment. If one of them has significant odds of paying a substantial portion of the principal payment if missed, while the odds are that the other will pay none, then the bond with the higher payment receives the higher rating. Bond rating services divide bonds into discrete classes. Table 18.8 shows Moody's classification of bonds and their discussion of what the various classifications mean.

Many organizations are restricted to buying bonds that have achieved at least a certain rating. These restrictions may be imposed by regulatory authority, by perception of legal requirements of prudent investment, or by organizational policy. In addition, many brokerage firms put together pools of bonds and then issue shares in these pools. These pools are normally restricted to A-rated bonds or better. These restrictions suggest the possibility of a segmented market between

Table 18.8   Key to Moody's Corporate Ratings

Aaa	Bonds which are rated Aaa are judged to be of the best quality. They carry the smallest degree of investment risk and are generally referred to as "gilt edge." Interest payments are protected by a large or by an exceptionally stable margin and principal is secure. While the various protective elements are likely to change, such changes as can be visualized are most unlikely to impair the fundamentally strong position of such issues.
Aa	Bonds which are rated Aa are judged to be of high quality by all standards. Together with the Aaa group they comprise what are generally known as high-grade bonds. They are rated lower than the best bonds because margins of protection may not be as large as in Aaa securities or fluctuation of protective elements may be of greater amplitude or there may be other elements present that make the long-term risks appear somewhat larger than in Aaa securities.
A	Bonds which are rated A possess many favorable investment attributes and are to be considered as upper medium-grade obligations. Factors giving security to principal and interest are considered adequate but elements may be present that suggest a susceptibility to impairment sometime in the future.
Baa	Bonds which are rated Baa are considered as medium-grade obligations (i.e., they are neither highly protected nor poorly secured). Interest payments and principal security appear adequate for the present, but certain protective elements may be lacking or may be characteristically unreliable over any great length of time. Such bonds lack outstanding investment characteristics and in fact have speculative characteristics as well.
Ba	Bonds which are rated Ba are judged to have speculative elements; their future cannot be considered as well assured. Often the protection of interest and principal payments may be very moderate and thereby not well safeguarded during both good and bad times over the future. Uncertainty of position characterizes bonds in this class.
B	Bonds which are rated B generally lack characteristics of the desirable investment. Assurance of interest and principal payments or of maintenance of other terms of the contract over any long period of time may be small.
Caa	Bonds which are rated Caa are of poor standing. Such issues may be in default or there may be present elements of danger with respect to principal or interest.
Ca	Bonds which are rated Ca represent obligations which are speculative in a high degree. Such issues are often in default or have other marked shortcomings.
C	Bonds which are rated C are the lowest rated class of bonds and issues so rated can be regarded as having extremely poor prospects of ever attaining any real investment standing.

higher rated bonds and lower rated bonds; however, we know of no conclusive evidence on this issue.

Moody's and Standard and Poor's classifications can be duplicated fairly accurately by utilizing a weighted average of firm characteristics as follows. A number of firm characteristics are hypothesized as influencing Moody's or Standard and Poor's classifications. These characteristics usually include variables such as the amount of earnings compared to the interest payments, the variability of earnings, the amount of debt in the capital structure, the net worth, and the amount of short-term assets compared to short-term liabilities. Data on these variables are

Table 18.9   Default Rates of Corporate Bonds during 1900–1943

Agency Rating[a]	Proportion of Bonds Defaulted			
	Railroads	Public Utilities	Industrials	Total
I	14.5	0.0	0.0	5.9
II	18.6	0.0	3.2	6.0
III	41.0	5.0	8.8	13.4
IV	36.0	14.0	18.5	19.1
V	70.7	32.5	31.9	41.1
VI–IX	69.0	45.7	37.5	50.1

[a]Median of various agency ratings at the time of offering: I is comparable to AAA, and so forth.

Source: H.G. Fraine and R.H. Mills, (22).

collected for a number of publicly traded bonds along with the classification of each bond by one of the bond rating services. Mathematical techniques exist for finding the combination of firm variables that best duplicates the classification of the rating agency. The combination is best in the sense that it most accurately reproduces the ratings. Once the best combination is determined, it is then tested using data on other publicly traded bonds to see how well it classifies them. Accurate classification of 70 to 80% of the bonds is not uncommon, with most bonds being only one rating away from the published ratings.

Reproducing public ratings is useful in order that bonds not classified by the public rating services can be cheaply and accurately classified. The most obvious utilization of this system is in classifying private placements. Banks and insurance companies lend money to firms directly. These private placements are usually loans to small or medium-sized companies who wish to avoid the expenses of issuing publicly traded debt (e.g., SEC registration, brokerage costs). Analysts make judgments concerning the likelihood and size of loss, the appropriate interest rate on the potential loan, and the decision on whether to lend. When individual lending officers are judged in part by the volume of loans they make, they tend to be optimistic about the likelihood of the firm repaying the loan in the future. A scheme that fairly accurately reproduces public ratings is a check on this optimism. These schemes are frequently used to rate all loans under consideration. The analyst is then required to justify any difference in interest rates he or she wishes to offer compared to what is normal given the rating the bond receives.

How well do public rating systems predict default? Tables 18.9, 18.10 and 18.11 give a partial answer. The results shown in Table 18.9, while dated, are the most comprehensive we know of. Tables 18.10 and 18.11 give results over a more recent period. Note that Table 18.11 lists the number of bonds defaulting. There

Table 18.10   Default Rates of Corporate Bonds during 1970–1984

All bonds	0.116%
Low-rated debt[a]	2.54%

[a]Bonds rated below BBB by Standard and Poor's or below Baa 3 by Moody's.

Source: Altman and Nammacher [2].

Table 18.11   Number of Bonds in Default by Rating Category during 1970–1984

	Original Rating	Rating One-year Prior
AAA	0	0
AA	2	0
A	7	2
BBB	25	11
BB	21	14
B	40	53
CCC	17	43
CC	0	7
	112	130

Source: Altman and Nammacher [2].

are not the same number of bonds in each category, so that default rates can not be inferred from this table. However, it does indicate how few high-rated bonds default. At least in these studies, the rating agencies fairly accurately ranked bonds by default risk. Table 18.12 once again shows that agencies seem to be able to differentiate between bonds on the basis of expected loss. The results reported in the table are a little surprising in that realized return does not increase with decrease in rating class. One would expect a higher-risk premium as the rating of the bond declines. Table 18.12 does not substantiate this expectation. This may perhaps be explained by the fact that the study covers a period over which actual defaults were probably well in excess of expected.

Given that rating agencies accurately estimate the probability of loss, one would expect that promised return was very closely related to rating class. Table 18.13 shows the yield to maturity of bonds from 1973 through 1980. The data are for January of each year. In each year, promised yield was ordered by rating. This is what one should expect when default risk increases with a lower rating.

Instead of relating firm characteristics to ratings, and ratings to yield to maturity, one can directly explore the relationship between firm characteristics and yields. Fisher [21] did the most widely cited study of this type. Fisher argues that the difference in yield between a corporate bond and a government bond of the

Table 18.12   Quality Rating and Realized Yields during 1900–1943

Agency Rating (1)	Promised Yield (2)	Realized Yield		Loss Rate (5) (2) − (4)
		Hickman (3)	Fraine and Mills (4)	
I	4.5%	5.1%	4.3%	0.2%
II	4.5	5.1	4.3	0.2
III	4.9	5.0	4.3	0.6
IV	5.4	5.8	4.5	0.9
V	6.3	4.1	3.5	2.8
VI–IX	7.6	4.7	3.7	3.9

Sources: X. Hickman *Corporate Bond Quality and Investor Experience* (Princeton, N.J.: Princeton University Press, 1958); also Fraine and Mills (22).

Table 18.13 As Determined by Moody's Yield to Maturity from 1973 to 1980

	Rating			
	AAA	AA	A	BAA
Year	Yields			
1973	7.15	7.37	7.53	7.90
1974	7.83	8.00	8.17	8.48
1975	8.83	9.13	9.81	10.81
1976	8.60	9.13	9.54	10.41
1977	7.96	8.16	8.45	9.08
1978	8.41	8.59	8.76	9.17
1979	9.25	9.48	9.72	10.13
1980	11.09	11.56	11.88	12.42

same maturity is due to default risk and marketability. He argues that default risk is related to earnings variability, the length of time since the firm has missed a payment, and the equity debt ratio. Marketability is measured by the value of the firm's bonds outstanding. Fisher tested his hypothesis in five different years. The results are shown in Equation (18.2). R^2 is a measure that shows the percentage of the variations in the log of the difference in yield between government and corporate debt explained by his hypothesized variables. The amount explained is very high: 81%. The influence of the variables on yield differences is as expected. The greater the earnings variability, the greater is the yield difference. The longer the firm has been solvent, the smaller is the yield difference. The more equity in the capital structure, the smaller is the yield difference. Finally, the greater the number of bonds outstanding, the lower is the yield difference. It is also interesting to note that when the equation was estimated at different points in time, the coefficients were remarkably stable.

$$\begin{bmatrix} \text{Log of yield} \\ \text{difference} \end{bmatrix} = \text{constant} + .262 \begin{bmatrix} \text{log of earning} \\ \text{variability} \end{bmatrix} - .223 \begin{bmatrix} \text{log of period} \\ \text{of solvency} \end{bmatrix}$$

$$- .469 \begin{bmatrix} \text{log of } \dfrac{\text{equity}}{\text{debt}} \end{bmatrix} - .290 \begin{bmatrix} \text{log of bonds} \\ \text{outstanding} \end{bmatrix} \quad (18.2)$$

The empirical studies reviewed in this section of the chapter indicate that firm characteristics are useful in explaining both the quality ratings assigned by Standard and Poor's and Moody's and the differences between yield to maturity at which different corporate bonds sell.

Tax Effects

The cash flows from certain bonds have a tax advantage. These bonds should sell at a different yield to maturity than bonds without this tax advantage. The most obvious example of such bonds is municipal bonds. The coupon payments from municipal bonds are not subject to federal taxation and usually are not subject to tax in the state where they are issued. Because of the benefits of such favorable tax treatment, the yield to maturity on these bonds is less than the yield to maturity on comparable taxable issues. Generally the yield to maturity is 30% to 40% lower on municipal bonds than on similar taxable issues.

The second example of the effect of tax on bonds are the so-called flower bonds. Flower bonds were designated as such at time of issue. These bonds were originally issued at times of relatively low interest rates. Normally they would sell at a value well below face value so that their yield to maturity would be comparable to other bonds. However, they have a unique provision that substantially affects their value. Flower bonds are accepted at face value in payment of estate taxes. Thus a wealthy individual might find it attractive to add flower bonds to his or her portfolio if an imminent demise were anticipated. Because of this special provision, flower bonds will sell at much higher prices than they otherwise would, leading to lower yields to the investor.

While flower bonds are the most colorful bond with special tax treatment, the most common type of bond subject to special tax treatment is one with a sufficiently low or high coupon to cause it to sell at a price very different than its face value. For these bonds, capital appreciation or loss is a significant part of the investor's return in addition to interest income. Consider a low coupon bond. The coupon payments are subject to taxation at ordinary income tax rates. Low coupon bonds would have two components to their return: the return from the coupon plus the return from the price appreciation. The total return must be competitive with other bonds of similar characteristics. The portion of return from the price appreciation is taxable as a capital gain. For most investors the capital gain rate is lower than the income tax rate. Thus low coupon bonds have a tax advantage because a portion of their return receives favorable tax treatment. Given this tax advantage low coupon bonds should and do have a lower (before tax) yield to maturity. McCulloch [27] has estimated that bonds are priced consistent with investors being in a 20 to 30% tax bracket. This means that the after-tax yield on a low coupon versus a normal coupon bond with similar characteristics is the same as if flows were adjusted by assuming a 20 to 30% tax bracket.[2]

The tax bracket that is consistent with observed prices is important information to investors. If bonds are priced consistent with a 20 to 30% tax bracket, then investors in higher tax brackets will favor low coupon issues, all else held constant. Similarly, tax-exempt investors should primarily be holding the high coupon, high yield bonds.

Option Features of Bonds

Bonds sometimes contain a feature that constitutes an option for either the issuer of the bond or the holder of the bond. Since the valuation of options is discussed in detail in Chapter 20, we limit our discussion in this chapter to a

---

[2]High coupon bonds have a tax disadvantage. Coupon payments are subject to the high ordinary tax rate. The price decline is a long-term loss. Although laws change, at the time this book was written, the difference between the purchase price and the face value could be taken yearly as a loss in equal amounts. Thus on a bond with a 10-year maturity, 10% of the difference could be written off as a capital loss each year.

description of bond features that can be valued as options. Applying the option valuation formula to these features will not be specifically treated, although the option chapter together with the bibliography at the end of this chapter will allow the interested reader to pursue this subject.[3]

The most common option included in bond contracts is the possibility of a call by the issuing firm. The call privilege is the right by the issuing firm to repurchase the bond at a fixed price. The price is generally the par value (face value) of the bond plus a premium (called the call premium). For example, the bond might be callable at par plus 5% of par. Generally the call premium declines over time, making the likelihood of a call higher in the later years than in earlier years. For example, the call premium might be 5% in the first year, 4% in the second year, 3% in the third year, and so forth. In addition, it is common to preclude a call for a number of years. The possibility of a call reduces the value of the bond to the investor. An investor can assume that the firm will call at times when the bond without the call feature is worth more than the price at which it is actually called. This difference is a loss to the investor. The value of a comparable non-callable bond will lie above the call price when interest rates decline compared to the original issue price. Thus an investor wishing to lock up high interest rates by buying a bond at a time of high rates might find that he or she earns these rates only for a short time because the bond is called away when rates decline and the proceeds are invested at these lower rates. Many firms calculate return to the first time at which a bond is callable in order to compare return on callable and noncallable bonds. This procedure makes the unrealistic assumption that firms will call as soon as a bond is callable. This underestimates its value, just as a return to maturity that ignores the possibility of call is an overestimate of the expected return over this horizon. The only accurate way to estimate the value of the call is to use the option models discussed in Chapter 20.

Another option associated with bonds is the sinking fund option. Many bond issues require that part of the issue be retired over the life of the bond. For example, bond covenants may require that 5% of the issue be retired at the end of each year over the bond's ten-year life. The corporation has the option of purchasing the bonds directly or of calling the bonds it needs to meet its sinking fund obligation. Obviously it will meet its obligation in the cheapest way. Since the bonds are chosen in a random way, all investors have the risk of having their bonds called to meet the sinking fund obligation. The discussion of the call option is relevant in this case.

A third option found in certain bond contracts is the conversion option. This option benefits the bondholders. The bondholder has the option of converting the bond into common equity. The bond is used to pay for the equity. Assume a $1,000 par bond is convertible into 50 shares of common equity. Then the investor is paying $20 per share. The convertible bond can be viewed as a bond plus an option to buy 50 shares at $20 per share.

---

[3]See Black and Scholes [6] and Merton [38] for applications of the option pricing formula to bonds.

CONCLUSION

In this chapter, we have introduced bond terminology and the major features of bonds. The only principle feature we introduced but did not devote a section to was the effect of differing coupons. We did not devote a separate section to it because the effect of coupon payments has already been discussed in the tax and maturity sections. In the next chapter, we integrate bond management into portfolio theory.

APPENDIX

Estimating Spot Rates

As discussed in the text, very few pure discount government bonds exist for maturities longer than one year. Since spot rates are extremely important in bond valuation and investment decisions, it is necessary to estimate them. Three techniques have been discussed in the literature. We discuss two of them in this appendix. These two differ in that one of them estimates discrete rates and the other continuous rates.

Consider the following equation relating the price of a bond to the cash flows accruing to the bond holder.

$$P = \frac{c}{(1 + i_{01})} + \frac{c}{(1 + i_{02})^2} + \frac{c}{(1 + i_{03})^3} + \cdots + \frac{1,000 + c}{(1 + i_{0T})^T} \quad (A.1)$$

where

P is the price of the bond
c is the coupon
i_{0t} is the t period spot rate
T is the number of periods where there are coupon payments
$\$1,000$ is the principal payment

$$P = cD_1 + cD_2 + cD_3 + \cdots + (c + 1,000)D_T \quad (A.2)$$

where

$$D_t = \frac{1}{(1 + i_{0t})^t} \quad t = 1, \cdots, T$$

The price and the cash flows are known. Thus Equation (A.2) has the form of a multiple linear regression. D_1 through D_T are the regression coefficients to be estimated. In order to prevent estimates of forward rates being negative, it is normal to constrain the regression so that the D's are nonincreasing. Thus D_t is forced to be less than D_{t-1}. The spot rates estimated by this procedure are discrete. Since most bonds pay interest on a semi-annual basis, these are spot rates for cash flows six months apart. Thus i_{01} is the spot rate for the first 6 months, i_{02} is for the first 12 months, i_{03} for the first 18 months, and so on. Furthermore, they are rates between specific dates. For example, the 6-month intervals could be January to June and July to December. The difficulty with this procedure is that a large number of bonds pay interest on different dates and the spot rates must be interpolated in some way for use on these dates. Furthermore, bonds with different payment dates cannot be used in the estimation and thus a fair amount of data is discarded. Carleton and Cooper [12] suggested the just discussed procedure.

The alternative is to estimate a continuous discount function. The procedure just described estimates that $D(t) = 1/(1 + i_{0t})^t$ where the t has integer values such as 1, 2 or 3. $D(t)$ is called a discount function. Consider the following diagram. Discount rates for different 6-month intervals are plotted in the diagram.

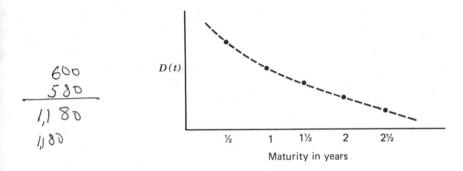

Maturity in years

Using the technique just discussed, all we obtain are the points shown. As an alternative the dashed line could be estimated. This would allow an estimation of discount functions for all maturities. There are several equations that could be used to approximate the relationship between $D(t)$ and maturity. Since we have assumed some curvature to the relationship, let us approximate it by a quadratic equation. We can write it as

$$D(t) = a_0 + a_1t + a_2t^2 \tag{A.3}$$

Once a_0, a_1, and a_2 are known, the spot rates for any time period are known. If the discount function for cash flow in 3½ months is required, then t is set as 3.5/12. The task is thus to estimate a_0, a_1, and a_2. The price of a bond is the present value of its coupon and principal payment. This was written in Equation (A.2) and can be written in compact form as

$$P = \sum_{t=1}^{T} c(t)D(t) \tag{A.4}$$

where $c(t)$ is the coupon payment for all periods before the horizon and the coupon plus principal at the horizon.

Substituting Equation (A.3) into Equation (A.4) yields

$$P = \sum_{t=1}^{T} c(t)(a_0 + a_1 t + a_2 t^2)$$

Rearranging,

$$P = a_0\left[\sum_{t=1}^{T} c(t)\right] + a_1\left[\sum_{t=1}^{T} tc(t)\right] + a_2\left[\sum_{t=1}^{T} t^2 c(t)\right]$$

Once again this is in the form of a linear regression. The terms in the brackets and the price are known and the a_i are regression coefficients. This is the procedure suggested by Schaefer [44] and McCulloch [32]. The discount function used by these authors is not exactly equal to that presented in Equation (A.3) but the general procedure is the same.[4]

QUESTIONS AND PROBLEMS

1. Given the following, does the law of one price hold? If not, what action should an investor take?

	Cash Flows in Period		
Bond	1	2	Price
A	½ 100	1,100	970
B	½ 80	1,080	936
C	90	1,090	980

2. Assume a bond with cash flows of $100 each year and a principal payment of $1,000 in five years and a current price of $960. What is:

A. Its current yield?

B. Its yield to maturity?

3. Given the following bonds and prices of bonds, what are the spot rates and forward rates?

Number	Price	1	2	3	4
A	900	1000			
B	820		1000		
C	725			1000	
D	675				1000

[4]Researchers have used a generalized polynomial curve fitting to estimate this relationship; we select a simple polynomial curve, the quadratic, to illustrate the procedure.

4. Given the cash flows shown below, does the law of one price hold? If not, what is the price of bond *C* that will make it hold?

	Cash Flows in Period		
Number	1	2	Price
A	80	1,080	982
B	1,100		880
C	120	1,120	1,010

5. Assume the data shown below. What tax rate would make the law of one price hold? Assume that the capital gains tax is one-half the ordinary income tax. Assume that capital gains and losss are paid at the end of period 2, that the tax rate on capital gains and losses is the same, and that there is a $1,000 principal on all three bonds.

Number	1	2	Price
A	80	1,080	985
B	1,100		900
C	120	1,120	1,040

BIBLIOGRAPHY

1. Alexander, Gordon J. "Applying the Market Model to Long-Term Corporate Bonds," *Journal of Financial and Quantitative Analysis*, **XV**, No. 5 (Dec. 1980), pp. 1063–1080.
2. Altman, Edward, and Nammacher, Scott. "The Default Experience on High Yield Corporate Debt," *Financial Analyst Journal* (July–Aug. 1985), pp. 25–41.
3. Ananthanarayanan, A.L., and Schwartz, Eduardo S. "Retractable and Extendible Bonds: The Canadian Experience," *The Journal of Finance*, **35**, No. 1 (March 1980), pp. 31–48.
4. Arak, Marcelle, and Silver, Andrew. "The Value of the Tax Treatment of Original-Issue Deep-Discount Bonds: A Note," *The Journal of Finance*, **39**, No. 1 (March 1984), pp. 253–260.
5. Black, Fischer, and Cox, John C. "Valuing Corporate Securities: Some Effects of Bond Indenture Provisions," *Journal of Finance*, **31** (May 1976), pp. 351–367.
6. Black, Fischer, and Scholes, Myron. "The Pricing of Options and Corporate Liabilities," *Journal of Political Economy*, **81** (May/June 1973), pp. 637–654.
7. Brennan, M.J., and Schwartz, E.S. "Convertible Bonds: Valuation and Optimal Strategies for Call and Conversion," *Journal of Finance*, **32** (Dec. 1977), pp. 1699–1715.

8. ———. "Conditional Predictions of Bond Prices and Returns," *The Journal of Finance*, **35**, No. 2 (May 1980), pp. 405–416.
9. ———. "An Equilibrium Model of Bond Pricing and a Test of Market Efficiency," *Journal of Financial and Quantitative Analysis*, **XVII**, No. 3 (Sept. 1982), pp. 301–330.
10. Buse, A. "Interest Rates, the Meiselman Model and Random Numbers," *Journal of Political Economy*, **LXXV** (Feb. 1967), pp. 49–62.
11. Cagan, Philip. *Changes in the Cyclical Behavior of Interest Rates* (New York: National Bureau of Economic Research, 1966).
12. Carleton, W.T., and Cooper, I.A. "Estimation and Uses of the Term Structure of Interest Rates," *Journal of Finance*, **31** (Sept. 1976), pp. 1067–1083.
13. Chambers, Donald R., Carleton, Willard T., and Waldman, Donald W. "A New Approach to Estimation of the Term Structure of Interest Rates," *Journal of Financial and Quantitative Analysis*, **19**, No. 3 (Sept. 1984), pp. 233–252.
14. Conard, Joseph W. *Introduction to the Theory of Interest* (Berkeley, Calif.: University of California Press, 1959.)
15. Constantinides, George M., and Ingersoll, Jonathan E., Jr. "Tax Effects and Bond Prices," *The Journal of Finance*, **37**, No. 2 (May 1982), pp. 349–351.
16. Cox, John C., Ingersoll, Jonathan E., and Ross, Stephen. "An Analysis of Variable Rate Loan Contracts," *The Journal of Finance*, **35**, No. 2 (May 1980), pp. 389–404.
17. Culbertson, John M. "The Term Structure of Interest Rates," *Quarterly Journal of Economics*, **LXXI** (Nov. 1957), pp. 485–517.
18. Fama, E. "Forward Rates as Predictors of Future Spot Rates," *Journal of Financial Economics*, **3** (Oct. 1976), pp. 361–377.
19. ———. "The Information in the Term Structure," *Journal of Financial Economics*, **13**, No. 4 (Dec. 1984), pp. 509–528.
20. ———. "Term Premiums in Bond Returns," *Journal of Financial Economics*, **13**, No. 4 (Dec. 1984), pp. 529–546.
21. Fisher, Lawrence. "Determinants of Risk Premiums on Corporate Bonds," *The Journal of Political Economy*, **67** (June 1959), pp. 217–237.
22. Fraine, H.G., and Mills, R.H. "The Effect of Defaults and Credit Deterioration on Yields of Corporate Bonds. *Journal of Finance*, **16**, (Sept. 1961), pp. 423–433.
23. Hansen, L.P., and Hodrick, R.J. "Forward Exchange Rates as Optimal Predictors of Future Spot Rates: An Econometric Analysis," *Journal of Political Economy*, **88** (Oct. 1980), pp. 829–853.
24. Johnson, Ramon, "Term Structure of Corporate Bond Yields as a Function of Risk of Default," *Journal of Finance*, **22** (May 1967), pp. 313–345.
25. Kessel, Reuben H. *The Cyclical Behavior of the Term Structure of Interest Rates* (New York: National Bureau of Economic Research, 1965).
26. Lang, Richard, and Rasche, Robert. "Debt-Management Policy and the Own Price Elasticity of Demand for U.S. Government Notes and Bonds," *Federal Reserve Bank of St. Louis Review*, **59** (Sept. 1977), pp. 8–22.
27. Lee, Wayne, Maness, Terry, and Tuttle, Donald. "Nonspeculative Behavior

and the Term Structure," *Journal of Financial and Quantitative Analysis,* **15** (March 1980), pp. 53–83.

28. Litzenberger, Robert H., and Rolfo, Jacques. "An International Study of Tax Effects on Government Bonds," *The Journal of Finance,* **39,** No. 1 (March 1984), pp. 1–22.

29. ———. "Arbitrage Pricing, Transaction Costs and Taxation of Capital Gains: A Study of Government Bonds with the Same Maturity Date," *Journal of Financial Economics,* Vol. 13 No. 3 (Sept. 1984), pp. 337–352.

30. Lutz, Friedrich A. "The Structure of Interest Rates," *Quarterly Journal of Economics,* **LV** (Nov. 1940), pp. 36–63.

31. Marsh, Terry. "Equilibrium Term Structure Models: Test Methodology," *The Journal of Finance,* **35,** No. 2 (May 1980), pp. 421–434.

32. McCulloch, J. Huston. "An Estimate of the Liquidity Premium." *Journal of Political Economy,* **83** (Feb. 1975), pp. 95–119.

33. McCulloch, J.H. "Measuring the Term Structure of Interest Rates," *Journal of Business,* **44** (Jan. 1971), pp. 19–31.

34. McCulloch, J.H. "The Tax-Adjusted Yield Curve," *Journal of Finance,* **30** (June 1975), pp. 811–830.

35. Malkiel, Burton G. "Expectations, Bond Prices, and the Term Structure of Interest Rates," *Quarterly Journal of Economics,* **LXXVI** (May 1962), pp. 197–218.

36. ———. *The Term Structure of Interest Rates* (Princeton, N.J.: Princeton University Press, 1966).

37. Meiselman, David. *The Term Structure of Interest Rates* (Englewood Cliffs, N.J.: Prentice-Hall, 1962).

38. Merton, Robert, "On the Pricing of Corporate Debt: The Risk Structure of Interest Rates," *Journal of Finance,* **29** (May 1974), pp. 449–470.

39. Modigliani, Franco, and Sutch, Richard. "Innovations in Interest Rate Policy," *American Economic Review,* **LVI** (May 1966), pp. 178–197.

40. ———. "Debt Management and the Term Structure of Interest Rates: An Empirical Analysis of Recent Experience," *Journal of Political Economy,* **75** (Supplement: Aug. 1967), pp. 569–589.

41. Pinches, G.E., and Mingo, K.A. "A Multivariate Analysis of Industrial Bond Ratings," *Journal of Finance,* **28** (March 1973), pp. 1–32.

42. Rao, Ramesh K.S. "The Impact of Yield Changes on the Systematic Risk of Bonds," *Journal of Financial and Quantitative Analysis,* **XVII,** No. 1 (March 1982), pp. 115–128.

43. Roll, Richard. *The Behavior of Interest Rates* (New York: Basic Books, 1970).

44. Schaefer, S.M. "Measuring a Tax Specific Term Structure of Interest Rates in the Market for British Government Securities," *Economic Journal,* **91** (June 1981), pp. 415–438.

45. ———. "Tax-Induced Clientele Effect in the Market for British Government Securities: Placing Bonds on Security Values in an Incomplete Market," *Journal of Financial Economics,* **X,** No. 2 (July 1982), pp. 121–160.

46. Shea, Gary S. "Pitfalls in Smoothing Interest Rate Term Structure Data:

Equilibrium Models and Spline Approximations," *Journal of Financial and Quantitative Analysis,* **19,** No. 3 (Sept. 1984), pp. 253–270.

47. Smith, Clifford, and Warner, Jerold. "On Financial Contracting: An Analysis of Bond Covenants," *Journal of Financial Economics,* **7** (June 1979), pp. 115–161.

48. Telser, L.G. "A Critique of Some Recent Empirical Research on the Explanation of the Term Structure of Interest Rates," *Journal of Political Economy,* **75** (Supplement: Aug. 1967), pp. 546–561.

49. Van Horne, James. "Interest-Rate Expectations, the Shape of the Yield Curve, and Monetary Policy," *Review of Economics and Statistics,* **XLVIII** (May 1966), pp. 211–215.

50. ———. "Interest-Rate Risk and the Term Structure of Interest Rates," *Journal of Political Economy,* **LXXIII** (Aug. 1965), pp. 344–351.

51. ———. "The Expectations Hypothesis, the Yield Curve, and Monetary Policy: Comment," *Quarterly Journal of Economics,* **LXXIX** (Nov. 1965), pp. 664–668.

52. Van Horne, James C., and Bowers, David A. "The Liquidity Impact of Debt Management," *The Southern Economic Journal,* **XXXIV** (April 1968), pp. 526–537.

53. Wood, John H. "Expectations, Error, and the Term Structure of Interest Rates," *Journal of Political Economy,* **LXXI** (April 1963), pp. 160–171.

54. Zwick, Burton. "Yield on Privately Placed Corporate Bonds," *The Journal of Finance,* **35,** No. 1 (March 1980), pp. 23–30.

Chapter 19

The Management of Bond Portfolios

In the previous chapter, we discussed the determination of interest rates and the characteristics of bonds that affect their return and value. In this chapter we discuss bond portfolio management. Modern portfolio theory has made less of an impact on bond management than it has on common equity management. Furthermore, some of the portfolio management techniques used in bond management are specific to the bond area and not outgrowths of modern portfolio theory. In this chapter we discuss the techniques specifically developed for the bond area as well as applications of general portfolio theory to the bond area.

The chapter is divided into three parts. First we discuss the major source of risk facing bond managers, changes in the yield curve, and measures used to examine a bond's sensitivity to this source of risk. Next we discuss ways of constructing a bond portfolio to insulate against this risk. These are normally referred to as passive portfolio strategies, although, as we will see, they generally involve actively adjusting the portfolio. Finally we will discuss bond management in a modern portfolio theory context, first discussing estimating expected return, then estimation of the variance-covariance structure.

DURATION

The return on a bond has two components: interest income and capital gains or losses caused by a change in price. A price change can come about because of the passage of time or as a result of a shift in the yield curve.

Price Change Due to Passage of Time

Consider first a price change due to the passage of time. Assume the following set of spot rates.

$$i_{01} = 10\%$$

$$i_{02} = 10\%$$

$$i_{03} = 10\%$$

These are annualized interest rates for one, two, and three years. Now consider a pure discount bond with three years to maturity. The price of a pure discount three-year bond that pays $1,000 at maturity is

$$P_3 = \frac{1{,}000}{(1 + i_{03})^3} = \frac{1{,}000}{(1.10)^3} = \$751.31$$

assuming that spot rates remain unchanged over the first year.[1] Then, at time 1 this bond must have the same yield as a two-year bond and thus have a price of

$$P_2 = \frac{1{,}000}{(1 + i_{02})^2} = \frac{1{,}000}{(1.10)^2} = \$826.45$$

This price change would occur over the year. The price change over the year is $P_2 - P_3 = \$75.14$, which results in a rate of return of

$$\frac{P_2 - P_3}{P_3} = 10\%$$

The effect of the passage of time on the price of a bond should be easy to understand for pure discount bonds. Since pure discount bonds do not pay any interest, the full return is due to a change in price. Coupon paying bonds also can have an expected price change due to the passage of time. There are a large number of bonds that are comparable in every way except that they offer different coupons. These bonds must offer similar returns to investors. Thus, for these bonds, there are anticipated price changes. For example, a 4% coupon bond will sell at a discount and offer an expected price increase if current interest rates for a similar bond are 10%. Most bonds include an anticipated price change as part of their return.

---

[1] This is the simplest example that can be constructed. It assumes a flat yield curve. The principle being demonstrated also holds under more complex shapes of the yield curve.

Unanticipated Price Change

The other cause of a price change is a change in future expectations concerning interest rates (an unanticipated shift in the yield curve). Assume that the yield curve shifts and the new spot rates are

$$i_{01} = 14\%$$

$$i_{02} = 14\%$$

$$i_{03} = 14\%$$

Further assume that the shift takes place immediately. In this case the three-year, pure discount bond would have a new price of

$$P'_3 = \frac{\$1,000}{(1.14)^3} = \$674.97$$

This results in a price change of

$$P_3' - P_3 = -\$76.34$$

If the yield curve remains constant over time or if expectations remain constant, the price change due to the passage of time is easy to calculate. The price change due to an unanticipated change in the yield curve is different.

If we knew how expectations concerning future interest rates would shift over time and others did not, then we would be able to calculate the price change of each bond and put all of our money into the bond with the highest total return. However, this is not possible; the best that we can do is to calculate the sensitivity of each bond to a shift in the yield curve.

Sensitivity to Shifts in the Yield Curve

In earlier chapters we calculated a measure called Beta to measure a common equity security's sensitivity to changes in an index. An analogous measure is calculated for bonds: it is called "duration." Duration is a measure of the sensitivity of the price of a bond to a change in interest rates. More specifically, minus duration times the proportional change in 1 plus the interest rate is equal to the unanticipated return due to a change in price.

In symbols:

$$R_u = -D \, \Delta i \qquad (19.1)$$

where

R_u is the unanticipated return due to a change in the interest rate
D is duration
Δi is the proportional change in 1 plus the interest rate

Note that we have dropped subscripts on the interest rate and have been referring to "the interest rate" as if there is a single rate that does not depend on maturity. This is in contrast to earlier sections where we were clearly specifying the time horizon of the interest rate. For simplicity we are assuming a single rate for all maturities. A single rate is an assumption of a flat yield curve. Shortly we will generalize the analysis.

To understand duration, consider a pure discount bond that matures in N years. Coupon paying bonds can be considered as combinations of pure discount bonds. Thus understanding duration for pure discount bonds will help us understand it for coupon bonds. Let P_0 be the current price of a pure discount bond that pays \$1,000 in T years. If i is the yearly interest rate, then

$$P_0 = \frac{\$1,000}{(1 + i)^T} \tag{19.2}$$

We derive the duration for this bond in the following section. The reader uninterested in the derivation can skip to the end of the dotted section.

....

Equation (19.2) can be written as

$$P_0 = (1,000)(1 + i)^{-T}$$

Recall that the derivative of X^N is $N X^{N-1} dX$. Thus

$$dP_0 = 1,000(-T)(1 + i)^{(-T-1)} d(1 + i)$$

Rearranging yields

$$dP_0 = \frac{-1,000T}{(1 + i)^T} \frac{d(1 + i)}{1 + i}$$

Note that $1,000/(1 + i)^T$ is the price of the bond P_0; thus,

$$dP_0 = -TP_0 \frac{d(1 + i)}{(1 + i)}$$

Dividing both sides by P_0 we have

$$\frac{dP_0}{P_0} = \frac{-TP_0}{P_0} \frac{d(1 + i)}{(1 + i)} = -T \frac{d(1 + i)}{(1 + i)}$$

The change in price divided by price dP_0/P_0 is the return due to an unanticipated change in the interest rate. $d(1 + i)/(1 + i)$ is the proportional change in 1 plus the interest rate.

If we define D as T then we have Equation (19.1). Thus the duration on a pure discount bond is its maturity.

$$P_0 = \frac{1,000}{(1+i) \cdot T}$$

For a pure discount bond such as presented in Equation (19.2), duration is equal to its maturity. Thus, given the assumption of a flat yield curve, the sensitivity of a pure discount bond to a change in the yield curve should be directly proportional to its maturity. When the change in the interest rate divided by 1 plus the interest rate is equal to 1%, the change in the price of a pure discount bond with a maturity of one year should be 1%, and the change in price of a pure discount bond with a maturity of five years should be 5%, and so on.

Table 19.1 illustrates these ideas. The bonds in Table 19.1 are pure discount bonds with the maturity shown in the first column. All bonds are assumed to return a principal of $1,000 at the horizon. The prices are shown in the next two columns under two alternative interest rate assumptions, 10% and 10.11%. The change in interest rate between the two columns is $0.1011 - 0.10$ or 0.0011. The percentage change in 1 plus the interest rate is $0.0011/(1.10)$ or 0.1%. The percentage change in price from the second to the third column should be minus duration times this 0.1 figure. Since for pure discount bonds, duration is maturity, the last column should be minus (0.1) times maturity, and it is. The analysis is derived for very small changes in interest rates and it holds exactly for a very small change in rates. For large changes in rates, the duration measure provides only an approximation of the actual percentage change in prices. However, the approximation is a good one.

Table 19.1   The Effect of a Change in Interest Rates on the Price of a Pure Discount Bond

Maturity (year)	Price		Percentage Change in Price
	$i = 10\%$	$i = 10.11\%$	
1	$909.09	$908.18	−0.1
2	$826.45	$824.80	−0.2
3	$751.31	$749.07	−0.3
4	$683.01	$680.29	−0.4
5	$620.92	$617.83	−0.5

Coupon paying bonds can be viewed as combinations of pure discount bonds. Consider a bond with two payments, one in 5 years and one in 10 years. If we consider each payment separately, and designate the return on the payment in 5 years due to an unanticipated change in interest rates as R_u^5 and the return on the payment in 10 years due to an unanticipated change in interest rates as R_u^{10}, we have

$$R_u^5 = -5 \Delta i$$

$$R_u^{10} = -10 \Delta i$$

The bond with two payments can be viewed as a portfolio of the 5-year payment and the 10-year payment. Let P_5 be the present value of the 5-year payment and P_{10} be the present value of the 10-year payment, P_0 be the value of the bond, and R_u be the unanticipated return on the portfolio.

In earlier chapters, we showed that the return on a portfolio is a weighted average of the return on the assets comprising that portfolio and that the weights are the fraction of the money invested in the asset. The same principles apply here. Thus, the unanticipated return on the portfolio is simply the sum of the fraction of the portfolio invested in each payment times the unanticipated return on the appropriate payment. The fraction invested in each payment is the present value of that payment divided by the price of the portfolio. Thus

$$R_u = \left(\frac{P_5}{P_0}\right) R_u^5 + \left(\frac{P_{10}}{P_0}\right) R_u^{10}$$

Substituting in for R_u^5 and R_u^{10} yields

$$R_u = \frac{P_5}{P_0} (-5 \Delta i) + \frac{P_{10}}{P_0} (-10 \Delta i)$$

$$= -\left[\frac{P_5}{P_0} (5) + \frac{P_{10}}{P_0} (10)\right] \Delta i$$

Thus the duration of a bond with two payments is a weighted average of the maturity of each payment where the weights are the proportion of the current value of the bond attributable to that payment. If the 5- and 10-year payment each contributed equally to the current value of the bond, then the duration would be 7½ years. This can be generalized to T payments. The present value of a payment made in period t is $C(t)/(1 + i)^t$ where $C(t)$ is the payment in period t. If P_0 is the price of the bond, then the fraction of the present value of each payment is $[C(t)/(1 + i)^t]/P_0$. Each weight is multiplied by the duration of the payment that is its maturity. Thus the duration of a T-period bond with payments in each period is

$$D = \frac{\frac{C(1)}{(1 + i)}}{P_0} 1 + \frac{\frac{C(2)}{(1 + i)^2}}{P_0} 2 + \cdots + \frac{\frac{C(T)}{(1 + i)^T}}{P_0} T$$

$$D = \frac{\sum_{t=1}^{T} \frac{tC(t)}{(1 + i)^t}}{P_0} \tag{19.3}$$

Notice that the duration for coupon paying bonds is less than the maturity. Up to now we have assumed that the yield curve is flat and that a shift takes place in the flat yield curve. There are many other assumptions that could be made. Different assumptions change the definition of duration. We have set out several of these in Appendix A at the end of the chapter. Researchers have compared these measures to see which seems to be the most accurate representation of a bond's sensitivity to a change in interest rates. The surprising result is that the one we have presented in this chapter, which was the first one ever derived and is certainly the simplest, seems to do about as well as any measure. Its performance helps explain why this measure is the one most widely used in practice.

Table 19.2 shows the duration on a number of bonds with different maturities and different coupons. Notice how the duration of a bond is much shorter than its maturity, especially for bonds with long maturities.

While this ends our presentation of the concept of duration, we return to duration and use it as a tool in bond portfolio management in the next section of the chapter.

Table 19.2   Duration of Bonds with Different Maturities and Coupons[a]

	Years to Maturity		
Coupon	3	5	10
4	2.88	4.57	7.95
6	2.82	4.41	7.62
8	2.78	4.28	7.04
10	2.74	4.17	6.76
12	2.70	4.07	6.54
14	2.66	3.99	6.36

[a]The analysis assumes $i = 10\%$ and annual payment of coupons.

PROTECTING AGAINST TERM STRUCTURE SHIFTS

Shifts in the term structure are viewed by most managers as the major sources of risk to bond portfolios. Just as shifts in the market systematically affect all equity prices, shifts in the term structure affect all bond prices.

Two techniques have been devised to try to insulate a portfolio from shifts in the term structure. These techniques are known as exact matching and immunization.

Exact Matching

Exact matching involves finding the lowest cost portfolio that produces cash flows exactly matching the outflows that are financed by the investment. For example, assume it is necessary to meet flows of $100, $1,000 and $2,000 over the next three years. These cash flows might be needed to meet pension payments. The bond portfolio is the investment used to meet these obligations. An exact matching program would determine a bond portfolio of one-, two-, and three-year bonds so that the coupons plus principal exactly match the three flows mentioned. In Appendix B, we discuss a procedure for determining a portfolio to accomplish this matching as well as variations on this procedure that can lead to lower cost portfolios. Exact matching programs are a passive investment program. Once the portfolio is determined, no additional changes are required even if the yield curve changes in dramatic ways. The performance of the portfolio is insensitive to interest rate shifts in the sense that it meets a fixed set of obligations regardless of changes in the yield curve. In practice, when the yield curve shifts there may well be profitable bond swaps, and a firm using an exact matching program would use the procedures of Appendix C to evaluate these swaps. Nevertheless, except for the possibility of a bond defaulting, the manager is reasonably assured of meeting the liabilities even with shifts in the yield curve.[2]

Immunization

The second category of techniques for protecting against interest rate shifts are immunization programs. Earlier we introduced duration as a measure of the sensitivity of a bond or a portfolio of bonds to interest rate shifts. Immunization theory attempts to eliminate sensitivity to shifts in the term structure by matching the duration of the assets to the duration of the liabilities. Thus, if duration is truly a measure of sensitivity to interest rate shifts, a shift in the term structure will have the same impact on the present value of both assets and liabilities and will leave unchanged the ability of the program to meet any obligations. If interest rates rise, the present value of assets and liabilities will fall by the same amount. Similarly, if interest rates fall, then the value of the assets and liabilities will rise by the same amount. Perhaps an analogy to Beta is helpful. If a liability had a Beta of 1.5, then purchasing an asset with a Beta of 1.5 would result in a zero Beta combination. This follows since the liability is an outflow and thus is a negative 1.5 Beta. The negative 1.5 Beta and the positive 1.5 Beta is a zero Beta combination insensitive to market movements.

To clarify further, consider a single liability of $100 at year 5. The goal of the investment program is to meet that liability. If a bond is purchased with a maturity of five years, the investor is certain about the value of the bond at the horizon but is uncertain about the rate at which coupon payments will be invested. If interest rates rise, the obligation will be more than met because the coupon payments will be invested at rates that were higher than anticipated. However, if interest rates fall, the obligation will not be met because the coupon payments will be invested at a rate below what was anticipated. If the investor purchases a bond with a maturity of longer than five years, the investor will also be uncertain about the value of the bond at year 5. Consider a rise in interest rates. With a rise in interest rates the aggregate value of the coupons at the horizon will be

---

[2]Many exact matching programs allow a cash carryover from one period to the next. In this case there is risk associated with the return to be earned on these funds. In addition, sinking fund provisions or callability can result in bonds no longer being part of the portfolio and thus are a source of risk.

higher than anticipated because of the coupon payments being invested at more favorable rates. However, because interest rates rose, the value of the bond at the horizon will be less. These influences work in the opposite directions. If the bond is selected properly, these effects will exactly balance one another. Similarly, consider a decline in interest rates. With a decline, the coupon payments will be invested at rates less than anticipated. The aggregate value of the interest payments at the horizon will be less. However, if interest rates decline, the value of the bond will rise. Once again it might be possible to choose a maturity so that these influences exactly offset one another.

The principles discussed in this part of the chapter are exactly why immunization works. At a point in time equal to the duration of the assets the change in reinvestment income will exactly match the change in the value of the bonds. Table 19.3 illustrates these ideas. Assume that interest rates are currently at 11% for all maturities. Further assume that the bond pays annual interest of 13.52% and has a maturity of five years. These are the flows shown in the first column of Table 19.3. The duration of this bond is four years. The value of this bond as of period 4 if interest rates remain at 11% is 165.946.

Table 19.3   The Value of a Bond with Changing Interest Rates

Time	Cash Flow	Value as of Period 4		
		11%	10%	12%
1	13.52	$13.52(1.11)^3$	$13.52(1.1)^3$	$13.52(1.12)^3$
2	13.52	$13.52(1.11)^2$	$13.52(1.1)^2$	$13.52(1.12)^2$
3	13.52	$13.52(1.11)^1$	$13.52(1.1)^1$	$13.52(1.12)^1$
4	13.52	13.52	13.52	13.52
5	113.52	$113.52(1.11)^{-1}$	$113.52(1.1)^{-1}$	$113.52(1.12)^{-1}$
		165.946	165.946	165.974

63.68

If interest rates decline to 10% the value as of period 4 is 165.946. The value is unchanged because the decrease in the value of the interest payments of 0.930 is exactly offset by an increase in the value as of period 4 of a payment of 113.52 in period 5. This increase is 0.930. If interest rates rise to 12%, the value of the coupon payments as of period 4 increases while the value as of period 4 of receiving 113.52 at period 5 decreases. Although these don't completely offset one another, they come close to doing so. This example illustrates the idea of immunization. If we had a liability at period 4, we could purchase a sufficient quantity of the bond to just meet the liability. For example, a $995 liability could be met with six bonds. Whether interest rates decrease or increase, the same liability could be met.

Why does the bond in Table 19.3 have these properties? The coupon for the bond in Table 19.3 was selected so that the bond has a duration of four years. Pure discount bonds have a duration equal to their maturity. Thus a pure discount bond with a maturity of four years also has a duration of four years. Earlier we argued that duration is a measure of sensitivity to interest rate changes. Two bonds with the same sensitivity have their value change by the same amount. If one bond could be swapped for a second before an interest change, it could also be swapped after the change. Since the pure discount bond has a constant value as of period 4, the bond that could be swapped for it would also have a constant value as of period 4.

Immunization strategies are widely used in order to mitigate the effect of interest rate changes. Extensive research has been done on designing immunized portfolios. We now discuss some implications of this research. The duration on a portfolio of bonds is a weighted average of the duration of the individual assets that comprise the portfolio.[3] Let X_i be the proportion of bond i in the portfolio, D_i be the duration of asset i, and D_P be the duration on the portfolio with N bonds.

$$D_P = \sum_{i=1}^{N} X_i D_i$$

There are obviously an enormous number of ways to construct a portfolio of a particular duration. For example, assume that a bond portfolio with a duration of 10 years is required. Further assume that four bonds are being considered with a duration of 6, 8, 10, and 12 years. Simply holding the bond with a duration of 10 years would meet the constraint. Alternatively one-sixth of the money could be invested in the bond with six years duration, one-fourth in the bond with 8 years duration, and the remaining seven-twelfths in the 12-year bond. This results in a duration of 10 years since

$$\left(\frac{1}{6}\right) 6 + \left(\frac{1}{4}\right) 8 + \left(\frac{7}{12}\right) 12 = 10$$

Two different strategies have been explored: a barbell strategy and a focused strategy. The focused strategy finds a portfolio of bonds with each bond having a duration close to the duration of the liability. For example, if the liability is 10 years, then the bonds might have a duration between 9 and 11 years. The bond portfolio is focused around the duration of the liability. The barbell strategy uses bonds with very different durations, for example, 5 and 15 years. The 10-year duration would be met by one-half in the 5-year duration bonds and one-half in the 15-year duration bonds. The advantage of a barbell strategy is that there is no necessity to construct individual bond portfolios to meet each liability. Instead, liabilities of different duration can be met by selecting different mixtures of the 5- and 15-year duration portfolios.

These two strategies have been explored to determine which one better meets the goal of having the asset and liability mix equally sensitive to changes in interest

---

[3] This is a property of almost all duration measures.

rates. The empirical evidence gives some support to the focused strategy. The reason seems to be as follows. All duration measures are approximations of the effect of the true shift in interest rate patterns. When individual assets and liabilities have similar durations, these errors are similar. When the individual assets in a portfolio have different durations from the liabilities even though the portfolio has the same duration, the error patterns can be very different. This latter pattern is what occurs with a barbell strategy. Thus inaccuracies in the duration estimate explain in part the evidence tending to support focusing.

Before closing this discussion, one more facet of immunization should be discussed. Immunization is often presented as a passive strategy, and therefore one by which a set of bonds is purchased and held to maturity. This impression is incorrect. Duration is calculated for a particular yield curve. As the yield curve shifts, duration changes and the assets and liabilities may no longer have the same duration. If the differences become large enough, restructuring is required. Furthermore, even if the yield curve stays constant, the duration of the assets and the liabilities will move apart unless both assets and liabilities have the same cash flow pattern. This also requires restructuring. Thus immunization is an active strategy.

In this section, we have presented techniques for protecting against interest rate shifts when the pattern of cash flows over the full horizon is important. In the next section, we discuss techniques for constructing portfolios when performance over a one-year period is being evaluated.

ACTIVELY MANAGED BOND PORTFOLIOS

In the prior sections we have discussed designing portfolios of bonds that are reasonably insensitive to changes in the yield curve. The return on these portfolios can fluctuate dramatically from period to period because the concern is meeting some future liability rather than period-by-period returns. Many managers are interested not in meeting some future liability but in the year-by-year return on the portfolio. Managers of bond funds and many managers of pension funds are concerned with year-by-year variability. For these managers modern portfolio theory can be of assistance. In the next two sections we discuss how the techniques discussed in earlier sections can be applied to the bond management area.

Estimating Expected Return

We start this section with a consideration of the simplest class of bonds: noncallable bonds issued by the federal government. Later we discuss expected return on nongovernment bonds and the impact of callability and tax considerations.

While any of the theories of the term structure of interest rates can be used to estimate the expected returns on a bond, let us start off illustrating the methodology with the simplest term structure theory: the expectations theory. Under the expectations theory, all bonds must give the same rate of return over any specific time horizon. Thus next period's expected return for any bond is simply the one-period spot rate.

This is modified if we recognize that bonds may be mispriced. Then the expected return will be a function of mispricing if it exists as well as the one-period spot rate. To see the impact of this on expected returns it is necessary to make an assumption about the period of time that elapses before the market corrects mispricing. We will follow common practice and assume that prices adjust to equilibrium within one period. This is the assumption implicit in most commercial services and seems consistent with empirical evidence.[4] To calculate the expected rate of return on a bond we need to calculate its expected equilibrium value one period in the future. Then, from the interest payment expected during the period and the expected capital gain (change in price), we can calculate the expected rate of return.

To get a price for a bond one period in the future, we need expectations about what spot rates or forward rates will be at that time. In the previous chapter we showed how to derive forward rates from the spot rates. If the expectation theory holds, forward rates are not expected to change over time. A hypothetical set of rates is shown in Table 19.4. Assuming these rates, let us examine the expected return on a bond that will mature in five years and pays interest of $8 per period. The bond has $100 principal payment and its current price is $82.

Table 19.4 Hypothetical Set of Rates

Period	Current One Period Forward Rate (%)	Expected Forward Rate in One Period (%)
1	10	
2	11	11
3	12	12
4	13	13
5	14	14

If the bond were priced in equilibrium at the initial period, its price would be

$$P_0 = \frac{8}{1.10} + \frac{8}{(1.10)(1.11)} + \frac{8}{(1.10)(1.11)(1.12)} + \frac{8}{(1.10)(1.11)(1.12)(1.13)}$$
$$+ \frac{108}{(1.10)(1.11)(1.12)(1.13)(1.14)}$$
$$= \$86.16$$

The expected price one period in the future is

$$P_1 = \frac{8}{1.11} + \frac{8}{(1.11)(1.12)} + \frac{8}{(1.11)(1.12)(1.13)} + \frac{108}{(1.11)(1.12)(1.13)(1.14)}$$
$$P_1 = \$86.77$$

---

[4]This is the assumption inherent in Barr Rosenberg's and most other bond pricing services.

Note that if the bond had been priced in equilibrium at time 0, the one-period cash flow would have been $8 in interest and 61¢ in capital gains for a total return of 8.61/86.16 or 10%. The 10% is, of course, the spot rate in the first period. If instead the bond could have been bought for $82, the return would be $8 in interest and $4.77 in capital gains or a return of 15.57%. This rate of return can be broken into its three components: 9.76% from interest income, 0.74% from the change in the equilibrium value of the bond, and 5.07% from the effect of mispricing.

If an alternative term structure theory is a better description of reality, there is a further element to expected return. However, the same techniques are applicable even if any of the other alternative term structure theories is a better description of reality. Consider the liquidity premium theory as an example. With the liquidity premium theory, the expected return is the one-period spot rate plus any adjustment so that the bond is priced in equilibrium plus the change in the liquidity premium. The same procedure can be used to value bonds as was discussed with the expectation theory, but the effect of the change in the liquidity premium has to be taken into account. Consider the example shown in Table 19.5

Table 19.5 is divided into two parts: calculations associated with the current period and calculations associated with one period in the future. The table shows forward rates in the current period. These one-period rates can be determined from spot rates using the techniques discussed in the prior chapter. In the second column is a set of hypothesized liquidity premiums. These are subtracted from the forward rates to arrive at the forward rates without the liquidity premium shown in the third column. These rates are assumed to remain unchanged. Thus the fourth column is the same as the third column. The column that is changed is the liquidity premium column. The liquidity premiums are the same; however, each premium is moved one period in the future. Thus the 0.1 liquidity premium that was the premium for two-year money as of the initial period appears in the third period rather than the second period since at time 1 two periods in the future is period 3.

Assume the same bond discussed previously: a bond with an 8% coupon and a $100 principal payment. Further assume that it sells for its equilibrium price. The forward rates shown in Table 19.5 as of the current period are identical to the rates in Table 19.4, and thus the equilibrium price is unchanged or

$$P_0 = \$86.16$$

The equilibrium price in one period using the rates shown in Table 19.5 is

$$P_1 = \frac{8}{1.109} + \frac{8}{(1.109)(1.119)} + \frac{8}{(1.109)(1.119)(1.129)}$$
$$+ \frac{108}{(1.109)(1.119)(1.129)(1.139)}$$
$$= \$87.05$$

Table 19.5 Assumed Forward Rates (in Percent)

	Current Period			Next Period		
	Forward Rates	Liquidity Premium	Forward Rate (Liquidity Premium Removed)	Forward Rate (Liquidity Premium Removed)	Liquidity Premium	Forward Rates
1	10		10			
2	11	0.1	10.9	10.9		10.9
3	12	0.2	11.8	11.8	0.1	11.9
4	13	0.3	12.7	12.7	0.2	12.9
5	14	0.4	13.6	13.6	0.3	13.9

Without an assumption of a liquidity premium, the equilibrium price in period 1 was $86.77. The difference between $87.05 and $86.77 is the effect of the additional capital gain due to bearing maturity risk. Total expected cash flow is interest income of $8, an expected capital appreciation without the liquidity premium of $86.77 − $86.16 or 61¢ and an effect of the liquidity premium applying to different cash flows of $87.05 − $86.77 or 28¢. Total expected return is (8 + 0.61 + 0.28) divided by $86.16 or 10.32%. The extra 0.32% is the liquidity premium effect. Any mispricing can be dealt with as discussed earlier for the expectations theory.

Up to now we have ignored the effect of default risk, callability, or tax effects in this discussion. Although there are many ways to deal with these influences, we will briefly discuss what has become the most widely used technique. To keep the discussion simple we will assume the expectations theory holds though the modifications for the liquidity premium theory are straightforward and follow from the discussion of how to deal with the liquidity premium presented before.

Let us look at callability. The future prices for noncallable government bonds are arrived at by the foregoing methods. Prices for callable bonds are arrived at by using the rates for noncallable bonds. The average difference between actual price for all callable bonds and the price arrived at for these bonds when they are priced as if they were noncallable bonds is then calculated. The theoretical price of any callable bond is arrived at by pricing as if it were a noncallable government bond and adding the average difference. Mispricing is the difference between the actual price and this theoretical price. This is obviously a crude procedure. A much more exact procedure would use the option pricing models of Chapter 20 to arrive at an estimate of the differential price due to callability. This differential price would be used to estimate possible mispricing. Taxes and default risk are evaluated in an analogous manner.[5]

---

[5]As an alternative to this procedure, some managers estimate spot rates and the effect of callability, default risk, and taxes simultaneously using a multiple regression and the techniques discussed in Appendix A at the end of the chapter. Once again an assumption is made that spot and forward rates remain unchanged and a new price is estimated one period in the future. This new price is used to calculate an expected return.

Index Models

In Chapters 5 and 6 we discussed methods of estimating the variance-covariance structure of common stock returns. The general principles discussed are equally as applicable to bonds as they are to stocks. However, there are special characteristics of bonds that suggest that some modification and respecification would be useful.

Single-index Models   In this section, we discuss the application of the single-index model to bond portfolio management. Consider first applying it to non-callable government bonds with no special tax effects. The return on government bonds can be divided into two parts: the anticipated return and the unanticipated return due to both changes in the yield structure and/or changes in the pricing of the bond in question relative to the yield structure. As discussed previously, if the expectations theory is correct and bonds are fairly priced, then all bonds should have the same expected return over the first period. If one of the other theories is correct or there is mispricing, then the bonds may have different returns and these returns will depend on the maturity of the bond. We will derive the single-index model under the assumption that the expectations theory holds.

The unanticipated return has two sources: a change in the yield curve or a change in the bond price relative to the yield curve. In the first section we showed that the return on a bond due to a shift in the yield curve was minus duration times a measure of interest rate change. We also emphasized that the duration measure is based on a simplified assumption about unanticipated shifts in the yield curve. Assume that the influence of shifts other than that assumed in deriving the duration measure is random. Further assume that shifts in the bond return relative to the yield curve are random. With these assumptions, the effect of these two influences on return are random and can be represented by e_i where the expected value of e_i is zero and the variance of e_i is represented by σ_{ei}^2.

Let us put these ideas together as follows.

$$\begin{matrix} \text{Total} \\ \text{return} \end{matrix} = \begin{matrix} \text{Expected} \\ \text{return} \end{matrix} + \begin{matrix} \text{Return due to an} \\ \text{unanticipated shift} \\ \text{in the yield curve} \end{matrix} + \begin{matrix} \text{Random} \\ \text{influence} \\ \text{on return} \end{matrix}$$

$$R_i = \overline{R}_i - D_i \Delta + e_i \tag{19.4}$$

where

R_i is the return on bond i

$\overline{R}_i$ is the expected return of bond i

D_i is the duration of bond i

Δ is the change in interest rate divided by 1 plus the interest rate

e_i is the random influence with a mean of zero and a variance of σ_{ei}^2

In Chapter 5 we expressed the single-index model in terms of an equity index. We can express the return on a bond in terms of a bond index. Let X_i^m be the proportion of bond i in the bond index. Then the return on the index called R_m is

$$R_m = \sum_i X_i^m R_i = \sum_i X_i \overline{R}_i - \sum_i X_i D_i(\Delta) + \sum_i X_i e_i$$

$$= \overline{R}_m - \sum_i X_i D_i \Delta + \sum_i X_i e_i$$

For a bond index with a large number of bonds $\Sigma_i X_i e_i$ should be approximately zero. This follows from assuming that the e_i are independent from one another. Define D_m as $\Sigma_i X_i D_i$ or the duration of the bond index. With these substitutions we have

$$R_m = \overline{R}_m - D_m(\Delta) \tag{19.5}$$

Solving (19.5) for Δ and substitutions into (19.4) yields[6]

$$R_i = \overline{R}_i + \frac{D_i}{D_m} (R_m - \overline{R}_m) + e_i \tag{19.6}$$

   To complete the analogy with the model discussed in Chapter 5, define β_i as D_i/D_m. With the assumption of e_i being independent of the bond index, β_i has the same meaning as in Chapter 5, that is, β_i is the covariance of R_i with R_m divided by the variance of R_m. However, there is no reason to estimate β_i using historical or modified historical data. Instead, it can be measured directly as the ratio of durations.

   Equation (19.6) is analogous to the single-index model presented for common stocks. If we make the assumptions of the single-index model that $E(e_i e_j) = 0$ for $i \neq j$ then we find

$$\text{cov} (R_i R_j) = \frac{D_i D_j}{D_m^2} \sigma_m^2$$

$$\text{var} (R_i) = \frac{D_i^2}{D_m^2} \sigma_m^2$$

This is not surprising since, as we have already stated, $\beta_i = D_i/D_m$. Single-index models have been used widely in stock selection. There is much less experience concerning their usefulness in the bond management area. Single-index models for bonds did not appear commercially until the 1980s. Similarly, there has been

---

[6]Using arbitrage pricing theory, this return generating process results in the following equilibrium model

$$\overline{R}_i = \overline{R}_z + \frac{D_i}{D_m} (\overline{R}_m - \overline{R}_z)$$

very little academic research of the applicability of single-index models to bond management. This is in contrast to the extensive research done in the common equity area.

Before leaving this discussion we want to mention some other influences affecting returns on bonds. These include liquidity premiums, tax effects, callability, and default risk. If the impact of all of these influences were constant over time, then the single-index model would be appropriate. However, if the premium for these influences changed over time, then bonds would have an added source of variance and covariance. These added influences might be an added source of covariance just like industry membership might be for common stocks. For example, two Aaa-rated bonds might move more alike than two bonds picked at random. This leads us logically to the next section of this chapter on multi-index models.

Multi-index Models   There are a number of reasons why a multi-index might be more relevant than a single-index model (several were discussed in the last section). The major reasons are:

1.   To more accurately measure the effect of interest rate changes.
2.   To reflect the variability introduced by the change in the yield spread between bonds of a particular risk class and governments.
3.   To reflect the variability introduced by the change in yield spread between bonds from various sectors: government, financial, and corporate.
4.   To reflect the variability introduced by the change in the value of a call.
5.   To reflect the variability introduced by changes in the importance of taxes.

Any of these influences could be important enough so that a multi-index model would reflect the covariance structure better than a single-index model. To be concrete let us consider one influence: the change in the yield spread between callable and noncallable bonds. Define S as the differential return on callable bonds due to this spread. Then the return on bond i could be represented by

$$R_i = \overline{R}_i + \frac{D_i}{D_m} (R_m - \overline{R}_m) + a_i S + e_i$$

where a_i is a constant representing the sensitivity of return on bond i to the yield spread S. This is a multi-index model like those described in Chapter 6. It is modified slightly because of its specific application to the bond area. However, the general analysis of Chapter 6 is equally applicable here. The covariance of return between two bonds that are both callable is

$$\text{cov} (R_i R_j) = \frac{D_i D_j}{D_m^2} \sigma_m^2 + a_i a_j \sigma_s^2$$

Similarly the covariance between a callable and a noncallable bond is

$$\text{cov}\ (R_i R_j) = \frac{D_i D_j}{D_m^2}\ \sigma_m^2$$

The spread risk just analyzed is one example of the application of the multi-index model as applied to the bond area. In the common stock area there is a fair amount of research on multi-index models. Some of this evidence was discussed in Chapter 6. In addition, in tests of arbitrage pricing theory there has been a great deal of work using multi-index models. The same is not true in the bond area. There is no evidence that we are aware of that analyzes the reasonableness of single- or multi-index models as estimating techniques for the covariance structure. Thus we must wait for further research before we can report on the relative merits of single- and multi-index models for bond portfolio management.

MANAGEMENT STYLES

Common equity managers are generally stock pickers. They try to pick stocks that will outperform other stocks of similar risk. While a few do try to time the market by changing the proportion of their portfolio invested in short-term cash, most keep fully invested. The amount invested in short-term cash is primarily a function of the needs to service their shareholders or of inflows temporarily invested before being put into common equity.

Bond managers in contrast are almost universally market timers. If they anticipate interest rates rising, they will sell long-term bonds and purchase short-term bonds. If they anticipate interest rates falling, they sell short-term bonds and purchase long-term bonds. Bond managers pay a price for this timing. Most bonds are not as liquid as common equities. Those bonds that have a large market and can be readily traded in a short period of time are primarily government bonds of certain special maturities. Restricting purchases to these bonds results in a lower expected return than purchasing corporate bonds with higher yields or bonds that are mispriced. In addition, folklore and possibly empirical evidence suggest that the bonds used in timing have a lower return due to their marketability. Finally, concentrating on a few government issues to facilitate timing results in a relatively undiversified portfolio.

No forecaster is accurate all of the time. For a forecast of future interest rates to be useful it has to be accurate and different from the consensus since the consensus is already reflected in existing rates. A forecaster should be correct in estimating whether interest rates will rise or fall 50% of the time by chance. A forecaster who is accurate 60% of the time in calling direction would be doing extremely well. Market timing involves one estimate each period: future interest rates. Since even a good forecaster will often be wrong, it will take a number of periods before it can be determined whether the manager has superior forecasting ability. Furthermore, even over a fairly long period of time, the manager has very few decisions, so that there is a reasonable probability of inferior performance even with forecasting ability. As just discussed, market timing involves structuring the portfolio in a way that incurs higher costs and involves holding types of issues that have lower average return. Thus forecasting has to be sufficiently good to cover these costs.

In general, selection involves a large number of decisions at one point in time. If an individual has superior forecasting ability, there is a reasonable chance that results will show superior performance. As the tools discussed in this chapter become more widely known, we expect to see more of this alternative style.

APPENDIX A

Duration Measures

There are at least a dozen different measures of duration. Duration measures the sensitivity of bond prices to a change in the yield curve. In the text we assumed that the yield curve was flat and there was a parallel shift in the yield curve. There are a large number of alternative assumptions that are possible. The yield curve could be upward or downward sloping, and the shift could be very different than parallel. Each of these alternative definitions results in a different measure of duration. In the text we derive one measure of duration. This is the measure most often used. The second most common is derived as follows.

1. Maculay's Second Measure

Assume that the yield curve is not flat but that spot rates vary. Let i_{0t} be the spot rate for a t-year bond. Consider a pure discount bond that pays \$1,000 at year t. Its price is

$$P_0 = \frac{1,000}{(1 + i_{0t})^t} = 1,000(1 + i_{0t})^{-1}$$

Its sensitivity to a change in $1 + i_{0t}$ is

$$dP_0 = 1,000(-t)(1 + i_{0t})^{-t-1}d(1 + i_{0t})$$

$$= \frac{1,000}{(1 + i_{0t})^t}(-t)\frac{d(1 + i_{0t})}{1 + i_{0t}}$$

Recalling that $P_0 = 1,000/(1 + i_{0t})^t$ and dividing through by P_0 yields

$$\frac{dP_0}{P_0} = -t\frac{d(1 + i_{0t})}{(1 + i_{0t})}$$

The key assumption of the second measure of duration is that the proportional change in the t-period spot rate is the same as the proportional change in the one-period spot or

$$\frac{d(1 + i_{0t})}{(1 + i_{0t})} = \frac{d(1 + i_{01})}{(1 + i_{01})}$$

Making this substitution yields

$$\frac{dP_0}{P_0} = -t \frac{d(1 + i_{01})}{(1 + i_{01})} \tag{A.1}$$

This equation holds for any t. A coupon paying bond can be considered a series of pure discount bonds. Let superscripts stand for the time of the flow, and let P_0^t be the current value of the tth-period flow. The price of a bond is the sum of the value of its components. Thus

$$P_0 = P_0^1 + P_0^2 + P_0^3 + \cdots + P_0^T$$

and

$$dP_0 = dP_0^1 + dP_0^2 + dP_0^3 + \cdots + dP_0^T$$

Dividing both sides by P_0 yields

$$\frac{dP_0}{P_0} = \frac{dP_0^1}{P_0} + \frac{dP_0^2}{P_0} + \frac{dP_0^3}{P_0} + \cdots + \frac{dP_0^T}{P_0}$$

or

$$\frac{dP_0}{P_0} = \frac{dP_0^1}{P_0^1}\frac{P_0^1}{P_0} + \frac{dP_0^2}{P_0^2}\frac{P_0^2}{P_0} + \cdots + \frac{dP_0^T}{P_0^T}\frac{P_0^T}{P_0} \tag{A.2}$$

Substituting in the equations for dP_0^1/P_0^1 through dP_0^T/P_0^T and recognizing that P_0^t is the present value of the payment in t yields

$$\frac{dP_0}{P_0} = \frac{\dfrac{C(1)}{(1 + i_{01})}}{P_0}(-1)\frac{d(1 + i_{01})}{(1 + i_{01})} + \frac{\dfrac{C(2)}{(1 + i_{02})^2}}{P_0}(-2)\frac{d(1 + i_{01})}{(1 + i_{01})}$$

$$+ \cdots + \frac{\dfrac{C(T)}{(1 + i_{0T})^T}}{P_0}(-T)\frac{d(1 + i_{01})}{1 + i_{01}}$$

$$= -\left[\frac{\displaystyle\sum_{t=1}^{T} t \frac{C(t)}{(1 + i_{0t})^t}}{P_0}\right]\frac{d(1 + i_{01})}{1 + i_{01}}$$

$$= -D_2 \frac{d(1 + i_{01})}{(1 + i_{01})}$$

D_2 measures the sensitivity of bond price to a change in the yield curve where the shift in the yield curve is such that the proportional change in all spot rates is the same.

2. Nonproportional Shift in Spot Rates

D_2 resulted from an assumption that the proportional change in all spot rates is identical. Empirical evidence suggests that long rates change less than short rates. Let $K(t)$ be the proportional change in the tth-period rate compared to the one-period rate. Then

$$\frac{d(1 + i_{0t})}{1 + i_{0t}} = K(t) \frac{d(1 + i_{01})}{1 + i_{01}}$$

One way of having long rates less volatile than short rates is if we define $K(t)$ as K^{t-1} and have K less than 1. With this definition the sensitivity of pure discount bonds to a change in interest rates is

$$\frac{dP_0}{P_0} = -tK^{t-1} \frac{d(1 + i_{01})}{1 + i_{01}} \tag{A.3}$$

For a coupon bond the proportional change in price is given by Equation (A.2). Substituting (A.3) into (A.2), recalling $P_0^t = C(t)/(1 + i_{0t})^t$ yields

$$\frac{dP_0}{P_0} = \frac{\frac{C(1)}{(1 + i_{01})^1}}{P_0} (-1) \frac{d(1 + i_{01})}{1 + i_{01}} + \frac{\frac{C(2)}{(1 + i_{02})^2}}{P_0} (-2) K^1 \frac{d(1 + i_{01})}{(1 + i_{01})}$$

$$+ \cdots + \frac{\frac{C(T)}{(1 + i_{0T})^T}}{P_0} (-T)K^{T-1} \frac{d(1 + i_{01})}{(1 + i_{01})}$$

or

$$\frac{dP_0}{P_0} = -\left[\sum_{t=1}^{T} \frac{tK^{t-1} \frac{C(t)}{(1 + i_{0t})^t}}{P_0} \right] \frac{d(1 + i_{01})}{(1 + i_{01})}$$

Define the term in the brackets as D_3. This is the third measure of duration. It measures the sensitivity of bond price to a shift in the yield curve, if the change in the tth-period spot rate is K^t times the change in the one-period spot rate.

Measures of duration have been developed for quite a few other possible changes in the yield curve. For instance, Bierwag has developed a measure of duration for additive changes in the yield curve, multiplicative changes in the yield curve, and the combinations of additive and multiplicative changes. Basically, any reasonable way in which the yield curve can change can give rise to another definition of duration. The problem is that each measure assumes that the yield curve can shift in only one pattern (additive, multiplicative, proportional, etc.), and that once we know the change in one spot rate (e.g., i_{01}) we know the change in all spot rates. In reality, shifts in the yield curve may not follow any set pattern. The true test of the definition will be how effectively it measures the actual changes in the prices of bonds due to a change in the yield curve.

APPENDIX B

Exact Matching Programs

One of the ways to reduce sensitivity to changes in interest rates is exact matching. Exact matching is an attempt to find the minimum cost portfolio such that the cash flows in each period are sufficient to cover all liabilities. Define the following elements.

1. $L(t)$ as the liabilities in time t.
2. $C(t,i)$ as the cash flows in period t from a bond of type i.
3. $P(i)$ as the price of bond i.
4. $N(i)$ as the number of bond of type i purchased.

The cost of the portfolio of bonds is the number of bonds of each type purchased times the price per bond summed over all bonds or $\Sigma_i N(i)P(i)$. This quantity is to be minimized. The aggregate cash flows from all bonds in time t is $\Sigma_i C(t,i)N(i)$. Note that some of these cash flows are coupon payments and some are principal payments. The restriction that cash flows be sufficient to meet liabilities is

$$\sum_i N(i)C(t,i) \geq L(t) \qquad \text{for all } t$$

The final constraint is that the investor cannot issue bonds. This requirement can be stated as $N(i) \geq 0$. Summarizing the exact matching problem is

$$\text{minimize } \sum_i N(i)P(i)$$

subject to

1. $\sum_i N(i)C(t,i) \geq L(t) \qquad$ for all t.

2. $N(i) \geq 0 \qquad$ for all i.

Note that liabilities are being met by coupon payments or maturing bonds. Bonds are not sold to meet cash flows. Thus the only risk is default risk. Adverse interest rate changes do not affect the ability to meet liabilities. Thus matching programs do not necessitate changes in a portfolio as interest rates change. The foregoing problem is a linear programming problem and can be solved with standard algorithms.

The major variation in this problem is to allow cash carryforward. If cash can be carried forward, then there are two possible sources of funds that can be used to meet liabilities: cash flows from the bond investment and cash carryover from the prior period.

Let S_t represent the amount of short-term investment and r be the one-period interest rate. Then in time t the value of the short-term investment is the prior period's investment S_{t-1} plus the interest on the investment or $S_{t-1}(1 + r)$. In each period sources of funds (cash from the bond portfolio and short-term investments) must be equal to uses of funds (liabilities plus cash to be carried forward).

$$\text{Sources of funds} = \text{Uses of funds}$$

$$\begin{bmatrix} \text{From bond} \\ \text{portfolio} \end{bmatrix} + \begin{bmatrix} \text{From prior short-} \\ \text{term investment} \end{bmatrix} = \begin{bmatrix} \text{Liabilities} \end{bmatrix} + \begin{bmatrix} \text{New one-period} \\ \text{investment} \end{bmatrix}$$

$$\sum_i N(i)C(t,i) + S_{t-1}(1 + r) = L(t) + S_t$$

With the addition of cash carryforward the problem becomes

$$\text{minimize} \sum_i N(i)P(i)$$

subject to

1. $\sum_i N(i)C(t,i) + S_{t-1}(1 + r) \geq L(t) + S_t$ for all t.

2. $N(i) \geq 0$ for all i.

3. $S_t \geq 0$ for all t.

4. $S_{-1} = 0$.

Once again liabilities are being met out of interest payments and principal payments so that bonds are not being sold. Thus the cash flows from the bond portfolio do not depend on the future course of interest rates. However, r is a future interest rate. If r is set sufficiently low, there will be very little chance that future interest rates will be lower and very little risk that cash flows will be insufficient to meet liabilities. Allowing cash carryforward cannot result in more cost than not doing so. Thus the formulation allowing cash carryforward (perhaps at zero interest) provides the better solution. Firms that offer this type of product usually find that competitive pressures force r to approximate current expectations about future short-term rates. In this case the bond matching program becomes much riskier and once again its feasibility depends on the actual course of future interest rates.

APPENDIX C

Bond Swapping Techniques

   In the second part of this chapter, we discussed methods of actively managing a bond portfolio. Techniques discussed in these sections allow for bond switches resulting from changes in perceptions of which bonds are over- or underpriced or resulting from changes in risk perceptions. Using the techniques discussed in the second part of this chapter is clearly an appropriate technique for determining bond swaps.

   An alternative procedure that makes many fewer assumptions is to attempt to find additional bonds that can be swapped for existing bonds that maintain the future cash flow pattern and yet earn immediate profit from the swap. This is the basic idea underlining a bond swap program. To be specific, define the following elements.

1. $P_B(i)$, the cost of buying bond i.
2. $P_S(i)$, the cash received from selling bond i.
3. $C(i,t)$, the cash flow of bond i in period t.
4. $N_B(i)$, the number of bonds of type i purchased.
5. $N_S(i)$, the number of bonds of type i sold.

With these definitions the cost of the bonds purchased is

$$\sum_i N_B(i)P_B(i)$$

The profit is the difference between the proceeds from the sale and the cost of the purchase or

$$\sum_i N_S(i)P_S(i) - \sum_i N_B(i)P_B(i)$$

The object of a bond swap program is to maximize this difference subject to not reducing cash flows. If the swap does not result in reduced cash flows, the bond portfolio will still meet any liabilities.

   To express this constraint we write

$$\sum_i N_B(i)C(i,t) \geq \sum_i N_S(i)C(i,t) \qquad \text{for all } t$$

One swap model is

$$\text{maximize} \sum_i N_S(i)P_S(i) - \sum_i N_B(i)P_B(i)$$

subject to

1. $\sum_i N_B(i)C(i,t) \geq \sum_i N_S(i)C(i,t)$ for all t.

2. $N_B(i), N_S(i) \geq 0$ for all i.

The ability to carry forward funds from an earlier to a later period can be added to the bond swap problem. This increases the risk since future interest rates are unknown. However, it increases the number of swap opportunities. Adding the ability to carry forward funds can be developed as follows. Let

1. S_t be the short-term investment in period t.

2. r be the one-period interest rate.

The value of the cash carried forward from period $t - 1$ is $S_{t-1}(1 + r)$. The investment in short-term cash in period t is S_t.

If short-term borrowing is not allowed, then S_t must be nonzero. The complete problem is

$$\text{maximize} \sum_i N_S(i)P_S(i) - \sum_i N_B(i)P_B(i)$$

subject to

1. $\sum_i N_B(i)C(i,t) + S_{t-1}(1 + r) \geq \sum_i N_S(i)C(i,t) + S_t$ for all $t = 1, \ldots, T$.

2. $N_B(i), N_S(i) \geq 0$ for all i.

3. $S_t \geq 0$ for all t.

4. $S_{-1} = 0$.

This is the standard bond swap problem.

QUESTIONS AND PROBLEMS

1. Consider a bond with semi-annual coupon payments of $50, a principal payment of $1,000 in 5 years, and a price of $1,000. Assume that the yield curve is a flat 10%. What is the duration of the bond?

2. Consider a bond with annual coupon payments of $100, a principal payment of $1,000 in 10 years, and a cost of $1,000. Assume a flat yield curve with a 10% yield to maturity. What is the duration of the bond? If the yield curve remains unchanged, what is the bond's duration in 3 years? In 5 years? In 8 years?

3. Given the following bonds

Bond	Duration
A	5
B	10
C	12

construct three different portfolios of the three bonds, each with a duration of 9 years.

4. Assume liabilities of $250, $500, and $550 must be met in periods 1, 2, and 3, respectively. Find a portfolio of the bonds shown below that meets these cash outflows. What is the cost of the portfolio? (*Hint:* The question does not require a least cost portfolio. Thus the linear programming procedure of Appendix B isn't necessary.)

Number	Price	Cash Flows in Period		
		1	2	3
A	950	50	1,050	
B	1,000	100	100	1,100
C	1,000	1,000		

5. Assume that the yield curve for the data of Problem 3 is 10%. Further assume that the three bonds are of equal value and the only bonds existing. Set up a single-index representation of their covariance. What is the covariance between all pairs of bonds?

BIBLIOGRAPHY

1. Bierwag, G.O. "Immunization, Duration and the Term Structure of Interest Rates," *Journal of Financial and Quantitative Analysis,* **12,** No. 4 (Dec. 1977), pp. 725–742.
2. Bierwag, G.O., and Kaufman, George. "Coping with the Risk of Interest Rate Fluctuations: A Note," *Journal of Business,* **50,** No. 3 (July 1977), pp. 364–370.
3. Bierwag, G.O., Kaufman, G.G., and Khang, C. "Duration and Bond Portfolio Analysis: An Overview," *Journal of Financial and Quantitative Analysis,* **13,** No. 4 (Nov. 1978), pp. 671–681.
4. Bierwag, G.O., Kaufman, George, G., and Toevs, Alden. "Single Factor Duration Models in a Discrete General Equilibrium Framework," *The Journal of Finance,* **37,** No. 2 (May 1982), pp. 325–338.

5. ———. "Immunization Strategies for Funding Multiple Liabilities," *Journal of Financial and Quantitative Analysis,* **XVII,** No. 1 (March 1983), pp. 113–124.

6. Boardman, Calvin M., and McEnally, Richard W. "Factors Affecting Seasoned Corporate Bond Prices," *Journal of Financial and Quantitative Analysis,* **XVI,** No. 2 (June 1981), pp. 193–206.

7. Boquist, J.A., Racette, G.A., and Schlarbaum, G. "Duration and Risk Assessment for Bonds and Common Stocks," *Journal of Finance,* **30,** No. 5 (1975), pp. 1360–1365.

8. Brennan, M.J., and Schwartz, E. "Savings Bonds, Retractable Bonds and Callable Bonds," *Journal of Financial Economics,* **5,** (1977), pp. 67–88.

9. Brennan, M.J., and Schwartz, E. "A Continuous Time Approach to the Pricing of Bonds," *Journal of Banking and Finance,* **3,** (1979), pp. 133–155.

10. Brennan, M.J., and Schwartz, E. "Conditional Predictions of Bond Prices and Returns," *Journal of Finance,* **35,** (1980), pp. 405–417.

11. Carr, J.L., Halpern, P.J., and McCallum, J.S. "Correcting the Yield Curve: A Re-interpretation of the Duration Problem," *Journal of Finance,* **29,** No. 4 (1974), pp. 1287–1294.

12. Constantinides, George M., and Ingersoll, Jonathan E., Jr. "Optimal Bond Trading with Personal Taxes," *Journal of Financial Economics,* **13,** No. 3 (Sept. 1984), pp. 299–351.

13. Cox, J.C., Ingersoll, Jr., J.E., and Ross, S.A. "Duration and the Measurement of Basic Risk," *Journal of Business,* **52,** No. 1 (Jan. 1979), pp. 51–61.

14. Dothan, U.L. "On the Term Structure of Interest Rates," *Journal of Financial Economics,* **6,** (1978), pp. 59–69.

15. Fisher, L., and Weil, R.L. "Coping with the Risk of Interest Rate Fluctuations: Returns to Bondholders from Naive and Optimal Strategies," *Journal of Business,* **44,** No. 3 (Oct. 1971), pp. 408–431.

16. Hessel, Christopher A., and Huffman, Lucy. "The Effect of Taxation on Immunization Rules and Duration Estimation," *The Journal of Finance,* **36,** No. 5 (Dec. 1981), pp. 1127–1142.

17. Ingersoll, J.E., Jr., Skelton, J., and Weil, R.L. "Duration Forty Years Later," *Journal of Financial and Quantitative Analysis,* **13,** (Nov. 1978), pp. 627–650.

18. Livingston, M., and Caks, J. "A 'Duration' Fallacy," *Journal of Finance,* **32,** (March 1977), pp. 185–187.

19. Macaulay, F.R. *Some Theoretical Problems Suggested by the Movements of Interest Rates, Bond Yields, and Stock Prices in the United States since 1856,* (New York: Columbia University Press, 1938).

20. Marshall, William J., and Yawitz, Jess B. "Lower Bounds on Portfolio Performance: An Extension of the Immunization Strategy," *Journal of Financial and Quantitative Analysis,* **XVII,** No. 1 (March 1982), pp. 101–114.

21. Niederhoffer, V., and Regan, P. "Earnings Changes, Analysts' Forecasts, and Stock Prices," *Financial Analysts Journal,* **28,** No. 3 (May–June 1972), pp. 65–71.

22. Redington, F.M. "Review of the Principles of Life-Office Valuations," *Journal of the Institute of Actuaries,* **18,** (1952), pp. 286–315.
23. Richard, S.F. "An Arbitrage Model of the Term Structure of Interest Rates," *Journal of Financial Economics,* **6,** (1978), pp. 33–57.
24. Richards, Malcolm. "Analysts' Performance and the Accuracy of Corporate Earnings Forecasts," *Journal of Business,* **49,** No. 3 (July 1976), pp. 350–357.
25. Schaefer, Stephen M., and Schwartz, Eduardo S. "A Two-Factor Model of the Term Structure: An Approximate Analytical Solution," *Journal of Financial and Quantitative Analysis,* **19,** No. 4 (Dec. 1984), pp. 413–421.
26. Spacek, Leonard. in Lorie, J., and Hamilton, M. [19], p. 146.

Chapter 20
Option Pricing Theory

The markets for options are among the fastest growing markets for financial assets in the United States. While option trading is not new, it experienced a gigantic growth with the creation of the Chicago Board of Options Exchange in 1973. The listing of options meant more orderly and thicker markets for these securities.

The growth in option trading has been accompanied by a trememdous interest among academics and practitioners in the valuing of option contracts. In this chapter we discuss alternative types of options, examine the effect of certain characteristics on the value of options, and present explicit models for valuing options.

TYPES OF OPTIONS

An option is a contract entitling the holder to buy or sell a designated security at or within a certain period of time at a particular price. There are a large number of types of option contracts, but they all have one element in common: the value of an option is directly dependent on the value of some underlying security. Options represent a claim against the underlying security and thus are often called contingent claim contracts. The two least complex options are called puts and calls. These are the most widely traded options. In addition, most other options either can be valued as combinations of puts and calls or can be valued by the methodology developed to value puts and calls. Consequently, we will begin this section with a discussion of puts and calls and then we will discuss other types of options and combinations of basic options.

Calls

The most common type of an option is a call. A call gives the owner the right to buy a fixed number of shares of a stock at a fixed price, either before or at some fixed date. Calls sold in Europe can generally be exercised only at a particular date. Thus, calls containing this provision are referred to as European calls. The right to exercise at any time up to the expiration date is a feature of calls sold in America and calls containing this provision are referred to as American calls. Take, as an example, a November 20 American call on Mobil at $70. This call gives the owner the right to buy a certain number of shares of Mobil at $70 a share any time on or before November 20. Calls are normally traded in units of 100 shares. Thus, one call would be a right to buy 100 shares of Mobil. Each characteristic of the call has a name. For example, the $70 price is called the exercise price. The final date at which the call can be exercised is the expiration date.[1]

One of the distinguishing characteristics of a call is that if it is exercised, the exchange of stocks is between two investors. One investor issues the call (called the call writer) and the other investor purchases the call. The call is a side bet between two investors on the future course of the security. Figure 20.1a shows the profit per share of stock for the holder of a call at the expiration date. The figure represents the pattern for a call originally purchased for $5 with an exercise price of $50. For a stock price below $50, it would not pay to exercise the call

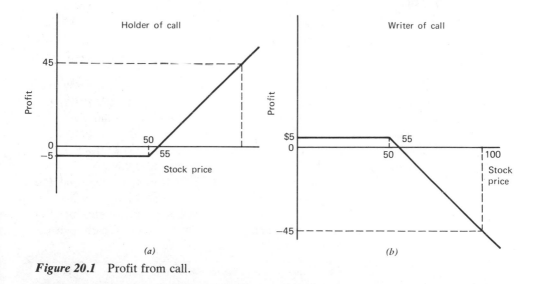

(a)   *(b)*

Figure 20.1   Profit from call.

---

[1]In the example we use an arbitrary date for expiration. For options not listed on the exchanges, any date is possible. However, options trading on the Chicago Board of Options have standardized expiration dates. Any single security will normally have options outstanding with three different expiration dates. These dates are three months apart (e.g., April, July, and October). These options expire at 10:59 A.M. Central Time on the Saturday after the third Friday of the month.

since shares could be purchased in the open market for less than the exercise price. For share prices above $50, it would pay to exercise the call and gain by the difference between the share price and exercise price. For example, if the share price is $54, then the holder of a call benefits from the ability to purchase the stock at $50 rather than $54. For share prices up to $55, the owner of the call loses money since the payoff from the stock purchase is less than the cost of the call. For a stock price above $55, there is a profit.

The position of the call writer is depicted in Figure 20.1*b*. The pattern of the profit is exactly opposite that of the call purchaser. For a stock price below $50 the call writer makes a profit equal to the $5 per share received from the issuance of the call; from $50 to $55 part of the $5 is lost by having to furnish the stock at a price below the market price; above $55, the call writer loses more than was received by selling the call.

Up to now we have referred to shares being traded between individuals as a result of exercise at the expiration of a call. We could have also discussed the exercise of a call before the expiration date. However, we have not done this so far since calls (even those that have an exercise price below the price of the stock) are rarely exercised before the expiration date.[2] For example, assume the share price is $60 and the exercise price is $50. Clearly, a profit can be made by exercising the option. There is a third alternative. Instead of exercising the option, sell it.

The sale may be to someone who does not currently maintain a position in the option or it may be to an investor who wrote an option and also wishes to liquidate his or her position.[3] The listing of options on exchanges facilitates these sales. With options listed on the exchange, the mechanics of the purchase or writing of an option becomes identical to the mechanics of the purchase or sale of a stock.

There are actions that a firm might take that will affect the value of its shares. For example, a two-for-one stock split would be expected to cut the price of a share in half. Stock dividends and cash dividends are two other examples. The value of an option is affected by these actions of the firm. Clearly, if there were no adjustment in the exercise price when a stock splits, the value of an option would be substantially reduced. Most options are protected against stock dividends and stock splits by automatic adjustments in the exercise price and the number of shares that can be purchased with one option. Cash dividends are not as frequently protected against. For example, there are no adjustments for cash dividends for options traded on the exchanges. The price of a stock on average

---

[2] In a later section of this chapter we will discuss the well-established proof that (except for possible exceptions associated with dividend payments) it never pays to exercise an American call prior to the expiration date. It is always better to sell it rather than exercise it.

[3] When an individual sells an option, the person purchasing it need not be the original writer. Rather, the individual purchasing the option is whoever happens to wish to buy the option on the day of sale. This is identical to what happens with any other security. When you buy a share of stock and subsequently sell it, the individual that you buy from or sell to is unknown and normally different.

decreases by slightly less than the amount of the dividend when a stock goes ex-dividend. Thus, all other things being equal, the price of an option should be lower on a stock that will go ex-dividend before the expiration date.

The next most common type of option is a put, which we will discuss in the next section.

Puts

A put is an option to sell stock at a given price on or before a particular expiration date. Consider, for example, a $50 General Motors put of December 18. The person who owned such a put would have the right to sell the General Motors stock to the person who issued the put at $50 a share on or before December 18. Puts, like calls, are traded in units of 100 shares. Thus, one put involves the right to sell 100 shares. If the exercise can take place only at the expiration date, it is called a European put. If the exercise can take place at any time on or before the expiration date, it is called an American put. A put, like a call, involves a transaction between two investors. Thus, the writing of puts has no effect on the value of the firm.

Figure 20.2 shows the profit at the expiration date for a put with an exercise price of $50 that originally cost $5. Figure 20.2a shows the profit to the owner of the put. Figure 20.2b shows the profit to the writer of a put. Consider Figure 20.2a. For prices about $50, the owner of the put would prefer to sell shares in the regular market rather than to the writer of the put, since the price received is greater. Thus, for prices above $50, the exercise value is zero. For prices above $45 but below $50, the owner of the put would prefer to exercise her option instead of selling her stock on the open market. However, the owner of the put

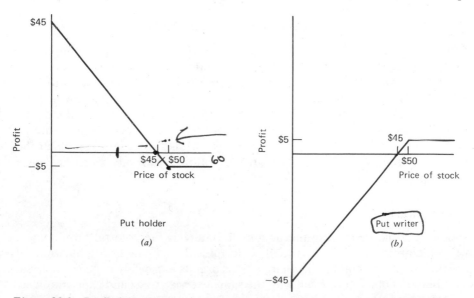

Figure 20.2   Profit from put.

loses money, since she paid more for the put than she gains from the sale at a higher price. Below $45, the owner of the put makes money, since the amount she gains from the sale at a more attractive price more than compensates for the cost of the put. The payoff pattern for the writer of the put is the exact opposite of the payoff pattern for the owner. For prices above $45, he makes money and for prices below $45, he loses.

Puts, like calls, are rarely exercised before expiration. Assume the share price in our example declined to $40. At $40, it clearly pays to exercise rather than to let the option expire. Instead of exercising the option, the owner could sell the right. While an American put is more likely to be exercised before expiration than an American call, we will show that it generally pays to sell rather than exercise a put, for the sale price will almost always be higher than the exericse value.

Warrants

A warrant is almost identical to a call. Like a call, it involves the right to purchase stock at an exercise price at or before an expiration date. A warrant differs from a call in one way: A warrant is issued by the corporation rather than another investor. This seemingly small difference is very important. There are two times when this difference has an effect on the value of the firm that issues the warrant. First, when the warrants are issued, the company receives the money for the warrant. Second, when the warrants are exercised, the following occurs:

1. The company receives the exercise price.
2. The number of shares of the firm that are outstanding goes up by the number of shares that are exercised.
3. The number of warrants still outstanding goes down.

Calls and puts are side bets by market investors and the corporation has no direct interest in transactions involving these options, either when they are created or exercised. Warrants, on the other hand, are used by the corporation to raise capital. The corporation and its shareholders have a definite interest in their issuance and exercise, since these transactions affect both the amount of cash the firm has raised and the ownership interest of its shareholders. Because the issuance and exercise of warrants affect the value of the security on which the warrant represents a contingent claim, the valuation of warrants becomes a more complex problem than the valuation of calls.

Combinations

Part of the fun of reading the options literature is the colorful terminology. One of the areas where it is especially colorful is the naming of combinations of options. An infinite number of combinations of puts and calls can be considered. A combination of a put and call with the same exercise price and expiration date is called a straddle. A similar combination of two puts and a call is a strip. If the combination is two calls and a put, it is called a strap. The payoff pattern at expiration is easy to detemine using the techniques discussed earlier. Likewise, the valuation can be accomplished using the techniques discussed later in this chapter.

Consider a straddle. Figure 20.3a shows the profit at expiration from the point of view of the purchaser of the option. Figure 20.3b is the profit from the point of view of the writer. As we can see from examining these diagrams, a straddle should be purchased by someone who believes the price of the shares will move substantially either up or down, without being sure of the direction, and who also believes that other investors have underestimated the magnitude of future price changes. For example, a straddle could be purchased by someone who knew that major information was about to be announced that would seriously affect the company's fortune, was unsure whether the information would be good news or bad news, and believed that other investors were unaware of the existence of this information. In contrast, the writer of a straddle is an investor who believes that the share price will trade at close to the exercise price, while others believe differently.

One of the interesting ways to trade options is in combination with the stock on which they represent a claim. The investor who combines stocks with contingent claims on the stocks has two assets with very strong correlations. Consider the writer of a call who also owns the shares.[4] Figure 20.4 shows the payoff pattern at expiration. The exercise price is assumed to be $50, the cost of the

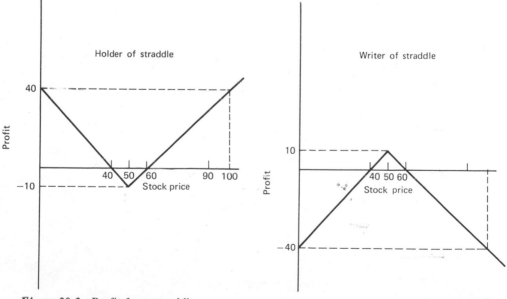

Figure 20.3   Profit from straddle.

---

[4]The writing of a call while owning the stock is called writing a covered call.

stock to the holder is also assumed to be $50, and the call is assumed to cost $5. Three separate lines are shown: one for the stock, one for the call, and one for the combination. As Figure 20.4 shows, an investor who writes a call and owns the stock rather than simply owning the stock increases the return at low stock prices at the expense of returns at the higher share prices.

As a final example, consider the ownership of a put plus the ownership of stock. Once again, assume an exercise price of $50, a stock cost of $50, and a put cost of $5. Figure 20.5 shows the payoff pattern. This combination reduces the return at higher stock prices in exchange for guaranteeing that if the stock declines in price, the portfolio will not decline below a lower limit.

Another type of combination is an option that can be purchased only in combination with another security. A convertible bond is an example of this combination. A convertible bond has the same characteristics as a normal bond and in addition can be converted into the shares of a company. Thus, the convertible bond can be considered a bond plus a call. However, the call has a special feature. Conversion of the bond into shares of stock involves giving up the bond, plus sometimes cash for the stock. Since the value of the bond changes over time, the exercise price changes over time.

We have discussed a number of combinations of options and options plus security positions in this section. There are many others that are possible. We leave it to our readers to determine the payoff pattern for those they find interesting.

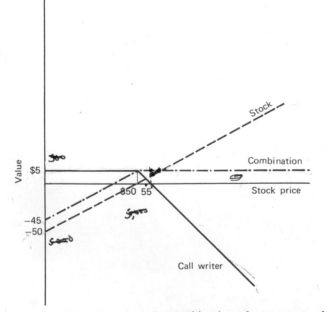

Figure 20.4 The value of a combination of common stock and a call.

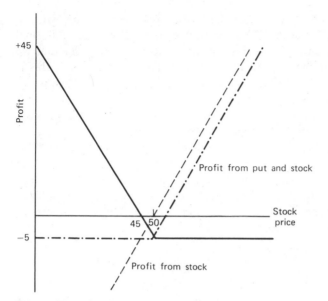

Figure 20.5 Profit from put and stock.

SOME BASIC CHARACTERISTICS OF OPTION VALUES[5]

In a short time we will examine formal option valuation models. However, before we do so we can infer the manner in which certain characteristics of options should affect their value in a rational market. Not only are these relationships interesting in themselves, they will also prove useful as a check on valuation models developed in the later sections. Any valuation model should be consistent with these basic relationships. It is interesting to note that some of the earlier option valuation models that were later proved incorrect were not consistent with these basic relationships.

Relative Prices of Calls with Alternative Characteristics

Recall that the European call gives the holder the right to purchase stock at the exercise price on a particular date (the expiration date). The American call differs from the European call in that it can be exercised at any time up to the expiration date. Since the American call is a European call with the added opportunity to exercise before the expiration date, it cannot be worth less than the European call. Thus, the first relationship established is that a European call with the same expiration date and exercise price as an American call cannot sell for more than the American call.

Consider two American calls with the same exercise prices and assume both

---

[5]The results in this section were developed by Merton [57].

calls are on the same stock. The one with the longer life offers the investor all the exercise opportunities of the one with the shorter life, plus some additional opportunities. Hence, it can't be worth less. It might bother the reader that we don't simply say that the longer lived call is more valuable. In general, this is true, but in some extreme cases (e.g., when both calls are worthless) this is not true. Hence the more cautious statement.

The next relationship concerns the exercise price. Consider two calls with the same expiration date written on the same stock. The one with the higher exercise price cannot be more valuable than the one with the lower exercise price. This is obvious, since the holder of the latter can be in the same position as the holder of the former, upon exercise, except that she will have cash left over.

While these relationships seem quite simple, as discussed earlier, not all valuation models that have been developed were consistent with these principles, hence they are worth keeping in mind.

Minimum Value of a European Call

In this section we will show that the value of a European call is at least the greater of zero and the difference between the stock price and the present value of the exercise price. To see this, consider two different portfolios. Portfolio A involves the purchase of a call and a bond that matures at the expiration date of the call and which at that date will have a value equal to the exercise price. If R is the interest rate between the time the call is valued and the expiration date, and if E is the exercise price, then bonds in the amount of $E/(1 + R)$ should be purchased. An alternative to portfolio A is the purchase of stock directly. Call this portfolio B. The key characteristics to these investments are shown in Table 20.1. S_1 is the stock price at expiration, S_0 is the current stock price, E is the exercise price, and C is the current price of the call. The payoffs at the expiration date are shown in the last two columns of the table.

If $S_1 > E$, then the payoffs from both portfolios are the same. However, if $S_1 \leq E$, the payoff from portfolio A is larger. Thus, portfolio A is at least as desirable as portfolio B, and if $S_1 \leq E$ at expiration is possible, A is more desirable.

Table 20.1   Payoffs from Alternative Holdings

		Value at Expiration Date	
Action	Investment	If $S_1 > E$	If $S_1 \leq E$
Portfolio A			
Buy call	$-C$	$S_1 - E$	0
Buy Bonds	$\dfrac{-E}{1 + R}$	E	E
Total	$-C - \dfrac{E}{1 + R}$	S_1	E
Portfolio B			
Buy stock	$-S_0$	S_1	S_1

Given that portfolio A is at least as desirable as B, it can't cost less than B; otherwise no one would purchase the stock (portfolio B). Therefore,

$$C + \frac{E}{1 + R} \geqslant S_0$$

or

$$C \geqslant S_0 - \frac{E}{1 + R}$$

The European call cannot sell for less than the stock price less the present value of the exercise price. Since the call cannot sell for a price below zero, we have completed the proof.

Early Exercise of an American Call

Probably the most surprising conclusion of modern option pricing theory is that it never pays to exercise an American call before the expiration date on a stock that doesn't pay dividends or whose exercise price is adjusted for dividend payments. Later we will present a simple proof. But before we do, it is worthwhile to discuss why this holds. The reason is simple but subtle. The American call is worth more alive than dead. It is worth more keeping the American call alive by not exercising it than killing it through exercise. Thus, an investor no longer wishing to hold the call is better off selling it than exercising it. Consider an example. Assume a stock is selling for $60 and an investor holds an American call with an exercise price of $50. Further, assume this investor believes that the stock price will decline between now and the expiration date. Clearly, the investor would prefer to exercise the call now rather than hold it and exercise it at a later date. There is another option: sell the call to another investor.

If the call has a market price higher than the $10 the investor makes on exercise ($60 stock price − $50 exercise price), selling the call is to be preferred. Why should the price of the call be more than $10? The American call has two sources of value: the value of an immediate call ($10) plus the value of the chance to call from now to the expiration date. As long as this latter opportunity has value, the American call should sell for more than $10. You might well ask why someone would wish to buy the call when the investor believes the stock price will decline. The answer is that this cannot be the general market belief or the stock price would have already declined. In other words, the aggregate market belief must be that the correct price is $60 and that at $60, the total return from the stock is competitive with securities of similar risk. Thus, the market must believe the return on the stock will be positive.

Now for the proof. Earlier, we argued that an American call cannot be worth less than a European call. We also showed that the European call was worth more than the maximum of zero and the difference between the stock price and the present value of the exercise price $[S_0 - E/(1 + R)]$. Thus, the value of the American call must be greater than the maximum of zero and $S_0 - E/(1 + R)$. However, if the call is exercised, its value is $S_0 - E$. Since $S_0 - E/(1 + R) > S_0 - E$, the call sells for more than its value if exercised.

The foregoing discussion assumed that the stock did not pay a dividend before the expiration date, or that the call was protected against dividends by having the exercise price adjusted by the amount of the dividend. If the stock is dividend paying or the call is not protected, early exercise is possible. Consider the example discussed earlier with a $60 stock price and a $50 exercise price. If the stock was about to pay a large dividend, then investors could rationally believe that the share price should be lower than $60 between the ex-dividend date and the expiration date and thus that the current difference is the best that can be obtained.[6]

Put Call Parity

A put and the underlying stock can be combined in such a way that the combination has the same payoff pattern as a call. Likewise, a call and the underlying equity can be combined so that they have the same payoff pattern as a put. This allows the put or call to be priced in terms of the other security.

This relationship is easiest to derive for European options. Furthermore, it is convenient to assume that the common equity will not pay a dividend in the period before the option expires. Define:

S_0 as the current stock price
S_1 as the stock price at the expiration date
E as the exercise price
C as the call price
P as the put price
R_B as the borrowing rate
R_L as the lending rate

Now consider a combination of a share of stock, a put, and taking a loan for an amount $E/(1 + R_B)$. If $E/(1 + R_B)$ is borrowed and if the interest rate between the purchase of the combination and the expiration date is R_B, then $[E/(1 + R_B)](1 + R_B) = E$ will have to be paid back. Thus, if $E/(1 + R_B)$ is borrowed, an amount equal to the exercise price will have to be paid back at the expiration date. The payoff of this combination at the expiration date is shown in Table 20.2. The payoff pattern is, of course, exactly the same pattern as for a call.

The investor has two possible investments: the call or the portfolio being discussed. Each investment has the same value at the expiration date. If they sell at different prices currently, then the investor can purchase the least expensive

---

[6]Stock prices are expected to drop by slightly less than the amount of the dividend when a stock goes ex-dividend.

Table 20.2 Payoffs of Portfolios Involving Puts

Security	Value at Expiration Date	
	If $S_1 > E$	If $S_1 \leqslant E$
Portfolio A		
Buy stock	S_1	S_1
Buy put	0	$E - S_1$
Borrow	$-E$	$-E$
Total	$S_1 - E$	0
Purchase of call		
Buy call	$S_1 - E$	0

investment and issue the more expensive investment. Since they have the same payoff pattern at the expiration date, the investor can use the proceeds of the one investment to meet the obligations of the other. If they have different costs, a guaranteed profit can be made. Assuming the portfolio is less expensive than the call, then the investor would write the call and purchase the portfolio. If the call is more expensive than the portfolio, this combination then yields a guaranteed profit. The guaranteed profit is immediate and has zero risk. Such a possibility cannot last long in any efficiently functioning market. Thus, the call can't be more expensive than the portfolio, and writing the call plus purchasing the portfolio can't be profitable. Writing a call involves a cash inflow of C and purchasing portfolio A involves flows of $-S_0 - P + E/(1 + R_B)$. This implies

$$C - S_0 - P + \frac{E}{1 + R_B} \leqslant 0$$

or

$$S_0 + P - \frac{E}{1 + R_B} \geqslant C$$

Consider what happens if the call is less expensive than the portfolio. In this case, the investor would wish to issue the portfolio and buy the call. The flows would be $-C$ for the call and $S_0 + P - E/(1 + R_L)$ for portfolio A.

These flows closely resemble those discussed earlier, but R_L has replaced R_B. Since we assume the investor is short selling the portfolio rather than purchasing it, the investor is lending rather than borrowing and R_L is assumed to be the lending rate.

If the call is less expensive than the portfolio, then this combination yields a guaranteed profit. A guaranteed profit with no risk can't last long in the market, so buying the call and issuing the portfolio cannot be a profitable combination. This implies that

$$S_0 + P - \frac{E}{1 + R_L} - C \leqslant 0$$

or

$$C \geq S_0 + P - E/(1 + R_L)$$

Putting the equations together yields

$$S_0 + P - \frac{E}{1 + R_B} \geq C \geq S_0 + P - \frac{E}{1 + R_L}$$

If $R_L = R_B$, the inequalities above become equalities and we have the put call parity relationship.

Some comment on the two different arbitrage combinations is in order. The first combination was appropriate if the call was more expensive than the portfolio. This strategy involved buying stock and a put, borrowing, and writing a call. All of these are feasible, and the combination is a full description of the necessary actions.[7] The other combination was appropriate when the call was less expensive than the portfolio. This involved selling the stock short, writing a put, lending, and buying a call. The analysis assumed that the proceeds of the short sale were immediately available. This is unrealistic in general, as discussed earlier. However, it would represent a realistic situation for an investor who currently owned the shares and who engages in a transaction identical to a short sale by selling his or her existing shares. Since there are likely to be many of these investors, the put call parity theorem should hold reasonably well.

The previous analysis examined the payoff pattern at the expiration date of the option. This is, of course, the only relevant date to examine for European options. With American options, other dates are potentially relevant. One of the components of the portfolio is a put. It can be shown that it may pay to exercise a put before expiration, and the value of the American put may be higher than shown in the prior tables.[8] The issuance of an American put involves the risk of premature exercise and the arbitrage discussed earlier need no longer hold. Another problem with applying the prior analysis is the possibility of the payment of dividends. The payment of dividends would, of course, affect the payoffs depicted earlier. If the dividends are already announced, then the stock price can be adjusted by reducing it by the present value of the dividends. With this adjustment, dividends don't affect the prior analysis except insofar as they affect the probability of exercising a put. If dividends are not announced, then adjusting by the expected dividends is reasonably satisfactory. All these issues mean that the put call parity relationship may not hold perfectly for American options. Nevertheless, it should be a close approximation to market relationships. This is

---

[7]The only margin required is the margin on the call. The ownership of the stock is sufficient to meet this requirement.

[8]See Merton [57].

exactly what the empirical results (see Klemkosky and Resnick [42] and Gould and Galai [32]) have shown.[9]

VALUATION MODELS

In this section we will present and discuss two widely used option valuation models. The models we will present are for the European call. From the last section the reader will recall that it never pays to exercise an American call before its expiration date if it is either dividend protected or the stock will not pay dividends before the expiration date. An American call that meets these conditions will not be exercised before it expires and thus it can be valued as a European call. In the previous section we derived the relationship between the value of puts and calls. Thus, the valuation formula for a call can also be used to value puts.

The differences in modern valuation formulas stem from the alternative assumptions made about how share price changes over time. In this section we will present two models. One assumes that the percentage change in share price follows a binomial distribution; the other assumes it follows a log normal distribution.

Binomial Option Pricing Formula

The simplest of the option pricing formulas is the binomial option pricing formula.[10] Since the implications of the formula are similar to those of more complicated formulas and since the formula is easy to derive and understand, we will present a detailed derivation in this section.

Assume that a call is being valued one period before expiration. Further assume that the stock is currently selling at $50 and will either increase to $75 or decrease to $25. Further assume that the borrowing and lending rate is 25%. Under these conditions, what is the current value of a call with an exercise price of $50?

To answer this question, consider the portfolio shown in Table 20.3.

The way the portfolio is constructed, the investor receives nothing at period one whether the stock sells at $25 or $75. This suggests that the investment should cost nothing or that $2C - 50 + 20 = 0$ or that $C = \$15$. To confirm this, consider two other values of C: $C = \$10$ or $C = \$20$. If $C = \$10$, then the call is underpriced. This suggests buying the call, shorting the stock, and lending will lead to an instantaneous profit. Let us examine this combination in Table 20.4.

No matter which share price occurs at period one, there are no net flows. The only flow occurs at zero and is a plus $10. This is a guaranteed return with no

---

[9]The arbitrage involving the short sale of stock is sometimes profitable empirically. This part of the put call relationship has less empirical support.

[10]The earliest derivation of this formula is in Stone [82]. Recently, Sharpe [75], Cox and Ross [19], and Rendleman and Bartter [66] have independently derived the formula.

Table 20.3

	Flows at 0	Flows at 1	
		$S_1 = 25$	$S_1 = 75$
Write 2 calls	$+2C$	0	-50
Buy 1 share stock	-50	$+25$	$+75$
Borrow $20	$+20$	-25	-25
		0	0

risk and as investors purchase the combination of securities shown before, prices will adjust until the profit disappears.

Now consider the case $C = \$20$. At this price, the call is overpriced and the investor issues the call, borrows, and buys stock. The flows are shown in Table 20.5.

Once again, there are no net flows at period 1, so that if this situation existed, the investor would have a guaranteed return with no risk. Such opportunities should disappear quickly if they exist, and the three securities should be so priced that riskless profits cannot occur. The call must sell at $15. Let's generalize this example.

The portfolio was constructed so that payoffs from the call plus the stock were the same, no matter what the value of the stock at time period 1. Then, by lending or borrowing, the payoff of the portfolio of calls, stock, and riskless bonds can be made to have zero return at time 1. In the example given a combination of two calls and one share of stock yielded 25—no matter what happened at period 1—and served the purpose. The number of shares of stock per call that makes the payoff from the combination independent of share price is called the hedge ratio. Let:

$(1.50)(50)$

S_0 = the stock price at period zero

(50) E = the exercise price of the option

u = one plus the percentage change in stock price from time 0 to time 1, if the stock price increases

1.50 d = one plus the percentage change in stock price from time 0 to time 1 if the stock price decreases

C = the call price

α = the number of shares of stock purchased per share of the call

Table 20.4

	Flows at 0	Flows at 1	
		$S_1 = 25$	$S_1 = 75$
Purchase 2 calls	-20	0	$+50$
Short 1 share stock	$+50$	-25	-75
Lend $20	-20	$+25$	$+25$
	$+10$	0	0

Table 20.5

	Flows at 0	Flowsat 1	
		$S_1 = 25$	$S_1 = 75$
Write 2 calls	+40	0	−50
Buy 1 share of stock	−50	+25	75
Borrow $20	+20	−25	−25
	+10	0	0

C_u = the value of the call if the stock increases in value (the maximum of $uS_0 - E$ or 0)

C_d = the value of the call if the stock decreases in value (the maximum of $dS_0 - E$ or 0)

Consider Table 20.6. For this to be a hedged portfolio the flows at period 1 must be independent of the value of the stock. Thus

$$-C_u + \alpha u S_0 = -C_d + \alpha d S_0$$

or

$uS_0 - E$

$$\alpha = \frac{C_u - C_d}{S_0(u - d)}$$

In the previous example, $C_d = 0$, $C_u = 25$, $S_0 = 50$, $u = 1.5$, and $d = .5$. Thus,

$$\alpha = \frac{25 - 0}{50(1.5 - .5)} = \frac{25}{50} = \frac{1}{2}$$

Thus, to have the call plus the stock have the same payoffs, no matter what value the stock has at period 1 we must purchase one-half as many shares of stock as we write calls. Two calls and one share of stock, the hedged position used in the previous example, is consistent with this ratio. Utilizing a hedge ratio of α means that the flows at time 1 are the same or $-C_u + \alpha u S_0 = -C_d + \alpha d S_0$. To make the portfolio flows at one equal zero, we borrow an amount such that we owe $(C_d - \alpha d S_0)$ at time 1 (or, equivalently, $C_u - \alpha u S_0$). If r is one plus the interest rate, we borrow $(C_d - \alpha d S_0)/r$. This results in the flows shown in Table 20.7.

Table 20.6

Action	Flows at 0	Flows at 1	
		$S_1 = uS_0$	$S_1 = dS_0$
Write call	C	$-C_u$	$-C_d$
Buy α shares of stock	$-\alpha S_0$	$\alpha u S_0$	$\alpha d S_0$

Table 20.7

		Flows at 1	
Action	Flows at 0	Price = uS	Price = dS
Write call	C	$-C_u$	$-C_d$
Buy α stock	$-\alpha S_0$	$\alpha u S_0$	$\alpha d S_0$
Borrow	$\dfrac{-C_d + \alpha d S_0}{r}$	$C_d - \alpha d S_0 = C_u - \alpha u S_0$	$C_d - \alpha d S_0$
Total	$C - \alpha S_0 - \dfrac{C_d - \alpha d S_0}{r}$	0	0

As discussed earlier, if the flows at period 1 on the portfolio are zero, the investment also must be zero. Thus:

$$C - \alpha S_0 - \frac{C_d - \alpha d S_0}{r} = 0 \quad \text{or} \quad C = \frac{\alpha r S_0 + C_d - \alpha d S_0}{r} \quad (20.1)$$

Substituting for α yields

$$C = \frac{\left(\dfrac{(C_u - C_d)}{S_0(u - d)}\right) r S_0 + C_d - \left(\dfrac{C_u - C_d}{S_0(u - d)}\right) d S_0}{r}$$

or

$$C = \frac{\dfrac{(C_u - C_d)r + C_d(u - d) - d(C_u - C_d)}{u - d}}{r}$$

or

$$C = \frac{C_u \dfrac{(r - d)}{(u - d)} + C_d \dfrac{(u - r)}{(u - d)}}{r}$$

This is the formula for the value of the call with one period remaining until it expires. It can be further simplified by defining $P = (r - d)/(u - d)$. With this definition

$$(1 - P) = 1 - \frac{r - d}{u - d} = \frac{(u - d) - (r - d)}{u - d} = \frac{u - r}{u - d}$$

Making these substitutions into the previous formula, we have

Value of Call:
$$C = \frac{C_u P + C_d (1 - P)}{r}$$

Binomial Option Pricing Formula

where

$$P = \frac{r - d}{u - d}$$

Before proceeding, one comment is in order. Notice that in this derivation we were never concerned with the probability of an up or down movement. We have never even discussed what it might be. P and $1 - P$ are not probabilities; rather, they are numbers that depend on the magnitude of the up and down movements and the riskless rate of interest. What does the value of the call depend on? Examining the formula shows that it depends on C_u, C_d, r, u, and d. However, C_u and C_d depend on the exercise price, the size of u and d, and the current stock price S_0. For example, if an up movement in the stock involves an exercise, then $C_u = uS_0 - E$. Thus, in a two-period example the call price ultimately depends on·

u, the size of the up movement

d, the size of the down movement

E, the exercise price

r, one plus the riskless rate of interest

S_0, the current stock price

The type of factors that affect the call price carry over to the more complicated model discussed later.

There is a second way this formula can be derived that yields useful insight into the valuation of options. If we use the value of α derived earlier as the ratio of stocks to calls, then no matter whether the stock goes up or down, we get the same return. An investment that has the same outcome no matter what happens is riskless and should yield the riskless rate of interest. Thus, if we buy the stocks while writing sufficient calls to maintain the hedged position given by α, the return on the investment must be r.

$$(\text{investment}) \; r = \text{outcome}^{11}$$
$$(\alpha S_0 - C)r = \alpha dS_0 - C_d$$

A glance at Equation (20.1) shows that it is identical to the expression above. To move from Equation (20.1) to the option pricing formula involved substituting

---

[11] The outcome could alternatively have been written as $\alpha u S_0 - C_u$.

for α and rearranging. Thus, both procedures lead to the same result. The idea of valuing options by forming a riskless hedge carries over to models of more complicated stock movements that will be examined in a later section of this chapter.

The formula for pricing a call when there is more than one period to the expiration is a simple extension of the one-period formula just derived. Figure 20.6 shows what can happen to the share price when there are two periods to go to expiration.

The formula just derived allows us to determine the value of the call with one period to expiration (e.g., at period 1). However, knowing the value at time 1 allows the calculation of the value at time 0 by acting as if there is one period to go. In this iterative manner the binomial valuation can be derived. In Appendix A at the end of the chapter we go through a detailed derivation and show that the value of the call with n periods to go is

$$C = S_0 B[a,n,P'] - Er^{-n}B[a,n,P]$$

where

$$P = \frac{r-d}{u-d} \quad P' = \frac{u}{r}P$$

and

S_0 is the current stock price
E is the exercise price

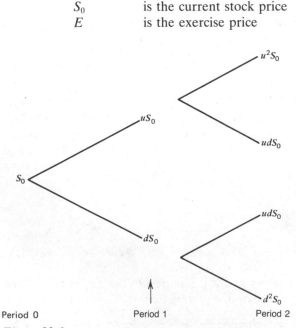

Period 0   Period 1   Period 2

Figure 20.6

n	is the number of periods to expiration
r	is one plus the riskless rate of interest
a	is the lowest number of upward moves in price at which the call takes on a positive value at expiration
$B[a,n,P']$	is the probability of a number of up moves in share price equal to or greater than a occurring out of n movements where the probability of an up move is P'. The probability is obtained from the binomial formula or can be looked up in a table of the binomial formula.
u and d	remain as defined earlier.

Some additional comment on $B[a,n,P']$ or $B[a,n,P]$ is warranted. First, a is determined by examining the current price, the exercise price, and the expiration date. Assume, for example, that the current stock price was \$50, the exercise price was \$60, $u = 1.50$, $d = .80$, and $n = 10$. A little calculation will show that if there are four or more increases in share price, the stock price will exceed \$60 by the expiration date. Thus, $a = 4$ in this example.[12] The second comment necessary is that although in order to calculate $B[a,n,P']$ or $B[a,n,P]$ we act as if P' or P are probabilities, in actuality they have nothing to do with probabilities. P and P' depend on the size of the up and down movements and the risk-free rate. They are not connected with the probabilities of these up and down movements taking place. We refer to them as probabilities solely because we employ them as if they were probabilities in using the binomial formula.

Note that each of the factors that we demonstrated as affecting call price in the two-period model also affect call prices in the multiperiod model. The call is a function of the size of the up movement, the size of the down movement, the exercise price, the current share price, and the riskless rate of interest. In addition, the multiperiod model is a function of n, the number of periods remaining until expiration.

The binomial formula just derived can be utilized to derive two other valuation formulas that allow a continuous change in the share price. This is accomplished by letting the length of the period between up or down movements become very small, and hence the number of periods is very large. The most popular of these models is due to Black and Scholes, and is developed in the next section.

The Black–Scholes Option Valuation Formula

In the previous section of this chapter we derived an option pricing formula under the assumption that the rate of return on the underlying stock followed a binomial formula. Under certain conditions, the binomial distribution converges to the normal distribution.

If we assume that a stock's continuously compounded rate of return follows a

---

[12]$50(1.50)^4(.80)^6 = 66.35$, whereas $50(1.50)^3(.80)^7 = 35.39$. More formally, a can be defined as the number for which $u^{a-1}d^{n-(a-1)}S_0 < E \leq u^a d^{n-a}S_0$.

normal distribution, then the option pricing model developed in the preceding section reduces to the Black–Scholes option pricing formula presented below.[13]

$$C = S_0 N(d_1) - \frac{E}{e^{rt}} N(d_2) \tag{20.1a}$$

$$d_1 = \frac{\ln(S_0/E) + (r + \frac{1}{2}\sigma^2)t}{\sigma\sqrt{t}} \tag{20.1b}$$

$$d_2 = \frac{\ln(S_0/E) + (r - \frac{1}{2}\sigma^2)t}{\sigma\sqrt{t}} \tag{20.1c}$$

where

r	= the continuously compounded riskless rate of interest
C	= the current value of the option
S_0	= the current price of the stock
E	= the exercise price of the option
e	= 2.7183
t	= the time remaining before the expiration date expressed as a fraction of a year
σ	= the standard deviation of the continuously compounded annual rate of return
$\ln(S_0/E)$	= natural logarithm of S_0/E
$N(d)$	= the value of the cumulative normal distribution evaluated at d

The Black–Scholes formula can be used to value any option. In the next section of this chapter we will discuss how to use it. Before we do, we will discuss the variables that affect the valuation of calls as well as the relationship of this formula to that discussed earlier.

Perhaps the most interesting aspect of the Black–Scholes model is a variable that does *not* appear as a determinant of the value of a call. This variable is the expected rate of return on the stock. Any of the option models determines the price of the option in terms of the price of the underlying stock. The stock price, in fact, acts as the numeraire in which call prices are expressed. Expected return enters the model insofar as it determines current share price, but given current share price, it does not affect the value of the call.

The impact of the other variables on the value of the call can be seen by examining the properties of the Black–Scholes model as each changes. In general, the results are as follows: the higher the ratio of the current price of the stock to the exercise price of the call, the higher the value of the call. This is reasonable, for the higher this ratio, the less the price of the stock must increase for the call to have a value on its expiration date. The longer the time to maturity on the

---

[13]See Cox and Ross [19].

call, the higher the value of the call. This again is sensible, for the longer the time to maturity, the more the stock's price is likely to deviate from its present level at maturity. Since the payoff from deviations from price are asymmetrical, the longer time to maturity increases the value of the call.[14] Finally, the higher the riskless rate of interest, the greater the value of the call. This follows logically from the fact that the higher the riskless rate, the lower the present value of the amount that must be paid to exercise the call. The reader should note that these conclusions are consistent with the general statements we said must hold in a rational option pricing formula. They are also consistent with the conclusions we derived when we discussed the binomial formula.

Using the Black–Scholes Model

In examining the Black–Scholes formula we saw that the only data we needed to value an option were the current price of the stock, the exercise price of the option, the time remaining before expiration of the option, a cumulative normal probability table, the riskless rate of interest, and the standard deviation of the continuously compounded annual rate of return on the stock. All of these, except for the standard deviation, are easily observable.[15] One way to estimate the standard deviation of the continuously compounded annual rate of return on a stock is to use historic data on stock returns.[16] The Black–Scholes model was derived under the assumption of identically distributed rates of return over time. If this assumption in fact were strictly true over all periods, then estimates of the variance from historical data would be very good. As an example of this procedure, assume that we wish to estimate the appropriate variance for some stock using one year of historical weekly data. The price relative for each stock is simply the price at the end of the week plus any dividends divided by the price at the beginning of the week. The natural logarithm of the price relative is the continuously compounded rate of return per week. The standard deviation of the continuously compounded rate of return can easily be computed by applying the standard formula to the sequence of continuously compounded rates of return. For example, standard deviation is

$$= \left(\sum_{i=1}^{N} \left(\frac{(X_i - \overline{X})^2}{N} \right) \right)^{1/2}$$

---

[14]For example, if the price of the stock is below the exercise price, then decreases in price up to the exercise time would result in the same value, zero, at the exercise time. In contrast, a rise in price could lead to a positive value for the call at the exercise time.

[15]The continuously compounded riskless rate of interest is usually found by taking the rate on a government security that has a maturity date equal to (or as close as possible to) the expiration date on the call.

[16]In the next section of this chapter we will discuss another method that uses the Black–Scholes model itself to prepare estimates of the standard deviation.

To convert the continuously compounded weekly standard deviation to a yearly standard deviation, simply multiply by the square root of 52.

Once inputs for the Black–Scholes valuation formula have been defined, one can easily solve for the value of a call option. Perhaps this can best be illustrated with an example.

$$
\begin{aligned}
S_0 &= 90 \\
E &= 100 \\
t &= .5 \text{ (6 months)} \\
\sigma &= .5 \\
r &= .10
\end{aligned}
$$

Then d_1 and d_2 can be easily computed as follows:

$$
d_1 = \frac{\ln(90/100) + (.10 + \tfrac{1}{2}(.25))(.5)}{.5\sqrt{.5}} \approx .02
$$

$$
d_2 = \frac{\ln(90/100) + (.10 - \tfrac{1}{2}(.25))(.5)}{.5\sqrt{.5}} \approx -.33
$$

From any table of the cumulative normal distribution, we can compute:

$$
N(d_1) = N(.02) = .5080
$$

$$
N(d_2) = N(-.33) = .3707
$$

The value of the call is

$$
45.72 \ - \ 35.26
$$

$$
C = 90(.5080) - \frac{100}{e^{.10(.5)}}(.3707) = \$10.46
$$

Using the Black–Scholes formula we now have a theoretical value for the call of $10.46. Assume that the call was selling at $9.50. If the Black–Scholes formula is correct, the call is undervalued in the market. The investor can take advantage of this by buying the call directly. Alternatively, the investor could be protected against adverse stock price changes by buying the call and selling the stock short. Recall from the previous section that this combination is a riskless hedge.[17] It can be shown that if we accept the Black–Scholes option pricing fromula as correct, the appropriate hedge ratio is given by $N(d_1)$ or, in our example, .5080.

---

[17] In the section discussing the binomial formula we derived a hedge ratio. A similar argument in the Black–Scholes model shows that the hedge ratio is $N(d_1)$. Examining d_1 shows that it should be expected to change over time and thus the hedge ratio also changes.

This means that for every call option purchased, .5080 or slightly more than half of the share of stock should be sold short.

IMPLICIT ESTIMATES OF STOCK'S OWN VARIANCE FROM OPTION FORMULAS

In the previous section of this chapter we discussed the input needed to use option valuation models. All of the model input variables were easily observed except for one — the variance of the instantaneous rate of return on the stock. Up to now, we have assumed that the value of this variable is inferred from historical data. However, there is a second way in which option valuation formulas such as the Black–Scholes formula can be used. If we believe that option prices are such that the Black–Scholes model holds on average, then the market price of the option can be substituted for C in the model. The only remaining unknown in the formula is the instantaneous rate of variance of the stock.[18] Since we have one equation and one unknown, a formula like the Black–Scholes formula can be used to determine the variance of the stock. If the assumptions behind the Black–Scholes model are completely valid, and the model holds on average, then the variance implied by the Black–Scholes model should be a good estimate of the market's expectation about the variance of a stock's return. On any one stock there are likely to be many calls outstanding, and these calls will probably have different exercise prices and expiration dates. From each of these calls we can obtain an estimate of the standard deviation of the stock's continuously compounded rate of return. The efficiency of the estimate should be improved if we combine several independent estimates. Ways of doing this will now be discussed.

The simplest way to find an estimate of σ is to take an average of the estimates obtained from each call outstanding on the stock. If there are N calls outstanding, and if σ_j is the estimate of the standard deviation arrived at by employing data for the jth call, then

$$\sigma = \frac{1}{N} \sum_{j=1}^{N} \sigma_j$$

Not all authors weight the estimates equally. Many authors place less weight on estimates obtained from calls that have prices less sensitive to σ. This weighting scheme would place less weight on calls where the stock price is far from the exercise price, and more weight on calls where the stock price and exercise price are close. There are several variants of this weighting.[19] Some authors simply discard estimates from calls where the stock price is very different from the

---

[18]The Black–Scholes formula cannot be explicitly solved for variance. However, an iterative procedure can be used to find the implied variance for any stock that is consistent with this formula. See [44] for a discussion of search procedures.

[19]See [9] and [72] for additional suggestions as to plausible weighting schemes.

exercise price. Other authors have suggested weighting by the relative sensitivity of the call price of the option to changes in the standard deviation.[20]

Although calculating weights in the manner just discussed is only one of a large number of weighting techniques that have been advocated for arriving at estimates of the variance of a stock's return, it is one of the few subject to empirical tests. Latane and Rendleman [44] have used a weighting scheme similar to that described earlier to investigate the ability of estimates of variance from the Black–Scholes model to serve as forecasts of the future. To judge the usefulness of this technique, Latane and Rendleman perform two sets of tests. One set looks directly at whether better forecasts of actual future variance are achieved when (1) forecasts are prepared by computing variance over a historical period or (2) forecasts are prepared from the Black–Scholes model. They conclude that forecasts from the Black–Scholes model are more accurate. As a second test, they examine whether larger profits are earned by arbitraging mispriced calls where the value of the call is computed by using the variances arrived at in (1) or (2). They again conclude that the use of variances inferred from the Black–Scholes model leads to a better valuation of assets (a higher excess return) than does the forecastings of variances from historical data.

While this technique for estimating variance has important implications for the pricing of options, it also can be important for portfolio selection. In earlier chapters, we have discussed how estimates of expected returns, variances, and correlation coefficients are necessary inputs to the portfolio selection process. We have devoted two chapters to estimating correlation coefficients. We have also mentioned that estimates of expected returns must come from security analysts and that analysts can be trained to produce estimates of variances. The latter is much more difficult than the former. The option literature seems to provide either a useful alternative measure of variances or, at the least, a useful benchmark to help the analysts in their estimation process.

Artificial or Homemade Options

One of the existing insights in modern option theory is that an appropriate mixture of treasury bills and a security creates a payoff pattern identical to the pattern of an option on the underlying security. This is exciting because options are written only on a limited number of securities and artificially created options can produce the payoff pattern of an option on securities or portfolios where actual options don't exist. Consider, for example, an arbitrary portfolio. Assume

---

[20]This technique was used by [44]. Defining $\partial C_j / \partial \sigma_j$ as the change in the call price of call j to a change in standard deviation of call j, then the weight on the jth estimate of standard deviation (W_j) is

$$W_j = \frac{\partial C_j}{\partial \sigma_j} \bigg/ \sum_k \frac{\partial C_k}{\partial \sigma_k}$$

and

$$\sigma = \sum_{j=1}^{N} w_j \sigma_j$$

Table 20.8

	Value at Expiration Date	
	If Stock Price is 40	If Stock Price is 50
Buy put	5.00	0.00
Short ½ share of stock	−20.00	−25.00
Buy T-bills	25.00	25.00
Sum	5.00	0.00

further that the portfolio does not resemble an index. In this case options would not exist on the portfolio. Assume further the portfolio has a value of $100.00. A homemade put at $105.00 can be created. This eliminates the risk of returns below 5% for the portfolio. Of course, homemade puts, like traded puts, have a cost. In the case of an artificial put, the cost comes in the form of a reduction in returns when returns on the portfolio are above 5%. Thus a homemade put changes the return distribution of the portfolio by eliminating returns below 5% and reducing the returns above 5% in the same manner as a traded put would. Whether this is desirable or not depends on the investor's taste for risk and return. The creation of an artificial put on a portfolio goes by the name of "portfolio insurance" since the portfolio is insured against returns below 5%.

Let's examine in more detail the construction of an artificial put. The first row of Table 20.8 shows the payoff pattern of a put if the stock price can end up at $50.00 or $40.00 in one period and if the exercise price is $45.00. Rows 2 and 3 show a combination of shorting the stock and buying T bills that has the same payoff pattern as the put. If the put doesn't exist, then shorting the stock and owning T bills creates a homemade put that has the same payoff pattern as a publicly traded put.

Note that when a homemade put is written in conjunction with a portfolio or asset, the investor is not literally short. Consider a pension portfolio and an artificial put. The short sale is accomplished by selling off part of the portfolio. Holding less of the portfolio is equivalent to owning the portfolio while simultaneously being short part of it.

Note also that the homemade put is created by selling off less than one share of stock. In the example it was one-half share. If there were more than one period, the fraction of shares sold short would change over time. Thus the creation of homemade options involves frequent readjustment of the combination of the underlying security and T bills in order that the payoff pattern resemble that of an option. Early implementation of this idea involved literally selling and buying shares of an asset or portfolio. In order to replicate the payoff pattern of an option, frequent transactions were called for. Since frequent sales and purchases meant substantial transaction costs, shares were traded less frequently and the payoff pattern deviated substantially from that of an option. As discussed in the next chapter, futures have substantially lower transaction costs. Furthermore, futures can be used to construct an asset like stocks or bonds. Thus the growth of futures markets has been a spur to the creation of artificial options.

CONCLUSION

In this chapter we have examined the characteristics and valuation of contingent claim contracts. The development of a set of models for pricing contingent claims is a fairly recent and important contribution. We have explored the theory behind these models and their use in valuing options. In addition, we have shown how such models can be used to develop estimates of the variance of the return on the stocks against which they represent a claim. This may be an important input to portfolio management models.

APPENDIX A

Derivation of the Binomial Formula

In the text we showed that with one period to go, the value of the call was

$$C = \frac{PC_u + (1 - P)C_d}{r} \tag{A.1}$$

Now consider the possibilities with two periods to go. These are represented in the diagram shown below:

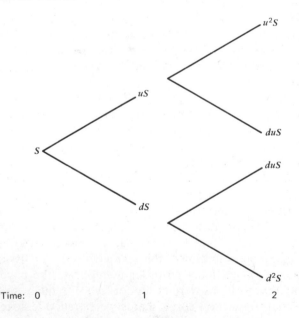

where

1. C_u^2 as the value at expiration if there are two up movements in the stock $= \text{maximum } [u^2S - E, 0]$

2. C_{ud} as the value at expiration if there is one up and one down movement in the share price = maximum $[udS - E, 0]$
3. C_{d^2} as the value at expiration if there are two down movements in the share price = maximum $[d^2S - E, 0]$

Applying Equation (A.1) we can determine the value of the calls at period 1 if the share price is uS at period 1 as

$$C_u = \frac{PC_{u^2} + (1 - P)C_{ud}}{r}$$

Again, by applying Equation (A.1) we can determine the value at period 1 if the share price is dS at period 1 as

$$C_d = \frac{PC_{ud} + (1 - P)C_{d^2}}{r}$$

Now consider period 0. Knowing the value at period 1, we can act as if there is only one period to go. This is shown as follows:

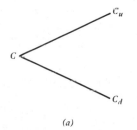

(a)

Applying Equation (A.1) again yields

$$C = \frac{P\dfrac{PC_{u^2} + (1 - P)C_{ud}}{r} + (1 - P)\dfrac{PC_{ud} + (1 - P)C_{d^2}}{r}}{r}$$

Simplifying,

$$C = \frac{P^2C_{u^2} + 2P(1 - P)C_{ud} + (1 - P)^2C_{d^2}}{r^2} \tag{A.2}$$

In exactly the same way we can derive the formula for the three-period case. The possible movements of the share price are shown in Figure 20.7.

Notice in this case that two periods before the expiration date the stock price is either uS or dS instead of S, as it was in the two-period example. If it is uS,

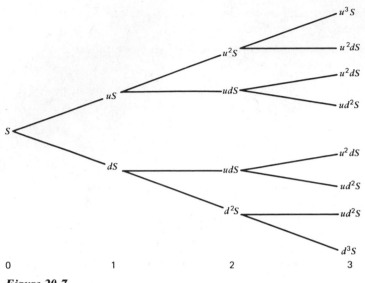

Figure 20.7

then from Equation (A.2) the value at time 1 is simply

$$C_u = \frac{P^2 C_{u^3} + 2P(1 - P)C_{u^2 d} + (1 - P)^2 C_{ud^3}}{r^2}$$

If the price of the stock were dS in period 1, then

$$C_d = \frac{P^2 C_{u^2 d} + 2P(1 - P)C_{ud^2} + (1 - P)^2 C_{d^3}}{r^2}$$

where $C_{u^n d^R}$ = the value expiration if there are n up movements and R down movements. Applying Equation (A.1) yields the value of the call at time zero; we have

$$C = P\frac{\dfrac{P^2 C_{u^3} + 2P(1 - P)Cu^2 d + (1 - P)^2 C_{ud^2}}{r^2} + (1 - P)\dfrac{P^2 C_{u^2 d} + 2P(1 - P)C_{ud^2} + (1 - P)^2 C_{d^3}}{r^2}}{r}$$

Simplifying,

$$C = \frac{P^3 C_{u^3} + 3P^2(1 - P)C_{u^2 d} + 3P(1 - P)^2 C_{ud^2} + (1 - P)^3 C_{d^3}}{r^3}$$

Recalling the determination of the value of the call at the horizon and examining the form of the above equations shows that for n periods before the horizon the value of the call is

$$C = \frac{\left[\sum_{j=0}^{n} \frac{n!}{j!(n-j)!} P^j(1-P)^{n-j}\max[0, u^j d^{n-j} S_0 - E]\right]}{r^n}$$

We can simplify the expression by defining a as the minimum number of up movements necessary for it to pay to exercise the option at the expiration date. For sequences with fewer than a up movements, the call will not be exercised and the value at expiration will be zero. Thus, the summation need start only at a. Furthermore, for more than a up movements we know that exercise pays. Thus, when the lower limit on the summation is a, the maximum can be rewritten as $u^j d^{n-j} S_0 - E$.

With these changes we have

$$C = \frac{\sum_{j=a}^{n} \frac{n!}{j!(n-j)!} P^j(1-P)^{n-j}(u^j d^{n-j} S_0 - E)}{r^n}$$

Rearranging,

$$C = S_0 \left[\sum_{j=a}^{n} \frac{n!}{j!(n-j)!} \frac{(Pu)^j[(1-P)d]^{n-j}}{r^n}\right]$$

$$- Er^{-n}\left[\sum_{j=a}^{n} \frac{n!}{j!(n-j)!} P^j(1-P)^{n-j}\right]$$

The second expression in brackets is the binomial formula with P serving the role of a probability and can be represented as $B[a, n, P)$. The first expression in brackets also turns out to be a binomial formula. To see this, first write part of it as

$$\frac{(Pu)^j[(1-P)d]^{n-j}}{r^n} = \left(\frac{Pu}{r}\right)^j \left(\frac{(1-P)d}{r}\right)^{n-j}$$

Define P' as $(Pu)/r$. Then if $1 - P' = (1 - P)d/r$ we would have a binomial formula with P' serving the role of probability. A little algebra demonstrates that this is appropriate. Recall $P = (r - d)/(u - d)$. Thus,

$$1 - P' = 1 - \frac{Pu}{r} = 1 - \frac{u(r-d)}{r(u-d)} = 1 - \frac{ur - ud}{ur - dr} = 1 - \frac{ur - dr - ur + ud}{ur - dr}$$

$$= \frac{d}{r}\left[\frac{u - r}{u - d}\right] = \frac{d}{r}\left[\frac{u - d - r + d}{u - d}\right] = \frac{d}{r}\left[1 - \frac{r - d}{u - d}\right]$$

$$= \frac{d}{r}[1 - P]$$

This last expression is what we wanted to show. Thus, the first term in the brackets has the form

$$\sum_{j=a}^{n} \frac{n!}{j!(n-j)!} P'^{j}(1 - P')^{n-j}$$

This can be represented as $B[a,n,P']$. Substituting the two expressions for binomials in the basic equation for a call yields

$$C = S_0 B[a,n,P'] - Er^{-n}B[a,n,P]$$

APPENDIX B

Derivation of the Black–Scholes Formula

The derivation of the Black–Scholes formula starts out in a similar manner to the derivation of the binomial formula. First, a portfolio is constructed that has the same return, no matter how well the stock performs. This portfolio, as in the case of the binomial formula, consists of writing a call and buying the stock. For simplicity, consider buying one share of stock. Then it can be shown that the amount of calls to write is one divided by the change in the value of the call with a unit change in the value of the stock.

The following example will clarify this. Assume that the call changes by one-half of the amount of the stock change. Thus, the rule just described says to write two calls. If the stock increased by $1, the ownership of the stock would cause an increase of $1 in the value of the hedge. However, if two calls are written, each call should increase in value by $.50 or the two calls by $1. Since the hedge involves a writing of two calls, this causes a loss of $1 in the value of the hedge.

Thus, the portfolio value is unchanged by a change in the share price. Such a riskless portfolio should yield the riskless rate of interest. Let

V_H be the initial value (cost) of the hedge
S be the market price of a share of stock
C be the value of a call
Q_s be the quantity of stock owned
Q_c be the quantity of calls owned
r be the riskless rate of interest

Then the value of the hedge is

$$V_H = Q_s S + Q_c C \tag{B.1}$$

and the change in the value of the hedge is

$$dV_H = Q_s dS + Q_c dC$$

This hedge is riskless and thus should yield the riskless rate of interest per each unit of time. Thus,

$$rV_H dt = Q_s dS + Q_c dC$$

Substituting for V_h from Equation (B.1), and recalling that if the hedge is formed in terms of writing calls,

$$Q_S = +1 \quad \text{and} \quad Q_C = \frac{-1}{\partial C / \partial S},$$

we have

$$r \left[S - \frac{C}{\partial C / \partial S} \right] dt = dS - \frac{1}{\partial C / \partial S} dC$$

Rearranging,

$$dC = \frac{\partial C}{\partial S} dS - r \frac{\partial C}{\partial S} \left[S - \frac{C}{\partial C / \partial S} \right] dt = \frac{\partial C}{\partial S} dS - rS \frac{\partial C}{\partial S} dt + rCdt \quad \text{(B.2)}$$

What is required next is a model of stock price and call price changes. The assumption that Black and Scholes make is that the instantaneous change in stock price follows a normal distribution.

$$\frac{dS}{S} = \mu dt + \sigma dZ$$

μ is the instantaneous expected return, σ is the instantaneous variance, and dZ is the zero mean unit standard deviation normally distributed variate. Given the stock price process described before, the change in the call price is well known from theorems in stochastic calculus.[21]

$$dC = \frac{\partial C}{\partial S} dS + \frac{\partial C}{\partial t} dt + \frac{1}{2} \frac{\partial^2 C}{\partial S^2} \sigma^2 S^2 dt$$

This expression should look somewhat familiar. The first two terms on the right-hand side are the terms that would be obtained in standard calculus if you take a total derivative of the value of a call. The last term arises because of the

---

[21]The equation follows from Ito's Lemma. See [8].

stochastic element in S. Substituting for dC in Equation (B.2) yields

$$\frac{\partial C}{\partial S} dS + \frac{\partial C}{\partial t} dt + \frac{1}{2} \frac{\partial^2 C}{\partial S^2} \sigma^2 S^2 dt = \frac{\partial C}{\partial S} dS - rS \frac{\partial C}{\partial S} dt + rC dt$$

Subtracting the term $(\partial C/\partial S)\, dS$ from each side, noting that there is a dt in each remaining term and thus that it can be eliminated by dividing by dt, and rearranging yields

$$\frac{\partial C}{\partial t} = rC - rS \frac{\partial C}{\partial S} - \frac{1}{2} \frac{\partial^2 C}{\partial S^2} \sigma^2 S^2 \qquad\qquad \text{(B.3)}$$

This is a differential equation. At the horizon, the value of the call is

$$C = \begin{array}{ll} S - E & S > E \\ 0 & S \le E \end{array}$$

Solving the differential equation and using the value at the horizon as the boundary condition yields the expression shown in the text.

QUESTIONS AND PROBLEMS

1. A registered representative recently advised one of his clients to sell calls on all the stock he owned. He explained that the client wouldn't lose money, but would benefit by what he got paid for the call. Sounds foolproof. What's wrong?

2. Consider the purchase of a combination of two puts and a call. Assume that the call costs $5, the put $6, and the exercise price for the put or call is $50. Plot the profit versus the stock price at the expiration date.

3. Consider two calls, one with an exercise price of $40 and one with an exercise price of $45. Assume that the call with the $40 exercise price sells for $8 and the call with the $45 exercise price sells for $5. Assume that they have the same expiration date. Consider the strategy of issuing two $45 calls and purchasing one $40 call. Plot the profit versus the share price at the expiration date.

4. Assume the binomial pricing model. Assume that the share price is $50, the exercise price is $60, $u = 1.2$, $d = .9$, $r = 1.1$, and $N = 10$. What is the value of α? What is the call value?

5. Determine the value of the following call using the Black–Scholes model. The stock currently sells for $95 and the instantaneous standard deviation of the stock's return is .6. The call has an exercise price of $105, and has 8 months to go before expiration. The continuously compounded riskless rate of interest is 8%.

BIBLIOGRAPHY

1. Arditti, Fred D., and John, Kose. "Spanning the State Space with Options," *Journal of Financial and Quantitative Analysis,* **XV,** No. 1 (March 1980), pp. 1–10.
2. Baesel, Jerome B., Shows, George, and Thorp, Edward. "The Cost of Liquidity Services in Listed Options: A Note," *The Journal of Finance,* **38,** No. 3 (June 1983), pp. 989–996.
3. Ball, Clifford A., and Torous, Walter N. "A Simplified Jump Process for Common Stock Returns," *Journal of Financial and Quantitative Analysis,* **XVIII,** No. 1 (March 1983), pp. 53–66.
4. ———. "Bond Price Dynamics and Options," *Journal of Financial and Quantitative Analysis,* **XVIII,** No. 4 (Dec. 1983), pp. 517–532.
5. ———. "On Jumps in Common Stock Prices and Their Impact on Call Pricing," *The Journal of Finance,* **40,** No. 1 (March 1985), pp. 155–174.
6. Bhattacharya, Mihir. "Empirical Properties of the Black–Scholes Formula under Ideal Conditions," *Journal of Financial and Quantitative Analysis,* **XV,** No. 5 (Dec. 1980), pp. 1081–1106.
7. Bhattacharya, Sudipto. "Notes on Multiperiod Valuation and the Pricing of Options," *The Journal of Finance,* **36,** No. 1 (March 1981), pp. 163–181.
8. Black, Fischer, and Scholes, Myron. "The Pricing of Options and Corporate Liabilities," *Journal of Political Economy,* **81,** No. 3 (May/June 1973), pp. 637–654.
9. Boyle, Phelim. "Options: A Monte Carlo Approach," *Journal of Financial Economics,* **4,** No. 3 (May 1977), pp. 323–338.
10. Boyle, Phelim, and Ananthanarayanan, A. L. "The Impact of Variance Estimation in Option Valuation Models," *Journal of Financial Economics,* **5,** No. 3 (Dec. 1977), pp. 375–387.
11. Boyle, Phelim P., and Emanuel David. "Discretely Adjusted Option Hedges," *Journal of Financial Economics,* **8,** No. 3 (Sept. 1980), pp. 259–882.
12. Bracken, Jerome. "Models for Call Option Decisions," *Financial Analysts Journal,* **24,** No. 5 (Sept.–Oct. 1968), pp. 149–151.
13. Breeden, Douglas, and Litzenberger, Robert. "Prices of State-Contingent Claims Implicit in Option Prices," *Journal of Business,* **51,** No. 4 (Oct. 1978), pp 621–651.
14. Brennan, Michael, and Schwartz, Edwardo. "The Valuation of American Put Options," *Journal of Finance,* **XXXII,** No. 2 (May 1976), pp. 449–462.
15. Brennan, M. J., and Solanki, R. "Optimal Portfolio Insurance," *Journal of Financial and Quantitative Analysis,* **XVI,** No. 3 (Sept. 1981), pp. 279–300.
16. Brenner, Menachem, and Galai, Dan. "On Measuring the Risk of Common Stocks Implied by Options Prices: A Note," *Journal of Financial and Quantitative Analysis,* **19,** No. 4 (Dec. 1984), pp. 403–412.
17. Courtadon, George. "The Pricing of Options on Default-Free Bonds," *Journal of Financial and Quantitative Analysis,* **XVII,** No. 1 (March 1982), pp. 75–100.

18. ———. "A More Accurate Finite Difference Approximation for the Valuation of Options," *Journal of Financial and Quantitative Analysis,* **XVII,** No. 5 (Dec. 1982), pp. 697–700.

19. Cox, Stephen, and Ross, Stephen. "A Survey of Some New Results in Financial Option Pricing Theory," *Journal of Finance,* **XXXI,** No. 2 (May 1976), pp. 383–402.

20. ———. "The Valuation of Options for Alternative Stochastic Processes," *Journal of Financial Economics,* **3,** No. 112 (Jan.–March 1976), pp. 145–166.

21. Dimson, Elroy. "Instant Option Valuation," *Financial Analysts Journal,* **33,** No. 3 (May–June 1977), pp. 62–69.

22. ———. "Option Valuation Nomograms," *Financial Analysts Journal,* **33,** No. 6 (Nov.–Dec. 1977), pp. 71–74.

23. Fischer, Stanley. "Call Option Pricing When the Exercise Price Is Uncertain, and the Valuation of Index Bonds," *Journal of Finance,* **XXXIII,** No. 1 (March 1978), pp. 169–176.

24. French, Dan W. "The Weekend Effect on the Distribution of Stock Prices: Implications for Option Pricing," *Journal of Financial Economics,* **13,** No. 4 (Dec. 1984), pp. 547–560.

25. Galai, Dan. "Tests of Market Efficiency of the Chicago Board Options Exchange," *Journal of Business,* **50,** No. 2 (April 1977), pp. 167–197.

26. ———. "On the Boness and Black–Scholes Models for Valuation of Call Options," *Journal of Financial and Quantitative Analysis,* **XII,** No. 1 (March 1978), pp. 15–27.

27. Galai, Dan, and Masulis, R. "The Option Pricing Model and the Risk Factor of Stock," *Journal of Financial Economics,* **13,** No. 1/2 (Jan.–March 1976), pp. 53–81.

28. Geske, Robert. "The Pricing of Options with Stochastic Dividend Yield," *Journal of Finance,* **XXXIII,** No. 2 (May 1978), pp. 617–625.

29. Geske, Robert, and Roll, Richard. "On Valuing American Call Options with the Black–Scholes European Formula," *The Journal of Finance,* **39,** No. 2 (June 1984), pp. 443–456.

30. Geske, Robert, and Johnson, H. E. "The American Put Option Valued Analytically," *The Journal of Finance,* **39,** No. 5 (Dec. 1984), pp. 1511–1524.

31. Geske, Robert, and Shastri, Kuldeep. "Valuation by Approximation: A Comparison of Alternative Option Valuation Techniques," *Journal of Financial and Quantitative Analysis,* **XX,** No. 1 (March 1985), pp. 45–72.

32. Gould, J. P., and Galai, Dan. "Transactions Costs and the Relationship Between Put and Call Prices," *Journal of Financial Economics,* **1,** No. 2 (July 1974), pp. 105–130.

33. Gultekin, N. Bulent, and Rogalski, Richard J. "Government Bond Returns, Measurement of Interest Rate Risk, and the Arbitrage Pricing Theory," *The Journal of Finance,* **40,** No. 1 (March 1985), pp. 43–62.

34. Halpern, Paul J., and Turnbull, Stuart M. "Empirical Tests of Boundary Conditions for Toronto Stock Exchange Option," *The Journal of Finance,* **40,** No. 2 (June 1985), pp. 481–500.

35. Hausman, W. H., and White, W. L. "Theory of Option Strategy Under Risk Aversion," *Journal of Financial and Quantitative Analysis*, **111,** No. 3 (Sept. 1968), pp. 343–358.

36. Hilliard, Jimmy, and Leitch, Robert. "Analysis of the Warrant Hedge in a Stable Paretion Market," *Journal of Financial and Quantitative Analysis*, **XII,** No. 1 (March 1977), pp. 85–103.

37. Ho, Thomas S.Y., and Macris, Richard G. "Dealers Bid-Ask Quotes and Transaction Prices: An Empirical Study of Some AMEX Options," *The Journal of Finance*, **39,** No. 1 (March 1984), pp. 23–46.

38. Jarrow, Robert, and Rudd, Andrew. "Approximate Option Valuation for Arbitrary Stochastic Processes," *Journal of Financial Economics*, **10,** No. 3 (Nov. 1982), pp. 347–370.

39. Johnson, H.E. "An Analytic Approximation for the American Put Price," *Journal of Financial and Quantitative Analysis*, **XVIII,** No. 1 (March 1983), pp. 141–162.

40. Jones, E. Philip. "Option Arbitrage and Strategy with Large Price Changes," *Journal of Financial Economics*, **10,** No. 4 (March 1984), pp. 91–114.

41. Kassouf, Sheen. "Warrant Price Behavior — 1945 to 1964," *Financial Analysts Journal*, **24,** No. 1 (Jan.–Feb. 1968), pp. 123–126.

42. Klemkosky, Robert C., and Resnick, Bruce G. "Put-Call Parity and Market Efficiency," *The Journal of Finance*, **34,** No. 5 (Dec. 1979), pp. 1141–1157.

43. ———. "An Ex Ante Analysis of Put-Call Parity," *Journal of Financial Economics*, **8,** No. 4 (Dec. 1980), pp. 363–378.

44. Latane, Henry, and Rendleman, Richard. "Standard Deviations of Stock Price Ratios Implied on Option Prices," *The Journal of Finance*, **XXXI,** No. 2 (May 1976), pp. 369–381.

45. Leabo, Dick, and Rogalski, Richard. "Warrant Price Movements and the Efficient Market Model," *The Journal of Finance*, **XXX,** No. 1 (March 1975), pp. 163–177.

46. Leland, Hayne E. "Who Should Buy Portfolio Insurance?" *The Journal of Finance*, **35,** No. 2 (May 1980), pp. 581–594.

47. Litzenberger, Robert, and Sosin, Howard. "The Theory of Recapitalization and the Evidence of Dual Purpose Funds," *The Journal of Finance*, **XXXII,** No. 5 (Dec. 1977), pp. 1433–1455.

48. MacBeth, James C., and Merville, Larry J. "Tests of the Black–Scholes and Cox Call Option Valuation Models," *The Journal of Finance*, **35,** No. 2 (May 1980), pp. 285–300.

49. Manaster, Steven, and Rendleman, Richard J., Jr. "Option Prices as Predictors of Equilibrium Stock Prices," *The Journal of Finance*, **37,** No. 4 (Sept. 1982), pp. 1043–1058.

50. Margrabe, William. "The Value of an Option to Exchange One Asset for Another," *The Journal of Finance*, **XXXIII,** No. 1 (March 1978), pp. 177–198.

51. McDonald, Robert, and Siegel, Daniel. "Option Pricing When the Under-

lying Asset Earns a Below-Equilibrium Rate of Return: A Note," *The Journal of Finance,* **39,** No. 1 (March 1984), pp. 261–266.

52. McGuigan, James, and King, William. "Security Option Strategy Under Risk Aversion: An Analysis," *Journal of Financial and Quantitative Analysis,* **VIII,** No. 1 (Jan. 1973), pp. 7–15.

53. ———. "Evaluating Alternative Stock Option Timing Strategies," *Journal of Financial and Quantitative Analysis,* **IX,** No. 4 (Sept. 1974), pp. 567–578.

54. Merton, Robert. "The Impact on Option Pricing of Specification Error in the Underlying Stock Price Returns," *The Journal of Finance,* **XXXI,** No. 2 (May 1976), pp. 333–350.

55. ———. "Option Pricing When Underlying Stock Returns Are Discontinuous," *Journal of Financial Economics,* **3,** No. 1/2 (Jan./March 1976), pp. 125–144.

56. ———. "The Relationship Between Put and Call Option Prices: Comment," *The Journal of Finance,* **XXVIII,** No. 1 (March 1973), pp. 183–184.

57. ———. "Theory of Rational Option Pricing," *Bell Journal of Economics and Management Science* (Spring 1973), pp. 141–183.

58. Merton, Robert, Scholes, M., and Gladstein, M. "The Returns and Risk of Alternative Call Option Portfolio Investment Strategies," *Journal of Business,* **51,** No. 2 (April 1978), pp. 183–242.

59. Parkinson, Michael. "Option Pricing: The American Put," *Journal of Business,* **50,** No. 1 (Jan. 1977), pp. 21–36.

60. ———. "Empirical Warrant-Stock Relationships," *Journal of Business,* **45,** No. 4 (Oct. 1972), pp. 563–569.

61. Perrakis, Stylianos, and Ryan, Peter J. "Option Pricing Bounds in Discrete Time," *The Journal of Finance,* **39,** No. 2 (June 1984), pp. 519–526.

62. Peterson, Richard. "Investor Preferences for Future Straddles," *Journal of Financial and Quantitative Analysis,* **XII,** No. 1 (March 1977), pp. 105–120.

63. Phillips, Susan M., and Smith Clifford W., Jr. "Trading Costs for Listed Options: The Implications for Market Efficiency," *Journal of Financial Economics,* **8,** No. 3 (June 1980), pp. 179–189.

64. Protopapadakis, Aris, and Stoll, Hans R. "Spot and Futures Prices and the Law of One Price," *The Journal of Finance,* **38,** No. 5 (Dec. 1983), pp. 1431–1456.

65. Reback, Robert. "Risk and Return in CBOE and AMEX Option Trading," *Financial Analysts Journal,* **31,** No. 4 (July–Aug. 1975), pp. 42–52.

66. Rendleman, Richard, and Bartter, Brit. "Two-State Option Pricing," *The Journal of Finance,* **34,** No. 5 (Dec. 1979), pp. 1093–1110.

67. ———. "The Pricing of Options on Debt Securities," *Journal of Financial and Quantitative Analysis,* **XV,** No. 1 (March 1980), pp. 11–24.

68. Rubinstein, Mark. "Displaced Diffusion Option Pricing," *The Journal of Finance,* **38,** No. 1 (March 1983), pp. 213–217.

69. ———. "A Simple Formula for the Expected Rate of Return of an Option over a Finite Holding Period," *The Journal of Finance,* **39,** No. 5 (Dec. 1984), pp. 1503–1510.

70. ———. "Nonparametric Tests of Alternative Option Pricing Models Using All Reported Trades and Quotes on the 30 Most Active CBOE Option Classes from August 23, 1976 through August 31, 1978," *The Journal of Finance,* **40,** No. 2 (June 1985), pp. 445–480.

71. Rubenstein, Mark, and Cox, John. *Option Markets* (Englewood Cliffs, N.J.: Prentice-Hall, 1985).

72. Schmalensee, Richard, and Trippi, Robert. "Common Stock Volatility Expectations Implied by Option Primia," *The Journal of Finance,* **XXXIII,** No. 1 (March 1978), pp. 129–148.

73. Schwartz, Eduardo S. "The Pricing of Commodity-Linked Bonds," *The Journal of Finance,* **37,** No. 2 (May 1982), pp. 525–538.

74. Sears, R. Stephen, and Trennepohl, Gary L. "Measuring Portfolio Risk in Options," *Journal of Financial and Quantitative Analysis,* **XVII,** No. 3 (Sept. 1982), pp. 391–410.

75. Sharpe, William. *Investments* (Englewood Cliffs, N.J.: Prentice-Hall, 1978.)

76. Smith, Clifford. "Option Pricing: A Review," *Journal of Financial Economics,* **3,** No. 1/2 (Jan.–March 1976), pp. 3–51.

77. Smith, Keith. "Option Warrant and Portfolio Management," *Financial Analysts Journal,* **24,** No. 3 (May–June 1968), pp. 135–138.

78. Stapleton, R. C., and Subrahmanyam, M. G. "The Valuation of Options When Asset Returns Are Generated by a Binomial Process," *The Journal of Finance,* **39,** No. 5 (Dec. 1984), pp. 1525–1540.

79. Sterk, William E. "Test of Two Models for Valuing Call Options on Stocks with Dividends," *The Journal of Finance,* **37,** No. 5 (Dec. 1982), pp. 1229–1238.

80. Stoll, H.R. "The Relationship between Put and Call Option Prices," *The Journal of Finance,* **XXIV,** No. 5 (Dec. 1969), pp. 801–824.

81. ———. "Reply," *The Journal of Finance,* **XXVIII,** No. 1 (March 1973), pp. 185–187.

82. Stone, Albert. *Option Models.* Ph.D. Dissertation, New York University, 1969.

83. Stulz, René M. "Options on the Minimum or the Maximum of Two Risky Assets: Analysis and Applications," *Journal of Financial Economics,* **X,** No. 2 (July 1982), pp. 161–186.

84. Weinstein, Mark I. "Bond Systematic Risk and the Option Pricing Model," *The Journal of Finance,* **38,** No. 5 (Dec. 1983), pp. 1415–1430.

85. Whaley, Robert E. "Valuation of American Call Options on Dividend-Paying Stocks: Empirical Tests," *Journal of Financial Economics,* **X,** No. 1 (March 1982), pp. 29–58.

Chapter 21

The Valuation and Uses of Financial Futures

Forward contracts are commitments entered into by two parties to exchange a specific amount of money for a particular good or service at a specified future time. While the price is decided upon at the time of the agreement, no cash changes hands at that time. However, either or both parties to the transaction often have to post some funds to guarantee fulfillment of the contract. Forward contracts are a part of everyday life. When one orders a car not in stock from a dealer, one is buying a forward contract for the delivery of a car. The price and description of the car are specified. In this case the delivery date might not be exact. In addition, a deposit is often required to guarantee that the buyer will take delivery and pay the agreed-upon price.

In this chapter we will be primarily concerned with financial futures, though we will say a few words about other types of futures. Financial futures are similar to, but slightly different from, forward contracts. The name "financial future" is very descriptive. "Financial" means that the good to be delivered is a financial instrument (e.g., a stock or bond). The word "future" as opposed to "forward" reflects the fact that on these contracts, profits and losses are computed and settled on a day-to-day basis rather than at the end of the contract. This is called "marking to the market" and we will have more to say about it shortly. In addition, contracts for financial futures are traded on organized exchanges that set standard terms for the contracts.

This chapter is divided into four sections. In the first section we describe in more detail the characteristics of financial futures. In the second section we show how these contracts can be valued. In the third section we discuss how financial futures can be used in the investment process. Finally in the fourth section we briefly discuss commodity futures and commodity funds.

DESCRIPTION OF FINANCIAL FUTURES

A financial futures contract calls for the delivery of either a specific financial instrument or a member of a set of financial instruments at a specific date or during a specific period of time for an agreed-upon price. Financial futures are traded on organized exchanges and have standardized contract terms. The exact terms differ from financial future to financial future. Table 21.1 lists some of the financial instruments on which financial futures are being or have been traded. We can categorize these instruments as debt instruments, stock indexes and foreign currencies.

The terms of a futures contract are always specified in detail. These include:

1. The amount and type of asset to be delivered — exactly what asset or set of assets must be delivered and in what quantities.

2. The delivery date or maturity date — the date or period of time at which the exchange is to be consummated.

3. The exact place and process of delivery.

In addition, the exchanges often place certain restrictions on trading. For example they set

1. Margin, the amount of funds that must be put up to ensure that each party will follow through with his or her side of the transaction.

2. Limits on the size of price changes that can occur within a trading day and the size of positions that can be taken.

These restrictions are imposed to ensure orderly markets.

Let's start by discussing the profits or losses from trading futures. Then we will return to an examination of some of the attributes of financial futures that affect their performance.

Profits and Losses from Futures Contracts

Futures contracts are traded on organized exchanges and have prices determined at any moment in time just as do stocks and bonds. In the next section of this chapter we will examine how these prices are determined in the market-

Table 21.1 The Underlying Instruments with Financial Futures

Debt Instruments	Stock Indexes	Currencies
Treasury bills	S&P 500 Index	British Pound
Bank certificate of deposit	S&P 100 Index	Canadian Dollar
Euro dollars	NYSE Composite Index	Japanese Yen
GNMA's	Value Line Index	Swiss Franc
Treasury notes	NASDAQ 100 Index	West Germany Mark
Treasury bonds	S&P OTC 250 Index	
Municipal bonds		

place. For now, let us consider the profit and loss that accrues to the parties to a futures contract. The purchaser of a futures contract is said to be long a contract. The purchaser agrees to take delivery of a certain financial instrument at a certain time. The seller is said to be short the contract; the seller agrees to deliver the instrument at a certain time. We will first examine the case of the purchaser of a specific contract.

Let us consider one contract of government bonds for delivery in 10 days. Government bond contracts are traded in amounts of $100,000 face value. Assume the settlement price series is as shown in Table 21.2. The price is per $1,000. Thus 66 represents $66,000.

For a moment, let us assume that these prices were on a forward contract, rather than on a futures contract. For a forward contract gains and losses are settled at the maturity date. At the maturity, time 0, the forward price must be the same as the price for immediate delivery since the forward and spot contract each require immediate delivery of the same instrument. The original buyer of the forward contract has the right (obligation) to buy the bond at $66. At maturity, bonds cost $68. The profit to the buyer of the contract is $2 times the $1,000, or $2,000. Correspondingly, the seller of the contract is selling a bond at $66 when the market price is $68. This is a loss of $2 times $1,000, or $2,000.

Note that the profit to the purchaser is equal to the loss of the seller. Forwards and futures are zero-sum games; the profits (or loss) of the purchaser plus the loss (or profit) to the seller equals zero.

The cash flow pattern from the viewpoint of a buyer or seller of a futures contract is different from and more complex than the cash flow pattern from a forward contract. This is because, as mentioned earlier, futures contracts are marked to the market on a daily basis. At the close of each trading day, the gain or loss from the price change that occurred over that day is immediately credited or debited to the accounts of the individuals who are long or short. Furthermore, all contracts are rewritten so that the price at which parties are obliged to buy

Table 21.2

Day	Settlement Price*	Cash Flow if Long 1 Forward	Cash Flow if Short 1 Forward	Cash Flow if Long 1 Future	Cash Flow if Short 1 Future
−9	66				
−8	67	0	0	+1,000	−1,000
−7	67	0	0	+1,000	−1,000
−6	65	0	0	−3,000	+3,000
−5	64	0	0	−1,000	+1,000
−4	66	0	0	+2,000	−2,000
−3	64	0	0	−2,000	+2,000
−2	68	0	0	+4,000	−4,000
−1	67	0	0	−1,000	+1,000
0	68	+2,000	−2,000	+1,000	−1,000
Total Cash Flow		+2,000	−2,000	+2,000	−2,000

*Prices are quoted in thousands of dollars to the nearest 1/32 of a thousandth.

and sell the financial instrument is the price of the future at the close of the day. This repricing is referred to as "marking to the market" and the price used to mark to the market is called the settlement price. The aggregate profit or loss from the contract over the life of the contract would be the same whether it is a forward or a futures contract, namely $2,000, but the timing of the cash flows is very different.

As just discussed, the person who shorted (wrote) a foward contract with the price behavior displayed in Table 21.2 would have one cash flow of −$2,000 on day 0. The person who wrote a futures contract would have a much more complex pattern. On day −8, the futures price is $67. So the writer of the futures contract would then be debited by $1,000 on day −8. The writer of the futures contract would then be considered to have a contract at $67. The contract is marked to the market. On day −7, futures go to $68. Since the contract is implicitly at $67, the loss is again $1,000. The writer will have the account debited by $1,000 and the price of the contract will be specified at $68. Thus the writer of the futures contract has the series of intermediate cash flows shown in Table 21.2. If the reinvestment rate were zero, an investor wouldn't care whether a future or forward contract was held. However, the potential of receiving cash or having to come up with cash on a daily basis makes futures contracts different from forward contracts.

Some Important Attributes of Futures Contracts

In this section we discuss three aspects of financial futures that can impact their performances. These are margin, limits, and delivery.

Margin   To purchase or sell a future is actually to enter into a promise to take a future course of action with associated cash flows over time. This is not a traditional investment because, at the time a futures position is bought or sold, no cash changes hands between the two parties. However, in order to ensure that the parties can fulfill their obligation, an initial margin or good faith deposit must be made with the broker. The size and terms of the good faith deposit vary from future to future. They are generally related to the size of the contract and the variability in the daily value of the contract. Relating to daily variability makes sense since the purpose of the good faith deposit is to see that contracts are fulfilled and that contracts are adjusted for profits or losses (marking to the market) on a daily basis. Margins for futures are small relative to other types of markets. For example, the initial margin needed to buy a future on one million dollars face value of T bills is $1,000. Furthermore, the margin can be put up in the form of earning assets such as T bills or letters of credit. Nowadays, every futures market has a maintenance margin level, usually 75 to 80% of the initial margin level. If margin drops below the maintenance level due to marking of the market, then the investor must come up with additional funds to bring the account back to the original margin level. The cash flows needed to do so are called variation margin and this added margin must be put up in the form of cash. If the investor doesn't deposit the added margin, the broker can liquidate the position at the going market price. The investor is liable for any shortfall that occurs when his portfolio is liquidated.

Limits   Another aspect of futures markets that should be discussed is the existence of limits. Most financial futures markets have limits on the size of the position any investor can take. Of more interest is that they have limits on the size of the price change that is allowed to take place during any day. For example, price moves on the one million dollar 90-day T bill contract are limited to $1,500 per day. When the price moves up or down by that amount during a day, trading essentially stops. What this can mean (and in fact has meant in the futures market for silver among others) is that a position can't be closed out during a period of time at any price. There have been periods of time where price has moved down by the limit for a number of days in a row and no one has traded at that price. Thus for a number of days it was literally impossible to trade on organized exchanges. While these limits were imposed to ensure orderly markets, they constitute an added risk to investing in futures markets.

Delivery   The delivery options of financial futures contracts are well specified. However, the person who has shorted the future often has several options as to which of several financial instruments to deliver and sometimes an option on exactly what day to deliver. For example, in dealing with the futures on Treasury Bonds, the investor who has shorted such a future can deliver any government bond with more than a 15-year maturity and more than 15 years to first call. There are many bonds in the market at any time that fit the description and hence can be delivered. The amount of any bond that must be delivered to satisfy the contract is well specified. A set of "conversion factors" have been determined to ensure that a delivered bond would have the same yield to maturity or, if callable, yield to first call as an 8% coupon bond. The attempt was to make a large number of bonds equivalent for delivery. However, over most periods of time, these bonds are not equivalent. Generally, at any point in time there is a bond that is "cheapest" to deliver. This option to deliver any bond, along with the option to deliver at any point over a short period of time, adds value to the position of the future seller and correspondingly subtracts it from the value of the buyer. However, the seller always wants to deliver the cheapest bond. This bond has been stable over long periods of time. Thus the reader should not overemphasize the value of the option.

Not all financial futures are settled by delivery of an asset. Some (e.g., stock index futures) are always settled for cash. In this case, the final settlement price of the futures contract is set equal to the market price of the underlying assets on the last trading day of the contract.

Delivery of an asset rarely takes place, even for those contracts that are theoretically settled by delivery of an asset. Almost all futures positions are settled by an offsetting trade rather than by delivery. For example, a buyer of a June Treasury bond contract can close out that position at any time by selling a June Treasury bond contract. Less than 1% of all futures contracts traded are settled by delivery of the underlying asset.

VALUATION OF FINANCIAL FUTURES

The valuation of financial futures is greatly simplified by understanding the relationship between futures prices and the current (or spot) price of the underlying financial instrument. As we will show, a particular relationship must exist, for if it fails to hold, then an immediate riskless profit could be made. Since there are many individuals continuously looking for opportunities to profit from just such a failure, these basic relationships are reasonably descriptive of real markets. We will examine the relationship between spot and future prices for each of the major financial futures. All of the pricing relationships are derived from the ability to hold a financial instrument directly or to create a second instrument with almost identical cash flows by buying or selling futures contracts.

Treasury Bill Futures

Consider an investor who wants to hold a 151-day T bill. The investor could do so in either of two ways. First, the investor could purchase it directly by simply buying the 151-day T bill. Alternatively, the investor could purchase it indirectly. The investor could buy a forward contract on a 91-day T bill for delivery in 60 days. Simultaneously, the investor could purchase a 60-day T bill that matures for an amount exactly sufficient to take delivery of the forward contract. As we will show below, the resulting cash flows are identical. Both investments involve an immediate cash outlay and an inflow of the same size in 151 days. Since the future cash flows are the same, the price (initial cash flow) must be the same. Let's look at the two ways to purchase a 151 day T bill in more detail.

1. *Directly.* Buy a 151-day Treasury bill at a cost of P.
2. *Indirectly.* Buy a forward contract that will lead to delivery in 60 days of a 91-day T bill. Let's define F as the price the holder of a forward contract must pay to take delivery of bills in 60 days. Buy a 60-day T bill that will have a value equal to F at the delivery date. This will cost $F/(1 + R)$, where R is the rate of interest on a 60-day T bill.

The cash flows for these two strategies are shown in Table 21.3. Both of these strategies produce identical future cash flows (equivalent to that of holding a 151-day instrument). Since they have identical cash flows, they should have the same cost. Thus

$$F/(1 + R) = P \qquad (21.1)$$

That two identical instruments should sell at the same price is known as the "law of one price."

If the prior relationship does not hold, then there are profit opportunities. The presence of such profit opportunities should lead reasonably alert investors to try to exploit them and in the process cause the relationship to hold. There are three types of profit opportunities that should force Equation (21.1) to be an equality.

Table 21.3

Action	0	60	151
Direct			
Buy 151-day T bill	P_0		1,000,000
Indirect			
Buy forward contract and take delivery		$-F$	1,000,000
Buy 60-day T bill	$F/(1 + R)$	$+F$	
Sum	$F/(1 - R)$		1,000,000

Buy the Cheapest Instrument   The real 151-day T bill and the homemade 151-day T bill are identical instruments. Anyone who wished to hold a 151-day instrument should buy the least expensive of the two. This will bid up the price of the cheaper and cause the more expensive to decrease in price. To buy either of the two, the investor would incur transaction costs. If there are a sufficient number of investors with a desire to buy a 151-day instrument, the return of the two instruments could be affected only by the difference in transaction costs between the direct and the indirect purchase of a T bill, and these should be exceedingly small. Thus Equation (21.1) should be extremely accurate.

Swap   Assume that the homemade 151-day T bill is cheaper than the traded bill. In this case, anyone holding the 151-day T bill would earn an immediate profit equal to the difference in their prices less transaction costs by selling the 151-day T bill and purchasing the homemade 151-day T bill. Such a trade will involve transaction costs on the purchase and on the sale. If the return differential is greater than two transaction costs, an alert investor will undertake the swap. This should force Equation (21.1) to be close to an equality. Since transaction costs in the T bill and futures markets are very small, the equality should be very closely approximated.

Pure Arbitrage   The final force causing the law of one price to hold is pure arbitrage. Arbitrage involves selling short the more expensive instrument and using the proceeds of the sale to purchase the cheaper. Since subsequent cash flows are identical, this involves an immediate profit. The transaction costs are on the purchase and sale. In addition, the short seller usually incurs a $\frac{1}{2}$ of 1% cost on the short position. This last force causing the law of one price to hold is the most powerful in the sense that there are a large number of alert arbitrageurs prepared to take advantage of any discrepancies in the market. At the same time, since transaction costs are higher, the difference between a 151-day T bill and a homemade 151-day T bill can be larger without it paying to eliminate the differences.

Which of these three profit opportunities sets prices is still an open question. However, any of them should cause the returns of the 151-day T bill and the homemade 151-day T bill to be close and Equation (21.1) to be a reasonable equation for pricing forward treasury bills.

There are several simplifications in our analysis. We used a forward contract in our discussion. However, futures contracts are the contracts that are available to most investors. The reason we used forward contracts was to avoid the intermediate cash flows associated with marking futures contracts to the market. Futures contracts, of course, involve marking to the market. Thus the homemade 151-day T bill has intermediate cash flows. However, marking to the market does not have much of an impact for T bill futures. Elton, Gruber, and Rentzler [15] found that marking to the market affected cash flows on a million dollar T bill position by an average of only four dollars. A difference in cash flows due to marking to the market in the range of plus or minus ($31) occurred 75% of the time. To put these numbers in context, recall that T bill futures are sold in million dollar denominations, so that over 60 days at 9% interest the total cash flow is close to $15,000. Thus the effect of marking to the market is trivial and Treasury bill futures can be sensibly treated as if they were forwards. Elton, Gruber, and Rentzler [15] did an extensive analysis of the difference in returns of the actual bill and homemade bill. There were differences and any strategy that involves selling futures generally offered the higher return. While this is evidence that the law of one price does not hold exactly, and the market is not perfectly efficient, the differences were quite small.

Treasury Bond Futures

Treasury bills are government debt of one year or less to maturity. In addition, they are pure discount instruments with no intermediate cash flows. Treasury bills sell for less than their value at maturity. The increase in value from the time of the sale to the maturity provides the return to the investor. Treasury bonds, in contrast, have original maturities longer than one year and provide a periodic coupon payment as well as potential capital appreciation or loss. A futures market exists for treasury bonds that have at least 15 years to maturity and are either noncallable or if callable are not callable for at least 15 years. There are a large number of different government bonds that meet this criteria and any of them can be delivered to settle a treasury bond futures contract. The standard bond to be delivered is an 8% coupon bond. Conversion factors have been computed for bonds with different coupon rates. Bonds with a different coupon are worth some fraction (for higher coupon bonds, a fraction greater than one) of the standard 8% bond. When the conversion factors were created, the hope was that there would be many different issues that would be equivalent and could be delivered. In practice there is generally a single bond that is cheapest to deliver and will be delivered if actual delivery takes place. This particular issue that is cheapest to deliver is fairly stable over time. Thus the bond that would be potentially delivered is fairly well known at the time the futures contract is written. There are two ways an investor who wished to purchase a government bond could do so:

1. *Purchase directly.* The investor purchases the bond at a current spot price, which can be represented as *P*.

2. *Purchase with delay.* The investor buys a Treasury bond future with a delivery price of *F* and simultaneously buys a Treasury bill with a face

value of F that matures at the delivery date on the futures contract. The cost of the Treasury bill is $F/(1 + R)$ where R is the T bill rate for the time until the future is delivered.

If the bond does not pay interest before the delivery of the future, these are equivalent positions, and if the law of one price holds, they should have the same cost. Thus,

$$F/(1 + R) = P \qquad (21.2)$$

If the Treasury bond has an interest payment before the delivery date, then the price of direct purchase should be reduced by the present value of this payment. If I is the payment and $PV(I)$ is the present value of the payment, then the law of one price implies

$$F/(1 + R) = P - PV(I) \qquad (21.3)$$

Once again we are ignoring marking to the market. In addition, the foregoing analysis assumes we know which bond will be delivered. Historically, the bond that will be delivered, the so-called cheapest deliverable instrument, has remained stable over long periods of time, so that this assumption holds reasonably well in practice. In addition, all of the earlier discussion on what causes the law of one price to hold still follows. Thus Equation (21.2), while a very good estimate of the futures value, should be be expected to hold exactly.

There are other debt instruments with futures markets available. At the time this chapter was written, futures existed on GNMA's (mortgage pools with a government guarantee of interest), bank CD's (short-term bank debt), and Treasury notes (intermediate-term government debt). Futures markets are developing rapidly, and we expect that futures will become available on additional instruments over time. The reader should be able to modify the preceding analysis to value these alternative instruments.

Stock Index Futures

Futures exist on a number of stock market indexes such as the S&P 500 Index, the S&P 100 Index, the Value Line Index, and the NYSE Composite Index. The NYSE Composite is a value-weighted index of all the stocks on the New York Stock Exchange. Its return is equivalent to the capital appreciation on a portfolio of all stocks listed on the New York Stock Exchange where the weights in the portfolio are proportional to the market value of the stock (number of shares times price per share). The S&P 100 and 500, as the names imply, have 100 or 500 firms in the index, and these are generally the largest firms on the New York Stock Exchange. They are also value-weighted indexes. The Value Line Index has a peculiar construction and, given its unimportance in the futures market, will not be discussed further here. The introduction of stock index futures was delayed by the lack of deliverable instruments. What facilitated their introduction was the acceptance of a cash settlement. For most stock index futures, the future is marked to the spot when the future expires. Cash is then transferred at that point in time; no instrument is ever delivered. While there are lots of ways to arrive at the value of stock futures, the easiest way is to assume that an investor looks at the following alternatives: buy an index fund leveraging the position so that the expected cash flow prior to a particular date is zero; or buy T bills and futures so the same purchase of the index fund is accomplished at maturity.

1. *Direct purchase of an index fund, taking action to eliminate intermediate cash flows.* Assume the index fund can be bought for P dollars and the expected dividend on this amount of the fund is D. Let $PV(D)$ be the present value of the expected value of the future dividend stream. Borrow enough money so that the debt is repaid with the dividend. That is, borrow $PV(D)$ and use these borrowed funds to pay for part of the index fund. Thus the amount of cash that must be put up is $P - PV(D)$.

2. *Indirect purchase.* Buy futures that will represent the same amount of the index fund for an amount of money, F, and simultaneously buy a T bill that will mature at a value F. The treasury bill costs $F/(1 + R)$. Since the amount of the index fund purchased is the same, and since the divided flows are used to repay the borrowing, the cost must be the same or:

$$F/(1 + R) = P - PV(D)$$

or

$$F = P\left[(1 + R) - \frac{PV(D)}{P}(1 + R)\right] \qquad (21.3)$$

There are arbitrageurs who continually monitor this relationship and take action if it is out of line. Who are the arbitrageurs? One group is index fund managers. Brokerage firms continually monitor the relationship between stock index values and stock index futures prices. When the futures are cheap, they offer to buy a part of an index fund and to sell the fund Treasury bills and futures. Since the stock trading is not based on a belief that individual shares are mispriced, the brokerage firm believes that the shares can be rapidly resold and thus can offer very low transaction costs; $\frac{1}{8}$ of a dollar is not unusual. Likewise, if futures become overpriced, the reverse trade is made. In terms of our earlier discussion of how the law of one price comes about, this is considered a swap. In addition, there are arbitrageurs in the market who have constructed a small portfolio that is highly correlated with the index. This portfolio is bought or sold short depending on the value of Equation (21.3) with a corresponding action taken in the futures market.

Figure 21.1 is taken from a Salomon Brothers report. It shows the difference in the theoretical value of the stock index future compared to the actual value of the index. The theoretical value depends on Salomon's forecast of dividends.

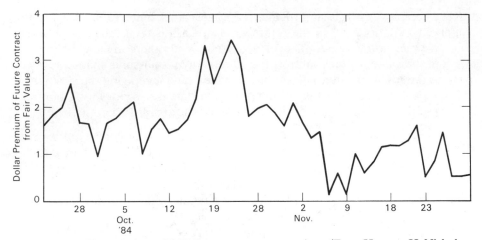

Figure 21.1   The premium of S&P futures contract over time. (From Hanson, H. Nicholas, and Margolis, Louis, "Using Stock Index Futures to Create Synthetic Money Market Instruments," Salomon Brothers, Inc., February 1985, p. 2.)

Over time, futures have been systematically underpriced. At least one index fund has taken advantage of this relative cheapness and has consistently been invested in Treasury bills and futures. The performance of this fund has been superior to standard index funds, indicating that apparent inefficiencies are truly inefficiencies and can be used to earn an excess return.

Before leaving this section, it is appropriate to once again emphasize the factors that might cause the formula not to fit exactly. The formula depends on a forecast of dividends. However, these are dividends on an index, so they are relatively easy to forecast. Nevertheless, there is some small amount of risk in dividend forecasts and this could introduce some added risks when attempting to duplicate the performance of an index fund with futures. The formula also ignores any effect of marking to the market. In the case of stock index futures, and insofar as a stock index is a proxy for a market portfolio in a CAPM sense, these flows may be correlated with the market and consequently may introduce systematic risk. We will now turn to a discussion of foreign currency futures.

Foreign Currency Futures

Futures exist on the major currencies. Table 21.1 showed the exact currencies for which futures contracts exist. Once again two equivalent instruments can be created that allow the valuation of the futures contract. The two equivalent instruments in this case are riskless domestic debt and riskless foreign debt. Foreign riskless debt is held as follows: convert dollars to a foreign currency, for example pounds. Invest the money in the foreign riskless debt. Guarantee the rate of conversion back to dollars with financial futures. This is accomplished by writing a futures contract converting pounds to dollars at the maturity of the foreign T bill for an amount equal to the maturity value of the T bill. Since the conversion to dollars is at a known rate, the foreign investment is riskless. Futures are quoted in number of dollars per pound. Let S be the initial number of dollars that can be bought with one pound. The initial conversion is to convert dollars to pounds. To convert dollars to pounds we use one over the rate or $1/S$. For example, if the rate is \$2 per 1£, one dollar is worth half a pound (1/2). Finally let F be the futures price of one pound and R^B be the foreign (British) riskless rate. Consider an investment in British riskless debt. Then the number of pounds bought per dollar invested is $1/S$. The value of the debt at maturity is $(1 + R^B)/S$. Finally the value at the maturity in dollars is

$$\frac{(1 + R^B)}{S}F$$

and the return is

$$\left[\frac{(1 + R^B)}{S}F\right] - 1$$

If the law of one price holds, all riskless debt should have the same return. If R^D is the rate of return on domestic debt then,

$$R^D = [(1 + R^B)F/S] - 1$$

or

$$F = [(1 + R^D)/(1 + R^B)]S \qquad\qquad (21.4)$$

Equation (21.4) is known as interest rate parity. Empirically, interest rate parity seems to hold fairly well. The risk element besides marking to the market is a fear of exchange controls. Governments can and do restrict conversion from one currency to another. In addition, governments can tax the returns to foreign investors. This affects the relative return and can be one element of risk insofar as a change in the tax law can occur during the time of the hedge.

In this section, we have discussed the valuation formula for commonly traded financial futures. The same principles should hold for the financial futures we have not discussed here.

THE USES OF FINANCIAL FUTURES

The growth in financial futures trading has been astronomic in recent years. For example, the dollar volume of shares commanded by futures contracts traded on the S&P index on an average day exceeds the dollar volume of direct trading in these shares. The major markets for financial futures are liquid and involve low transaction costs. Transaction costs are only a fraction of those involved in trading the underlying assets commanded by futures contracts. The combination of liquidity with low transaction costs has meant that there are a large variety of uses for financial futures contracts. We will attempt to review only a few of them here. We find it helpful to divide the uses to which financial futures can be put into three categories: hedging, investment management, and investment products. There is overlap between these categories, but they do serve as a useful characterization.

Hedging

The use of financial futures as a hedging mechanism has received the most attention in the financial literature. Hedging refers to the use of financial futures to reduce a type of risk to which the buyer or seller is subject. For example, the corporation about to sell a long-term issue of bonds (or the underwriter of such an issue) can eliminate most of the risk of interest rate movements by selling a future on a like amount of long-term government bonds. By doing so the corporation in essence locks in the current interest rate. If interest rates go up, the corporation will have to pay a higher interest rate to sell its bonds, but it will find that the value of its short position in futures has gone up by a similar amount. Unfortunately, this may not be an exact dollar-for-dollar movement because of basis risk. Basis risk is the risk that the spot price of the firm's corporate bonds and the futures price of government bonds do not move exactly alike. Corporate bonds and government bonds do move in similar but not identical ways over time. For example, when interest rates go up, the price of both long-term government bonds and long-term corporate bonds go down, but the amounts by which they go down need not be exactly the same because the spread in rates between the two instruments can change. However, the divergence of these rates over time is very small relative to the effect on the prices of either instrument as the level of rates changes.

As another example of hedging, consider a corporate treasurer who expects to receive a large sum of money in three months to invest in Treasury bills. By buying T bill futures now, he or she can lock up a known rate on T bills. In fact, if the treasurer takes delivery, the return will be certain.

Finally, consider an investor due to retire who is worried about the value of that portion of the pension fund that is invested in common stocks. By selling futures on a widely diversified portfolio like the S&P index, the investor can hedge away the risk that the stock market will go up or down between now and the time of retirement.

Changing Investment Policy

Financial futures have transaction costs that are dramatically less than those on stocks and bonds. This implies that they are likely to be the preferred way to change the risk exposure of individual assets or categories of assets. In addition, the use of financial futures allows a direct measure of the value added or subtracted by the policy change. Finally, using financial futures allows a wider choice of assets because of an ability to change risk exposure without having to buy and sell the individual assets in the portfolio. The ideas just presented need elaboration. The elaboration is best done with a few examples.

Changing the Market Exposure of a Stock Portfolio   Consider a manager of a mutual fund with a particular exposure to changes in market level. Assume for a moment that the Beta on the portfolio is 1.5. Thus a 1% move in the market should be expected to lead to a 1.5% change in the rate of return on the portfolio. Assume further that the manager is pessimistic about the future course of the market and wishes to reduce the exposure. Without financial futures the manager would sell high Beta stocks and purchase lower Beta stocks or Treasury bills with the proceeds. With financial futures the Beta on the portfolio can be reduced in an alternative manner. If the manager sells stock index futures, the combination of the existing portfolio and the stock index futures will have a reduced Beta. By selling sufficient stock index futures, the manager can reduce the Beta to any level desired. Conversely, if the manager wished to increase the Beta on the portfolio, financial futures could be purchased.

There are a number of advantages in using futures to control the risk exposure of the portfolio to market fluctuations. First, transaction costs on futures are dramatically less than transaction costs of selling stock and purchasing T bills, or of using stock swaps to change the portfolio beta. Second, if the firm feels that it has the ability to select individual stock issues, then changing the market exposure by selling stock and purchasing T bills reduces the contribution of selection ability to the performance on the overall portfolio.

For example, if a manager who felt that the return on a particular stock portfolio would be 1% above equilibrium reduced its market exposure by being half in T bills, the return on the full portfolio should be $\frac{1}{2}$ of 1% above equilibrium. By contrast, if futures were used to control risk exposure, the full 1% would generally be earned on the portfolio. Likewise, if the manager controls market risk exposure on the overall portfolio by constraining the Beta to be a particular level, then the performance should be reduced if there is forecasting ability because less promising stocks must be selected in order to maintain a promised risk level. The final advantage of using futures is that they allow a direct evaluation of timing. Managers often try to vary their market risk exposure because of a belief in their ability to anticipate market moves. If the manager uses futures to time, then profits and losses on the futures position are a direct measure of the manager's timing ability. The use of futures separates performance due to timing from performance due to selection.

Changing Interest Rate Exposure on Bonds   In prior chapters we discussed the concept of bond duration. Bond duration is a measure of the sensitivity of a bond portfolio to changes in interest rates. Most bond managers are timers. They forecast the future course of interest rates. If they feel rates will rise more than they had previously anticipated, they shorten the maturity of their portfolio. If they feel rates will fall more than they had anticipated, then the maturity will be lengthened. Transaction costs across bonds can vary dramatically. The transaction costs of very liquid government bonds are substantially less than those of thinly traded government or corporate bonds. Because of this, timers generally hold very liquid governments as a large part of their portfolio. Thus, timers are giving up the greater expected return of corporates and less liquid governments in order to have lower transaction costs.

Futures can accomplish the same purpose without constraining the investor to holding lower return securities. The duration on a portfolio can be changed by buying or selling futures. If the manager wishes to shorten the duration, then futures are sold. For example, consider the issuance of a one-year future on a Treasury bond when Treasury bonds are held in the portfolio. The Treasury bond could be delivered against the future in a year. Thus the maturity of the bond has switched from long term to one year with a corresponding change in the duration. If the manager wishes to lengthen the maturity of the portfolio, then futures are bought.

There are a number of advantages in using futures to change interest rate exposure. These are the same reasons discussed earlier in using stock index futures. However, they bear repeating here. First, the transaction costs are substantially less. Second, using futures allows the manager to make the selection decision independent of the duration decision. Thus if the manager feels that certain sectors or bonds are especially attractive, these bonds can be selected even if they are illiquid and can be sold only with large transaction costs. Even if the manager does not profess to have selection ability, bonds that are illiquid but promise higher returns such as corporates can be selected. The reader should note that the manager can be exposed to basis risk by using futures on instruments that differ from those held in the portfolio to change duration. However, the impact on returns due to instrument types that are not perfectly matched should be small compared to the impact of interest rate changes on portfolios of different durations. Finally, profits and losses on the futures are a direct measure of the timing ability and the value added by the timing ability, if any exists. Many managers profess to have timing ability, but it is difficult to measure. Using futures gives a direct measure.

Before leaving this section one other issue will be briefly discussed. When interest rates were extremely high, the duration on even long-term bonds was fairly short. The problem was that the liabilities of many institutions (e.g., pension funds) had longer durations than even the longest maturity bond. Thus immunization, the matching of the duration on assets and liabilities, was infeasible using bonds alone. Futures can be used to change duration. A mixture of bonds and futures could be constructed with an arbitrarily long duration. Thus in periods of higher interest rates, employing futures was the only way that immunization was possible for many liabilities.

Changing the Bond–Stock Mix   Consider a manager of a balanced fund. One of the decisions that must be made is the relative exposure to the stock market and to the bond market. If the manager decides that the exposure to the stock market should be increased, it should be obvious from the prior sections that this change can be accomplished with futures. Purchasing stock index futures will increase the Beta on the stock portfolio and increase the stock market exposure. Selling bond futures decreases the duration and reduces the exposure to interest rate changes. All of the advantages of futures discussed in prior sections still hold for this use of futures. In particular, the use of futures lowers transaction costs, allows security selection to be independent of the market exposure decision, and gives an unambiguous measure of timing ability.

Creating New Products

Futures have been used to create products that could not exist or were inordinately expensive before futures existed. One such product is an Alpha fund. The idea behind such a fund is to capture the stock selection ability of a set of analysts without being subject to market risks. The implementation of the concept simply involves selling enough futures on the S&P index so that the sum of the Betas on the futures and the fund's stock portfolio equals zero. Thus the fund has a Beta of zero. Assume that the stock portion of the fund has a Beta of one. Then the amount of futures to be written equals the value of the fund. From an earlier section we know that the futures price is the spot price adjusted up by the risk-free rate and down by the dividend rate. If the stock portfolio has the same dividend rate as the S&P index, its dividend rate will match the minus dividend term in the equation valuing futures. Thus the return on the fund should be equal to the return on Treasury bills plus any Alpha or greater than equilibrium return earned on its stock portfolio. Such funds are called Alpha funds.

A second set of products involving futures stems from the fact that futures can be used to (almost) replicate puts and calls as well as to replicate stocks and bonds. In the section of this chapter on pricing, we have shown how futures are priced by their ability to replicate existing financial instruments. Holding T bills and buying futures on the S&P index is almost the same as investing in the S&P index.[1] Similarly, selling T bills and selling futures on the S&P index is almost the same as shorting the S&P index.

We showed in previous chapters that puts and calls can be replicated by dynamically changing the mix of instruments in a portfolio. For example, a put on a stock could be replicated by buying T bills and shorting the stock. But now we know that shorting the stock can be replicated by borrowing and selling futures on the stock. Thus the put or call may be replicated by using futures in combination with lending and borrowing. This is particularly important in artifical puts (portfolio insurance) constructed through dynamic portfolio rebalancing. This rebalancing can take place at a much lower cost using futures than it can through changing the bond–stock mix. This has lead to the creation of products using futures that attempt to replicate holding

1. T bills plus calls on long-term bonds.
2. T bills plus calls on stocks.
3. Long-term bonds or bond portfolios plus puts on these bonds.
4. Stocks or stock portfolios plus puts on these stocks.

---

[1]The word *almost* is used because of the effect of marking to the market and the uncertainty of the dividend stream on stocks.

In closing we should mention that just as a position in futures plus a position in the underlying instrument plus T bills can be used to replicate calls and/or puts, calls and/or puts can be used in combination with a position in the underlying instruments to replicate futures.

NONFINANCIAL FUTURES AND COMMODITY FUNDS

This chapter is primarily concerned with a discussion of financial futures. Before closing, though, we should mention that there are a tremendous number of nonfinancial commodity futures. Futures exist on a range of additional assets, from those that are thought of as being close to financial assets like silver and gold to those that are almost never thought of as financial futures like hog bellies. In the late 1960s and 1970s, with the tremendous increase in inflation in the American economy, interest grew in both commodity futures and financial futures as hedges against inflation. Actually, returns on commodity futures should reflect only unanticipated inflation as anticipated inflation should already be incorporated in the pricing of the commodity futures. One has to be cautious about interpreting the returns on commodity futures. Commodity futures are used heavily to hedge away the risk faced by producers and manufacturers of products; hence supply, demand, and prices, are heavily affected by end product demand and prices. Roll [33] recently found that orange juice futures prices were affected by and predictive of weather. In addition, since price is affected by unanticipated inflation rather than inflation itself, to decide on the timing of purchases of futures one has to predict unanticipated inflation. In other words one has to be a better predictor of inflation than the aggregate of investors (the market). Finally, there is the problem of computing a rate of return on a position in futures. Recall that no money changes hands when futures are bought or sold. Only a margin is posted and that can often be posted in the form of T bills. Very little evidence exists on the rate of return on futures investing. That which does exist makes arbitrary assumptions about the way to compute rates of return and studies a period of time when inflation went from close to zero to over 10%. While it is worthwhile examining these results, one should be somewhat cautious about generalizing from them. Bodie [3] and Bodie and Rozansky [4] have studied the performance of an equally weighted portfolio of 23 commodity futures during the period of 1950 through the 1980s. Their data show that over the period the return and risk characteristics of financial futures were very close to that of the S&P 500, but because of a negative correlation between stocks and futures, a portfolio composed of long positions in commodity futures should be included in an investor's optimum portfolio.

There is another approach to the problem of the return on futures and that is to study the performance of publicly traded commodity funds. That is the subject to which we now turn.

In the 1980s, there has been an explosion of public commodity funds. These funds are similar to mutual funds in the sense that investors buy shares and the

Table 21.4 Returns and Risk of Different Investment, June 1979–June 1984

Instrument	Average Monthly Returns	Standard Deviation of Monthly Returns
Common stocks	.0118	.0434
Shearson bond index	.0063	.0304
Commodity funds	.0046	.1064

From Elton, Gruber, and Rentzler [16].

proceeds are pooled and managed by a professional manager. Commodity funds invest in financial futures as well as commodity futures. Managers can and will go short as well as long. Thus commodity fund managers are trying actively to guess the course of futures prices rather than taking a passive strategy. Table 21.4 shows the return characteristics of these funds relative to some standard market indexes. The S&P index and the Shearson index can be considered to be respectively the return on an index fund of stocks and the return on an index fund of bonds. The striking feature of this table is the high variability of the return. The standard deviation of the commodity funds is $2\frac{1}{2}$ to 3 times that of either bond funds or stock funds. The correlation of commodity funds with the stock and bond index is small. Over this period the correlation was $-.12$ with common equity and was $-.11$ with the Shearson bond index. Given the low realized returns and the high standard deviation of returns on these funds, evidence in this period indicates that an average commodity fund should not be added to a stock or bond portfolio despite the low correlation. Past return may not be predictive of future returns but the characteristics shown in Table 21.4 would suggest that commodity funds are not useful additions to a bond or stock portfolios.

BIBLIOGRAPHY

1. Anderson, Ronald W., and Danthine, Jean-Pierre. "Hedging and Joint Production: Theory and Illustrations," *The Journal of Finance,* **35,** No. 2 (May 1980), pp. 487–497.
2. Black, Fischer. "The Pricing of Commodity Contracts," *Journal of Financial Economics* (Jan.–March 1976), 167–179.
3. Bodie, Ziv. "Commodity Futures as a Hedge Against Inflation," *The Journal of Portfolio Management* (Spring 1983), pp. 12–17.
4. Bodie, Ziv, and Rosansky, Victor. "Risk and Return in Commodity Futures," *Financial Analysts Journal* (May 1980).
5. Breeden, Douglas T. "Consumption Risk in Futures Markets," *The Journal of Finance,* **35,** No. 2 (May 1980), pp. 503–520.
6. Callier, Philippe. "One Way Arbitrage, Foreign Exchange and Securities Markets: A Note," *The Journal of Finance,* **36,** No. 5 (Dec. 1981), pp. 1177–1186.
7. Capozza, Dennis, and Cornell, Bradford. "Treasury Bill Pricing in the Spot and Futures Markets," *Review of Economics and Statistics* (Nov. 1979).

8. Chang, Eric C. "Returns on Speculators and the Theory of Normal Backwardation," *The Journal of Finance,* **40,** No. 1 (March 1985), pp. 193–208.
9. Cornell, Bradford. "Taxes and the Pricing of Treasury Bill Futures Contracts: A Note," *The Journal of Finance,* **36,** No. 5 (Dec. 1981), pp. 1169–1176.
10. Cornell, Bradford, and Reinganum, Marc R. "Forward and Future Prices: Evidence from the Foreign Exchange Markets," *The Journal of Finance,* **36,** No. 5 (Dec. 1981), pp. 1035–1046.
11. Cornell, Bradford, and French, Kenneth R. "Taxes and the Pricing of Stock Index Futures," *The Journal of Finance,* **38,** No. 3 (June 1983), 675–694.
12. Cox, John C., Ingersoll, Jonathan E., and Ross, Stephen A. "The Relation between Forward Prices and Future Prices," *Journal of Financial Economics* (1981), pp. 321–346.
13. Dusak, Katherine. "Futures Trading and Investor Returns: An Investigation of Commodity Market Risk Premiums," *Journal of Political Economy* (Nov.– Dec. 1973), pp. 1306–1387.
14. Ederington, Louis. "The Hedging Performance of the New Futures Market," *The Journal of Finance* (March 1979), pp. 157–170.
15. Elton, Edwin, Gruber, Martin, and Rentzler, Joel. "Intra-day Tests of the Efficiency of the Treasury Bill Futures Market," *Review of Economics and Statistics* (Feb. 1984), pp. 129–137.
16. Elton, Edwin, Gruber, Martin, and Rentzler, Joel. "Professionally Managed Publicly Traded Commodity Funds," forthcoming *Journal of Business.*
17. Fama, Eugene. "Forward Rates as Predictors of Future Spot Rates," *Journal of Financial Economics* (Oct. 1976).
18. Feder, Gershon, and Ross, Knud. "Risk Assessments and Risk Premiums in the Eurodollar Market," *The Journal of Finance,* **37,** No. 3 (June 1982), pp. 679–692.
19. Figlewski, Stephen. "Futures Trading and Volatility in the GNMA Market," *The Journal of Finance* (May 1981).
20. Forsythe, Robert, Palfrey, Thomas R., and Plott, Charles R. "Futures Markets and Informational Efficiency: A Laboratory Examination," *The Journal of Finance,* **39,** No. 4 (Sept. 1984), pp. 955–982.
21. Gay, Gerard D., and Manaster, Steven. "Hedging against Commodity Price Inflation: Stocks and Bills as Substitutes for Futures Contracts," *Journal of Business* (July 1982).
22. Gay, Gerald D., and Manaster, Steven. "The Quality Option Implicit in Futures Contracts," *Journal of Financial Economics,* **13,** No. 3 (Sept. 1984), pp. 353–370.
23. Hilliard, Jimmy E. "Hedging Interest Rate Risk with Futures Portfolios Under Term Structure Effects," *The Journal of Finance,* **39,** No. 5 (Dec. 1984), pp. 1547–1570.
24. Ho, Thomas S.Y. "Intertemporal Commodity Futures Hedging and the Production Decision," *The Journal of Finance,* **39,** No. 2 (June 1984), pp. 351–376.
25. Hsieh, David A., and Kulatilaka, Nalin. "Rational Expectations and Risk

Premia in Forward Markets: Primary Metals at the London Metals Exchange," *The Journal of Finance,* **37,** No. 5 (Dec. 1982), pp. 1199–1208.

26. Jacobs, Rodney L. "The Effect of Errors in Variables on Tests for a Risk Premium in Forward Exchange Rates," *The Journal of Finance,* **37,** No. 3 (June 1982), pp. 667–678.

27. Jagannathan, Ravi. "An Investigation of Commodity Futures Prices Using the Consumption-Based Intertemporal Capital Asset Pricing Model," *The Journal of Finance,* **40,** No. 1 (March 1985), pp. 175–192.

28. Jarrow, Robert A., and Oldfield, George S. "Forward Contracts and Futures Contracts," *Journal of Financial Economics* (Dec. 1981), pp. 373–382.

29. Kilcollin, Thomas Eric. "Difference Systems in Financial Futures Markets," *The Journal of Finance,* **37,** No. 5 (Dec. 1982), pp. 1183–1198.

30. Park, Soo-Bin. "Spot and Forward Rates in the Canadian Treasury Bill Market," *Journal of Financial Economics,* No. 1 (March 1982), pp. 107–114.

31. Rendleman, Richard, and Carabini, Christopher. "The Efficiency of the Treasury Bill Futures," *The Journal of Finance* (Sept. 1979), pp. 895–914.

32. Richard, Scott F., and Sundaresan, M. "A Continuous Time Equilibrium Model of Forward Prices and Futures Prices in a Multigood Economy," *Journal of Financial Economics* (Dec. 1981), pp. 347–72.

33. Roll, Richard. "Orange Juice and Weather," *American Economic Review* (Dec. 1985), pp. 861–881.

PART 4

EVALUATING THE INVESTMENT PROCESS

Chapter 22

Evaluation of Portfolio Performance

An integral part of any decision-making process should be the evaluation of the decision. This is equally true whether investors make their own investment decisions or employ a manager to make them.

A large percentage of investments are made by professional managers. Professionally managed funds include mutual funds, pension funds, college endowments, and discretionary accounts, among others. It is important for an investor utilizing one of these managers not only to evaluate how well the fund has done relative to other funds, but also to understand the fund's general policies and to be able to tell how well the fund has followed them. How diversified is the fund? How actively does it try to pursue short-run aberrations in prices? What is the bond–stock mix and how much does it vary? In order for the individual investor to understand the risks he or she is undertaking, the fund's policies and how strictly the manager adheres to them must be known. For the institution that has engaged a professional manager, examining the manager's policies enables the institution to evaluate not only the risks they are undertaking, but also the costs of any restrictions they might have placed on the fund manager.

Evaluation is important, not only to the individual or institution who engages a professional money manager, but also to the individual who invests personal funds. Once again, evaluation involves more than rating how well the investor has performed compared to others. To the individual making investment decisions, it is important to understand what caused the performance. Were there extra benefits from market timing or only extra transaction costs? Was stock selection superior?

Portfolio evaluation has evolved dramatically over the last ten years. The acceptance of modern portfolio theory has changed the evaluation process from crude return calculations to rather detailed explorations of risk and return and the sources of each. Furthermore, ten years ago evaluation was not an integral part of many organizations. This has changed (in part from external pressure) so that at this time most investment organizations incorporate evaluation as an integral part of their decision-making process.

This chapter discusses the current state of portfolio evaluation principles. It is divided into four sections. In the first section we go through the measurement of the overall fund performance. In the second section we analyze how the overall evaluation can be decomposed into those factors that affect the overall performance. In the third section we examine whether there are general characteristics associated with managers that have performed well. Finally, in the last section we examine whether fund performance is predictible.

EVALUATION TECHNIQUES

The evaluation of portfolio performance is essentially concerned with comparing the return earned on some portfolio with the return earned on one or more other portfolios. It is important that the portfolios chosen for comparison are truly comparable. This means that they not only must have similar risk, but also must be bound by similar constraints. For example, an institution that restricts its managers to investing in bonds rated AA or better should not evaluate its managers by comparing their performance to the performance of portfolios that are unconstrained. Although such a comparison would be useful in evaluating the relevance of the constraint, it would not be relevant for evaluating the manager.

Often the return earned by a fund is compared to the return earned by a portfolio of similar risk. In other comparisons an explicit risk–return trade-off is developed so that comparisons can be made across funds with very different risk levels. In either case, it is necessary to be more precise about what is meant by risk and return.

Measures of Return

In earlier chapters when we computed return, we calculated the capital gains plus dividends from an initial investment. Thus, if a security paid dividends of $3.00 and had a capital gain of $7.00 on an investment of $100, the return was

$$\frac{7 + 3}{100} = 0.10 = 10\%$$

The 10% return was the return over the period in which the capital gain occurred.

When evaluating a portfolio, generalizing our simple idea of return requires care. A problem occurs because there are many inflows and outflows of funds to the portfolio and very different amounts of money are invested at different points in time. To illustrate this, consider the example shown in Table 22.1. The

Table 22.1

	Period			
	0	1	2	3
1. Value before inflow or outflow	$100	$110	$231	$55
2. Inflow (outflow)	0	$100	($181)	
3. Amount invested	$100	$210	$ 50	
4. Ending value	$110	$231	$ 55	

portfolio has increased in value by 10% in each period, yet the ending value is less than the beginning value because of net outflows. To determine the rate of return by comparing the ending value to the beginning value would not reflect these changes.

As a second example, consider Table 22.2. This table shows two different patterns of inflows and outflows. In both cases, over the entire period, the inflows equal the outflows. Furthermore, the rate of return earned by each fund is identical in each period. However, the ending value is very different because the fund manager of Fund *A* had the good luck to have the funds in the period that was highly profitable.

If we just looked at the ending value, compared to the beginning value over the full period, Fund *A*'s performance would look superior. However, the period by-period return is identical and (ignoring risk for the moment) so is the manager's performance. *Unless* the inflows and outflows are under the control of the manager (and in most cases they are not), the manager should not be rewarded or penalized for the good or bad fortune of having extra funds available at a particular time.

We eliminate the effect of having different amounts of funds available if we calculate the rate of return in each time period and then compound the return to determine it in the overall period. When the rate of return is calculated this way, it is called the *time weighted rate of return*. For Fund *A* the return in the

Table 22.2

	Period			
	0	1	2	3
Rate of return earned by each manager	20%	−10%	10%	
Fund *A*				
1. Value before inflow or outflow	100	240	126	$138.60
2. Inflow (outflow)	100	(100)	0	0
3. Amount invested	200	140	126	
4. Ending value	240	126	138.60	
Fund *B*				
1. Value before inflow or outflow	100	120	198	$107.80
2. Inflow (outflow)	0	100	(100)	0
3. Amount invested	100	220	98	
4. Ending value	120	198	107.80	

first period is $(240 - 200)/200 = 20\%$. In the second period the return is $(126 - 140)/140 = -10\%$. In the third period the return is $(138.60 - 126)/126 = 10\%$. The overall return is the product of 1 plus each of the three one-period returns minus 1, or $(1.20)(0.90)(1.10) - 1 = 0.188$, or 18.8%. This return is the same for A and B. Since the manager's performance was identical, this is appropriate. Also, in the first example, the time-weighted rate of return would show the actual 10% return that was earned for each period. It would not penalize the manager for the net outflows encountered.

To calculate the time-weighted rate of return requires knowledge of the value of the fund any time there is a cash inflow or an outflow. For a fund with frequent transactions, this involves substantial calculations. If the inflows and outflows are not related to the market performance, then less frequent calculations may yield a reasonable approximation. Often funds are sold in units. Inflows and outflows affect the number of units but any one unit reflects the same initial investment. In this case tracing the performance of one unit is equivalent to determining the time-weighted rate of return.

Having examined return, it is necessary to look at risk.

Measures of Risk

There are two possible measures of risk that can be used: total risk or non-diversifiable risk. Consider a college endowment fund. Clearly, the appropriate risk is the risk on the total assets. The college will find very little comfort in the fact that part of the risk could be diversified away if they held other assets when the portfolio under consideration contains their total assets. As an alternative, consider the pension fund of a large corporation. For example, at one time AT&T allocated its pension funds to 125 separate managers. The contribution to the risk of the pension fund as a whole from the portfolio under supervision of any of these managers is primarily the nondiversifiable risk. AT&T, in evaluating its managers, should look at return relative to nondiversifiable risk.

As discussed in earlier chapters, total risk is normally measured by standard deviation of return whereas nondiversifiable risk is normally measured by the Beta coefficient. Having discussed risk and return, it is appropriate to look at techniques for examining portfolio performance.

Direct Comparisons

As discussed before, one way to compare portfolios is to examine the return earned by alternative portfolios of the same risk. This is the procedure used by Friend, Blume, and Crockett [12] in their examination of mutual funds. Mutual funds have been evaluated by academics more than any other group of investment vehicles. This attention, which may well be unwelcome, is due, primarily, to the fact that data on mutual funds' portfolios are publicly available. Throughout this chapter we illustrate the discussion of performance measurement with reference to mutual fund studies.

Table 22.3 from the Friend, Blume, and Crockett study shows the mean return

Table 22.3 Characteristics of Investment Performance of Mutual Funds and Random Portfolios with Variance as a Measure of Risk (Jan. 1960–June 1968)

Risk Class	Number in Sample		Mean Variance		Mean Return	
	Mutual Funds	Equally Weighted Random Portfolios[a]	Mutual Funds	Equally Weighted Random Portfolios[a]	Mutual Funds	Equally Weighted Random Portfolios[a]
Low risk	43	62	0.00120	0.00118	0.102	0.128
Medium risk	25	51	0.00182	0.00184	0.118	0.142
High risk	18	50	0.00280	0.00279	0.138	0.162

[a]NYSE stocks only, assuming an equal investment as of beginning of period in each stock included.

Source: Friend, Blume, and Crockett [12].

earned by a group of mutual funds compared to randomly generated portfolios. In this table variance was used as a measure of risk. The mutual funds were divided into three risk categories (high, medium, and low risk). Random portfolios with risks approximating the risk of the mutual funds were generated. The columns under mean variance show how closely they matched. The last two columns show the return on each group of random portfolios and mutual funds. In this period and for this measure, mutual funds did worse than randomly selected portfolios.

Friend, Blume, and Crockett repeated this analysis using Beta as a measure of risk. Table 22.4 illustrates this comparison. Once again, they divided mutual funds into low, medium, and high risk and matched these funds with randomly selected portfolios. The last four columns show the mean return on the mutual funds and three groups of random portfolios.

The three groups of random portfolios differ in how the stocks were selected and how they were weighted. Equally weighted random portfolios are constructed by randomly selecting securities from the New York Stock Exchange in a manner so that the odds of selecting any security is the same as the odds of selecting any other security. The stocks, once selected, are weighted equally. Proportionally weighted, variant 1 are random portfolios where the odds of selecting any one stock are proportional to the amount of the stock outstanding, but, once selected, an equal dollar amount is placed in each security. Finally, in variant 2, the odds of selecting any stock are equal, but, once selected, the amount invested in any stock is proportional to the dollar amount of that stock outstanding.

There is nothing special about the particular way each of these portfolios was constructed, but the variation illustrates an important point. Earlier we discussed that it is important to compare managers' performances with relevant alternatives. If a manager is restricted from undertaking certain types of investments, then the return on these investments should not be used to evaluate performance.

Mutual funds tend to invest in securities of large corporations and when they do purchase the securities of smaller companies, they tend to purchase them in

Table 22.4 Comparison of Investment Performance of Mutual Funds and Random Portfolios (Jan. 1960–June 1968)

	Number in Sample		Mean Beta Coefficient		Mean Return			
Risk Class	Mutual Funds	Equally Weighted Random Portfolios[a]	Mutual Funds	Equally Weighted Random Portfolios	Mutual Funds	Equally Weighted Random Portfolios	Proportionally Weighted Random Portfolios, Variant 1	Proportionally Weighted Random Portfolios, Variant 2
Low risk ($\beta = 0.5-0.7$)	28	17	0.614	0.642	0.091	0.128	0.116	0.101
Medium risk ($\beta = 0.7-0.9$)	53	59	0.786	0.800	0.106	0.131	0.097	0.084
High risk ($\beta = 0.9-1.1$)	22	60	0.992	0.992	0.135	0.137	0.103	0.092

[a]Approximately the same number in a group for each of the variants.

Source: Friend, Blume, and Crockett [12].

small amounts. If this underrepresentation of small firms by mutual funds is by choice, then it is perfectly reasonable to use small firms in the evaluation, and the equally weighted random portfolios are a relevant alternative. However, the underrepresentation may not be by choice. Mutual funds are restricted by law from holding more than 5% of the shares of any one company. This may in fact mean that the mutual funds cannot invest as much in a small firm as they do in a large one. Thus, in evaluating whether mutual fund managers have outperformed random selection, variant 1 or 2 might well be the correct alternative.

There is an alternative viewpoint from which the relevancy of the three alternative randomly selected portfolios should be examined: the investor's viewpoint. If the investor is facing a choice as to whether or not to entrust funds to a mutual fund, then the equally weighted scheme may be relevant since the investor can make equally weighted investments even if the mutual fund cannot invest equally.

An examination of Table 22.4 shows that the method used to construct random portfolios affects the conclusions concerning mutual fund performance. During this period small firms had a higher return than large firms. Random portfolios with greater representation in these small firms performed best. During the period studied mutual funds were dominated by equally weighted random portfolios but not by the other two variants.

We have just shown that performance can be measured by comparing the return of any portfolio with the return on other portfolios with the same risk. Another possibility is to develop an explicit risk–return trade-off. In the next section we examine some techniques for measuring portfolio performance that allow a comparison of funds with differing risk.

One-parameter Performance Measures

There are four different one-parameter performance measures that have been proposed in the literature. We will discuss each measure in turn. These measures differ in their definition of risk and their treatment of the ability of the investor to adjust the risk level of any fund in which he or she might invest.

The Excess Return to Variability Measure   Consider the original portfolio problem. Figure 22.1 plots the return risk opportunities with riskless lending and borrowing.

As shown in Chapter 3, all combinations of a riskless asset and a risky portfolio lie along a straight line (in expected return standard deviation space) connecting the riskless asset and the risky portfolio. Thus, the line $R_F A$ represents mixtures of the riskless asset and risky portfolio A, and $R_F B$ represents mixtures of the riskless asset and risky portfolio B. As we argued earlier, all investors would prefer portfolio A to B because combinations along $R_F A$ always give a higher return for the same risk. This idea can be and has been used for mutual fund evaluation.

Consider Figure 22.2. Portfolio A is being compared to portfolio B. If a riskless rate exists, then all investors would prefer A to B because combinations of A and the riskless asset give higher returns for the same level of risk than combi-

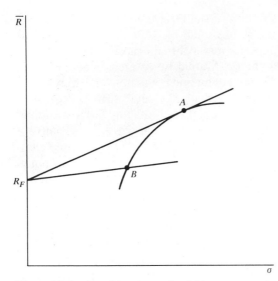

Figure 22.1   Combinations of a riskless asset and
a risky portfolio.

nations of the riskless asset and B. All combinations of any portfolio and the
riskless asset lie in a ray that intersects the vertical axis at R_F. The preferred
portfolio is that which lies on the ray passing through R_F, which lies furthest in
the counterclockwise direction. In Figure 22.2 the portfolios are ranked alpha-
betically. Stating that the preferred portfolio lies on the most counterclockwise
ray is equivalent to stating that the slope of the ray is the highest. In Chapter 4
we showed that the slope of the line was $(\overline{R}_p - R_F)/\sigma_p$. This ratio is one of the

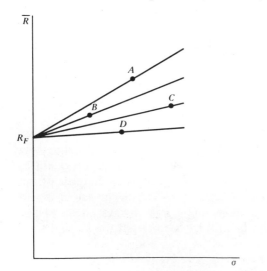

Figure 22.2   Combinations of a riskless asset and
some mutual funds.

measures first utilized in portfolio evaluation and is called the Sharpe measure. An examination of the ratio shows that funds are ranked by the fund's return above the risk-free rate (excess return) divided by the standard deviation of return. This ratio is often referred to as an excess return to variability measure.

Table 22.5 applies this measure to mutual funds. The table is taken from Sharpe [46]. Column 1 is the return less a riskless rate of 3%. Sharpe chose 3% as his

Table 22.5 Performance of 34 Mutual Funds, 1954–1963

Mutual Fund	Average Annual Excess Return (%)	Variability of Annual Return (%)	Reward-to-Variability Ratio $(R/V)^a$
Affiliated Fund	11.6	15.3	0.75896
American Business Shares	7.0	9.2	0.75876
Axe-Houghton, Fund A	7.5	13.5	0.55551
Axe-Houghton, Fund B	9.0	16.3	0.55183
Axe-Houghton, Stock Fund	8.9	15.6	0.56991
Boston Fund	9.4	12.1	0.77842
Broad Street Investing	11.8	16.8	0.70329
Bullock Fund	12.7	19.3	0.65845
Commonwealth Investment Company	7.9	13.7	0.57841
Delaware Fund	11.4	21.4	0.58253
Dividend Shares	11.4	15.9	0.71807
Eaton and Howard, Balanced Fund	8.0	11.9	0.67399
Eaton and Howard, Stock Fund	12.2	19.2	0.63486
Equity Fund	11.6	18.7	0.61902
Fidelity Fund	13.4	23.5	0.57020
Financial Industrial Fund	11.5	23.0	0.49971
Fundamental Investors	13.0	21.7	0.59894
Group Securities, Common Stock Fund	12.1	19.1	0.63316
Group Securities, Fully Administered Fund	8.4	14.1	0.59490
Incorporated Investors	11.0	25.5	0.43116
Investment Company of America	14.4	21.8	0.66169
Investors Mutual	8.3	12.5	0.66451
Loomis-Sales Mutual Fund	7.0	10.4	0.67358
Massachusetts Investors Trust	13.2	20.8	0.63398
Massachusetts Investors — Growth Stock	15.6	22.7	0.63687
National Investors Corporation	15.3	19.9	0.76798
National Securities — Income Series	9.4	17.8	0.52950
New England Fund	7.4	10.2	0.72703
Putnam Fund of Boston	10.1	16.0	0.63222
Scudder, Stevens & Clark Balanced Fund	7.7	13.3	0.57893
Selected American Shares	11.4	19.4	0.58788
United Funds — Income Fund	13.1	20.9	0.62698
Wellington Fund	8.3	12.0	0.69057
Wisconsin Fund	10.8	16.9	0.64091

$^a R/V$ ratio = (Average return − 3.0 percent)/variability. The ratios shown were computed from original data and thus differ slightly from the ratios obtained from the rounded data shown in the table.

Source: Sharpe [46].

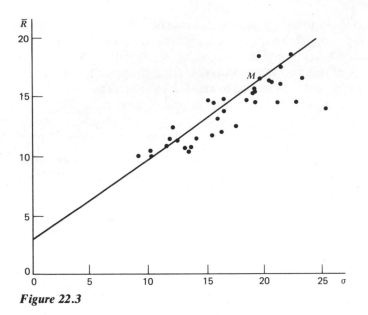

Figure 22.3

estimate of the riskless lending and borrowing rate. Column 2 is the standard deviation. Column 3 is column 1 divided by column 2, which is the Sharpe measure of mutual fund performance or excess return to variability. Figure 22.3 is a plot of these data and the Dow-Jones Index (designated by the symbol M). The ray connecting the risk-free asset and the Dow-Jones Index is shown on the diagram. Most of the mutual funds have a lower reward-to-variability index than the Dow-Jones Index. This implies that most mutual fund managers in this period did worse than they would have done if they had simply invested in the Dow-Jones Index and lent or borrowed to obtain their preferred risk.

The Sharpe measure looks at the decision from the point of view of an investor choosing a mutual fund to represent the majority of his or her investment. An investor choosing a mutual fund to represent a large part of his or her wealth would likely be concerned with the full risk of the fund, and standard deviation is a measure of that risk. Furthermore, if the investor desired a risk different from that offered by the fund, he or she would modify the risk by lending and/or borrowing. The relevant definition of performance may change if the problem is examined from the point of view of the fund manager. This leads directly to our second measure of performance.

Differential Return with Risk Measured by Standard Deviation   Let us assume for the moment that we are evaluating the manager of an all-equity portfolio who has the risk level determined by the client and that the manager is the only equity manager so that total risk is important. Such a situation is not atypical and may represent the situation for the manager of the equity portion of a pension fund. Pension funds often choose separate managers for the equity and bond portions of their portfolio and give target risk levels to each. What should be evaluated in this case is the ability of the manager to pick securities and combine them into a portfolio, given the risk level at which he is constrained to operate. The pension fund manager could obtain a portfolio of the desired risk through the naive strategy of placing part of the money in the market portfolio and part in the riskless asset (and, indeed, should have done so if the manager had no special selection skills). Thus, a measure of the manager's performance is how much better he did than this naive strategy. Consider Figure 22.4 and let A designate the fund being evaluated.

If the manager had followed the naive strategy of investing in the riskless asset and the market portfolio to obtain the same risk as A, a portfolio with the risk and return of A' would result. The differential return at the manager's chosen risk level (the distance AA') is a measure of how much better or worse the manager did than the naive strategy.[1]

The slope of the ray connecting R_F and M is, of course, $(\overline{R}_M - R_F)/\sigma_M$ and the intercept is R_F. Thus, the equation of the line is

$$\overline{R}_i = R_F + \left(\frac{\overline{R}_M - R_F}{\sigma_M}\right)\sigma_i$$

The return on portfolio A' is determined by substituting the standard deviation of A in the foregoing formula and solving for the return of A'. The differential

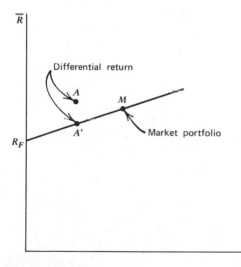

Figure 22.4

---

[1]The measure just discussed is usually presented in return and Beta space and we will do so shortly. Depending on the relevant measure of risk, it may be more appropriate in standard deviation space.

return is the difference, in return, between A and A'. For example, given

1. $R_F = 5\%$
2. $\overline{R}_M = 10\%$
3. $\sigma_M = 20\%$
4. $\sigma_i = 15\%$
5. $\overline{R}_A = 10\%$

then,

$$\overline{R}_{A'} = 5 + \left(\frac{10 - 5}{20}\right)15 = 8.75\%$$

and the differential return

$$\overline{R}_A - \overline{R}_{A'} = 10 - 8.75 = 1.25\%$$

With this measure, funds are ranked by their differential return with the best performing fund the one with the highest differential return.

Figure 22.5 illustrates this measure with mutual fund data. It is taken from the Sharpe study and is exactly the same as Figure 22.3. The differential return for each fund is shown by the vertical lines. Table 22.6 lists the differential return. Both the Sharpe measure and the differential return measure will list the same mutual funds as performing better or worse than the market index. If a fund lies above line R_FM in Figure 22.5, it will have a positive differential return and lie

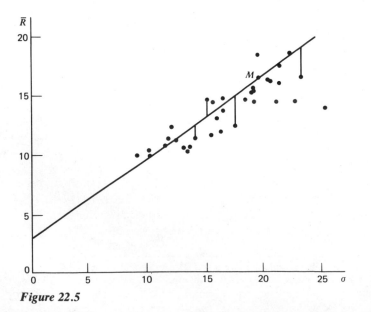

Figure 22.5

Table 22.6   Differential Returns with Standard Deviation as a Measure of Risk

	Average Annual Return	Return on a Portfolio of the Same Risk[a]	Differential Return
Affiliated Fund	14.6	13.20	1.40
American Business Shares	10.0	9.14	0.86
Axe-Houghton, Fund A	10.5	12.00	−1.50
Axe-Houghton, Fund B	12.0	13.87	−1.87
Axe-Houghton, Stock Fund	11.9	13.40	−1.50
Boston Fund	12.4	11.07	1.33
Broad Street Investing	14.8	14.21	0.59
Bullock Fund	15.7	15.87	−0.17
Commonwealth Investment Company	10.9	12.14	−1.24
Delaware Fund	14.4	17.27	−2.87
Dividend Shares	14.4	13.61	−0.79
Eaton & Howard, Balanced Fund	11.0	10.94	0.06
Eaton & Howard, Stock Fund	15.2	15.81	−0.61
Equity Fund	14.6	15.47	−0.87
Fidelity Fund	16.4	18.67	−2.27
Financial Industrial Fund	14.5	18.34	−3.80
Fundamental Investors	16.0	17.47	−1.47
Group Securities, Common Stock Fund	15.1	15.74	−3.64
Group Securities, Fully Admin. Fund	11.4	12.40	−1.00
Incorporated Investors	14.0	20.01	−6.01
Investment Company of America	17.4	17.54	−0.14
Investors Mutual	11.3	11.34	−0.04
Loomis-Sales Mutual Fund	10.0	9.94	0.06
Massachusetts Investors Trust	16.2	16.87	0.67
Massachusetts Investors — Growth Stock	18.6	18.14	0.46
National Investors Corporation	18.3	16.27	2.03
National Securities — Income Series	12.4	14.87	−2.47
New England Fund	10.4	9.80	−0.60
Putnam Fund of Boston	13.1	13.67	0.57
Scudder, Stevens & Clark Balanced Fund	10.7	11.87	−1.17
Selected American Shares	14.4	15.94	−1.54
United Funds — Income Fund	16.1	16.94	−0.84
Wellington Fund	11.3	11.00	0.30
Wisconsin Fund	13.8	14.27	−0.47

[a]Obtained by a mixture of market and risk-free rate.

Source: Sharpe [46].

on a ray with a higher slope than $R_F M$. The converse is true for funds that lie below the line $R_F M$. However, the relative ranking of the funds is affected by the choice of performance measure. This can be seen by comparing Table 22.6 with Table 22.5. Figure 22.6 illustrates why. The Sharpe measure would rank B as better than A since an investor through mixing the riskless asset and portfolio B would get a higher return for any level of risk than could be obtained by combining A with the riskless asset. The differential return index would rank A better than B. This is because the distance $A–A'$ is greater than the distance $B–$

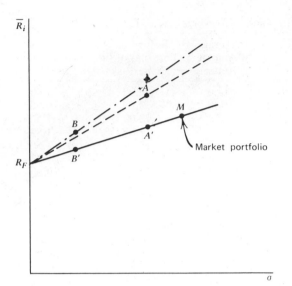

Figure 22.6

B'. This means that manager A was able to outperform a mixture of the market portfolio and lending with the same risk as A by more than manager B could outperform a mixture of the market portfolio and lending at the same risk level as B.

Each of the two measures just discussed have their counterparts when nondiversifiable risk (Beta) is chosen as the appropriate measure of risk.

Excess Return to Nondiversifiable Risk   Consider portfolios in expected return Beta space. It is easy to show that all combinations of a riskless asset and a risky portfolio lie on a straight line connecting them. Furthermore, the slope of the line connecting the risky asset A and the risk-free rate is $(\overline{R}_A - R_F)/\beta_A$. Once again, an investor would prefer the portfolio on the most counterclockwise ray emanating from the riskless asset.[2] In Figure 22.7 the portfolio ranking is alphabetical.

---

[2]Designate the Beta on a portfolio of the riskless asset and portfolio A as β_p. Designate the Beta on portfolio A as β_A and the Beta on the riskless asset as β_F. The Beta on a portfolio is a weighted average of the Beta on the individual securities. Thus $\beta_p = X\beta_A + (1 - X)\beta_F$. But the Beta on a riskless asset is zero or $\beta_F = 0$. Therefore, $X = \beta_p/\beta_A$. The expected return on a portfolio is a weighted average of the expected return on the individual assets. Thus, $\overline{R}_p = X\overline{R}_A + (1 - X)R_F$. Substituting β_p/β_A for X, we have

$$\overline{R}_p = \frac{\beta_p}{\beta_A} \overline{R}_A + \left(1 - \frac{\beta_p}{\beta_A}\right)R_F$$

Rearranging yields

$$\overline{R}_p = R_F + \left(\frac{\overline{R}_A - R_F}{\beta_A}\right)\beta_p$$

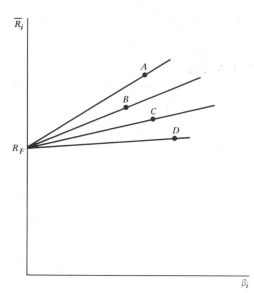

Figure 22.7

This measure of portfolio performance was first suggested by Treynor [56] and is often called the Treynor measure. The final risk measure examines differential return when Beta is the risk measure.

Differential Return When Risk Is Measured by Beta   Consider the line connecting the riskless rate and the market portfolio. A manager could obtain any point along this line by investing in the market portfolio and mixing this with the riskless asset to obtain the desired risk level. If the manager's choice is to actively manage the fund, then one measure of the manager's performance is the difference in return earned by actively managing the fund, compared to what would have been earned if the manager had passively invested in the market portfolio and riskless asset to achieve the same risk level. The slope of the line connecting the riskless asset and the market portfolio is $(\overline{R}_M - R_F)/\beta_M$ and the intercept must be the riskless rate. The Beta on the market portfolio is one. Thus, the equation of the line is

$$\overline{R}_p = R_F + (\overline{R}_M - R_F)\beta_p \tag{22.1}$$

The differential return is the actual return less the return on the portfolio of identical Beta, but lying on the line connecting the riskless asset and the market portfolio. This return is calculated, using the equation stated before, along with the Beta of the portfolio being evaluated.

Assume the market return is 10% and the risk-free rate is 5% and the Beta on the portfolio being evaluated is 0.8. Then a mixture of the market portfolio and the riskless asset to obtain a Beta of 0.8 would have an expected return of

$$\overline{R}_p = 5 + (10 - 5)(0.8) = 9\%$$

The differential return is the difference between the return on the portfolio and the 9% just calculated.

This measure was first proposed by Jensen [21] and is often referred to as the Jensen differential performance index. As an illustration of its use, consider Table 22.7 taken from the Security and Exchange Commission study of mutual funds. As seen from this table, mutual funds over the period 1960–1969 seemed to outperform the passive strategy. By looking at the lower part of the table, which splits the period into two subperiods, it is easy to see that this is due to superior performance in the second subperiod.

The Jensen measure has a special appeal because of its relationship to the capital asset pricing models discussed in Chapters 11–13. We presented the Jensen model as a comparison between the return on the mutual fund and the return on a portfolio constructed by mixing the riskless asset and the market portfolio to obtain the same risk. There is an alternative way of viewing the Jensen measure. Equation (22.1) is, of course, the capital asset pricing line discussed in Chapter 11. The differential return can be viewed as the difference in return earned by the fund compared to the return that the capital asset pricing line implies should be earned. Viewed in this way, the Jensen measure becomes a special case of a large number of measures that could be used.

Chapters 11 and 12 discussed a number of different capital asset pricing models. Any of these could be used in calculating the differential return. The empirical evidence supporting the various CAPM models, discussed in Chapter 13, can help the reader decide which might be most relevant.

For example, assume that the zero Beta version of the CAPM seems most reasonable. As discussed in Chapter 12, this implies that the expected return on portfolio i is given by

$$\overline{R}_i = \overline{R}_z + (\overline{R}_M - \overline{R}_Z)\beta_i$$

This formula is used to calculate the expected return implied by the zero Beta CAPM for a portfolio with the same risk as the portfolio being evaluated. The differential return is the return on the portfolio being evaluated, less the return implied by the zero Beta CAPM.

Viewing the Jensen measure in this way also has implications for mutual fund evidence discussed earlier. Recall, when we were discussing the evidence on the CAPM, that empirical estimates of the CAPM have a higher intercept and a lower slope than the simple CAPM would suggest. In Figure 22.8 we have drawn these two lines. If the empirical line truly represents the risk–return opportunities available in the marketplace, then viewing the Jensen measure as a comparison to the CAPM line would imply that the differential returns should be calculated

Table 22.7   Performance Summary — All Funds with Complete Data for 1960–1969
period

Evalua-tion Period	Beta Range	No. Funds	Average Values (Unweighted)				
			Number of Observations (months)	Monthly Fund Return (%/month)	Aver-age Beta	Monthly Market Return (%/month)	Differ-ential Return
Jan. '60 to Dec. '69	0–0.4	3	120	0.43	0.23	0.77	0.007
	0.4–0.8	35	120	0.63	0.68	0.77	0.004
	0.8–1.0	44	120	0.79	0.91	0.77	0.066
	1.0–1.2	30	120	0.86	1.07	0.77	0.056
	1.2+	13	120	1.05	1.33	0.77	0.130
	Total	125	120	0.78	0.91	0.77	0.051
Jan. '60 to Dec. '64	0–0.4	4	60	0.60	0.16	1.05	0.245
	0.4–0.8	47	60	0.83	0.65	1.05	0.064
	0.8–1.0	43	60	0.82	0.91	1.05	−0.157
	1.0–1.2	22	60	0.73	1.11	1.05	−0.415
	1.2+	9	60	1.14	1.30	1.05	−0.162
	Total	125	60	0.82	0.85	1.05	−0.107
Jan. '65 to Dec. '69	0–0.4	3	60	0.17	0.26	0.49	−0.250
	0.4–0.8	22	60	0.46	0.69	0.49	0.001
	0.8–1.0	46	60	0.68	0.91	0.49	0.194
	1.0–1.2	30	60	0.73	1.08	0.49	0.236
	1.2+	24	60	1.20	1.41	0.49	0.673
	Total	125	60	0.74	0.99	0.49	0.252

Source: SEC study [45].

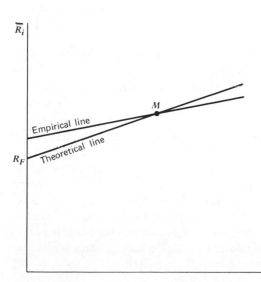

Figure 22.8

relative to the empirical line. Utilizing the empirical line rather than the theoretical line would result in portfolios with Betas less than one having smaller differential returns (if the differential returns are positive) and portfolios with Betas greater than one having larger differential returns. Most mutual funds have Betas less than one. Therefore, calculating the differential returns from the empirical line would result in mutual funds being judged as having poorer performance. Utilizing the empirical CAPM might result in negative differential returns even though they were positive if the theoretical line is used.

We have presented the four single-index performance measures currently in use. The choice between them depends on the appropriate measure of risk and the appropriate viewpoint. In the next section we examine techniques for evaluating specific aspects of portfolio performance.

DECOMPOSITION OF OVERALL EVALUATION

In the previous section we examined a number of overall measures of performance. There have been a number of attempts to examine various aspects of performance that might affect overall performance. In this section we discuss these techniques.

One of the most widely referenced decompositions is one proposed by Fama [9]. Figure 22.9 shows Fama's decomposition. The line plotted in Figure 22.9 is the line representing all combinations of the riskless asset and portfolio M. As discussed earlier, one possible strategy for a manager with a desired risk level is to achieve this level by holding a portfolio composed of the riskless asset and the market. Line $R_F M$ plots the return on all such combinations. The Jensen measure of performance is, of course, the height above the line, or $A-A'$ in Figure 22.9. Fama calls this distance return from selectivity.

Portfolios A and A' have the same Beta and thus the same nondiversifiable risk. However, A and A' do not have the same total risk. All of the risk of the naive strategy comes about because of fluctuations in the market portfolio and thus the risk of portfolio A' is completely nondiversifiable. Portfolio A, however, is not strictly a market portfolio, or its return would lie on $R_F M$. In the process of earning extra return, diversifiable risk was incurred.

If this portfolio is a small part of the holdings of investors, this does not matter because diversifiable risk will wash out in looking at their total holdings. If the portfolio represents their entire portfolio, it does matter. The relevant question becomes, is the extra return worth the extra risk? These considerations are exactly the considerations discussed earlier when we discussed whether Beta or standard deviation was the appropriate measure of risk for evaluating portfolio management. If total risk is the appropriate measure of risk, then the easiest solution is to use one of the measures discussed earlier. However, many authors prefer working in the expected return Beta framework and the same analysis can be done in that framework. Instead of comparing A with a naive portfolio with the

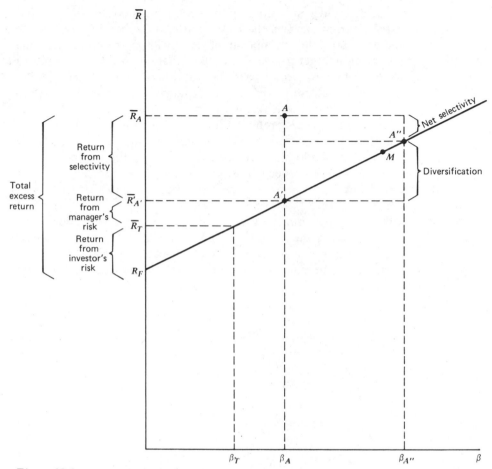

Figure 22.9

same nondiversifiable risk, compare it with a naive portfolio with the same total risk. On Figure 22.9, portfolio A'' is such a portfolio.[3]

The quantity $\overline{R}_A - \overline{R}_{A''}$ is a measure of the extra return earned on portfolio A compared to a naive portfolio with the same total risk. It is the same size, of course, as would have been determined if we had used standard deviation directly as a measure of risk. Fama calls the distance $\overline{R}_A - \overline{R}_{A''}$ net selectivity. He calls the distance $\overline{R}_{A''} - \overline{R}_{A'}$ diversification, decomposing $\overline{R}_A - \overline{R}_{A'}$, into $\overline{R}_A - \overline{R}_{A''}$, and $\overline{R}_{A''} - \overline{R}_{A'}$ is his first decomposition.

---

[3]How can A'' be determined? As an example, assume total risk σ^2 is 20. Since the risk on the naive portfolio is totally nondiversifiable, its risk is $\beta^2 \sigma^2_M$, where σ^2_M is the variance of portfolio M. If $\sigma^2_M = 15$, then equating total risk $20 = 15\beta^2$, or the Beta on the naive portfolio with the same total risk as portfolio A is

$$\beta_{A'} = \sqrt{20/15}.$$

The second part of the decomposition is to decompose the return $\overline{R}_{A'} - R_F$, which is the extra return earned on the naive portfolio for bearing risk. There are a large number of possible decompositions. One will be presented. Assume the manager was given a target risk level, say, β_T. Then the difference in return between the naive portfolio with risk β_T and the risk-free rate could be considered the extra return that the investor expected to earn, given the risk the investor was willing to bear. Fama calls this return, shown as $\overline{R}_T - R_F$, the return due to "investor's risk." The remaining return is $\overline{R}_{A'} - \overline{R}_T$. This is the return earned because the manager chose a different risk level than the target.

Decomposing $\overline{R}_{A'} - R_F$ into $\overline{R}_T - R_F$ and $\overline{R}_{A'} - \overline{R}_T$ is the second part of Fama's decomposition. The total decomposition is shown in Figure 22.9. We now examine in more detail specific aspects of portfolio performance that have been analyzed.

One aspect of portfolio performance generally measured is diversification. How much of the risk incurred by the portfolio is due to market movements and how much is due to unique movements of the individual securities in the portfolio? Diversification is usually measured by the percentage of total risk that can be

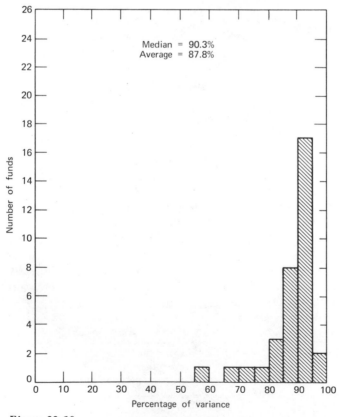

Figure 22.10

accounted for by market movements. If, for the moment, we assume that an index like the Dow-Jones Index represents the market, then the first step is to correlate the returns on the Dow-Jones Index with the returns on the portfolio. The square of the correlation coefficient represents the percentage of total variation in portfolio returns explained by movements in the Dow-Jones Index. Almost all evaluation services provide this measure and most academic studies also utilize this measure. Figure 22.10 presents this measure for 34 mutual funds. As can be seen by examining the figure, most mutual funds are well diversified and the majority of the risk they incur is risk of market movements. However, there are a number of mutual funds shown in Figure 22.10 that bear substantial nonmarket risk. If the mutual fund represents a substantial portion of the investor's portfolio, then the investor also bears the nondiversifiable risk. For the extra risk to be worthwhile, there needs to be substantial extra return. The mutual fund evidence reviewed in the earlier section would indicate that most mutual funds do not earn sufficient return to justify incurring this extra risk. In addition, there is no evidence to suggest that superior performance is related to a lack of diversification. Thus, the mutual funds that have substantial amounts of non-market risk are generally poor investments for individuals for whom the mutual fund represents their principal investment.

A second aspect of mutual fund performance that is often examined is timing. The question is, how successful have mutual funds been in timing market movements and how is timing measured? Managers use one of two techniques in an attempt to improve performance through timing. The first is to change the percentage committed to bonds and stocks in anticipation of market changes. If the market is expected to increase, then the manager increases the amount invested in common equities. If the market is expected to decline, then the manager

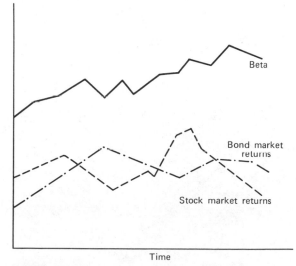

Figure 22.11

switches from common equity to bonds. The alternative way managers attempt to market time is to adjust the average Beta on the portfolio in anticipation of changes in the market. Thus, when the market is expected to increase, the manager increases the Beta on the portfolio to obtain a portfolio with a greater responsiveness to market changes. When the manager feels the market might decline, high Beta securities are sold and low Beta securities purchased to reduce the Beta on the portfolio and make the portfolio less responsive to market movements.

Both the changes in the bond–stock mix and the changes in Beta on the common equity portion of the portfolio are attempts to change the average Beta on the total portfolio. Attempts to measure successful timing are best done utilizing Beta since Beta captures both changes simultaneously. Nevertheless, both the bond–stock mix and the Beta on the common equity portion of the portfolio have been used as indications of timing ability.

The easiest way to examine the effectiveness of attempts to market time is to graphically examine market movements versus the bond–stock mix or average Beta. Figure 22.11 is an example using Betas. For this fund very little evidence of successful timing is present. If the fund has a well specified policy regarding the average Beta or the bond–stock mix, then it is more illuminating to examine the relationship between deviations from the policy and changes in the market. Figure 22.12 is an example of this type of analysis.

Another measure of a manager's timing ability is to look at a plot of portfolio Beta or bond–stock mix compared to the market return. If there is significant timing ability, then there should be a relationship between these variables and this should be apparent from the plot.

A third way to measure market timing is to look directly at the fund return compared to the market return. If the fund did not engage in market timing, then the average Beta on the overall portfolio should be fairly constant. If there

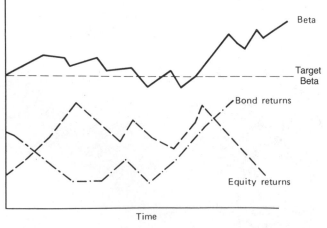

Figure 22.12

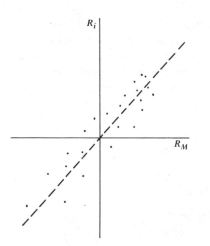

Figure 22.13

was no diversifiable risk in the portfolio, then the portfolio return would be a constant fraction of the market return. A plot of market return compared to portfolio return would be a straight line. On an actual portfolio there is usually some diversifiable risk and some changes in both Beta and the bond–stock mix. If there was no successful timing, then these differences would simply cause the relationship between market return and portfolio return to be a scatter of points around a straight line, such as that shown in Figure 22.13. Assume a fund was able to engage in successful timing through changing Beta. In this case, when the market increased substantially, the fund would have a higher than normal Beta and would tend to do better than it would have otherwise done. This would cause the points to be above the normal line in Figure 22.13 for large market changes. Likewise, if the manager were able to anticipate a market decline, he

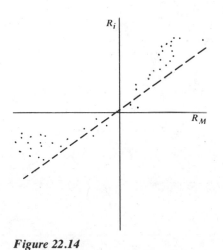

Figure 22.14

or she would reduce the Beta and have a portfolio that declined less than it would otherwise. This would mean that for low market returns points would tend to scatter above the normal relationship. The points above the normal relationship for low and high market returns would give a curvature to the scatter of points if there were successful timing. An example is shown in Figure 22.14. Treynor and Mazuy [55] utilized this to analyze the timing ability of mutual funds. They found that only one fund out of the 37 they examined exhibited any significant timing ability. They did not examine the odds that one would observe one such fund when no timing ability existed.

PROBLEMS IN PORTFOLIO MEASUREMENT

For most individuals and institutions, riskless or near riskless investments are available. The purchase of the government bond of the appropriate maturity is riskless except for some potential risk on the rate to be earned on reinvested interest.[4] Similarly, for individuals, savings accounts are essentially riskless. Note, however, that the single-parameter portfolio evaluation techniques, in general, assume lending and borrowing at the same riskless rate.

As an example, consider the Sharpe measure where portfolios are ranked by the slope of the ray connecting the risk-free asset and the portfolio being evaluated. Using this measure, we would say that portfolio A in Figure 22.15 dominated portfolio B, which dominated portfolio C, which dominated portfolio D.

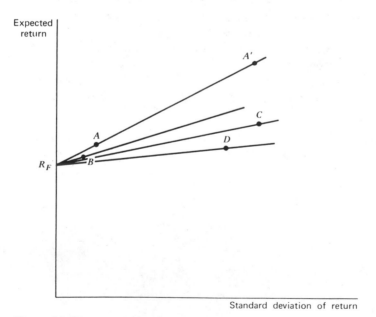

Figure 22.15

To move out on the ray $R_F A$ beyond portfolio A required borrowing at the riskless rate and investing more than 100% in A. The argument of why A dominates C is that an investor desiring a portfolio with the risk of C would be better off holding A and borrowing to move to A'. If borrowing at the riskless rate is not possible, then it is no longer clear that A dominates C. If the borrowing rate is higher than the lending rate, say, R'_F, then the investor follows the line $R'_F A$ to move beyond A. The situation is depicted in Figure 22.16. In this case A dominates C for risk levels to A'', but beyond A'' portfolio C and lending (up to the risk level associated with C) or C and borrowing (for risk levels beyond C) dominate A and borrowing.

In many cases the choice is unambiguous. Clearly A dominates B in Figure 22.15, even if the borrowing rate is different from the lending rate. Combinations of lending or borrowing and A have higher return than lending and borrowing and B. This would be true for any portfolio that had lower risk than A. Portfolios with more risk than A may, or may not, be dominated by A. From the efficient set theorem A dominates D in Figure 22.15 since it has both higher return and less risk than D. Combining lending or borrowing with A or D will not change this relationship.

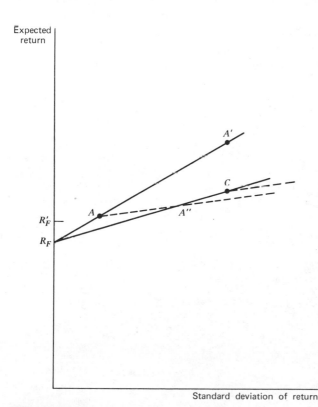

Figure 22.16

The portfolios that A would dominate can be seen from Figure 22.17. A dominates all portfolios that lie below $R_F AA''$.

Although the foregoing discussion utilized the Sharpe measure as an example, the same sort of issues are present with the other measures. It is left to the reader to trace through the implications for the other models.

The second problem with implementing single-parameter risk measures is caused by changing risk levels. One style followed by managers is to try to earn an excess return by trying to anticipate market cycles and adjusting the portfolio accordingly. The standard method is to sell securities and purchase bonds in anticipation of a market decline and to sell bonds and purchase stocks in anticipation of a market increase. An alternative method utilized by some managers is to change the average Beta on the portfolio in anticipation of market movements by changing the type of stock held. If the market is expected to increase, the portfolio manager increases the average Beta on the portfolio in order to increase the sensitivity of the portfolio to the market. If the market is expected to decline, the manager decreases the Beta on the portfolio in order to make the portfolio less sensitive to market movements.

Many managers adopt one or more of these strategies in order to consciously adjust the risk on the portfolio. For many other portfolios, the risk changes as a by-product of adjustments in the portfolio's composition because of changes in expectations concerning individual security performance. In either case, the risk level of the portfolio is changing through time. Changing the risk level of the portfolio causes problems in the evaluation process. Most mutual fund evaluation

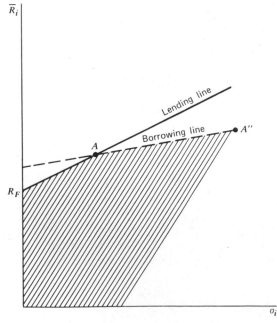

Figure 22.17

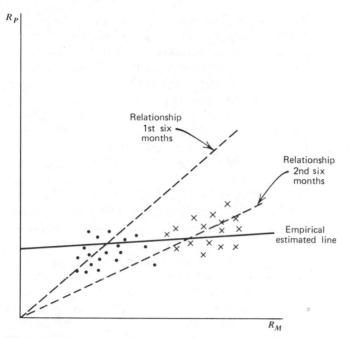

Figure 22.18

studies and many portfolio evaluation services calculate the risk on the portfolio by examining the past sequence of returns for the portfolio. If the risk level of the portfolio has been changing through time, this procedure can lead to an estimate of risk very different from what it was at any point in time.

Perhaps this can best be illustrated by examining a possible set of circumstances when Beta is used as a measure of risk. Let us assume that the composition of a portfolio is unchanged for a six-month period. After the sixth month, the firm decides that the market is likely to go down and so it lowers the Beta on the portfolio for the next six months. Figure 22.18 shows the Beta that would be arrived at by using each of the six months of data separately and the overall Beta that would be found for the period.[5]

Notice that the Beta for the year need bear no fixed relationship to the Beta for any six-month period. In this case, the Beta for the year is measured as being lower than the actual Beta on the portfolio at any point in time. The important point to keep in mind here is that estimating risk from a historical series of returns on a portfolio can produce a risk measure that bears no resemblance at all to the risk on the portfolio at any point in time.

We have raised an important problem. It would be convenient if we could

---

[5]The reader might note that the return in the market was higher in the second six months than the first six months. This can be seen by noting that the points representing the second six months are farther to the right on the horizontal axis.

produce a solution. Fortunately, we can. The risk on a portfolio at any point in time can be estimated by examining the risk of the individual securities and combining them using actual investment proportions to obtain the risk on the portfolio. For example, the Beta on a portfolio at a point in time can be found by estimating the Beta on each stock in the portfolio (using one of the techniques discussed in Chapter 5), and the risk on the portfolio found by taking a weighted average of the individual stock Betas. The weights are the fraction of the portfolio each stock represents. The differential return can then be found by measuring the returns between each portfolio change and compounding for the entire period.

A third possible problem has been emphasized by Roll. Roll points out that Beta is not an unambiguous risk measure. The Beta when using the S&P Index is not the same as the Beta calculated using the Dow-Jones Index as the market. Changing the definition of the market portfolio can change both the Beta and the ranking of portfolios. This is one more example of the principle we emphasized throughout this chapter. In evaluation one must be very careful to determine what is the purpose and what are the relevant alternatives. In this case it may pay the user to evaluate performance under several alternative definitions of the market portfolio. If the performance is robust (e.g., it appears good under a reasonable set of alternative market definitions), the user can feel confident in the result. If it is not robust, the user must either decide that performance is ambiguous or decide which market definition is the most relevant for judging performance in the particular problem under study.

Having examined some of the problems in single-parameter measures, it is worthwhile summarizing some of the mutual fund evidence discussed earlier.

MUTUAL FUND PERFORMANCE

In the earlier section we discussed mutual fund studies to illustrate some of the performance measurement techniques. In this section we intend to summarize the results.

When examining mutual fund performance figures, it is important to be careful to state the purpose of the evaluation. One purpose is to evaluate them as an alternative to individual direct investment, and this is the question we initially address. There are three types of transaction costs incurred directly or indirectly by investors in mutual funds. Mutual funds incur costs when they buy and sell securities. Second, mutual funds charge a yearly management fee. The typical size of this fee is ½% of net asset value. Finally, mutual funds often charge an initial fee to the purchaser of the fund's shares. This is typically 8% of the purchase made. Not all funds make this additional charge. Those that do not are referred to as no-load funds; those that do are referred to as load funds.

All of the tables in the earlier part of this chapter were prepared by deducting transaction costs of purchasing and selling the securities and the management fee from returns. However, the front load is not deducted. The argument for this choice is as follows. The alternative to mutual fund investment is direct investment. This involves a transaction cost for the initial purchase and final sale. Not deducting the front load is roughly equivalent to these transactions costs. This procedure is a rough approximation. It clearly distorts, somewhat, the relative performance of load compared to no-load funds. Since no-load funds do not involve an initial purchase charge, the return or no-load funds is understated, relative to the return on an investor's direct purchase. Since the normal front load funds charge 8%, and 8% is larger than normal transaction costs, the return for load funds is overstated, relative to individual direct purchase. Although this slightly affects the comparison between these types of funds, it probably has little effect on the overall conclusions concerning mutual fund performance.

The Evidence

A review of the previous tables shows that, in general, mutual funds performed worse than a naive strategy of random selection or mixing the market with the riskless asset. This conclusion is broadly consistent with the evidence reviewed earlier and the other mutual fund studies that we did not examine of McDonald [33], Williamson [58], and Cranshaw [5]. There are exceptions. The SEC study showed one period of superior performance, and the Friend, Blume, and Crockett [12] study showed good mutual fund performance compared to certain types of random selection.

As one might expect, these studies have not been happily received by the mutual fund industry. Is there any justification in light of these studies for an investor using mutual funds?[6] Mutual funds do provide substantial diversification. Figure 22.10 taken from the Sharpe study shows that about 88% of the total variance of return of mutual funds was due to market movements, leaving 12% diversifiable risk. Merrill Lynch, in their analysis of funds using their service, found that funds diversified away all but about 10% of the risk. Elton and Gruber [7] show that for an equally weighted randomly selected portfolio to be 90% diversified, 48 securities are required.[7]

For an investor with limited capital, very large transaction costs are required to obtain the same degree of diversification. Thus, for small investors, mutual funds, even with slightly poor performance, still provide a reasonable alternative to direct purchase. If mutual funds are at times a good investment vehicle, a reasonable question to ask is: Are there any characteristics of mutual funds that are associated with superior performance?

The first variable to examine is sales charges. Table 22.8 shows such an examination. On average, the funds with low sales charge outperformed funds with medium or large sales charges. The apparent exception is that the low-risk high-charge funds outperformed the low-risk low-sales charge funds.

However, there are only three funds involved in this group and this is not enough evidence from which to draw firm conclusions. Recall that this comparison

---

[6]The advantages discussed shortly apply equally well to closed end funds. Malkiel [32] suggests these funds may be more appropriate investment vehicles.

[7]A careful selection of stocks can reduce this number significantly.

Table 22.8 Comparison of Investment Performance of Mutual Funds with Different Sales Charges (Jan. 1960–June 1968)

	Number in Sample			Mean Return		
Risk Class (Beta Coefficient)	Below 8.25%[a]	8.25 to 8.5%	Over 8.5%	Below 8.25%[a]	8.25 to 8.5%	Over 8.5%
Low Risk ($\beta = 0.5-0.7$)	9	15	3	0.090	0.091	0.099
Medium risk ($\beta = 0.7-0.9$)	20	28	4	0.112	0.104	0.094
High risk ($\beta = 0.9-1.1$)	6	13	3	0.151	0.129	0.135

[a]Sales charges at end of 1967 as percentage of sales price. No-load funds are included in the below-8.25% group.

Source: Friend, Blume, and Crockett [12].

is being made without deducting the sales charges (front load) from the returns. If we deducted this cost, which an investor pays when purchasing the fund, the results would be even more striking. Many of the low-sales charge funds are no-load funds. Examining these results would indicate that no-load funds have superior performance to load funds before deducting the sales charge and, clearly, are even better after the deduction. This evidence suggests that an investor interested in obtaining diversification, via mutual funds, would be best to use no-load funds.

The next three variables we examine are concerned with the techniques for managing mutual funds as well as characteristics that investors might use in selecting funds. First, do funds with high turnover have superior performance? Table 22.9 examines this question. This table indicates that funds with high

Table 22.9 Comparison of Investment Performance of Mutual Funds with Different Stock Portfolio Turnover Ratios (Jan. 1960–June 1968)

	Number in Sample			Mean Return		
Risk Class (Beta Coefficient)	Below 25%[a]	25 to 50%	Over 50%	Below 25%[a]	25 to 50%	Over 50%
Low Risk ($\beta = 0.5-0.7$)	10	11	6	0.087	0.094	0.094
Medium risk ($\beta = 0.7-0.9$)	18	16	9	0.106	0.105	0.111
High risk ($\beta = 0.9-1.1$)	1	6	10	0.092	0.112	0.148

[a]These are averages of turnover ratios for the years 1966–1968, inclusive. The turnover ratio in each year is defined as the lesser of purchases or sales of portfolio stock divided by the average market value of stockholdings at the beginning and end of the year.

Source: Friend, Blume, and Crockett [12].

Table 22.10   Comparison of Investment Performance of Mutual Funds with Different Management Expense Ratios (Jan. 1960–June 1968)

Risk Class (Beta Coefficient)	Number in Sample			Mean Return		
	Below 0.60%[a]	0.60 to 0.75%	Over 0.75%	Below 0.60%[a]	0.60 to 0.75%	Over 0.75%
Low Risk ($\beta = 0.5\text{–}0.7$)	7	9	7	0.093	0.085	0.093
Medium risk ($\beta = 0.7\text{–}0.9$)	14	17	19	0.103	0.102	0.114
High risk ($\beta = 0.9\text{–}1.1$)	0	11	10	. . .	0.126	0.140

[a]Management expenses in 1960 as percentage of average assets during year.

Source: Friend, Blume, and Crockett [12].

turnover seem to outperform funds with low turnover. The additional stock transactions lead to superior performance. However, other studies such as that of Sharpe [46] show the opposite, that the transaction costs of the larger turnover are larger than any additional performance. Additional study is necessary to determine which result better describes reality.

The second variable that has been examined is the ratio of expenses to assets. Expenses are the annual management fee. Table 22.10 lends some support to the hypothesis that the funds with greater expenses have superior performance. Other studies have found different results, however, so some caution is in order.

Another variable that has been examined is fund size. The argument can go either way. Large funds have an advantage in that they have more to spend for information and analysis. On the other hand, large funds may have more impact on the market when they engage in purchase and sales. When investigators examined this variable, they were not able to find any impact of size on per-

Table 22.11   Comparison of Investment Performance of Mutual Funds in Different Asset Size Groups (Jan. 1960–June 1968)

Risk Class (Beta Coefficient	Number in Sample				Mean Return			
	$10 to 50[a]	$50 to 100	$100 to 500	$500 and over	$10 to 50[a]	$50 to 100	$100 to 500	$500 and over
Low risk ($\beta = 0.5\text{–}0.7$)	8	5	14	1	0.088	0.093	0.092	0.105
Medium risk ($\beta = 0.7\text{–}0.9$)	11	12	18	12	0.101	0.111	0.105	0.110
High risk ($\beta = 0.9\text{–}1.1$)	3	3	13	3	0.125	0.153	0.131	0.146

[a]Asset size in millions of dollars as of the end of 1967.

Source: Friend, Blume, and Crockett [12].

Table 22.12   Relationship Between Stated Investment Objectives and Mutual Fund
Volatility, 125 Funds

	Investment Objective				
Volatility Range	Capital Gain	Growth	Growth Income	Income	Total
0– .4	0	0	0	3	3
.4– .8	0	5	18	12	35
.8–1.0	2	7	33	2	44
1.0–1.2	5	21	4	0	30
1.2+	8	5	0	0	13
Total	15	38	55	17	125

Source: S.E.C. study [45].

formance. Table 22.11 taken from Friend, Blume, and Crockett shows typical results.

There is another issue worth examining. Mutual funds have different stated objectives with respect to risk. If the actions of the funds differed from the stated objectives, then this would be an additional source of risk to the investors. Table 22.12 taken from the SEC study is typical. It shows that, in general, funds' stated objectives and performance are closely related.

A final question concerns the consistency of mutual funds performance. Do funds that outperform other funds in one period outperform them in a second? Table 22.13 taken from the SEC study provides a tentative "yes" to this question.

A second objective in examining mutual fund performance was to examine strong form efficiency. It is to this task that we now turn.

Strong Form Efficiency

In examining strong form efficiency, we are attempting to determine whether a group of investors, in this case mutual fund managers, is able to obtain superior performance using whatever information and selection techniques it wishes to employ.

In examining this question it is relevant to look at performance after the transaction costs involved with the purchase and sale of securities. The ques-

Table 22.13   Continuity of Performance

Number of Consecutive Years Fund's Performance Had Positive Differential Return	Proportions of Group with Positive Differential Return in Subsequent Year
1	50.4
2	52.0
3	53.4
4	55.8
5	46.4

tionable transaction cost is the fee for management service. The management fee covers two types of cost. First, it covers analysis and bookkeeping costs. This is the cost of obtaining information about securities, processing the information, and maintaining information about the portfolio. The second component of the management fee is the profit. In testing strong form efficiency, one should deduct only costs of operating the fund (including management and analysis costs). This is a transaction cost of investing in the stocks, and the market should be efficient only after deducting such costs. Profit should, of course, not be deducted.[8] The

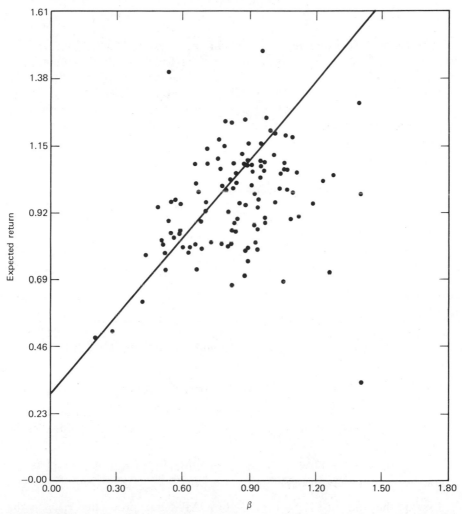

Figure 22.19

---

[8]Opportunity costs of alternative employment should be deducted. Some argue that these are small enough to be ignored.

difficulty arises because it is impossible, in general, to separate these costs. The usual procedure is to examine the returns after payment of the management fee. Figure 22.19 is taken from Jensen and is the result most often quoted. The scatter around the line is reasonably uniform, indicating, on average, that mutual funds do not possess superior selection ability relative to other groups of managers. In addition, they seemingly do not earn extra returns sufficient to cover the portion of the management fee that represents analysis costs.[9] Thus, Jensen's evidence supports strong form efficiency.

CONCLUSION

In this chapter we examined the state of the measurement and analysis of portfolio performance. We discussed alternatives for the overall evaluation of portfolios, as well as diagnostics to see what managers were doing and how well they accomplished their goals. Along the way we examined the actual performance of mutual funds and pointed out some deficiencies in the way that portfolio evaluation techniques are used.

QUESTIONS AND PROBLEMS

1.   Below are data on five mutual funds:

Fund	Return	Standard Deviation	Beta
A	14	6	1.5
B	12	4	0.5
C	16	8	1.0
D	10	6	0.5
E	20	10	2

   What is the reward-to-variability ratio and the ranking if the risk-free rate is 3%?

2.   For the data in Problem 1, what is the Treynor measure and ranking?

3.   For the data in Problem 1, what is the differential return if the market return is 13%, the standard deviation of return is 5%, and standard deviation is the appropriate measure of risk?

4.   For the data in Problem 1, what is the differential return if Beta is the appropriate measure of risk?

5.   Assume that the zero Beta form of the CAPM is appropriate. What is the differential return for the funds shown in Problem 1 if $R_z = 4\%$?

---

[9]Mains [31] has shown that Jensen's results are biased against mutual funds. He argues that this reverses Jensen's results. However, he does not include any transaction costs. As discussed before, some must be included to appropriately judge strong form efficiency.

6. For Funds A and B in Problem 1, how much would the return on B have to change to reverse the ranking using the reward-to-variability measure?

BIBLIOGRAPHY

1. Arditti, Fred. "Another Look at Mutual Fund Performance," *Journal of Financial and Quantitative Analysis,* **VI,** No. 3 (June 1971), pp. 909–912.
2. Barineau, III, John. Critique of [49]: "Does 'Good Portfolio Management' Exist?" *Management Science,* **15,** No. 6 (Feb. 1969), pp. B322–B324.
3. Carlson, Robert. "Aggregate Performance of Mutual Funds: 1948–1967," *Journal of Financial and Quantitative Analysis,* **V,** No. 1 (March 1970), pp. 1–32.
4. Cohen, Kalman, and Pogue, Jerry. "Some Comments Concerning Mutual Fund Versus Random Portfolio Performance," *Journal of Business,* **41,** No. 2 (April 1968), pp. 180–190.
5. Crenshaw, T.E. "The Evaluation of Investment Performance," *Journal of Business,* **50,** No. 4 (Oct. 1977), pp. 462–485.
6. Dietz, Peter. "Components of a Measurement Model, Rate of Return, Risk and Timing," *Journal of Finance,* **XXIII,** No. 2 (May 1968), pp. 267–275.
7. Elton, Edwin J., and Gruber, Martin J. "Risk Reduction and Portfolio Size: An Analytical Solution," *Journal of Business,* **50,** No. 4 (Oct. 1977), pp. 415–437.
8. Fabozzi, Frank J., Francis, Jack C., and Lee, Cheng F. "Generalized Functional Form for Mutual Fund Returns," *Journal of Financial and Quantitative Analysis,* **XV,** No. 5 (Dec. 1980), pp. 1107–1120.
9. Fama, Eugene. "Components of Investment Performance," *Journal of Finance,* **XVII,** No. 3 (June 1972), pp. 551–567.
10. Fisher, Larry, and Weil, Roman. "Coping with the Risk of Interest Rate Fluctuations: Returns to Bondholders from Naive and Optimal Strategies," *Journal of Business,* **44,** No. 4 (Oct. 1971), pp. 408–431.
11. Friend, Irwin, and Blume, Marshall. "Measurement of Portfolio Performance Under Uncertainty," *American Economic Review,* **LX,** No. 4 (Sept. 1970), pp. 561–575.
12. Friend, Irwin, Blume, Marshall, and Crockett, Jean. *Mutual Funds and Other Institutional Investors* (New York: McGraw-Hill, 1970).
13. Gaumnitz, Jack E. "Appraising Performance of Investment Portfolios," *Journal of Finance,* **XXV,** No. 3 (June 1970), pp. 555–560.
14. Gepfert, Alan. Critique of [49]: "Does 'Good Portfolio Management' Exist?" *Management Science,* **15,** No. 6 (Feb. 1969), pp. B322–B324.
15. Gibb, J. William. "Critical Evaluation of Pension Funds," *Journal of Finance,* **XXIII,** No. 2 (May 1968), pp. 337–343.
16. Gordon, M., Paradis, G., and Rorke, C. "Experimental Evidence on Alternative Portfolio Decision Rules," *American Economic Review,* **LXII,** No. 1 (March 1972), pp. 107–118.
17. Grant, Dwight. "Portfolio Performance and the 'Cost' of Timing Decisions," *Journal of Finance,* **XXXII,** No. 3 (June 1977), pp. 837–838.

18. Gumperz, Julian, and Page, Evertee. "Misconceptions of Pension Fund Performance," *Financial Analysts Journal,* **26,** No. 3 (May–June 1970), pp. 30–37.

19. Guy, James. "The Performance of the British Investment Trust Industry," *Journal of Finance,* **XXXIII,** No. 2 (May 1978), pp. 443–455.

20. Jensen, C. Michael. "The Performance of Mutual Funds in the Period 1945–1964," *Journal of Finance,* **XXIII,** No. 2 (May 1968), pp. 389–415.

21. Jensen, Michael. "Risk, the Pricing of Capital Assets, and the Evaluation of Investment Portfolios," *Journal of Business,* **42,** No. 2 (April 1969), pp. 167–247.

22. Jobson, J.D., and Korkie, Bob. "Potential Performance and Tests of Portfolio Efficiency," *Journal of Financial Economics,* **X,** No. 4 (Dec. 1982), pp. 443–466.

23. ———. "On the Jensen Measure and Marginal Improvements in Portfolio Performance: A Note," *The Journal of Finance,* **39,** No. 1 (March 1984), pp. 245–252.

24. Joy, Maurice, and Porter, Burr. "Stochastic Dominance and Mutual Fund Performance," *Journal of Financial and Quantitative Analysis,* **IX,** No. 1 (Jan. 1974), pp. 25–31.

25. Klemkosky, Robert. "The Bias in Composite Performance Measures," *Journal of Financial and Quantitative Analysis,* **VIII,** No. 3 (June 1973), pp. 505–514.

26. Kon, Stanley, and Jen, Frank. "Estimation of Time-Varying Systematic Risk and Performance for Mutual Fund Portfolios: An Application of Switching Regression," *Journal of Finance,* **XXXIII,** No. 2 (May 1978), pp. 457–475.

27. Kroll, Yoram, and Levy, Haim. "Sampling Errors and Portfolio Efficient Analysis," *Journal of Financial and Quantitative Analysis,* **XV,** No. 3 (Sept. 1980), pp. 655–688.

28. Lee, Cheng, and Jen, Frank. "Effects of Measurement Errors on Systematic Risk and Performance Measure of a Portfolio," *Journal of Financial and Quantitative Analysis,* **XIII,** No. 2 (June 1978), pp. 299–312.

29. Levitz, Gerald. "Market Risk and the Management of Institutional Equity Portfolios," *Financial Analysts Journal,* **30,** No. 3 (Jan./Feb. 1974), pp. 53–60.

30. Levy, Haim. "Portfolio Performance and Investment Horizon," *Management Science,* **18,** No. 12 (Aug. 1972), pp. B645–B653.

31. Mains, Norman. "Risk, the Pricing of Capital Assets, and the Evaluation of Investment Portfolios: Comment on [21]," *Journal of Business,* **50,** No. 3 (July 1977), pp. 371–384.

32. Malkiel, Burton. "The Valuation of Closed and Investment Company Shares," *Journal of Finance,* **XXXII,** No. 2 (June 1977), pp. 847–886.

33. McDonald, John. "Objectives and Performance of Mutual Funds: 1960–1964," *Journal of Financial and Quantitative Analysis,* **IX,** No. 3 (June 1974), pp. 311–333.

34. Meyer, Jack. "Further Applications of Stochastic Dominance to Mutual Fund

Performance," *Journal of Financial and Quantitative Analysis,* **XII,** No. 3 (June 1977), pp. 235–242.

35. Miller, Tom W., and Gressis, Nicholas. "Nonstationarity and Evaluation of Mutual Fund Performance," *Journal of Financial and Quantitative Analysis,* **XV,** No. 3 (Sept. 1980), pp. 639–654.

36. Mills, D. Harlan. "On the Measurement of Fund Performance," *Journal of Finance,* **XXV,** No. 5 (Dec. 1970), pp. 1125–1131.

37. Monroe, Robert, and Trieschmann, James. "Portfolio Performance of Property-Liability Insurance Comapnies," *Journal of Financial and Quantitative Analysis,* **VII,** No. 2 (March 1972), pp. 1595–1611.

38. Peterson, David, and Rice, Michael L. "A Note on Ambiguity in Portfolio Performance Measures," *The Journal of Finance,* **35,** No. 5 (Dec. 1980), pp. 1251–1256.

39. Pohlman, R., Ang, J., and Hollinger, R. "Performance and Timing: A Test of Hedge Funds," *Journal of Portfolio Management,* **4,** No. 3 (Spring 1978), pp. 69–72.

40. Rothstein, Marvin. "On Geometric and Arithmetic Portfolio Performance Indexes," *Journal of Financial and Quantitative Analysis,* **VII,** No. 4 (Sept. 1972), pp. 1983–1992.

41. Sarnat, Marshall. "A Note on the Prediction of Portfolio Performance from Ex-Post Data," *Journal of Finance,* **XXVII,** No. 3 (June 1972), pp. 903–906.

42. Schlarbaum, Gary. "The Investment Performance of the Common Stock Portfolios of Property-Liability Insurance Companies," *Journal of Financial and Quantitative Analysis,* **IX,** No. 1 (Jan. 1974), pp. 89–106.

43. Schlarbaum, Gary, Lewellen, W., and Lease, R. "Realized Return on Common Stock Investments: The Experience of Individual Investors," *Journal of Business,* **51,** No. 2 (April 1978), pp. 299–325.

44. ———. "The Common-Stock Portfolio Performance Record of Individual Investors: 1964–70." *Journal of Finance,* **XXIII,** No. 2 (May 1978), pp. 429–441.

45. Securities and Exchange Commission. *Institutional Investor Study,* U.S. Government Printing Office, Washington, D.C., 1971, Part 2, pp. 325–347.

46. Sharpe, William. "Mutual Fund Performance," *Journal of Business,* **39,** No. 1, Part 2 (Jan. 1966), pp. 119–138.

47. Sharpe, W.F. "Reply to [57]," *Journal of Business,* **41,** No. 2 (April 1968), pp. 235–236.

48. Shick, Richard, and Trieschmann, James. "Some Further Evidence on the Performance of Property-Liability Insurance Companies' Stock Portfolio," *Journal of Financial and Quantitative Analysis,* **XIII,** No. 1 (March 1978), pp. 157–166.

49. Simon, Julian. "Does 'Good Portfolio Management' Exist?" *Management Science,* **15,** No. 6 (Feb. 1969), pp. B308–B319.

50. Simonson, Donald. "The Speculative Behavior of Mutual Funds," *Journal of Finance,* **XXVII,** No. 2 (May 1972), pp. 381–391.

51. Smith, Keith. "Is Fund Growth Related to Fund Performance?" *Journal of Portfolio Management,* **4,** No. 3 (Spring 1978), pp. 49–55.
52. Smith, Keith, and Tito, Dennis. "Risk-Return of Ex Post Portfolio Performance," *Journal of Financial and Quantitative Analysis,* **IV,** No. 4 (Dec. 1969), pp. 449–471.
53. Swadener, Paul. "Comment: Portfolio Performance of Property-Liability Insurance Companies," *Journal of Financial and Quantitative Analysis,* **VII,** No. 2 (March 1973), pp. 1619–1623.
54. Tehranian, Hassan. "Empirical Studies in Portfolio Performance Using Higher Degrees of Stochastic Dominance," *The Journal of Finance,* **35,** No. 1 (March 1980), pp. 159–220.
55. Treynor, Jack, and Mazuy, M. "Can Mutual Funds Outguess the Market?" *Harvard Business Review,* **44,** No. 4 (July/Aug. 1966), pp. 131–136.
56. Treynor, Jack. "How to Rate Management of Investment Funds," *Harvard Business Review,* **43,** No. 1 (Jan./Feb. 1965), pp. 63–75.
57. West, Richard. "Mutual Fund Performance and the Theory of Capital Asset Pricing: Some Comments," *Journal of Business,* **41,** No. 2 (April 1968), pp. 230–234.
58. Williamson, Peter. "Measurement and Forecasting of Mutual Fund Performance: Choosing an Investment Strategy," *Financial Analysts Journal,* **28,** No. 5 (Nov./Dec. 1972), pp. 78–84.

Chapter 23

Evaluation of Security Analysis

The selection of a portfolio of securities can be thought of as a multistage process. The first stage consists of studying the economic and social environment and the characteristics of individual companies in order to produce a set of forecasts of individual company variables. The second stage consists of turning these forecasts of fundamental data about the corporation and its environment into a set of forecasts of security prices and/or returns and risk measures. This stage is often called the valuation process. The third and last stage consists of forming portfolios of securities based on the forecast of security returns. Although, as we have seen in the last chapter, a great deal of attention has been paid, both in the academic literature and in practice, to evaluating how well the entire process works, almost no attention has been paid to evaluating the component parts of the process. This is particularly surprising because the bulk of the evidence seems to indicate that the overall process does not work very well. The lack of extraordinary performance could be due to any of several causes, such as a lack of forecast ability, an inability to turn good forecats of fundamental company data into good forecasts of returns, or a lack of ability to turn good forecasts of return into efficient portfolios. For example, it is perfectly possible that an organization has superior forecasting ability with respect to fundamental firm variables but does not capitalize on this information in forming portfolios.

In this chapter we are concerned with methods of analyzing how well an organization forecasts fundamental economic variables and how well it turns these forecasts into meaningful measures of security returns. To value a stock correctly, an organization must analyze and predict a large number of fundamental variables relating to each firm and the economy. In point of fact, the analysts at most institutions spend most of their time forecasting earnings (or growth in earnings). Because of this and because of the key role played by future earnings in any valuation scheme (see Chapter 16), we have selected forecasts of earnings per share as the fundamental firm variable examined in this chapter. The reader should keep in mind that the techniques we discuss for examining the accuracy of earnings estimates can be applied with a little imagination to forecasts of any fundamental variable. We start this chapter with a brief discussion of the sensitivity of price to earnings, and an overall look at the accuracy of earnings estimates. Then we present techniques that should be useful in evaluating and diagnosing the errors in earnings forecasts. Finally, we study some techniques for examining the valuation process itself.

WHY THE EMPHASIS ON EARNINGS?

In Chapter 16 we saw that a firm's value was generally considered to be a function of dividends, growth, and risk. Forecasts of future dividends are usually prepared by applying a forecasted payout ratio to forecasted earnings. At least in the short run payout ratios are easy to forecast and, to the extent they vary from historical levels, they usually do so as a function of earnings changes. We have already devoted a large amount of material to the analysis and forecasting of risk (Chapters 5 and 6). Thus the key remaining variable is the forecast of future earnings.

In Chapter 17 we showed that an ability to forecast future earnings can allow an excess return to be earned, even in the absence of a complex valuation model. For example, we saw that the 30% of firm that had the largest increase in earnings offered the investor a risk-adjusted excess return of 7.48% over a 13-month period, while those in the lower 30% offered a risk-adjusted excess return of -4.93%.[1]

The ability to earn an excess return by correctly forecasting earnings implies that the market's forecast of earnings (which determines price) is not perfectly accurate. Further evidence of this is supplied by the fact that the excess return we can earn from a perfect forecast of earnings becomes smaller and smaller as the end of the fiscal year approaches.[2] This is consistent with the market's estimate of future earnings becoming more and more accurate as information is released during the fiscal year.

A very good proxy for market expectation of future earnings is the consensus forecasts of security analysts. If the average forecast of security analysts is close to market expectations, then one should not be able to purchase stock on the basis of these expectations (e.g., forecasted growth) and make an excess return. Empirical evidence strongly suggests that this is, in fact, true.[3]

---

[1]See Elton, Gruber, and Gultekin [5].

[2]See Elton, Gruber, and Gultekin [5] for evidence of this.

[3]See Elton, Gruber, and Gultekin [5].

On the other hand, if the consensus forecasts are a good proxy for market expectations and one can forecast with more accuracy than the average analyst, then one should be able to make an excess return. In Chapter 17 we saw that this was, in fact, true. The next logical question to ask is how large has the error in consensus forecasts been. The answer is, quite large. If we examine forecasts made nine months before the end of the fiscal year, we find that for the 30% of the companies for which analysts most overestimated growth in earnings, their average error in forecasting growth was 63.6%. If we examine the 30% of the companies for which analysts most underestimated growth, we find their estimates were off, on average, by −38.9%. As the end of the fiscal year approaches, these errors shrink. But three months before the end of the fiscal year, they were still quite large: +26.4% and −27.0%, respectively.

It would be interesting to see how well individual analysts have performed compared to the consensus estimates. Unfortunately, no such studies exist. However, there are three studies of how accurately individual analysts' forecast compared to simple extrapolations of past earnings.

Cragg and Malkiel [3] analyzed predictions of long-term (five-year) growth rates prepared on each of a large sample of firms by analysts at five leading institutions. They concluded that there seems to be no clear-cut ability of the institutions examined to outperform simple extrapolations of historical growth rates.

Elton and Gruber [4] analyzed the ability of the analysts at three financial institutions to predict earnings nine months before the end of the fiscal year. They found that, of the three institutions examined, one performed slightly worse than historical extrapolation of past earnings, two performed slightly better, but none of the differences was statistically significant at even the 10% level. Recently, Brown and Rozeff [1] investigated the performance of Value Line estimates of earnings, once again comparing them with historical extrapolation methods. They found that Value Line outperformed the extrapolation techniques at a statistically significant level. A reasonable conclusion to draw from this evidence is that, while it is not easy to outperform historical extrapolation, there are individuals and perhaps institutions that might be able to do so. It may also be true that there are individuals and institutions that can outperform the consensus forecasts.

It is surprising, in light of the impact of the accuracy of earnings forecasts on stock selection and in light of the tremendous resources that financial institutions devote to the preparation of earnings forecasts, that more resources have not been devoted to the evaluation of earnings estimates. This is the subject with which the next section of this chapter deals.

THE EVALUATION OF EARNINGS FORECASTS

Although very little has been written about the evaluation of the estimates of security analysts, there is a broad literature in economics on the evaluation of forecasts. We draw heavily on this literature and, in particular, on the work of

Henri Thiel in this section. We start by examining a meaningful overall measure of the accuracy of earnings forecasts. Then we look at both graphical and numerical techniques for diagnosing the sources of forecast error. We will end this section with an argument that any evaluation of earnings forecasts should be performed relative to the consensus (average) forecast of earnings. Anticipating this discussion and to provide a benchmark against which to measure analysts' performance, we provide data on the performance of the consensus forecast for several error measures discussed in this section.[4]

Overall Forecast Accuracy

In order to evaluate earnings forecasts in an exact manner, one should really have a loss function that measures the loss caused by any size error in the forecast. While this is indeed desirable, in many fields the evaluation of estimates must be performed in the absence of an explicit loss function. The most frequently assumed loss function is the quadratic, and the most frequently assumed measure of loss is the mean squared error.[5]

The mean squared forecast error for any set of forecasts can be easily computed as

$$\text{MSFE} = \frac{1}{N} \sum_{i=1}^{N} (F_i - A_i)^2$$

where

    MSFE is the mean squared forecast error
    F_i is a forecast of the earnings per share for firm i
    A_i is the actual earnings per share that occurs for firm i

The mean squared forecast error is often developed in terms of the change in earnings. Define

    P_i as the predicted change in earnings
    R_i as the realized change in earnings
    H_i as the level of earnings at the time the forecast was made

Then,

$$P_i = F_i - H_i$$

$$R_i = A_i - H_i$$

---

[4]The data used for the results reported in this chapter were extracted from the I/B/E/S data base compiled by Lynch, Jones, and Ryan. We include the consensus forecasts for all corporations with a December fiscal year, which were followed by three or more analysts for the years 1976, 1977, and 1978. Most tables are based on a total of 1,242 consensus forecasts.

[5]See Thiel [7, 8].

The mean squared error in terms of the change in earnings can be written as

$$\text{MSFE} = \frac{1}{N} \sum_{i=1}^{N} (P_i - R_i)^2$$

The same MSFE results whether we perform the analysis in terms of the predicted change in earnings or the predicted level of earnings.[6]

It will prove convenient for error diagnosis to examine the forecast error as the error in forecasting the change in earnings. The mean squared forecast error can be used to rank forecasting techniques. However, it would be useful to scale the MSFE so that its value has a natural interpretation. One useful way to scale it has been suggested by Thiel [7, 8]. This measure, often referred to as Thiel's inequality coefficient (TIC), involves dividing the MSFE by the sum of the squared change in earnings, or

$$\text{TIC} = \left(\sum_{i=1}^{N} (P_i - R_i)^2 \right) \Big/ \left(\sum_{i=1}^{N} R_i^2 \right)$$

Notice that two values of this measure have an easily interpreted economic meaning. If the predicted change in earnings always equaled the realized change in earnings (perfect forecasting), then the numerator would be zero and TIC would be zero. Thus, a value of TIC equal to zero implies perfect forecasting ability. If the predicted change in earnings always equaled zero, then P_t would equal zero and TIC would equal one. A value of TIC equal to 1 implies that the forecasts are exactly as accurate as a forecast of no change in next period's earnings. TIC allows us to obtain a sense of how well a forecaster performs, even before comparisons are made with other forecasters. A value below 1 indicates that the forecaster outperforms the naive no-change model. A value larger than 1 indicates that the forecasts could not outperform the most naive of all forecasting models.

Table 23.1 presents the values of TIC for the consensus estimates over the three years 1977, 1978, and 1979. Notice that 11 months before the last consensus forecast, the average analyst has a TIC value of .75, indicating that the performance of the consensus forecast is slightly better than the naive forecast. By the time analysts prepare their last forecast, the value of TIC has fallen to .15, indicating a great deal of accuracy. Table 23.1 also shows an extremely regular decrease of TIC for successive forecasts. The coefficient of determination between

---

6

$$\text{MSFE} = \frac{1}{N} \sum_{i=1}^{N} (P_i - R_i)^2 = \frac{1}{N} \sum_{i=1}^{N} [F_i - H_i - (A_i - H_i)]^2 = \frac{1}{N} \sum_{i=1}^{N} (F_i - A_i)^2$$

Examination of the last term makes it clear that the MSFE of the change in earnings is identical to MSFE in terms of level of earnings.

Table 23.1　TIC over Time

Months before final forecast	11	10	9	8	7	6	5	4	3	2	1	0
TIC		.75	.70	.62	.54	.49	.44	.41	.35	.28	.26	.20	.15

TIC and time is .99. As Elton, Gruber, and Gultekin [6] show, this same pattern occurs in each year, as well as on average over the entire period.

Before leaving this section we should mention an alternative to examining forecasts in terms of the error in forecasting earnings. Some researchers have suggested that forecasts be examined in terms of the *percentage* error in forecasting earnings. Ultimately, the test of which is correct depends on whether losses or gains are a function of the amount or the percentage by which earnings are misestimated. While this decision is up to the user, he or she should be aware that if percentage errors are used, results tend to be dominated by the huge percentage errors usually found in companies with very small earnings. Very small size earnings (a small denominator in the percentage calculation) make misestimation of any size appear quite serious. A problem also arises when the company has zero or negative earnings.[7] The analysis in this section can easily be recast in terms of percentage earnings error. The reader must decide which is the most relevant criterion.

Diagnosis of Forecasting Errors

There are infinitely many ways to examine forecast errors to learn more about them and perhaps correct future forecasts for their deficiencies. In this section we first present a diagrammatic scheme that can be used to learn a great deal about the pattern of forecast errors, and then we present some numerical techniques for computing diagnostics.

Graphical Analysis　One of the simplest, and yet most revealing, techniques for examining the pattern in forecast errors is the Prediction Realization Diagram (PRD) proposed by Thiel [7, 8]. This diagram is simply the plot of the predicted change in earnings against the realized change. The predicted change is plotted along the line that lies at a 45 degree angle to the horizontal axis and actual change is plotted along a line that lies at a minus 45 degree angle to the horizontal axis. This is shown in Figure 23.1.

If we plot in this space the forecasted change in earnings versus the realized change, we can learn quite a lot about the type of forecast errors being made. Notice that if a point lies on the horizontal straight line, it indicates that the forecast change was exactly equal to the actual change. To the extent that points lie above the horizontal straight line, it indicates that estimates were too high. To the extent that points lie below the horizontal line, it indicates that estimates were too low. Now let us take a closer look at what each section of the graph

---

[7]When earnings are zero, the percentage change in earnings will be infinite. When earnings are negative, the meaning of percentage changes in earnings is ambiguous.

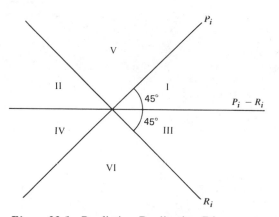

Figure 23.1 Prediction Realization Diagram.

represents. A point lying in section I of the PRD indicates that the forecaster successfully predicted that earnings would increase, but that the size of the increase was overestimated. A point lying in section II indicates that the analyst successfully predicted a decrease in earnings but that the size of the decrease was underestimated (earnings were overestimated). If a point lies in section V, it indicates that the analyst predicted the wrong direction for the change in earnings. That is, the analyst predicted they would increase when they, in fact, decreased. Section III, IV, and VI are analogous to sections I, II, and V. Section III represents a successful prediction of an increase in earnings but an underestimate of the size of the increase. Section IV represents a successful prediction of a decrease but an overestimate of the size of the decrease. Finally, a point in section VI represents a forecast of a decrease in earnings when they actually increased. Sections V and VI indicate that the analyst misestimated the direction of the change in earnings movements whereas the other sections indicate the analyst got the direction right but the size wrong.

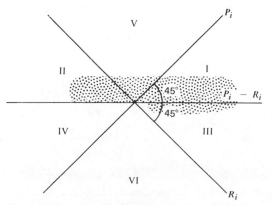

Figure 23.2 Prediction Realization Diagram: optimistic forecaster.

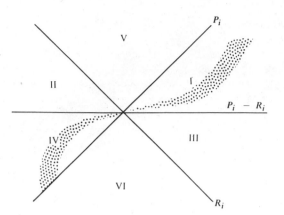

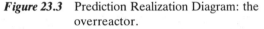

Figure 23.3　Prediction Realization Diagram: the overreactor.

Examination of a group of forecasts on the PRD can reveal quite a lot of information about the source of error in analysts' forecasts. In Figures 23.2 and 23.3 we have constructed two hypothetical patterns that might be observed. Figure 23.2 presents the case where a forecaster is consistently optimistic. The forecaster consistently overestimates earnings changes when they were positive (section I) and consistently underestimates the size of a negative change (section II) or actually predicts a positive change when changes are negative (section V).

A more interesting pattern is revealed in Figure 23.3. In this diagram we find the profile of an analyst who is excellent at predicting the direction of change. However, the analyst overreacts to change by becoming overoptimistic as large positive changes are expected and overpessimistic as large negative changes are expected. This can be seen by the fact that estimates lie further and further from the horizontal axis as the actual level of earnings change increases.

These are only two of the many potential patterns of forecaster behavior that can be seen through the PRD. The reader is encouraged to construct other series of points on this diagram and to interpret their meaning.

Numerical Analysis　While the graphical analysis of forecast errors is extremely useful, there are also several analytical decompositions of the mean squared forecast error that can provide useful insight into the sources of forecasting error. Let us take, as an example, a firm that has a collection of analysts making forecasts of a broad group of stocks in the economy. We discuss two meaningful decompositions of these errors. The first is based on the level of aggregation at which errors occur, while the second looks at the forecast error in terms of the characteristics of the forecasters.

Errors Decomposed by Level of Aggregation　It would be extremely useful to determine at what level of aggregation errors in the forecasts occurred. One scheme for analyzing the level separates earnings errors into three components.

This scheme is shown below.

$$\text{MSFE} = \frac{1}{N} \sum_{i=1}^{N} (P_i - R_i)^2$$

$$= (\overline{P} - \overline{R})^2 + \frac{1}{N} \sum_{i=1}^{N} [(\overline{P}_a - \overline{P}) - (\overline{R}_a - \overline{R})]^2$$

$$+ \frac{1}{N} \sum_{i=1}^{N} [(P_i - \overline{P}_a) - (R_i - \overline{R}_a)]^2$$

where
$\overline{P}$ = mean value of P_i across all stocks followed by all analysts
$\overline{R}$ = mean value of R_i across all stocks followed by all analysts
$\overline{P}_a$ = mean value of P_i for industry a to which i belongs. Each industry will have a different value of $\overline{P}_a$
$\overline{R}_a$ = mean value of R_i for each industry in turn

The first term measures how much of the forecast error is due to inability of the analysts, in total, to predict what average earnings will be for the economy. This term is simply the squared difference between the average predicted change in earnings and the average realized change in earnings. The second term is a measure of how much of the total error is due to the individual analysts misestimating the differential performance of particular industries from the average for the economy.

Let us examine this term in more detail. For each firm (i) the difference between the mean predicted change in earnings for the industry to which it belongs ($\overline{P}_a$) and the mean predicted change in earnings for all firms ($\overline{P}$) is calculated. The same term is calculated for actual change in earnings ($\overline{R}_a - \overline{R}$). The difference between the two is squared and summed for all firms. Then the average value of this term is taken. The third term measures how much of the error is due to analysts not being able to predict the difference in performance of the individual stocks they follow from the appropriate industry average. The first part of this term is the difference between the predicted change in earnings for an individual stock P_i and the average predicted change for a stock in the industry to which i belongs. The second part has the same meaning, but deals with realizations. These differences are squared, summed, and then averaged.

By dividing through both sides of the equation by the MSFE, we express each source of error as a fraction of the total mean squared forecast error. Diagnosing the source of the error can be of great significance to the firm. For example, if the major source of error arises from misestimated aggregate earnings, then the company should concentrate more effort on preparing its forecasts of the general economy. If the analysts are provided with better information about the aggregate

Table 23.2 Percentage Error in Earnings Change by Level of Aggregation

	Economy	Industry	Company
January	1.7	36.5	61.8
February	1.8	36.4	61.8
March	1.9	35.6	62.4
April	1.9	33.7	64.4
May	2.4	33.4	64.2
June	2.7	31.8	65.6
July	2.8	31.7	65.5
August	2.8	30.9	66.2
September	3.0	28.2	68.9
October	2.7	27.2	70.1
November	2.2	23.6	74.3
December	1.9	17.6	80.5

level of earnings and are explicitly encouraged to use this information, then improvement should occur in the firm's forecasting effort. Assuming that each analyst follows one industry or a group of closely related industries (economic sector), then a large value for the second term points to an error in understanding the economics of alternative industries. Large values of the third term indicate that errors are associated with being unable to differentiate between the performance of individual companies even when mistakes in forecasts of the level of the economy and industries are removed.

Obviously, this same type of decomposition can be repeated for all individual analysts with their error decomposed into their misestimate of how the stocks they follow will do, on average, and their inability to differentiate the performance of the companies they follow.

In Table 23.2 we have presented the decomposition of the mean square error by level of aggregation for the set of consensus forecasts discussed earlier. Perhaps the most striking aspect of this table is the small percentage of error that is due to misestimating the performance of the economy (the average company). This source of error never exceeds 3% of the total mean squared error. The percentage of error due to industry misestimates starts at 36.5% in January and declines continuously to 17.6% by the end of the fiscal year. Consequently, the error due to misestimating individual companies grows from 61.8% to 80.5% over the year. We have already seen that the size of analyst's errors shrinks over the year. Now we see that while analysts become more accurate in forecasting both industry and company errors, their ability to forecast industry influences grows relative to their ability to forecast company performance over the year.

Errors Decomposed by Forecast Characteristics There is a second type of decomposition of forecast errors that is meaningful to management. This decomposition looks for the pattern of mistakes and is a numeric analogue to the graphical analysis presented earlier. We can write this decomposition as

$$\text{MSFE} = \frac{1}{N} \sum_{i=1}^{N} (P_i - R_i)^2$$

$$\text{MSFE} = (\overline{P} - \overline{R})^2 + (1 - \beta)^2 \sigma_P^2 + (1 - \rho)^2 \sigma_R^2$$

where

β is the slope coefficient of the regression of R on P
ρ is the correlation of P and R
σ_P^2 is the variance of P
σ_R^2 is the variance of R

The first term in this equation $(\overline{P} - \overline{R})$ represents bias. This is the tendency of the average forecast to either overestimate or underestimate the true average. The second term represents inefficiency or the tendency for forecasters to be systematically overoptimistic (or insufficiently optimistic) about good (or bad) events. If the Beta of actual earnings on forecasted earnings is greater than 1, then forecasts are overestimates of earnings at high values and underestimates at low values of actual earnings. If Beta is less than 1, then analysts underestimate earnings when they are high and overestimate earnings when they are low. The final component of this equation is the random disturbance term.

When we apply this decomposition to consensus estimates, we find some interesting results. The vast majority of analysts' errors are random rather than systematic in nature. In all months over 91%, and in one-half of the months over 94%, of the MSFE arise from random error. Inefficiency as well as bias contribute very little to MSFE. Furthermore, Betas are close to one and vary randomly around one. There does not seem to be a systematic tendency of analysts to get overexcited or overly cautious about potentially good performance on the part of firms.

The Evaluation of Earnings Forecasts — Again

While it is important to examine the accuracy of earnings estimates and to diagnose where errors are being made, there is another step that should be taken. Forecast errors can more meaningfully be judged relative to some bench mark than they can on an absolute basis. The need for a bench mark is easy to see. It is less difficult to forecast earnings for some stocks and for some industries than it is for others. For example, the earnings of public utilities are more stable and easier to forecast than are the earnings for electronics manufacturers. If a bench mark is not used, the forecaster who follows utilities or the firm that specializes in utility stocks will be judged a better forecaster (if its ability is about the same) than the forecaster who follows electronics stocks.

Thus, one quality we would like a bench mark to have is to adjust for the difficulty of the forecasting process. A second quality we would like a bench mark to have is to represent an absolute base such that forecasting ability above the bench mark can be potentially transformed into superior security selection while performance below the bench mark is unlikely to lead to superior security selection. Fortunately, a bench mark exists that satisfies both these criteria. It is the consensus forecast introduced in Chapter 17. The accuracy of the consensus forecast reflects how easy or difficult it is to forecast the earnings for a particular company or group of companies. In addition, as we have already seen, the price of any stock reflects (incorporates) the consensus forecast. The ability to forecast with no more accuracy than the consensus should not lead to a superior return, while the ability to forecast with more accuracy should.

Thus, we propose that the bench mark against which all analysts and forecasts be judged should be the consensus forecast. As a first step in analyzing the performance of any analyst or group of analysts (institution), their mean squared forecast error can be computed and compared directly with the mean squared forecast error for the consensus forecast. The consensus mean squared forecast error should be computed over that same set of corporations for which the analyst or institution prepared forecasts. Then each of the diagnostics discussed earlier in this chapter can be computed for the consensus forecasts and compared directly with the diagnostics of the institution's forecasts. Alternatively, consensus forecasts can be used as the bench-mark forecast and individual forecasts compared against it. This would involve defining realizations as the consensus forecast of change in earnings.

EVALUATING THE VALUATION PROCESS

The valuation process converts a set of forecasts about company fundamentals and economic data into a set of forecasts of market variables or a recommended course of action to take with respect to individual securities. The number of books and articles written about the valuation of securities far exceeds the number of publications on modern portfolio theory. It is surprising that, given the large number of publications on how to value securities, almost nothing has been written about how to value the valuation process itself.

Before turning to an evaluation of the valuation process, let us spend a little time thinking about what form the output from the valuation process should take. The problem becomes rather simple when we realize that the output from the valuation process is the input to portfolio analysis. We know what we need to perform portfolio analysis. We need estimates of the expected return for each stock, the variance of the return on each stock, and the correlation of returns between each pair of stocks. Chapters 5 and 6 dealt with alternative models for predicting correlations between securities as well as techniques for evaluating these alternative models. We mentioned at that time that we felt it unlikely that the analyst would ever produce direct estimates of correlation coefficients.

What analysts can produce are estimates of expected returns, perhaps variances, or estimates of the parameters of at least one of the models from Chapter 5 and 6 that can be used to estimate variance and covariances. For illustrative purposes, let us assume that analysts are preparing estimates of expected returns and Betas. Their estimates of Beta may well involve subjective modification of historical or fundamental Betas.

The question then remains, given that analysts produce estimates of the relevant risk and return parameters, how do we evaluate the quality of these estimates?[8]

Evaluating the Valuation Process with a Full Set of Outputs

There are really three steps that can and should be taken in evaluating the valuation process:

1. How well does each output from the valuation process predict the future?

2. If the output is examined in a simple way, does the output lead to undervalued and overvalued stocks being correctly identified?

3. If the output is used in an optimal manner, does it produce good results?

Let us now examine each in turn. The first step is to see if there is any predictive content in the output for the valuation process. For example, one type of output should be the expected return for each security. One question to analyze is how well does expected return forecast future returns, and what are the sources of error in the forecast? We have already designed the system for analyzing this question in the first part of this chapter. For all of the evaluation procedures outlined in this part of the chapter, we can simply substitute expected rate of return for change in earnings. For the naive model against which to judge expected rate of return, we can substitute the historical average rate of return on the stock for the consensus forecast of earnings.

Any other individual output from the valuation process can be analyzed in an analogous manner. For example, Beta estimates could be used in any of the diagnostic procedures outlined in the first part of this chapter.

Let us assume that there is some predictive content in one or more of the outputs from the valuation process. Where do we go from there? The next step is to begin to analyze the output in combination. The simplest way to do this is to examine the output in expected return Beta space and to see how stocks that appear to be underpriced (or overpriced) perform in subsequent periods. To be more specific, assume that analysts as of December 31, 1985, have forecasted the expected return and Beta for a group of stocks for the year 1986. Based on expectations about returns and Betas for the year 1986, an expected security market line could be constructed. The distance that a particular security lies

---

[8]In this section we really are presenting techniques for the evaluation of the valuation process given the quality of inputs to the valuation process. This should not be disturbing, since the previous section dealt with evaluating these inputs.

above this line is a measure of its attractiveness as a candidate for purchase. The distance above or below the expected security market line is usually referred to as a stock expected Alpha. This is a measure of how much more or less than its equilibrium return a stock is expected to earn. At the end of 1986, the actual return and Beta for each stock can be measured as well as the security market line for 1986. This allows the computation of an actal Alpha for each stock for 1986. The expected Alpha for each stock can now be compared with the Alpha that occurred for each stock. In particular, the predictive power of expected Alpha can be compared with the naive prediction of all future Alphas equal to zero. If the expected Alphas predict better than this model, there is informational content in the valuation process.

The final step in evaluating the output from the valuation process is to see if employing this output with the portfolio optimization rules of Chapters 4 and 7 lead to the selection of portfolios that perform well. Using the appropriate techniques from Chapters 4 and 7, we select that portfolio that would be optimum if the input from the valuation process were correct. We can then use any of the techniques outlined in the previous chapter to evaluate the portfolio we have selected. Hopefully, this portfolio will outperform naive strategies such as buying an index fund with the same risk.

Although we could end the discussion of evaluation of the valuation process at this point, there is one more step that should be taken. Using the techniques of the previous chapter, the portfolio discussed earlier should be compared with the portfolio actually held by the institution performing this analysis. If the institution's portfolio does not perform as well, it indicates that the portfolio manager is not making optimum use of the information supplied to him. If the manager's portfolio performs better, it indicates that he or she is introducing additional information not contained in the output of the valuation process.

Evaluating the Output of the Valuation Process: Incomplete Information

To perform portfolio analysis properly, one needs a full range of inputs on expected return, variances, and covariances. While more and more firms are recognizing this and encouraging their analysts to provide data in this form, the majority of firms have a much simpler form for output from the valuation process.

Many firms have their analysts provide data to portfolio managers (or provide data to the firm's clients) in terms of a recommendation to either buy, sell, or hold particular stocks.[9] This is less satisfactory than output provided, in terms of rate of return forecasts. It forces the analyst to compress a continuous rating of securities into a three-point scale. This prevents the analyst from passing along information to the portfolio manager or, perhaps worse, gives the analyst an excuse for not developing the information. The best evaluation that can be done in a case like this is to examine the performance of each of the three groups of stocks to see if the groupings contain information.

---

[9]Some firms use a five-point scale rather than a buy-sell-hold recommendation, but the evaluation will be similar to that described in this section.

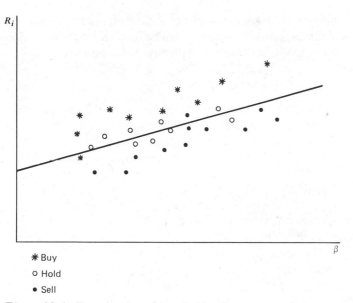

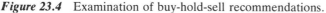

* Buy
o Hold
• Sell

Figure 23.4 Examination of buy-hold-sell recommendations.

An an example of the type of analysis that might be done, let us assume that we have a group of stocks for which buy-sell-hold recommendations have been made as of December 31, 1985. The firm has a one-year time horizon and it is now December 31, 1986. Then the returns on each stock for the year 1986 can be plotted in return Beta space. Furthermore, the best estimate of the security market line that existed in 1986 can be plotted on the same diagram. The alphas or distances above and below the line could be computed for each stock.[10] Figure 23.4 illustrates this analysis.

Hopefully the majority of the buy recommendations lie above the line and the majority of the sell recommendations lie below the line. The difference between the rate of return on the stock and the return expected on each stock given the security market line can be calculated for each buy recommendation, as well as for each hold and sell recommendation.[11] The average for each group can be computed. It should be positive for the buy recommendations, close to zero for the hold, and negative for the sells. Notice that, even in computing the average distances for each group, we have implicitly made an assumption. The assumption is that in putting together a portfolio, the portfolio manager will place an equal dollar amount in each buy and an equal dollar amount in each sell. This is not an optimal course of action, even if the buy and sell ratings are perfectly accurate. There are bound to be differences in the relative rankings of stocks within each

---

[10]The estimate of the security market line should be made from all stocks, not just from those stocks followed by the firm.

[11]This distance is simply the vertical distance between the line and the point.

category, and this procedure fails to take account of these differences. However, the naive procedure of assuming equal investment can be used to get an indication of whether there is information in the estimates of buy, hold, and sell.[12]

CONCLUSION

Almost all the emphasis in the evaluation process has been placed on evaluating the performance of portfolios held by financial institutions. In light of the fact that the performance of these portfolios has been unsatisfactory, it is important to start examining the steps in the portfolio management process to see if there is information that is not being used. In this chapter we have suggested a series of steps for doing so. The first step is to examine the forecasts of fundamental data on corporations to see if they contain information. The second step is to evaluate the output from the valuation process to see if it has taken advantage of any information contained in the security analyst's basic forecast. The final step is to compare portfolios selected in an optimal fashion from the output of the valuation process with portfolios selected by portfolio managers to analyze what the portfolio manager adds to the process. It is only by breaking the portfolio selection and management process into stages that a firm can find what it does well and what it does poorly in the hope of improving portfolio performance.

QUESTIONS AND PROBLEMS

1.   Assume that a brokerage firm concentrates on a few closely related industries. It has produced a set of estimates of earnings for 1985 and subsequently recorded the earnings that actually occurred. This data is given below:

Industry	Firm	Previous Earnings	Estimated Earnings	Actual Earnings
A	1	1.05	1.10	1.05
	2	1.32	1.37	1.35
	3	3.50	4.25	3.25
B	4	2.06	2.10	2.12
	5	2.08	2.13	2.12
	6	2.60	3.25	2.80
	7	1.07	1.06	1.06
C	8	2.00	2.70	2.40
	9	.55	.52	.54
	10	1.18	1.16	1.20

   A.   Plot these points on a Predictive Realization Diagram. What can we learn about the forecast pattern of this firm from the PRD?

---

[12]This naive procedure is necessary if one wishes to isolate the effect of information in the buy, hold, or sell recommendations. If one wished to simultaneously evaluate risk variables, a more complex procedure is possible.

B. Calculate the mean square forecasted error for this firm.

C. Decompose the error by level of aggregation. That is, determine what percentage of the error was due to the inability to forecast earnings for this sector of the economy, what percent was due to an inability to forecast each industry, and what percent was due to inability to forecast differences for each firm.

D. Examine another level of decomposition. Assume that there are three analysts, each following one industry. What is the mean squared error of each analyst? How much of the error of each analyst is due to the analyst's inability to predict the future of the industry followed, and how much is due to an inability to differentiate between the firms in the industry?

E. Decompose the error by forecast characteristics. Find what percentage of the error is due to bias, what percentage is due to variance, and what percentage is due to covariance.

BIBLIOGRAPHY

1. Brown, Lawrence, and Rozeff, Michael. "The Superiority of Analysts' Forecast as Measures of Expectations: Evidence from Earnings," *Journal of Finance,* **XXXIII,** No. 1 (March 1978), pp. 1–16.
2. Brown, Stephen J., and Warner, Jerold B. "Measuring Security Price Performance," *Journal of Financial Economics,* **8,** No. 3 (Sept. 1980), pp. 205–258.
3. Cragg, J. G., and Malkiel, B. G. "The Consensus and Accuracy of Some Predictions of Growth of Corporate Earnings," *Journal of Finance,* **23,** No. 1 (March 1968), pp. 67–84.
4. Dybvig, Philip H., and Ross, Stephen A. "Performance Measurement Using Differential Information and a Security Market Line," *Journal of Finance,* **40,** No. 2 (June 1985), pp. 383–400.
5. ———. "The Analytics of Performance Measurement Using a Security Market Line," *The Journal of Finance,* **40,** No. 2 (June 1985), pp. 401–416.
6. Elton, Edwin J., and Gruber, Martin J. "Earnings Estimates and the Accuracy of Expectational Data," *Management Science,* **18,** No. 2 (April 1972), pp. 409–424.
7. Elton, Edwin J., Gruber, Martin J., and Gultekin, Mustafa. "Expectations and Share Prices," *Management Science,* **27,** No. 9 (Sept. 1981).
8. ———. "Professional Expectations: Accuracy and Diagnosis of Errors," working paper, New York University (1983).
9. Thiel, Henri. *Applied Economic Forecasting* (Amsterdam: North-Holland, 1966).
10. ———. *Optimal Decision Rules for Government and Business* (Amsterdam: North-Holland, 1964).

Chapter 24
A Brief Retrospective

The reader who has just finished this book may find himself or herself in somewhat of a quandary. The careful reader of Chapters 11, 12, 13, 14 and 15 may conclude that capital markets are efficient and in equilibrium. If all available information is included in market prices, except perhaps for some minor anomalies, why hire and pay money to security analysts? If markets are efficient, why bother with the first part of this book on portfolio analysis? Shouldn't this material be relegated to the circular file, and, in fact, shouldn't that part of the financial community that deals with security selection or portfolio management be dismissed and their products replaced by a gigantic passive portfolio (index fund)? This solution is not without its advocates in both the business and academic community. Obviously, we should not have put you through the "pleasure" of reading all of this book if we believed that the solution to the investment problem was this simple.

Perhaps we should step back at this point and review two opposite approaches that are taken to the investment process. We have labeled the first approach the modern version of the traditional approach. We inserted the word "modern" both because this approach has evolved over the years and also because often anything labeled "traditional" is immediately suspect. The second approach has been called the efficient market approach, though it could equally well be called the passive portfolio approach.

MODERN VERSION OF THE TRADITIONAL APPROACH

The modern version of the traditional approach is outlined diagrammatically in Figure 24.1. This approach starts with the premise that the forecasts of at least some security analysts contain information that is not completely incorporated

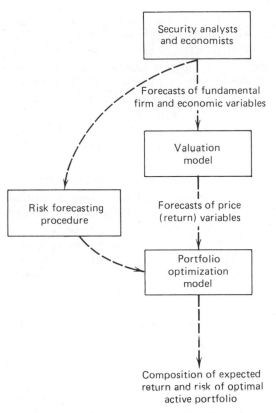

Security analysts
and economists

Forecasts of fundamental
firm and economic variables

Valuation
model

Risk forecasting
procedure

Forecasts of price
(return) variables

Portfolio
optimization
model

Composition of expected
return and risk of optimal
active portfolio

Figure 24.1 Modern version of traditional approach.

into market prices. It recognizes that there are differences in analysts' estimates and that some analysts, through superior investigation of and knowledge about the technology, economics, and management of selected companies and/or industries, can make better than average forecasts about the future earning power and risk of certain companies. The advocates of this approach recognize that, as pointed out in Chapters 17 and 22, the average or consensus forecast of company performance will be incorporated in price, but that superior forecasts may exist, may be able to be identified, and if identified, should allow superior returns to be earned. Any institution that hires security analysts and/or economists is implicitly or explicitly accepting this approach to the investment process.

The first job of the security analyst and/or economist is to produce forecasts of variables associated with the operations of the firm and of the economy. These forecasts almost always include estimates of future earnings per share and may include items such as an estimate of dividends, debt-to-equity ratios, earnings variability, and other risk measures. Any institution that hires security analysts and or economists to prepare forecasts of macroeconomic, industry, or firm variables must use a valuation model to convert these forecasts of fundamental data into forecasts of market prices. Sometimes the model is an explicit model such as the ones discussed in Chapter 16 for stocks or in Chapters 18 and 19 for bonds; sometimes it is an implicit model. Sometimes the output of a valuation model will be in terms of forecasted prices, sometimes forecasted returns, sometimes a ranking of stocks by expected returns, and sometimes a classification of stocks into some number of groups ranked by potential payoff. The key point is that investment decisions are made in terms of expected return including changes in market value and that a model is needed to convert forecasts of fundamental data into forecasts of market value.

The output from the valuation model also serves as part of the input to the model used to construct the investor's optimum portfolio. Chapters 2, 3, 4, 7, and 9 dealt with the properties of portfolio selection models. The portfolio selection model may be as complex as a full quadratic programming algorithm discussed in Chapter 4 or as simple as the "simple rules" discussed in Chapter 7. Expected return is a necessary input to any of these models. In addition, estimates of risk are necessary inputs. While estimates of return will be produced by valuation techniques such as those discussed in Chapters 16, 18, and 19, estimates of risk will most likely be produced by the techniques discussed in Chapters 5 and 6. These mechanical techniques are likely to be supplemented by analysts' subjective estimates, but the complexity of risk makes it unlikely that subjective estimates will replace the type of techniques discussed in the text.

The output from the portfolio selection model is the construction of the optimum portfolio and its expected return and risk.

THE EFFICIENT MARKET APPROACH

The efficient market approach to portfolio management starts with the premise that capital markets are perfectly efficient. Market prices perfectly reflect all available information, or at least any deviation of price from what it should be is completely random and unidentifiable. Analysis of individual firms, industries, or the economy cannot contribute to return and so such analysis, while having a cost, has no payoff. All we need to know about a security is its price and we really do not have to pay any attention to that since it is correct. The valuation model employed is a very simple one; the best estimate of value is the current price of the security.

If there is no further assumption of equilibrium, random selection of a well-diversified portfolio is appropriate. If one of the equilibrium models of Chapters 11, 12, or 14 is assumed to hold, then a more detailed specification of the optimum portfolio is possible. In the simplest case, where we accept the assumptions of the Sharpe–Lintner–Mossin general equilibrium model, all investors should simply hold the market portfolio. This conclusion may account in part for the increasing use of index funds by financial institutions for a large portion of their portfolios. If one believes in one of the more complex forms of the general equilibrium relationships, one simply holds a more complex passive portfolio. For example, if one accepts the presence of taxes (unfortunately neither one of us has been unable to avoid this assumption in our personal investing), one holds a dividend-tilted index fund.

If one accepts this framework, then Parts I and III of this book can be completely ignored except for those sections of Part I that were necessary to derive the results in Part II.

THE TWO APPROACHES: A RECONCILIATION?

The two approaches to portfolio management appear to be irreconcilable. This is one case where appearances are correct or at least almost correct. If markets are perfectly efficient, there is no payoff from careful security analysis and portfolio management. However, there appears to be increasing evidence that while markets are very efficient, they are not perfectly efficient. Several exceptions to perfect efficiency have been cited throughout this book, particularly in Chapter 15. Certain broad inefficiencies or anomalies have received a great deal of attention in recent years. These include the failure of prices to adjust completely and instantaneously to earning surprises, the small-firm effect, and end-of-year effects. We believe that the evidence is consistent with a concept of almost efficient markets rather than totally efficient markets. The question remains whether in almost efficient markets it pays to manage money actively. The answer lies in the ability of the individual or institution asking the question. On average, investors can do no better than the market portfolio, which after all represents the aggregate performance of all investors. Should a particular institution pursue active as opposed to passive management? One can answer the question only by applying the type of analysis outlined in Part IV of this book. One can consider the efficient market hypothesis the null hypothesis. It is the bench mark against which to judge investment performance. By employing the type of analysis presented in Chapters 22 and 23, an institution can determine if there has been a payoff from employing active management. Furthermore, the institution can determine if it produces real information at any stage in the investment process diagrammed in Figure 24.1 and if that information is capitalized on or dissipated at later stages in the process. Only by following the systematic approach to the investment process outlined in this book can any information in the forecasts of fundamental firm variables produced by security analysts be capitalized upon. However, if the input is bad, the output on even the most sophisticated valuation models and portfolio selection models will be bad. Tools exist and have been described for evaluating each step of the investment process. Portfolio optimization techniques exist for capitalizing on any information inherent in the forecasts of analysts. There is no excuse for an institution wanting to actively manage funds not to use these techniques to construct portfolios and to evaluate performance.

Index

Page numbers followed by *n* refer to footnotes or reference notes.